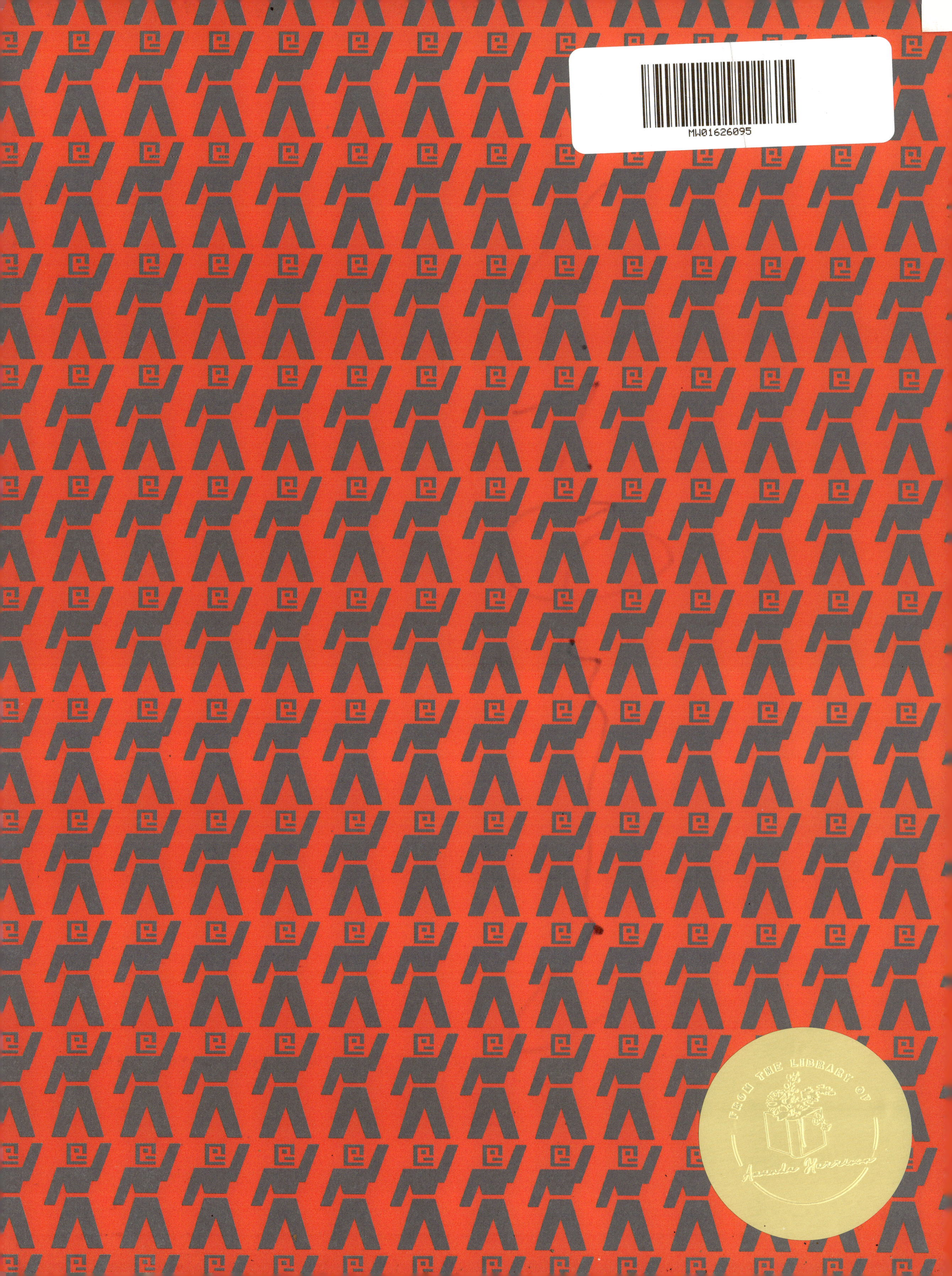
MW01626095
FROM THE LIBRARY OF

FOR ALIDA (POST)

VAN HAMERSVELD

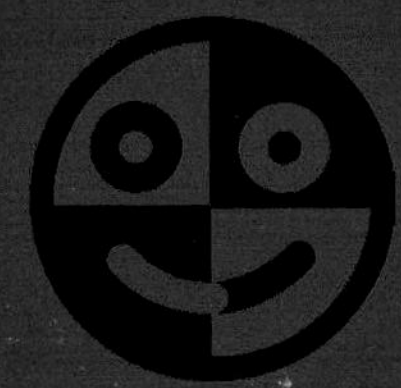

Coolhous Studio

ORIENTATION

THE COOLHOUS TRADEMARK

This book contains 50 years of images from 1961–2011.

What does "Coolhous" mean? It means "In The Mix!" During the late '90's, I had to submit an eight letter word for an internet email address. "Coolhous" as in a collage of sound, meaning... a style of electronic house-dance music, the music has been around since the early to mid-1990s, the music was infused into the mainstream pop and dance music worldwide. The graphic style of this book is a collage of images over time.

John Van Hamersveld

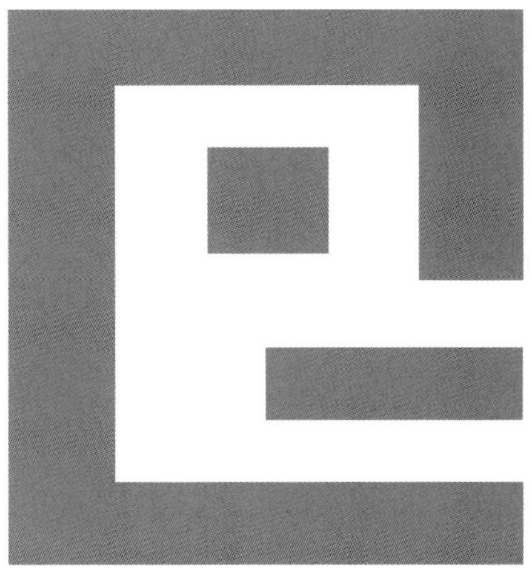

GINGKO
PRESS

PUBLISHED BY GINGKO PRESS IN ASSOCIATION WITH COOLHOUS STUDIO

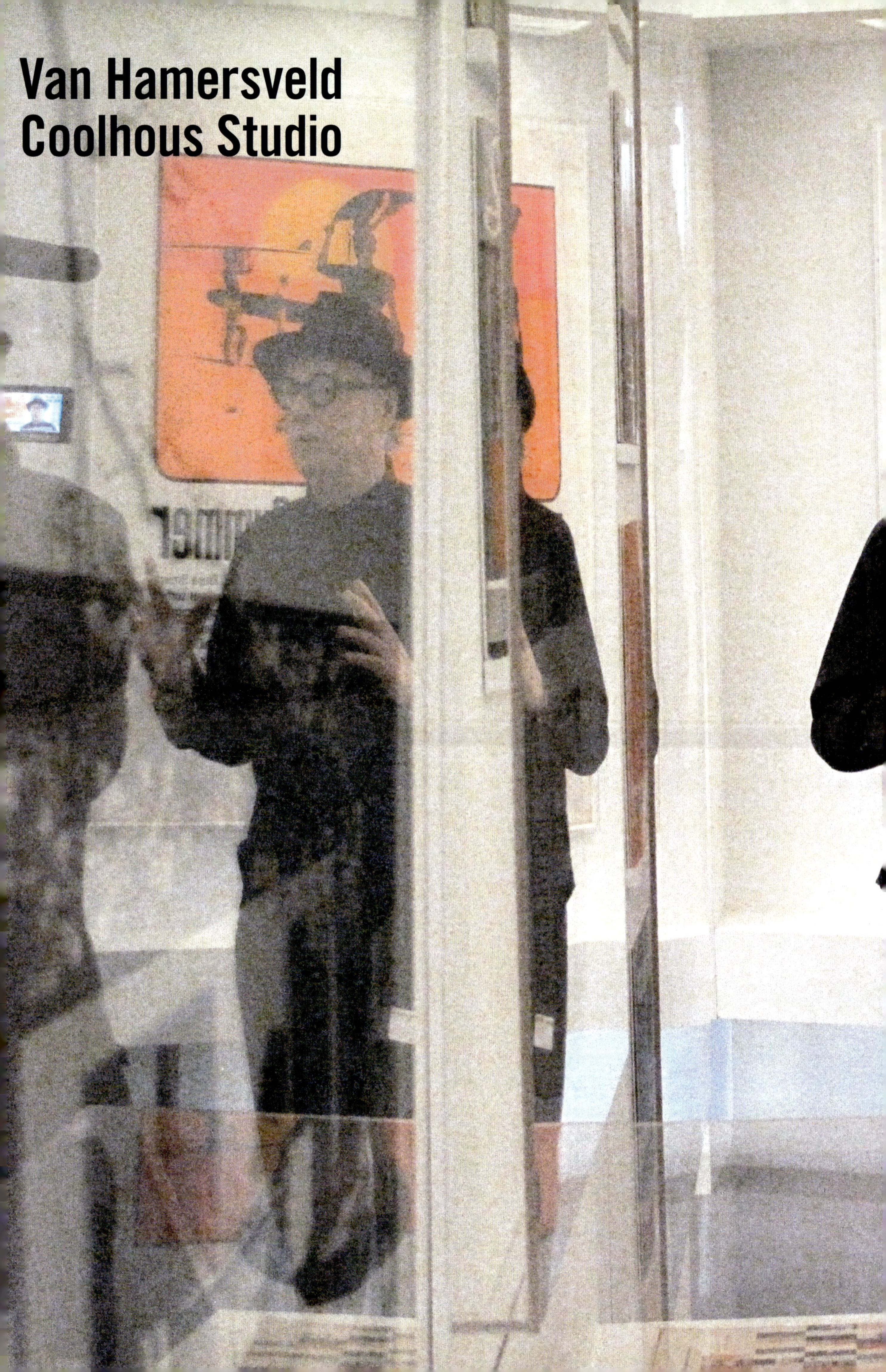

Van Hamersveld
Coolhous Studio

50 Years Of Graphic Design by John Van Hamersveld

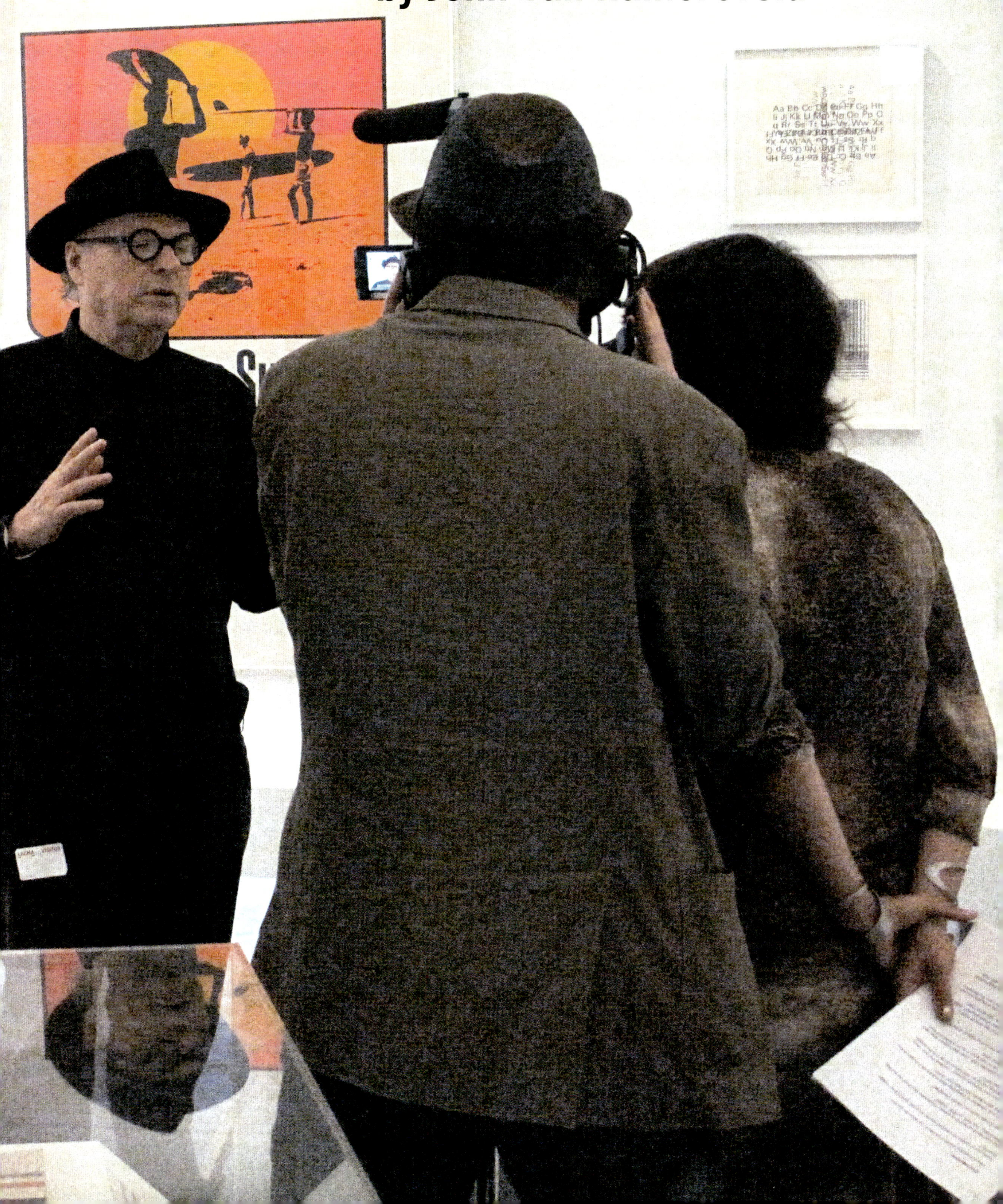

From Here...

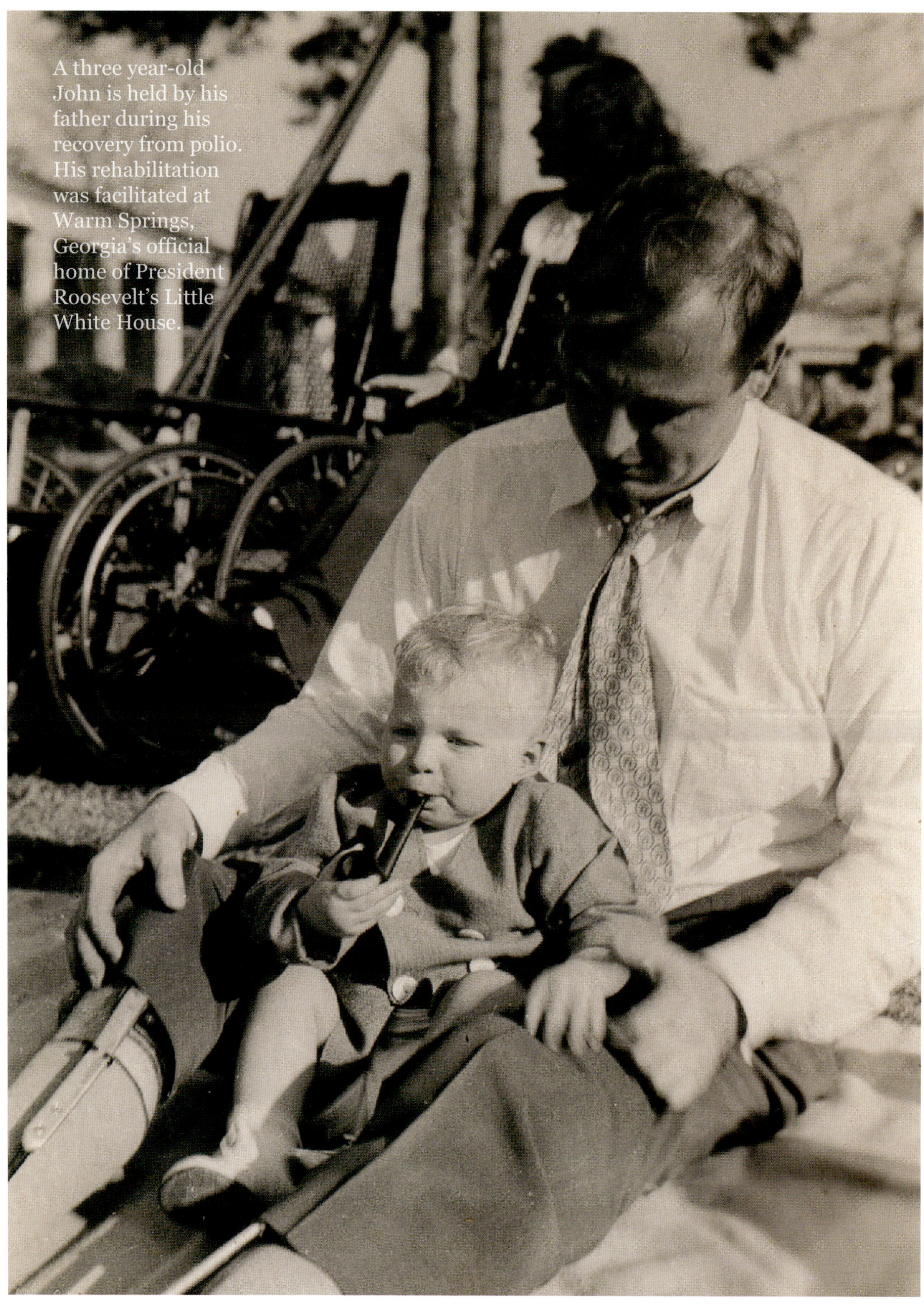

1945: FATHER AND SON, WARM SPRINGS, GEORGIA

...To Here!

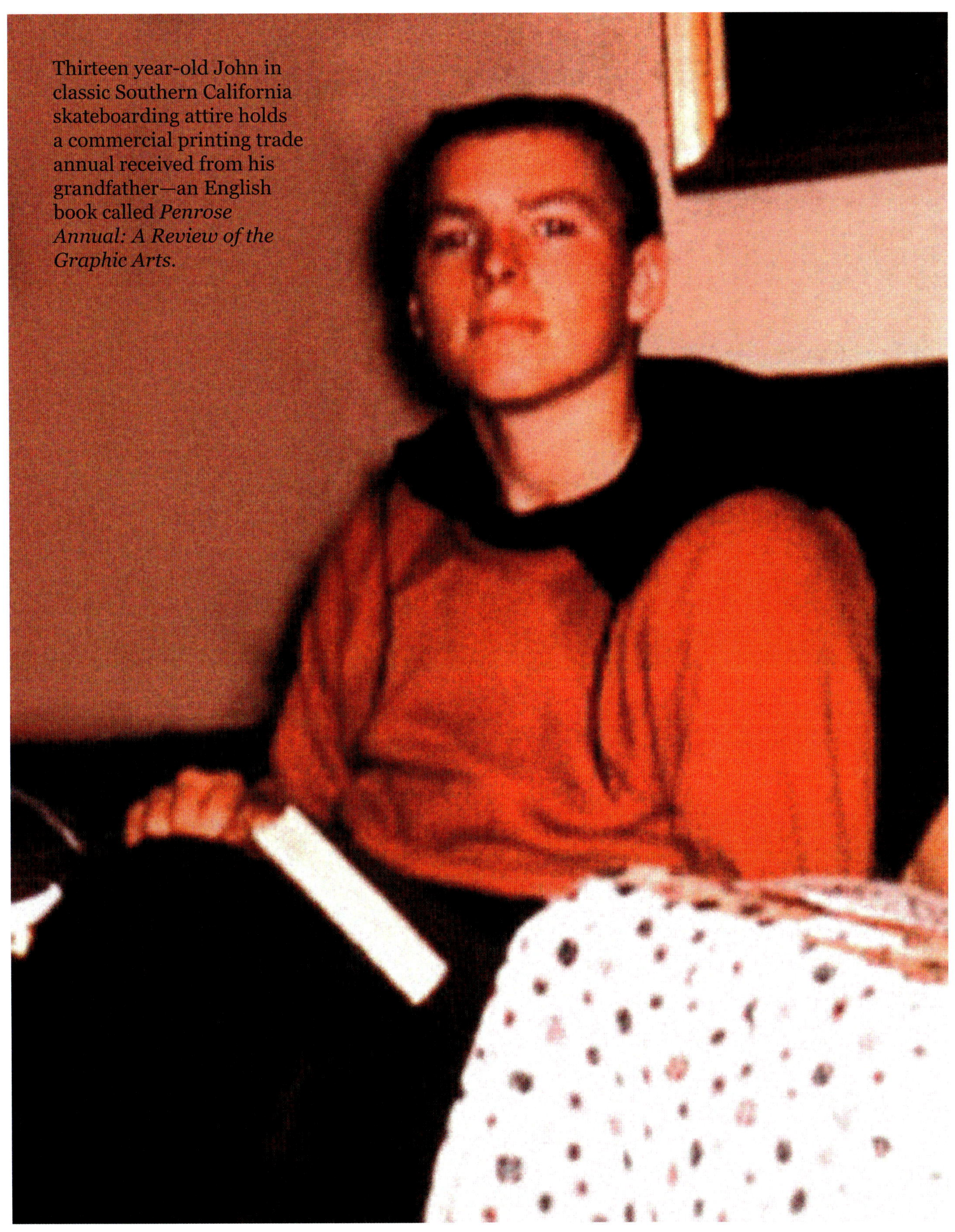

1954: CHRISTMAS, TEEN SURFER, PALOS VERDES ESTATES, CALIFORNIA

Looking for something?

304 p.

333 Pictures & Photos

50 Years of Graphic Design

T.C.

Foreword by Shepard Fairey

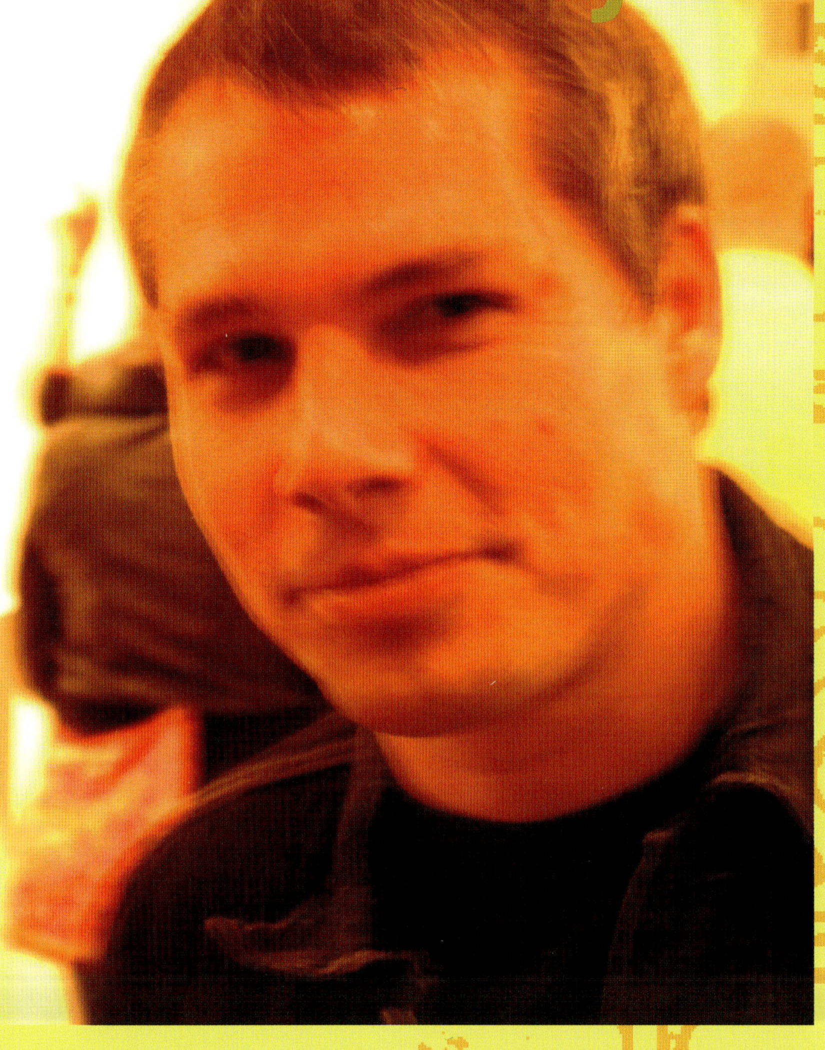

What makes a "perfect" image—one that can't be improved by rendering it differently, one that needs nothing added or subtracted?

Not only is a perfect image difficult to imagine any other way than it is, it's impossible to forget. The term "instant classic" is used far too loosely, but it does truly apply to a perfect image. Many people recognize a perfect image when they see one, even if only subconsciously. When I say "subconsciously," I mean that some people will acknowledge the power of a perfect image and it will subconsciously become the image that replaces anything similar that preceded it. For example, when I think of a banana, the image that comes to mind every time is Warhol's cover for *The Velvet Underground & Nico*. Frequently, a perfect image becomes a definition in and of itself—anyone who has seen the *Mona Lisa* will understand the term "Mona Lisa smile." There are few perfect images out there, and very few people ever make a single perfect image, much less several. John Van Hamersveld is the rare exception; he is an artist who has created several perfect images during his 50-year career.

Before discovering John Van Hamersveld's *Pinnacle Hendrix* poster, I had never thought consciously about what constituted, or how to make, a perfect image. John's iconic Hendrix poster gave me an epiphany that sharpened my focus as an artist. The Hendrix poster fit all of the aforementioned criteria: it's an illustration with the perfect balance of designed restraint and idiosyncratic, organic style. Though highly stylized, the image also conveys the essence of Jimi Hendrix himself. So much so that, like Warhol's banana, it has become the default image of Hendrix in my mind.

However, it goes beyond style. Through abstraction, the black-and-white image achieves something similar to a Rorschach inkblot test: it takes on the different interpretations projected by each viewer. I immediately saw a connection to Beethoven in John's rendering of Hendrix. I made the analogy of Hendrix's Afro to Beethoven's wig, and Hendrix's ascot to Beethoven's frilly frock. I've since seen this interpretation from other sources, and my assumption was that Hendrix was intentionally being recognized as having made a musical contribution to culture on the scale of Beethoven. When I spoke to John about the *Pinnacle Hendrix* image years later, he explained that the ascot was not inspired by Beethoven, but by Eric Clapton and Cream, who Hendrix admired for their music and fashion. However, the Beethoven comparison inspired John to illustrate a fantastic series of classical composers. Great images have the power to inspire consciously and subconsciously, creating a dialog and cycle of inspiration between artist and viewer.

The amazing thing about John Van Hamersveld is that he has not only created multiple perfect images during his career, but in multiple styles and with multiple mediums. John has created iconic images using illustration, graphic design, and photography all separately as well as using combinations of those techniques together. Though the *Pinnacle Hendrix* image was my introduction to John's art, I soon discovered that he had also created the seminal poster art for the surf movie *The Endless Summer.* The image, or one of the many mutations or derivations it has inspired, may be the most pervasive surf image ever created. Where the *Pinnacle Hendrix* image relies on illustration for its strength, *The Endless Summer* poster is pure graphic design. The poster depends upon the perfect balance of its elements—an iconic, high-contrast surf photo over a graphic horizon line and round setting sun in saturated red, yellow, and pink, with a stylish modernist movie title placed elegantly below. The sunset combined with the silhouetted abstraction of the surfers yields an image with an enduring connection to the romance of the surf lifestyle.

The *Pinnacle Hendrix* and *The Endless Summer* posters are two of John's most iconic and well-known images, but there are many more that people will know instantly but may not connect to his name. He created many well-known album covers, including the Beatles' *Magical Mystery Tour,* the Rolling Stones *Exile On Main St.,* Jefferson Airplane's *Crown of Creation,* the Grateful Dead's *Skeletons from the Closet,* Blue Cheer's *Vincebus Eruptum,* KISS's *Hotter Than Hell,* and Cream's *Royal Albert Hall.* In the world of corporate logos, John has made his mark for brands like fast-food chain Fatburger, '90s surf apparel company Gotcha, and shopping mall mainstay Contempo Casuals.

I could go on for ages about John's body of work, which would likely yield many "a-ha, I know that image!" responses, but I'll just let that unfold over the pages of this book. What I think is important to point out about John's career is that his diverse tastes and curiosity, which would seem to be virtues, may have been his Achilles heel. John has never been content sticking to one style or one arena to make his images. His forays into design, illustration, photography, painting, and signage for the worlds of clothing, surfing, music, and corporate design have left him with a body of work very difficult to package and brand. I think it would be more just if his name as an artist were known around the world, but the important thing is that his images are. John is still making beautiful work, and like the surfers from *The Endless Summer* searching for the perfect wave, John is still striving to make the perfect image.

ART SCHOOL (1961)

The Art Center instructors wore black suits as their formal wear uniform; a white shirt and thin black tie as if it were a James Bond movie of its time. George Harris was the color and design instructor who started the day for me at 9 a.m. sharp, once a week. There was a special flat sable hair brush with water-color paper for Winsor & Newton Designers' Gouache—a water-based, personal white tray you had to carry to class to mix your colors in. You had to have a tool box with all your supplies ready to go. There was a very small student store that had the scheduled list of the equipment needed to complete your project. Only problem was you had to be in the classroom to do the work, or else you were suspended. Three days of absence and you were out of the school. The Art Center simulated real life—without procrastination. It was all about discipline throughout a day and night schedule, with minimal sleep.

Introduction to the Rules:

SURVIVING ART SCHOOL
LEARNING ABOUT MEDIA
CREATING IDEAS
BEING AWARE
PUSHING PROMOTION
CREATING SALES
TRAVELING TO PLACES
BEING INSYNC WITH FANS
BRANDING THE LOOK
KNOWING YOUR CUSTOMER
THE EXPERIENCE

BY NIGHT

Coolhous Studio

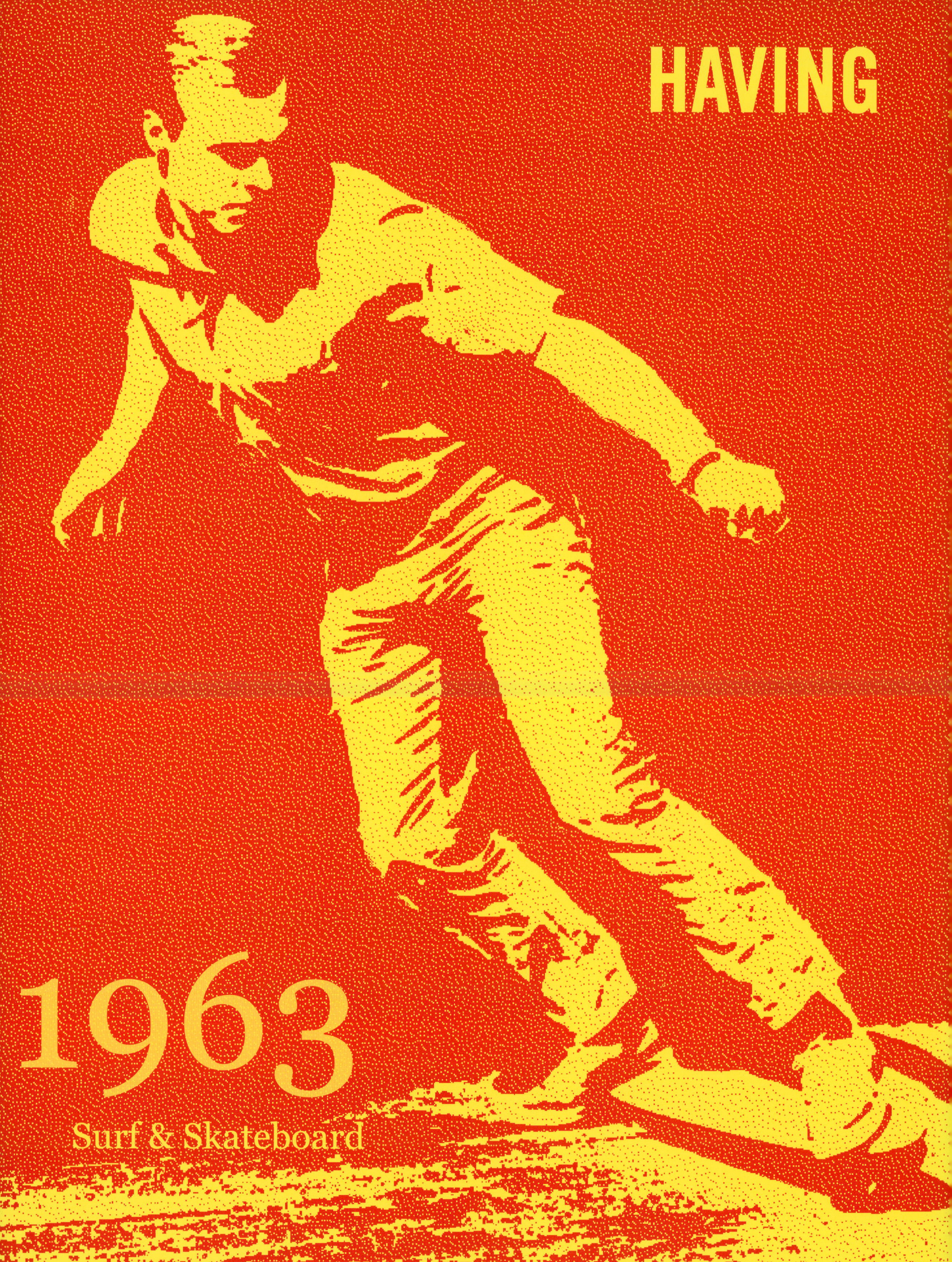
HAVING
1963
Surf & Skateboard

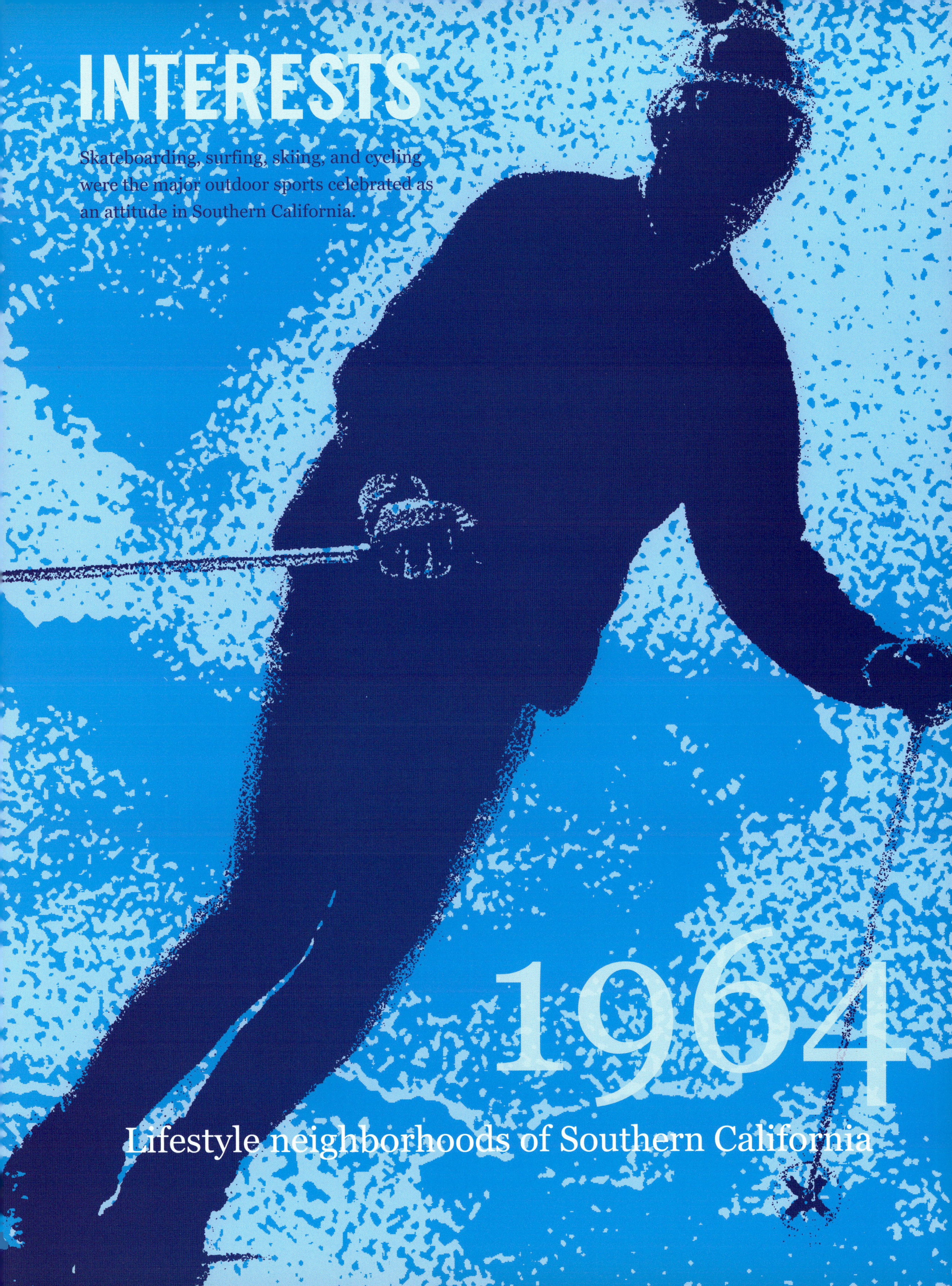
INTERESTS
Skateboarding, surfing, skiing, and cycling were the major outdoor sports celebrated as an attitude in Southern California.
1964
Lifestyle neighborhoods of Southern California

Beginnings at *Surfer* Magazine in 1962

"I was a surfer transitioning into a young graphic designer. Between getting a job at *Surfer magazine* and attending the Art Center College of Design, I created the *Endless Summer* poster on my kitchen table. Little did I know that I was creating an international cultural icon, while living and working in the small surf community of Dana Point, California.

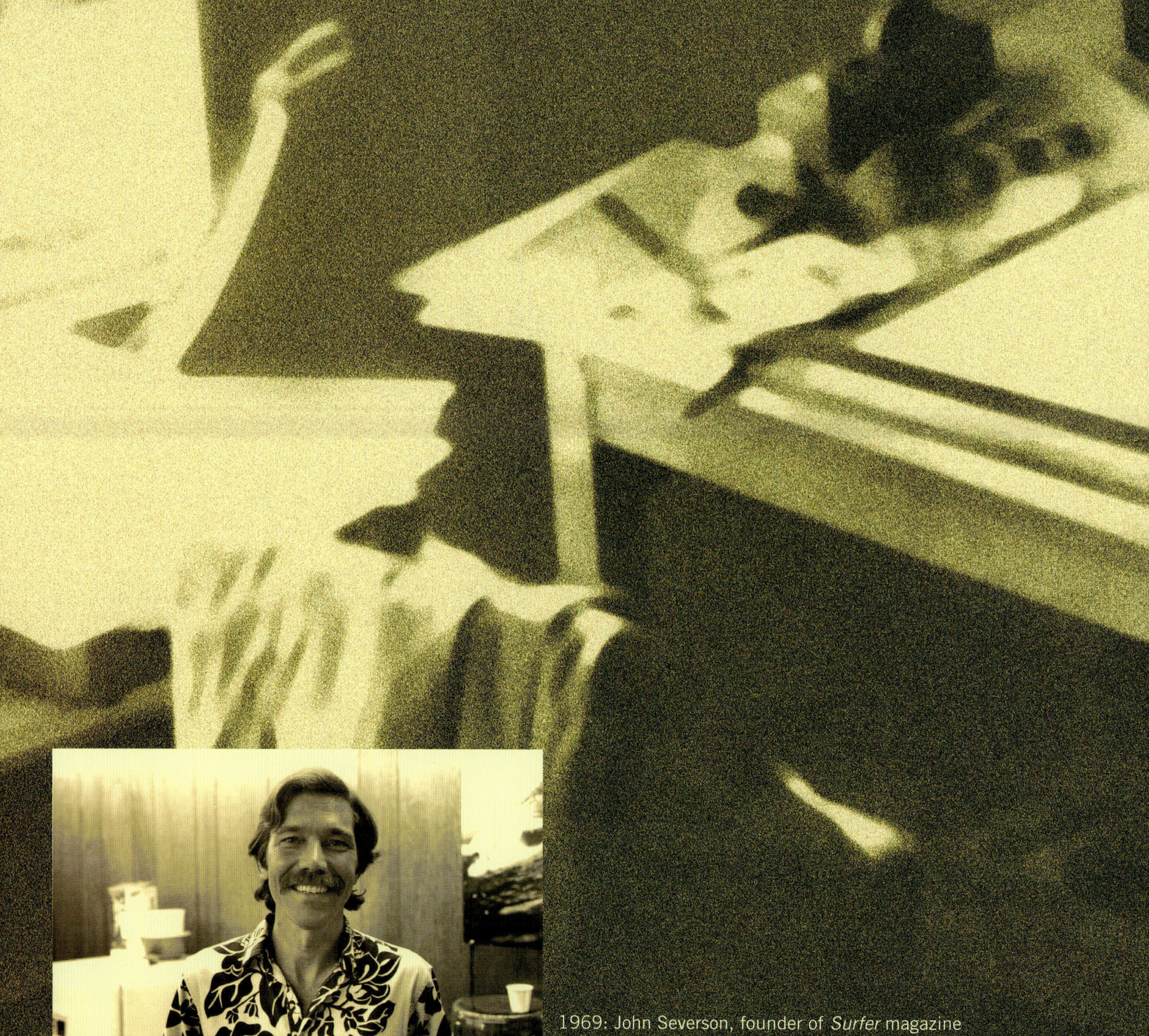

1969: John Severson, founder of *Surfer* magazine photographed in San Juan Capistrano, CA

SURFER

Between Art School and Industry

As I was finishing my first year at Art Center in 1962, my friendship as a surfer with Bing Copeland began to develop. We agreed in February that I would design a poster for him to distribute in the South Bay. This was my first poster design for the surf industry. The poster was made into an ad that was on the back cover of *Surfing Illustrated*, published in June of that same year. The image is now 50 years old. The next year, I designed the *Endless Summer* poster in a night class at the Art Center College of Design. This poster grew out of my relationship with Rick Griffin and our mutual admiration of surf imagery. I believe I would never have met Bruce Brown if Rick Griffin hadn't called John Severson in Dana Point on my behalf. Nor would I have had the chance to develop my graphic design career in New York, beginning in 1966, as Personality Poster distributed *The Endless Summer* around the world through the end of the decade.

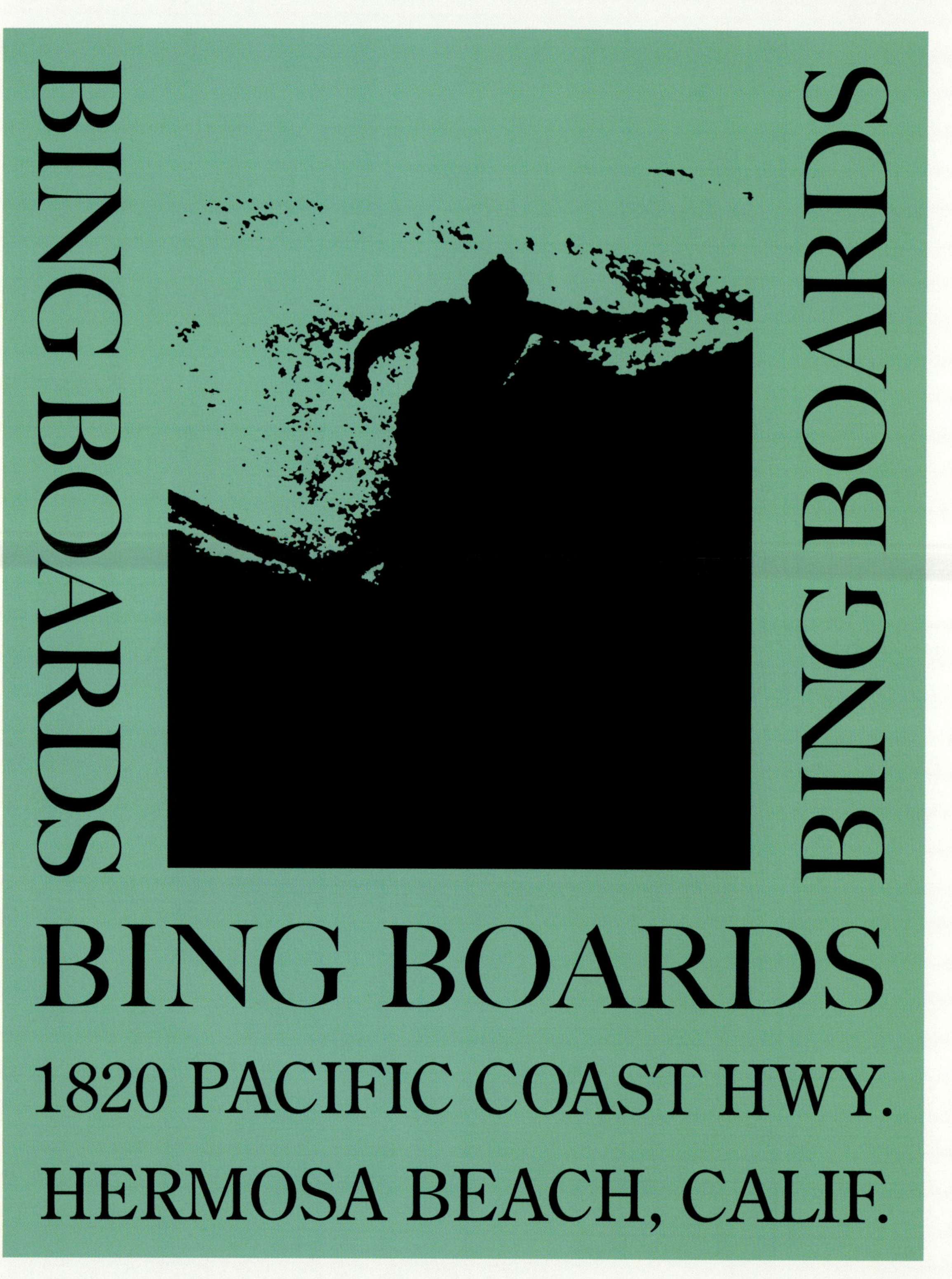

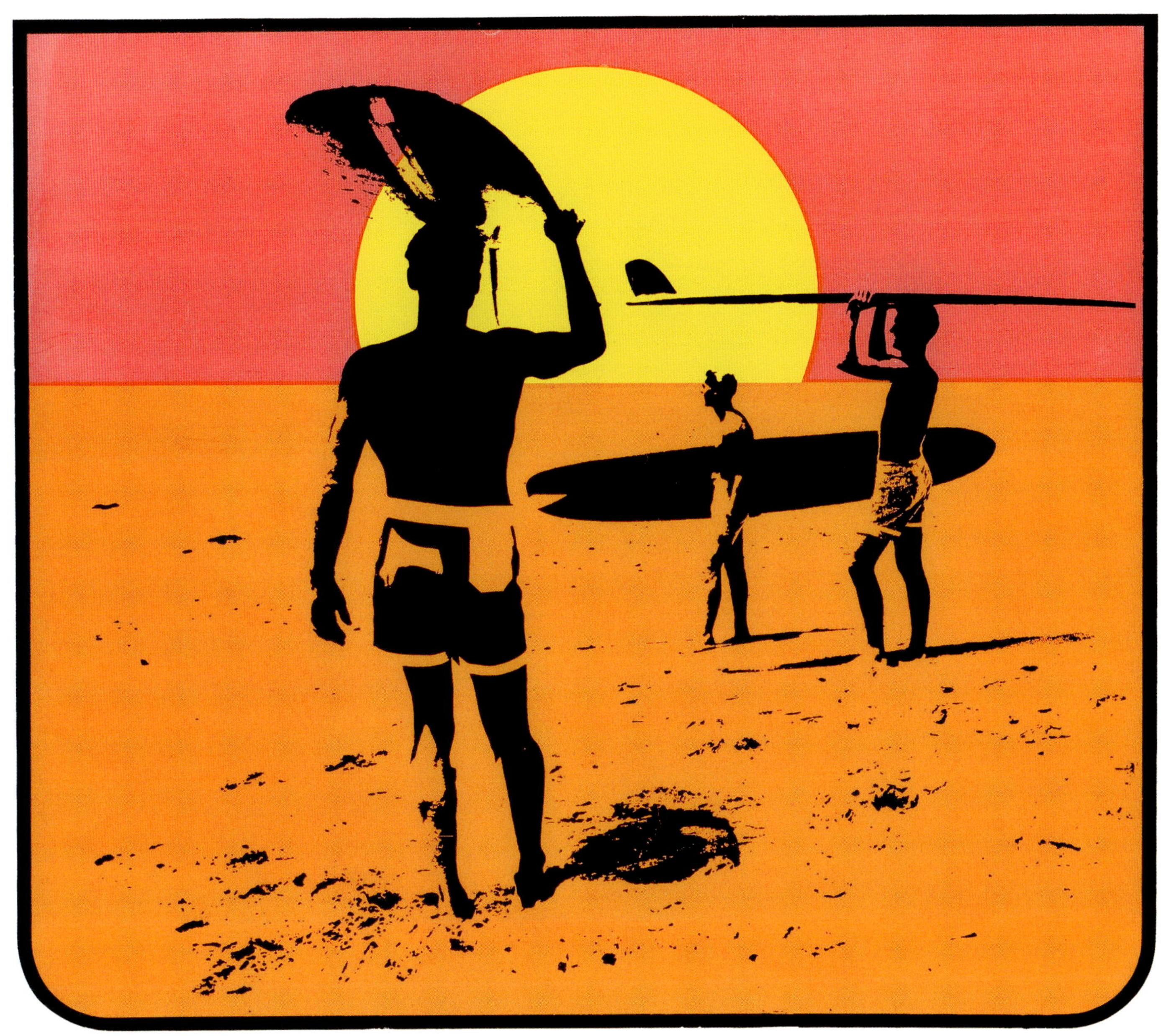

The Endless Summer

On any day of the year it's summer somewhere in the world. Bruce Brown's latest color film highlights the adventures of two young American surfers, Robert August and Mike Hynson who follow this everlasting summer around the world. Their unique expedition takes them to Senegal, Ghana, Nigeria, South Africa, Australia, New Zealand, Tahiti, Hawaii and California. Share their experiences as they search the world for that perfect wave which may be forming just over the next Horizon.

BRUCE BROWN FILMS

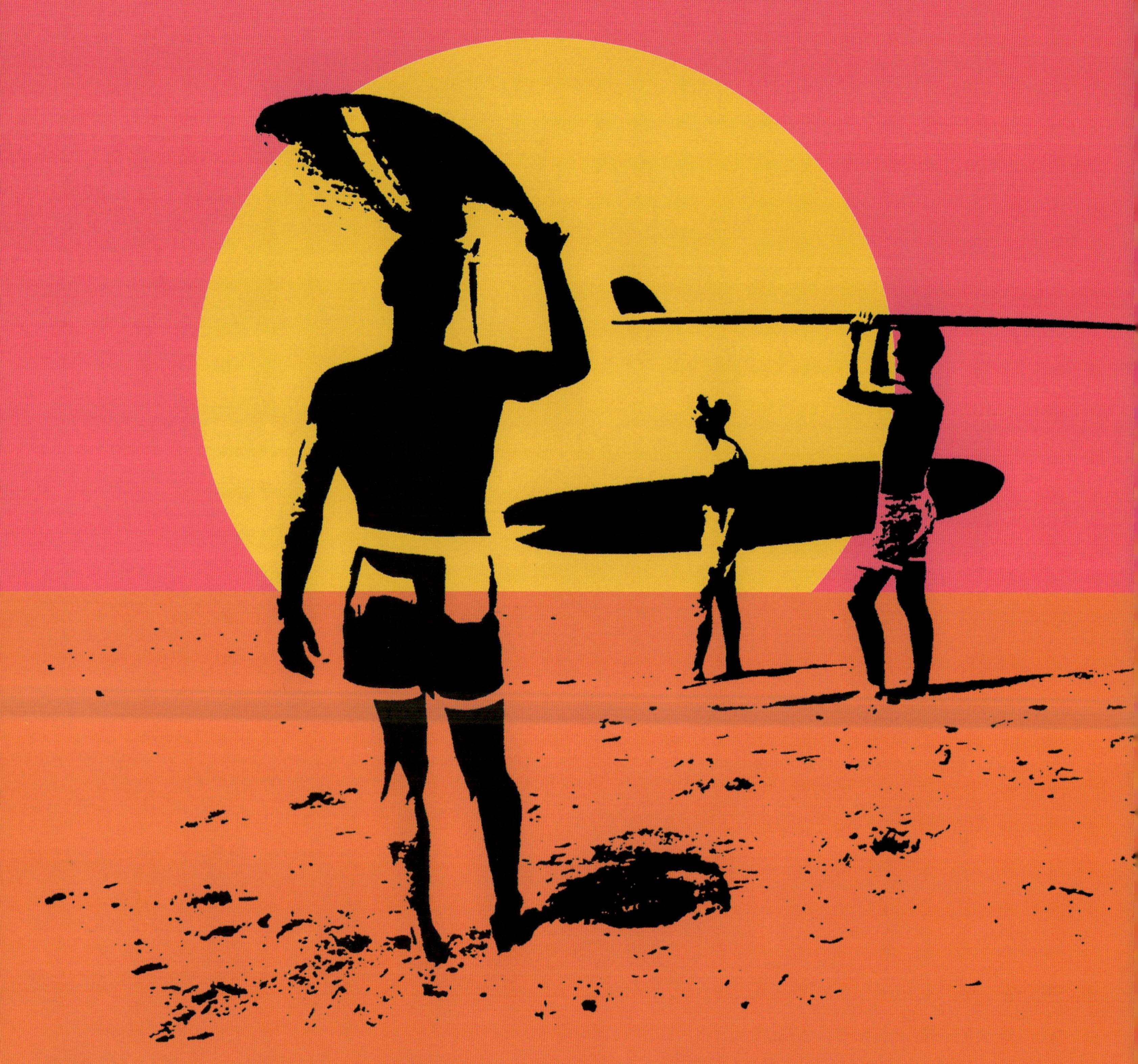

The Endless Summer

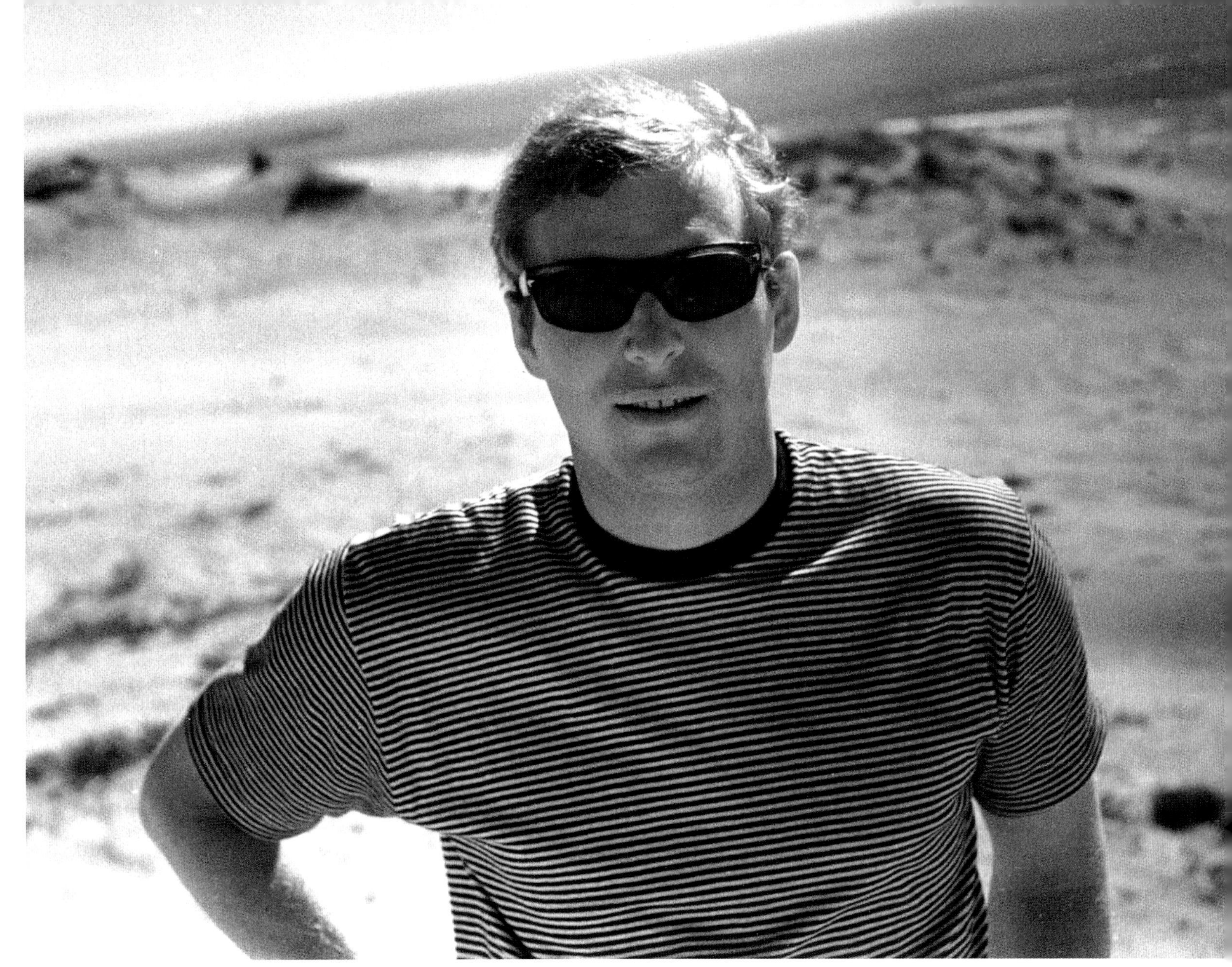

Surf Media Business (1966)

In New York City, it was blown-up into a one-sheet theater poster for the film's national distributor in 1966. The famous DayGlo poster was distributed throughout college campuses and headshops and became a national hit as a poster product.

"I WANT TO HOLD YOUR HAND."

My boss at the time was Brown Meggs, whom hired me to be the personal art director of the Capitol Records Distribution Company (CRDC) in March of 1967.

Los Angeles Times Archival for Friday, October 17, 1997:

Brown Meggs, the onetime chief executive of Capitol Records who signed the Beatles to their first American recording contract and who pioneered classical recordings at reduced prices, has died.

Meggs worked for Capitol Records, a subsidiary of EMI records, in the 1960s and early 1970s. Although he signed the most popular rock group of its time to a lucrative contract, he personally preferred classical music and opera.

His biggest professional accomplishment may have come in 1963, when he lured the Beatles to his label for American distribution. After Capitol rejected the group's first four singles, Beatles manager Brian Epstein persuaded Meggs, then the company's director of East Coast operations, to sign them by playing him an advance copy of "I Want to Hold Your Hand."

One of his major contributions to the industry was considered the establishment of Seraphim records, a budget line for Capitol's classical label, Angel...

—Burt Artfolk, Times Staff Writer

There's a fog upon L.A.
And my friends have lost their way
"We'll be over soon" they said
Now they've lost themselves instead.

—Lyrics from *Blue Jay Way*

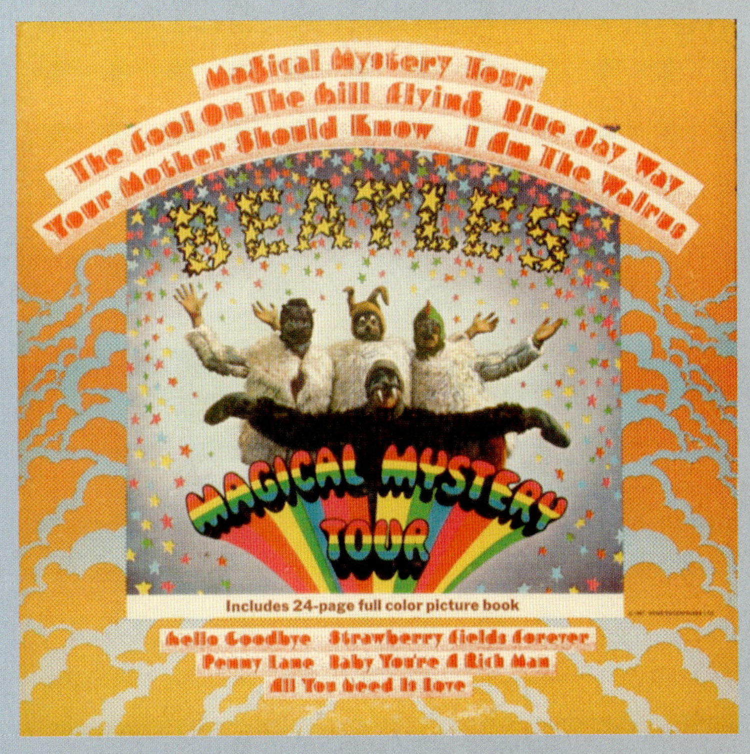

Brian Epstein, manager for the Beatles, died on the 27th of August, 1967. Around the time of his death, Brown Meggs sent me home to design the front cover of the *Magical Mystery Tour* album cover.

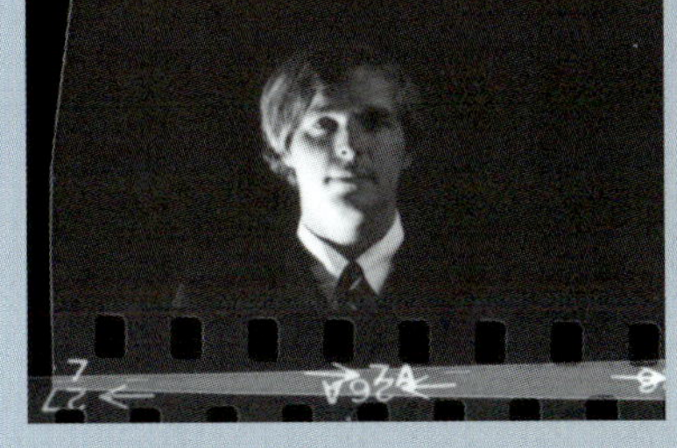

Eight hours at the Capitol office; eight hours at the Coronado Studio. Working in the pop culture dichotomy of its day, I lived two different lives.

1967

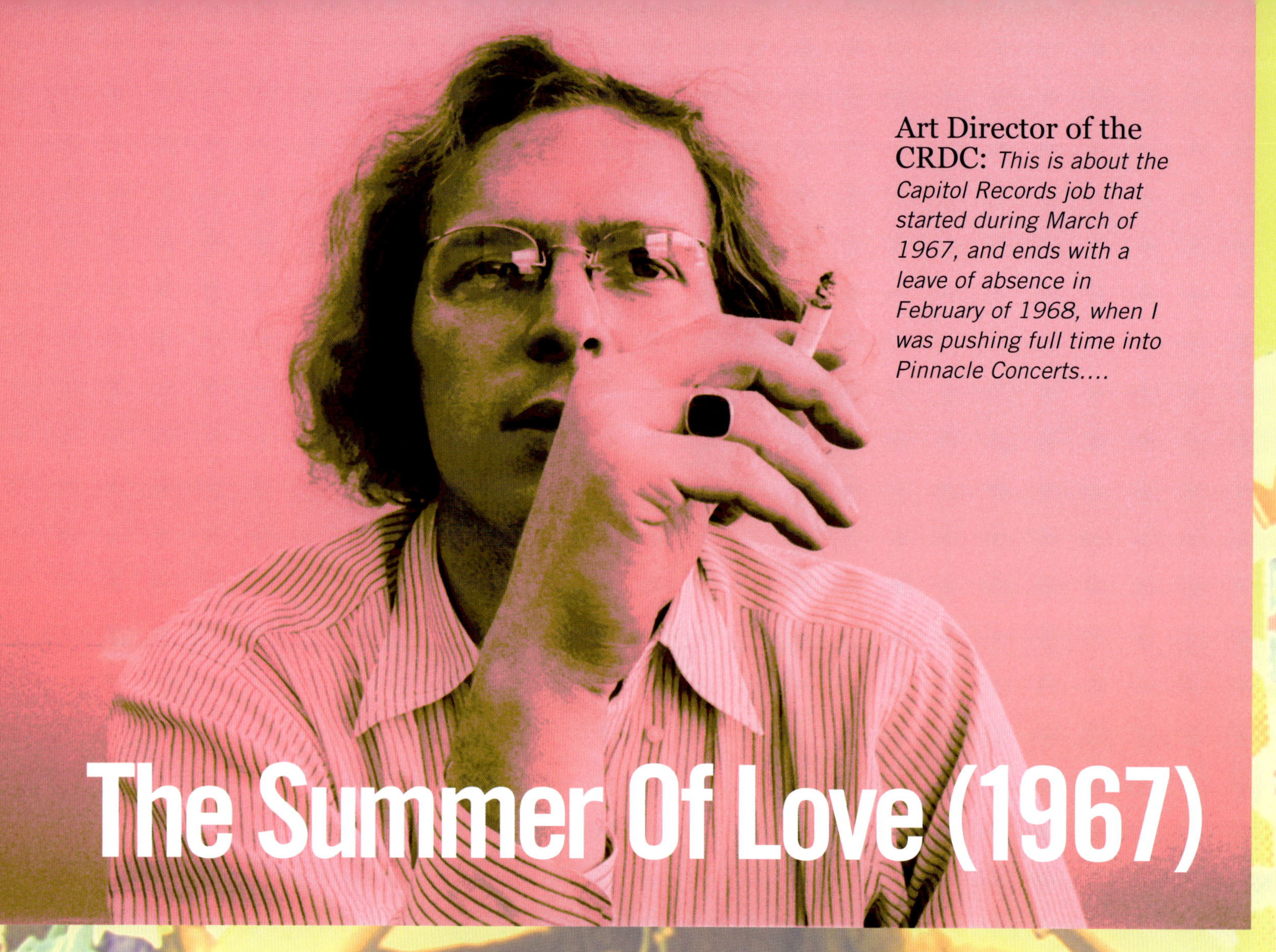

Art Director of the CRDC: *This is about the Capitol Records job that started during March of 1967, and ends with a leave of absence in February of 1968, when I was pushing full time into Pinnacle Concerts....*

The Summer Of Love (1967)

I met with Brown Meggs, vice president of Capitol Records, at his office on the eighth floor of the Capitol Records Building, just up from the corner of Hollywood Boulevard and Vine Street. He insisted that I take the job he was offering me, and he promised to pay me well. After I agreed, the job started right away. I got an office next to the creative services director, George Osaki. I went to DeVos, a clothing shop on Sunset Plaza, and purchased an Italian Baroni suit with boots, shirts, and ties. I wanted to be a hip, rock-star art director, as if I were an actual member of the Beatles or the Rolling Stones.

Then came the Beatles' *Magical Mystery Tour* album cover project in 1967.

First Project: Promotional Advertising for the Beatles' *Sgt. Pepper's Lonely Hearts Club Band:*

Brown Meggs gave me the job to create displays and advertising using the album package elements provided by EMI. The *Sgt. Pepper's* album is often referred to as the Beatles' *Mona Lisa*; being considered one of the most influential albums in existence by critics and publications worldwide. In 2003, *Sgt. Pepper's* was ranked by *Rolling Stone* magazine as "the greatest rock album of all time."

Around the same time, Brown Meggs sent me home to my Coronado studio from the Capitol Records office to explore a solution for the American release of the *Magical Mystery Tour*. Meggs handed a package to me and said, "Please make this work," and continued to talk about how disappointed they were with the cover photo without the Beatles' faces on the cover. Up until then, they had always marketed the product with photos of the members of the Beatles to showcase their personalities. I returned the next day with a solution that went directly to the printing manufacturer for distribution.

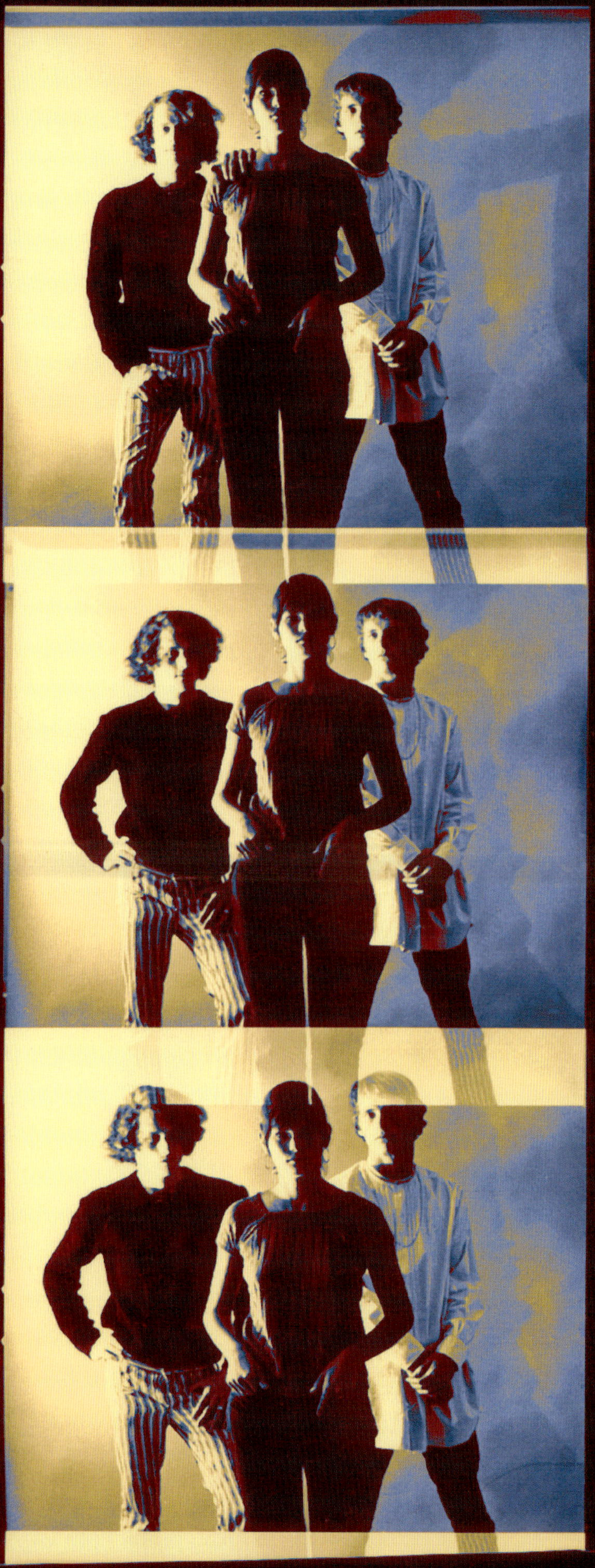

Pursuing My Photographs

Occasionally my friends would come as couples to the studio to pose for nude portraits. They came up the stairs to my apartment and into the front room where I had created a photo studio; it was empty, except for rounds of seamless backdrop paper. The couples had to go by the landlord's windows first, having parked in front of the building. The landlord peeping out his veiled windows in amazement, darting quickly from one window to another as they passed by. He would see the trendy models pass by with their boyfriends, the couple seeking to immortalize their vanity.

Photos of the Pinnacle Creative Community

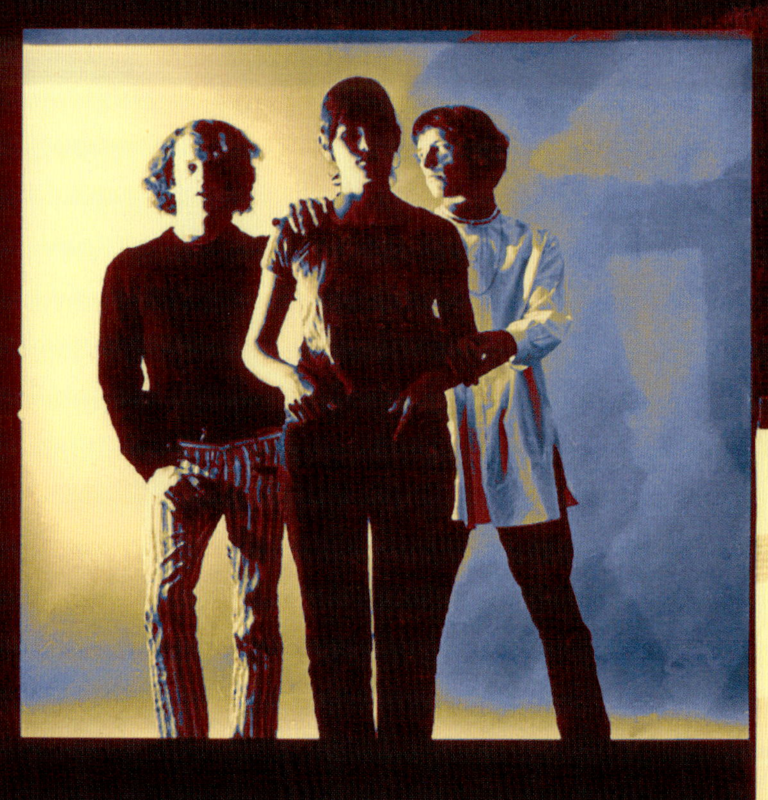

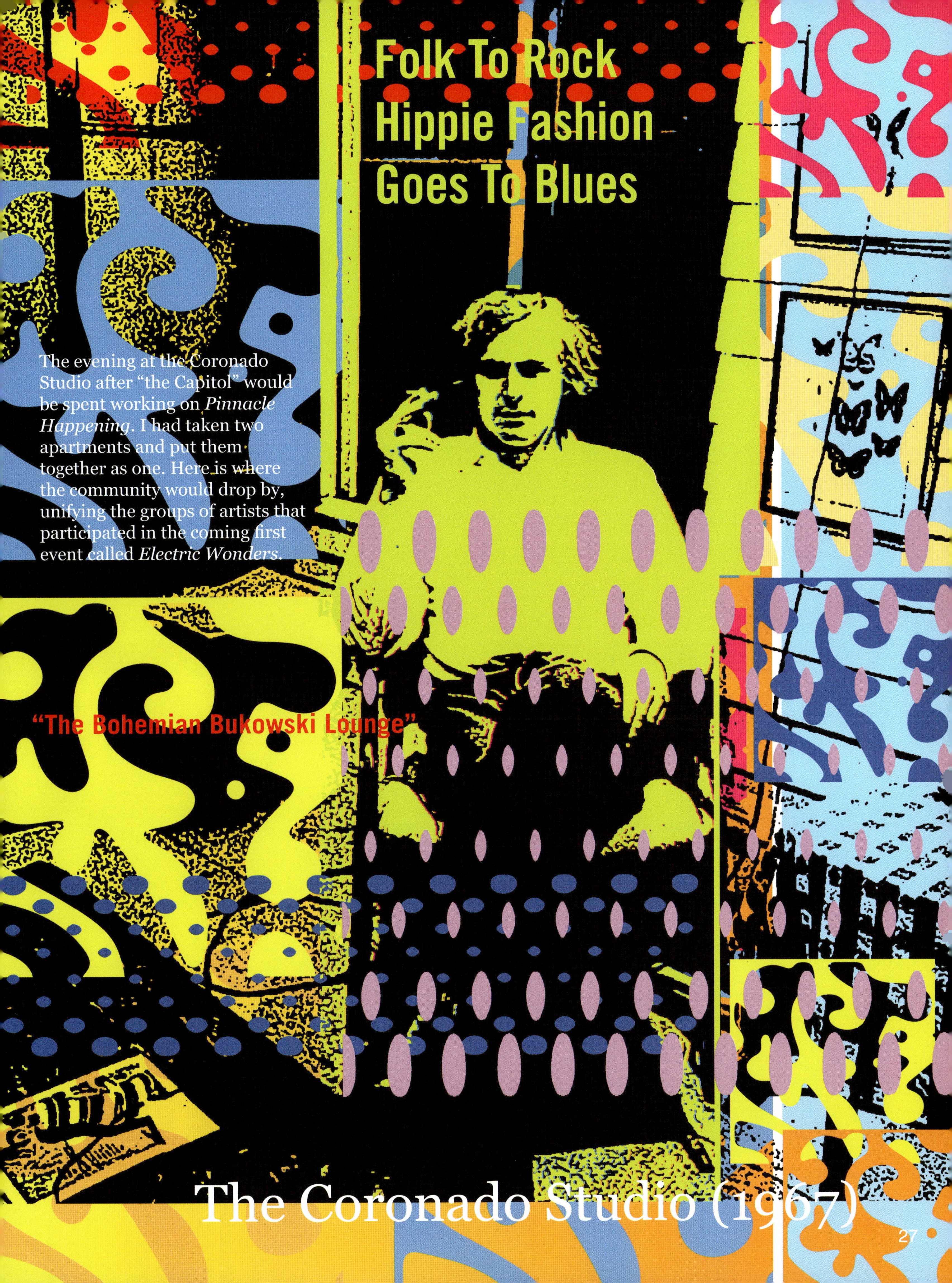

Folk To Rock Hippie Fashion Goes To Blues

The evening at the Coronado Studio after "the Capitol" would be spent working on *Pinnacle Happening*. I had taken two apartments and put them together as one. Here is where the community would drop by, unifying the groups of artists that participated in the coming first event called *Electric Wonders*.

"The Bohemian Bukowski Lounge"

The Coronado Studio (1967)

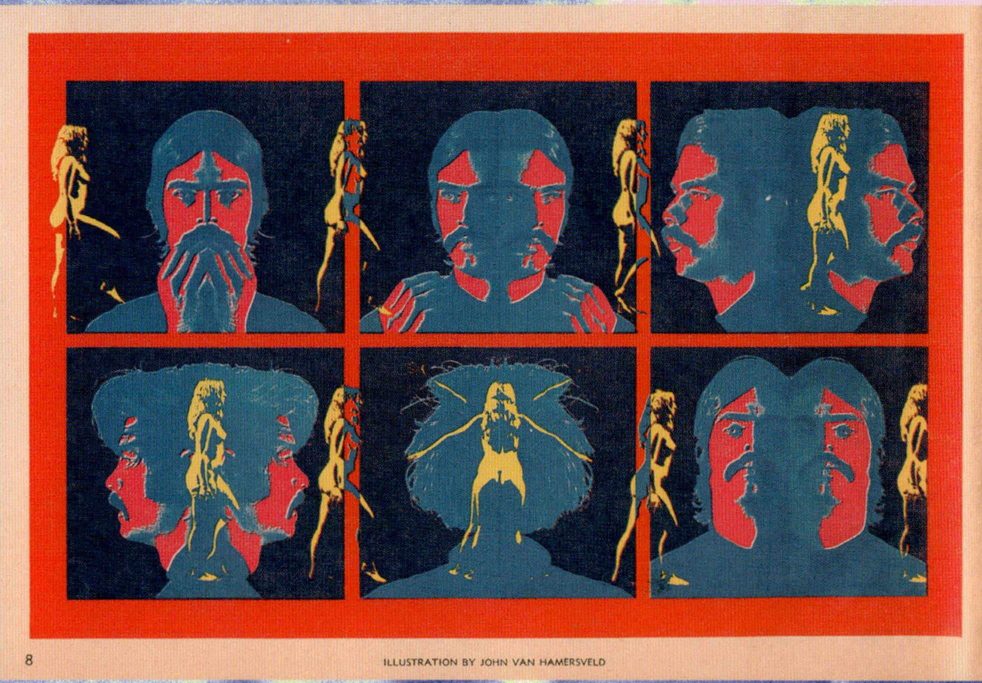

Pinnacle: The Art of Getting Higher

The above is a construction of photographs as an illustration for *The LA Times West* magazine, for the art director Mike Salisbury. The pictures are of my roomate Caleb Deschanel and my model friend Stevie portraying the use of LSD. These kind of jobs would be done at the Coronado Studio during the Pinnacle operation.

I was producing a lightshow section for Pinnacle with the creative community in the city to ensure the show would work with the audiences in order to create ideas and the uses of elements in artistic energy. The "music and the environment" helped create the "Happening" as a fashion dressed for the evenings.

Amongst the large team of people that assisted in this project were Burton Gershfield and Pat Oneil, an instructor at the UCLA Film School, who came around the studio one day with his experimental student film footage called *Now That the Buffalo's Gone*. Another part in carrying the first visuals after Electric Wonders were the Whitney Brothers; with Caleb Deschanel and artist Barry La Va, we formed the lightshow called *White Lightening*. We later added David Lebron and the Hog Farm, whom were friends with Hugh Romney. George Lucas and Charles Lipponcott, both USC film students, were also included. This introduced the visual arts budget, as well as the vivid lightshows. I designed the advertising and promotional information so the "Happenings" were both artistic and of value for coming to the events beyond their experience within the Pinnacle environment.

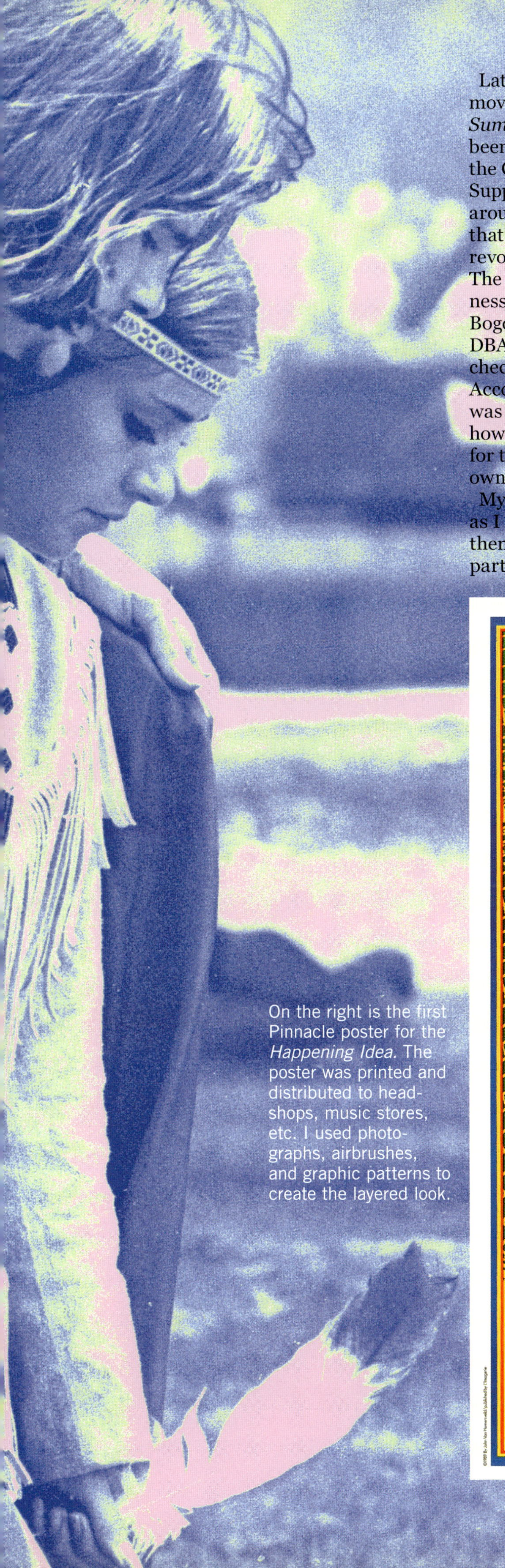

Late in the Summer of August 1967, after the Love-Ins in Griffith Park, I moved onto other projects. I settled into the first poster (after the *Endless Summer* hit big in New York City), and the Pinnacle campaign was to have been my next work. At the time, my commercial work would be formed at the Coronado Studio near 6th Street; across the street from Daniel's Art Supplies and a block behind of Otis Art Institute. I formed the group of us around my idea for a grant I had to pitch to Chouinard Art School. The idea that day was that we were going to be a part of the production business that revolved around my "Happening Idea" from Chouinard and San Francisco. The business would be named *PINNACLE* (which I had named). The business types we met with were Gary Perkins, who was representing Bob Bogdonavich and his StarKist Tuna family credit and assets. The California DBA had to be filed before starting the business partnership, and the checking acccount would have to be arranged for the funding of Pinnacle. Accompanying me was Honeya, my girlfriend; my friend Marc Chase, who was representing his mother's investment; and business student Sepp Donahower, who had some influence and connection to investor friends from USC for the Pinnacle Project. We all had to sign a business document, declare ownership, and then have things ready in order to be filed with the state.

My studio became the office for Sepp and Marc to work at during the time, as I had originated the name of the business to start the company. I was then the partner and creator of the visual image for Pinnacle, as was my part of the business relationship.

On the right is the first Pinnacle poster for the *Happening Idea.* The poster was printed and distributed to headshops, music stores, etc. I used photographs, airbrushes, and graphic patterns to create the layered look.

“Little did I know, this house would be an art scene heaven for meetings amongst late modernists, and a significant place in the city for LA’s modern movement.”

As I was standing there on the third floor of the new Kingsley Studio in 1968, I heard the ghosts discuss Jules’ curation of a nonfigurative painting group exhibit at the Los Angeles County Museum of Art.

Photo: Self-Portrait at the Kingsley Studio (February 1968)

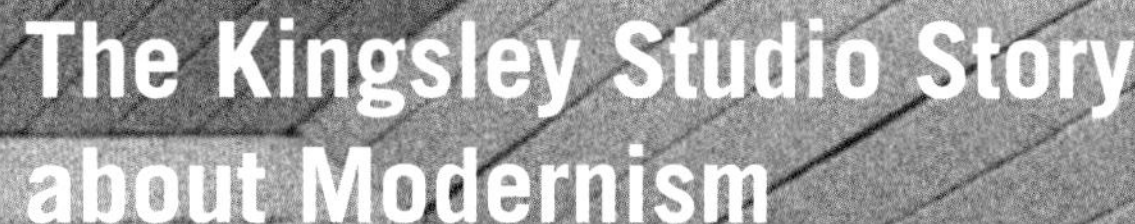

The Kingsley Studio Story about Modernism

Jules Langsner—a writer, curator, and Los Angeles Times art critic—had coined the term "hard-edge painting" with Peter Selz in 1959. This term describes the work of painters from California who, in reacting to the gestural forms of Abstract Expressionism, adopted a knowingly impersonal paint application with delineated areas of color using a particular sharpness and clarity. This approach to abstract painting became widespread in the 1960s, with California as the creative center.

On one nice February day, I spotted a "FOR RENT" sign while searching for a new studio. Stepping out of my car with my checkbook in hand, I noticed in the corner of my eye another person competitively following me towards the studio. As I got to the studio, I saw a woman sitting on the porch; she was the widow of Jules Langsner. I walked up the steps of the three story clap-board gray cottage, filled out the forms, and presented my check. Through a stroke of luck, she caught up to me and let the other person know that the building had been rented out. Little did I know, this house would be an art scene heaven for meetings amongst late modernists, and a significant place in the city for LA's modern movement.

Many people would be surprised to discover that the *Endless Summer* poster is a later modern image of twentieth century culture. The geometric forms have a modernist quality, but it is the color that pushes the image forward into the '60s.

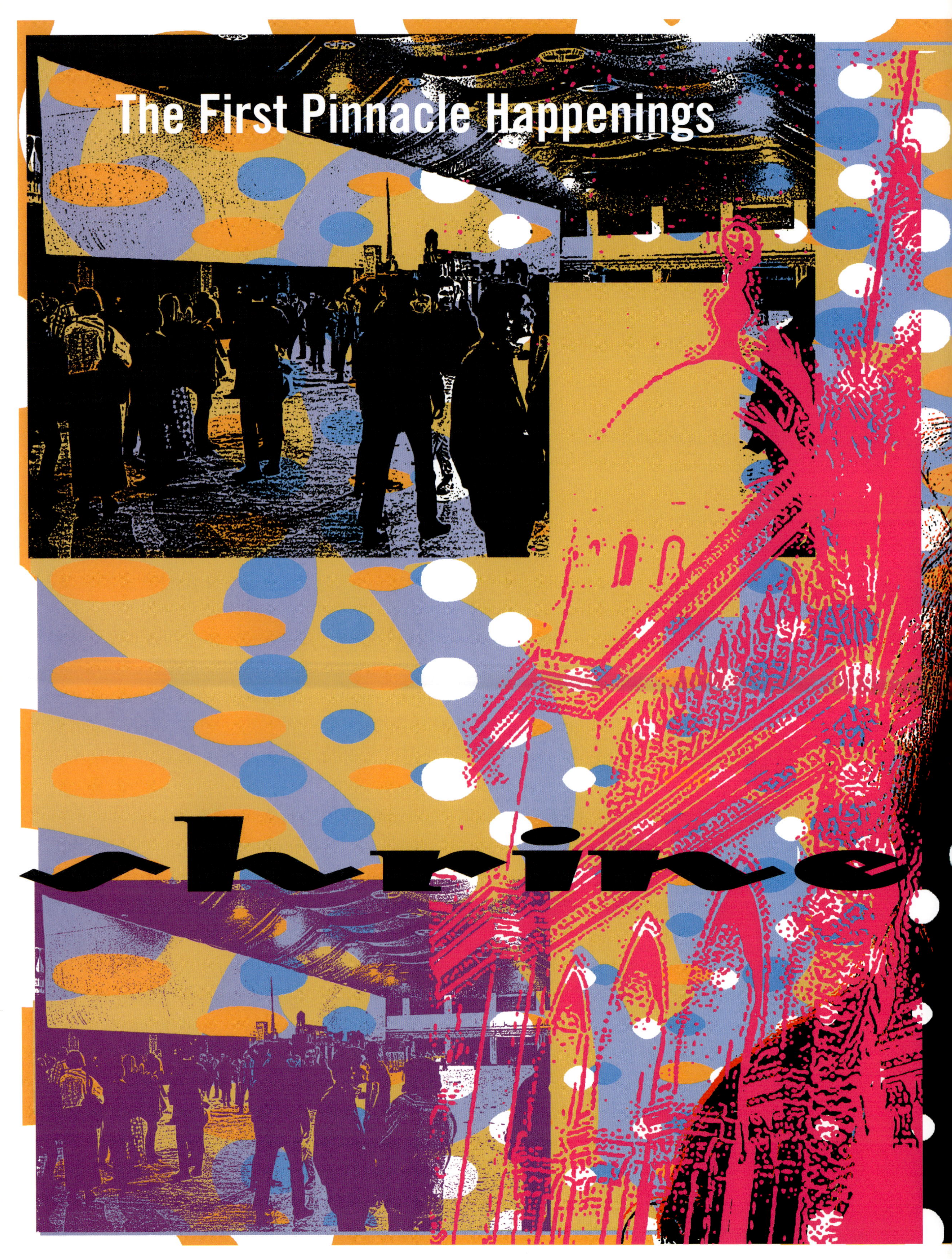
The First Pinnacle Happenings
shrine

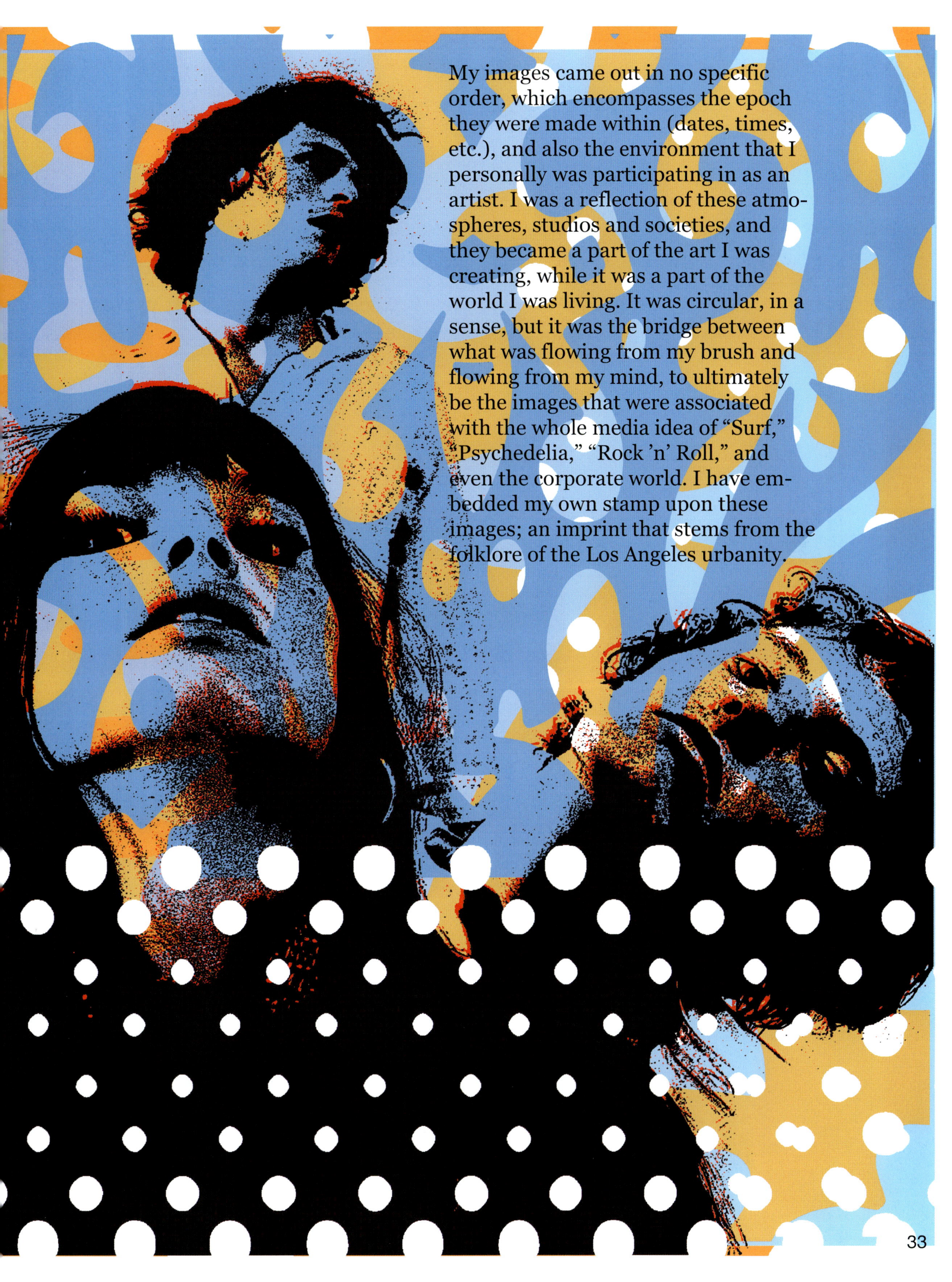

My images came out in no specific order, which encompasses the epoch they were made within (dates, times, etc.), and also the environment that I personally was participating in as an artist. I was a reflection of these atmospheres, studios and societies, and they became a part of the art I was creating, while it was a part of the world I was living. It was circular, in a sense, but it was the bridge between what was flowing from my brush and flowing from my mind, to ultimately be the images that were associated with the whole media idea of "Surf," "Psychedelia," "Rock 'n' Roll," and even the corporate world. I have embedded my own stamp upon these images; an imprint that stems from the folklore of the Los Angeles urbanity.

Pinnacle Culture

On January of 1967, the Human Be-In at San Francisco's speedway in Golden Gate Park placed hippie culture at the forefront of the press, making way for the legendary Summer of Love on the West Coast. The press described "Hippies" as people who created their own communities within Haight/Ashbury, enjoyed psychedelic rock, welcomed sexual revolutions, and partook in recreational drugs such as marijuana and lysergic acid diethylamide (LSD) to explore an alternative plane of existence.

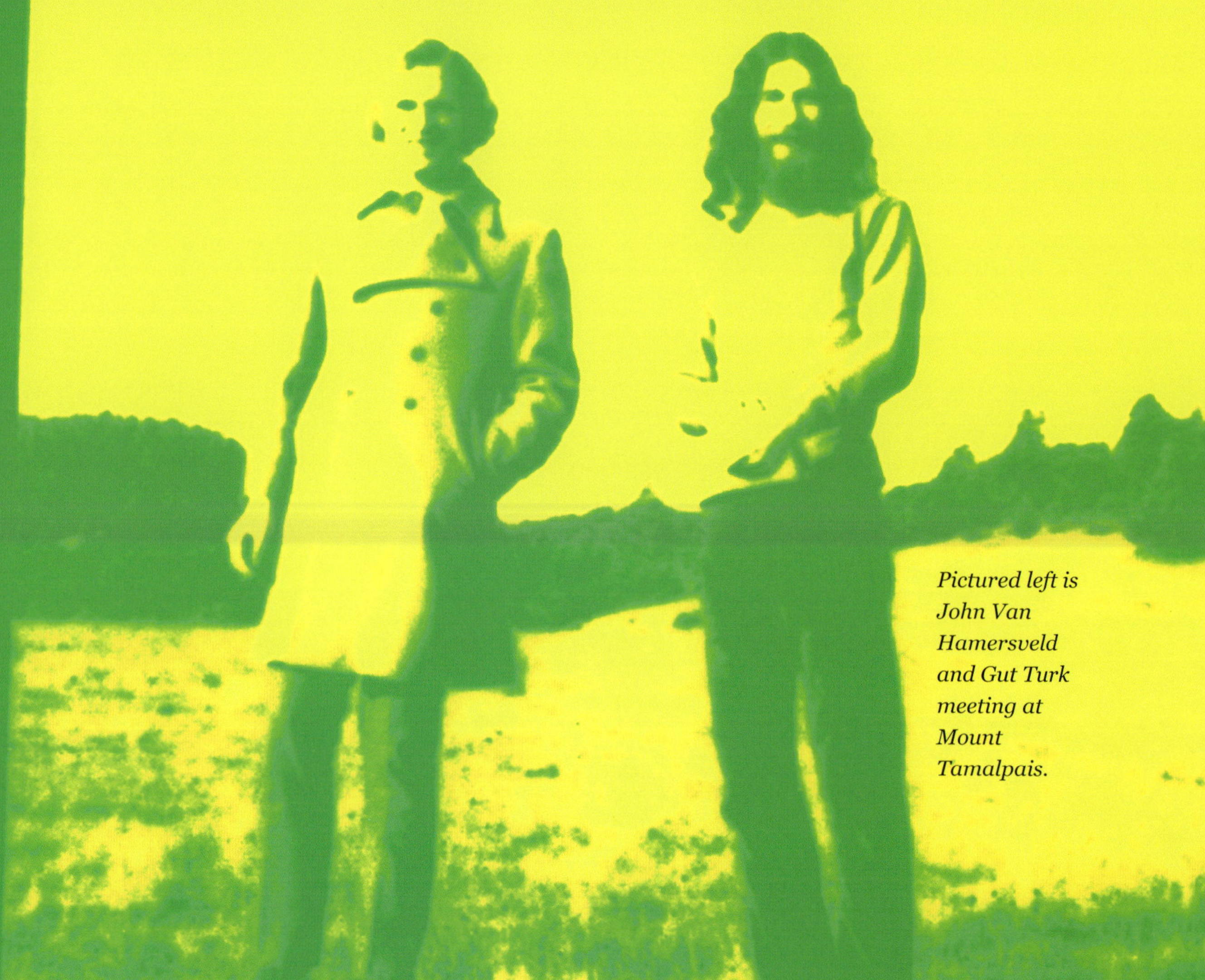

Pictured left is John Van Hamersveld and Gut Turk meeting at Mount Tamalpais.

I was in art school experiencing the rise of "Hippie Fashion," whose values had a major effect on culture, influencing popular music, television, film, literature, and the arts. Monterey Pop had organized the music of a new generation. The religious and cultural diversity espoused by the hippies had gained widespread acceptance, and Eastern philosophy and spiritual concepts reached a wide audience. Since the 1960s, many aspects of hippie culture were assimilated into mainstream society.

POSITION OF THE ESTABLISHMENT AND THE UNDERGROUND

Finding the Pinnacle Culture, 1967-1968:

My art school friends were involved in poetry and politics. They were reserved characters focused on the arts and were intensely creative, politically trying to position their ideas in galleries, museums, or happenings on the street or alternative sites. Within the art scene around the world grew a buzz with the underground idea; a sort of secondary society that wanted to have its own culture. The blur of subcultures were created like a postmodern idea where the fragmented factions of the population would assemble in amazement over issues like free love, free drugs, rock events, or even political issues. From those moments came the newly upward movement of hipsters, known as "Hippies."

Between the world of Bruce Brown (*The Endless Summer* success) and Brown Meggs (The Beatles) were the Establishment and the Coronado Studio. Both were positioned in the underground. There, inside of that downtown underground, came the event planned for the Shrine Exposition that would hold around 2,400 to 3,000 people in the building. We created a media campaign to sell tickets; security would charge $3.50 to attend. The first show attracted some people, but it took three to four events to get the people to show up and get the rock groups to play. As the gathering filled the hall, and people looked at each other, we attained critical mass.

Meanwhile, Brown Meggs was looking over my shoulder from weekend to weekend and couldn't believe I had to take a leave of absence from my work. The Underground had created a job for me to do promotional work at the studio. The Establishment had to wait, for I had created an idea that soon became the Pinnacle Culture. I entered into a new world with Gut as my guide.

Turk was from the San Francisco Underground. When we were introduced, he came with a résumé of being the ex-president of the San Bernardino Chapter for the Hell's Angels, and had been imprisoned for stealing cars. He became one of the managers for the band Blue Cheer, and as a friend of Rick Griffin, the subculture appeared before me.

PINNACLE SHOW AT THE SHRINE EXPOSITION HALL (1967)

Eric Albronda: *"Hi! At the time of the Pinnacle Concerts, my job was being the road manager and producer for Blue Cheer. The job description lines were so vague that I was really called upon to do whatever it took to make sure Blue Cheer appeared to be a responsible and reliable organization—and to ride herd over a great fun loving group of people. My first memory of anyone connected to Pinnacle was Sepp and Marc who came to the Eureka Street apartment in San Francisco. Their intention was to have us agree to play a concert of theirs at the Shrine Auditorium in Los Angeles. Blue Cheer at the time was an unsigned band, however we worked hard enough to capture a following before my record came out. Because of our popularity and because the new FM radio format would be playing unsigned bands, we were on the air in San Francisco and Los Angeles a whole lot. Maybe it was because Blue Cheer played loud crazy Rock and Roll, or maybe because John, Sepp, and Marc liked them so much we decided to give it a shot and OK the gig. I was also the booking agent for the band at the time. I was even the stand-by drummer should Paul Whaley turn up missing, or some other catastrophe (I held many different jobs in the band). Sepp showed up a few weeks later with a flat bed truck for loading Marshalls; it looked as if the hay had just been swept off, and the mud mixed in with who knows what just stuck to the hub caps. Now I knew I liked these guys at Pinnacle who appeared to be just like us—a real fun loving adventuresome bunch."*

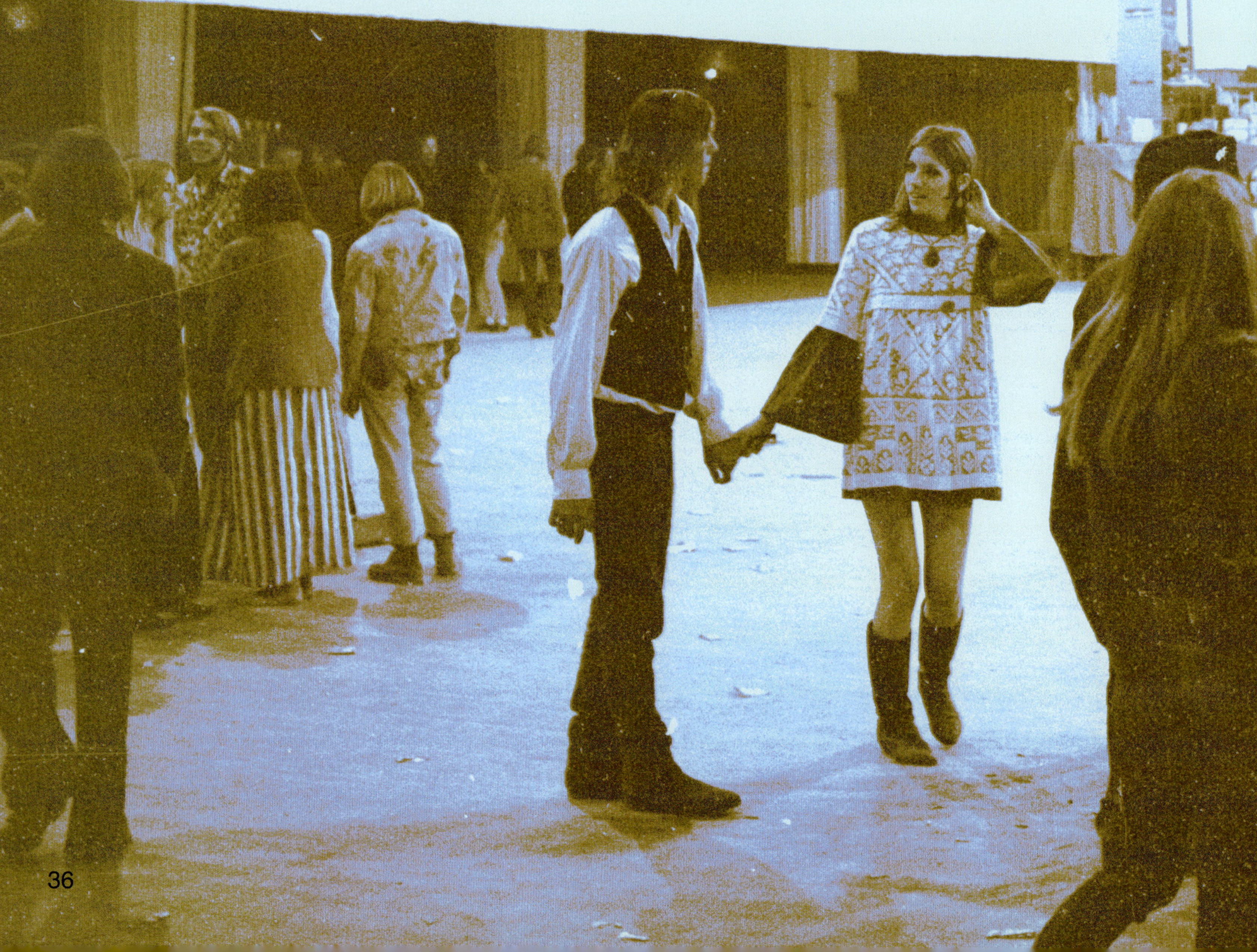

"Blue Cheer defined their onstage image as aviation mechanics working on a sound machine, being projected as the sound of jet engines taking off at the airport. Gut, one of the Blue Cheer managers, said they 'turned the air to cottage cheese.'"

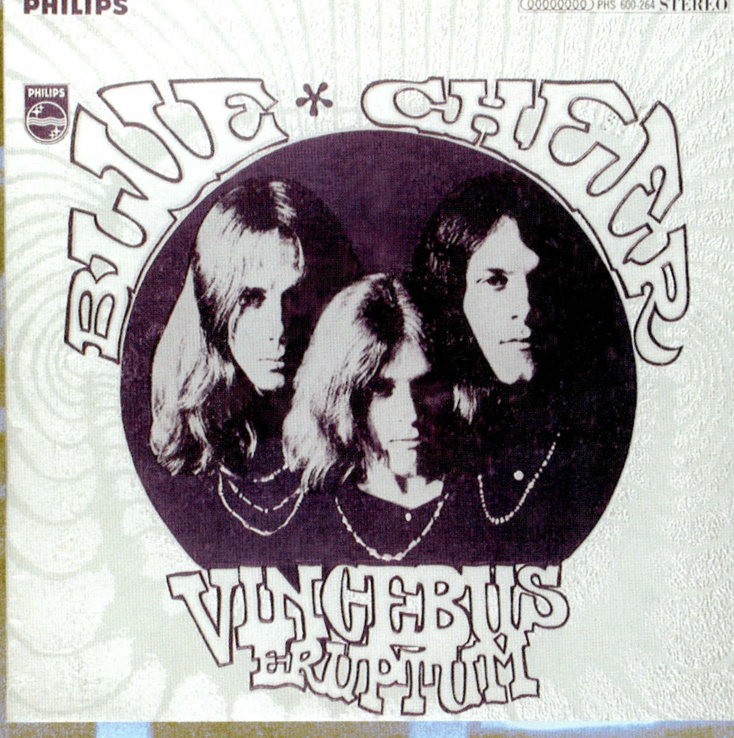

At the Coronado Studio I had a photo session with Blue Cheer. The art store, market and local restaurants gave me everything I needed to do my work. Capitol Records paid my studio bills while I created a scene for the community.

The Shrine Exposition Hall was down by USC. It's fun to look into the new world at the time, to see the people starting up in history and technology in motion projecting images on screens with loud noise. Stoned and numb, staring into the creative mixtures of images with the "Psychedelic Bombardment" of their time... Blue Cheer was set to be the loudest/heaviest rock band ever.

The audience would hear "Summer Time Blues" at full volume within the Blue Cheer's wall of Marshall amps, towering over their heads as if it were a cityscape. The vision of three musicians was dwarfed in scale, appearing as long haired characters moving around the stage with two guitars and drums. Blue Cheer defined their onstage image as aviation mechanics working on a sound machine, being projected as the sound of jet engines taking off at the airport. Gut, one of the Blue Cheer managers, said they "turned the air to cottage cheese."

San Francisco (1968) with Rick Griffin and John Van Hamersveld during the Psychedelic Era

From one week to the next, I found my interest level flattening out at my job as I was reaching the end of my tenure at Capitol Records with Brown Meggs, my mentor. I eventually left the company under a leave of absence. With money coming in, I was able to afford taking trips for as long as a day or two to see my friend Rick Griffin. My graphic works paid for the adventures. Pinnacle Dance Concert shows at the Shrine Exposition Hall created funding for the events, but I was on my own to make ends meet financially each month. At the Pinnacle events on weekends I met attorneys, promoters, managers, bands and groups within the entertainment business scene, as if I were a member of a band myself.

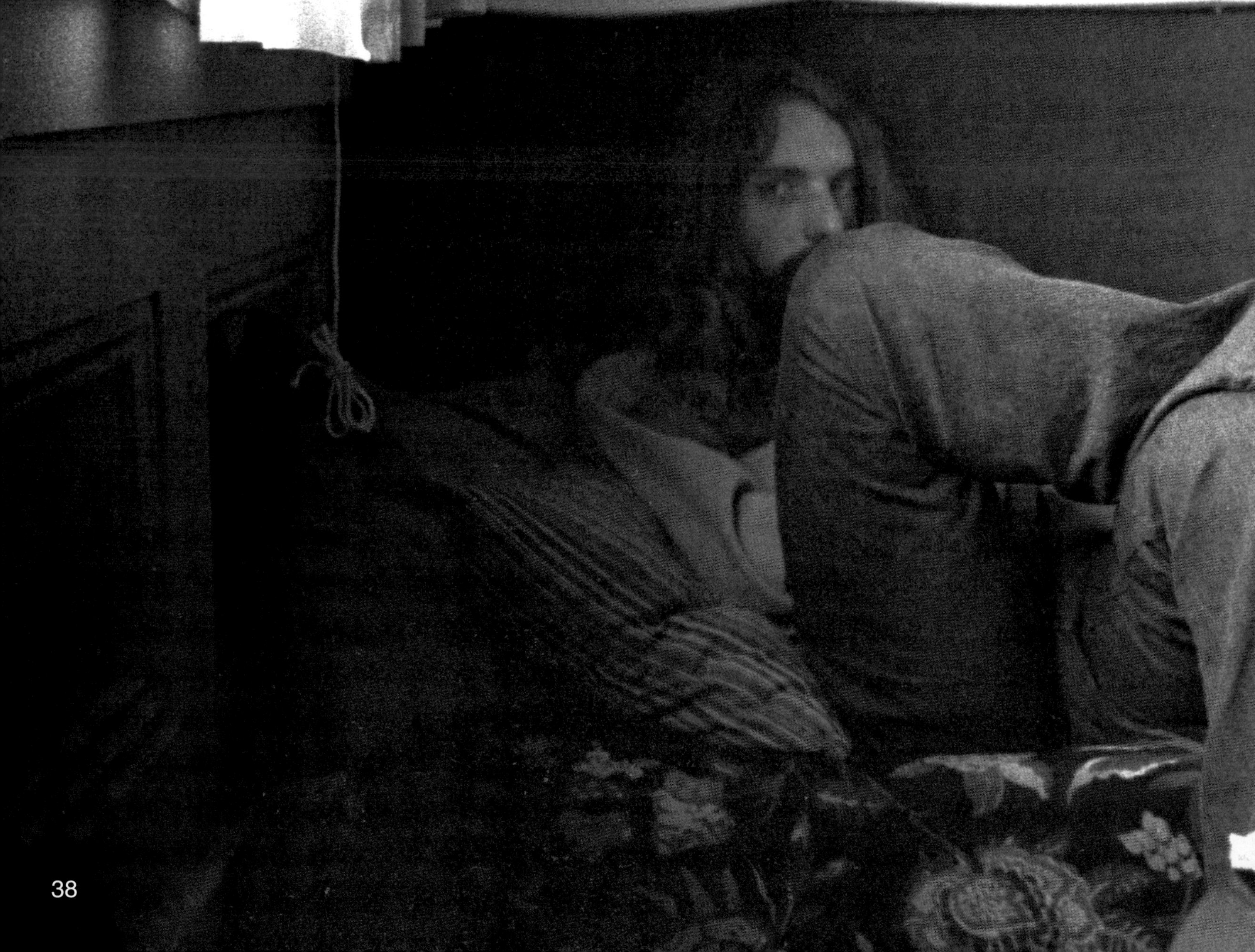

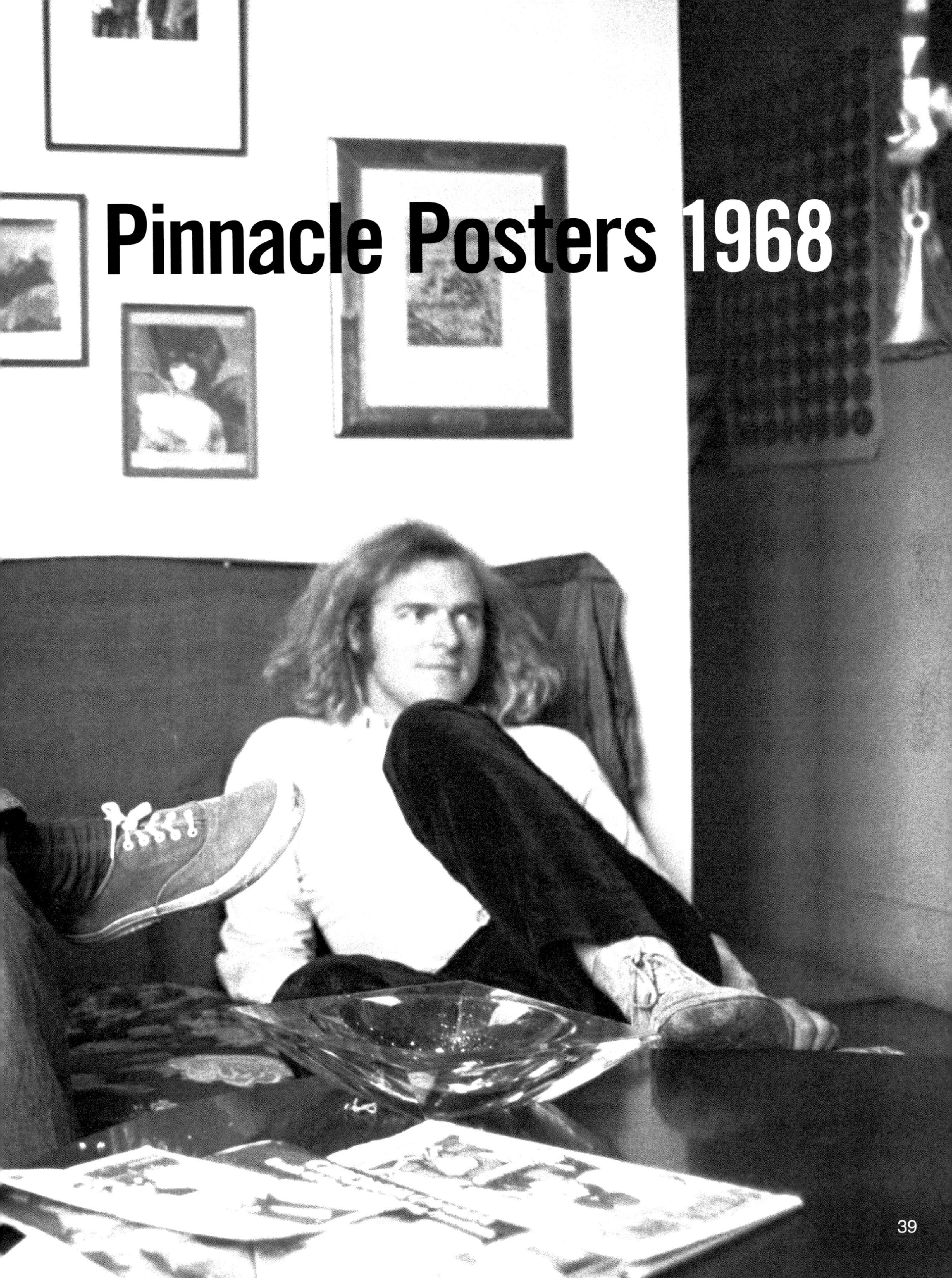

Pinnacle Posters 1968

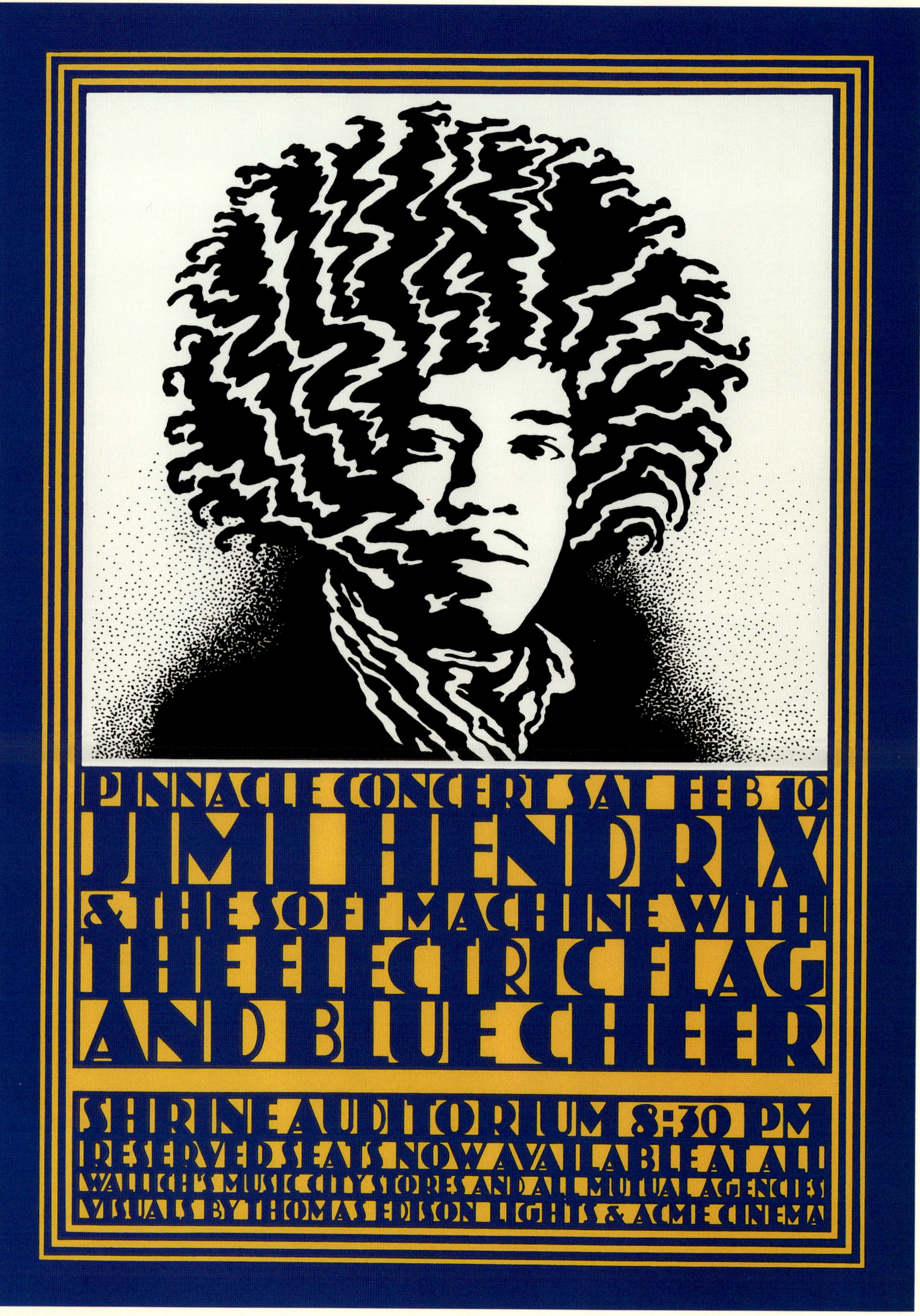

The Pinnacle Shrine Hendrix Poster (1968)

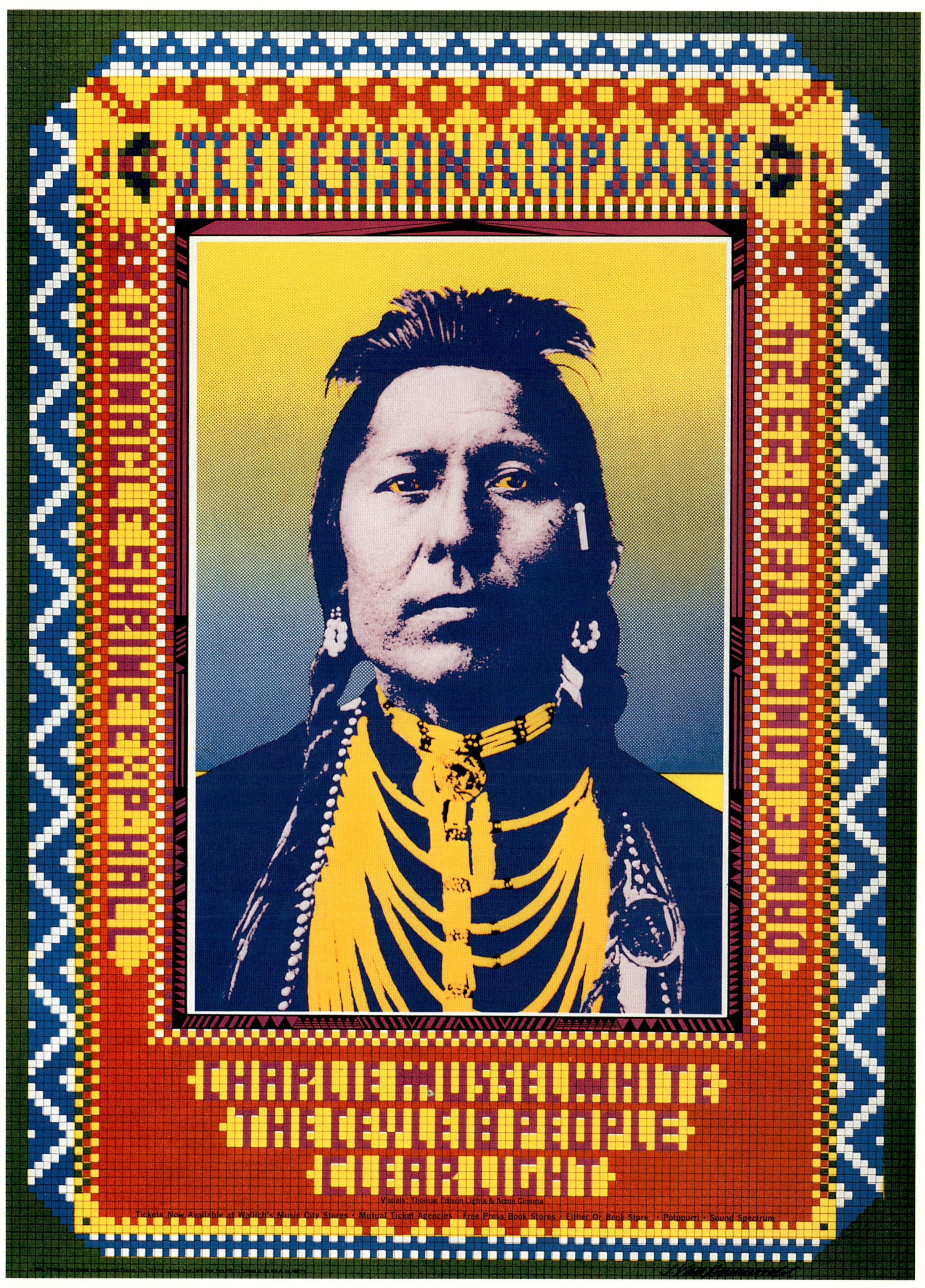

The Pinnacle Shrine Indian Poster (1968)

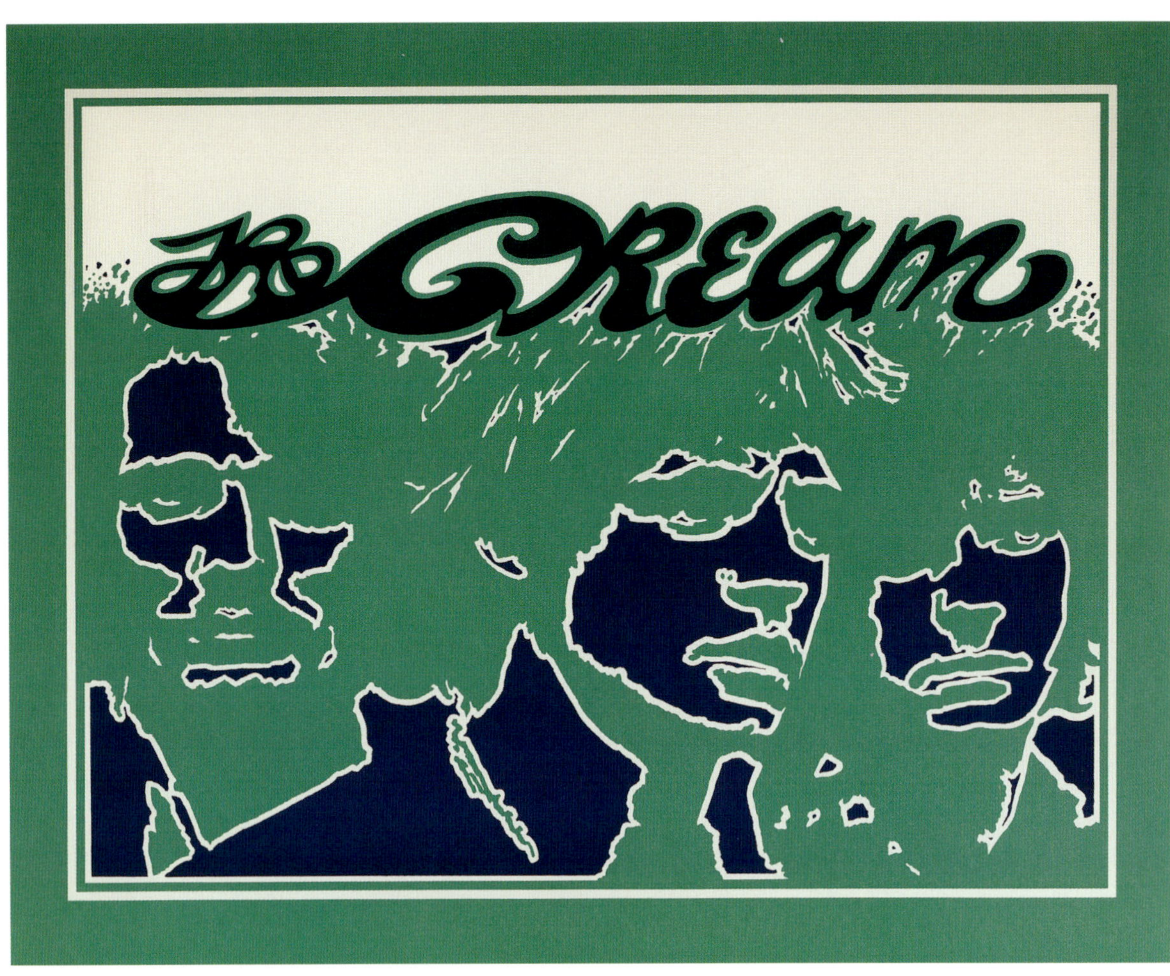

Below: The name "Pinnacle" was supposed to mean "getting higher." After the success of the shows and posters, I decided I wanted to make a sequence of connecting posters that did just that—when put together, they got "higher." These posters interlocked vertically into one big poster.

Right: One night in my studio, someone slipped me LSD. I got very sick and had intense hallucinations. During this trip, I found myself constructing the *Traffic* poster. I used nude photographs of a model to spell out the typography. Many said this poster felt like a Modernist design. Some thought it was a Dada-like poster design.

Above: *The Cream* poster was developed for a Northridge Junior College Show. Though it was not for a Pinnacle show, the poster was still made by Pinnacle. In 1987, I started selling prints of this poster.

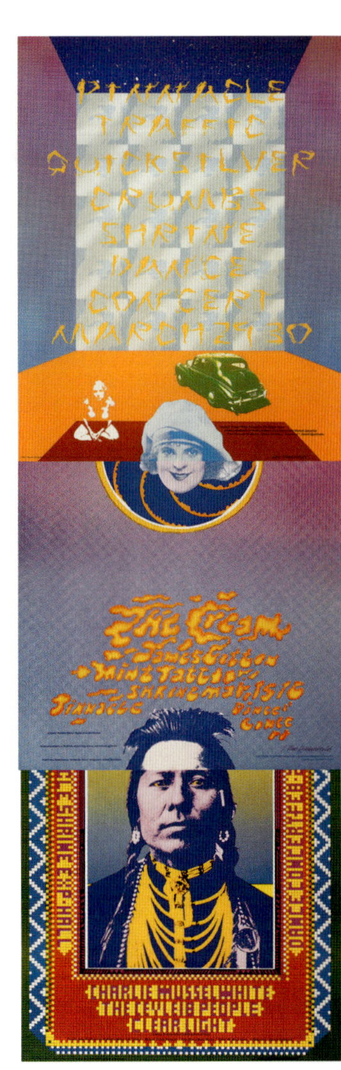

Straight Ahead: *"John Van Hamersveld was a founding member of Pinnacle, an organization that presented the JHE's February Tenth date at the Shrine Auditorium in Los Angeles. John remembers, 'In that day it was like every event was such a shocking thing to happen. The police, the campus police, and the city, everyone was really concerned. No one had really been able to break into that auditorium because it was so conservative. The (Hendrix) concert was one of the first of those kinds of shows that ever happened there.'*

'You had these dignitaries, they were in shock… relative to Blue Cheer and their performance, and the Electric Flag; and when Hendrix did come on, it was just a frenzy. He was such a good guitarist and he had that impeccable sense of timing, so he was able to pull a lot of attention and charisma into his show." A review of the concert mentions the light show displaying 'fitting images for the electronic cathedrals Hendrix constructed in the air.' "

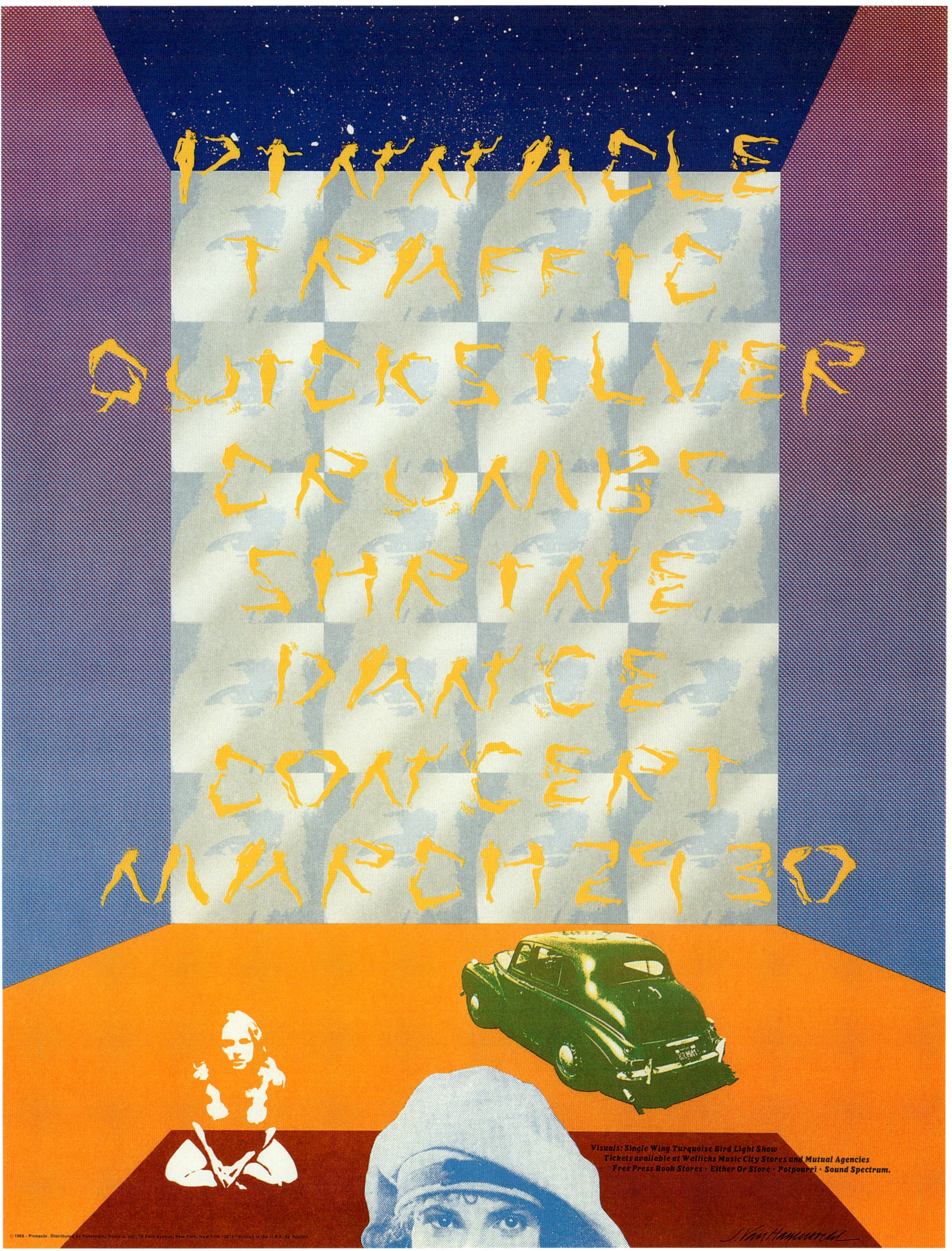
PINNACLE
TRAFFIC
QUICKSILVER
CRUMBS
SHRINE
DANCE
CONCERT
MARCH 29 30
Visuals: Single Wing Turquoise Bird Light Show
Tickets available at Wallichs Music City Stores and Mutual Agencies
Free Press Book Stores · Either Or Store · Potpourri · Sound Spectrum.
© 1968 - Pinnacle. Distributed by Personality Posters, Inc., 15 Fifth Avenue, New York, New York 10011 · Printed in the U.S.A. by Adprint

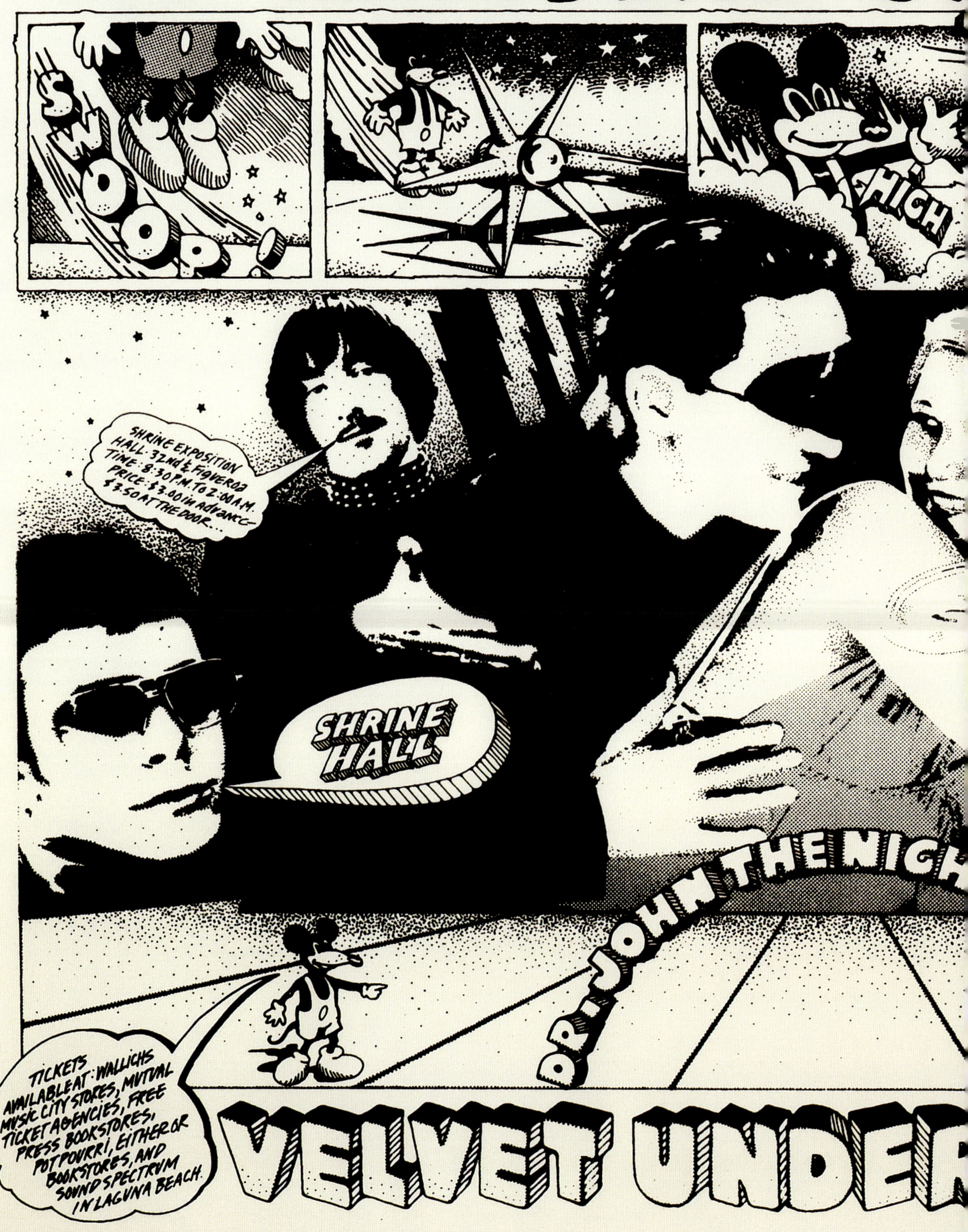
MAY CHAMBERS
SWOOP!
HIGH
SHRINE EXPOSITION HALL · 32nd & FIGUEROA TIME · 8:30 P.M. TO 2:00 A.M. PRICE · $3.00 IN ADVANCE- $3.50 AT THE DOOR...
SHRINE HALL
DR. JOHN THE
TICKETS AVAILABLE AT: WALLICHS MUSIC CITY STORES, MUTUAL TICKET AGENCIES, FREE PRESS BOOKSTORES, POT POURRI, EITHER OR BOOKSTORES, AND SOUND SPECTRUM IN LAGUNA BEACH.
VELVET

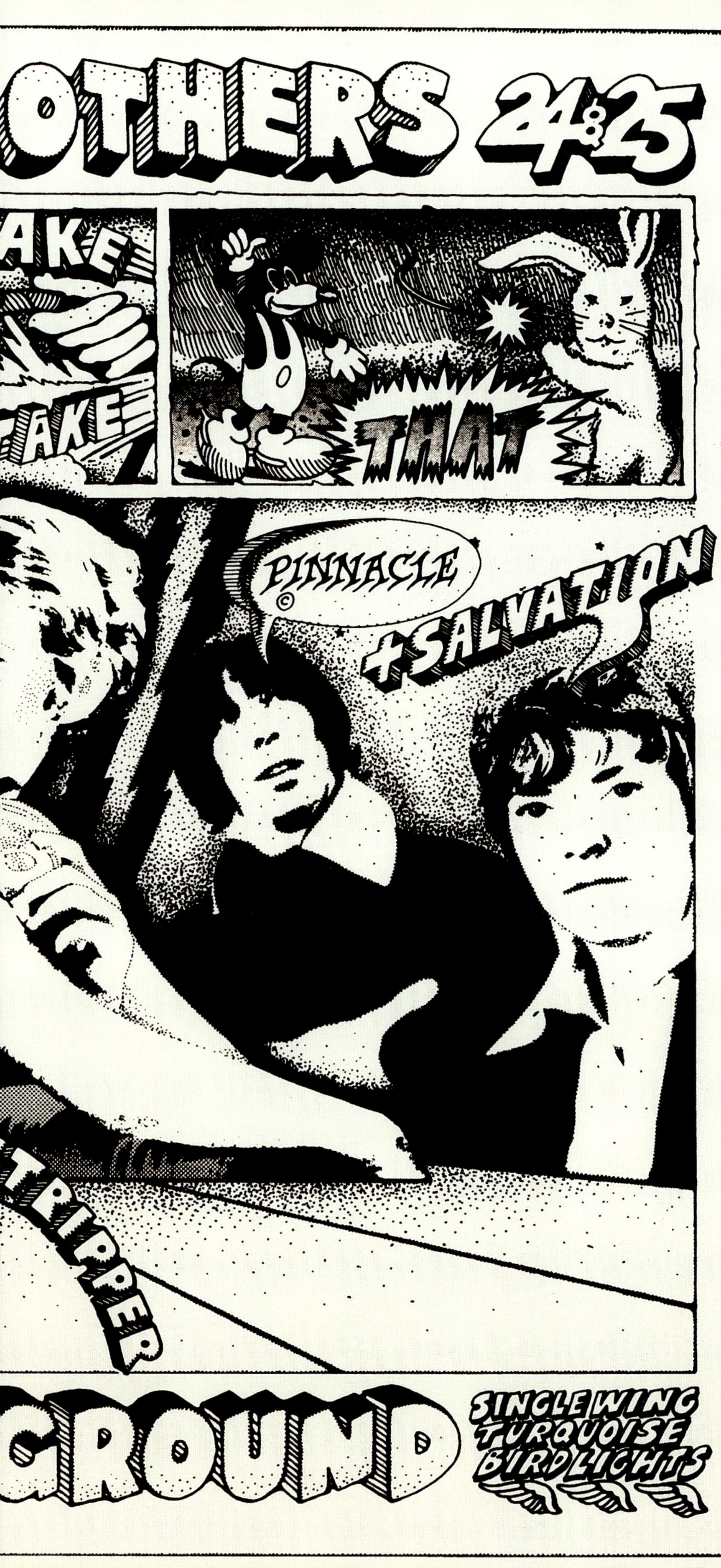

The Rock Poster Handbill As A Collector's Item

The Velvet Underground press kit had a photograph of the band all standing together. I took this image and cut out the photos of the band members. I took a scrap image found at a junk store and put it between the Velvet Underground band members in the center of the poster I was designing. To help integrate these two images I put Zap style illustrations around them.

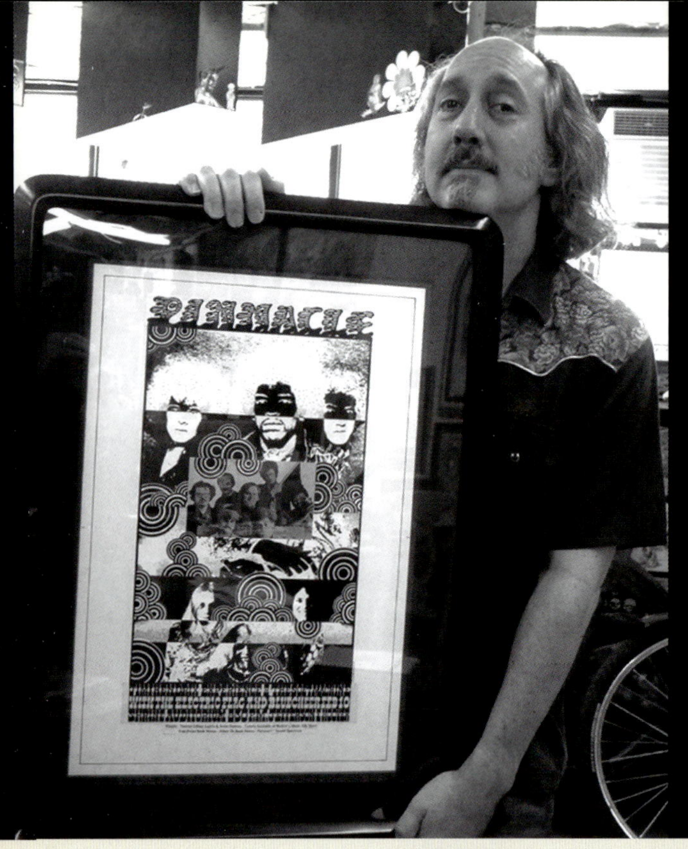

The Psychedelic Solution

Jacaeber Kastor, an art collector, owned a store called the Psychedelic Solution in New York. He possessed the original artwork for the *Pinnacle Hendrix Free Press Ad.* I signed it for him in 2008.

Photos and Drawings by John Van Hamersveld

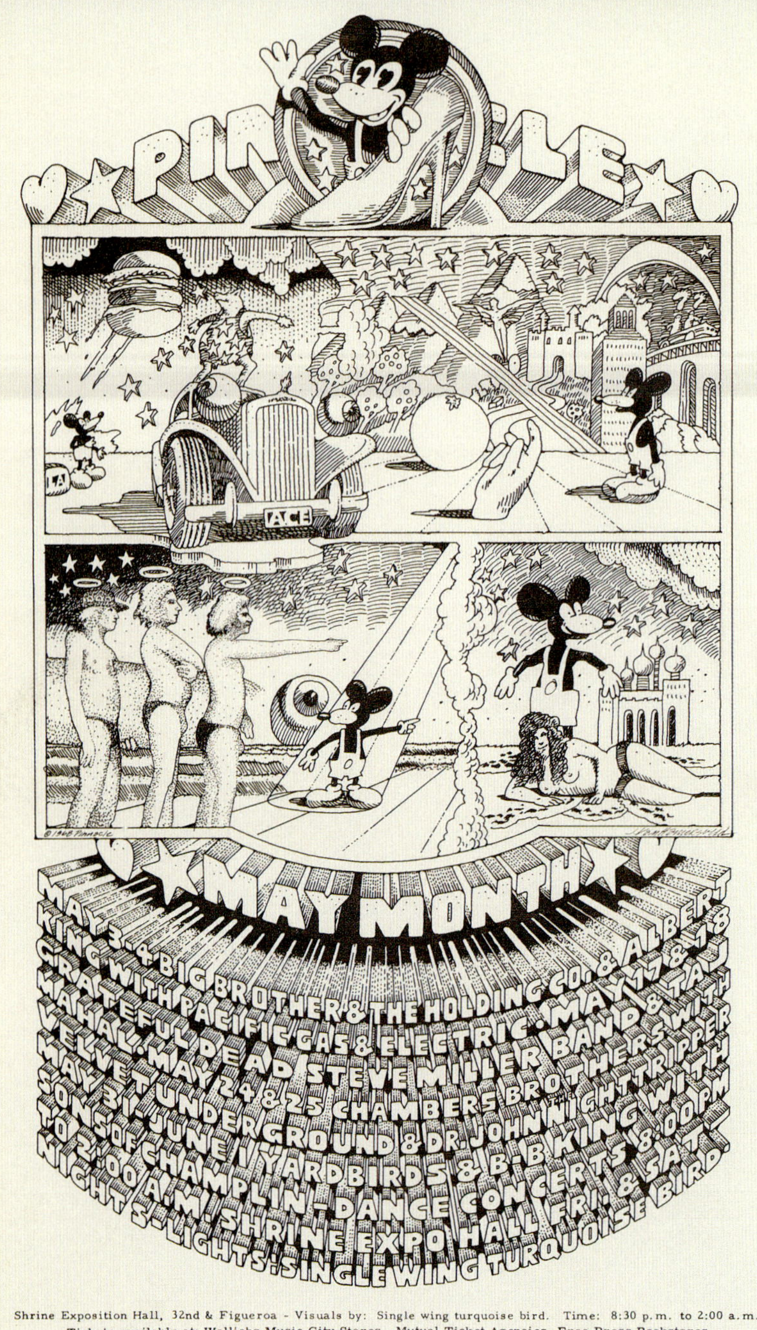

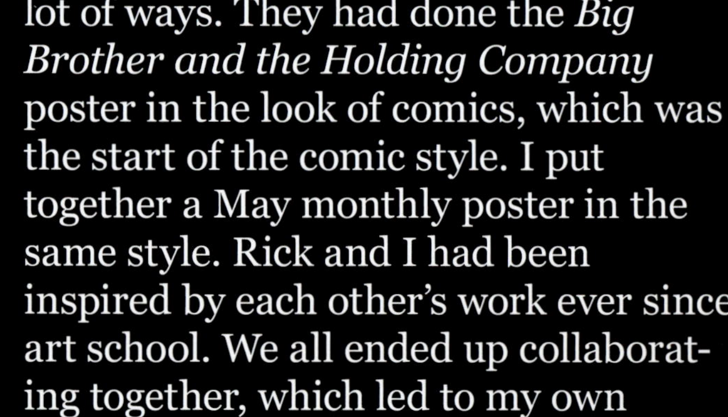

I would visit Victor Moscoso (shown in above photograph) in his studio. There was competition between all of us (Victor, myself, and Rick Griffin) in a lot of ways. They had done the *Big Brother and the Holding Company* poster in the look of comics, which was the start of the comic style. I put together a May monthly poster in the same style. Rick and I had been inspired by each other's work ever since art school. We all ended up collaborating together, which led to my own drawings which I never published.

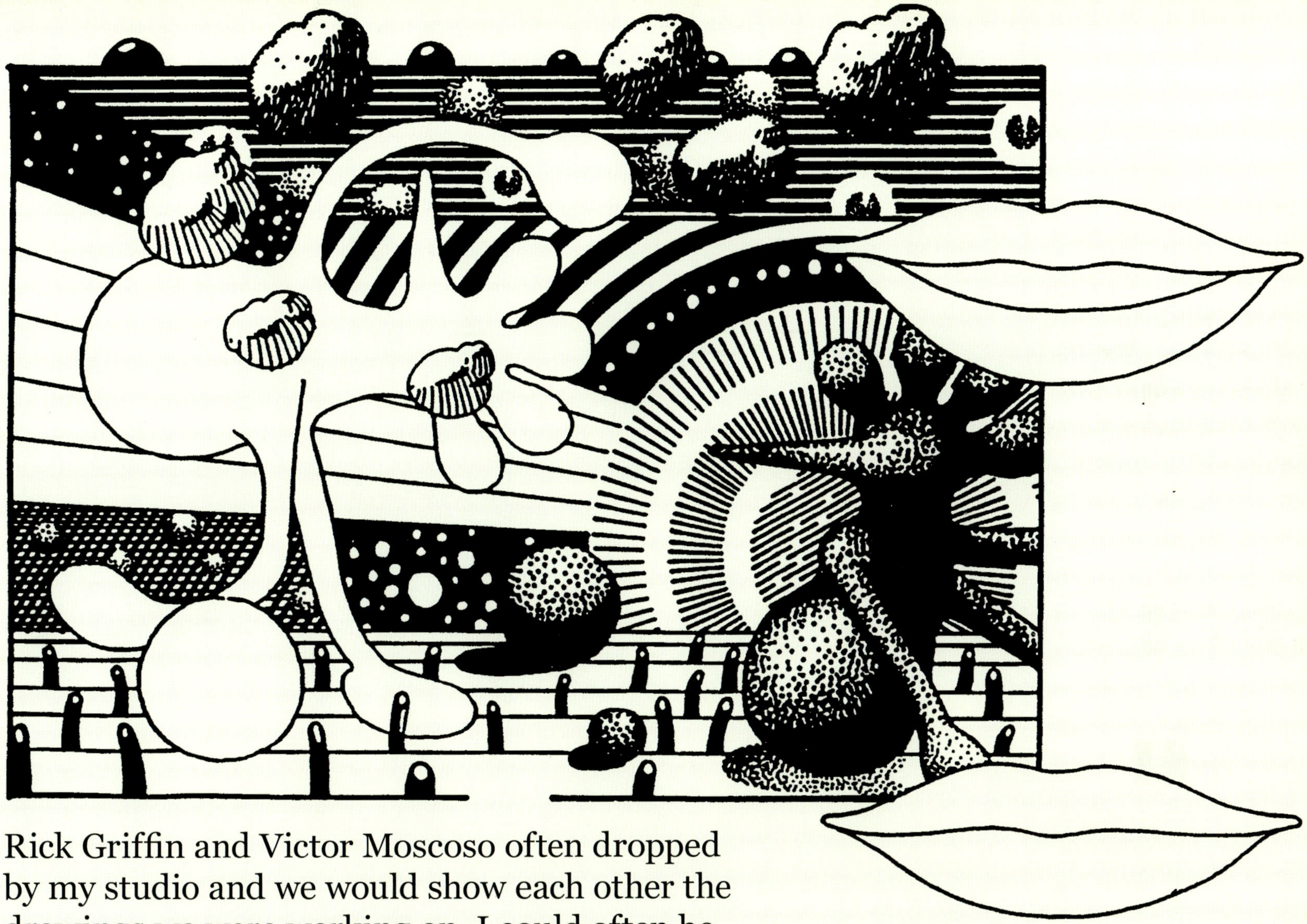

Rick Griffin and Victor Moscoso often dropped by my studio and we would show each other the drawings we were working on. I could often be found in my Kinsley studio—stoned—exploring the Zap style with my own mouse drawings.

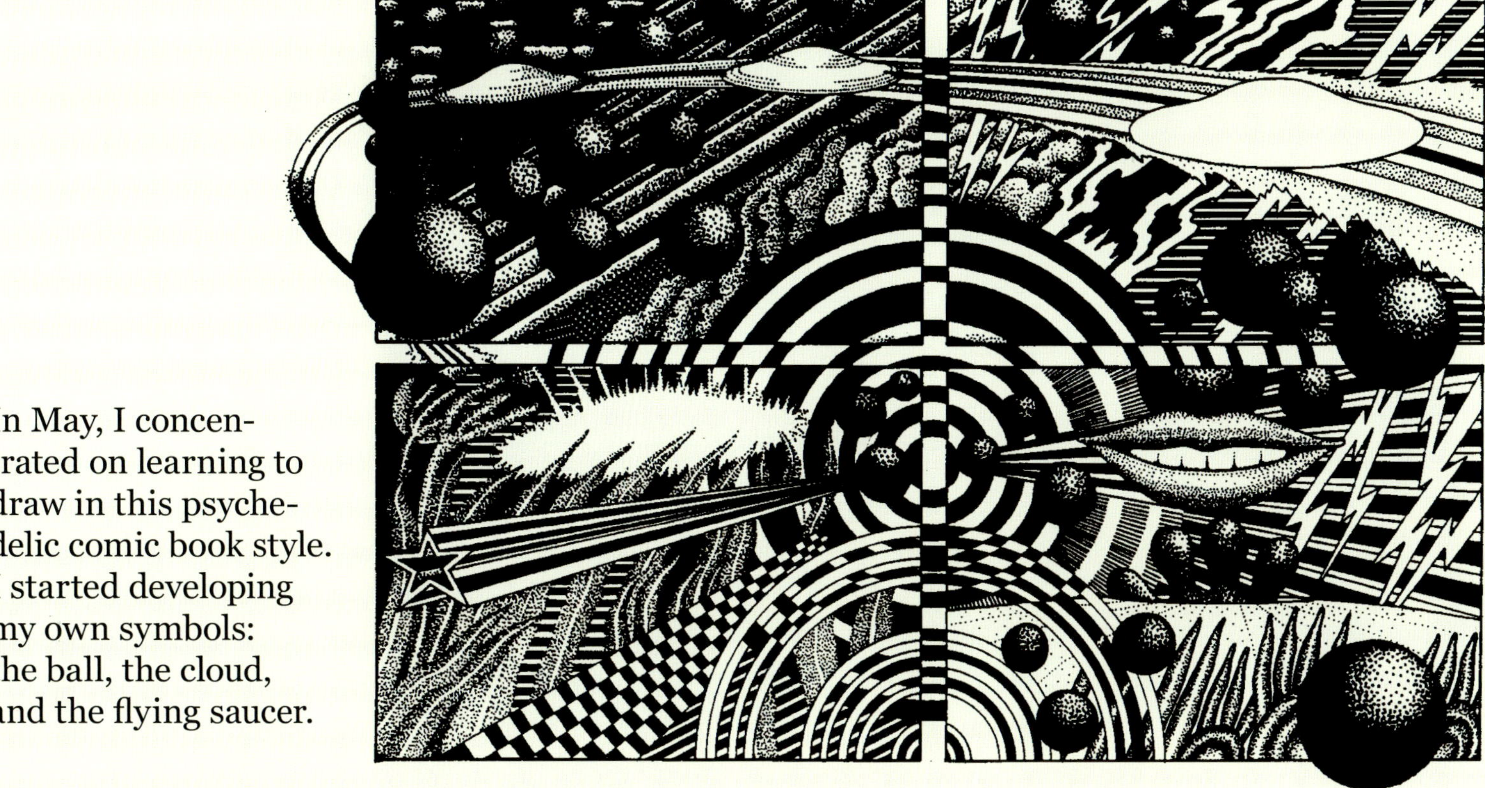

In May, I concentrated on learning to draw in this psychedelic comic book style. I started developing my own symbols: the ball, the cloud, and the flying saucer.

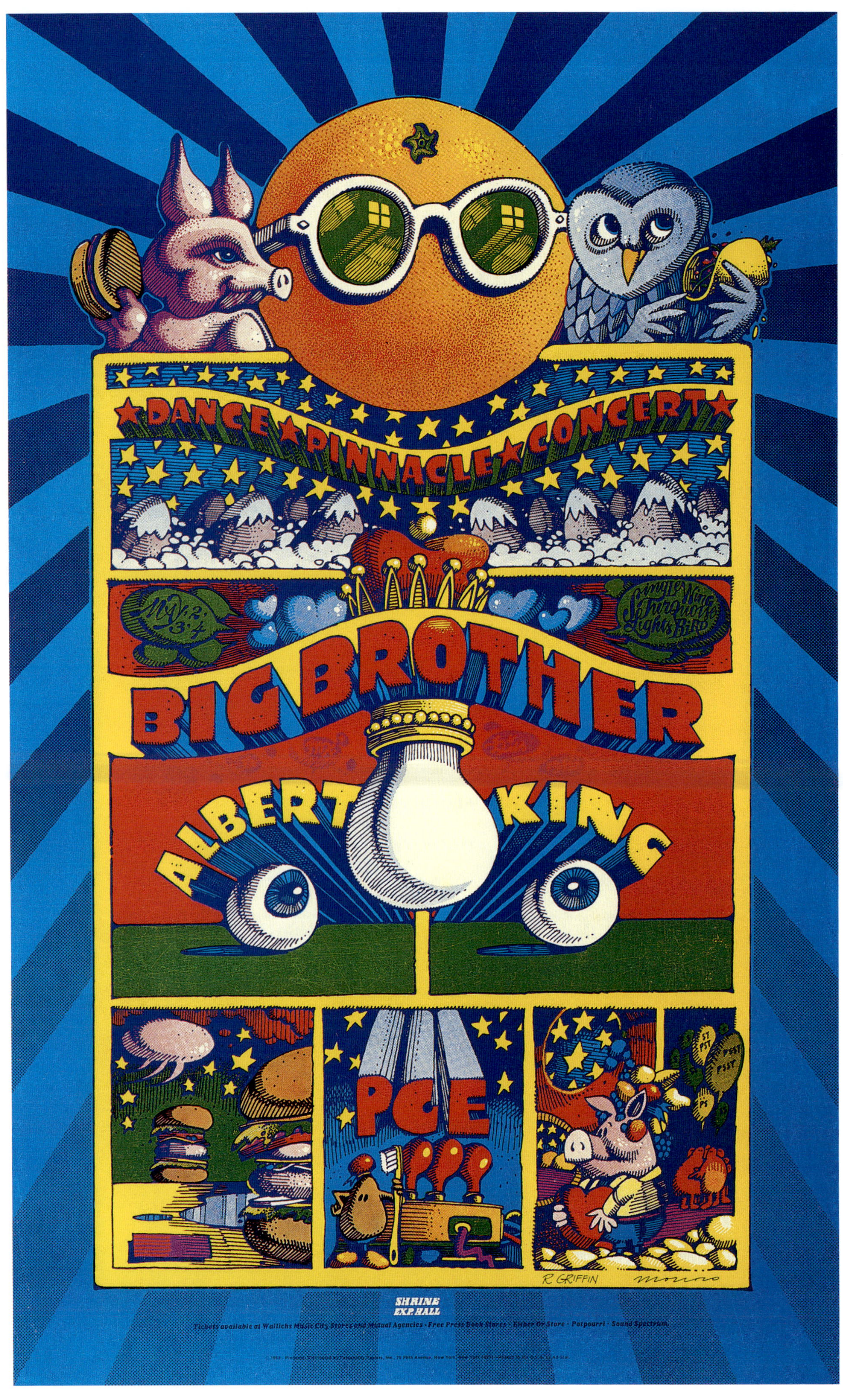
DANCE ★ PINNACLE ★ CONCERT
BIG BROTHER
ALBERT KING
PCE
R GRIFFIN
SHRINE
EXP. HALL
Tickets available at Wallichs Music City Stores and Mutual Agencies · Free Press Book Stores · Ember Or Store · Potpourri · Sound Spectrum

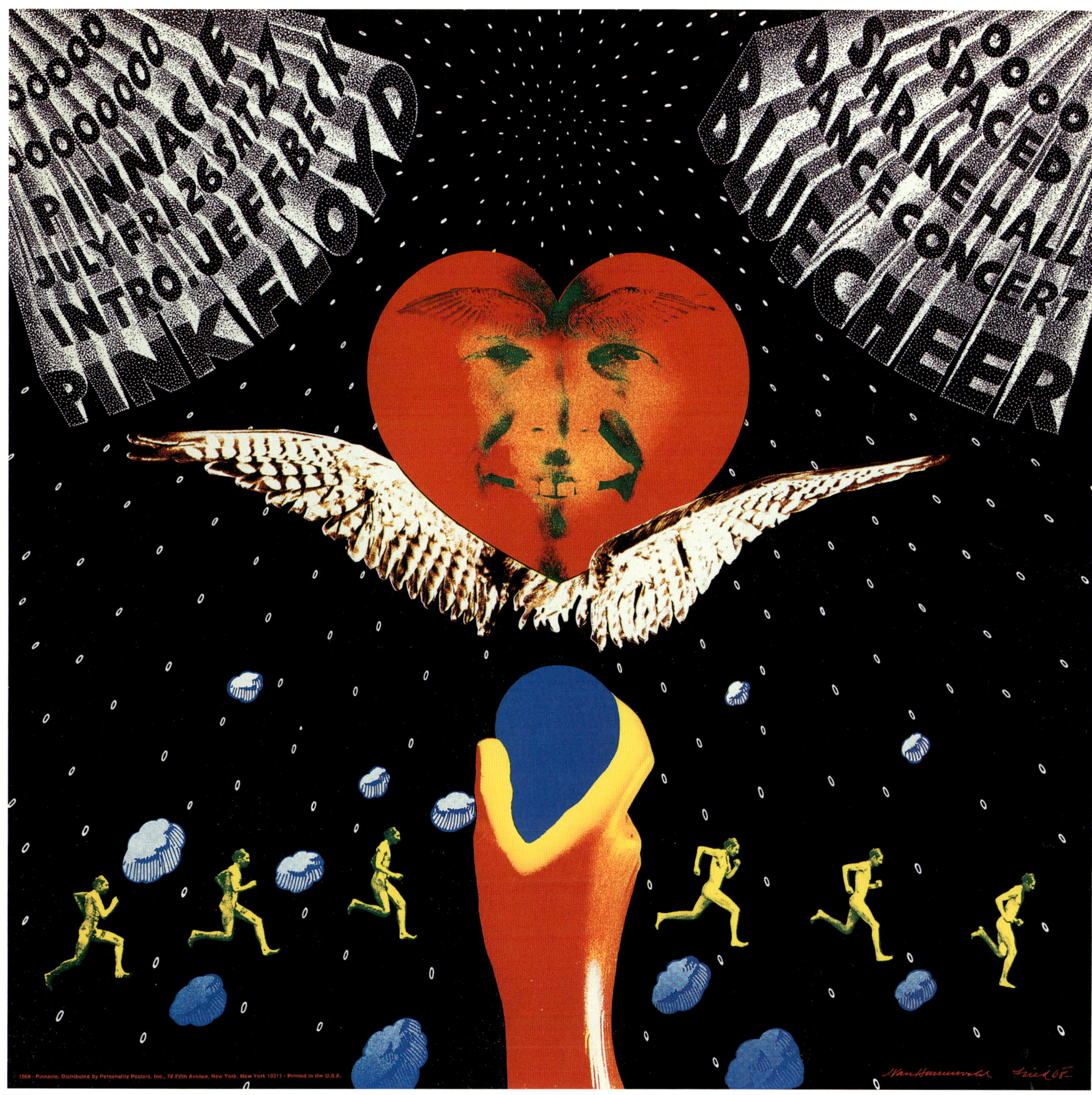

Poster Artist Collaborations

Left: San Francisco poster artists Rick Griffin and Victor Moscoso collaborated on the Big Brother Pinnacle *poster, bringing the fashionable cartoon strip drawing style to the design.*

Above: Bob Fried and John Van Hamersveld create and collage drawings and photography. The heart photo is the face of Van Hamersveld. The blue bulb and red plastic glove represents Pink Floyd.

A handful of artists, known as the "Big Five," were responsible for designing the majority of the best San Francisco psychedelic posters in the 1960s. Those five artists were Rick Griffin, Alton Kelley, Victor Moscoso, Stanley Mouse, and Wes Wilson, and they gained notoriety in *Life* and *Post* magazine in the New York media. Van Hamersveld invited the five into his Kingsley Studio in Los Angeles to collaborate on a few Pinnacle posters. The *Big Brother* poster, influenced by the cartoon style, led the two poster artists into the making of a cartoon strip for *Zap Comix* with R. Crumb. It was distributed widely to an American and international market.

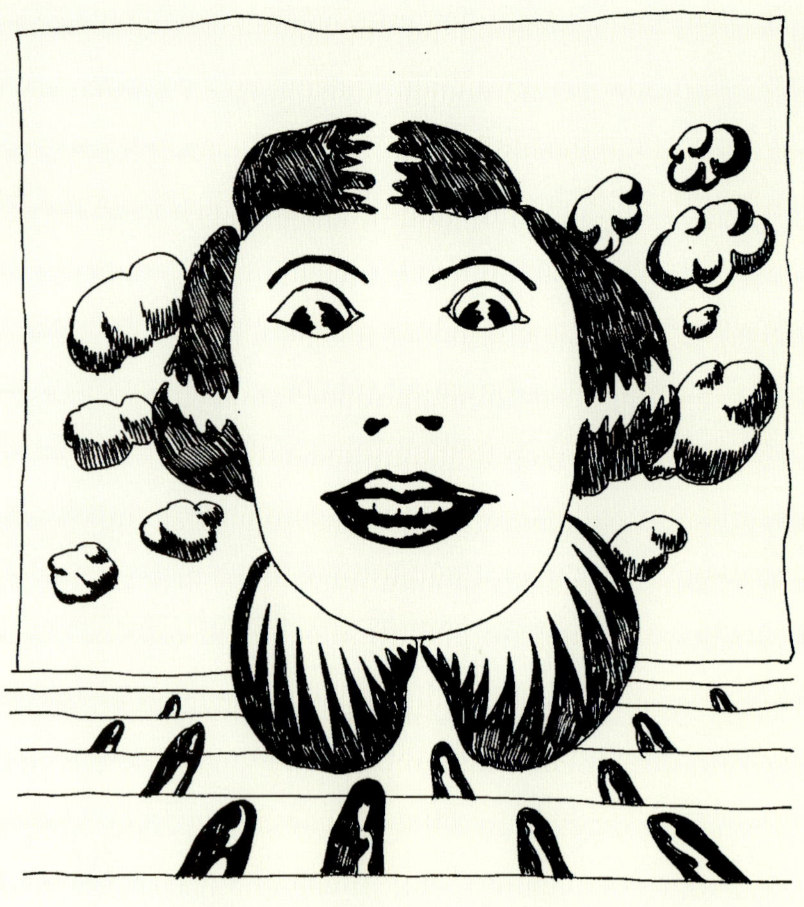

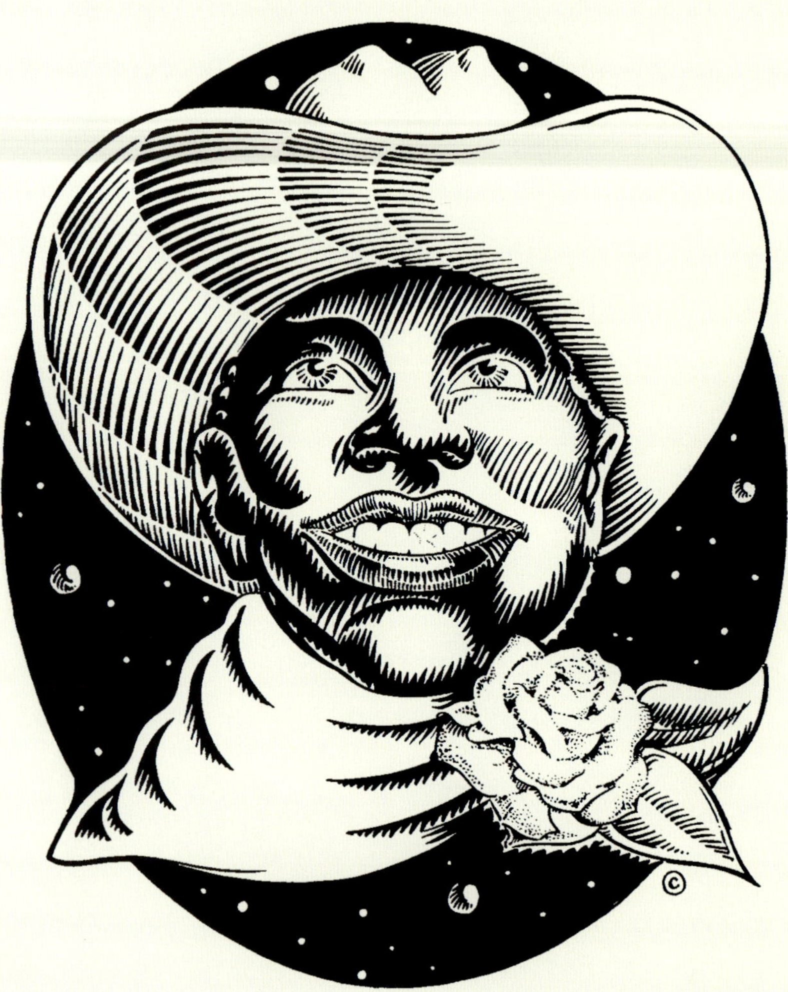

I visited San Francisco poster designers every Tuesday and would always invite them to stop by when they were in Los Angeles. The San Francisco poster artist Victor Moscoso came by many times since he was a good friend of Rick Griffin's. Bob Fried and his family spent a week with me during the summer. Bob Schnepf stayed with me in September while the Rose Bowl poster was being developed.

My art school girlfriend and I were living in the Kingsley studio at the time. The attic space on the third floor was where I did my drawings and met with my endless parade of friends and clients. One day my girlfriend came up the stairs while I was drawing and getting high. I drew a fun portrait drawing of her as we smoked pot. She had a big smile for the drawing. She had been in Texas that summer, and while she was there she bought me a cowboy hat. I ended up wearing it to keep my really long hair under control when I was out and about in the city. The fashion themes of antique clothes, Indians and cowboys, hippies, and old Blues musicians were present in the media and the music of the time.

The Rose Bowl poster idea started early one night when I composed the main elements of the poster as a design. The rose bud in the poster entered the image to fit in with the Cowboy/American Bluesman idea. Schnepf was staying with me the week of the poster deadline, so he was helping me by working on the hats and face. I drew the jellybean candy, added some clouds that I had done on several other posters, and then laid out the type I had set at the typographers for the billing of names.

When Schnepf woke up the next morning, the poster was done and ready for printing [at Cal Litho Printing] in San Francisco. I signed the poster on the left and Schnepf signed on the right; similar to how I did the Pink Floyd poster with Fried. I thought I gave up a lot to be friendly. I was the art director and one of the producers of the show and the ads and promotional campaign manager.

The American Music Show was the last Pinnacle event and poster. The drawing on the upper left was the sketch that created the idea for the poster. The finished image (lower left) was redrawn in 1996 for a t-shirt design. There were 3,000 of these posters printed that later disappeared from storage in 1968.

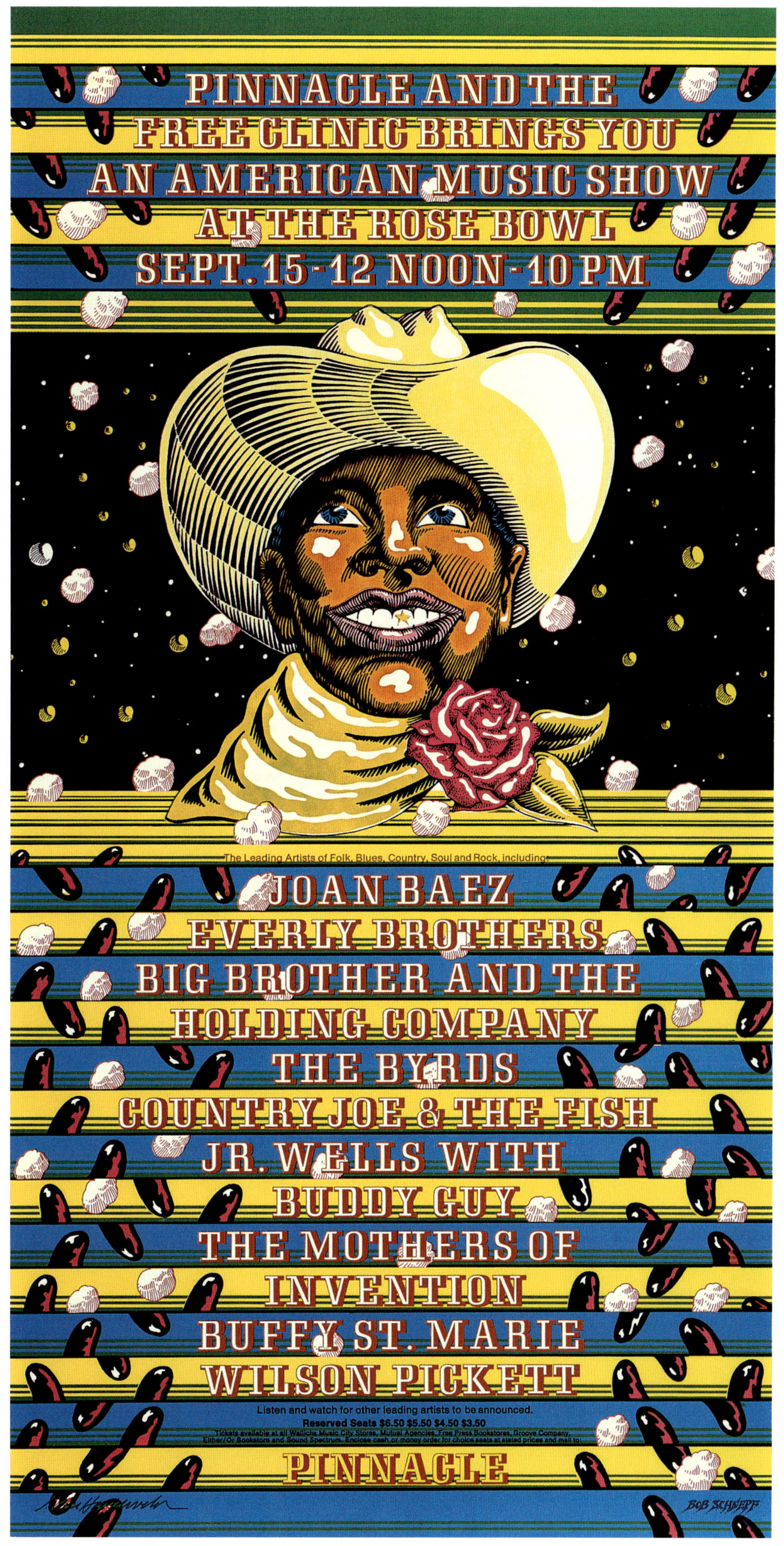
PINNACLE AND THE
FREE CLINIC BRINGS YOU
AN AMERICAN MUSIC SHOW
AT THE ROSE BOWL
SEPT. 15 - 12 NOON - 10 PM
The Leading Artists of Folk, Blues, Country, Soul and Rock, including:
JOAN BAEZ
EVERLY BROTHERS
BIG BROTHER AND THE
HOLDING COMPANY
THE BYRDS
COUNTRY JOE & THE FISH
JR. WELLS WITH
BUDDY GUY
THE MOTHERS OF
INVENTION
BUFFY ST. MARIE
WILSON PICKETT
Listen and watch for other leading artists to be announced.
Reserved Seats $6.50 $5.50 $4.50 $3.50
Tickets available at all Wallichs Music City Stores, Mutual Agencies, Free Press Bookstores, Groove Company,
Either/Or Bookstore and Sound Spectrum. Enclose cash or money order for choice seats at stated prices and mail to:
PINNACLE
BOB SCHNEPF

STEREO

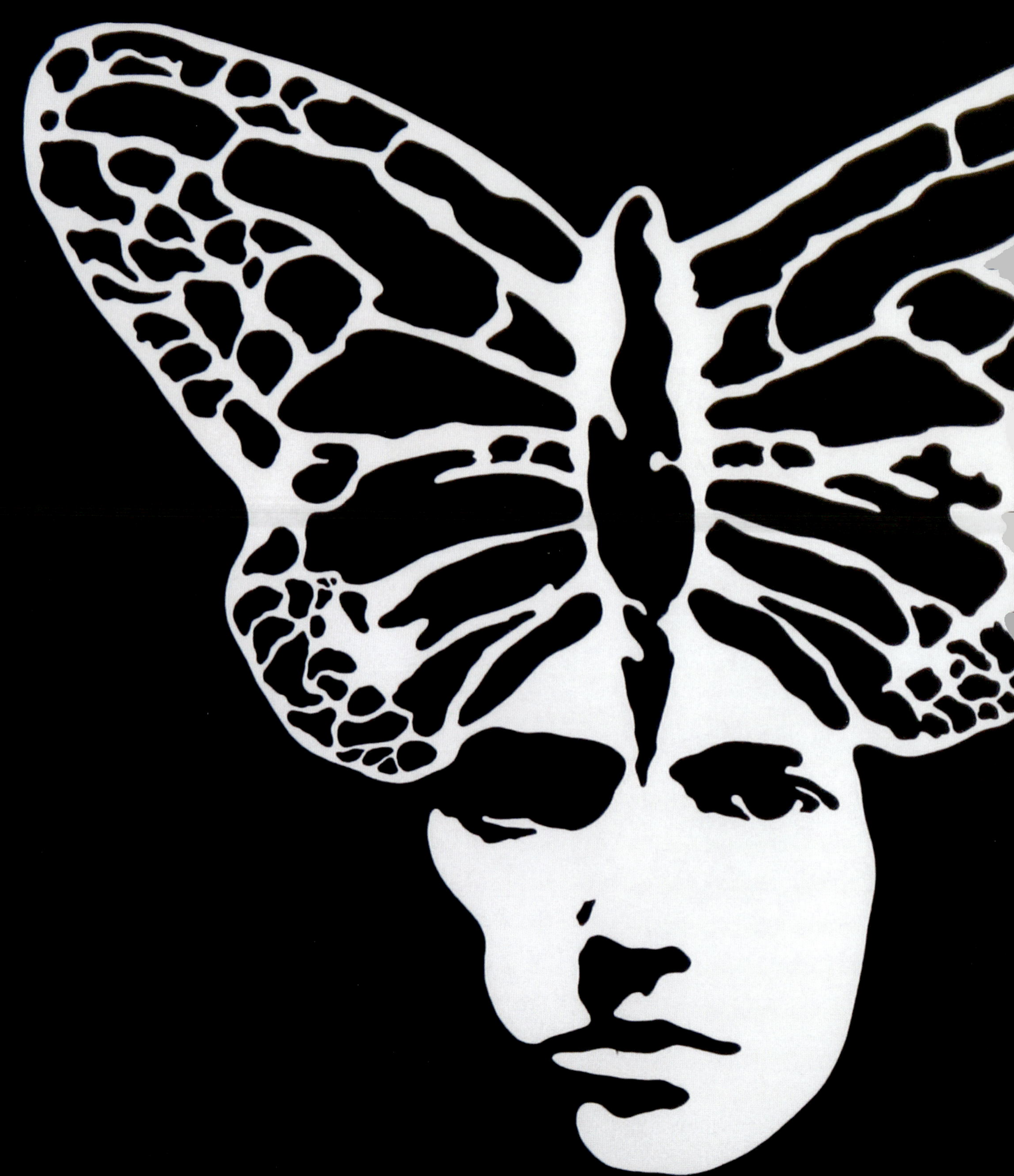

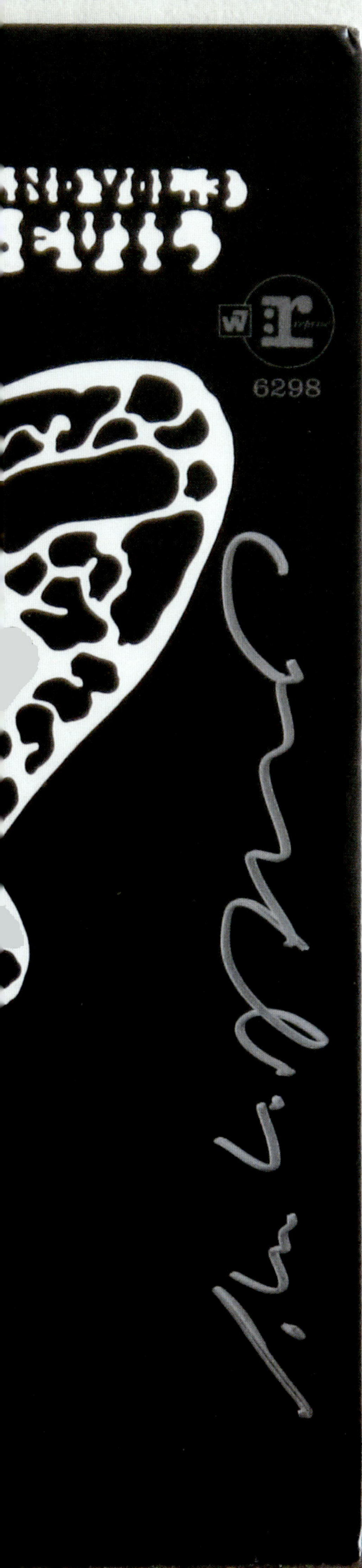

Black and white was also an issue in terms of dark and light karma.

As its title suggested, the work was a fusion of innocence and malice; the subject matter perfectly reflected in John Van Hamersveld's striking cover art work. If the "butterfly mind" represented both the transience of innocence and the psychedelic possibilities of a mind in free flight, its stark black and white setting rendered the image distinctly sinister. John recalls his work on A Child's Guide: *"Markley wanted a photograph of the band on the back so I took them up onto a hillside near Burbank and photographed them in colour with a Hasselblad camera and a wide angle lens. For the front cover I used the face from a photograph of Stevie, an artist friend who would pose nude for me. I combined my drawings and letterforms in black and white to create a stark contrast in the record racks. Black and white was also an issue in terms of dark and light karma. The butterfly's wings are a psychological symbol for reading into the mind, like an ink blot test by a psychologist, but as art. In this image, the head is thinking of the butterfly image—freedom from the karma in the well of darkness." It was surely one of the most powerful and iconic cover illustrations of its era.*

—From an interview with Tim Forster (1997)

Using the image of Stevie, I overlaid my drawings and letterforms in black and white to create a dark contrast. Stevie was also the model I used for the *Traffic* poster that I had made under the influence of LSD. On the right is the image of Stevie I used for the *Traffic* poster.

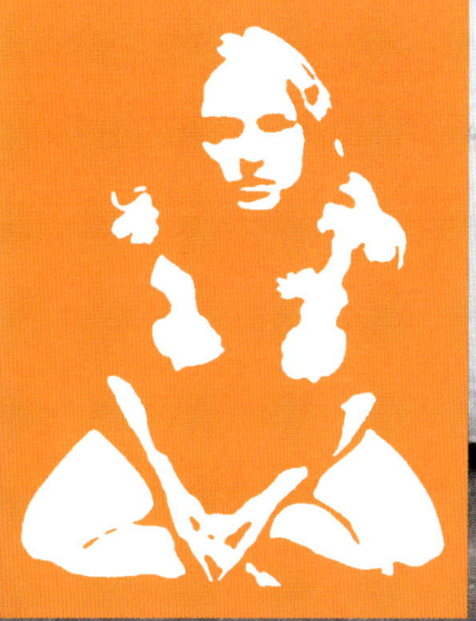

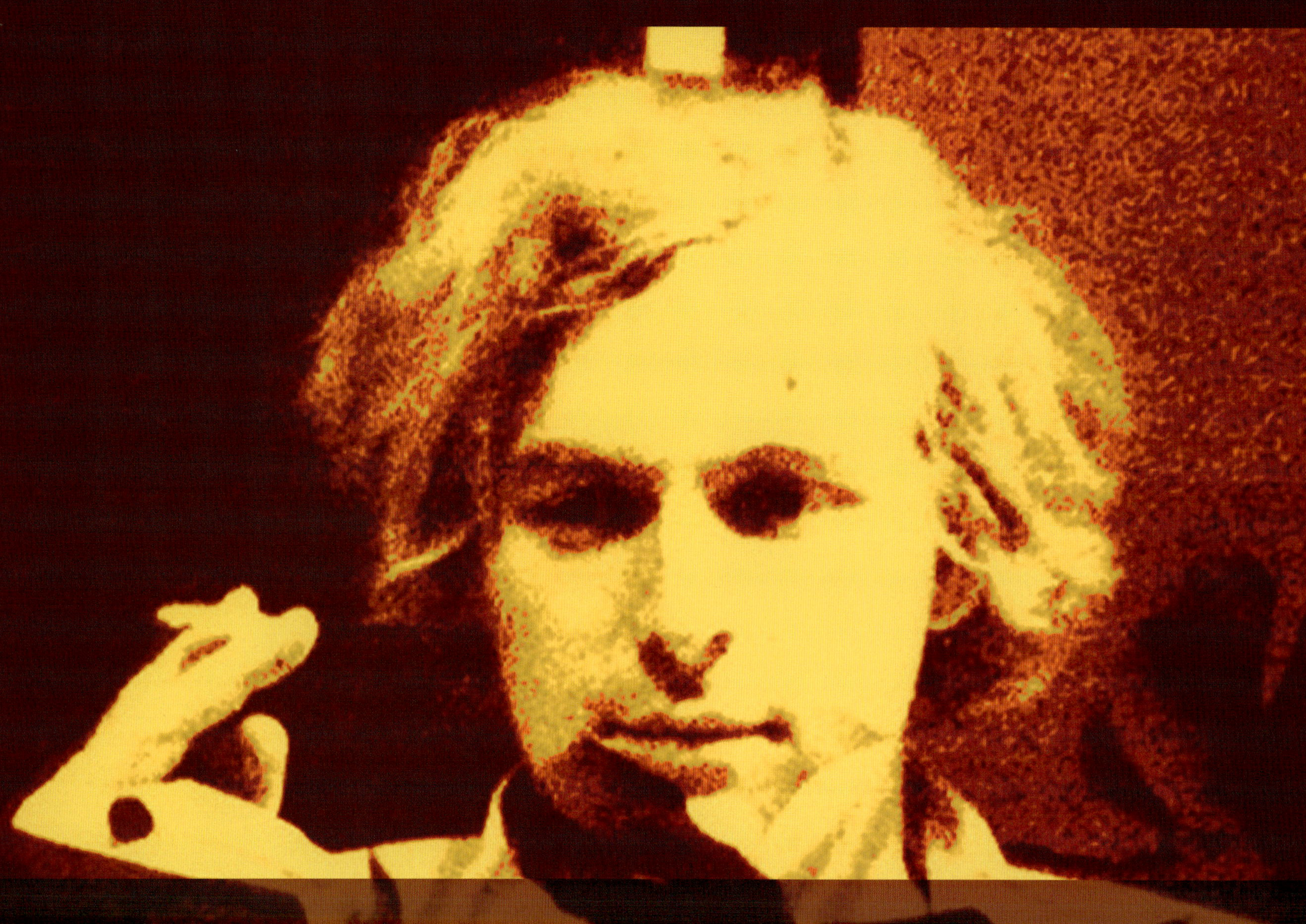

Getting Stoned With The Jefferson Airplane (1967)

December 31, 1967: The Winterland Ballroom, San Francisco. Bill Graham's Doors concert that evening. I was checking out the show backstage with the *Family Dog* poster artist Stanley Mouse. His best friend, Bob Seidemann, the man who captured Janis Joplin's most memorable images, arrived. He was escorting the rock goddess herself, Janis Joplin, along with the extraordinarily beautiful Grace Slick.

It was almost midnight. We slipped in between the curtains and created our own New Year's Eve party. Drinks and puffs were shared. We constantly checked our watches—when you're stoned, time is an easy thing to lose track of. As midnight arrived, the audience cheered and we all kissed and embraced. This was quite the memorable meeting with Grace Slick.

Baby Boomers!

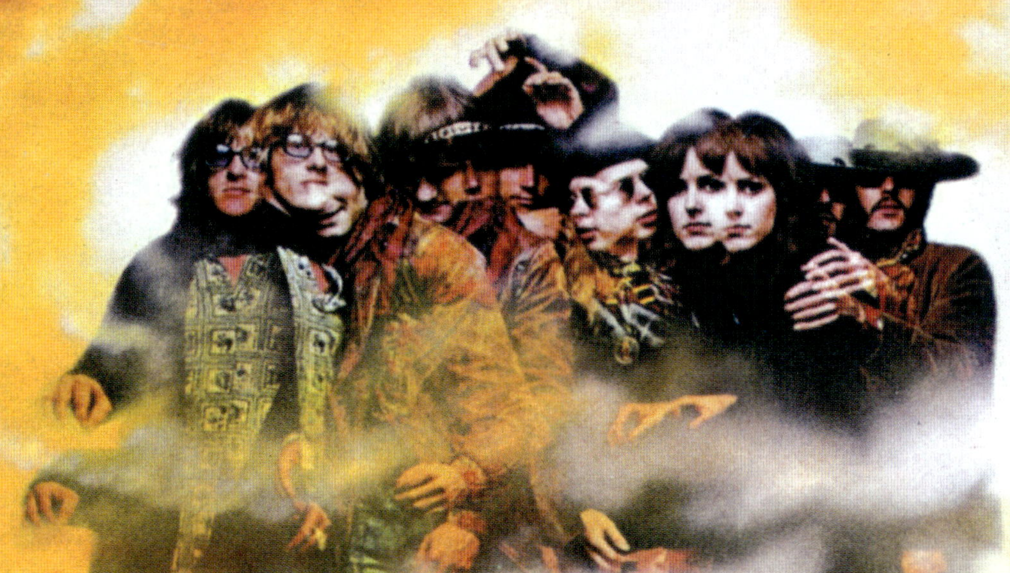

Bill Thompson, Jefferson Airplane's new band manager, called and told me he had photos of the band that were shot by Richard Avedon's assistant, Hiro. This was a breakthrough for me. Hiro was the young, hot, Japanese photographer of the moment. Ruth Ansel, the innovative art director at *Harper's Bazaar* magazine, had commissioned the shoot for a spread that, I think, never ran. Bill rushed over to the Kingsley studio with the goods. As I used the loop to examine the transparencies on the light box, the idea arose in my mind: "Let's get a photo of a bomb!" Another breakthrough? Bill quickly located a photograph of the mushroom cloud over Hiroshima (courtesy of the U.S. Army Air Corps) that we could use free of legal complications. First, I made dye transfer prints of the photographs. Then, a skilled airbrush artist meshed the two photographs into the singular image that I had so clearly in my mind—the fusion of Hiro's portrait with Hiroshima's explosion.

Do They Dig It?

"A joint burned in Paul's hand. He took a long puff."

Later on in the week, I was in San Francisco with the completed *Crown of Creation* album artwork. Bill escorted me to each of the band members' homes so I could present the *Hiro-Hiroshima* image to each member individually. Eventually, Bill and I arrived at Grace Slick and Paul Kantner's place, located in the Haight panhandle at Ashbury and Oak. Grace and Paul, who had the most creative influence in the band, lived in a Tiffany house, which was built at the turn of the century in an art nouveau style by the design firm Louis Comfort Tiffany. The sunlight came through the colored glass windows and cast a shimmering glow across this spacious antique palace. We went straight up the stairs to the top floor to meet with Grace and Paul in their inner sanctum. They sat on a sensuous, dark, bearskin bedspread. I showed them the album cover art. A joint burned in Paul's hand. He took a long puff. I saw *Crown of Creation* reflecting on the thick lenses of Paul's black-rimmed glasses as he gazed straight into the picture. Grace looked up at me. Her mesmerizing blue eyes nailed me to the wall. Grace and Paul looked at each other. Do they dig it? Do they even get it? I thought they liked it, but we were all so stoned, I couldn't tell what they were feeling. No one knew what their decision was. This process, it seemed, was a game to wear me down—an exercise worthy of a Venetian Doge. I was led off to another room and down the stairs. I passed by guitarist Jorma Kaukonen, who was wrapped in his long hair, and bassist Jack Casady, who appeared to be hiding behind little round sunglasses pasted on his face. They may have been masters of feedback on the guitar, but they offered me no kindness at that moment. Unfortunately, they reserved their comments for future meetings. I had no clue: I didn't know what the consensus of the band was or even if there was one! As I walked out the front door, Spencer Dryden, the drummer, who was always direct, said, "Hey, don't worry!"

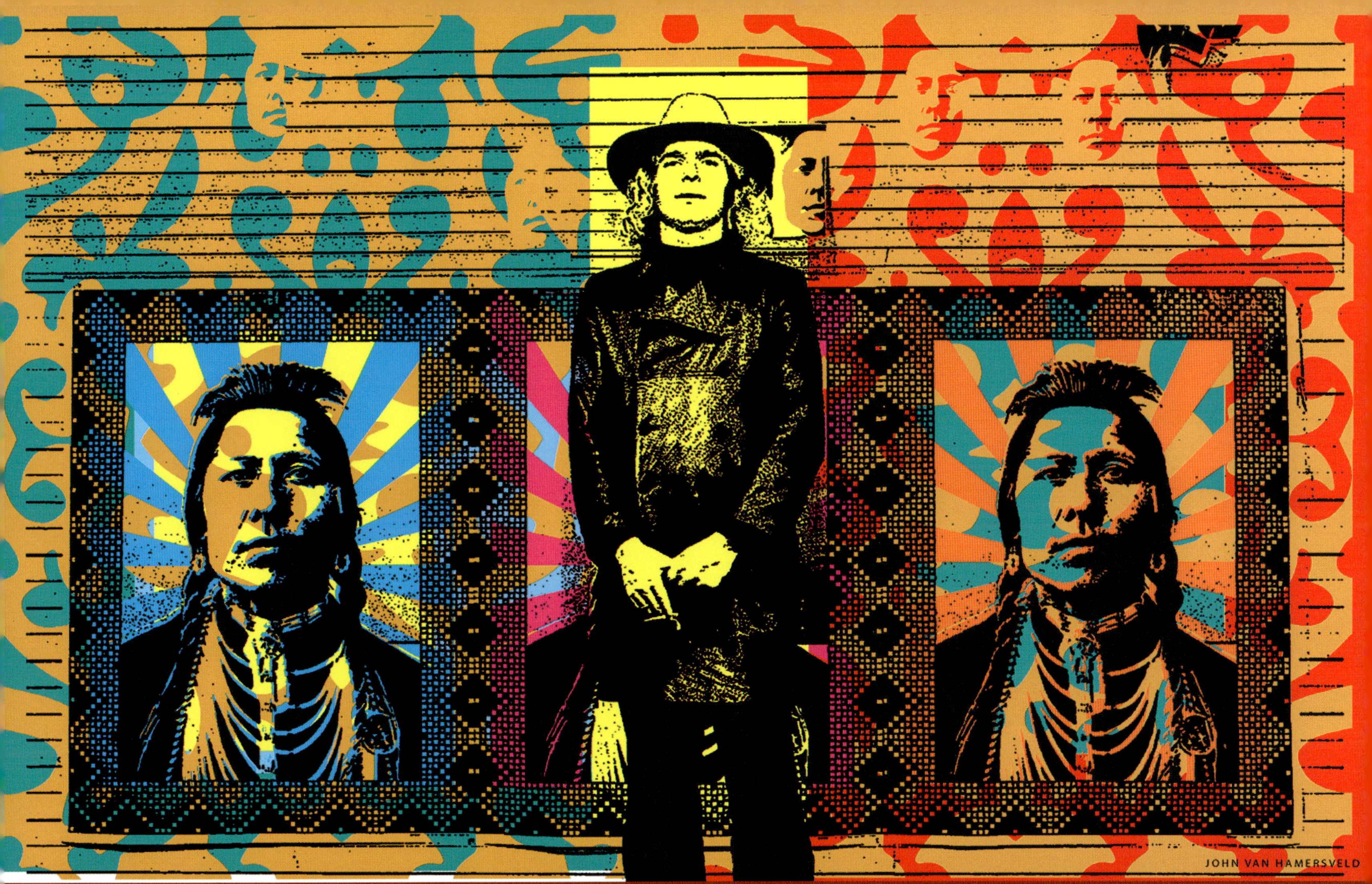

JOHN VAN HAMERSVELD

Finding The Indian

While living at the Coronado studio, I was involved with a girl name Honeya. She went to the Otis Art Institute, which was fairly near my studio. Sometimes Honeya and I would go down the block to the old antique stores and look through all the collected items. It was during one of those trips that I found the *Indian* photo. Later, when I was in the studio looking for an image for Jefferson Airplane, I could not think of any one image for them as a band, so I chose to enter from a subliminal level. Their audience was always stoned, so anything I used could be read into as intentional. I decided that I would think of the show as if it were a meeting of the northern and southern tribes of the new hippies, and out of the closet came the *Indian* photo. I combined this image with a beaded pattern for the typography, as a reference to the beaded belts that hippies would get at Indian trading outposts. I focused my typography in a myopic process, eventually having the words emerge like a beaded belt design. You could read it if you were stoned. The poster later transformed into a large print I made for exhibits.

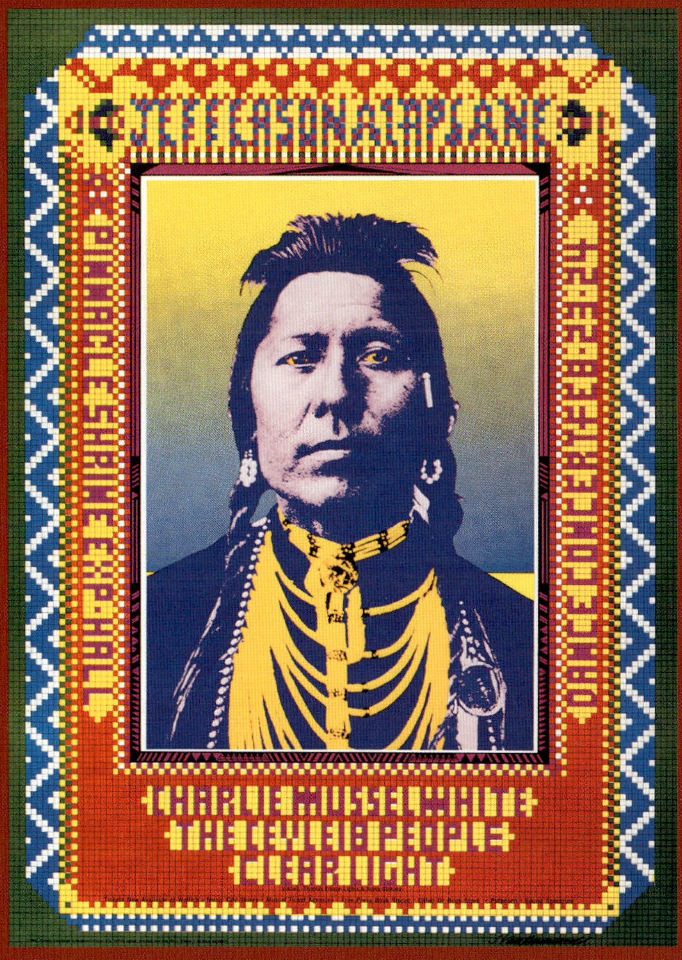

THE END OF AN ERA

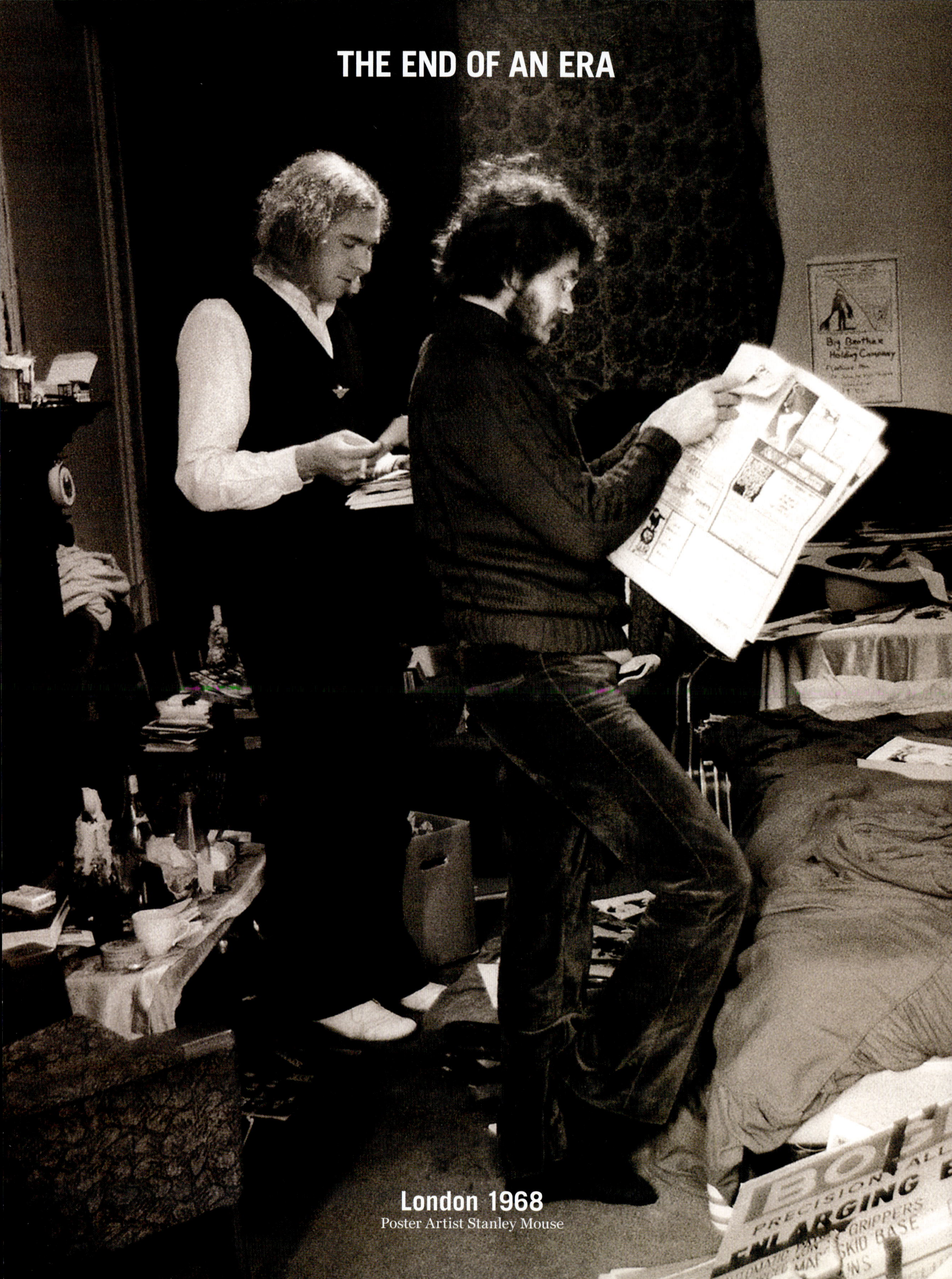

London 1968
Poster Artist Stanley Mouse

I was back from London in the Spring of 1969 and the media had recently lost interest in Rick and the "Five Psychedelic Poster Artists" as a result of the movement becoming very commercial and well distributed throughout the media. Now it was the character Robert Crumb, a tall nerdy cartoonist with an interest in social realism, who came forth to draw and discuss his view of the hippie society. A New York native with a career under way, he ended up in Potter Valley, California as a result of a following of "admirers" across the country. Whether he desired the attention is a question often raised, but always having a penchant for leaving a bad taste in the media's mouth would be his trademark—probably because he had something to say through his *Mr. Natural* comic book, or through the rest of his *Zap Comix*.

London to New York

It was April of 1969. I had just landed at Kennedy Airport for a two month stopover in New York City. I was returning from a four month stay in London, which was spent visiting the art and rock scene there. I was [re]tired, stoned, and confused after the hash parties, the Beatles' office on Seville Road, the Eric Clapton and Martin Sharp scene, tea time, Charlotte Rampling, and all the fascinating women in the night scene, the museum, galleries and new friends at the Royal College of the Arts.

Pop Art Surrealism

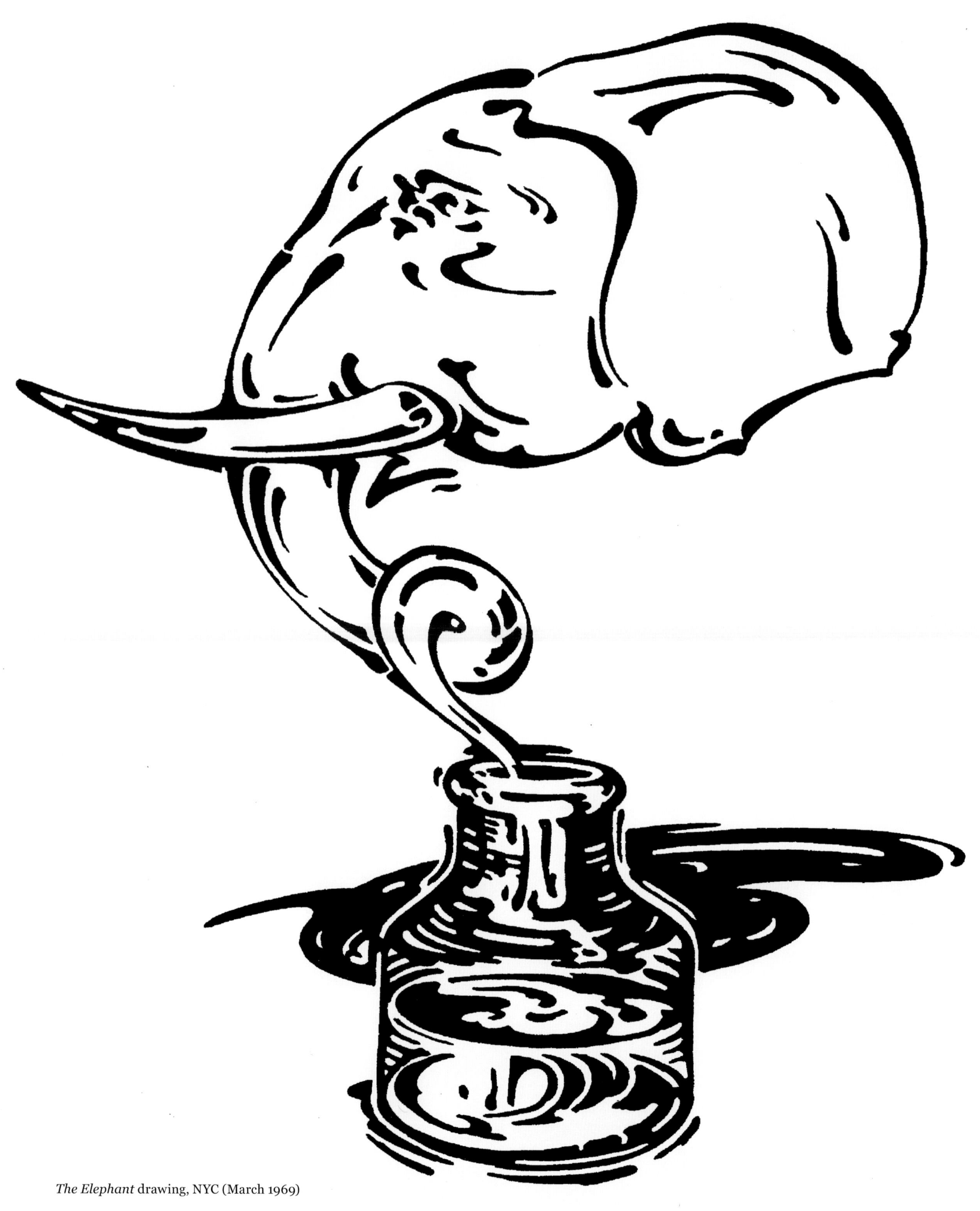

The Elephant drawing, NYC (March 1969)

MOUSE OUTSIDE THE BOX

At the Kingsley Studio the "Mouse Outside The Box" was created on the drawing board surface. The flat geometric shapes were designed in sections, like architecture. The drawing concept progressed months later.

THE SEVEN MOUSE DRAWINGS ON ST. MARKS PLACE

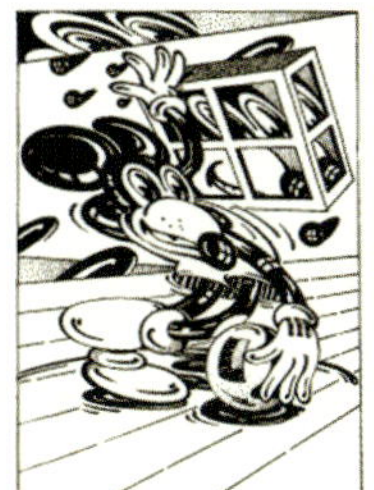
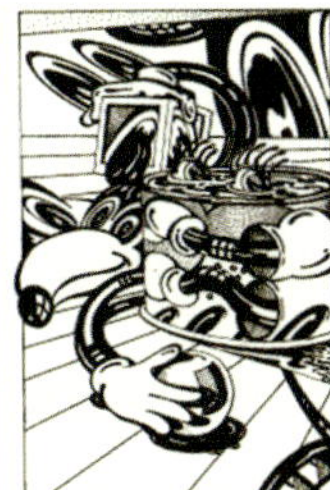
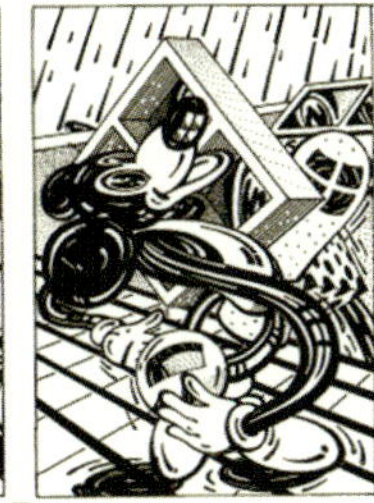
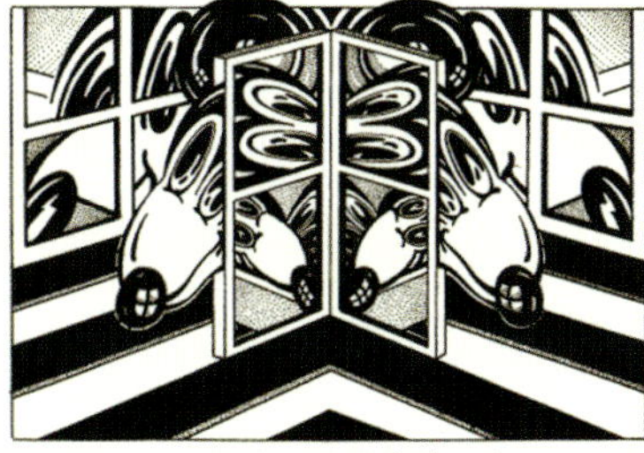
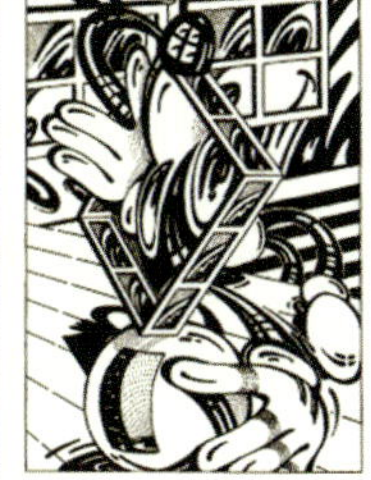
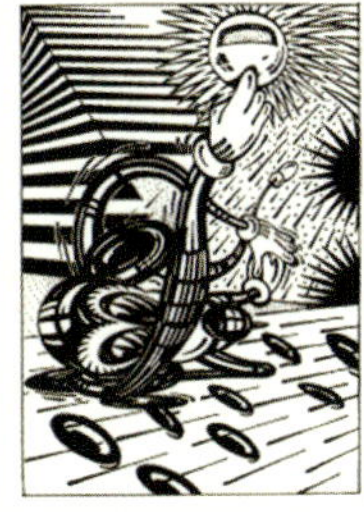
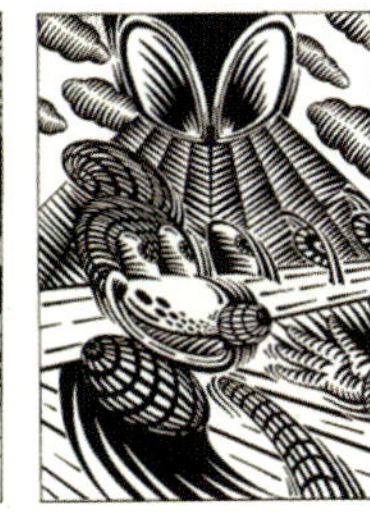

Mouse Drawigns 99 St Marks Place 1969

I had re-met the girl I knew from *Eye Magazine* in New York and moved in with her to find myself. She had some pot that my friend Marc had given her. I visited Martin Geisler to collect some royalties from the *Endless Summer* poster. He said he would give me $2400 in cash if I would create for him an *Endless Winter* poster. *The Endless Summer* had really made him a business over on 8th Street in the Village; his storefront signage read "Personality Posters" on the front of the building. Back at the girlfriend's I would hole up inside the small multi-room complex for days in the winter. The space was a 10' x 10' room, like a cube—empty, but with a mattress on the floor so her guests could crash. I sat on the floor with a pen and pad and began to draw my famous *Mouse* drawings. The light bulb overhead lit the drawing but also warmed the room throughout the day, as it was so very cold outside. I constructed my seven drawings through a gradual process of drawing a little each day over a period of a couple of months. These were called the "City Rat Drawings Inside Walls of Chaos."

The Small Portfolio Edition

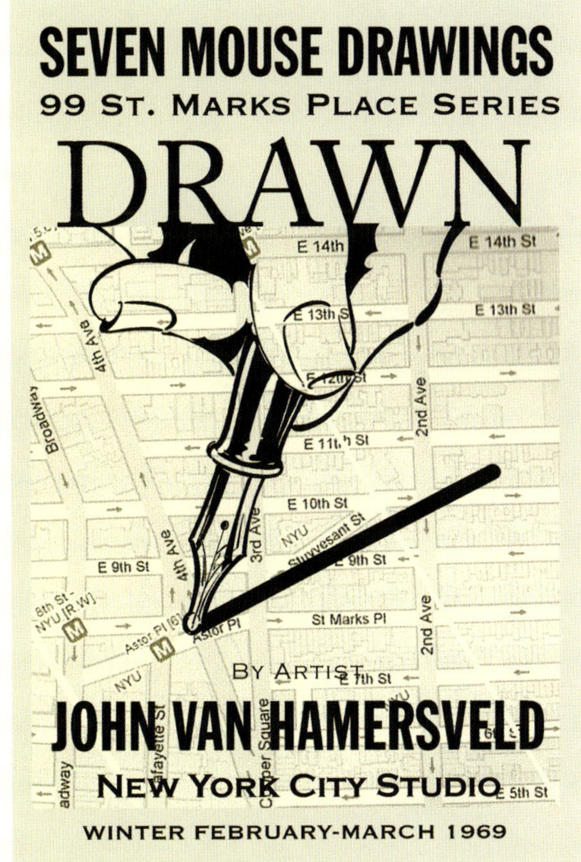

The drawn "Mouse" is created in shapes that become forms of abstraction within an object. Rick and Victor were the artist friends in my relationship with the cartoon. The "Mouse" image created a drawn vernacular, as their "Zap style" was created during our drawing meetings together.

The Drawing Table

Meetings Over Concepts

The Bellevue Studio near Bonnie Brae Avenue (1969)

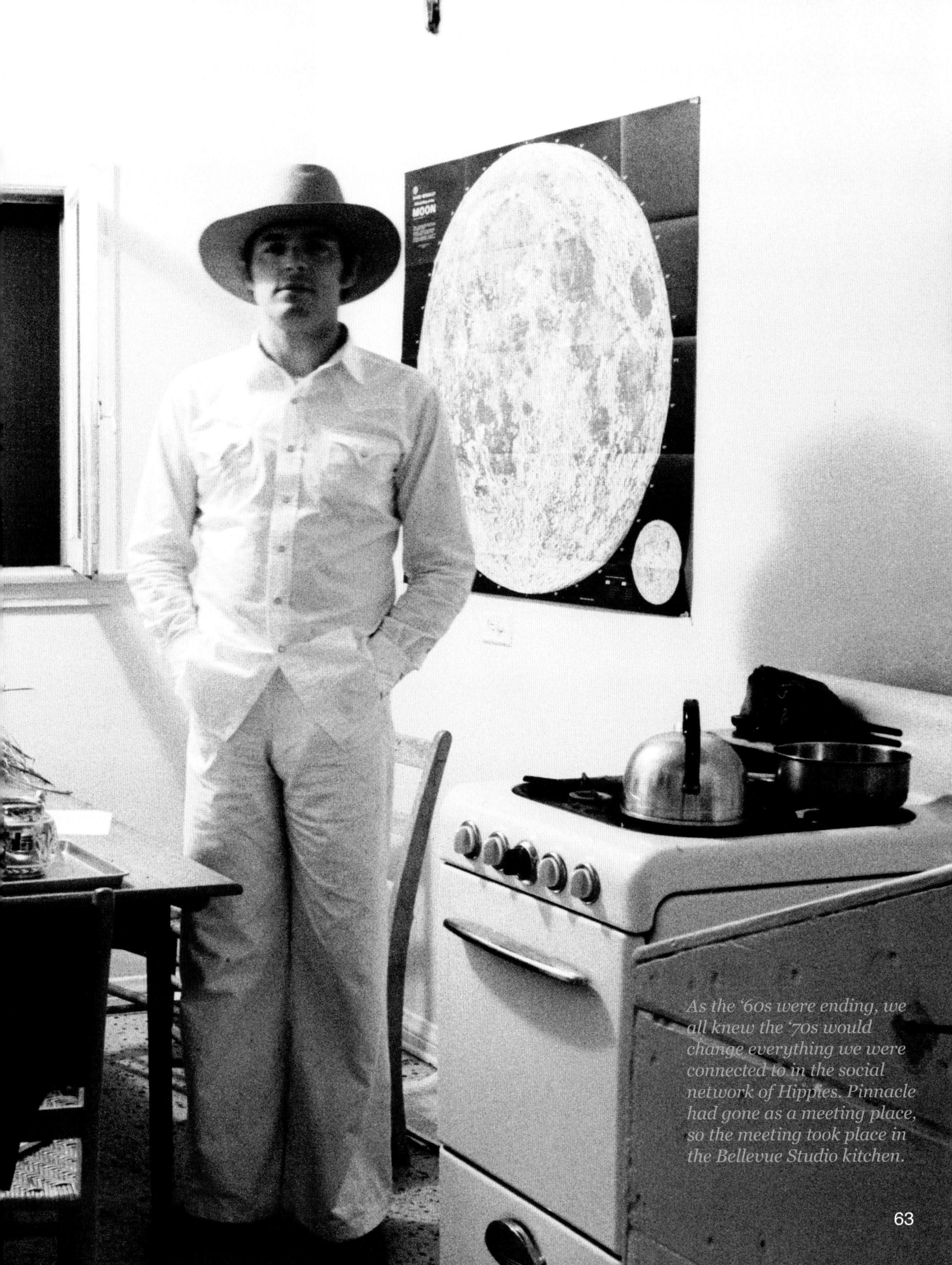

As the '60s were ending, we all knew the '70s would change everything we were connected to in the social network of Hippies. Pinnacle had gone as a meeting place, so the meeting took place in the Bellevue Studio kitchen.

The Bellevue Studio Days

My Bellevue studio was near the old Chouinard art scene [off Temple] of the early Sixties, where I had met with Rick Griffin before we had left for San Francisco and the Haight/Ashbury hippie scene there. This location was on the elevated enclaves of the Silverlake and Echo Park districts for artists. The small cottage-like house looked out over Los Angeles; I slipped through the day as I adjusted to the light coming into the windows and lighting my drawings. The sun was hot and gleamed into the living room studio house. The back bedrooms were lit nicely in the morning, but became darker as the sun moved west and lit the front living room until the dark of the night. There were the visitors from the past few years with the Pinnacle Experience. My perception had changed as it was created. The drug scene had transferred my innocence into the depressed; as passive characters smoking joints. I often was anxious and wandered around the house wondering what to do next.

I would think about work and how I had to go to Hollywood and find work at corporations now. The fun and excitement of Pinnacle was gone. I had a few different cars that often broke down, furthering the difficulty of getting around in my impoverished state. Sometimes I would go down Temple to take a bus over to Hollywood where I would sit and wait for another bus. Occasionally a carload of Chicanos would pass in a low slung car and heckle me about my long hair. The era was racial and territorial. I needed a haircut to work in the corporate world for money—to conform, as the conformist. Some said I should cut it myself. I found a barber and off it went... The end of an era.

Mescaline Experience

I remember my friend and I were sharing an afternoon joint at a second story studio apartment on Western Avenue, the antique district, where my friend's studio contained his famous interior design decor. He said, "I've got some Mescaline, in capsule form, do you want one?" I said to him, "I am so stoned already, I will split one with you." So I sat down on the floor and had my piece and kept smoking the number. We played some music and talked about new bands as we were listening to Blind Faith. After a while I said to my friend, "I don't feel too different. Hey, it's late and I think I'll go home and sleep this off in my own bedroom." Little did I know....

Take It to the Street

I left the apartment and went down the stairs and out the door, out onto Western Avenue, then across the street to the parking lane. I continued to walk up to my white '58 Comet station wagon. I walked along, step by step, up to the driver's side of the car door reaching for my car key as I felt a wind go by, with a swish. There, off to one side going up the street was a large gold car, as it skidded away to a halt and spun around in a u-turn, it came back towards me. As the car swerved by, in the window was this wildish face in a panoramic image smiling at me. The face was a character like a Pinnacle poster I had done of a black man with a big toothy smile and a gold star on his single front tooth. It scared me, but I was still able to open the door of the car and fall into the seat. I found my key and started the car to drive home, leaving my friend behind up there alone on the living room floor.

Going Out of the Smoke

I got back to Bellevue Studio, near Bellevue Avenue and Bonnie Brae, by driving through all the narrow back streets to find my way. I was so stoned and paranoid in the car I thought that the cops would pull me over for a bust. I reached the alleyway entrance to my building and stumbled into my bedroom. I stripped down and later laid down on the brass bed and buried my head in the comforter. I looked up and in front of me the wall opened into an illusion of large spirals turning into a world of exotic images, swirling in the space. I fell into a dream state and saw floating objects with Dali-like forms in a desert. I was so stoned I passed out on the pillow. The moment of clarity came the next day and never really went away. It was a turning point for me as I stopped smoking cigarettes. Everything remained sharp in my vision. I guess this is what happened to Indians when they experienced visions in sweat lodge ceremonies. Life goes on and the unconscious begins a dream, and the artist sketches from a new place where the visions unfold from his fingertips.

Rick Griffin's Inked Drawing (1969)

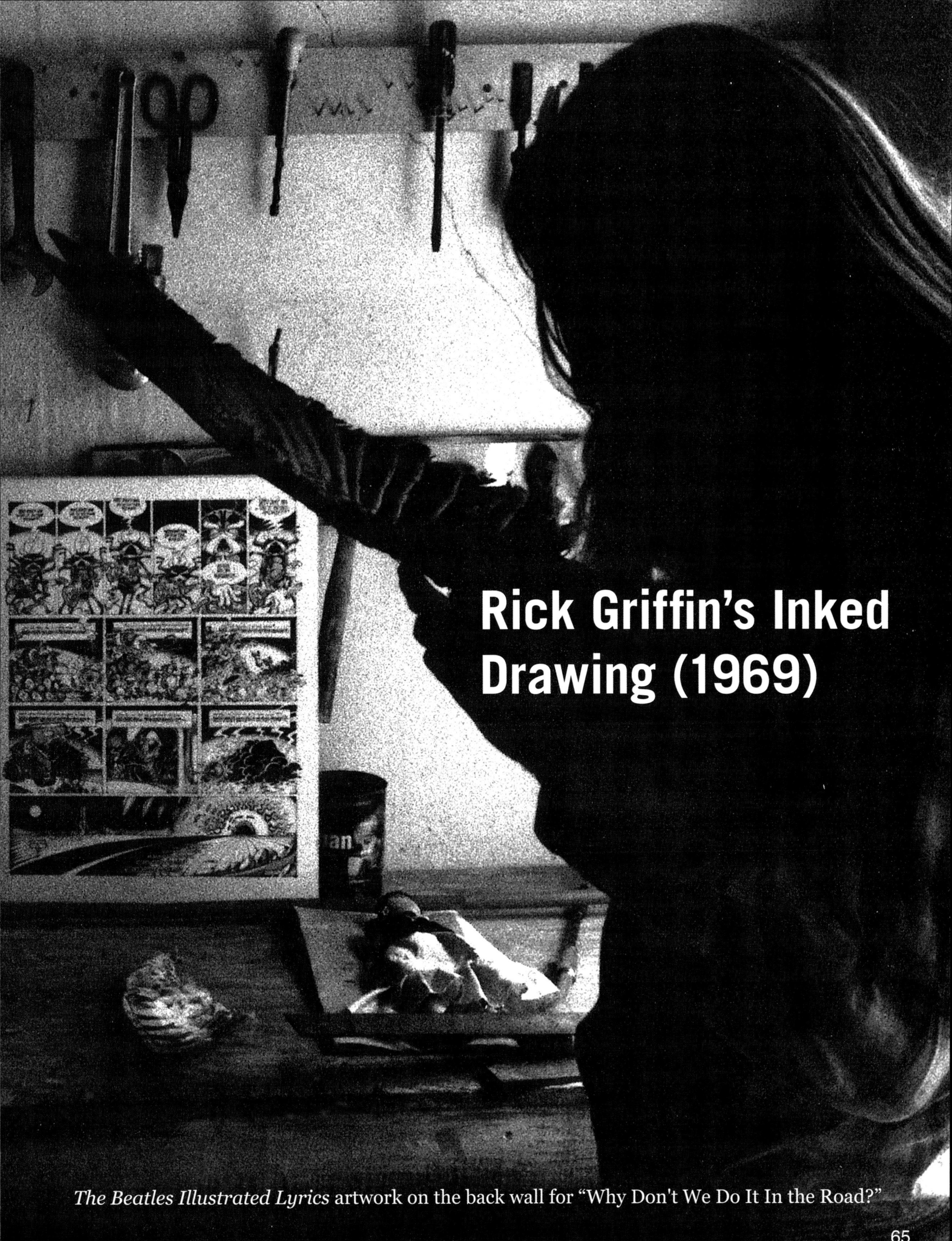

The Beatles Illustrated Lyrics artwork on the back wall for "Why Don't We Do It In the Road?"

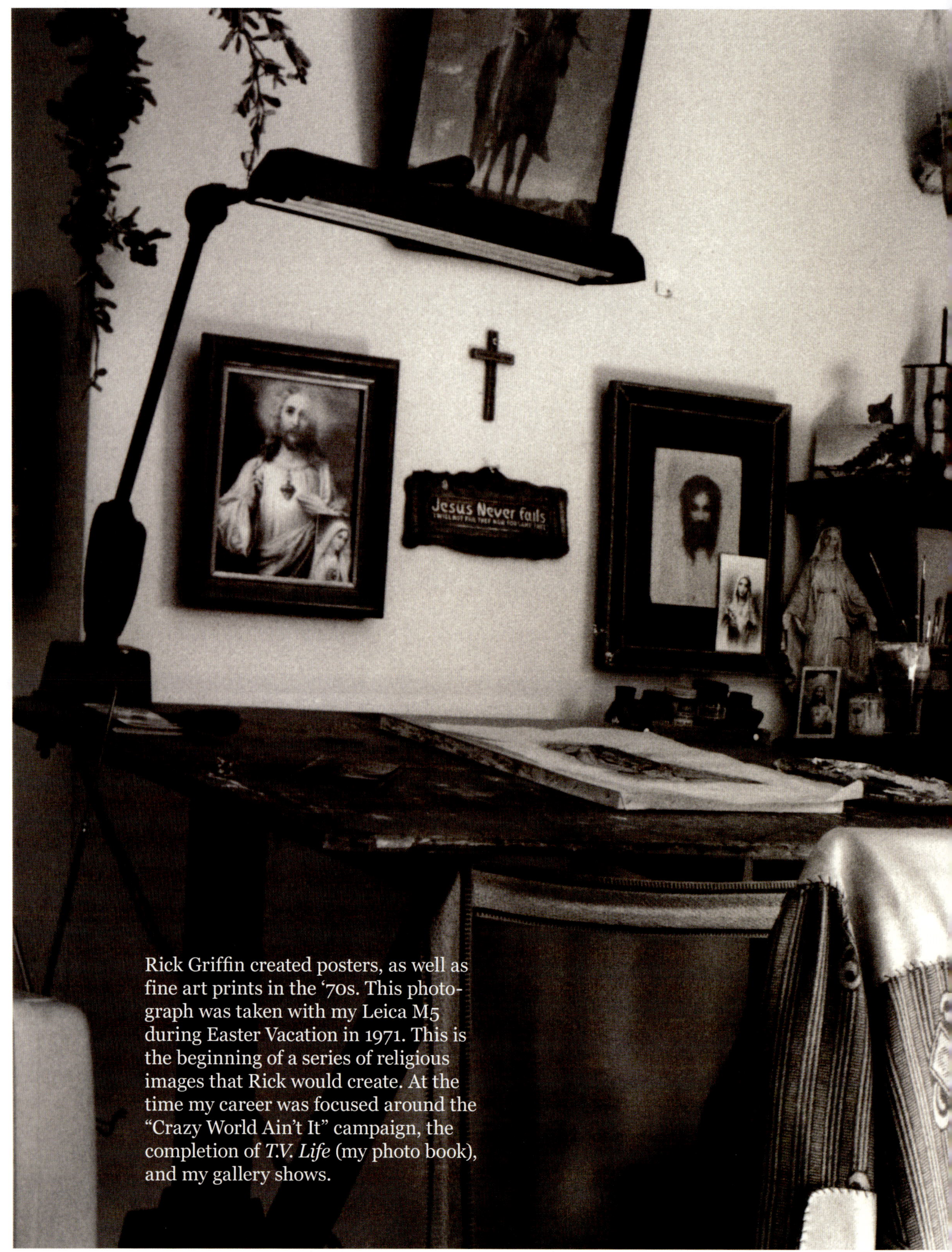

Rick Griffin created posters, as well as fine art prints in the '70s. This photograph was taken with my Leica M5 during Easter Vacation in 1971. This is the beginning of a series of religious images that Rick would create. At the time my career was focused around the "Crazy World Ain't It" campaign, the completion of *T.V. Life* (my photo book), and my gallery shows.

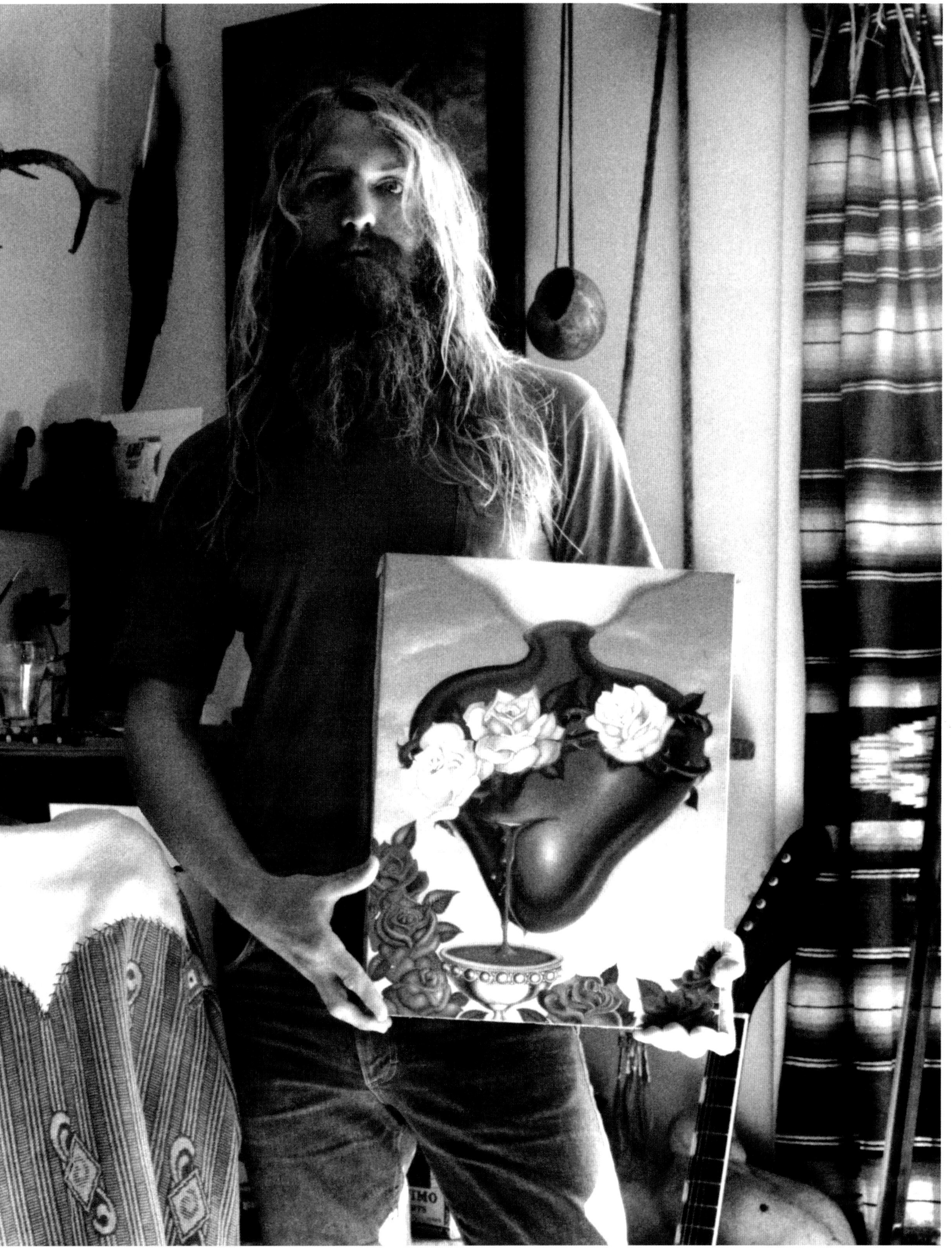

Chapman Park Studio Building (1970)

In 1970, I moved to the Chapman Park Studio building on 6th and Alexandria. It was a new decade and I had just finished the *Johnny Face* drawing. I published the black and red *Johnny Face* image on plastic paper called "Celestra Coat" paper. I made an edition of 400 copies; of this first edition of prints, I rounded up 80 posters and sent them to corporate art departments. When I later visited these corporate offices, I found that the poster was hung on the walls of their departments.

Johnny Face was a sign of the new decade and culture. It was my 1970s response to the Jimi Hendrix drawing done at the Kingsley Studio in 1968. *Johnny* was an instant hit in the 70s music scene. I made a pin of the image, which was then distributed by the Cherokee Book Store on Hollywood Boulevard, who also handled some of R. Crumb's *Mr. Natural* merchandise. The image was published again in 1990, in a compilation book of Los Angeles trademarks. Even today, people are enamored by *Johnny Face.*

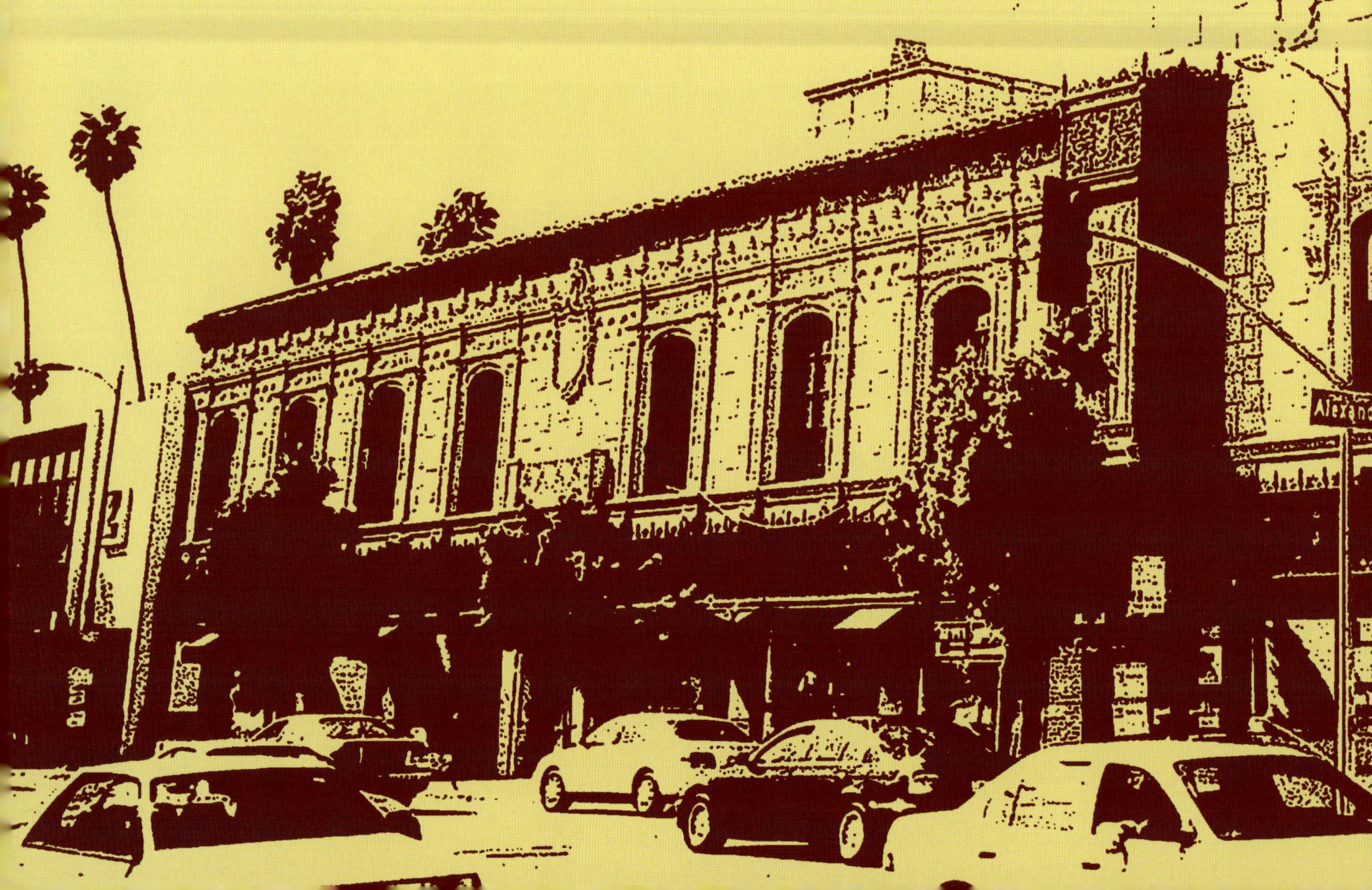

Johnny was very effective! Later on, the image and the *Crazy World Ain't It* logo pin showed up in Pasadena over at KRLA one day, and a salesman called me and wanted to do a billboard campaign. Foster and Klaiser, the outdoor advertising company, had done a media trade with KRLA. I guess I became the agency that day, and drew two faces of *Johnny* and the "she" version *Johnny Face* for the campaign. So in 1972, the two different outdoor billboards, "he and she," were booked at 250 sites in Los Angeles and Orange County. I asked to have 25 units of them placed near record labels and advertising agencies I knew. I had finished the album cover that month for the Rolling Stones' *Exile on Main Street* and the billboard on the Sunset Strip. This campaign tactic was enviable.

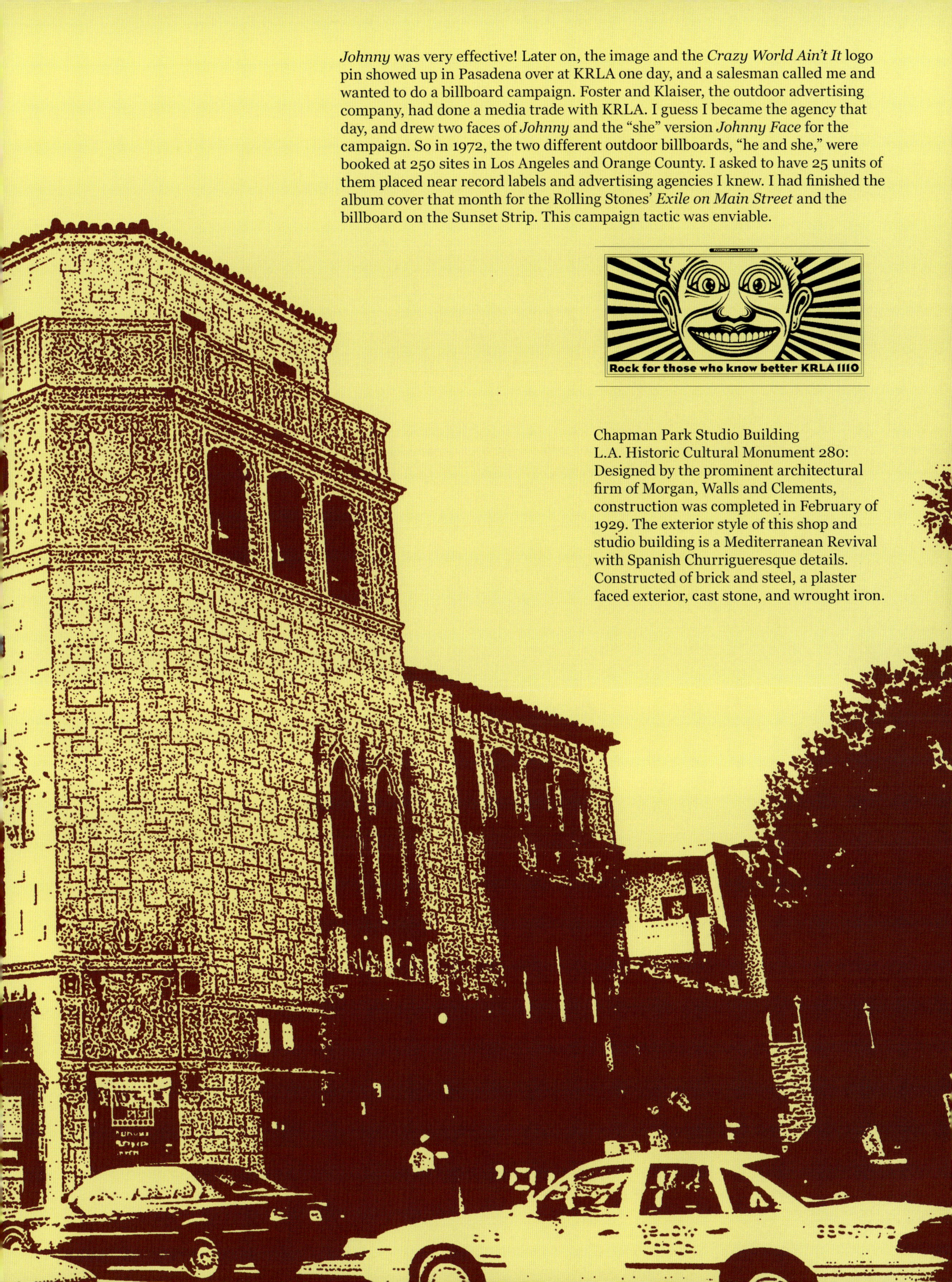

Chapman Park Studio Building
L.A. Historic Cultural Monument 280:
Designed by the prominent architectural firm of Morgan, Walls and Clements, construction was completed in February of 1929. The exterior style of this shop and studio building is a Mediterranean Revival with Spanish Churrigueresque details. Constructed of brick and steel, a plaster faced exterior, cast stone, and wrought iron.

Chapman Park Studio (1970)

The '60s were over for me after Chouinard, Capitol Records, Pinnacle Dance Concert promotion, and traveling to NYC and London. I returned in 1969 with my Leica camera, reminiscing about the end of the hippie age I knew as an art student. The hippie visitors of the studio days had to end with a few friends from the past. At the Bellevue Studio, they seemed out of touch with the new decade. One evening I went to see a Little Richard show at the Ambassador Hotel on Wilshire, where he was playing in the old Coconut Grove Room. After the show, I went out front and walked down the sidewalk of Alexander toward 6th Street. The moon was out that night, and I saw the Chapman Park Studio building under the moonlight. The Equitable Building that had just been built on Wilshire had a huge lighting system installed that made the slab-like structure look like something from Stanley Kubrick's *2001: A Space Odyssey*, which had just come out.

There, in Wilshire's corporate culture, the moon that night lit the facade of the building, but there was sky light where the moon lit the inside of Studio 15. I continued to walk down to the facade designed by Morgan, Walls & Clements, the architectural firm based in Los Angeles that worked in the Spanish Colonial revival and Mayan revival styles of the '20s. I loved the look because it looked like Europe, where I'd just been on vacation. I walked through an arched hallway and up the stairs to the second floor, went down the hallway and looked into an empty Studio 15.

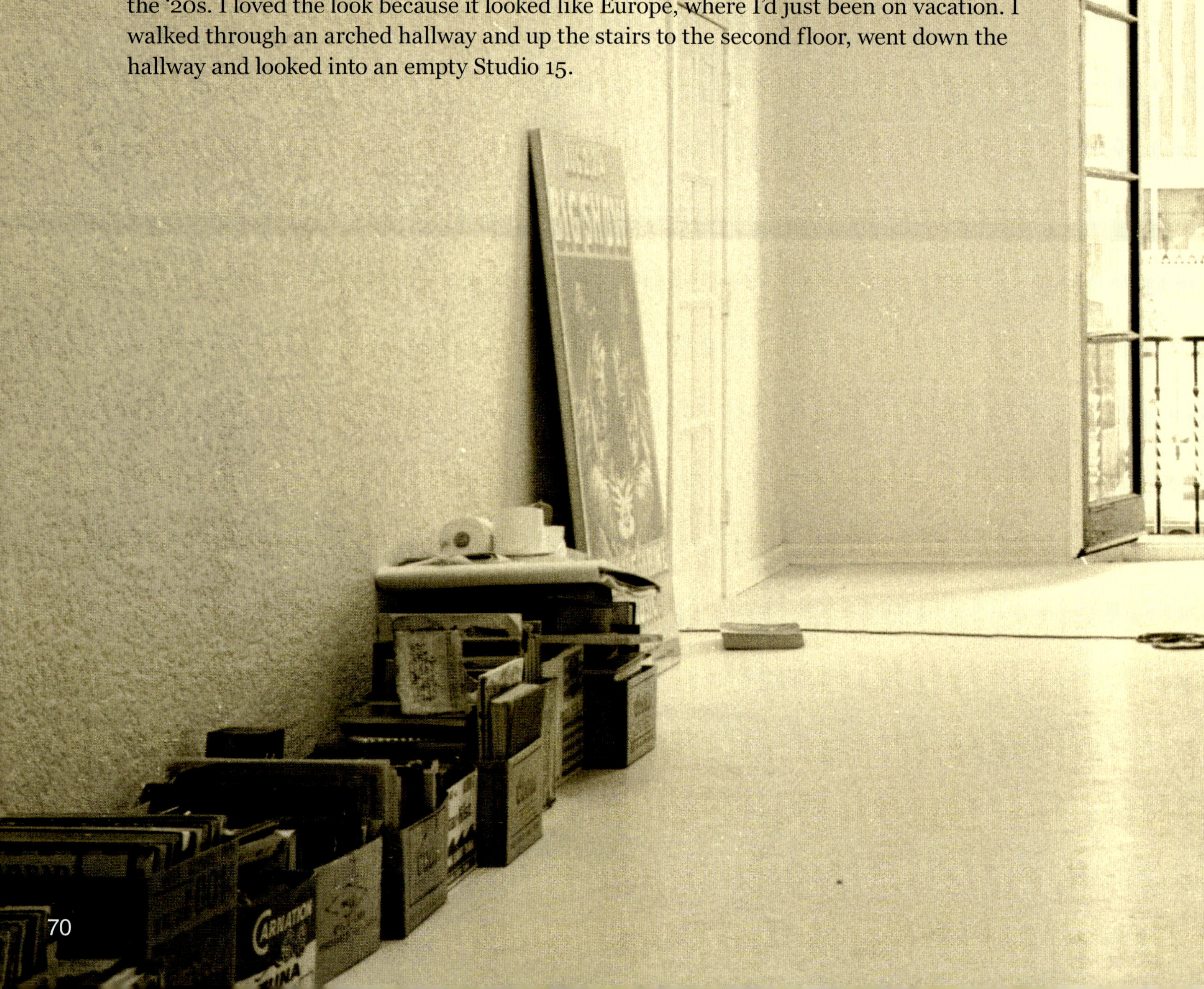

At that moment I had the vision of starting my first graphic design business. I had been doing freelance work in Hollywood and had the idea of selling my talent there and creating an independent art studio. So I rented the well-lit room; the loft had a 25 foot ceiling and space to live and work in. I had just quit smoking and started hanging out at the Ambassador Hotel pool that was a block away. I had a girlfriend and artists Billy Al Bingsten and Peter Alexander used to hang out at the pool too. Billy was the famous "Kahuna" of *Gidget's Story* about Malibu from my teen life, and the *Endless Summer* poster I designed had sold out from NYC. My surfer world from my teen years wasn't so useful anymore as an adult. I had to work now in the art & entertainment industry of Hollywood, creating communication work in line with Marshall McLuhan's concept, "the medium is the message." It seemed like a new world. New clients and a new kind of society, and there I was in the new decade, in line with McLuhan's belief: "We become what we behold. We shape our tools and then our tools shape us."

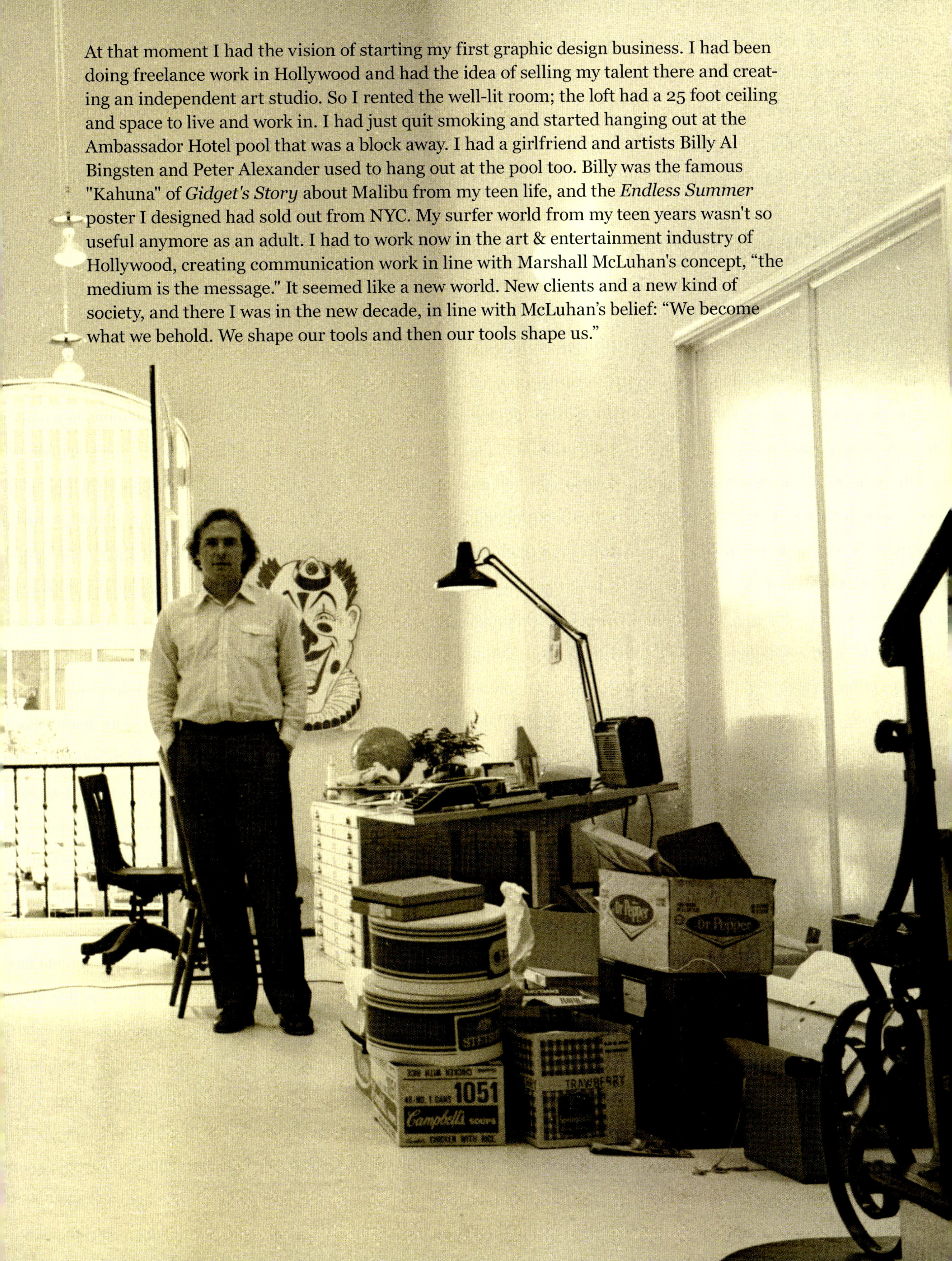

DRAWING A MASCOT FOR THE STUDIO WORKS

Beginning of the Chapman Park Studio Building (1970)

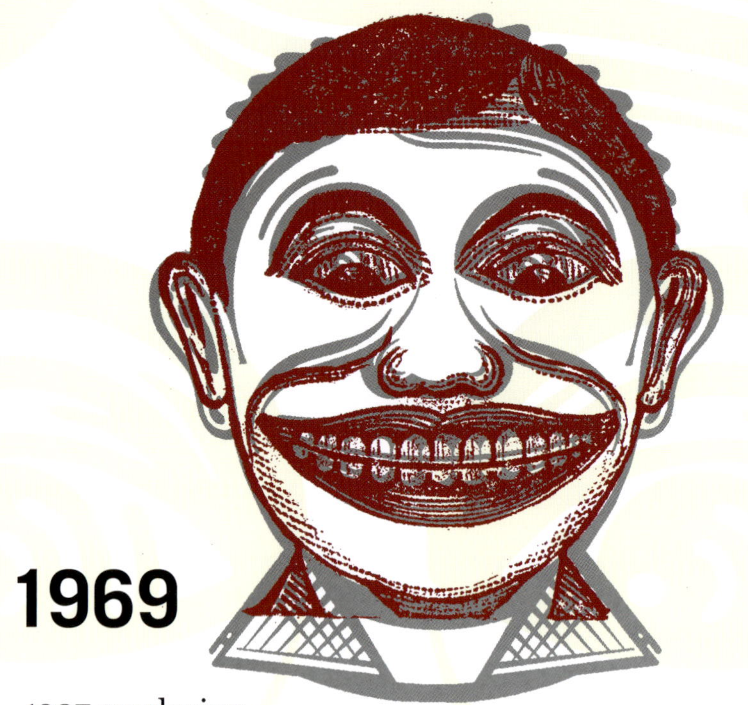

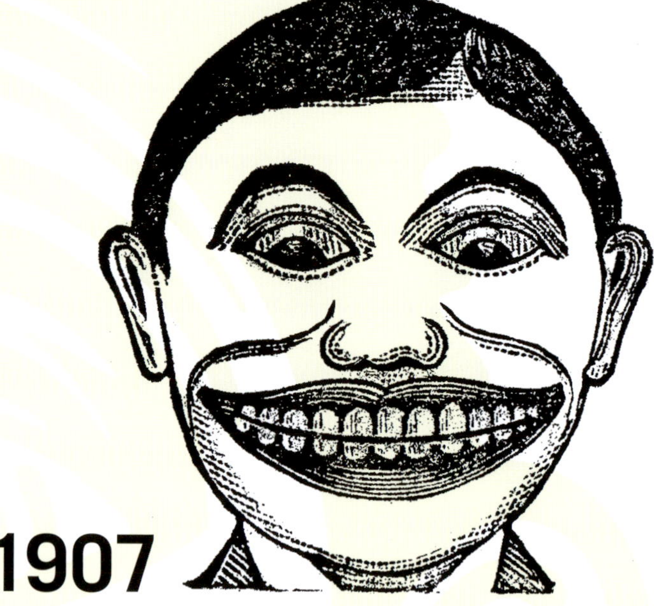

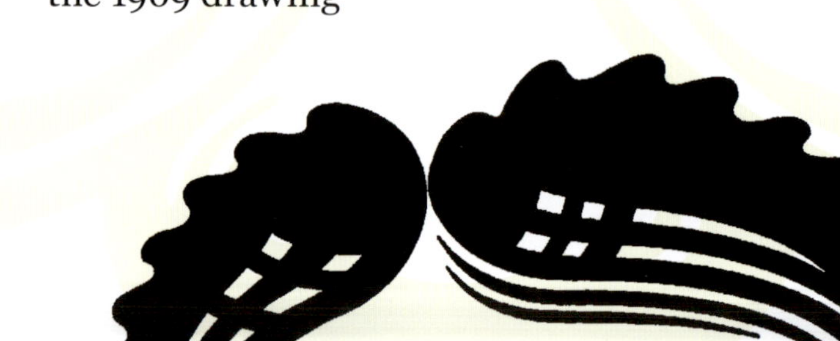

1969

1907

Found in *Wilshire Magazine;* published in 1907

1907 overlaying the 1969 drawing

IF YOU WANT FUN

Just get a full set of our **False Teeth** with **Punch and Judy** whistle attached. All for 10 cts. Make your mother-in-law laugh and scare off other evil spirits. Entertain a houseful all night. You can't eat with them, but you can chew the rag. By mail, 10 cents. **Postal Mfg. Co.,** Box 2656, Dept. 4, **Boston, Mass.**

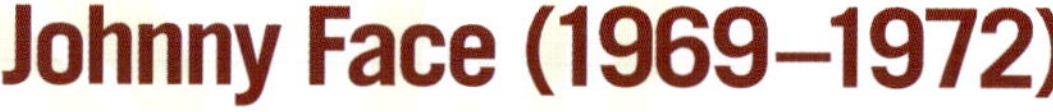

Johnny Face (1969–1972)

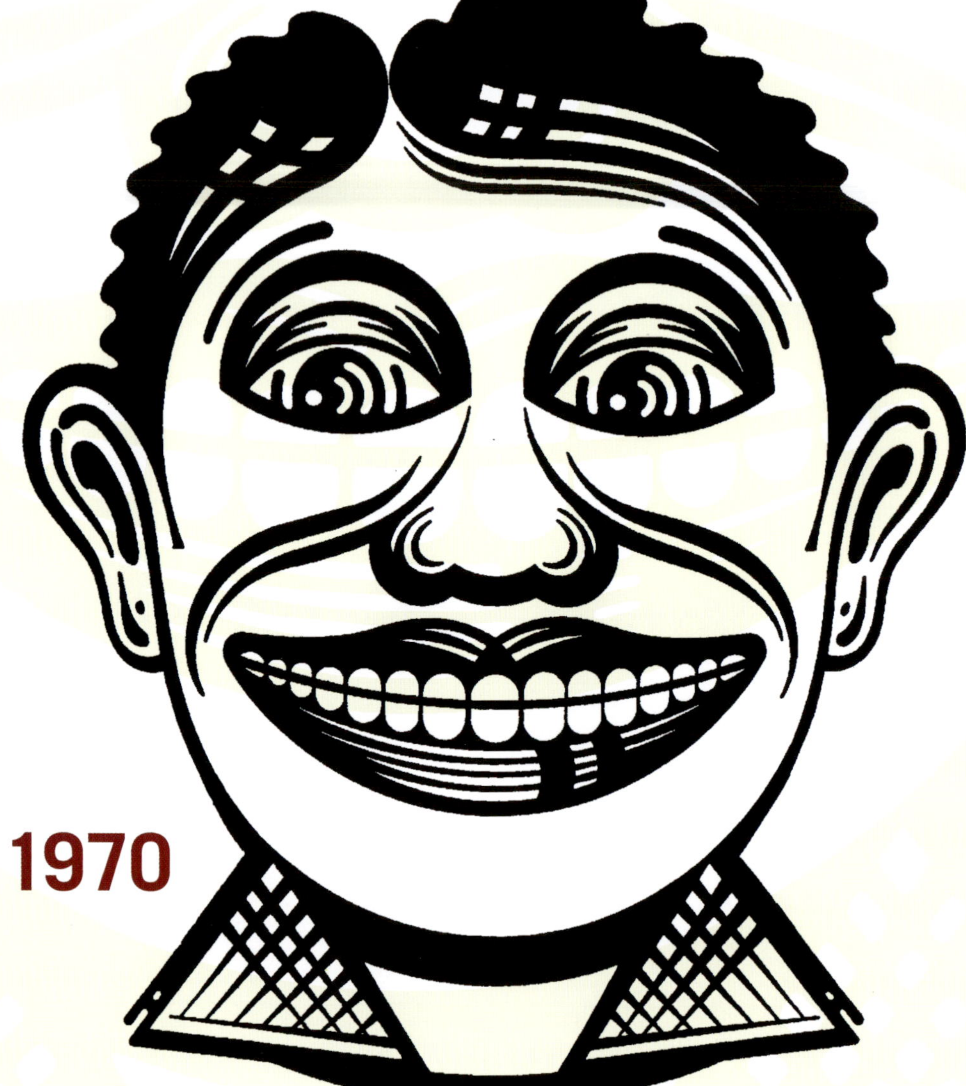

1970

In 1968, on the floor of the Willoughby Studio, I drew the portrait of my art school girlfriend Honeya, which led to the *Space Cowboy* image for the Rose Bowl American Music Show poster. Later, the mascot iconic image was the influence of a mescaline and marijuana jag, after which I was left with the enduring image of "a man's face with a big, toothy, glorious wide smile."

I came up with the *Johnny Face* logo the following year, which I used for promoting my own work. The mascot face was emblazoned across the famous chest of Mick Jagger in a 1972 *New Musical Express* feature on the Rolling Stones. It had a rich history. I transformed the *Crazy World* t-shirt into a suit covered in *Crazy World* buttons for a Los Angeles art directors club event.

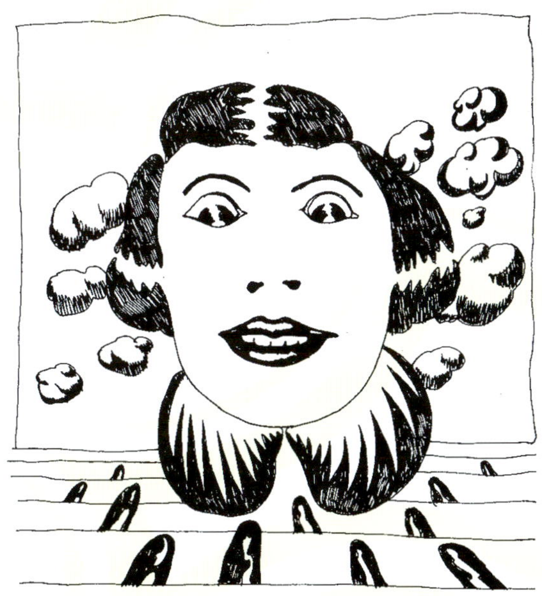

1968: The portrait of Honeya that helped shape the *Space Cowboy* (right)

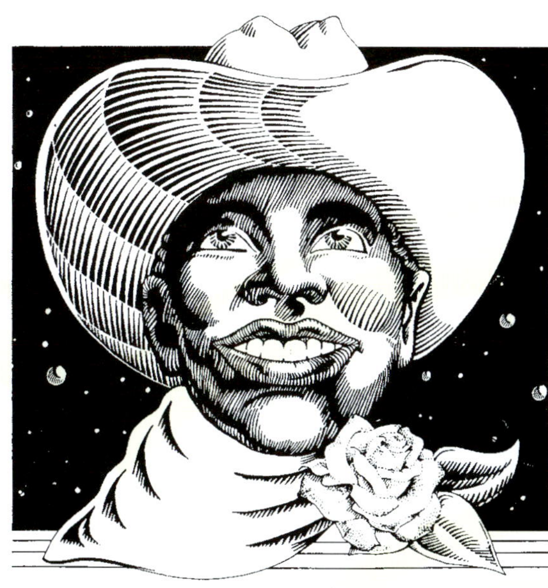

1968: At the Kingsley Studio, the portrait of Honeya led to this *Space Cowboy* image

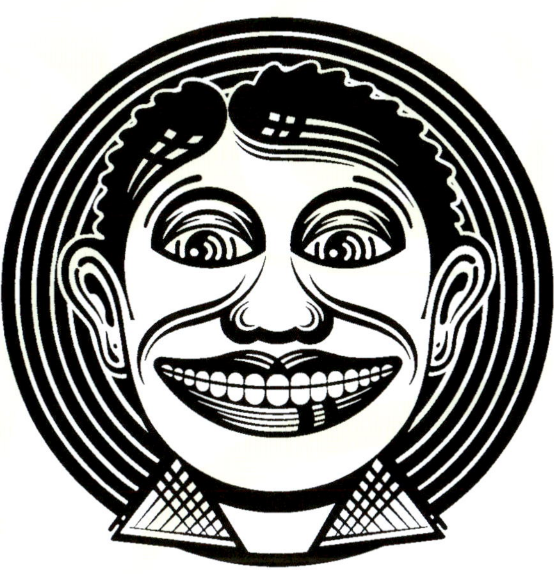

1970: The mascot drawing is designed for a red and black poster to promote the drawing

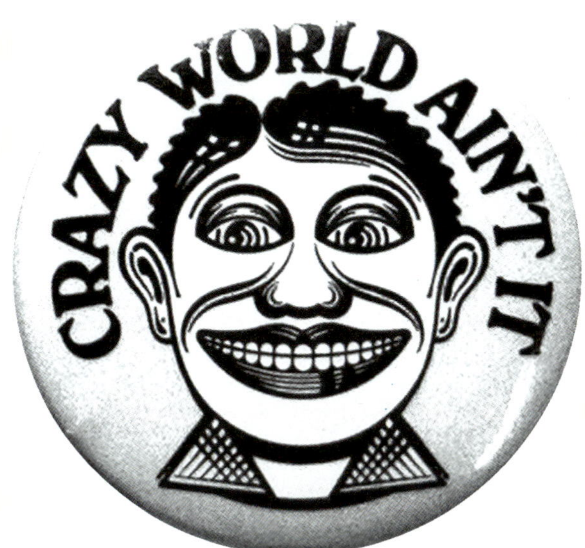

1971: The *Crazy World Ain't It* button is created and leads to the shirt promotion

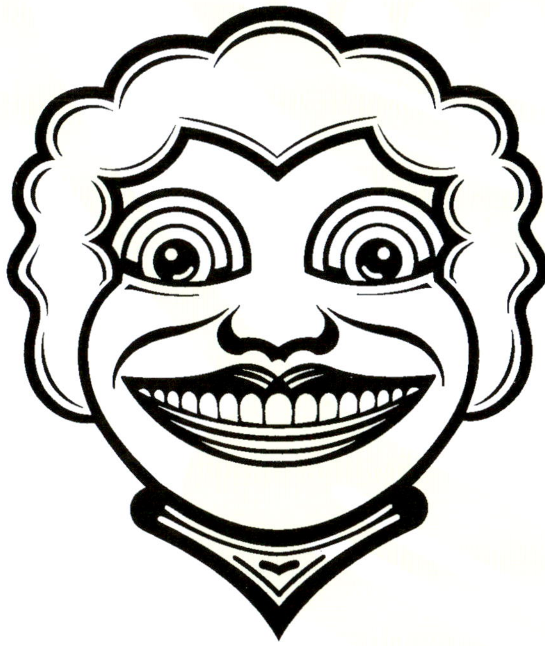

1972: The female version is created to be a companion to the male version of the *Johnny Face*

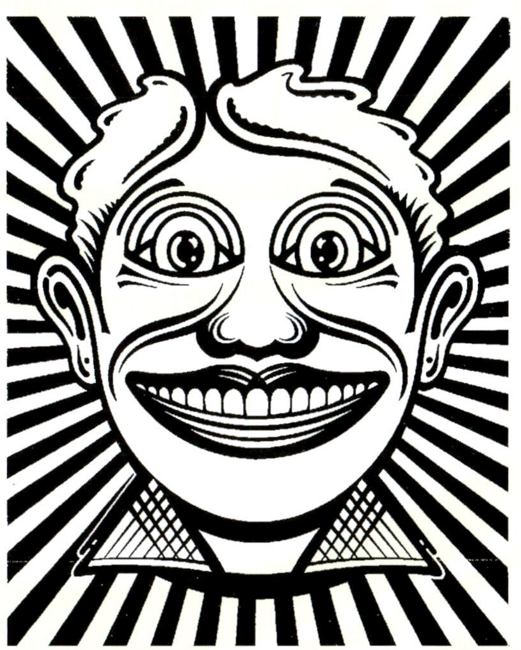

1972: The male version of the *Johnny Face* is adapted for a KRLA billboard project

The Johnny Mascot

Why not create your own corporate identity and go to the next level by designing a mascot to support your core message? I called it "Johnny!" I created a mascot character that was meant to support and enhance my art & entertainment business. I chose a paper on which I could print my two color poster, but the printer also had a plastic option called "Celestra Coat." Choosing the plastic surface meant that the paper would never get old.

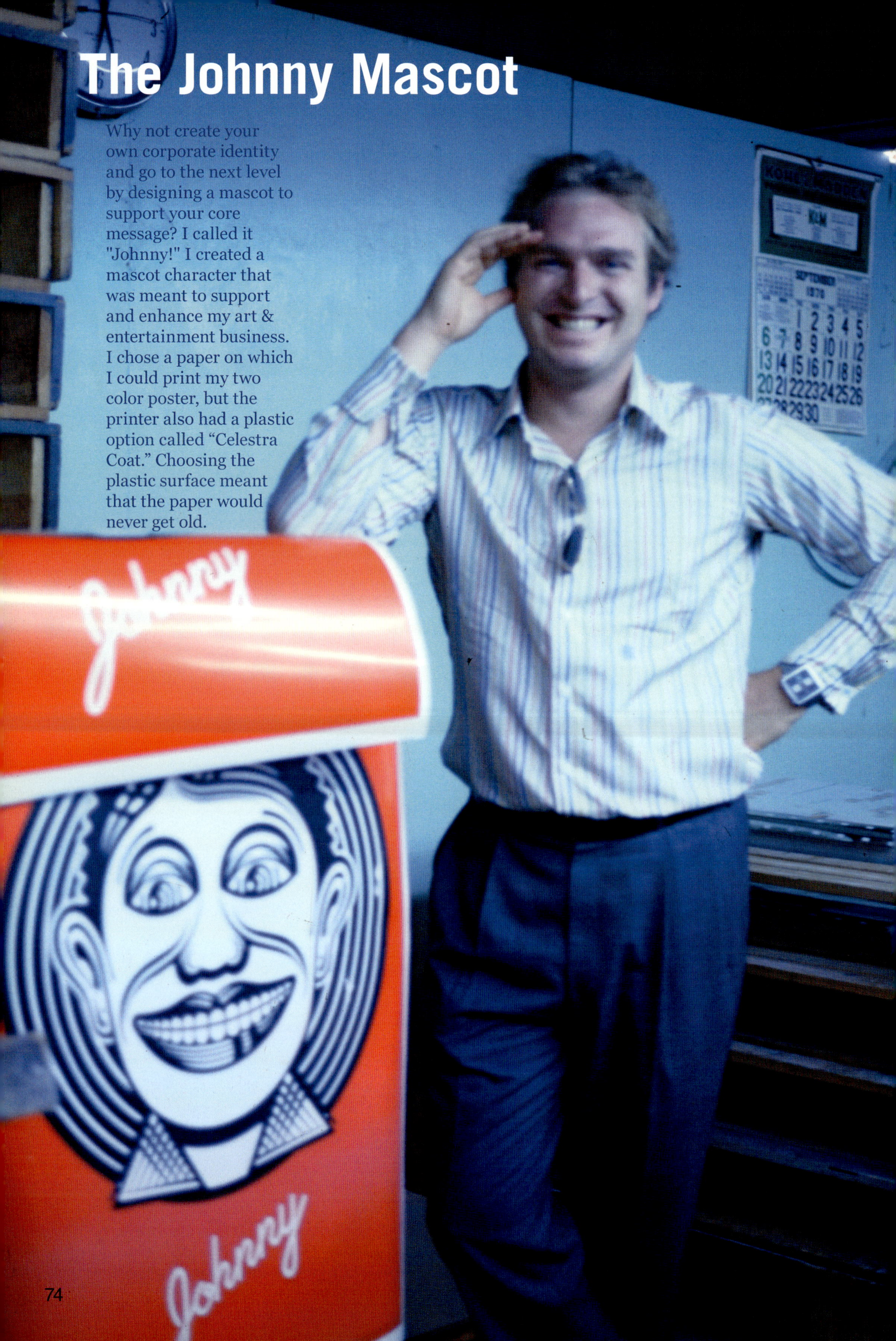

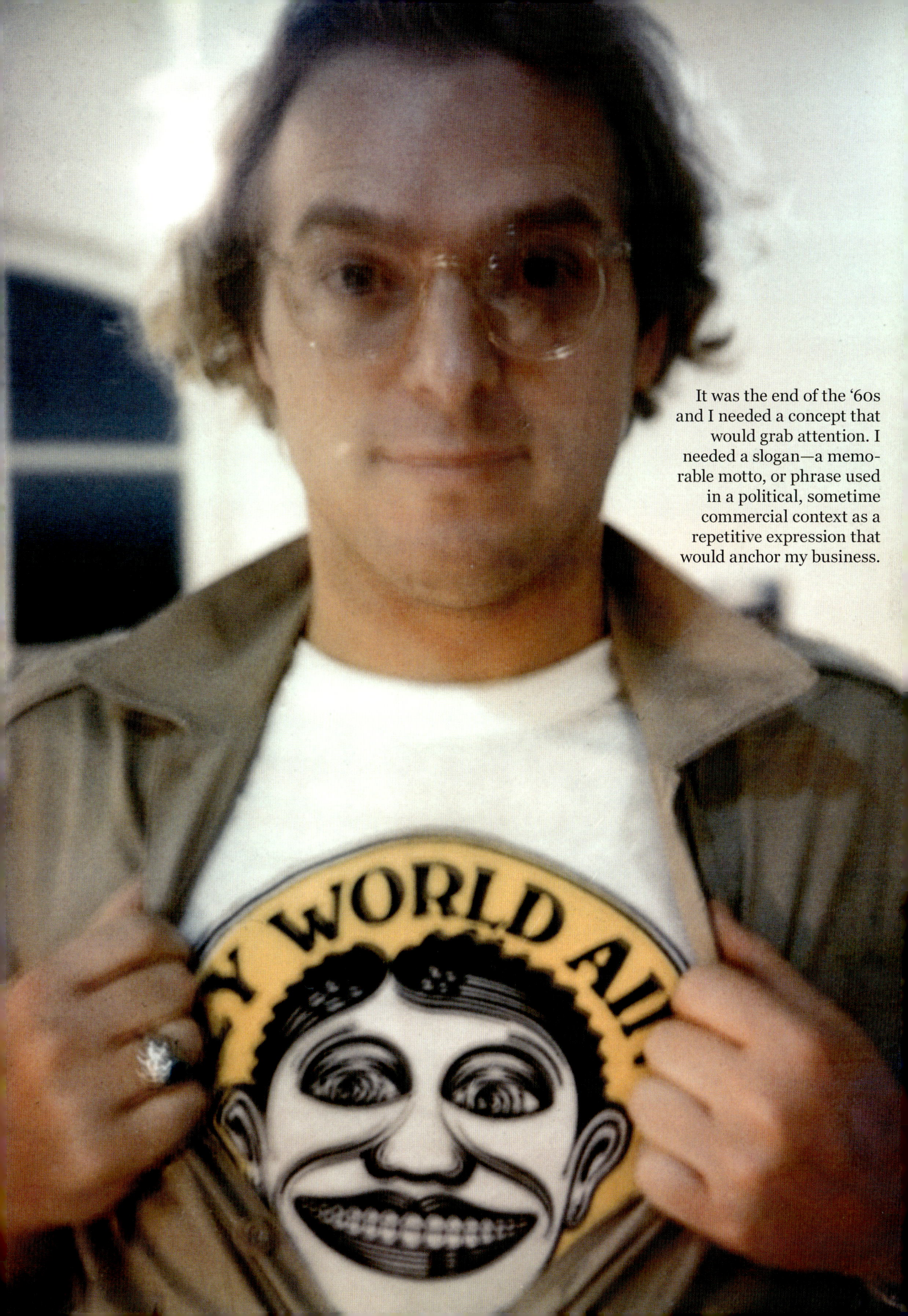

It was the end of the '60s and I needed a concept that would grab attention. I needed a slogan—a memorable motto, or phrase used in a political, sometime commercial context as a repetitive expression that would anchor my business.

Printed Images as Cultural Icons

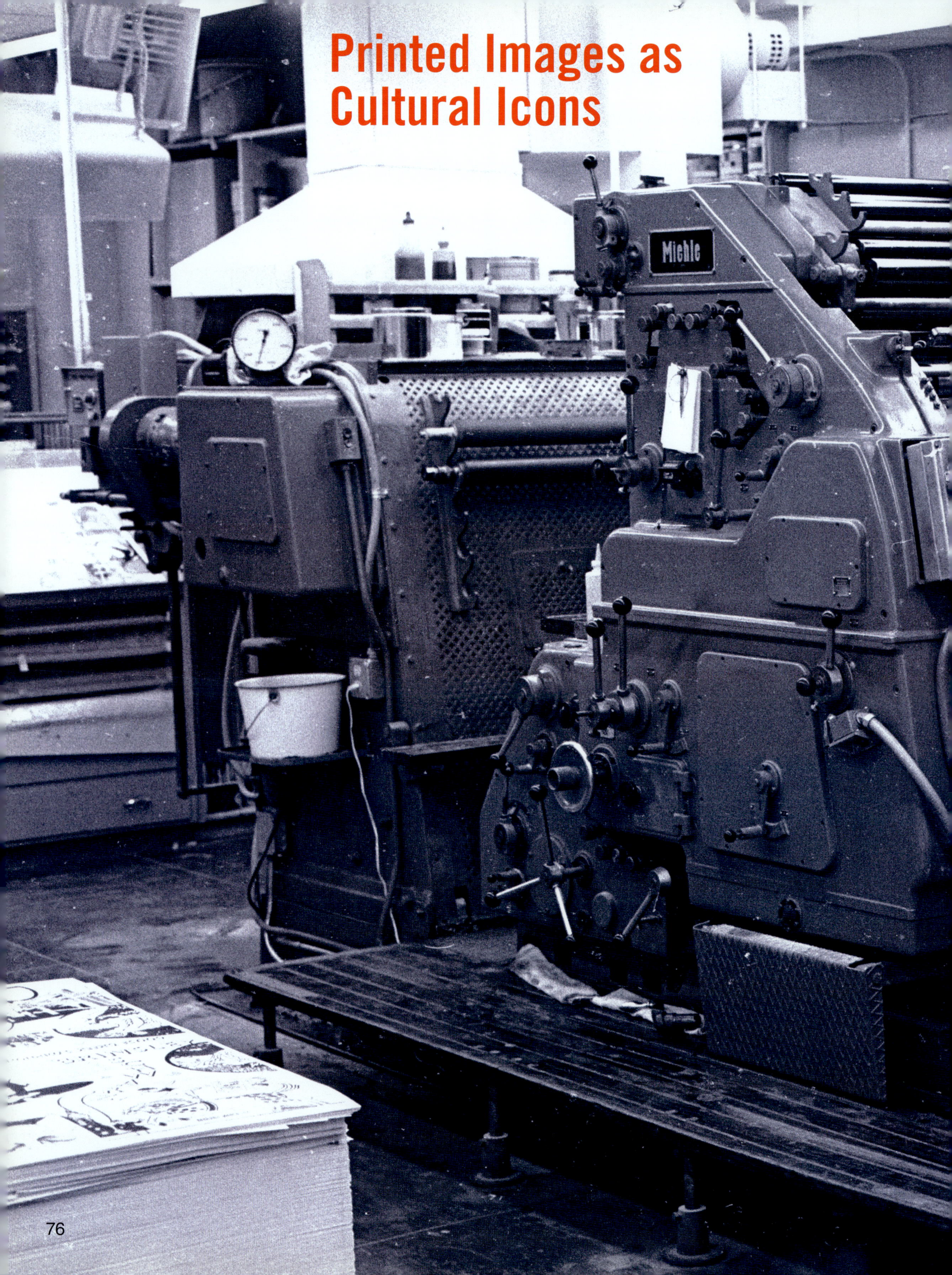

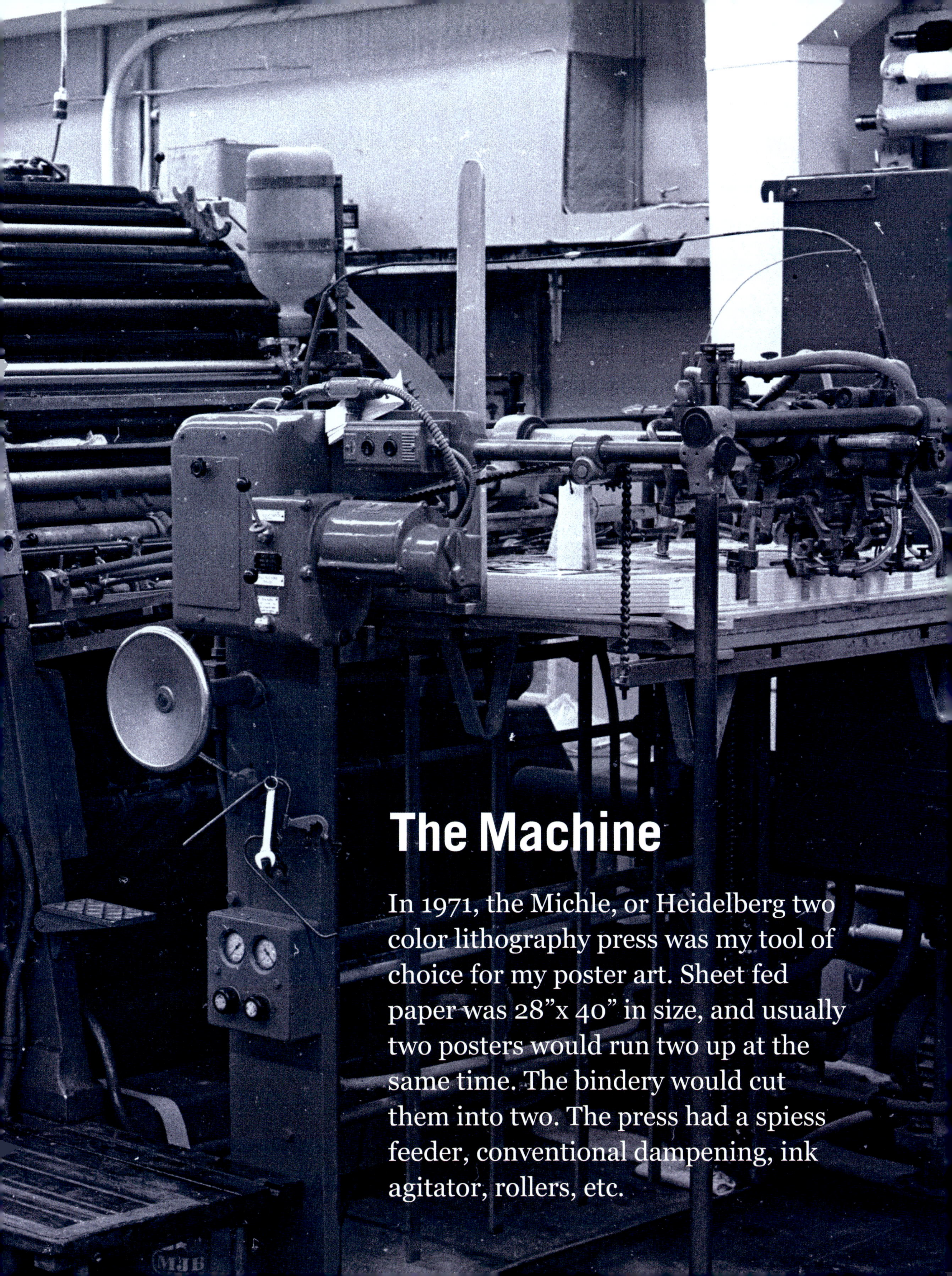

The Machine

In 1971, the Michle, or Heidelberg two color lithography press was my tool of choice for my poster art. Sheet fed paper was 28”x 40” in size, and usually two posters would run two up at the same time. The bindery would cut them into two. The press had a spiess feeder, conventional dampening, ink agitator, rollers, etc.

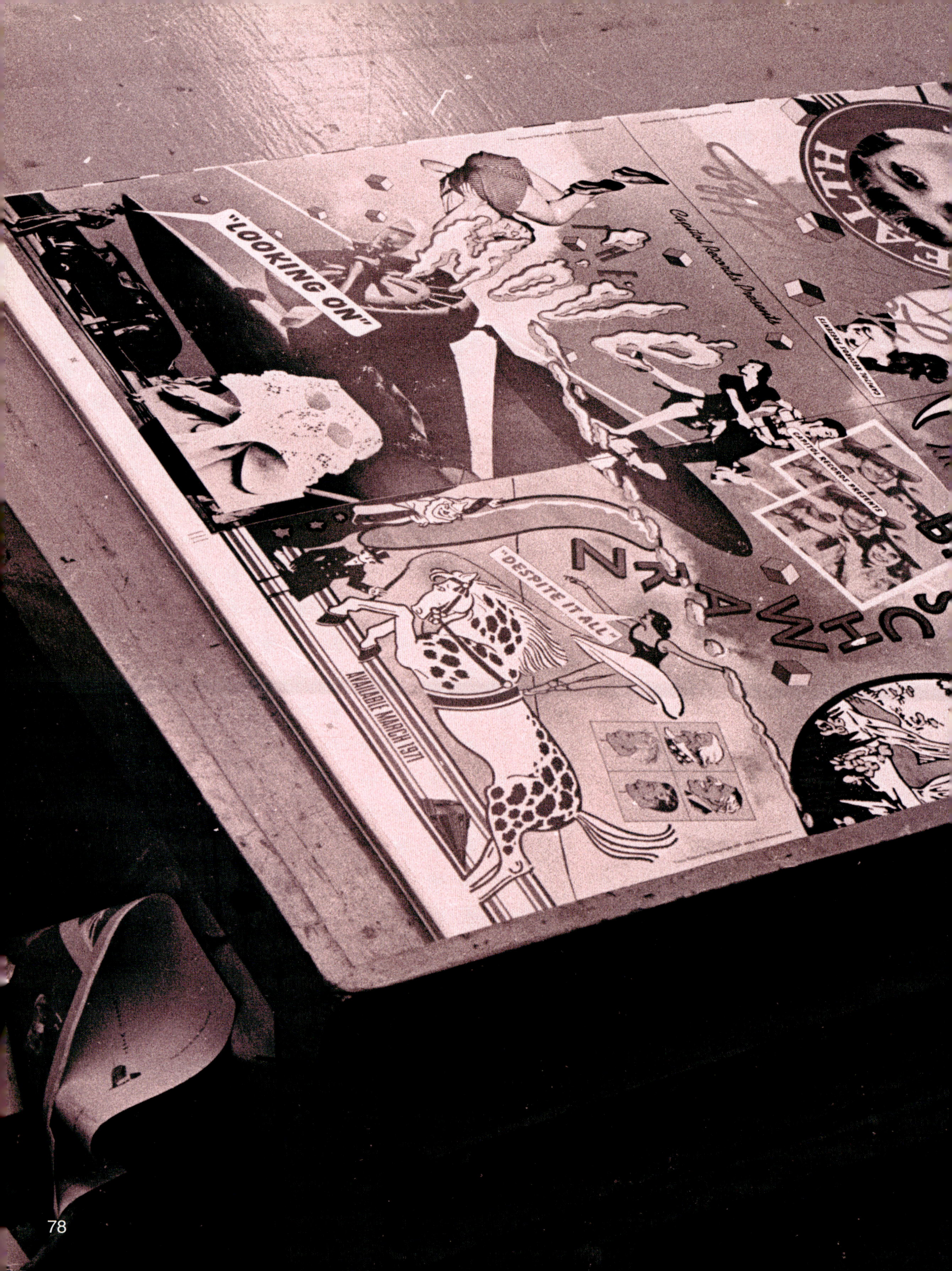
"LOOKING ON"
Capitol Records Presents
CAPITOL RECORDS PRESENTS
"DESPITE IT ALL"
AVAILABLE MARCH 1971

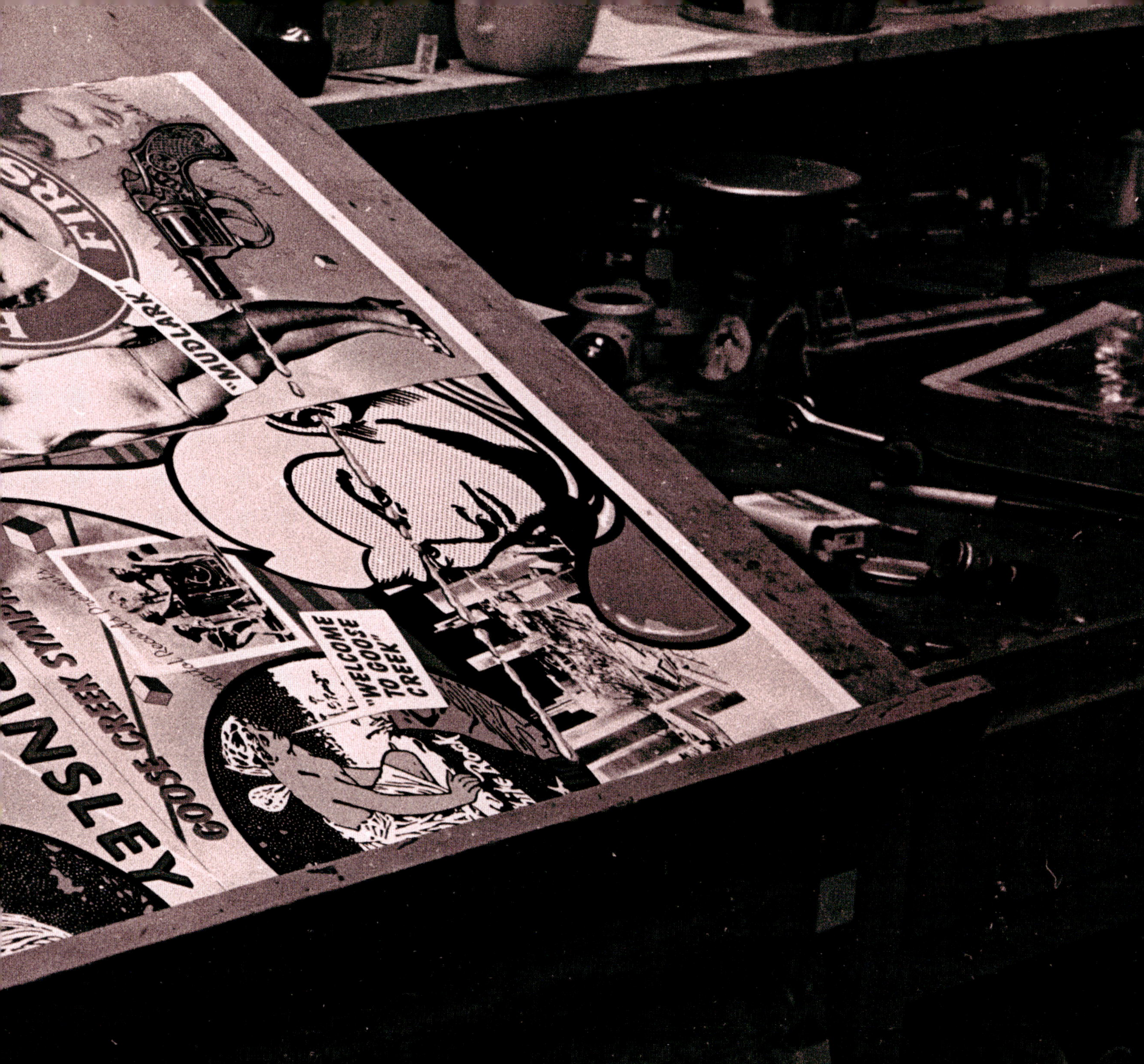

Corporate Culture: Making Iconic Communications

The underground surfaced as a recognizable icon in subsequent art & entertainment. The 12" x 18" poster of the '60s created in the early '70s became popular to market and promote as a music product for the Capitol distribution company. Designing and printing four different posters on one sheet all at the same time became a job for me in 1971. There were a few old two-color presses around me that I could use to cut waste and create a set of four posters in a row that hung on the horizon as a mural. The posters were distributed in four boxes at the record store as free collectibles promoting the four bands Capitol had just signed.

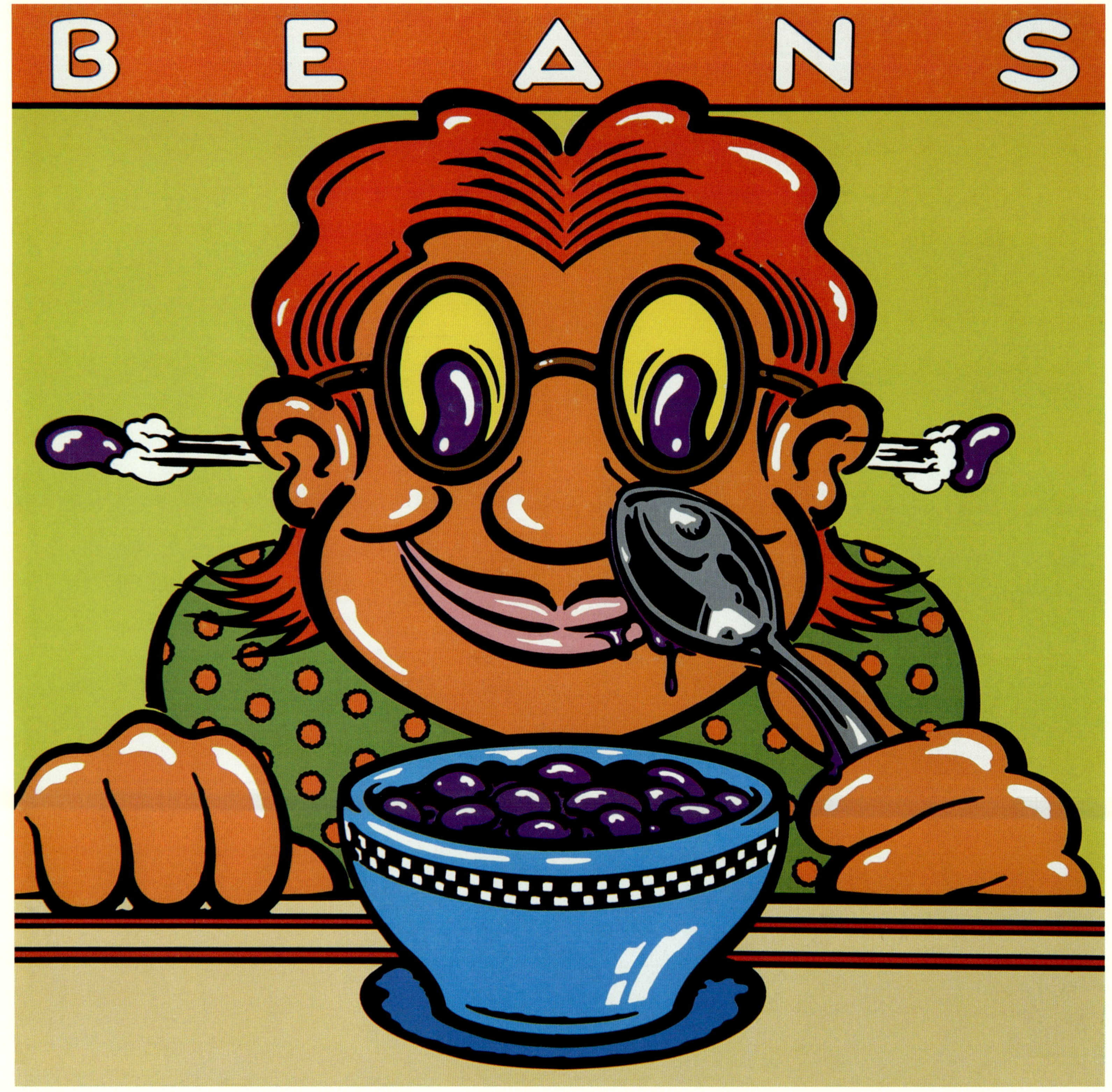

Beans Album Cover, 1971

The Beans were a band made up of high school friends from Phoenix, Arizona. Later, the Beans merged with the Red, White and Blues, creating a new band called the Tubes. The Tubes later grew to be a nationally known band.

I drew the album cover under the art direction of Norman Seef. There was a children's song that went, "Beans, beans, the musical fruit. The more you eat, the more you toot." This song ended up being the inspiration for the album art design. I drew a boy in front of a giant bowl of beans. His pupils are beans, as if signifying that all he can think about is eating the beans as his ears are "farting" out beans.

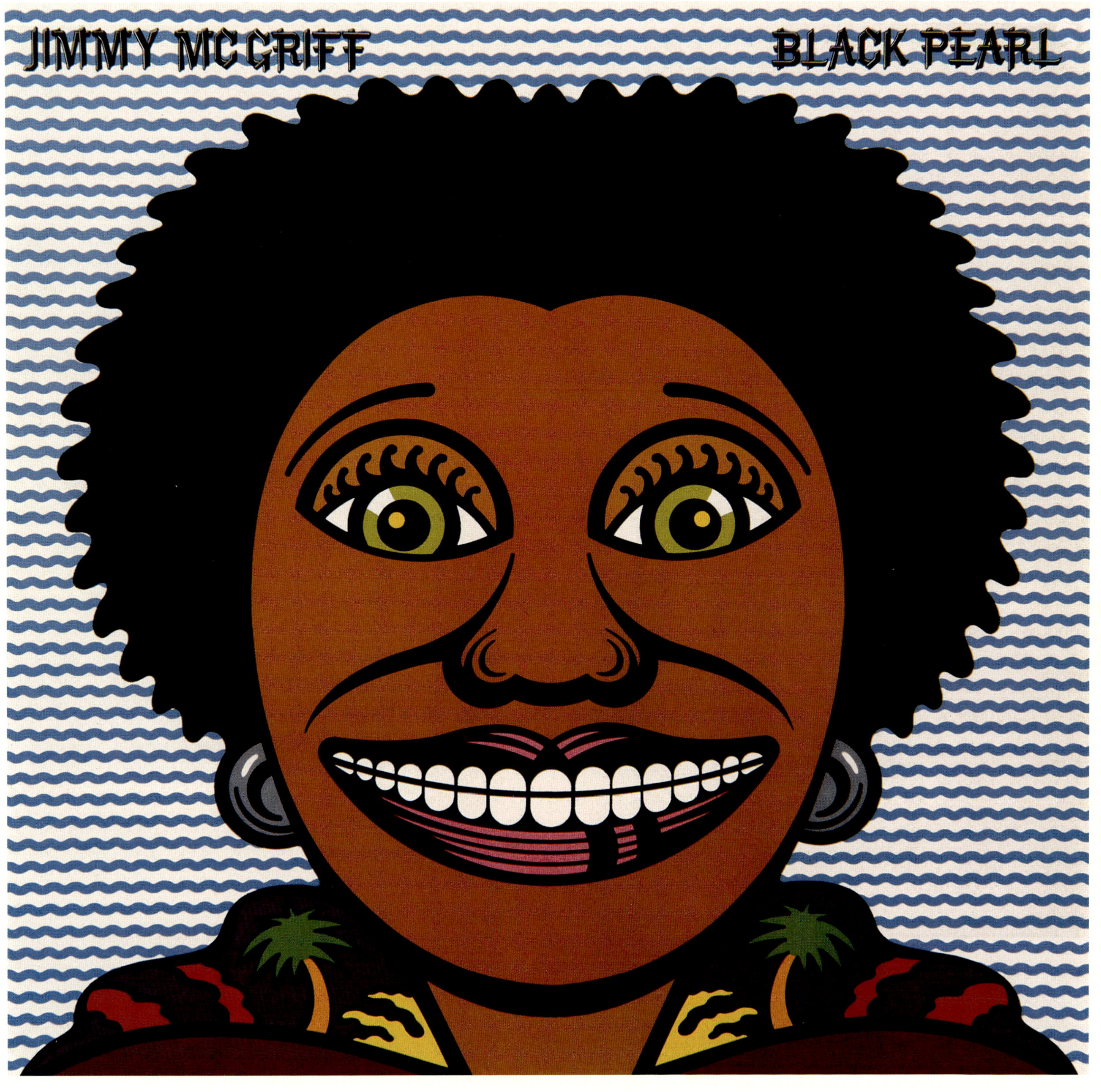

The Black Pearl Album Cover, 1972

The idea behind the *Black Pearl* album cover was to create an image that matched *Johnny Face*. By 1972, the KRLA billboards were all over LA. *Black Pearl* was set to come out, and I had just started preliminary work on the packaging for the Rolling Stones' *Exile on Main Street*, which went on to be a critically and commercially acclaimed album.

"While McGriff may be a good musician, I did not pick this album for that reason. I picked it simply for the brilliant attention grabbing art of John Van Hamersveld. While this is the first I have posted of his art, it will by no means be the last. You may not see the albums seen normally by him but you will see great art." –www.albumcoverart.wordpress.com

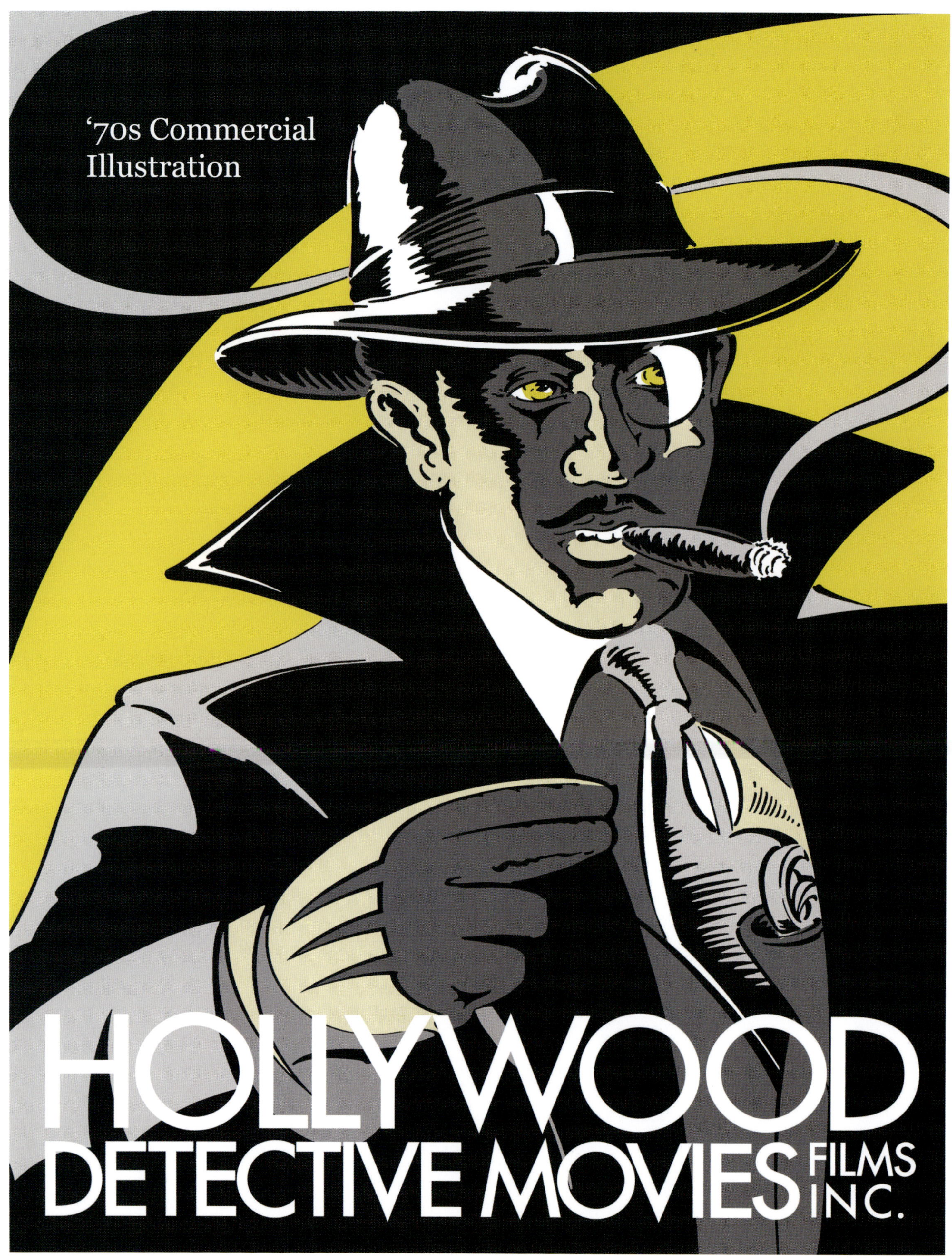

This Hollywood film poster was done for a company called Films Incorporated, based just outside of Chicago. Top Left: Neil Sedaka illustration for *Rolling Stone* magazine Top Right: Bonzo Dog Band, fire hydrant image. It has a definite phallic undertone. Bottom: Hollywood dragon, used for a Leon Russell song book.

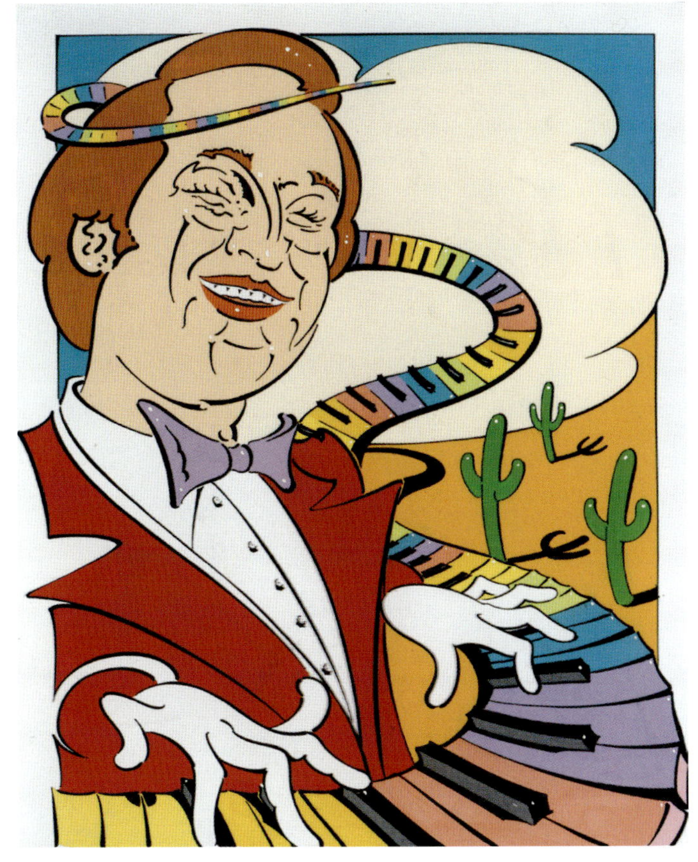

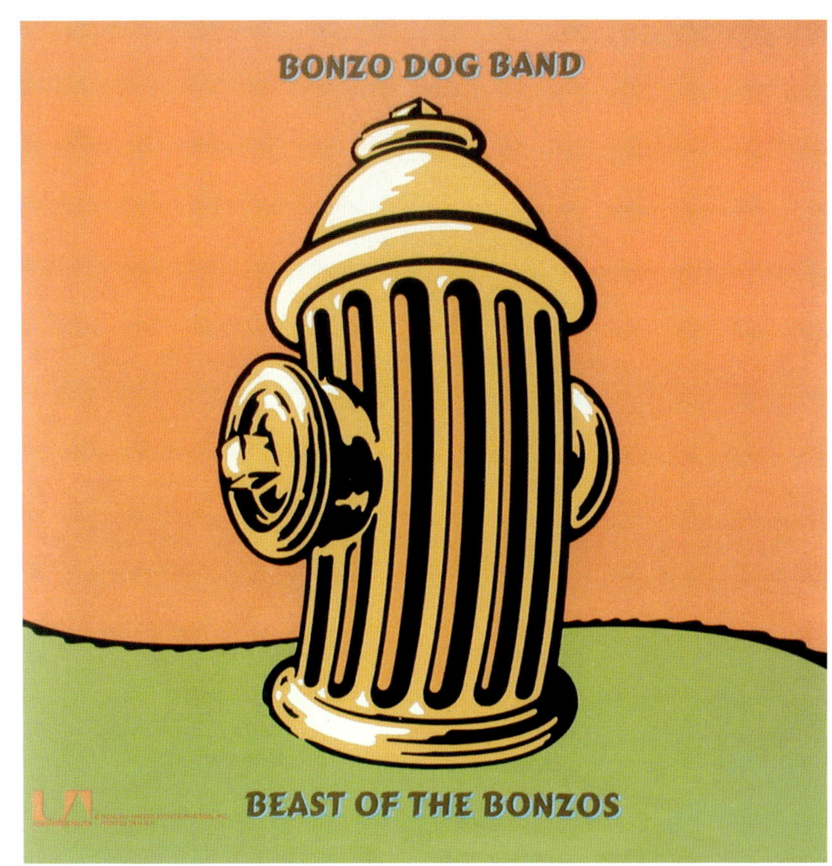
BONZO DOG BAND
BEAST OF THE BONZOS

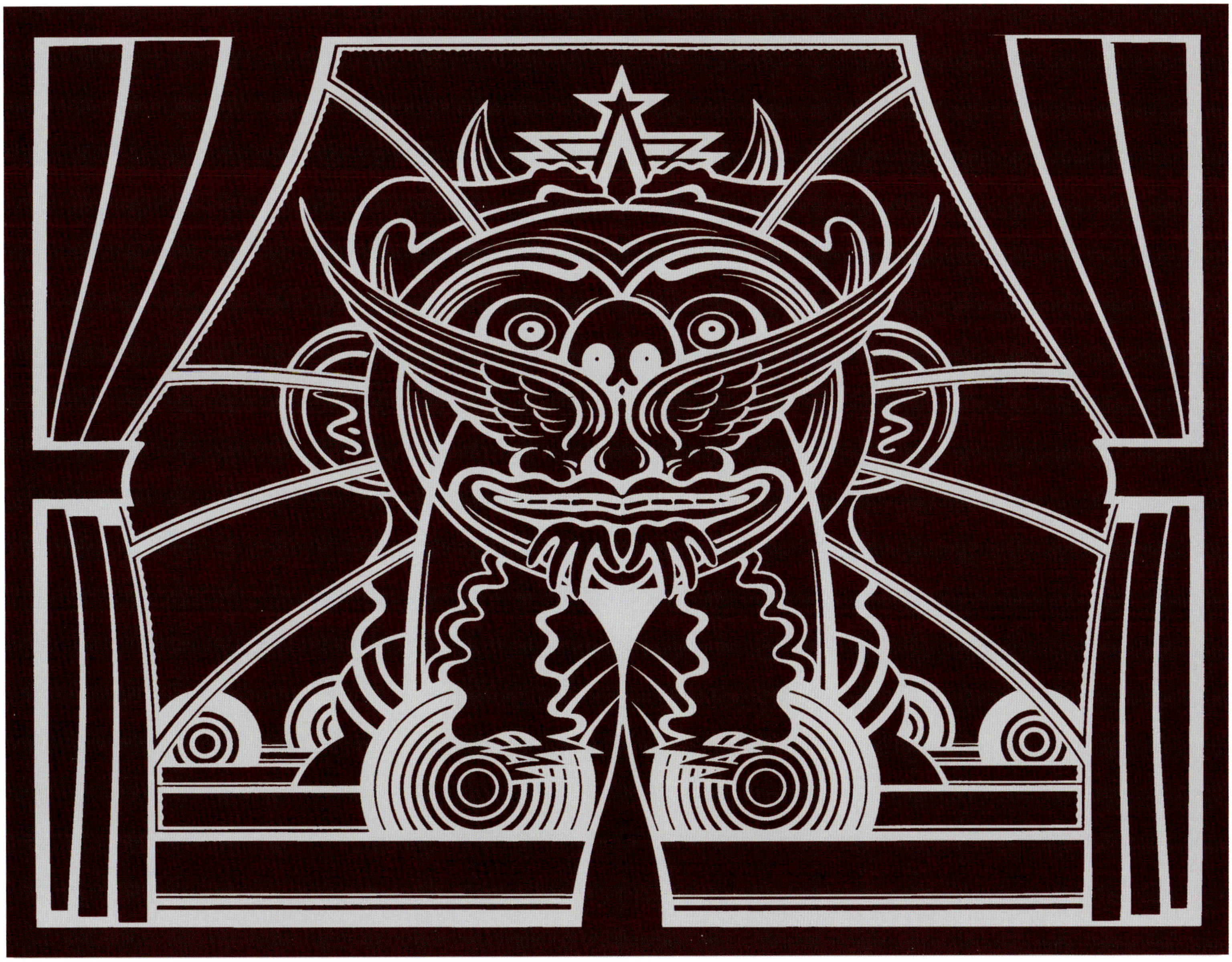

Achieving An Individual Identity

For Grant Green's live album, I tried to make use of all the skills I had learned over the years. For the background, I created a complex grid of panels that I sprayed with an airbrush. The repeating image of Grant Green's face highlighted the convergence of my knowledge of both photography and color. What this album became most famous for was the "neon" style typography. Due to the popularity of the font, I was able to license it out to several different type houses, such as Composition Arts (CA based) and Letter Graphics (NY based). Print magazines all featured the text on a cover, having it spell out the word "art" across the entire cover. This text was even included and critically acclaimed in a Swedish typography book. The first time I had played around with this style of "neon" type was on a promotional logo design I did of my name [J. Van Hamersveld].

BN-LA037-G2

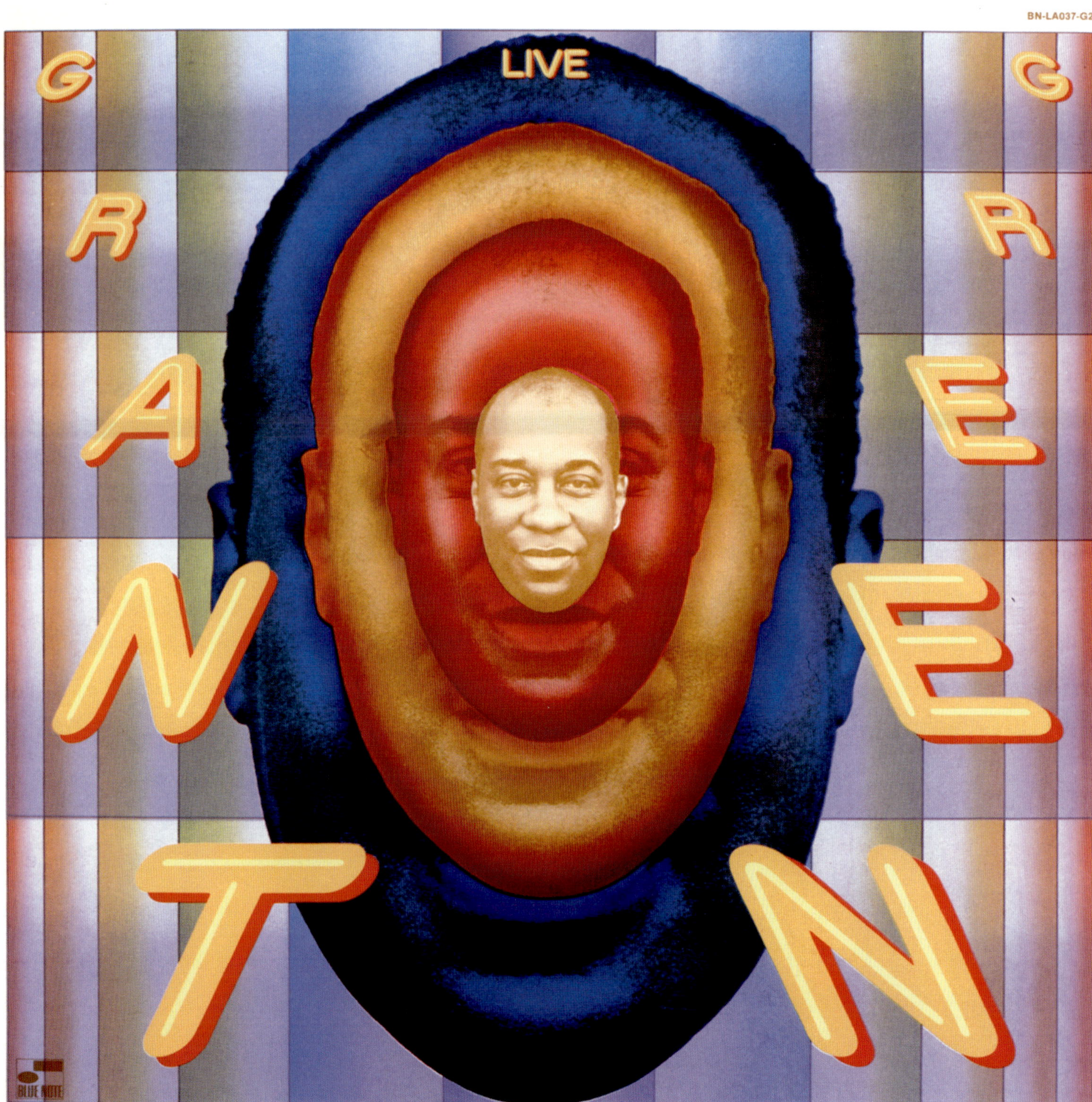

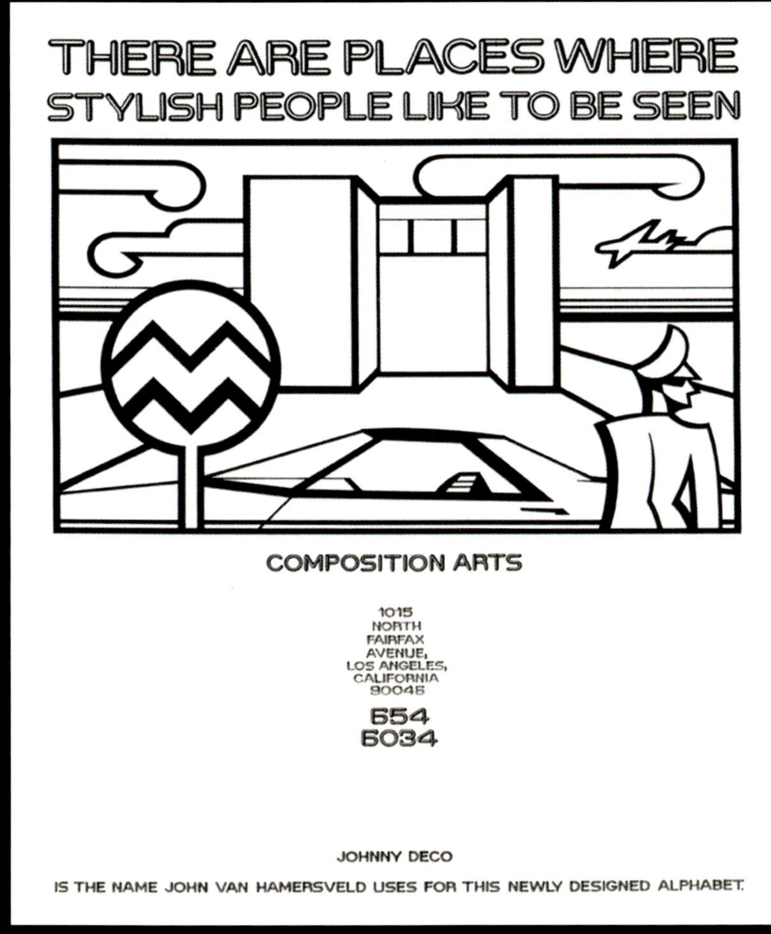

Typographic Company 1973

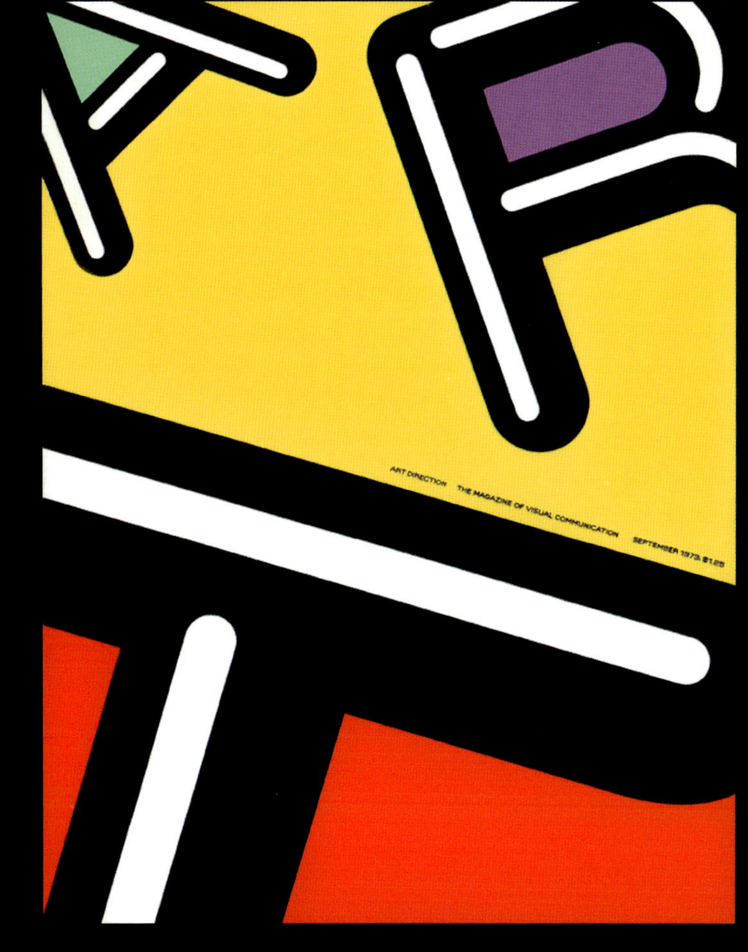

Trade Magazine 1973

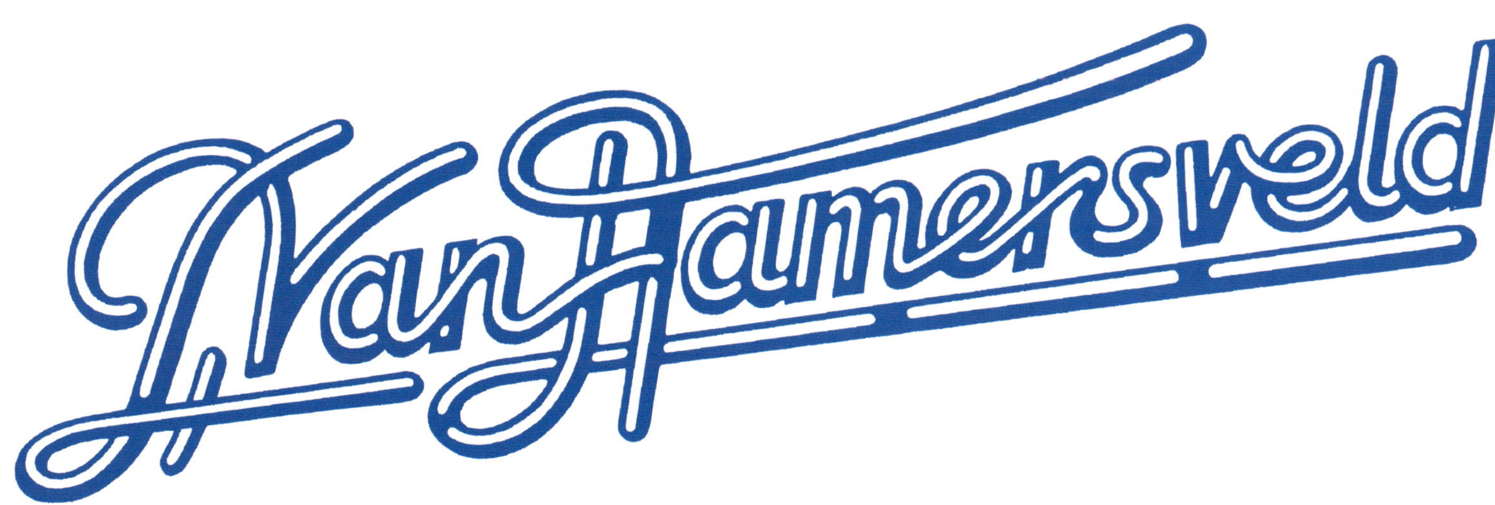

COMMERCIAL AND PRIVATE IDENTITY (1970)

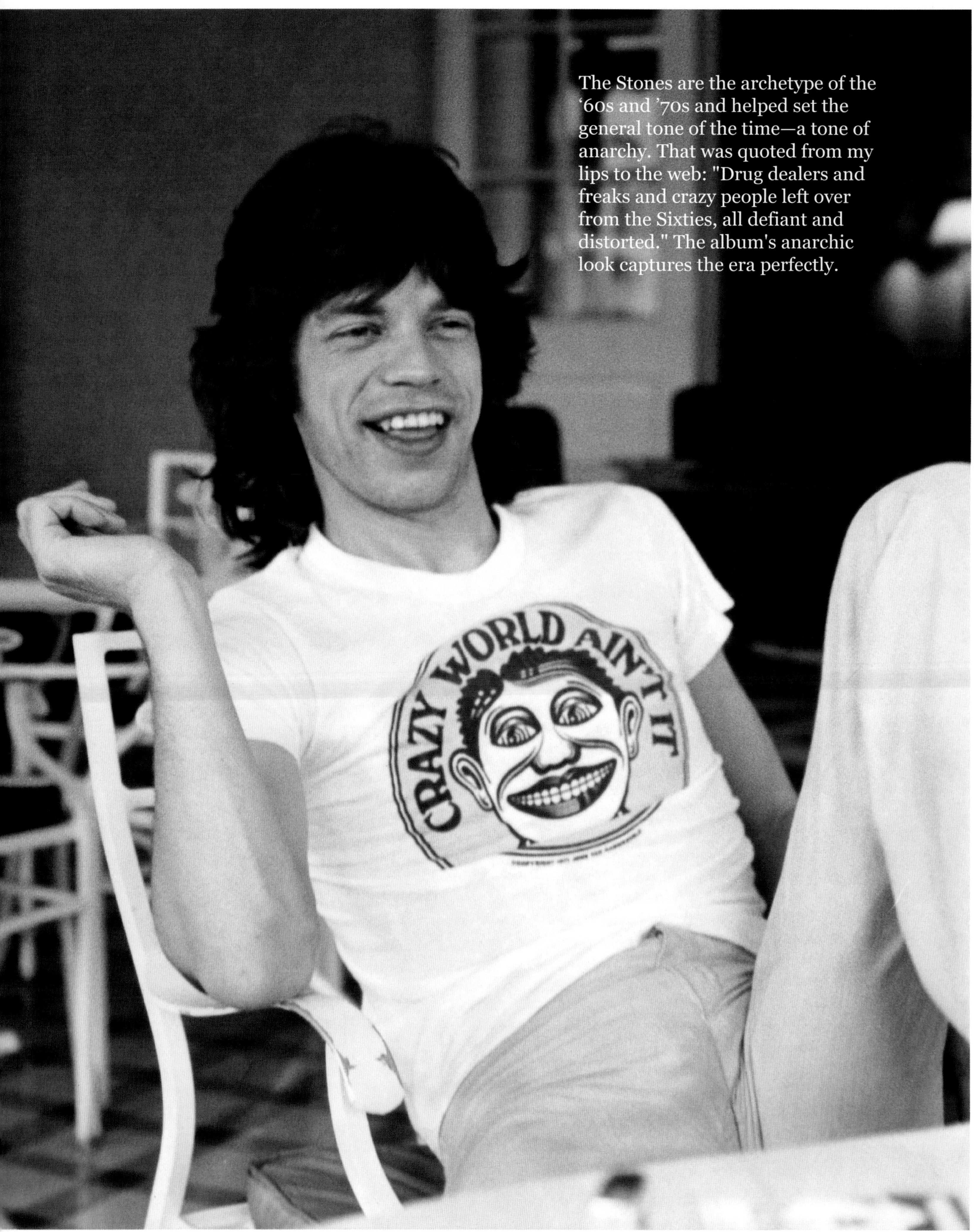

The Stones are the archetype of the '60s and '70s and helped set the general tone of the time—a tone of anarchy. That was quoted from my lips to the web: "Drug dealers and freaks and crazy people left over from the Sixties, all defiant and distorted." The album's anarchic look captures the era perfectly.

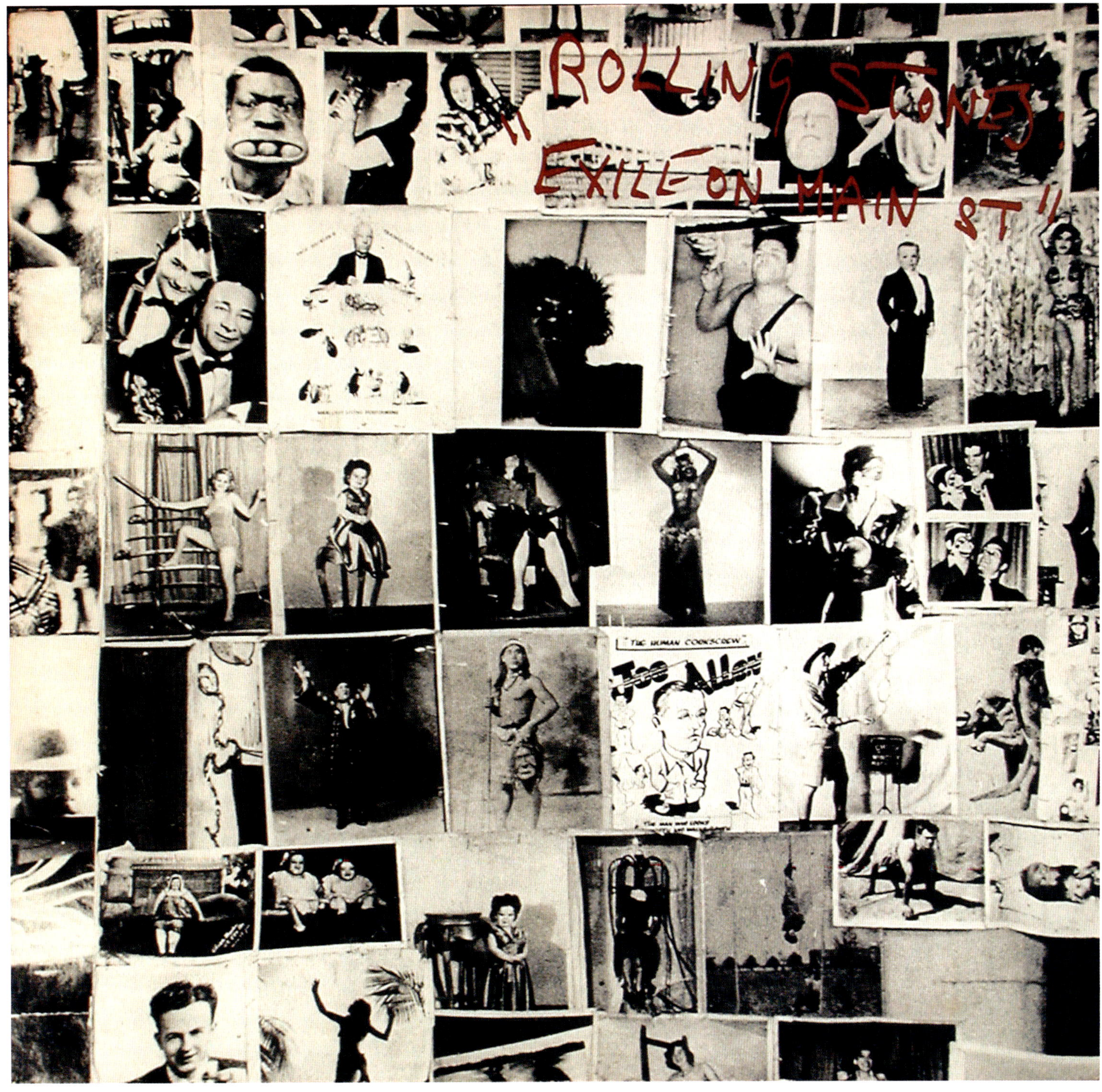

THE ROLLING STONES: EXILE ON MAIN STREET (1972)

When designing the *Exile* album cover, Mick Jagger and I sat side by side collaborating on the design. I later gave him six *Crazy World Ain't It?* t-shirts as a gift. Soon after, he was photographed for London based newspaper *New Music Express* while wearing one of the t-shirts I had given him.

The cover shot, which contained assorted pictures of circus freaks, is not a collage but a photo Robert Frank took in 1950 of the wall of a tattoo parlor somewhere on Route 66. The comparison to the notorious Stones—jet-setting tax exiles, cocaine-fueled satyrs, and perpetual outsiders—is clear. To drive the point home, an identical layout on the back cover features Frank's photos of the Stones themselves, shot on L.A.'s seedy Main Street (Frank's 1972 film documentary of the Stones, the unreleased *Cocksucker Blues*, would explicitly portray them as freaks). The inner sleeves were even more casually slapped together, with titles and credits hand lettered by Jagger himself. The layout perfectly compliments the sprawling, ramshackle sound of *Exile* itself.

PROMOTING "EXILE" TO THE STORES

Exzentriker

ON MAIN ST."

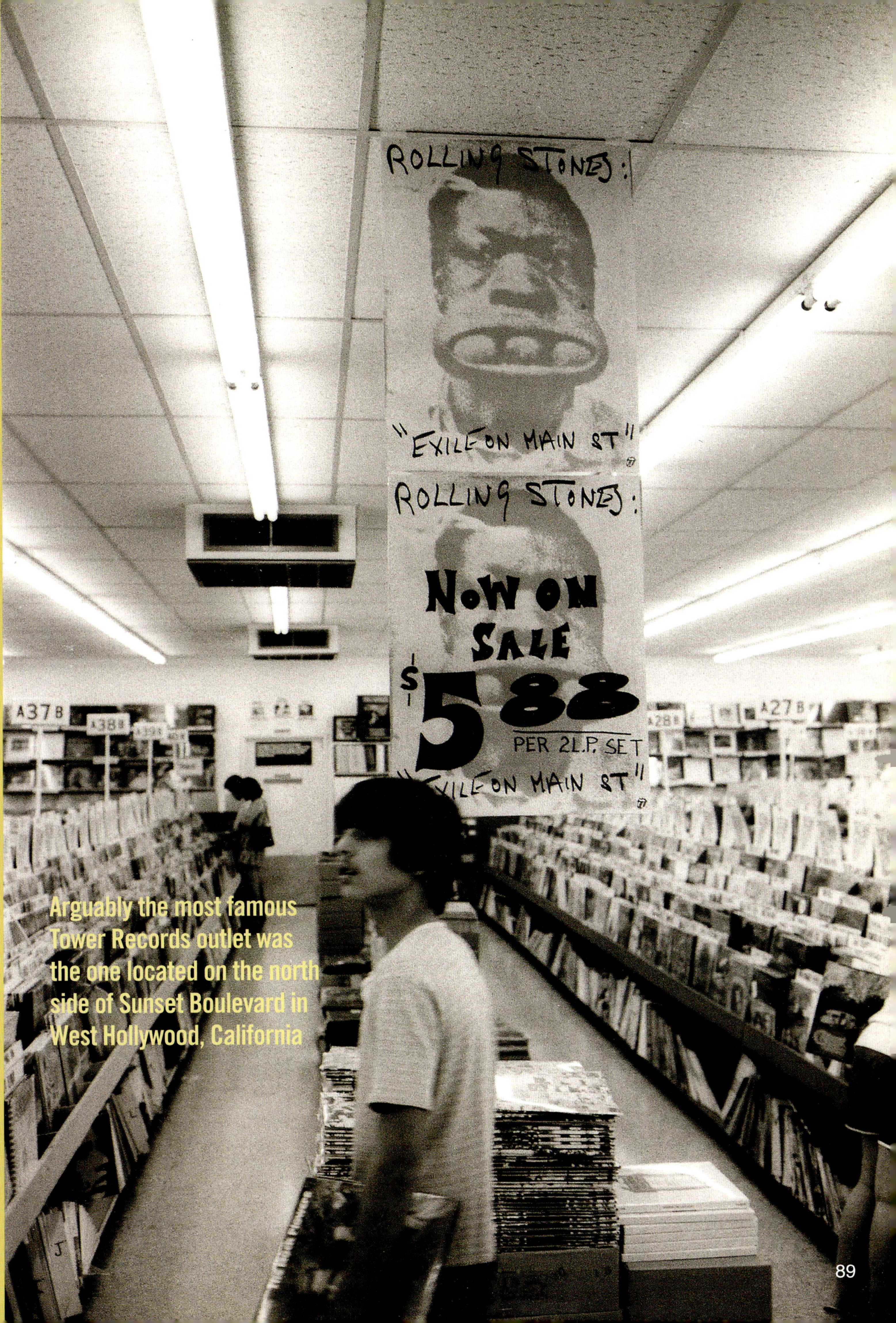

Arguably the most famous Tower Records outlet was the one located on the north side of Sunset Boulevard in West Hollywood, California

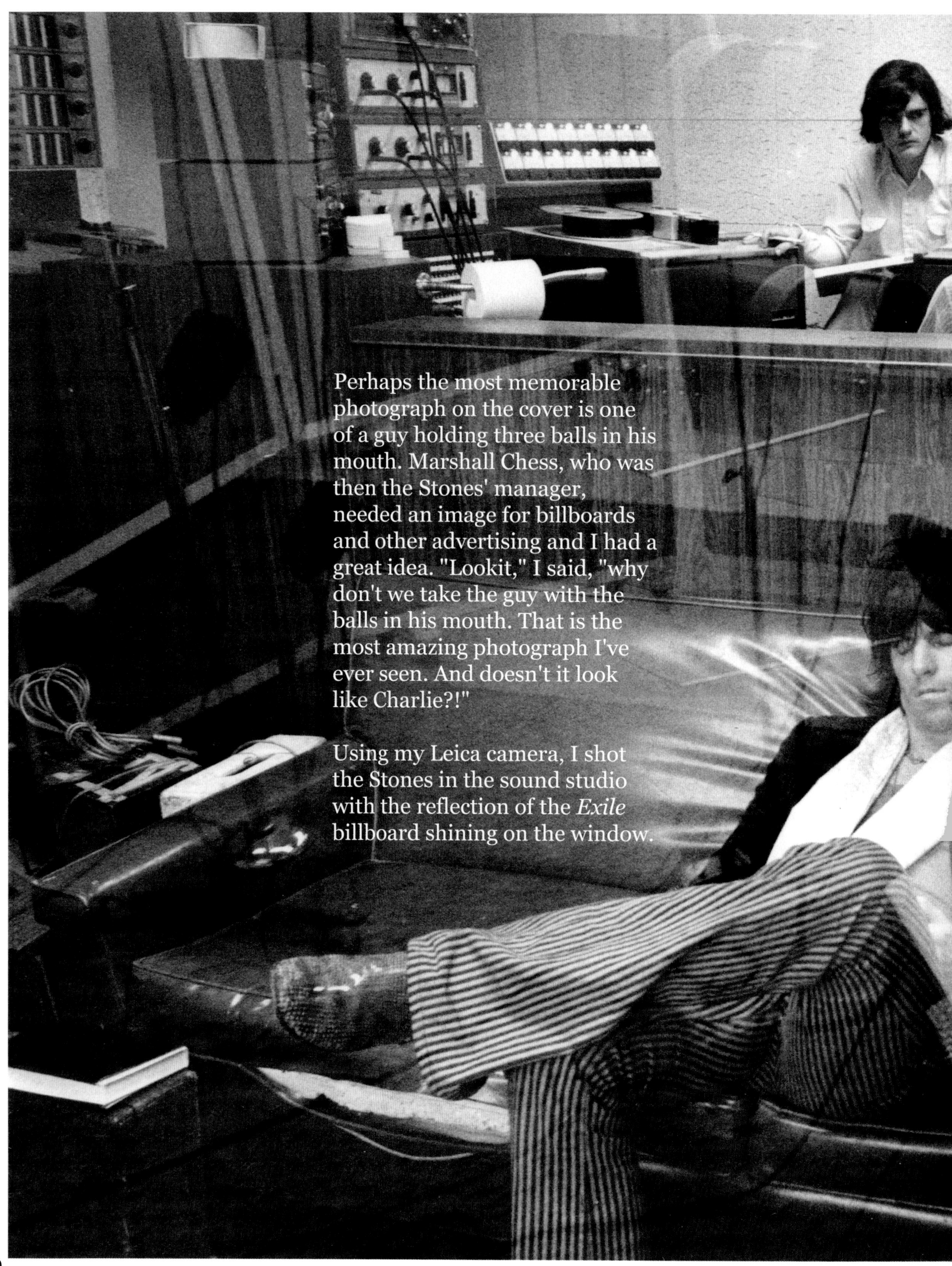

Perhaps the most memorable photograph on the cover is one of a guy holding three balls in his mouth. Marshall Chess, who was then the Stones' manager, needed an image for billboards and other advertising and I had a great idea. "Lookit," I said, "why don't we take the guy with the balls in his mouth. That is the most amazing photograph I've ever seen. And doesn't it look like Charlie?!"

Using my Leica camera, I shot the Stones in the sound studio with the reflection of the *Exile* billboard shining on the window.

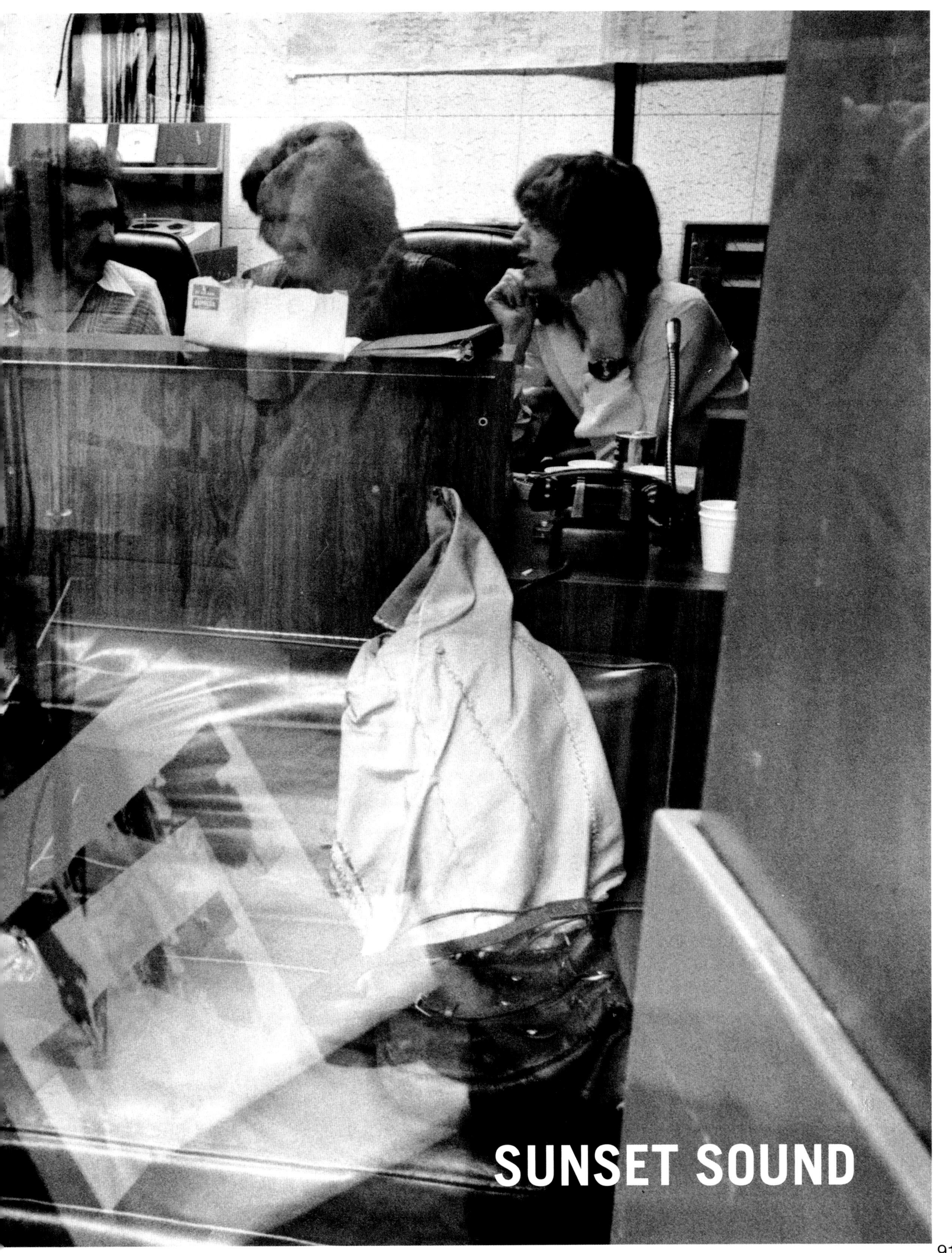

SUNSET SOUND

SUNSET STRIP BOULEVARD

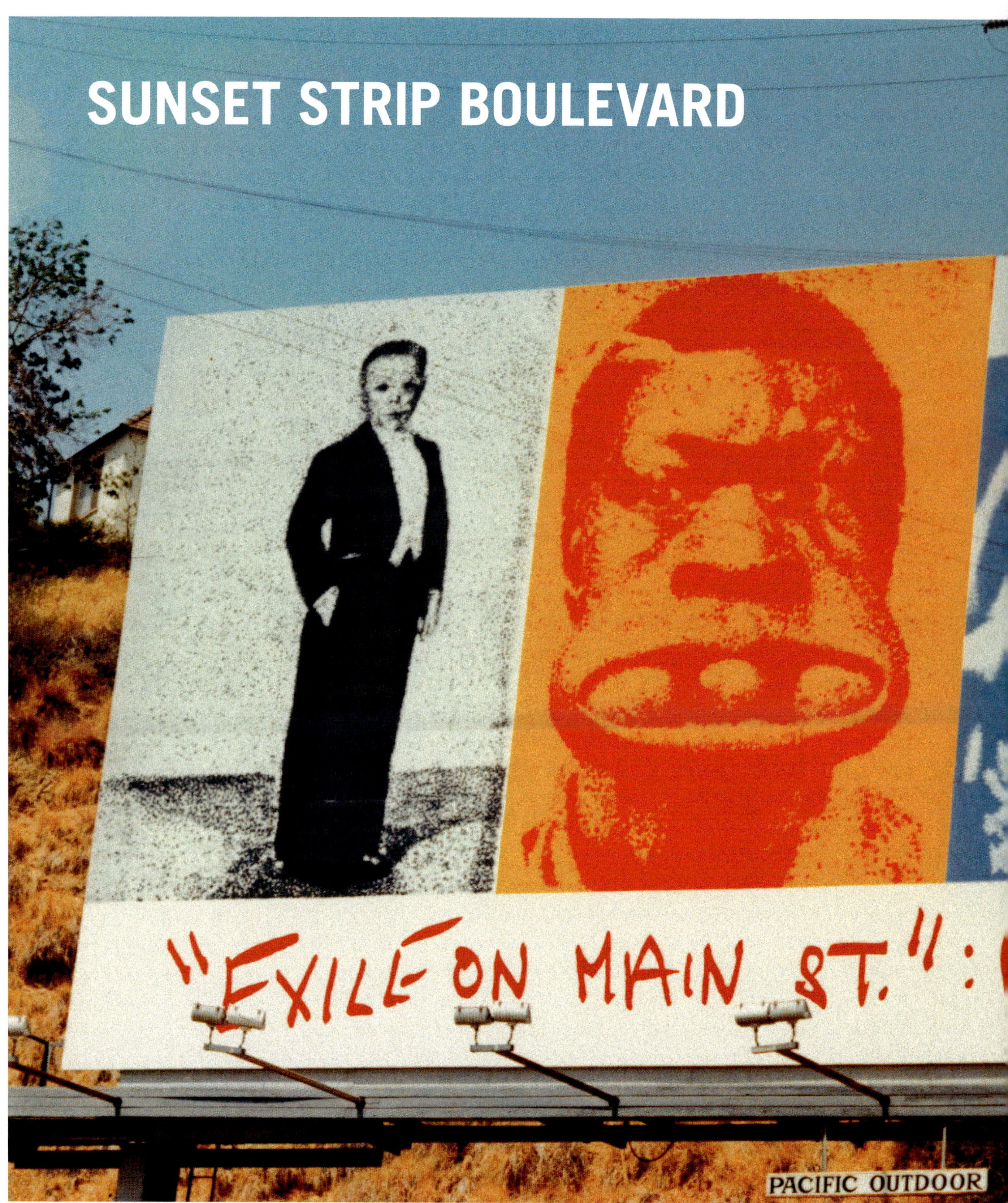

Surviving the test of time is the "vintage archival photograph" of the *Exile on Main Street* billboard available as a limited edition digital fine art print (2007). This 44 x 27.5 foot billboard was converted into a 40 x 23.5 inch color digital fine art print from an edition of 150, printed on a heavy watercolor paper stock and embossed with a printer's chopmark. It is signed and numbered in pencil by John Van Hamersveld.

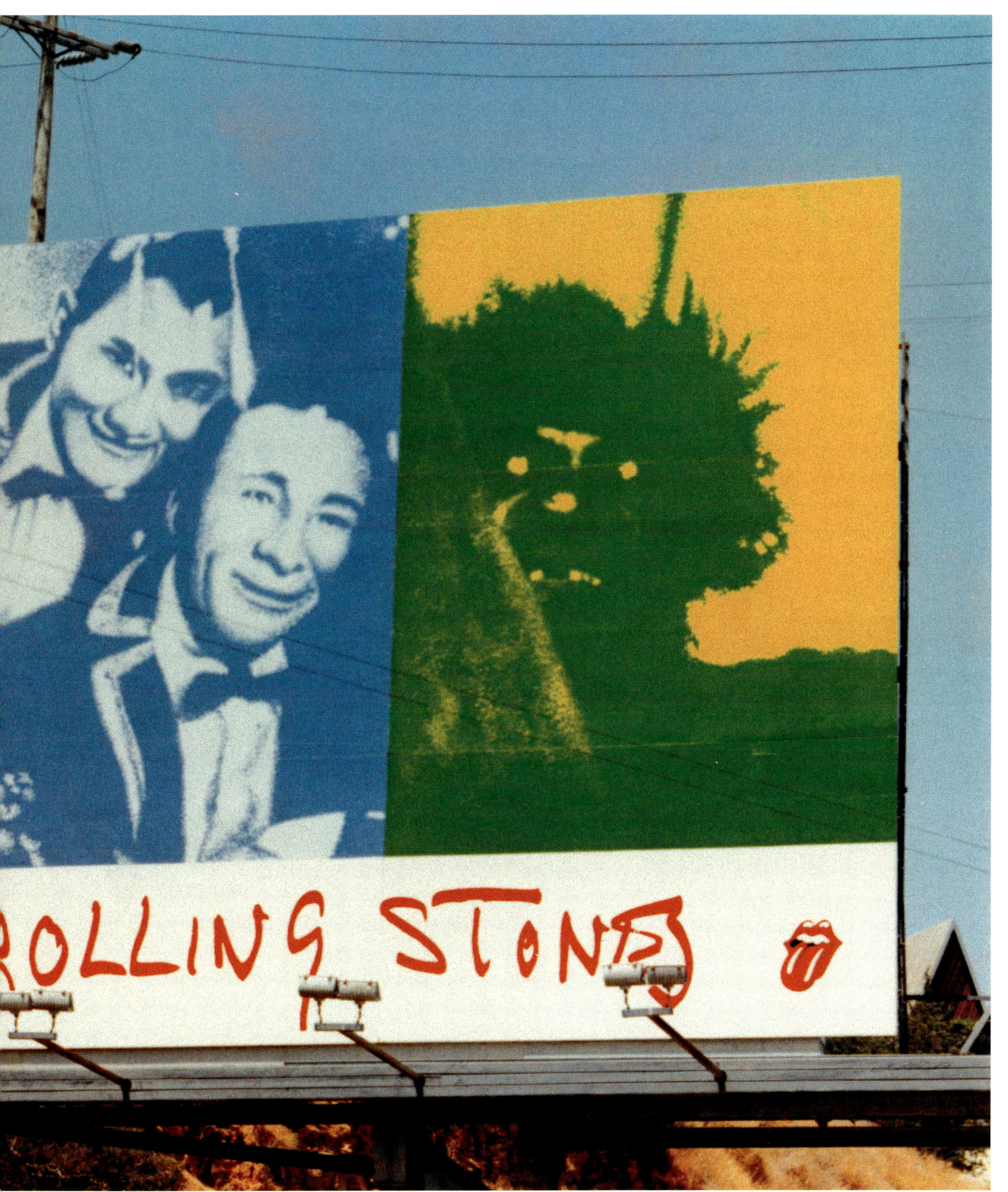

The collage (1972) is meant to be a depiction of the Rolling Stones. In left to right order: the butler is Mick Jagger, the man with three balls in his mouth is Charlie Watts, Bill Wyman and Mick Taylor are the two matadors, and Keith Richards is the sideshow freak.

Artist and Management (1974)

Since the 1920s blues era, musicians have always had their managers. The new artists of every generation need someone to book the shows and take care of organizing. Since musicians often rely so heavily on their managers, it's sometimes hard to separate musician from manager. Albert Grossman and Bob Dylan had this kind of relationship, as did Leo Kottke and Denny Bruce.

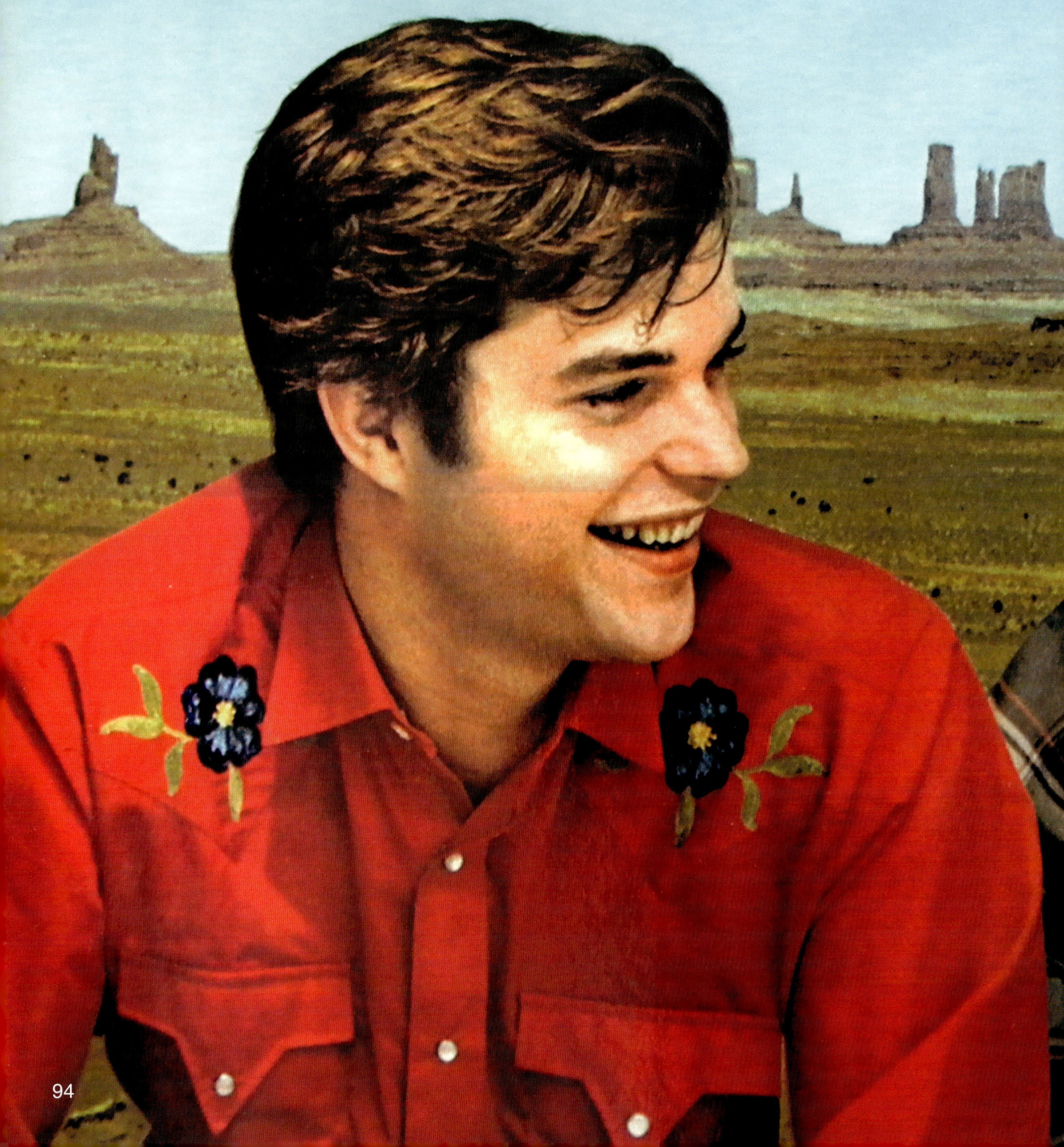

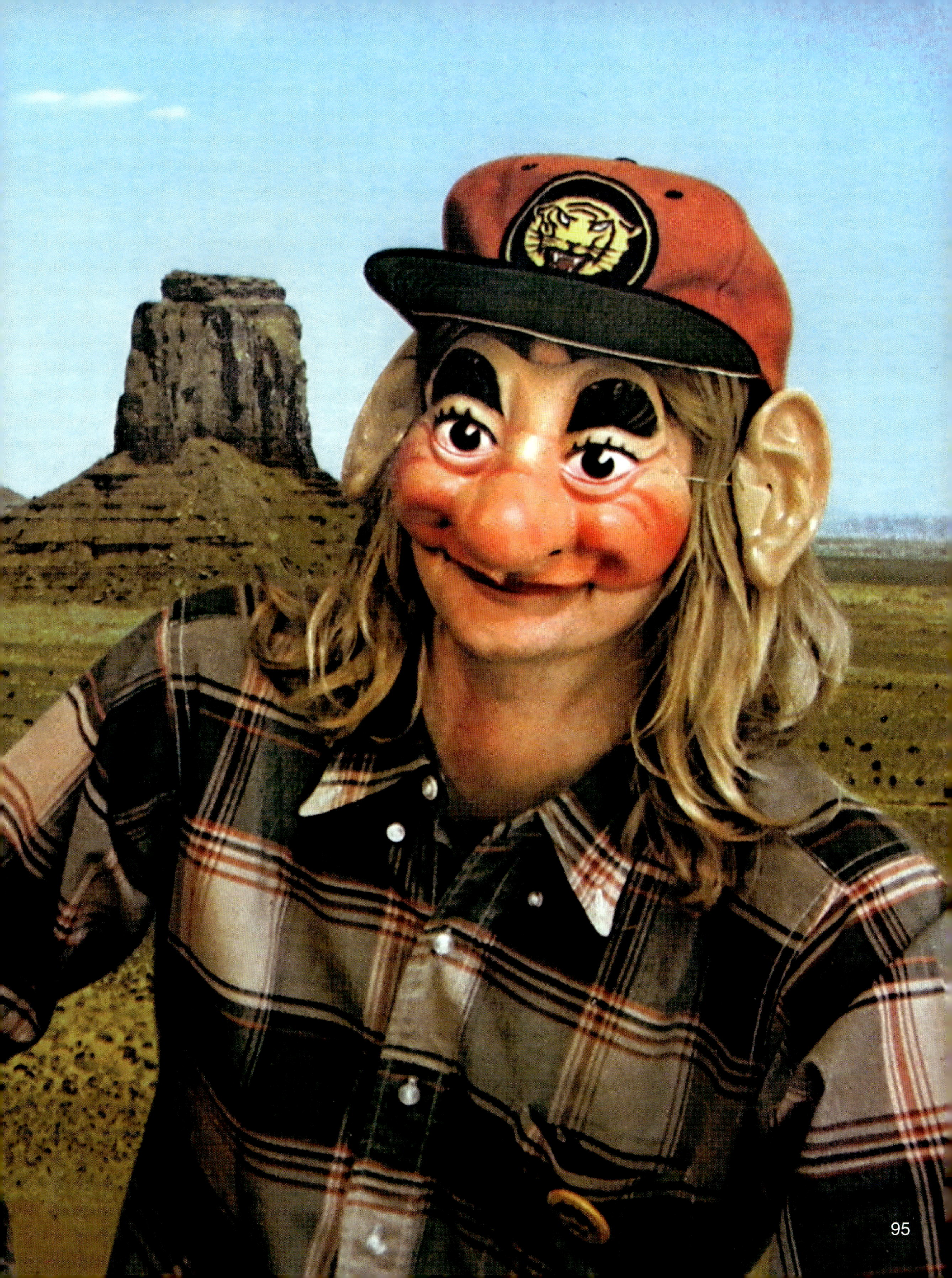

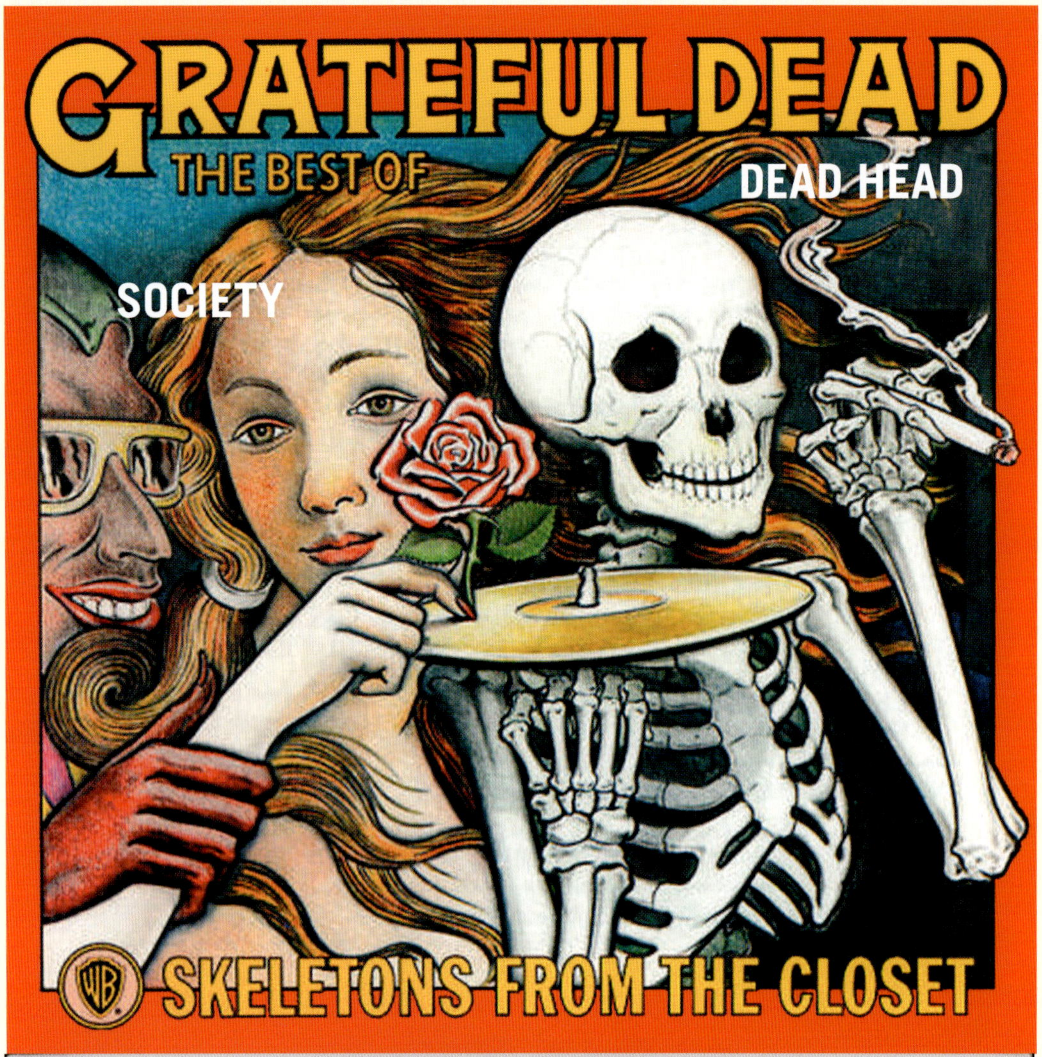

GRATEFUL DEAD
THE BEST OF
SKELETONS FROM THE CLOSET

DEAD HEAD

SOCIETY

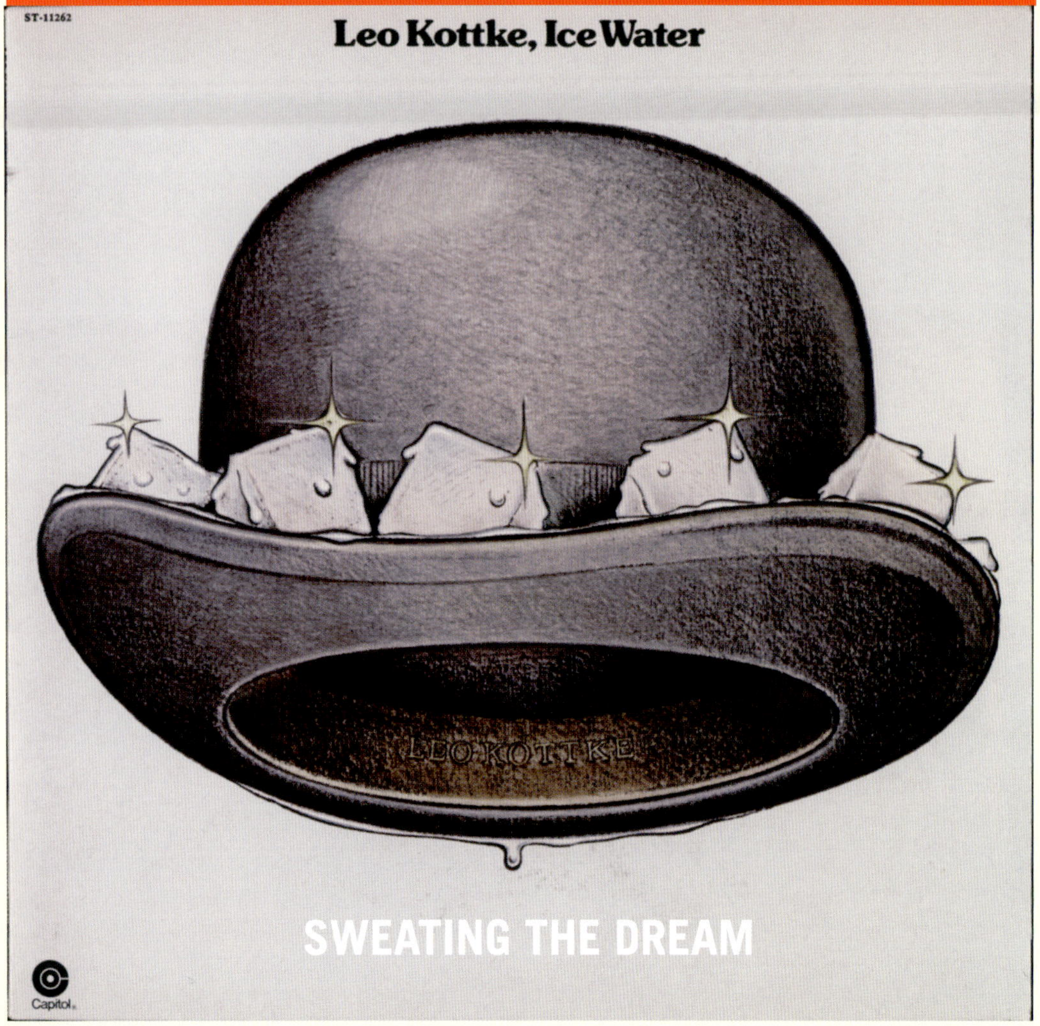

ST-11262
Leo Kottke, Ice Water
LEO KOTTKE
Capitol

SWEATING THE DREAM

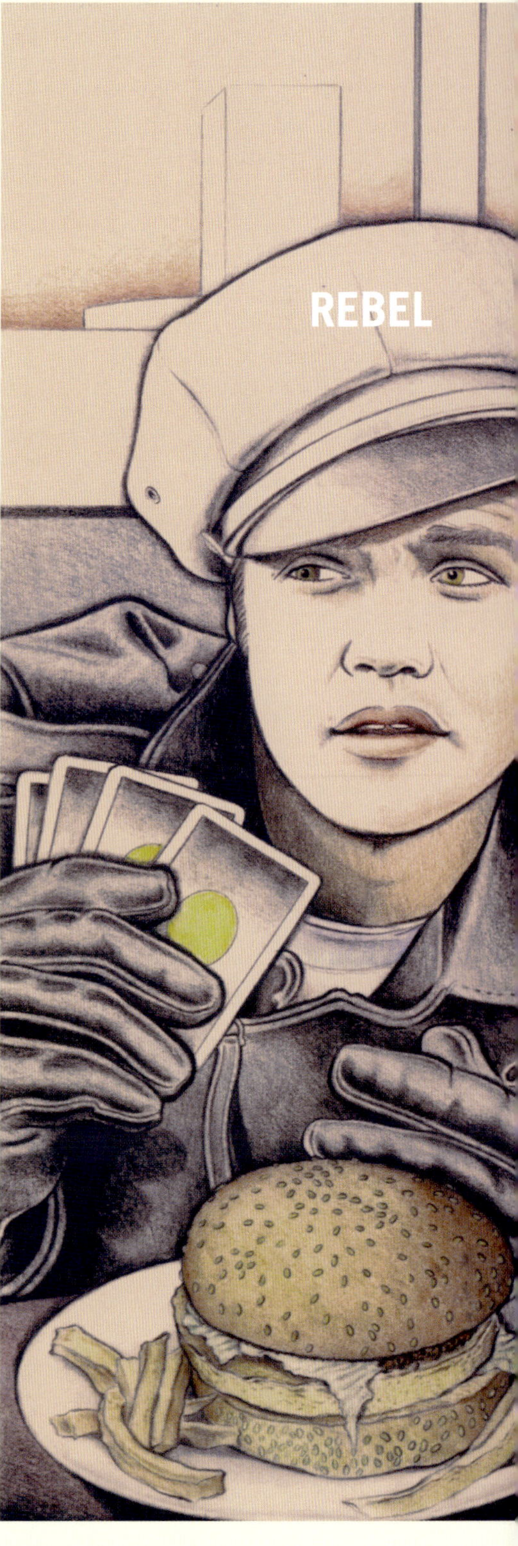

REBEL

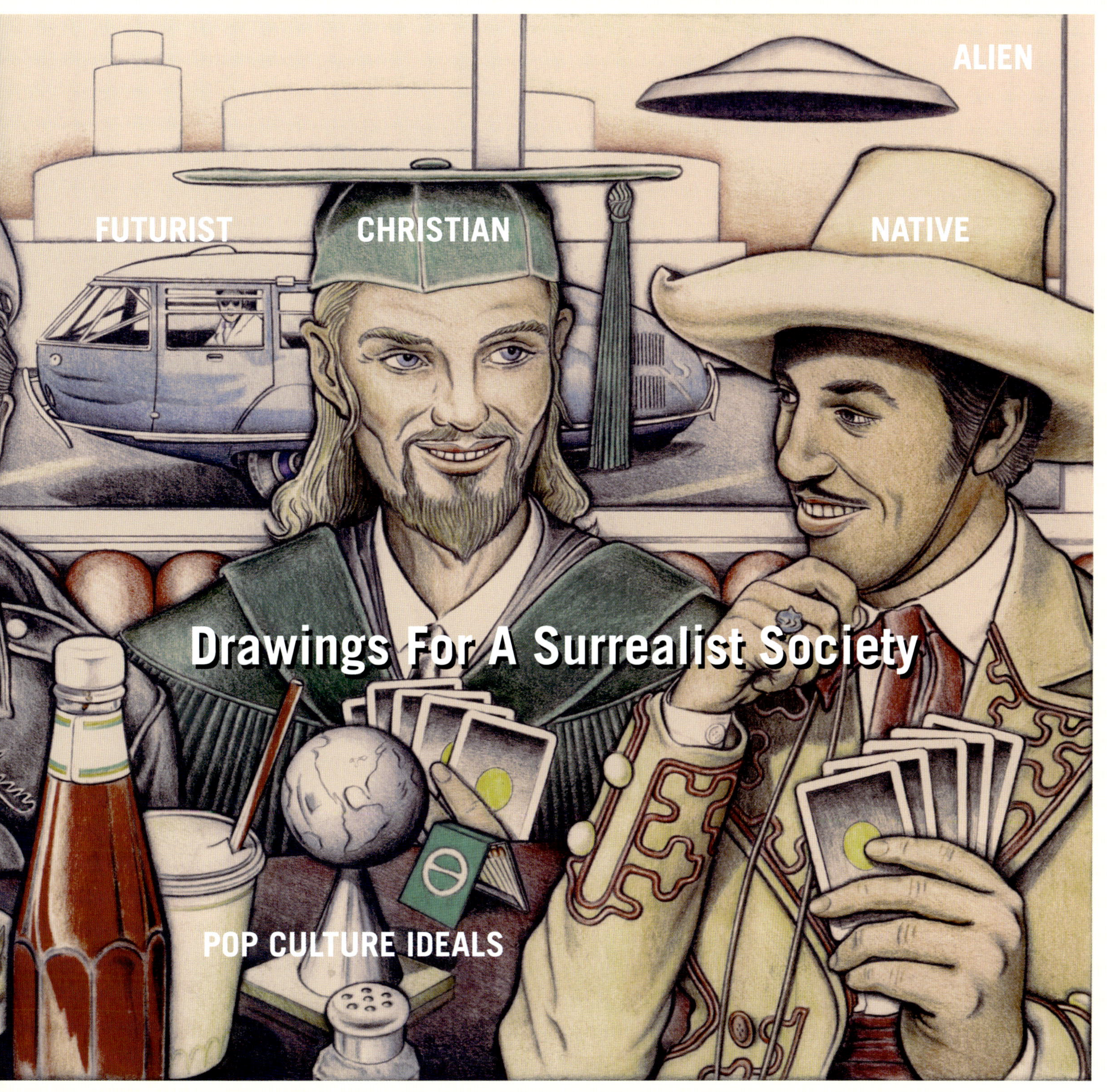

For a short period I had experimented with a very satirical and surreal approach. The '60s had boasted of a revolution (which never happened....) that had jaded me to some degree. This came out in my illustrations for *Skeletons from the Closet*, the Grateful Dead album cover. The character with the sunglasses is the devil and he is holding on to the hand of the *Birth of Venus*. Her hand is reaching out, holding a rose that is attached to the record needle, which sits on a skeleton's middle finger. In the skeleton's other hand, he is smoking a joint. These images create a domino effect—one thing leading to another. For Leo Kottke's album cover of *Ice Water*, I poked fun at the art world. I painted a Magritte bowler hat, draped in ice cubes. The idea is the cubes are literally cool, while the hat/Magritte are figuratively cool.

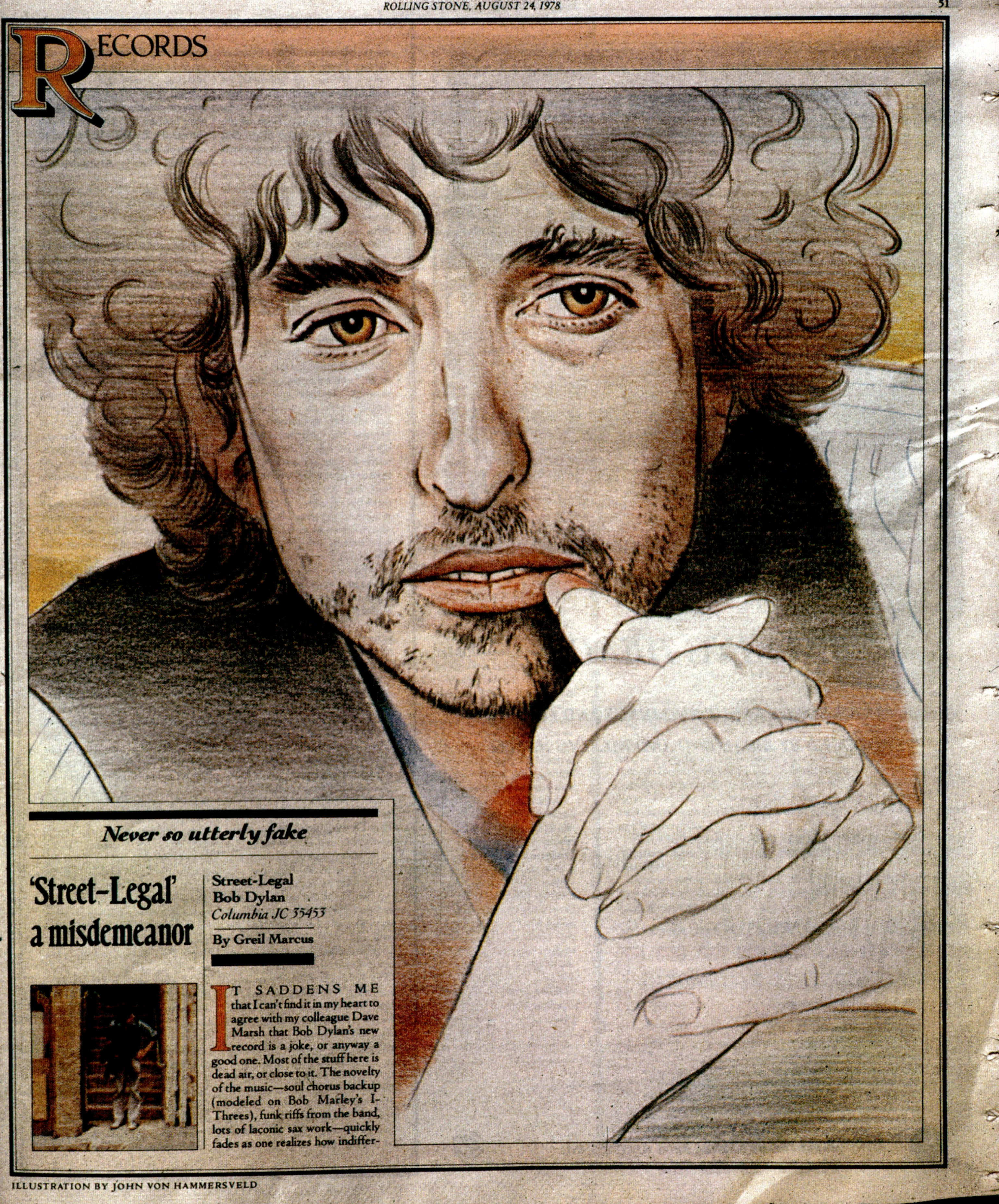

ROLLING STONE, AUGUST 24, 1978 51

RECORDS

Never so utterly fake

'Street-Legal' a misdemeanor

Street-Legal
Bob Dylan
Columbia JC 35453

By Greil Marcus

IT SADDENS ME that I can't find it in my heart to agree with my colleague Dave Marsh that Bob Dylan's new record is a joke, or anyway a good one. Most of the stuff here is dead air, or close to it. The novelty of the music—soul chorus backup (modeled on Bob Marley's I-Threes), funk riffs from the band, lots of laconic sax work—quickly fades as one realizes how indiffer-

ILLUSTRATION BY JOHN VON HAMMERSVELD

Two illustrations for *Rolling Stone* magazine. The James Dean portrait is the cover of the 1973 issue, the other is an illustration for Bob Dylan's record review in 1978.

SM14170

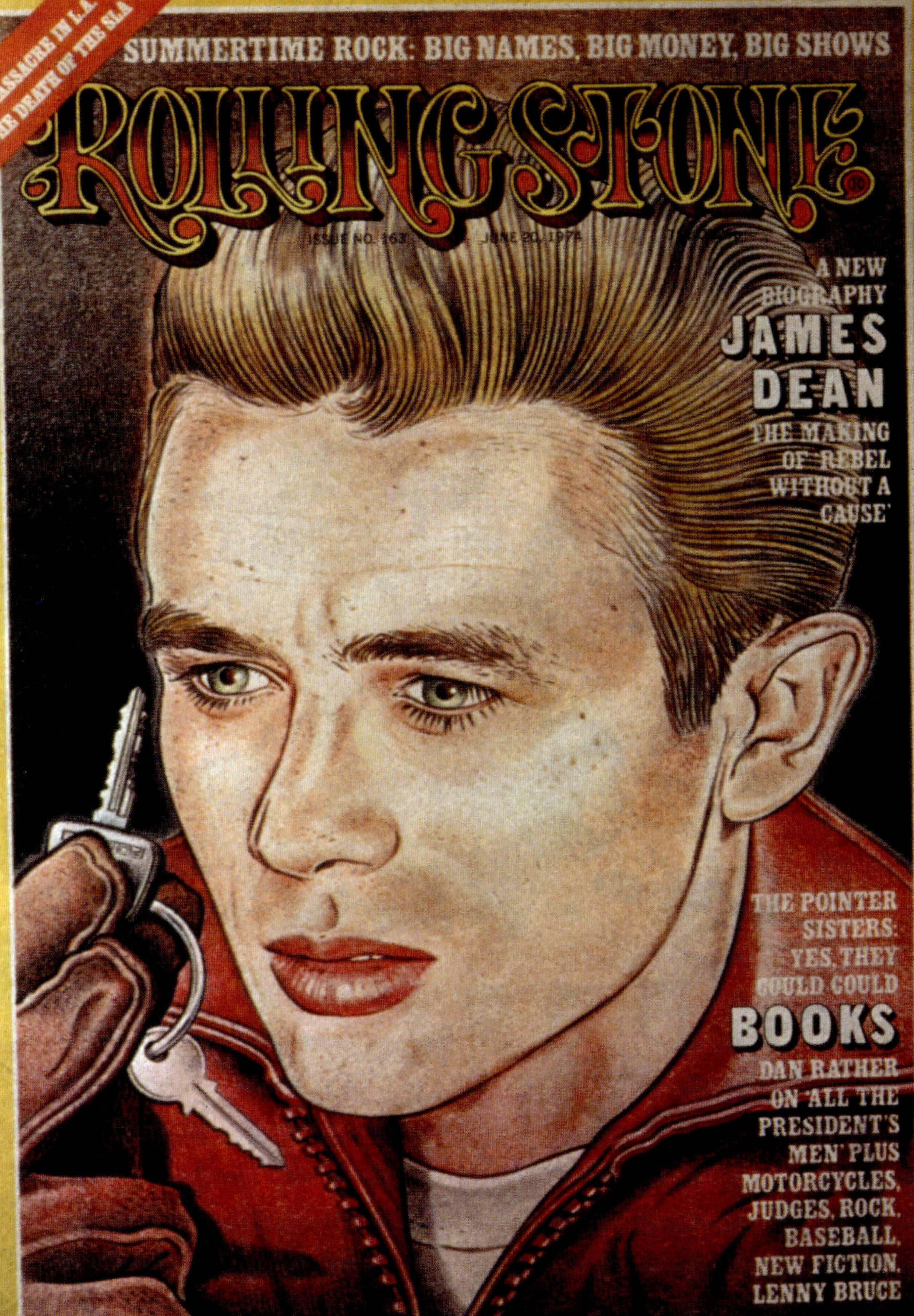
MASSACRE IN L.A.
THE DEATH OF THE SLA
SUMMERTIME ROCK: BIG NAMES, BIG MONEY, BIG SHOWS
ROLLING STONE
ISSUE NO. 163
JUNE 20, 1974
A NEW BIOGRAPHY
JAMES DEAN
THE MAKING OF 'REBEL WITHOUT A CAUSE'
THE POINTER SISTERS: YES, THEY COULD COULD
BOOKS
DAN RATHER ON 'ALL THE PRESIDENT'S MEN' PLUS MOTORCYCLES, JUDGES, ROCK, BASEBALL, NEW FICTION, LENNY BRUCE

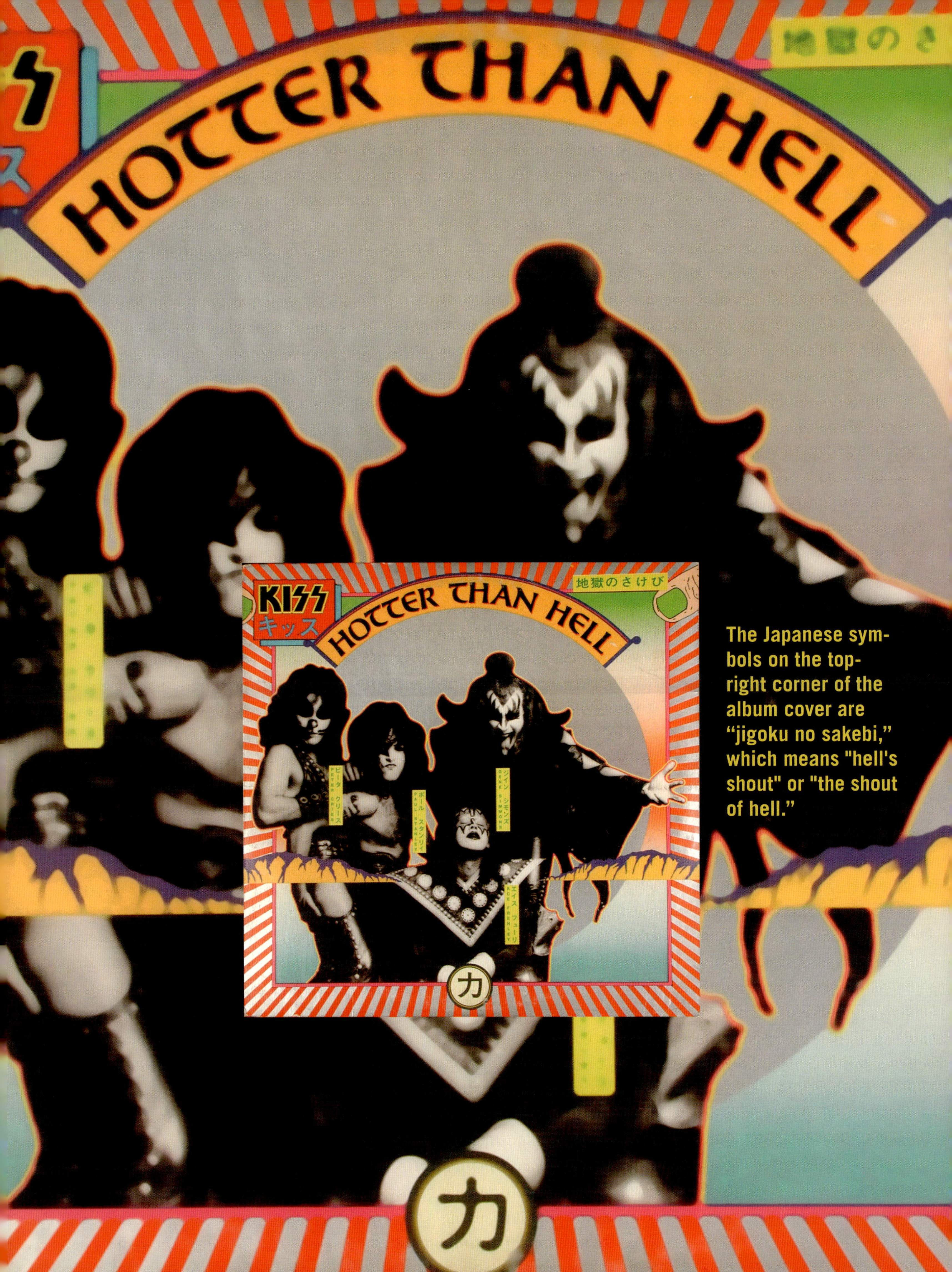

The Japanese symbols on the top-right corner of the album cover are "jigoku no sakebi," which means "hell's shout" or "the shout of hell."

Record Commerce

1974

A Commercial Disappointment

Despite the intense touring schedule Kiss maintained in 1974, *Hotter Than Hell* failed to outperform the band's first album. In fact, it did considerably worse. This was due partly to the fact that Casablanca Records' distribution deal with Warner Bros. Records had ended. The publicity push behind the album was not nearly what it was for the first album. One notable exception was a television commercial aired to promote the album. The only single released from the album, *Let Me Go, Rock 'n' Roll*, was distributed in low numbers and failed to chart. Less than three months after the album was released, Kiss was called back into the studio to record a follow up. *Hotter Than Hell* was certified Gold on June 23, 1977, when it sold 500,000 copies.

"Seeff gave me the Kiss photos. I had to create a solution for the images as a Japanese packaged product. I went down to Little Tokyo in LA, and collected up all the different elements I needed to make it a Japanese Style."
—JVH

Photography Session

The album is known for its striking cover: the front featured Japanese manga-influenced artwork, and the back cover showed individual band shots taken by Norman Seeff at a wild party, and a composite of all four band members' makeup designs. Everyone present at the session (with the exception of Simmons) was drunk for the entire photography session. Stanley was so drunk he had to be locked in his car. Paul's drunken state can easily be seen on the album's front cover as it appears Peter Criss is holding him up while Paul holds onto Peter's leg.

Detail About the Symbols

The Japanese character on the bottom of the album cover is called Chikara, which means "Power." It would later be used on various forms of Kiss material during the 1970s and 1980s, most prominently on Eric Carr's drum kit.

The Shout of Hell

The Japanese on the top-right corner of the album cover is "jigoku no sakebi," which means "hell's shout" or "the shout of hell."

"Knock'n On Heaven's Door"

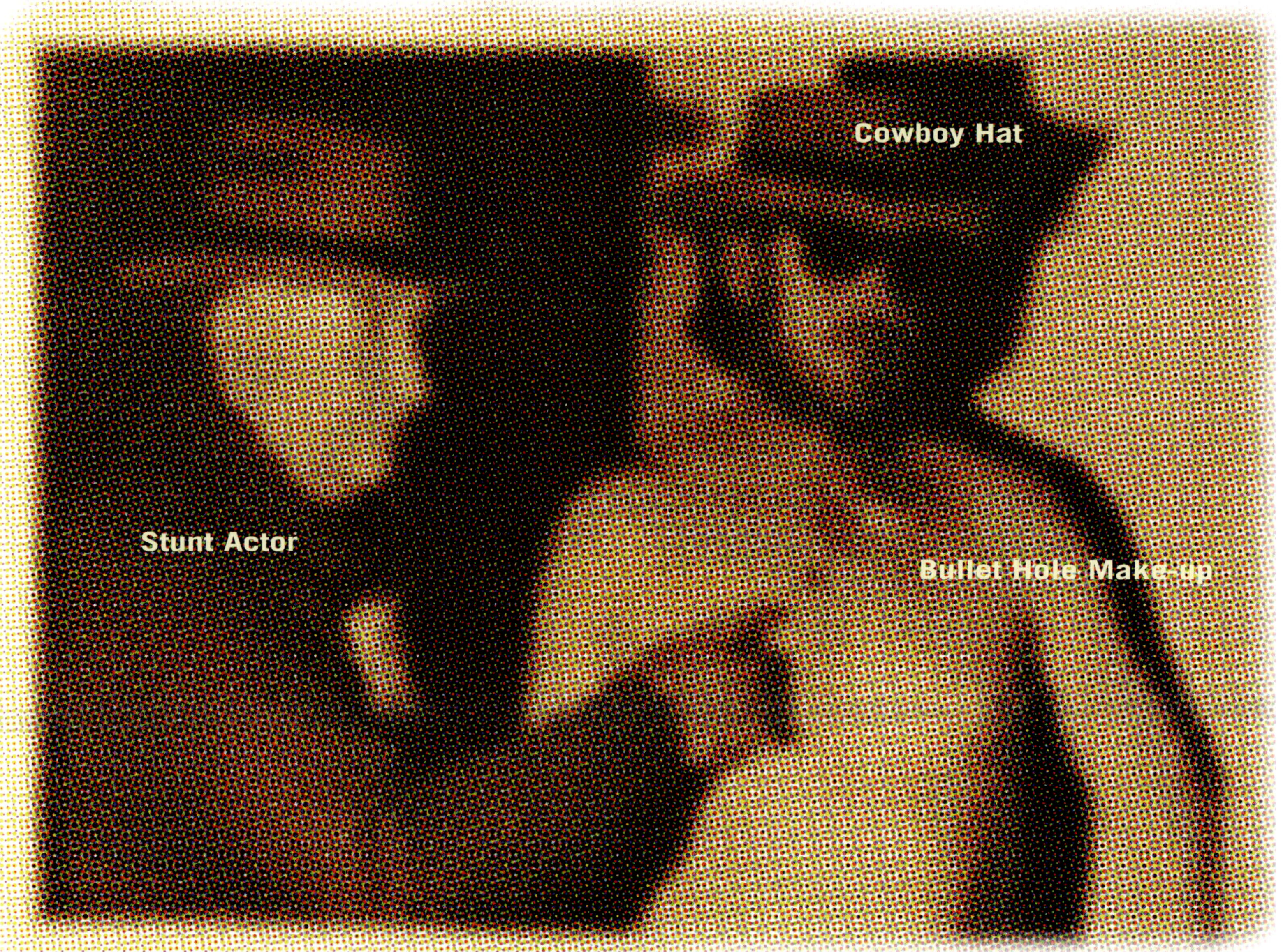

The Bob Dylan Story

"The corporation had made the decision, not Bob, when I had anticipated he would be the final vote."

The End Of Self Control

Pat Garrett & Billy the Kid is a soundtrack album released by Bob Dylan in 1973 for the Sam Peckinpah film

There Dylan stood in my doorway, dressed in a brown North Beach leather jacket with long fringed sleeves, bigger then life; as he moved, I watched with amazement. So many different famous people had been to this Chapman Park Studio complex, but this particular day was like no other. My obsession with his music and Beat-like manners led my interest to an apex in the preceding years. This was different than Jagger.

Jagger was always surrounded by heaps of people. With Dylan, it was just the two of us. One on one. Bob Dylan and myself. The phone rang and we moved to the large studio room next door. Bob sat down to take the call — it was his lawyer, David Braun. We sat down to have a discussion at a large table to focus on the packaging assignment.

I pull out a photograph pasted on a 12" x 12" paper, the size of an album cover. Dylan is looking at me as I carefully turn it for him to view. The white studio I was in was illuminating the two inch white border of the square; in the center of the composition was the photograph I collected for MGM, as 8" x 10" stills. The still was of a Mexican, cast as an extra in the Peckinpah film. The extra is waist high in the picture and brownish, with black hair combed back, wearing a cowboy hat. On the crest area the make-up person has embellished the image with a bullet hole. This heightens the view, making the image very visually exciting. Bob is entranced by the image. He looks at me and says, "This really works; the image has that Peckinpah sense of irony."

There is a knock at the door. I get up to peek through the blinds, and there is the face of producer Gordon Carroll in the door window. Gordon comes up, looks at the image, and cries out, "Not the Kennedy thing! Absolutely not!" Gordon makes his corporate move and says that he has both Bob and I by the balls. Gordon goes to the phone and starts his conversations. Bob and I are looking on as if we were two cut-out cartoon people standing in the culture with no real meaning. Gordon turns to look at us. We nod and out the door Gordon goes as if all was resolved. Bob left later and the room was empty. There I stood in the white room. The corporation had made the decision, not Bob, when I had anticipated he would be the final vote. You can now hear how the artists and their desires are not needed at this level of business any longer. In fact corporate faces bragged about the deals they did to fuck the dumb artists. They are in "control." This is marketing in 1973. They want nothing new, they want what will sell.

Al Capone once said, "You can get much farther with a kind word and a gun than you can with a kind word alone." I've always kind of felt that the kind word was the art, the experience, unadulterated by outside contamination. But the gun is what makes people move. It makes them follow commands. Mickey Dora was surfing amongst a couple hundred people in the early '50s. Bob Dylan was playing to a coffee shop barely full of listeners in the early '60s. But without exploitation, commercialism and promotion, Surf or Pop music would not have gone anywhere. I was naïve at the time. None of us knew we were creating archetypes. None of us knew that what we did would ever make a difference, or would be remembered even a few years after we did it. Least of all, none of us knew that we, the ones taking our Beatnik message and sharing it with the masses, would eventually be used by the machine for their exploitation. But that is the way it is.

Rosetta Brooks put it this way, "There are those who believe that Pop art died at the end of the '60s (both symbolically and actually with the shooting of Warhol by Valerie Solanis). Whether that is so or not, its afterlife, as represented by the works of the original exponents of American Pop during the past twenty years, now shows the sinister underside to those innocent dreams of the '60s."

T.V. LIFE

I self published my photography book *T.V. LIFE* in 1974. The printer made and bound 400 units. I passed them out to people I met. The photos start in 1967, when I bought my first NIKON camera. Near my job at Capitol Records was Schaefer's Camera. A salesman named "Cid" helped me over the counter with advice and information about cameras. First there was the NIKON, then the Hasselblad, then the Leica RSL, and then the Leica M5 with an automatic light meter. Later on was the small Leica CL, with a meter built in like a digital camera of today. As soon as I arrived at the store, I was always ready to learn about photography.

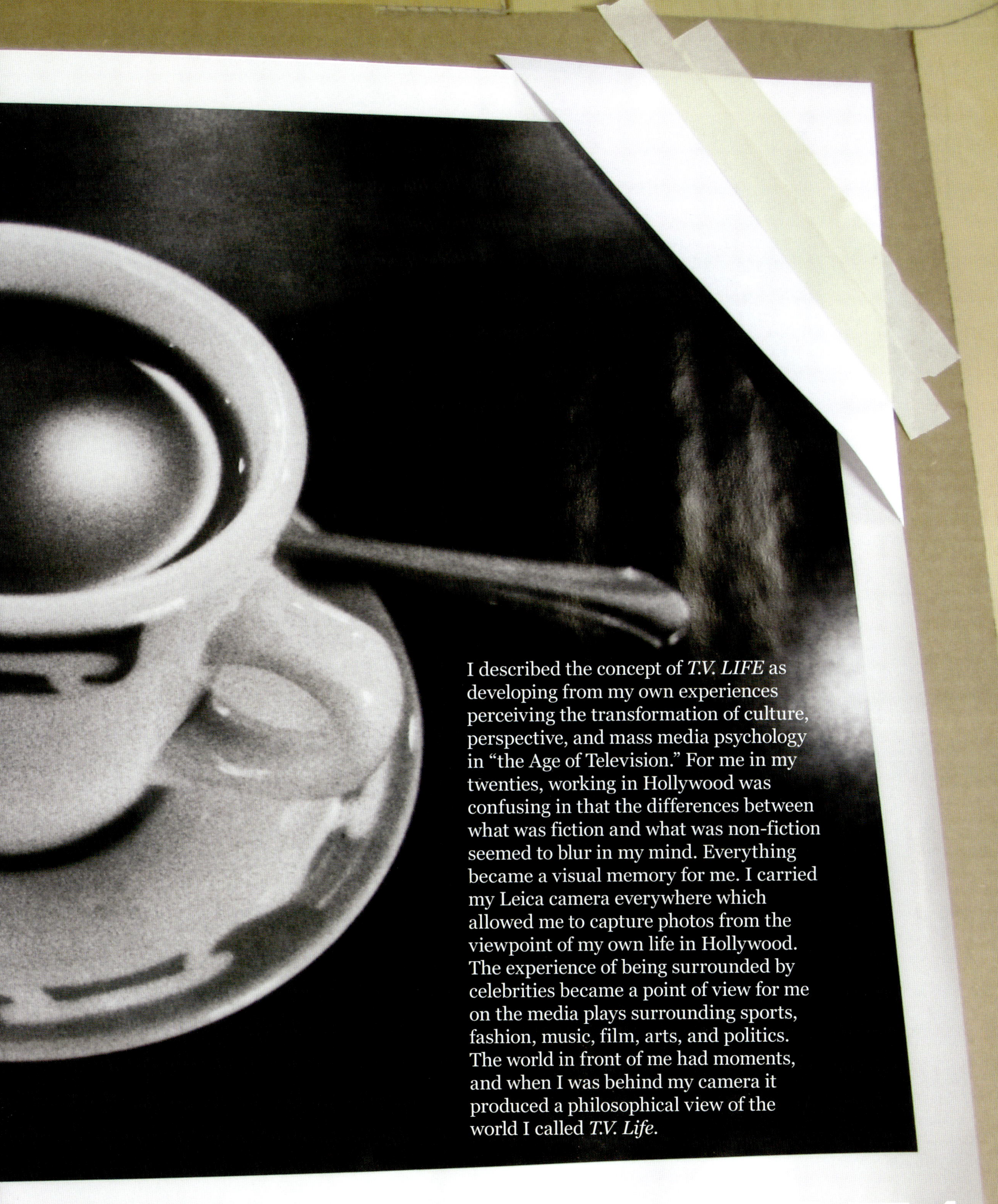

I described the concept of *T.V. LIFE* as developing from my own experiences perceiving the transformation of culture, perspective, and mass media psychology in "the Age of Television." For me in my twenties, working in Hollywood was confusing in that the differences between what was fiction and what was non-fiction seemed to blur in my mind. Everything became a visual memory for me. I carried my Leica camera everywhere which allowed me to capture photos from the viewpoint of my own life in Hollywood. The experience of being surrounded by celebrities became a point of view for me on the media plays surrounding sports, fashion, music, film, arts, and politics. The world in front of me had moments, and when I was behind my camera it produced a philosophical view of the world I called *T.V. Life*.

END OF AN ERA 1974

1978: At the opening of the East Building at the National Gallery of Art in Washington, D.C.

I had left my music business clients and become an instructor at the California Institute of the Arts, beginning a career as a designer—but more as a design consultant. I was also a self-made architect working on my studio house in Malibu as a developer and owner, and building a new business at my Willoughby studio in West Hollywood. I was transforming my design, working into forms and color. As I roamed the grounds of the National Gallery, it all seemed like my mouse drawing idea I had done in 1969 in New York City.

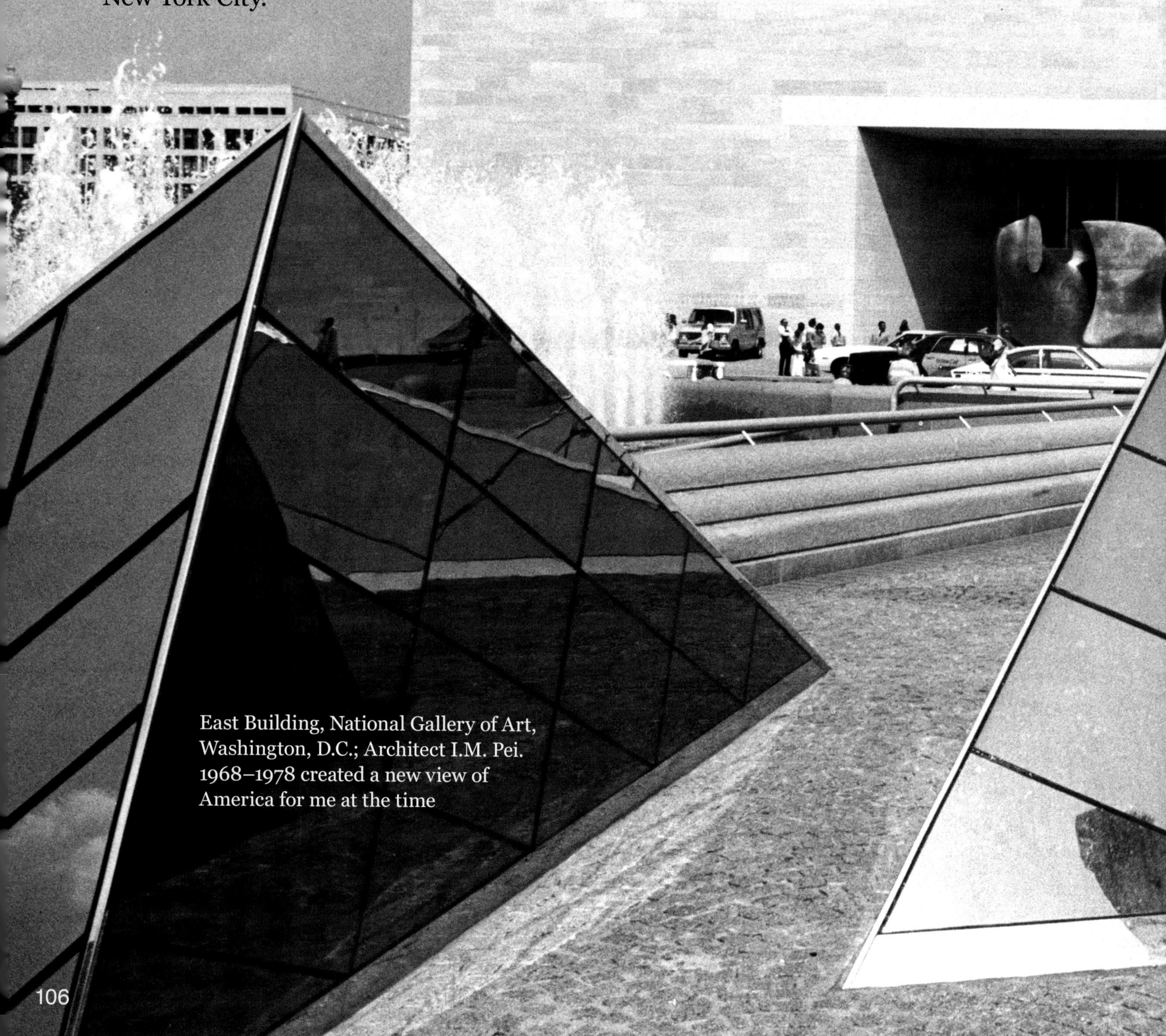

East Building, National Gallery of Art, Washington, D.C.; Architect I.M. Pei. 1968–1978 created a new view of America for me at the time

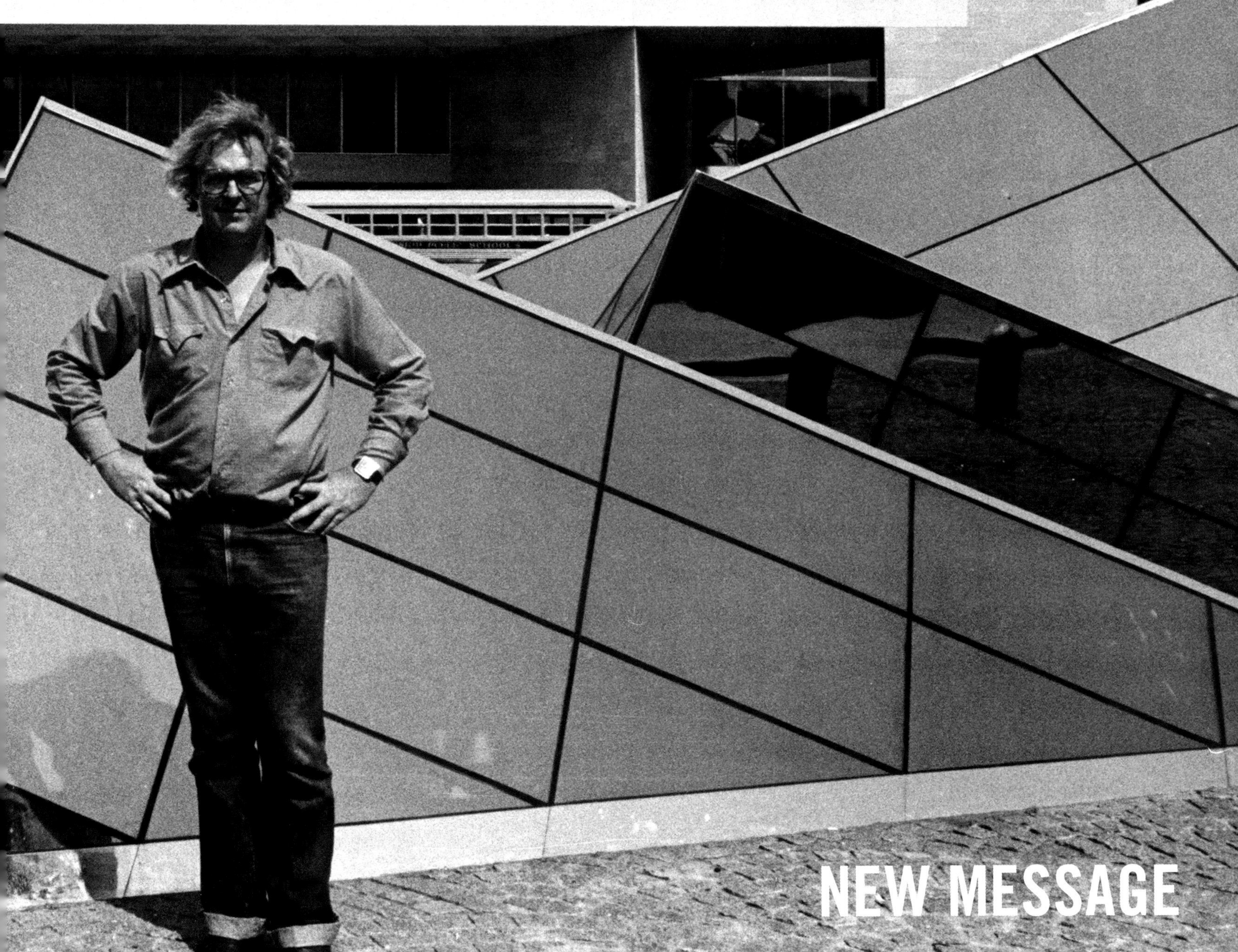

NEW MESSAGE

I moved to the Melrose District that had just opened as a fresh neighborhood. I was able to buy a 1927 steamboat design house from an elderly man and remodel the exterior and interior. It was located by an alley at Willoughby and La Cienega. This created a commercial and residential location where I could do my corporate design consulting. In 1975, L.A. Eyeworks was located on Mel-

I made a poster commenting on the times. Jim Benedict from NYC installed shows of my new work from 1976–1980.

The Melrose District

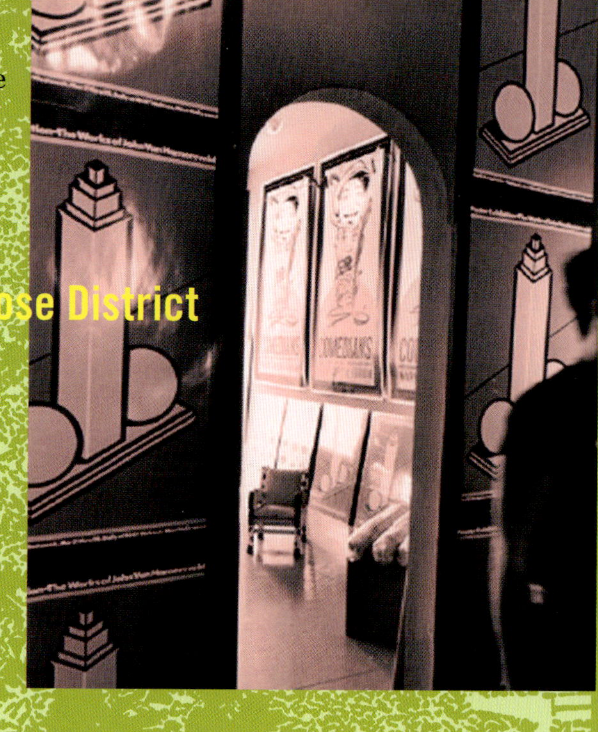

West Hollywood: The Willoughby Studio

rose Avenue, and across the street was the Industrial Revolution. Jim Benedict created a pop shop called Jolly Wall Graphics, where I showed my new fine art posters. The Pacific Design Center [designed by Ceasar Pelli] opened in 1975 for the contract furnishing business. The neighborhood responded by naming it the "Blue Whale." I created a poster announcement combining LA city hall and the "design center of arrogance."

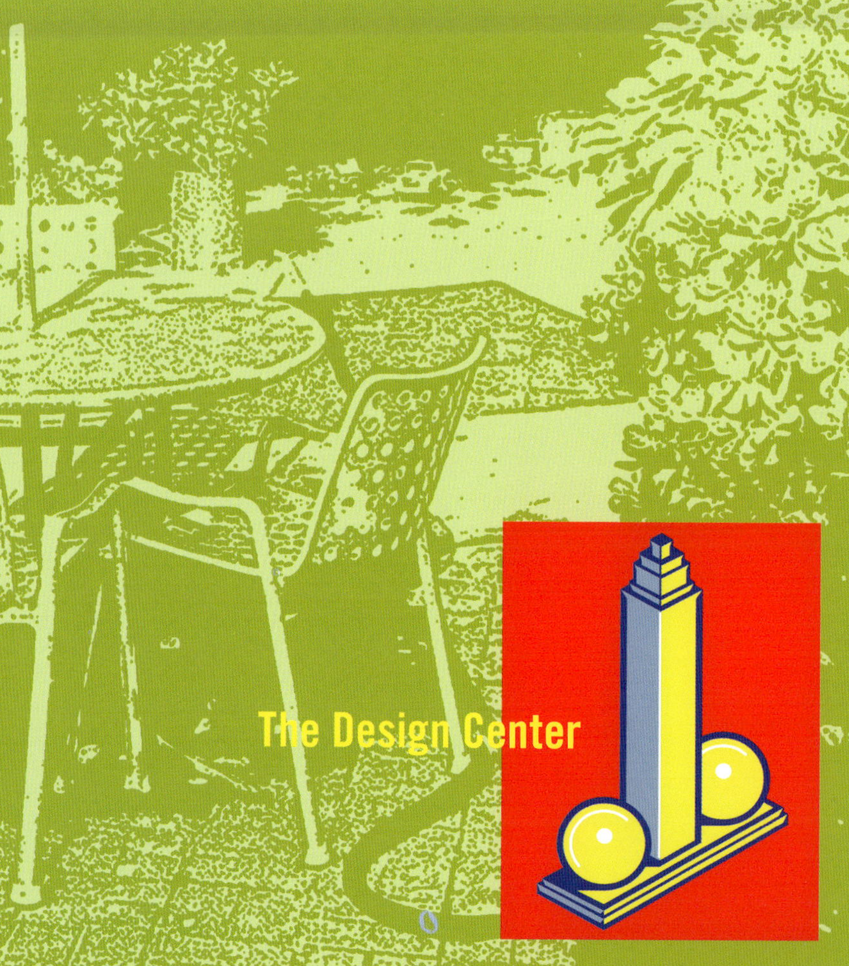

The Design Center

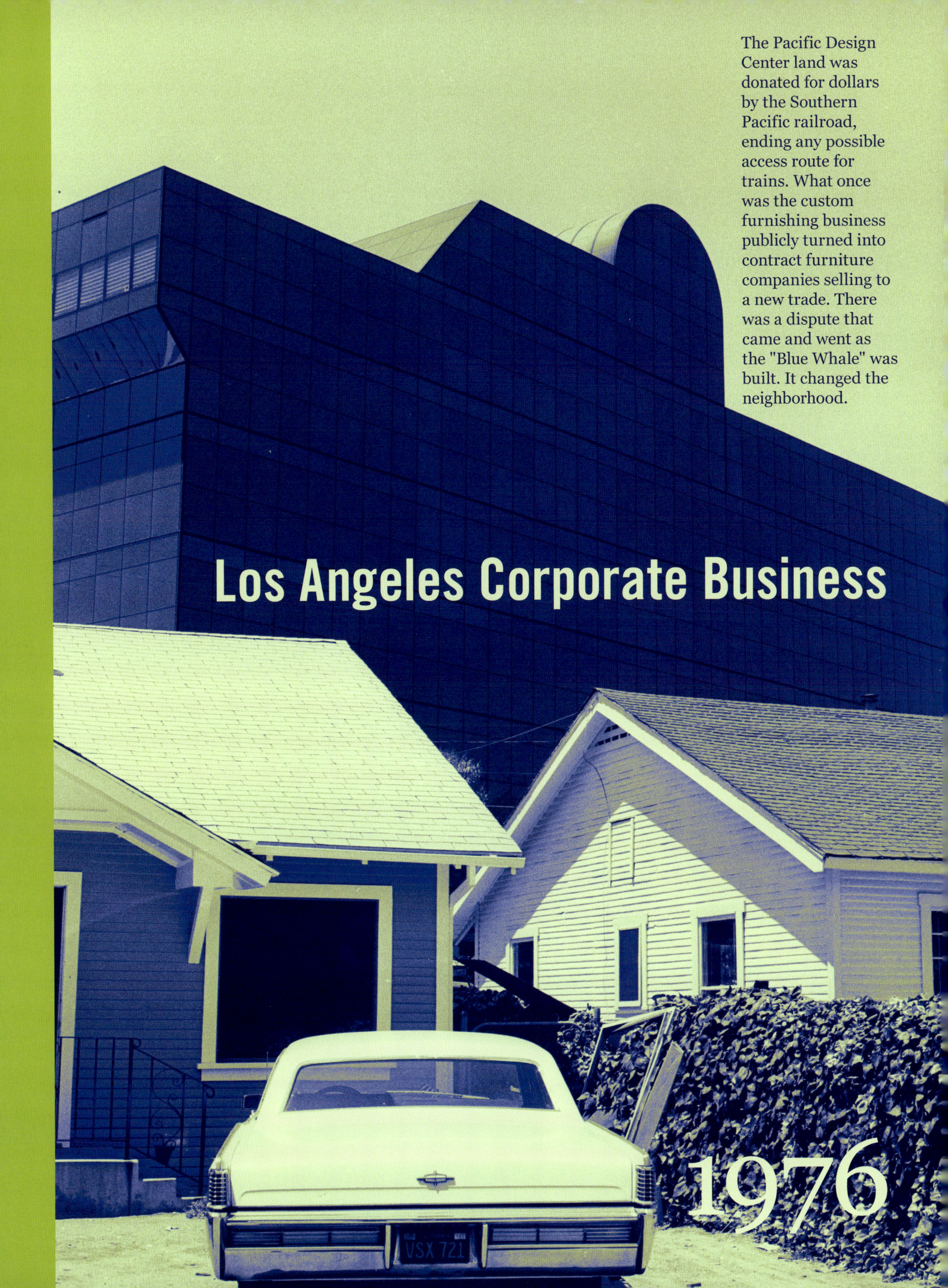

The Pacific Design Center land was donated for dollars by the Southern Pacific railroad, ending any possible access route for trains. What once was the custom furnishing business publicly turned into contract furniture companies selling to a new trade. There was a dispute that came and went as the "Blue Whale" was built. It changed the neighborhood.

Los Angeles Corporate Business

1976

Modernism and Postmodernism

I read Alvin Toffler's book *Future Shock,* and the following book *The Third Wave*. They were about the coming of the "Pro-sumers", with dialogue about the beginnings of the digital revolution on the horizon. I was an in-structor teaching design at CalArts. All seemed strange. Modernism had become an antiquity, and I lived in it. New machines were coming to make a new market, so down with Hippies and the environ-ment, up with automation.

The 1972 Willoughby Studio

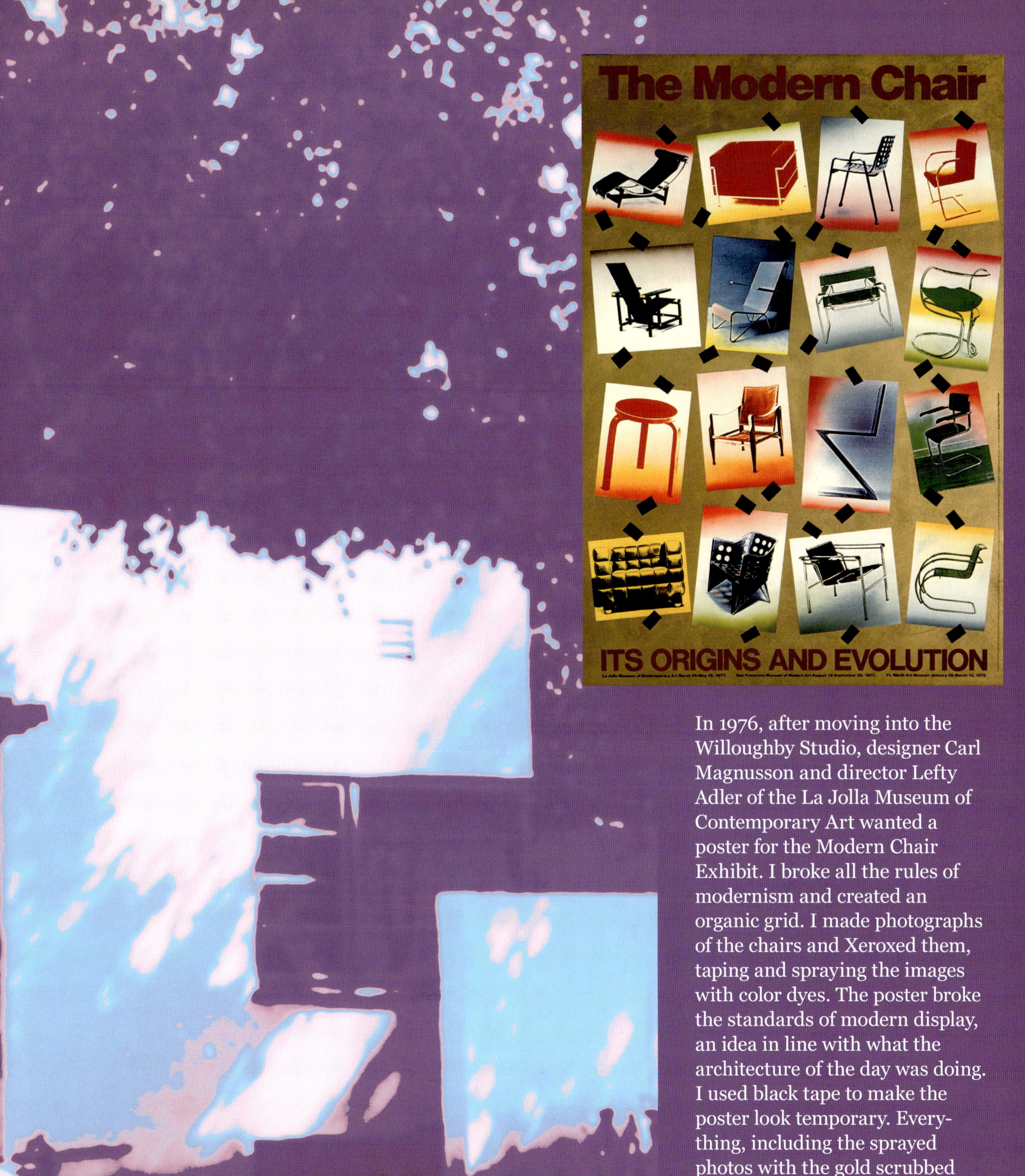

In 1976, after moving into the Willoughby Studio, designer Carl Magnusson and director Lefty Adler of the La Jolla Museum of Contemporary Art wanted a poster for the Modern Chair Exhibit. I broke all the rules of modernism and created an organic grid. I made photographs of the chairs and Xeroxed them, taping and spraying the images with color dyes. The poster broke the standards of modern display, an idea in line with what the architecture of the day was doing. I used black tape to make the poster look temporary. Everything, including the sprayed photos with the gold scrubbed background, was in contradiction with what people understood to be a classic and modernist poster.

In Contradiction

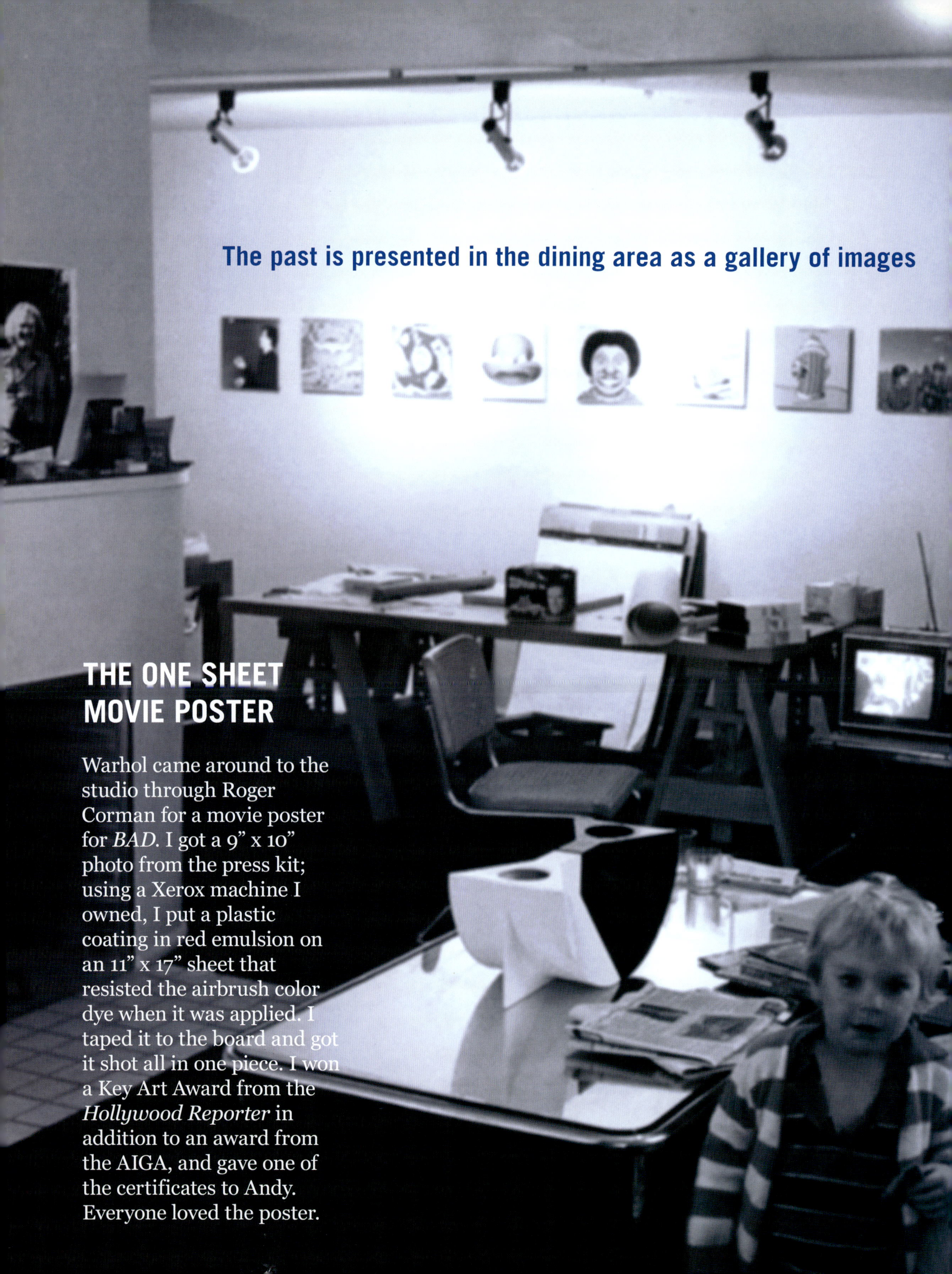

The past is presented in the dining area as a gallery of images

THE ONE SHEET MOVIE POSTER

Warhol came around to the studio through Roger Corman for a movie poster for *BAD*. I got a 9" x 10" photo from the press kit; using a Xerox machine I owned, I put a plastic coating in red emulsion on an 11" x 17" sheet that resisted the airbrush color dye when it was applied. I taped it to the board and got it shot all in one piece. I won a Key Art Award from the *Hollywood Reporter* in addition to an award from the AIGA, and gave one of the certificates to Andy. Everyone loved the poster.

THE WILLOUGHBY STUDIO POSTERS

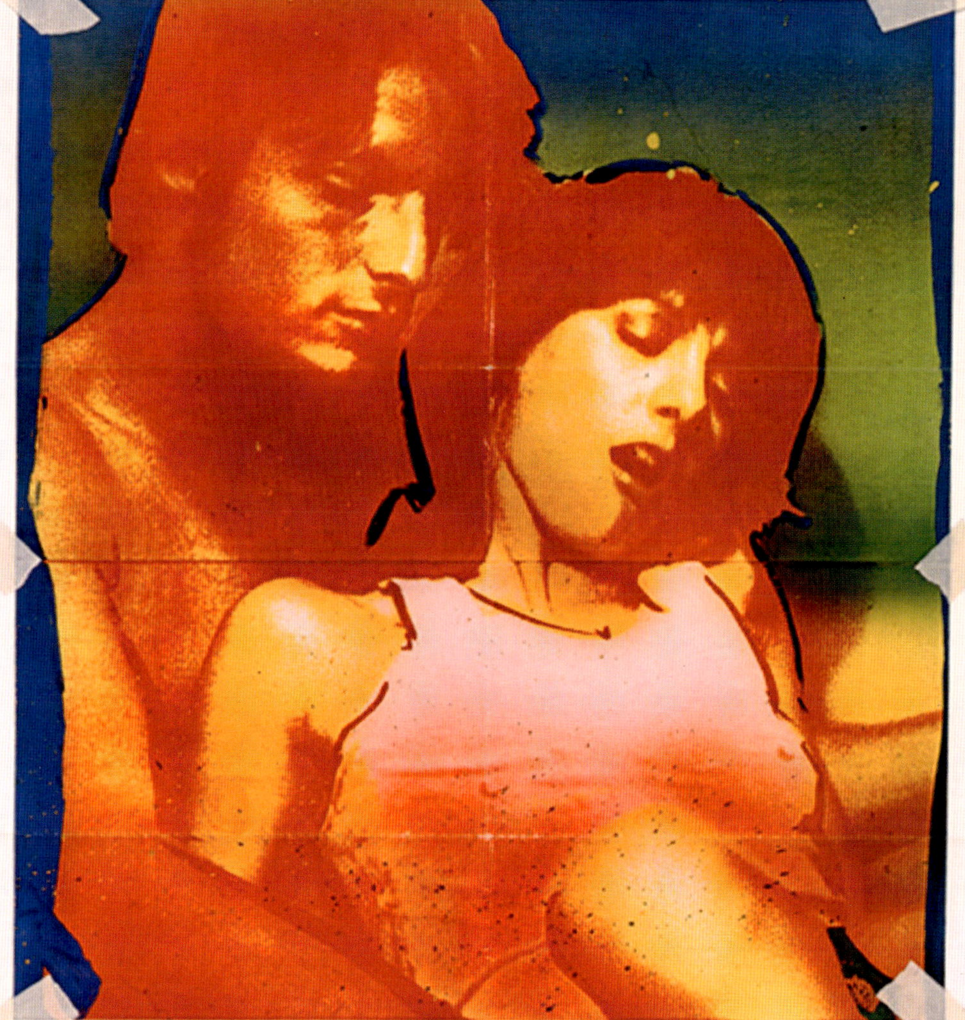

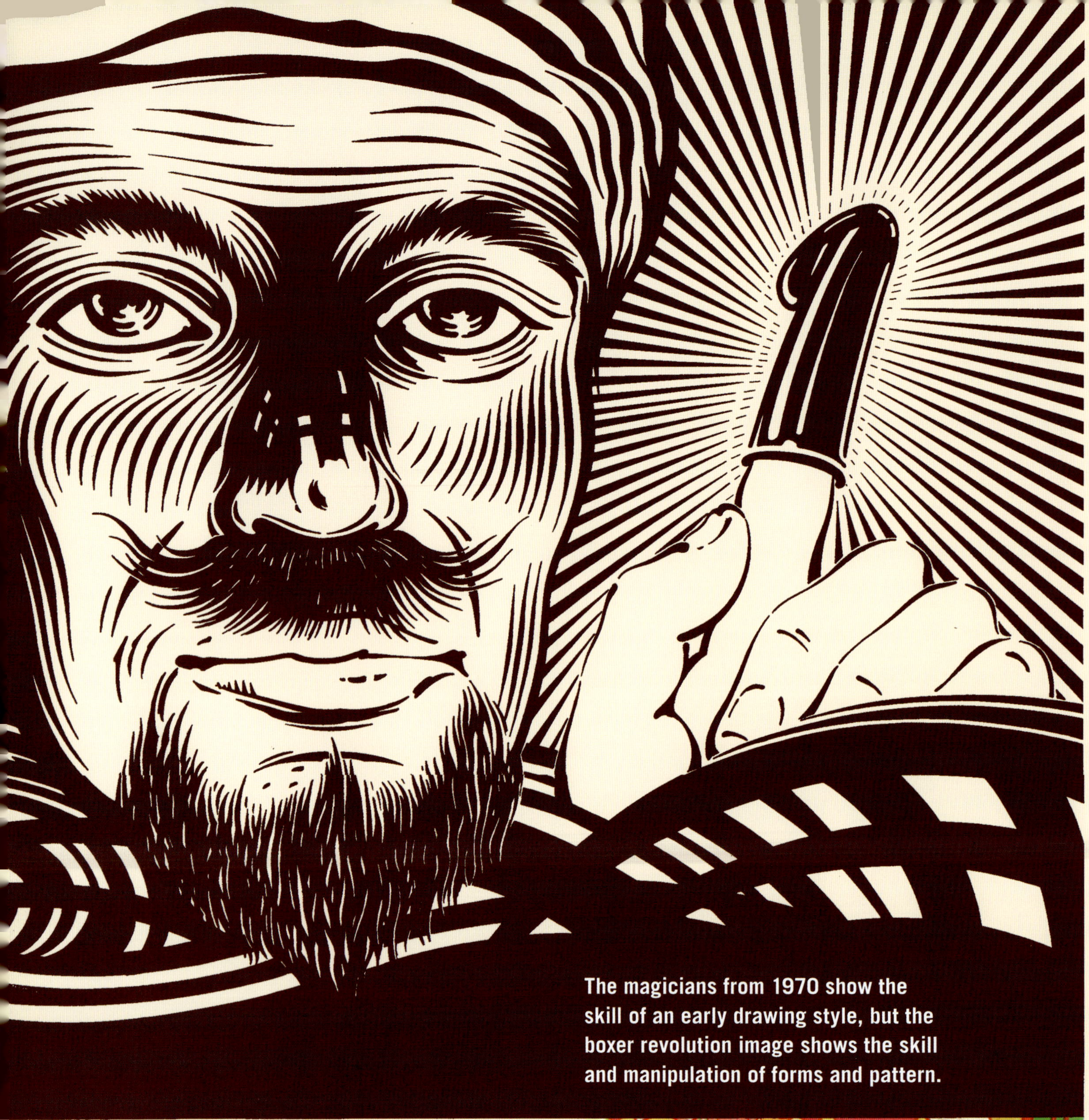

The magicians from 1970 show the skill of an early drawing style, but the boxer revolution image shows the skill and manipulation of forms and pattern.

At CalArts, drawing was not necessary in the program with all minds focused on conceptual art. I drew out my ideas in most cases because of the classical art education from my mother. So for me, drawing was like black magic. I could get that left hand out of my pocket and sit down and draw what was on my mind. That process is conceptual, although the outcome is an analog image on paper, or canvas. Though CalArts taught the students to go get someone to do the process, or manufacture the idea, I was there in contradiction to this lesson.

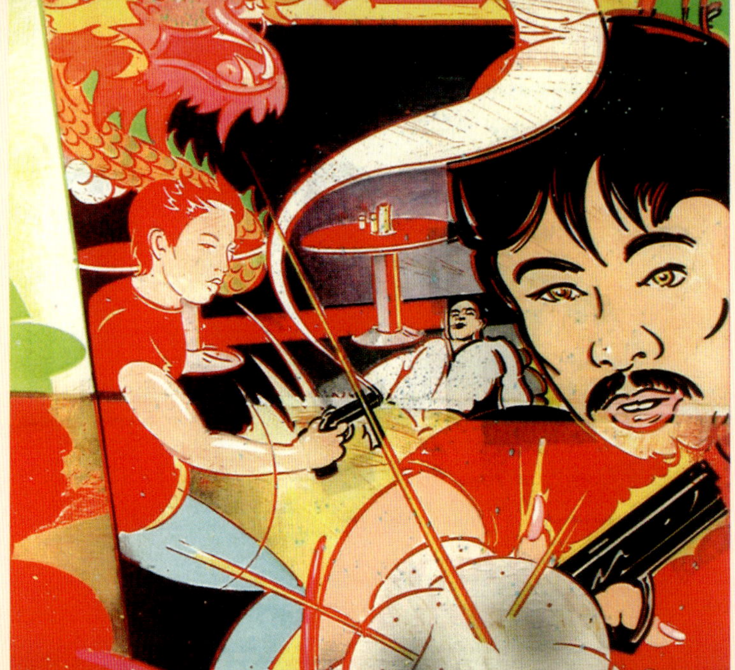

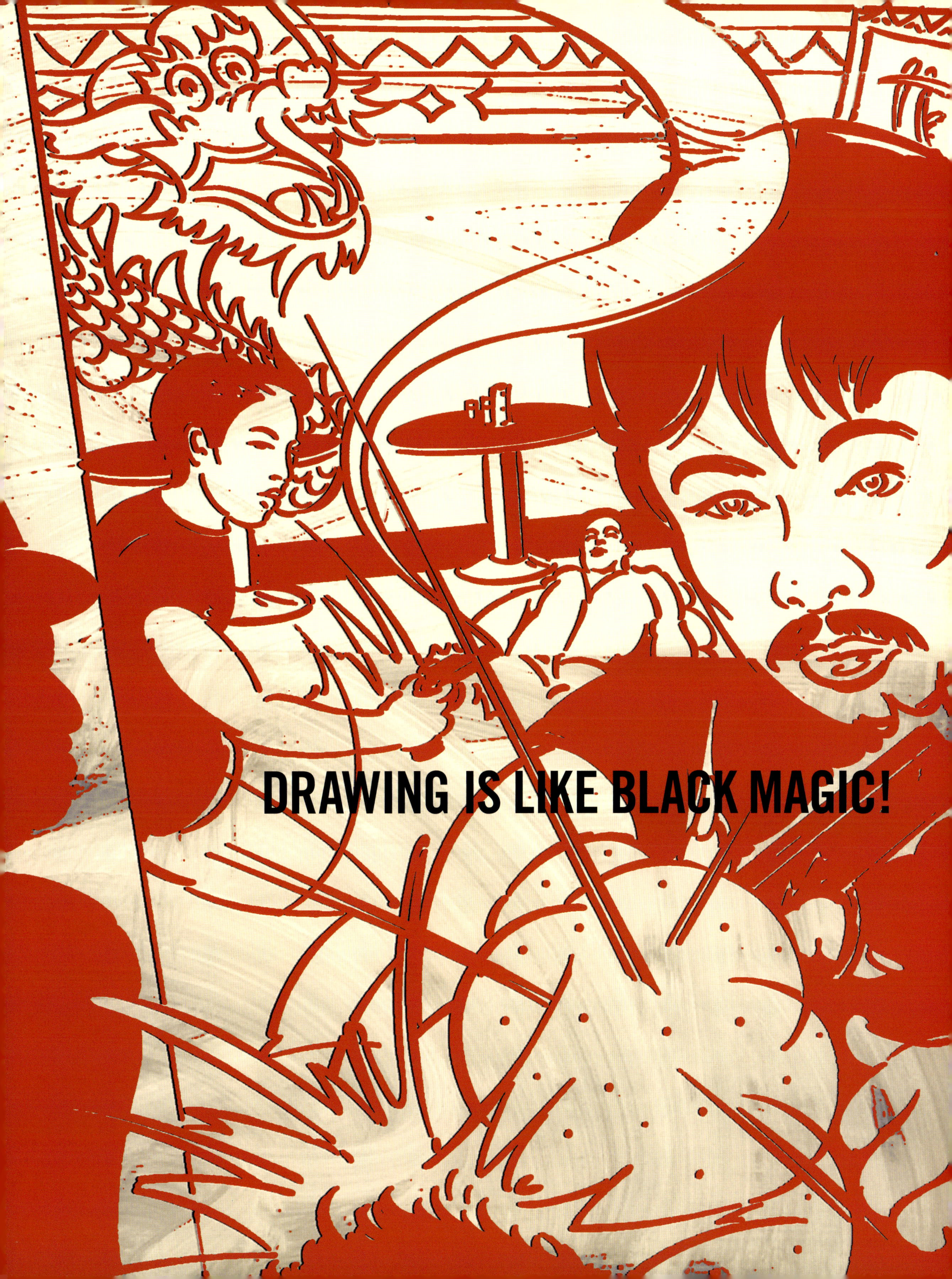
DRAWING IS LIKE BLACK MAGIC!

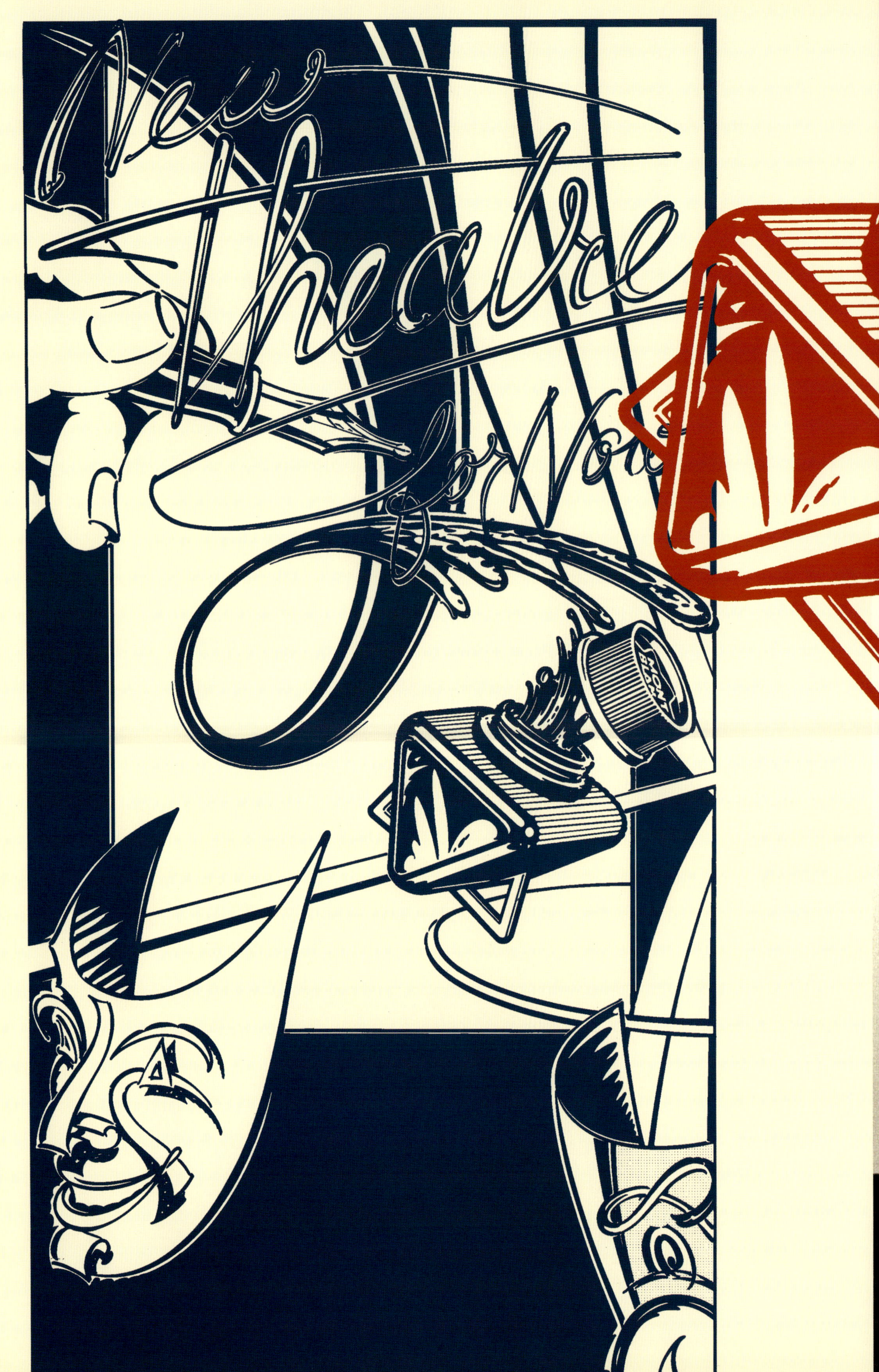
New
Theatre

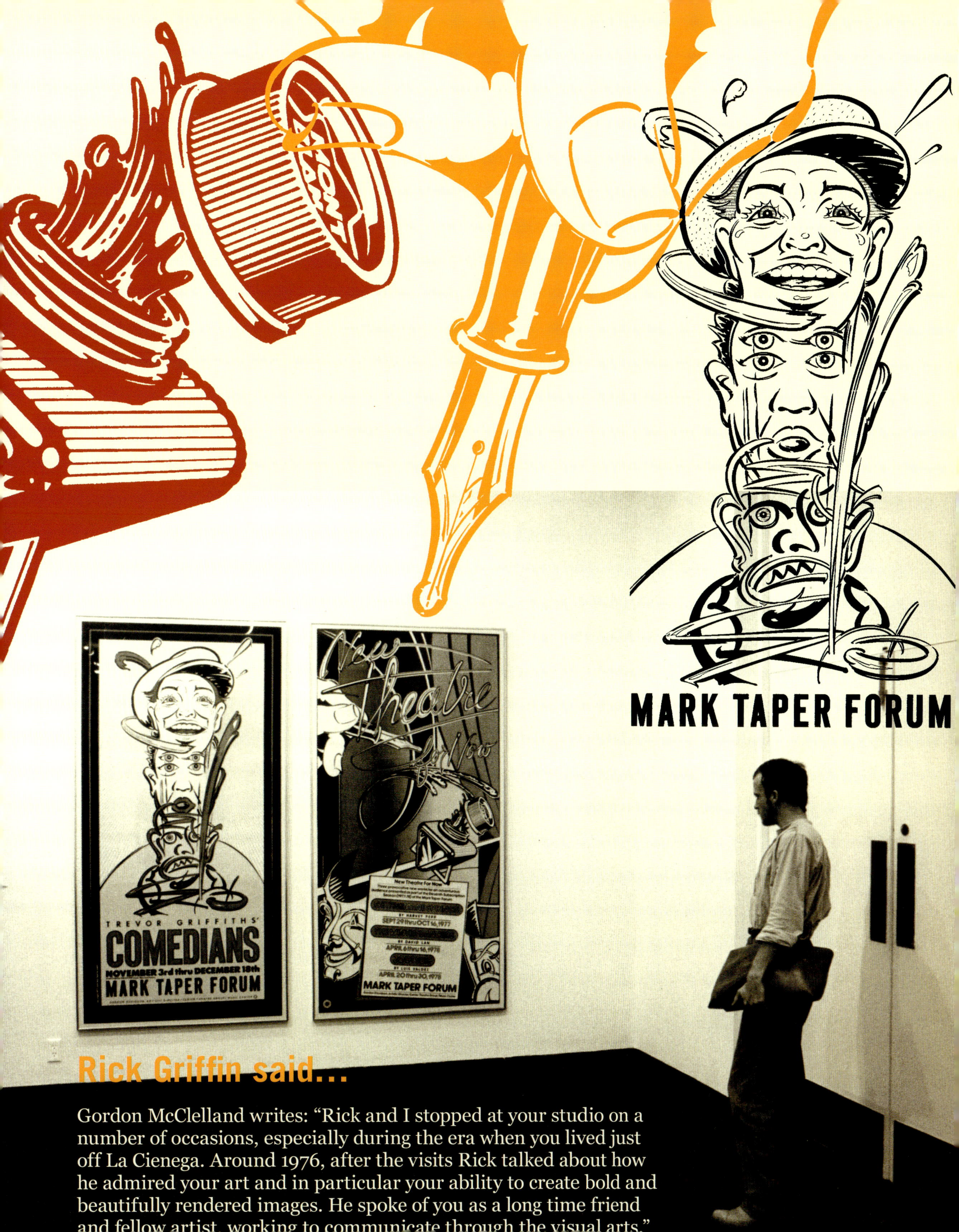

Rick Griffin said...

Gordon McClelland writes: "Rick and I stopped at your studio on a number of occasions, especially during the era when you lived just off La Cienega. Around 1976, after the visits Rick talked about how he admired your art and in particular your ability to create bold and beautifully rendered images. He spoke of you as a long time friend and fellow artist, working to communicate through the visual arts."

THE MELROSE DISTRICT

Elektra Records was just up the street on La Cienega. One day I was approached by the band at the studio to design the album cover and campaign for *An American Prayer: Jim Morrison Music by the Doors*. What most people don't understand is the album cover is only one part of a record's promotion. You had to meet them, exchange ideas, get photos—in this case, from photographers around the nation. Then a position and strategy was built with the company to make every aspect of the media and packaging work to sell the album.

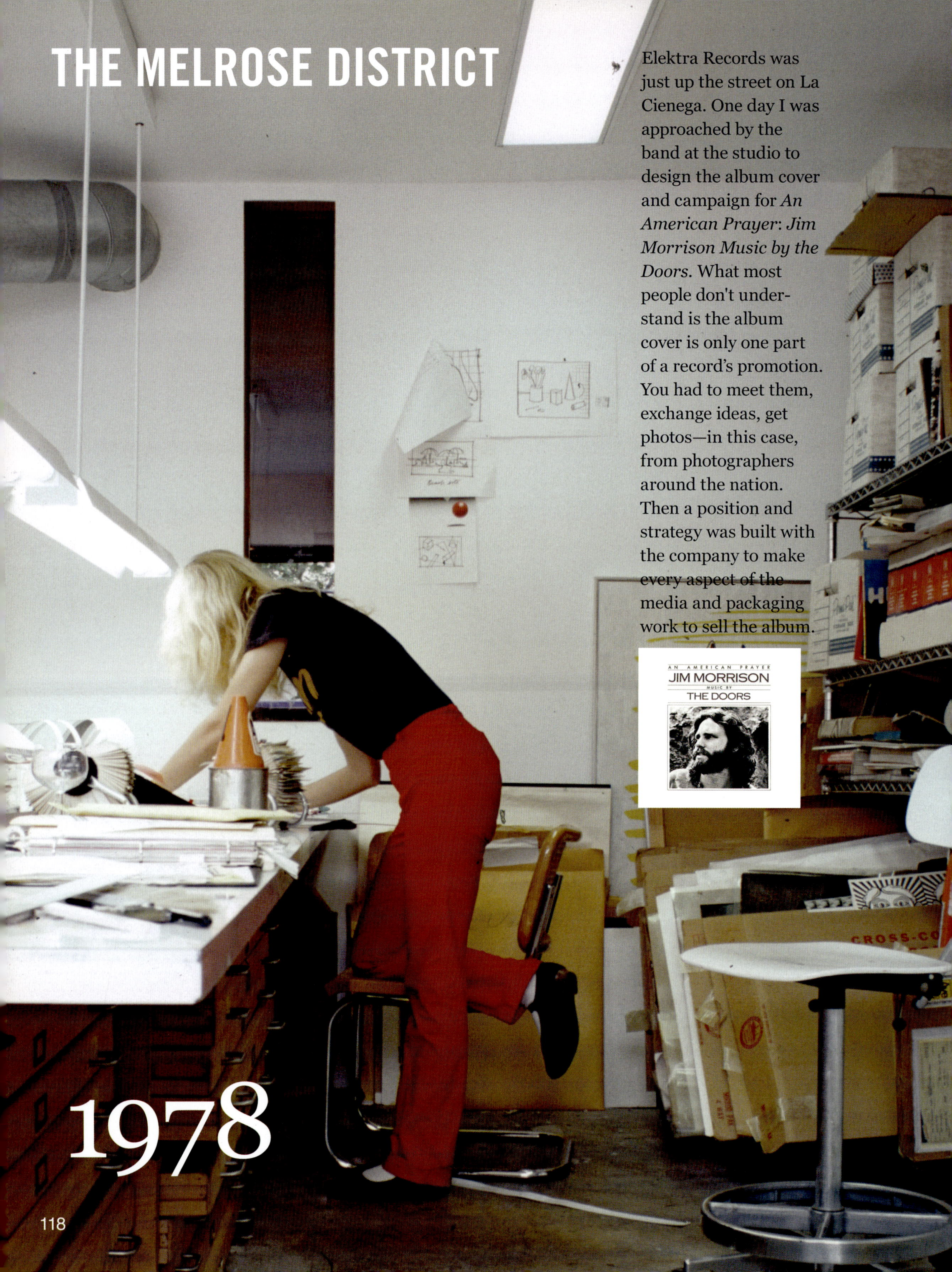

1978

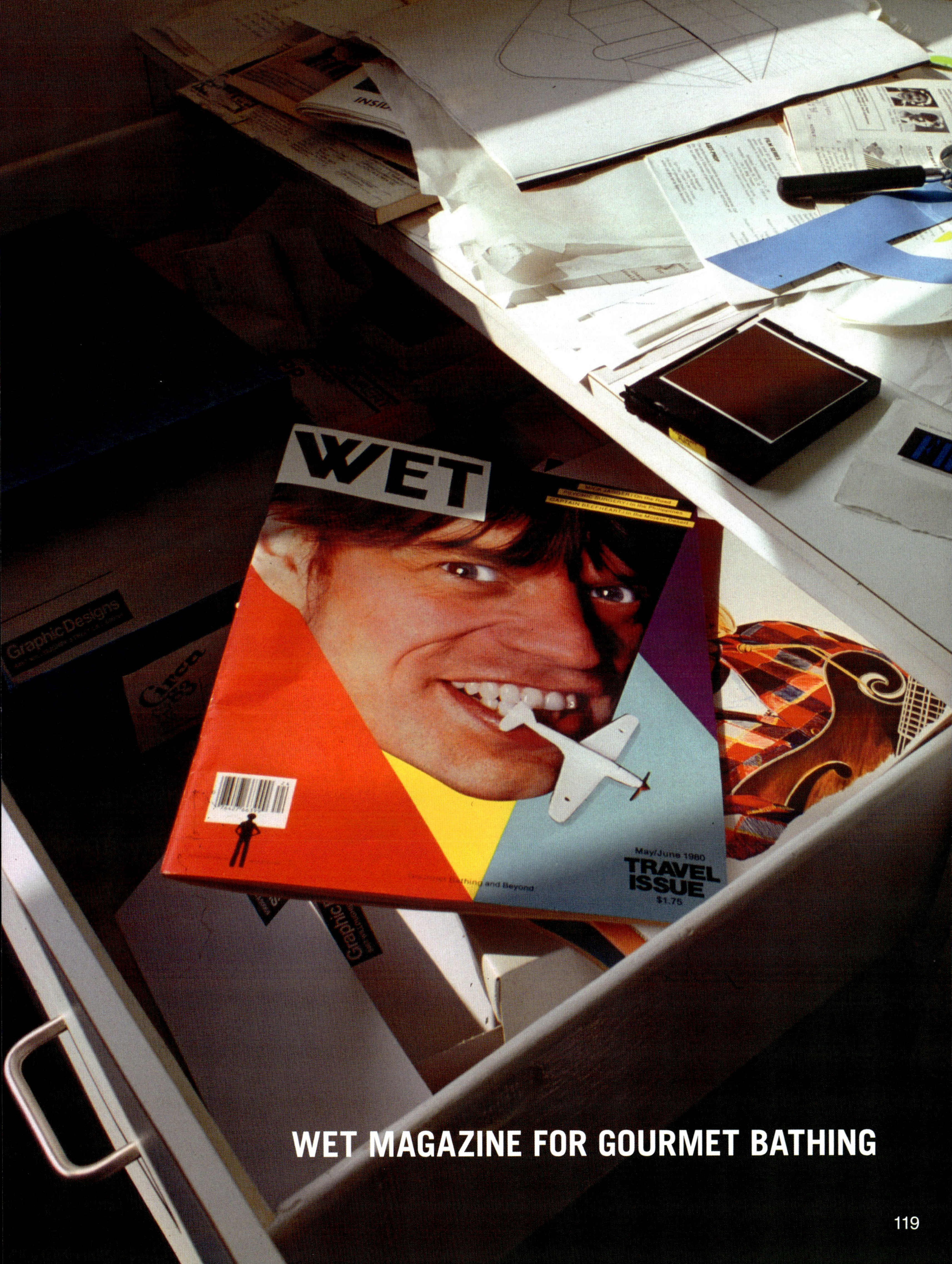

WET MAGAZINE FOR GOURMET BATHING

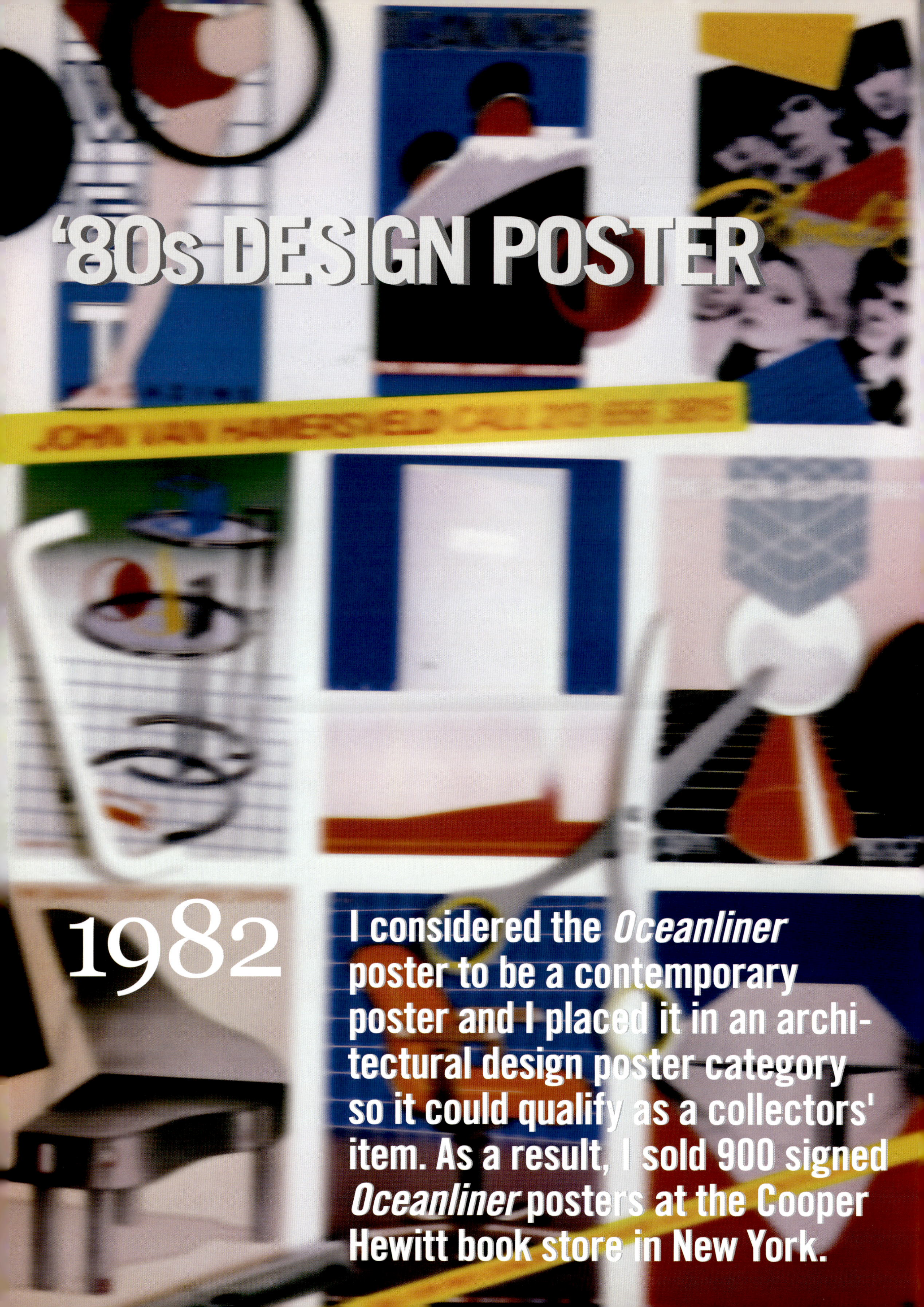

'80s DESIGN POSTER

1982

I considered the *Oceanliner* poster to be a contemporary poster and I placed it in an architectural design poster category so it could qualify as a collectors' item. As a result, I sold 900 signed *Oceanliner* posters at the Cooper Hewitt book store in New York.

Kathleen Eileen Moray Gray (1878–1976), also known as Eileen Gray, was a designer, architect and lacquer artist who helped spearhead modern design in the early 20th century. Despite her under the radar presence during the latter half of her career, her work is comparable to other modern design greats Le Corbusier and Mies van der Rohe and her designs are highly sought after by collectors and furniture enthusiasts around the world.

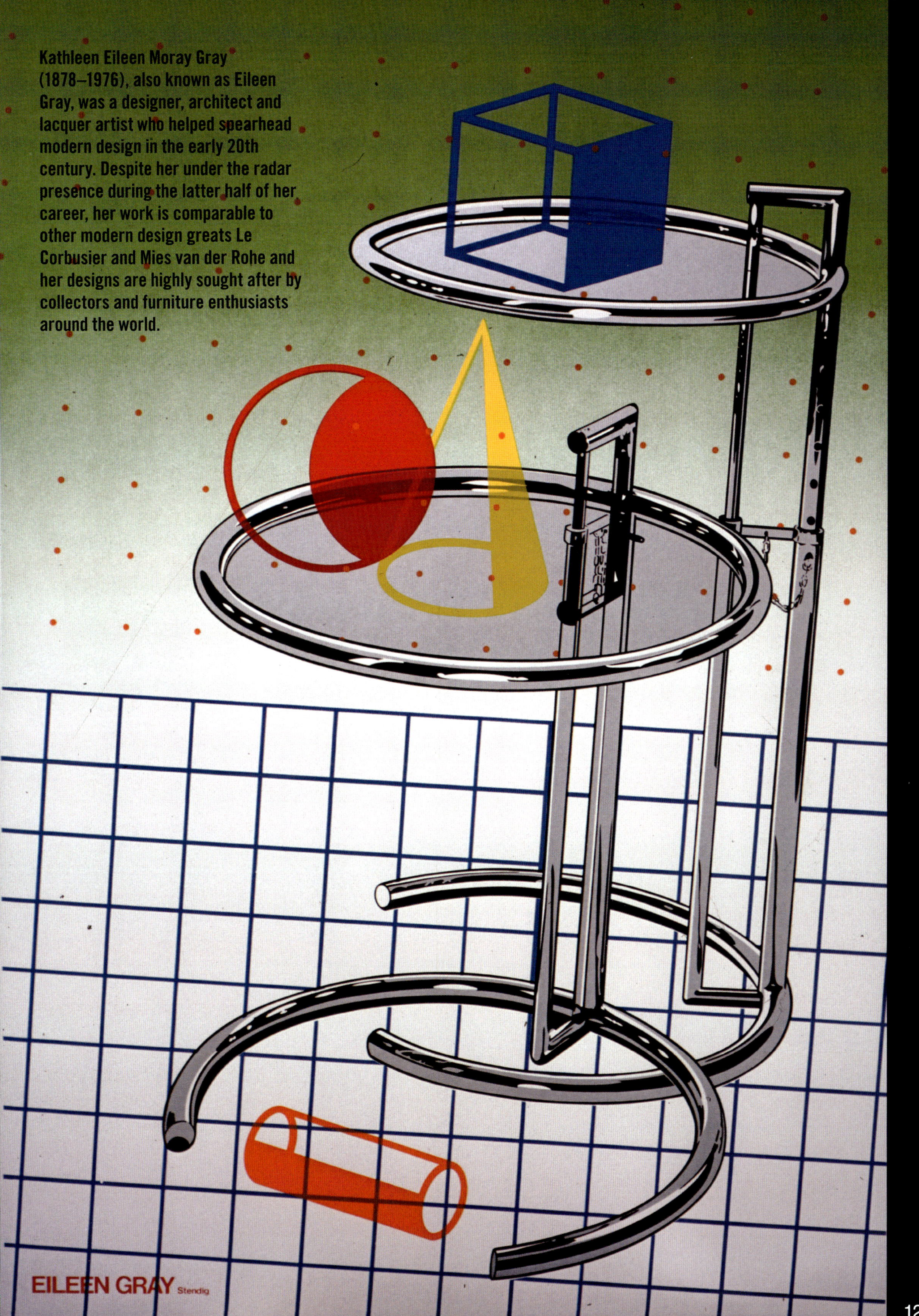

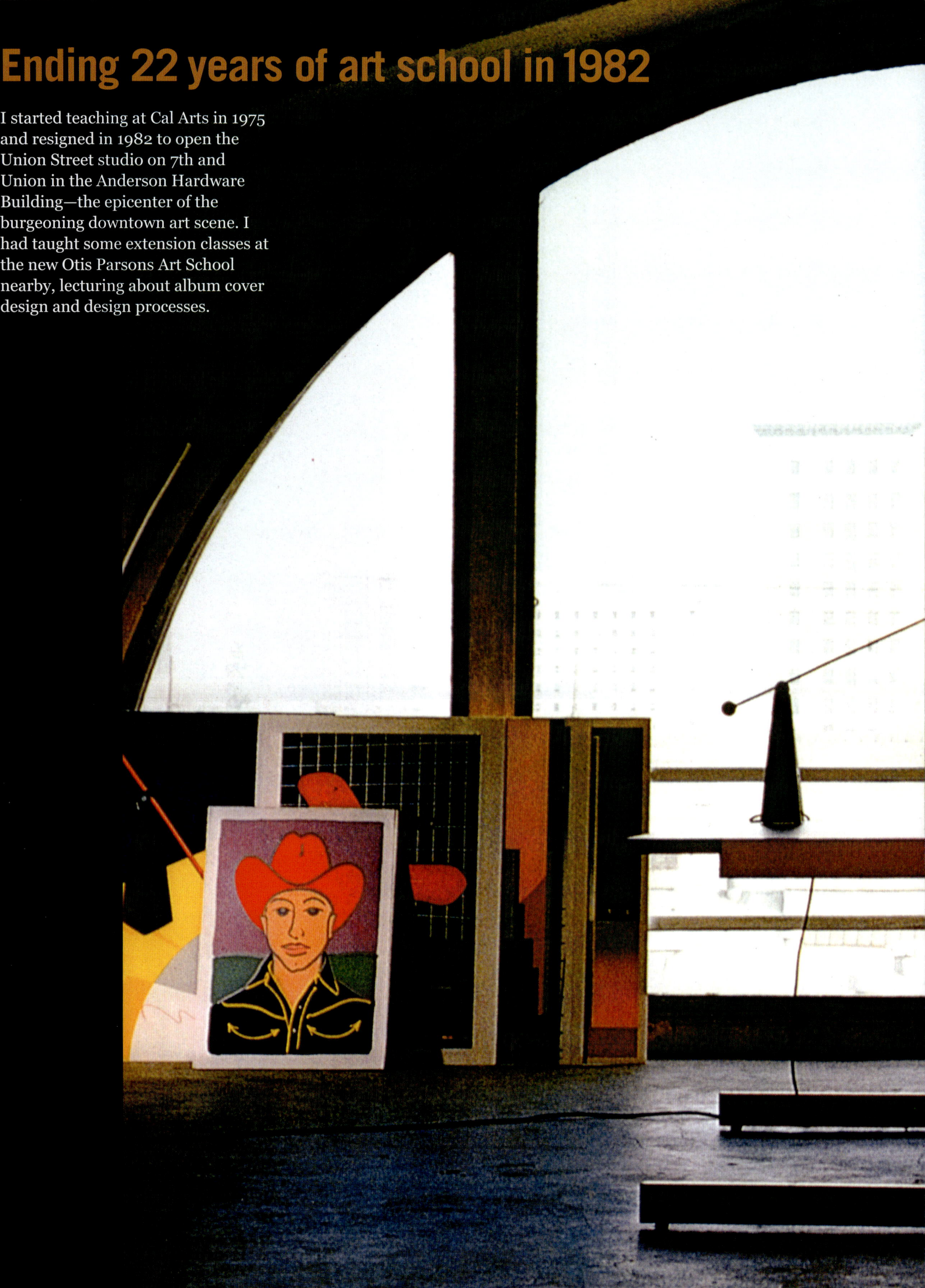

Ending 22 years of art school in 1982

I started teaching at Cal Arts in 1975 and resigned in 1982 to open the Union Street studio on 7th and Union in the Anderson Hardware Building—the epicenter of the burgeoning downtown art scene. I had taught some extension classes at the new Otis Parsons Art School nearby, lecturing about album cover design and design processes.

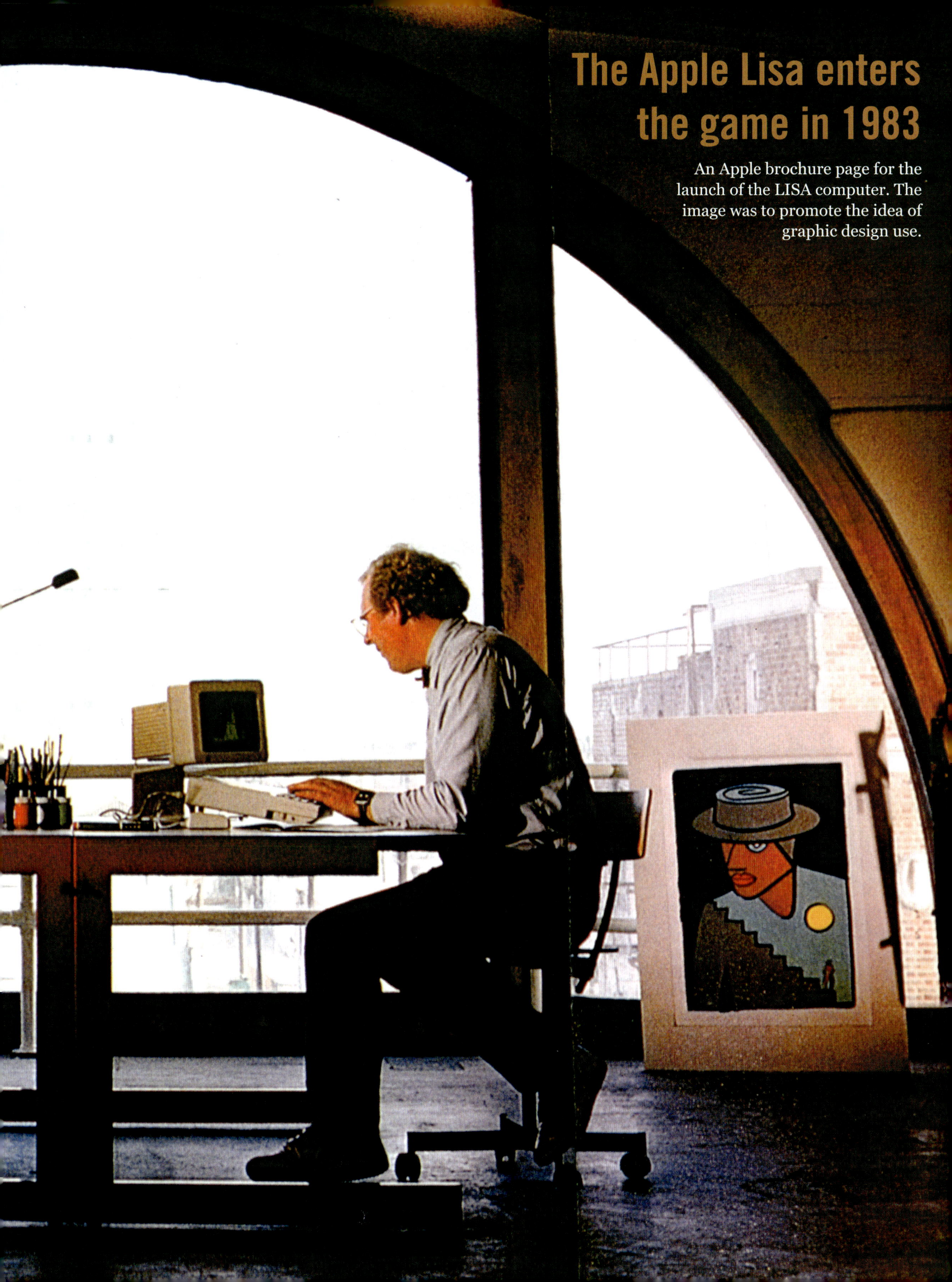

The Apple Lisa enters the game in 1983

An Apple brochure page for the launch of the LISA computer. The image was to promote the idea of graphic design use.

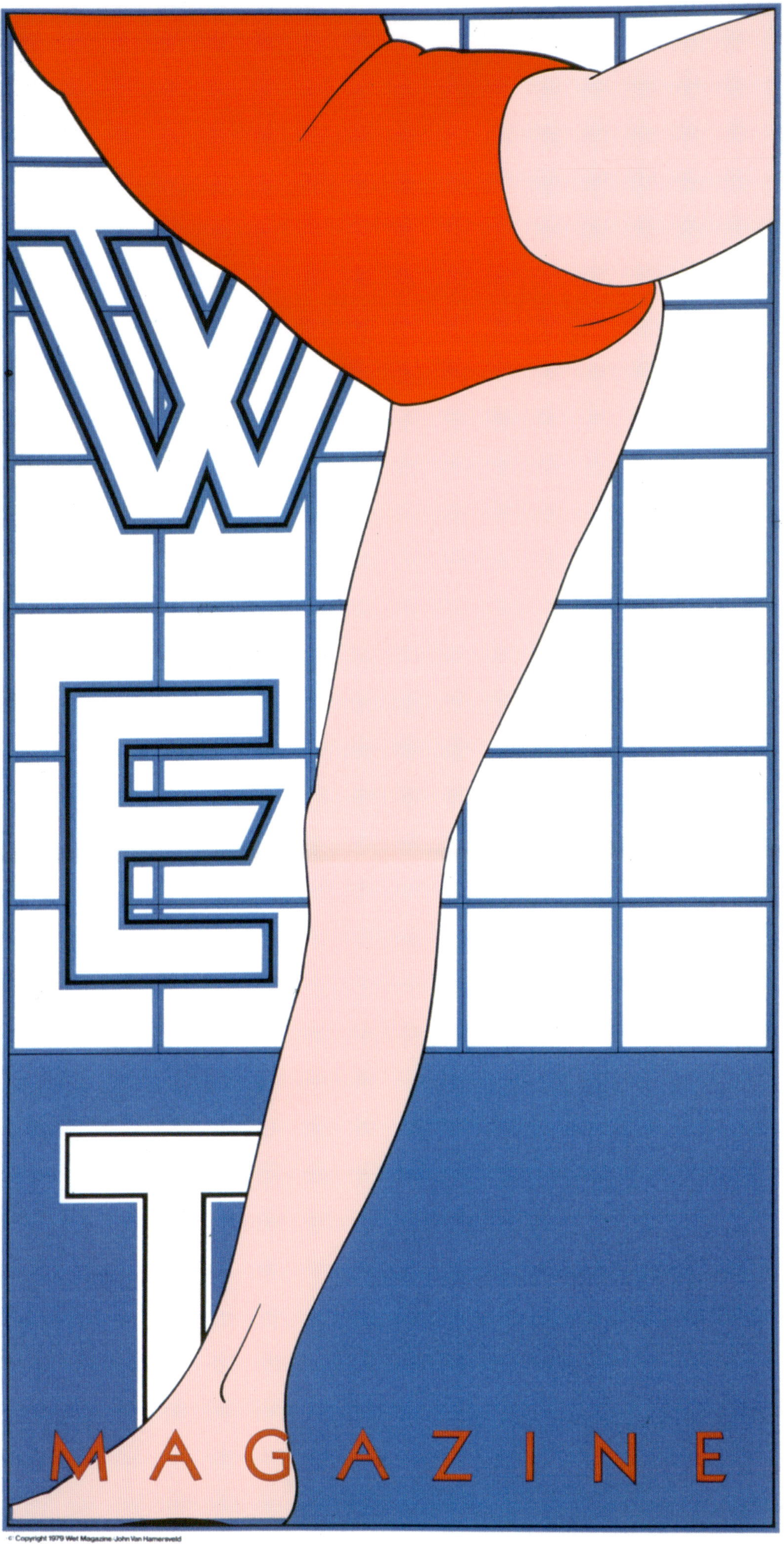
WET
MAGAZINE

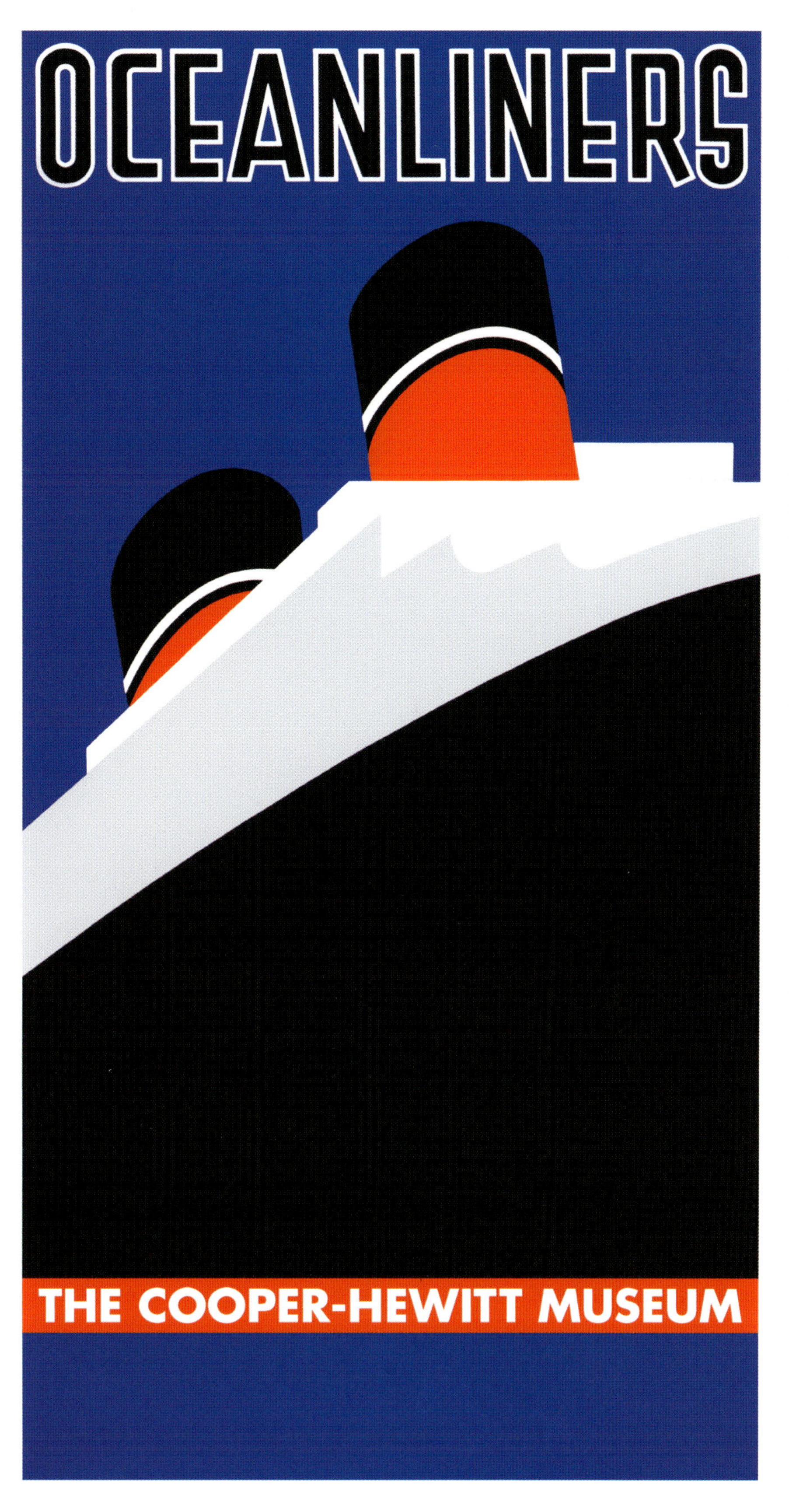

These posters were created to promote an exhibition for Oceanliner memorabilia at New York's Cooper Hewitt Museum, as well as a *Wet Magazine* subscription drive. Both the *Oceanliner* and *Wet Magazine* poster were sold at poster stores in the US; Mirage Editions published and distributed the posters for fifty dollars per print until the 1,500 unit edition sold out.

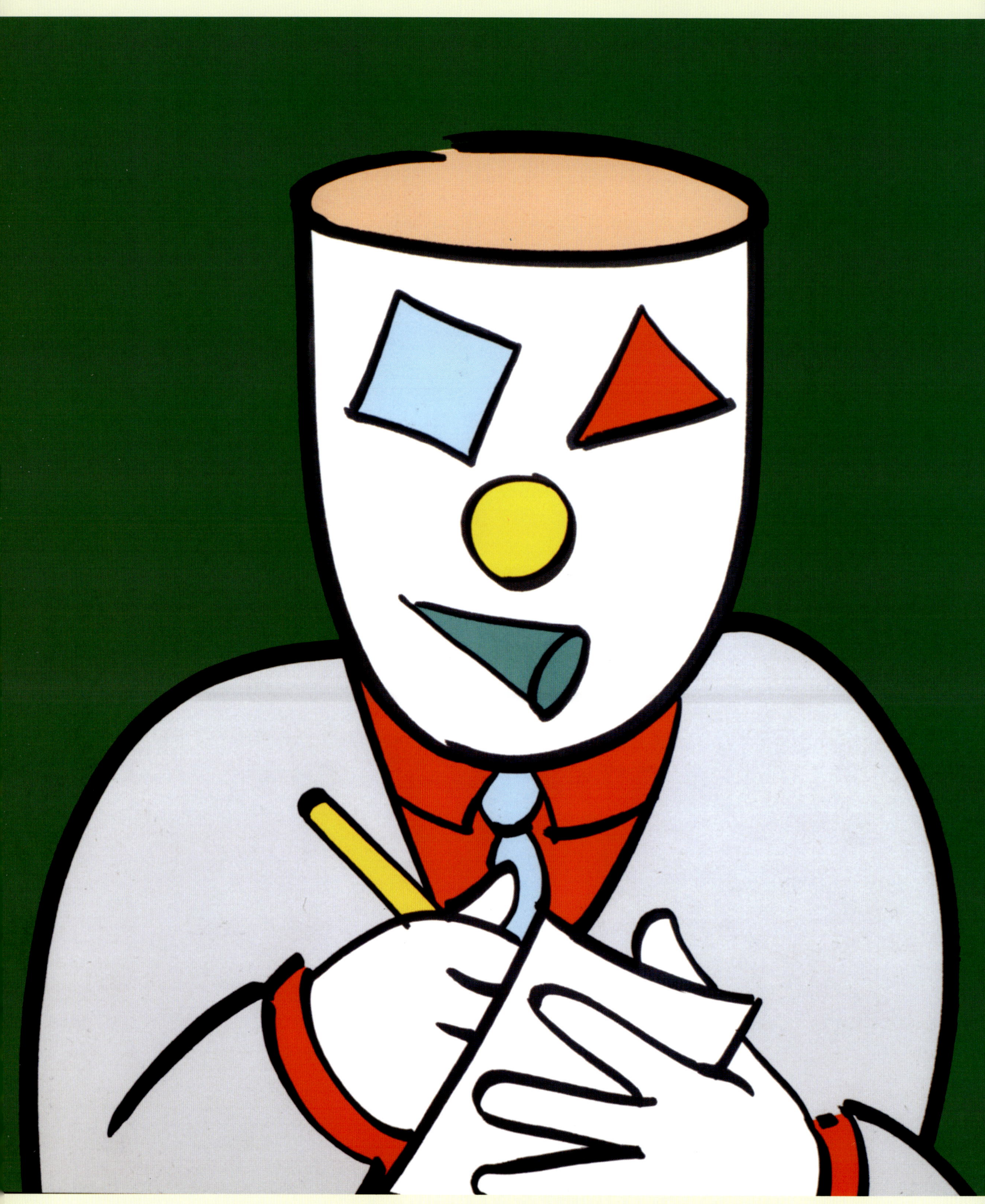

The Cal Arts Image (1980), "The Art Gangster"

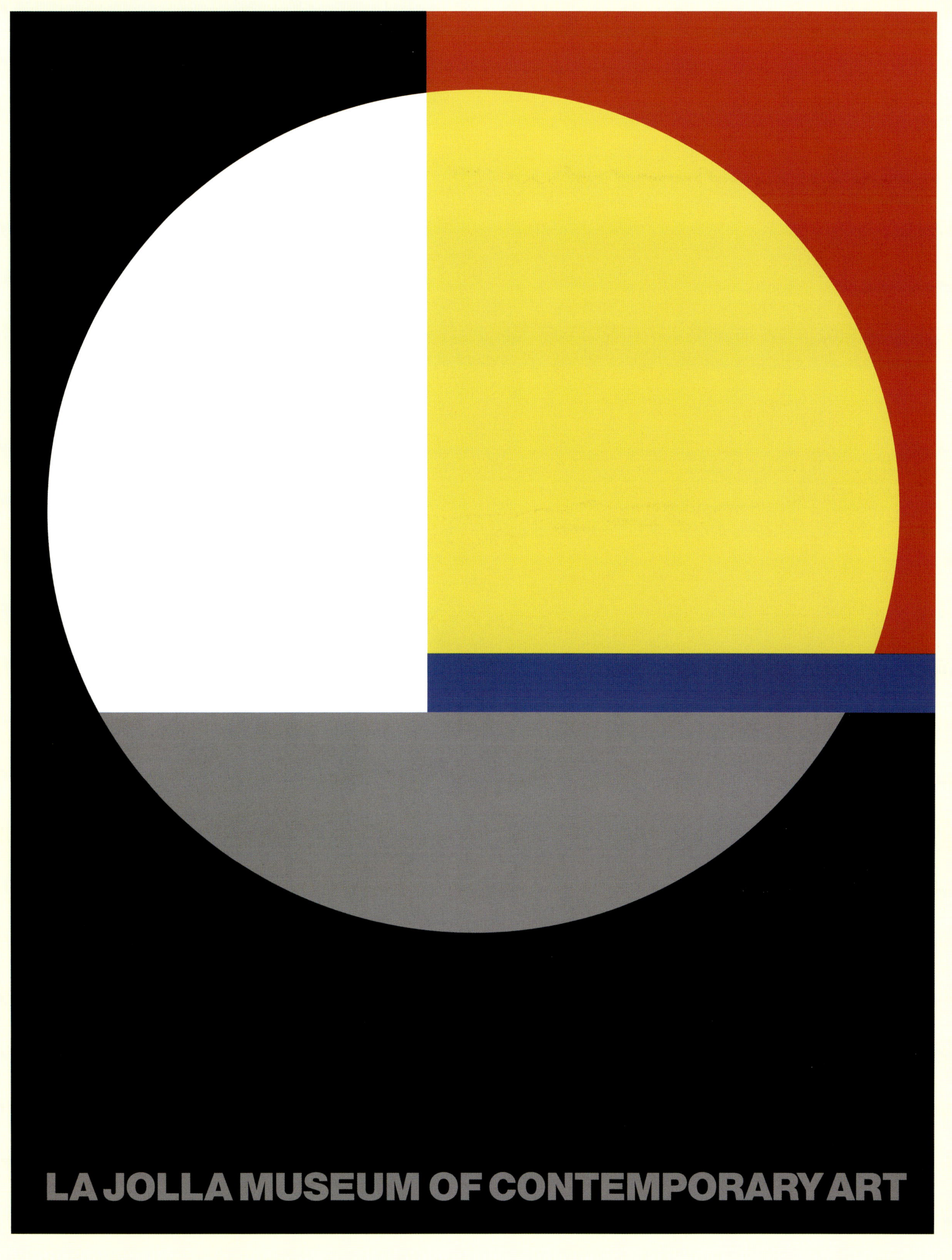
LA JOLLA MUSEUM OF CONTEMPORARY ART

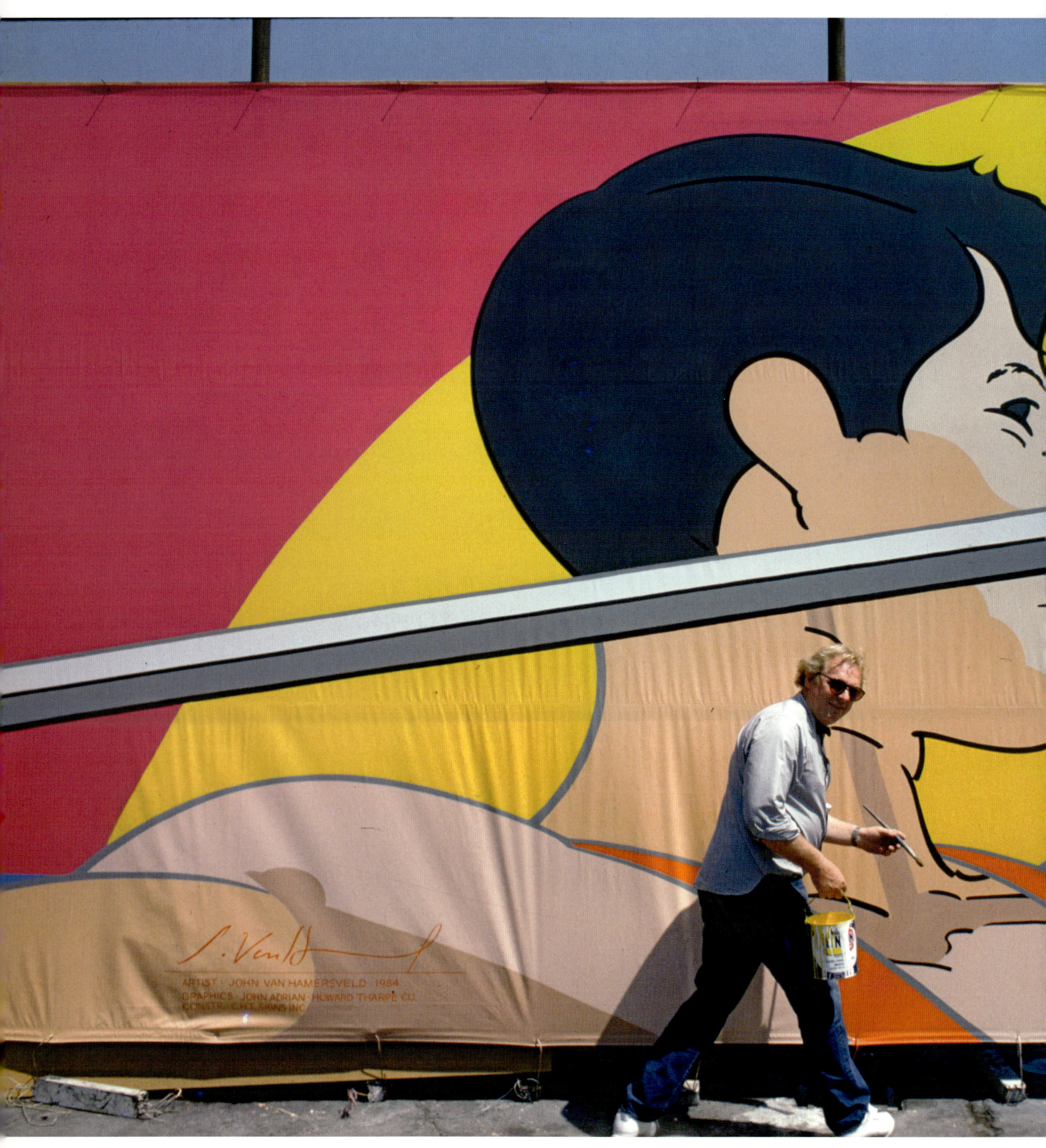

The Los Angeles 1984 Olympic Mural

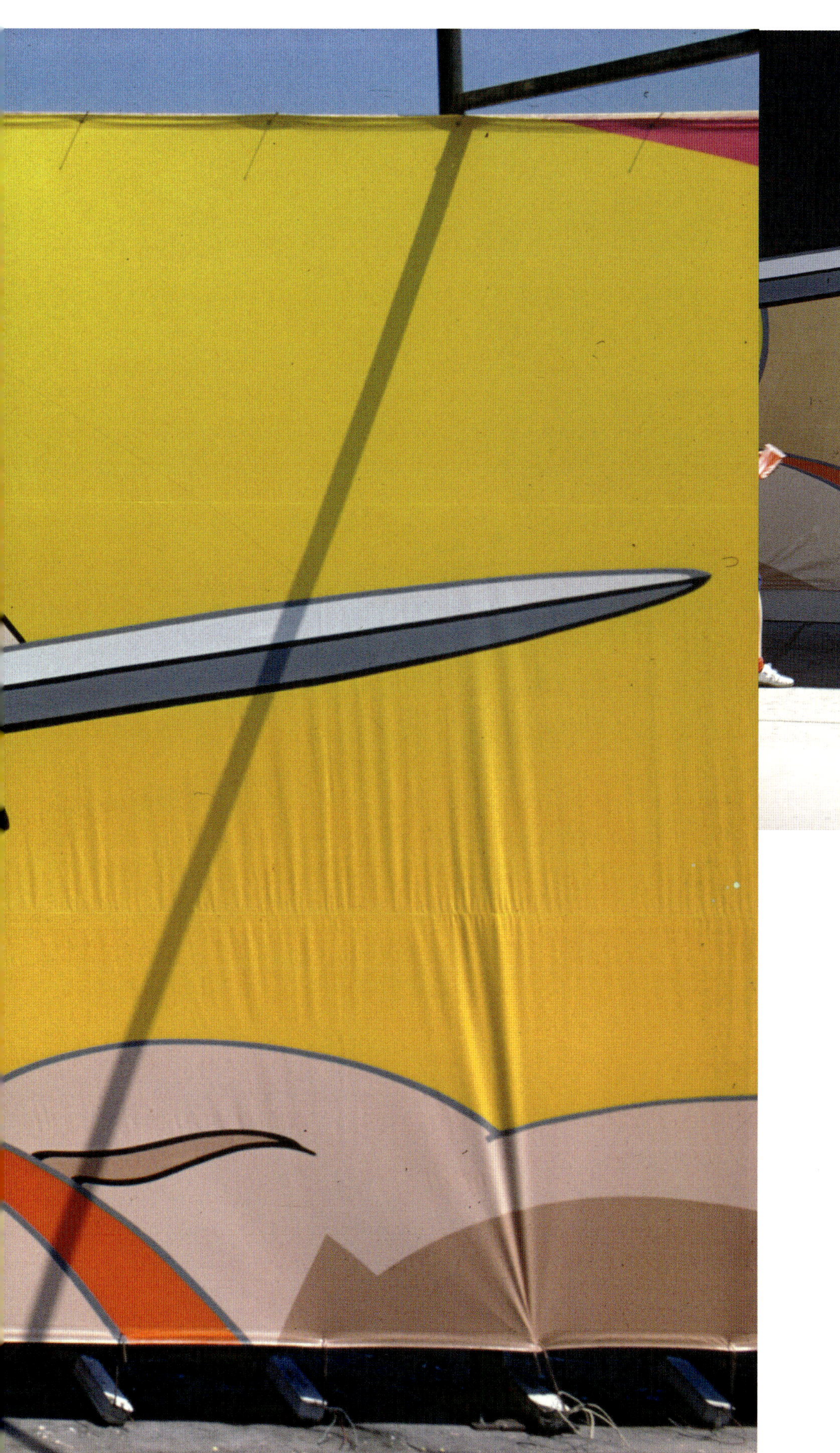

The Jerde Partnership was the developer of the placemaking and experiential philosophy for the design and planning of the 1984 Los Angeles Olympics. Jon Jerde's office commissioned a 360 foot mural design that wrapped halfway around the Los Angeles Coliseum Stadium. Converse Shoes sponsored the project. Saul Bass organized the Olympic Poster commissions.

In 1984, work began on a massive 360 foot Olympic mural in La Habra, a city in the northwestern corner of Orange County, California. The painters used a vinyl canvas material to create the 12' x 60' panels. Six giant panels were mounted around the lot to be painted. This shot shows the rough layout of the color palette I had assigned as the scheme. You can see the plywood backboard that served as the easel.

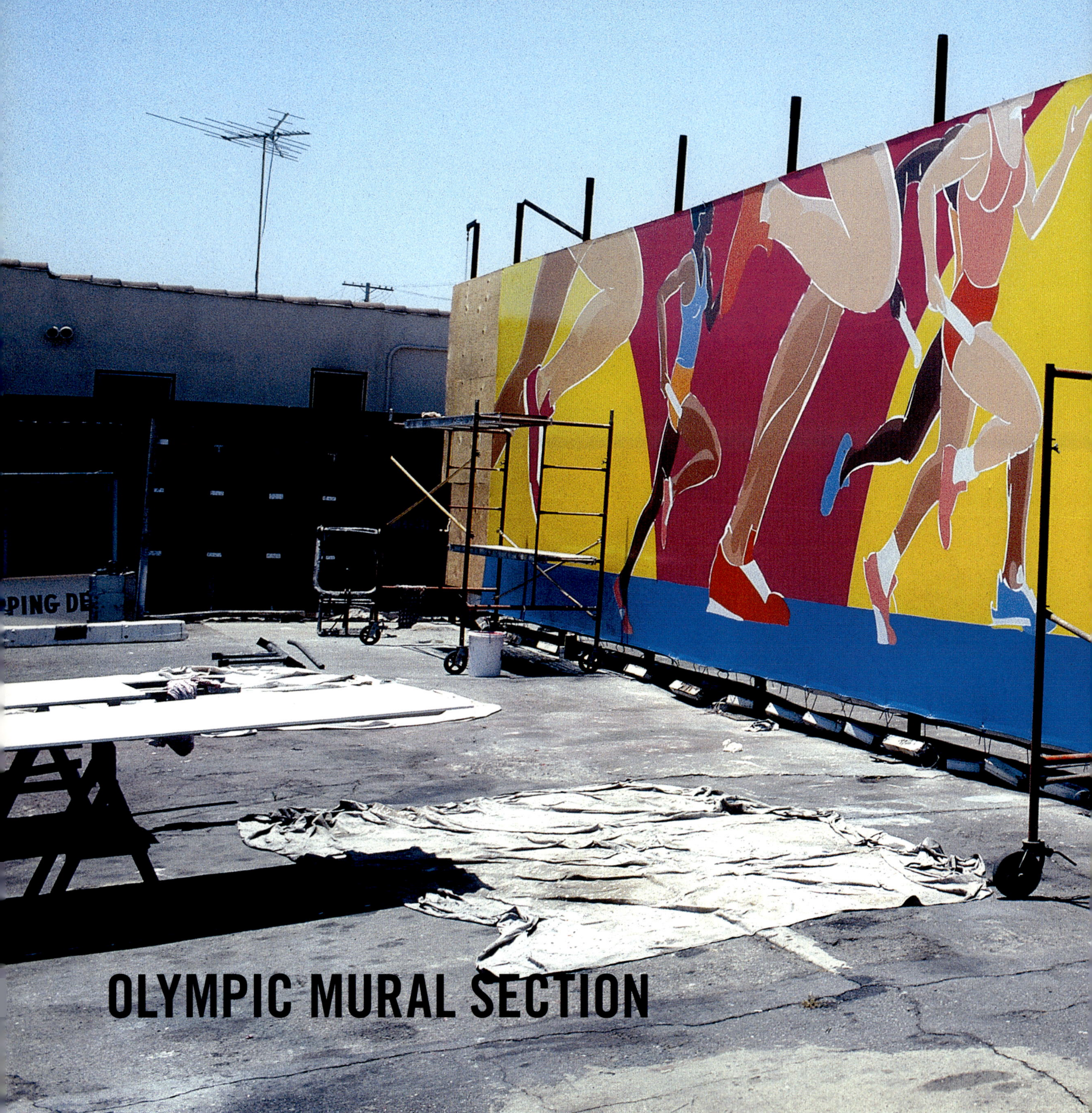

OLYMPIC MURAL SECTION

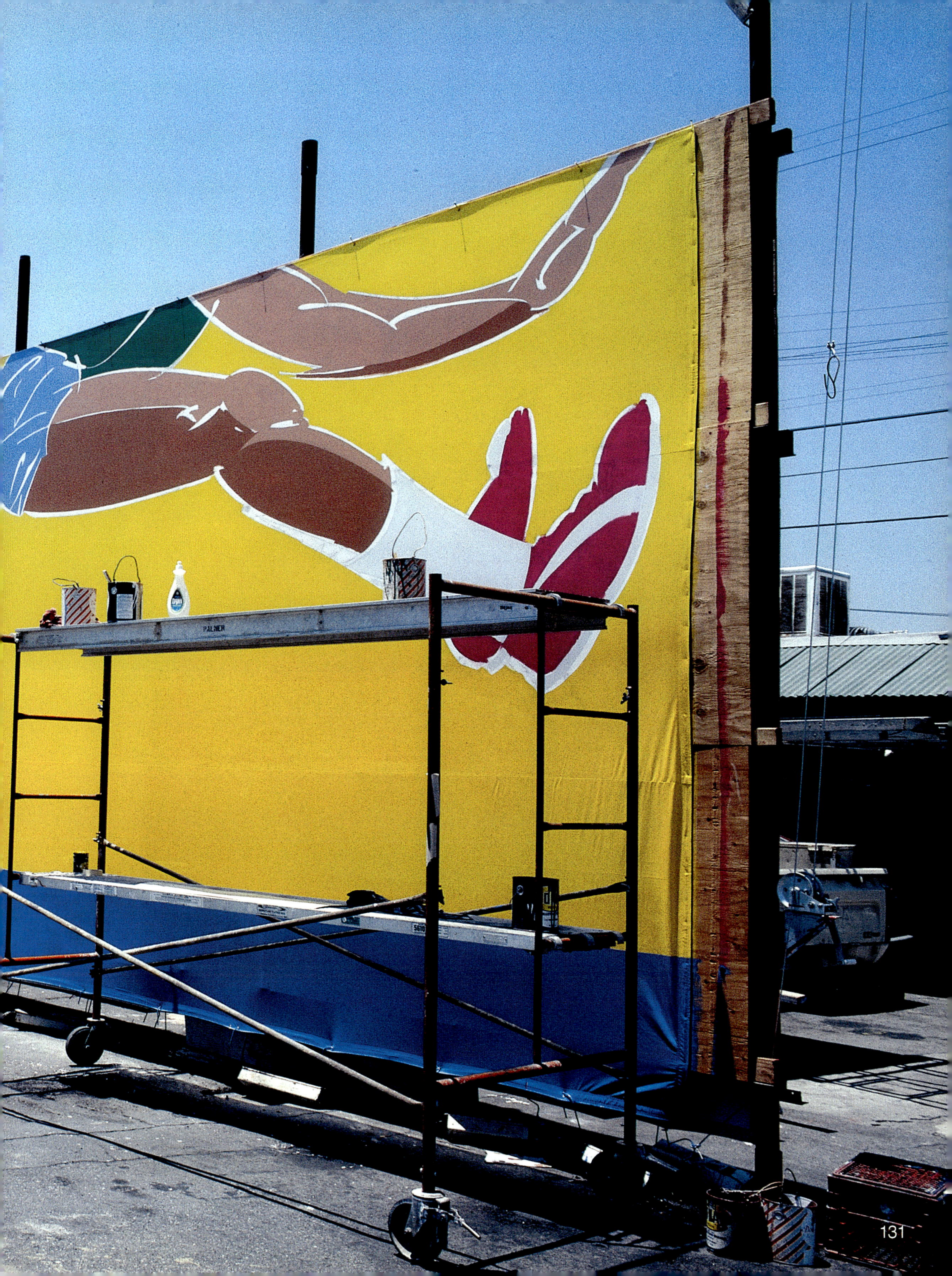

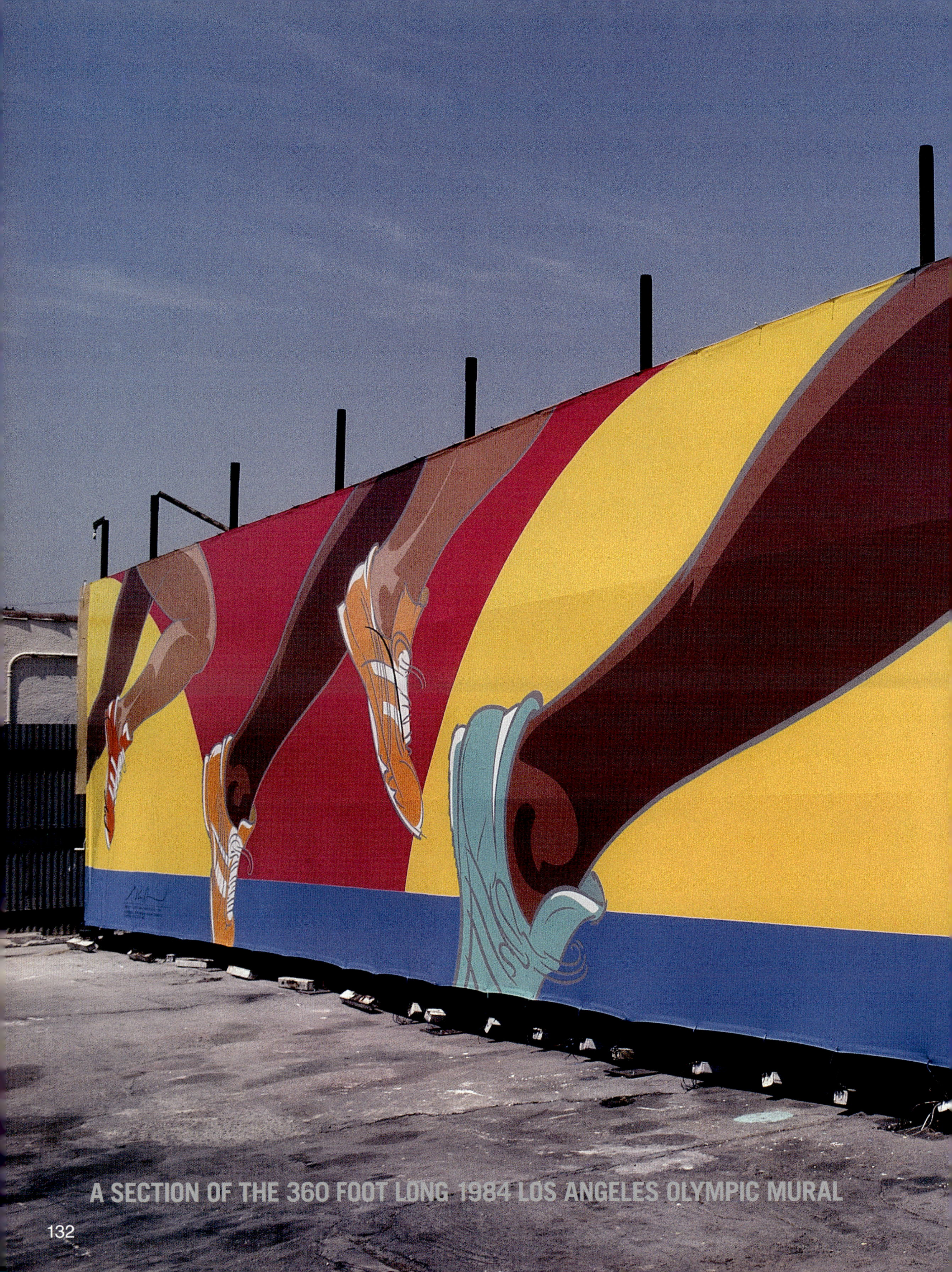

A SECTION OF THE 360 FOOT LONG 1984 LOS ANGELES OLYMPIC MURAL

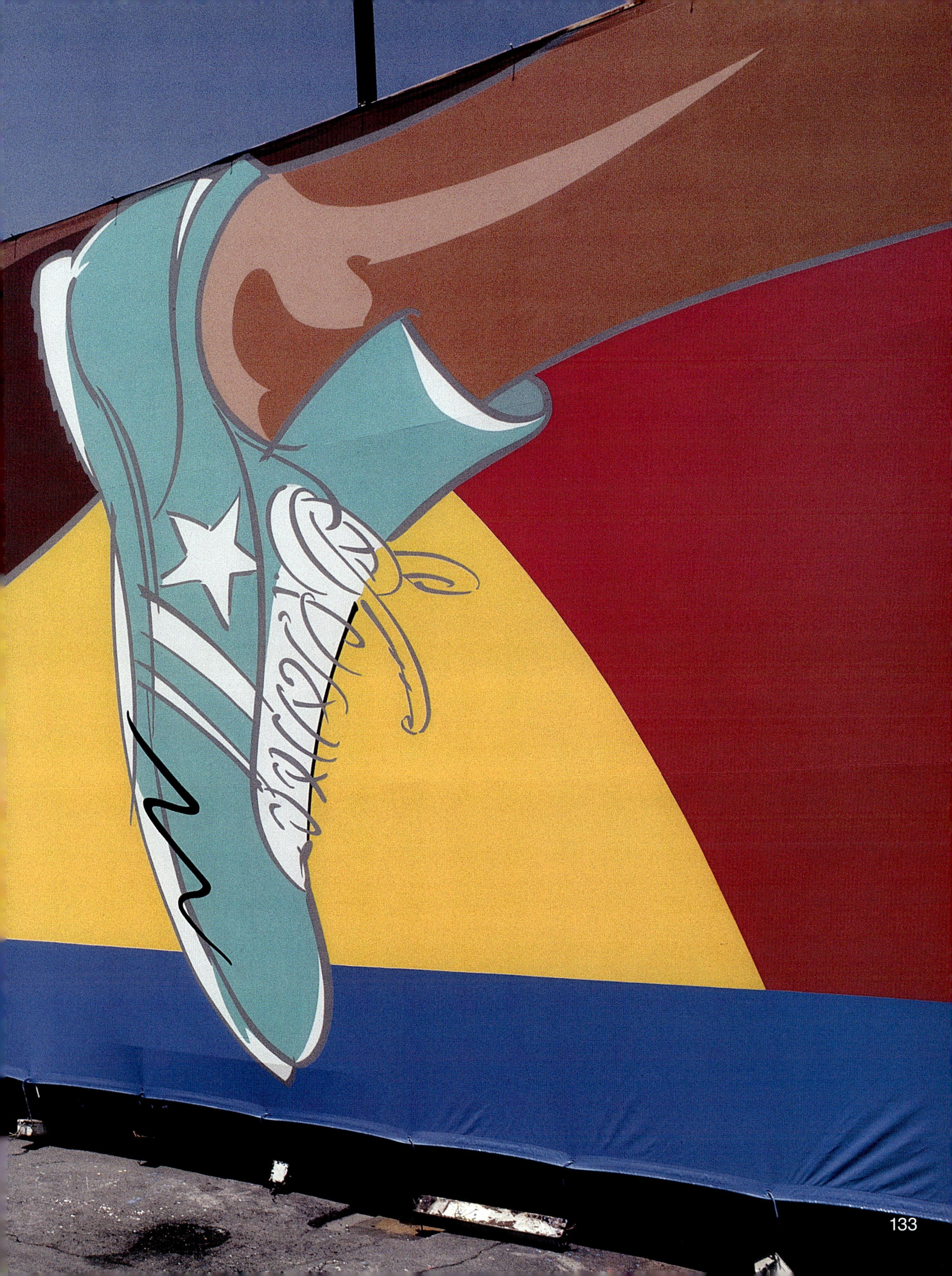

DRAWN AND DESIGNED AS A PICTOGRAM TRADEMARK

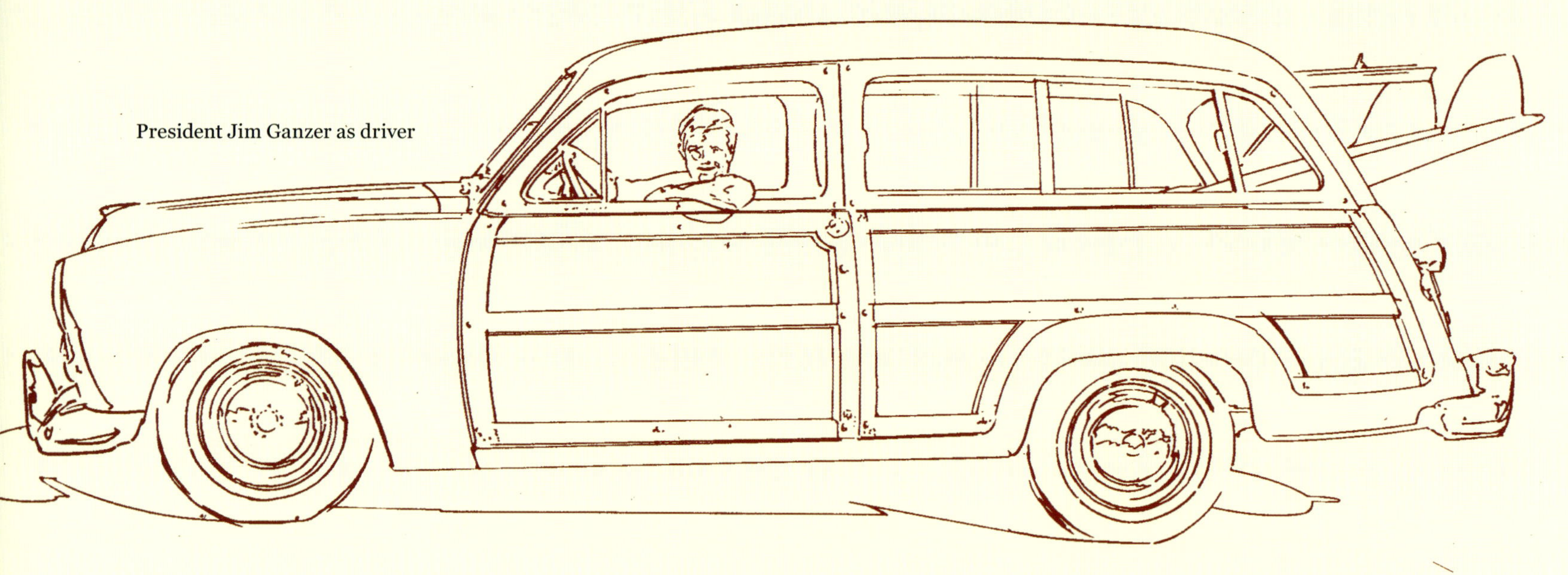

President Jim Ganzer as driver

The JIMMY'Z Phenomena of Eighties Surf Culture (1984–1992)

Through massive amounts of hype and grass-roots marketing/advertising within the local Malibu surf community, Jim Ganzer created JIMMY'Z. I was able to create a campaign that has managed to surpass the likelihood of copycats and corporate buyouts.

"E-Z IN, E-Z OUT"

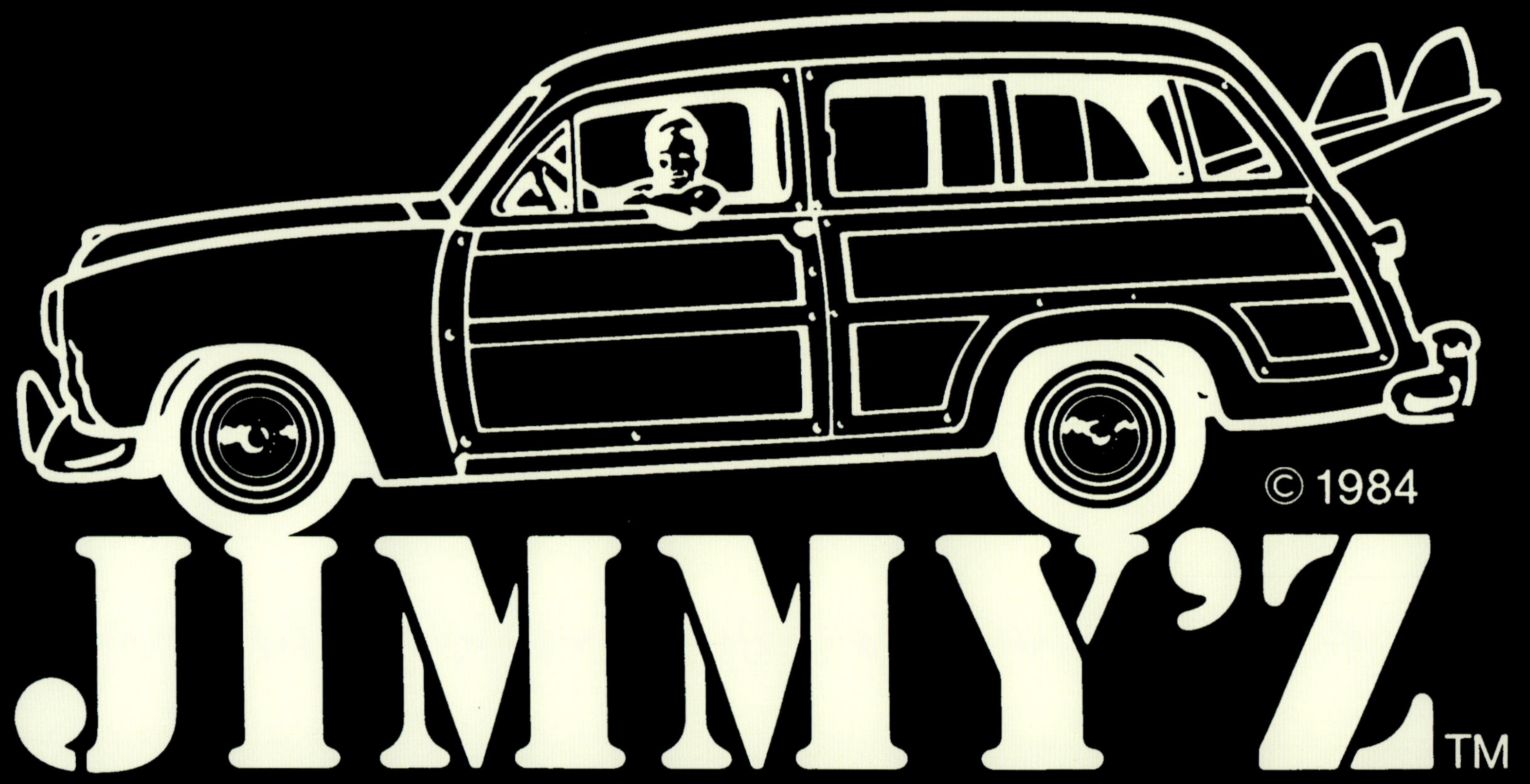

1984
Fashion Surfing

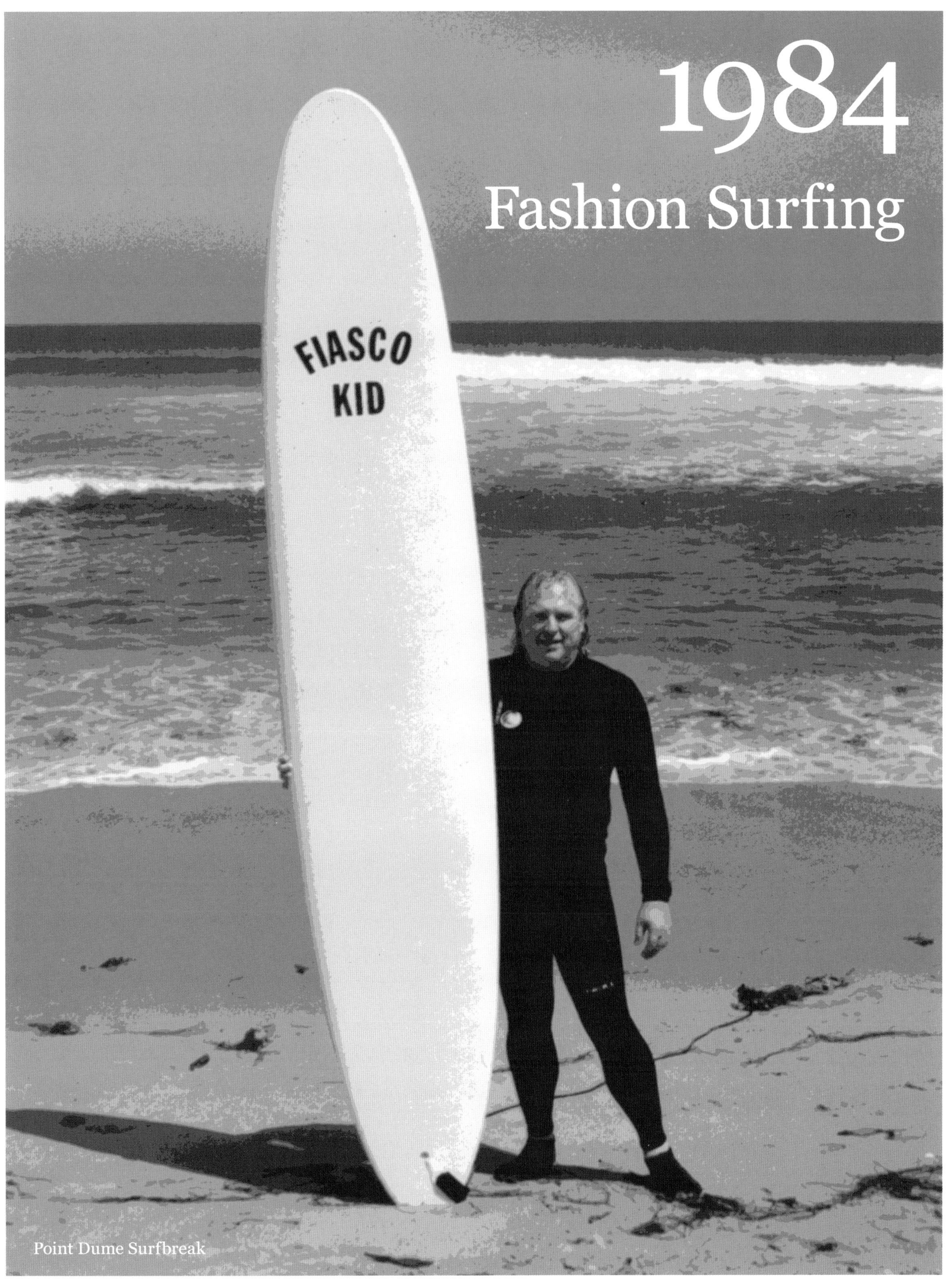

The Miki Dora's slogan "Fiasco Kid" of 1956 on a surfboard shaped by Phil Becker.

Malibu During the Fashionable Eighties Within the Surfer Industry

I moved my LA studio to Malibu in 1980, leaving the ailing record business behind. MTV had taken center stage, but I was surfing again and re-embracing my old surf world. I started up a license for the *Endless Summer* poster.

The Endless Summer

I met with Michael Tomson, the president of Gotcha, and he placed me in their design and advertising department. When we first started collaborating, I gave them the idea of using DayGlo colors for their clothing. The company went from 40 million to 75 million in sales as a result.

GOTCHA

That move helped create the JIMMY'Z account, logo, and advertising for the first two years as the brand grew. After I created the idea of a large singular 'Z' with something on top, the image reproduced on t-shirts became incredibly popular, defining their successful t-shirt business.

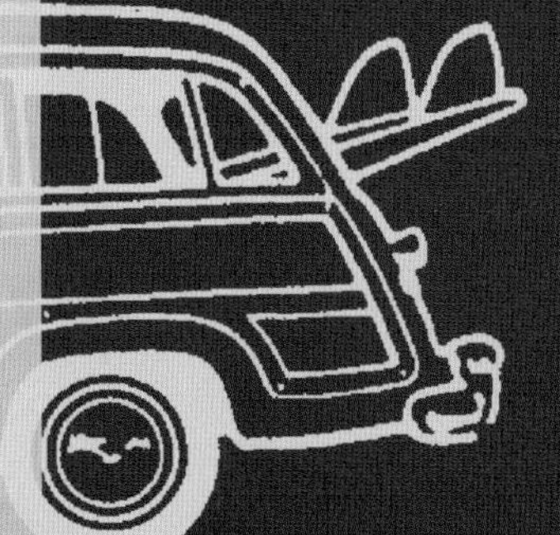

In the Malibu Studio we had cable services that came up the canyon, so I could have TV, fax, and Internet connections to the outside world. But I still went to town each day to see clients. Later I became the art director of *L.A. Style* magazine and designed a digital logotype, masthead and format for *Buzz* magazine.

THE MALIBU TECH HUT STUDIO 1986

The 12" x 12" Last Stand (1978–1980)

The Seventies bled into the punk/disco age with Blondie and Elvis Costello. I had a graphic relationship with Denny Bruce and Chrysalis Records. From the Willoughby Studio in West Hollywood, I could find projects in a never ending empire of the recording business. I was a photographer at times, and at other times I would find myself being able to draw or illustrate an image for a band. So as businessman, designer, and photographer, I would enter the design process as the art director of the image using different talents to solve each aspect of the image packaging.

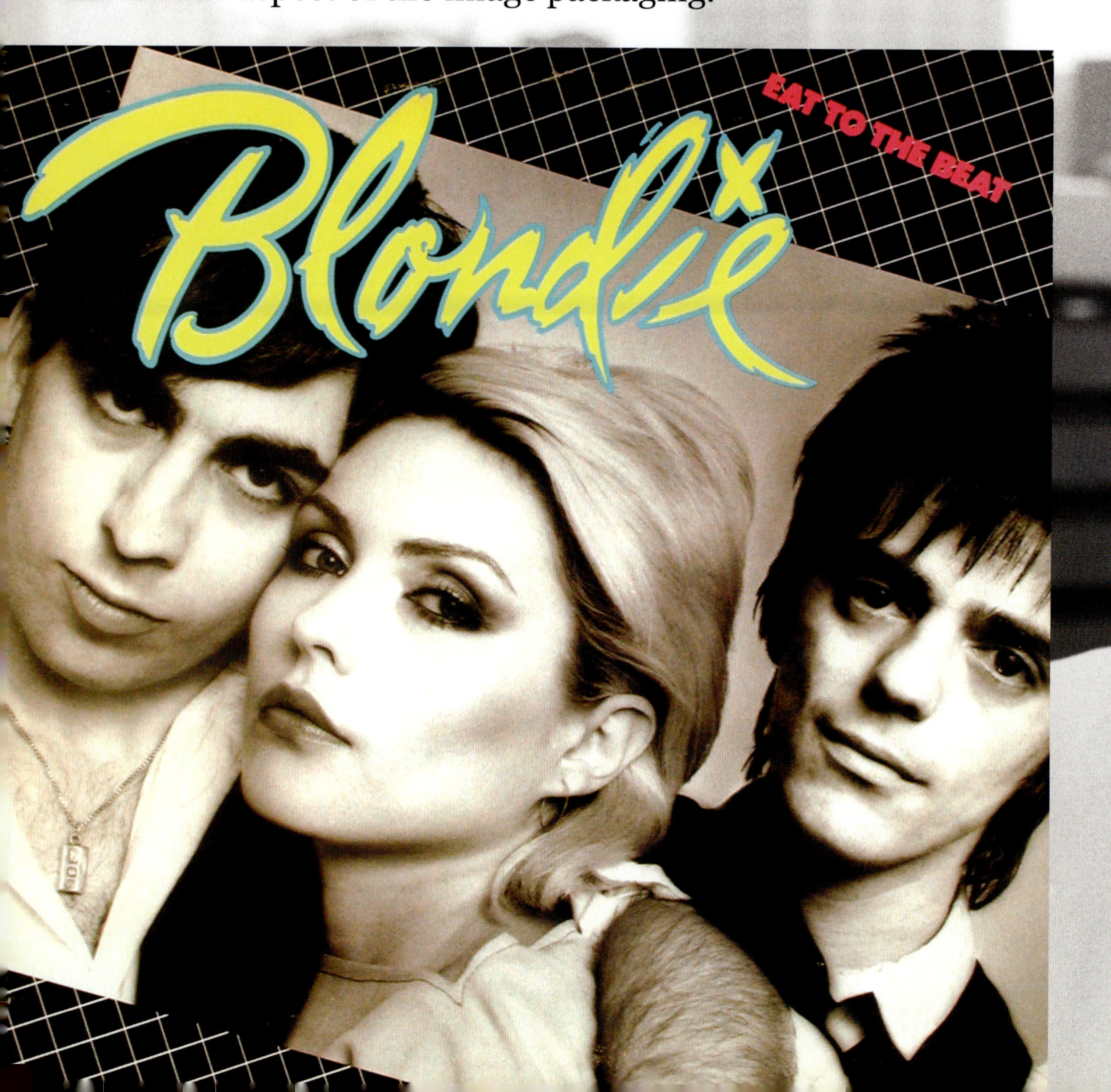

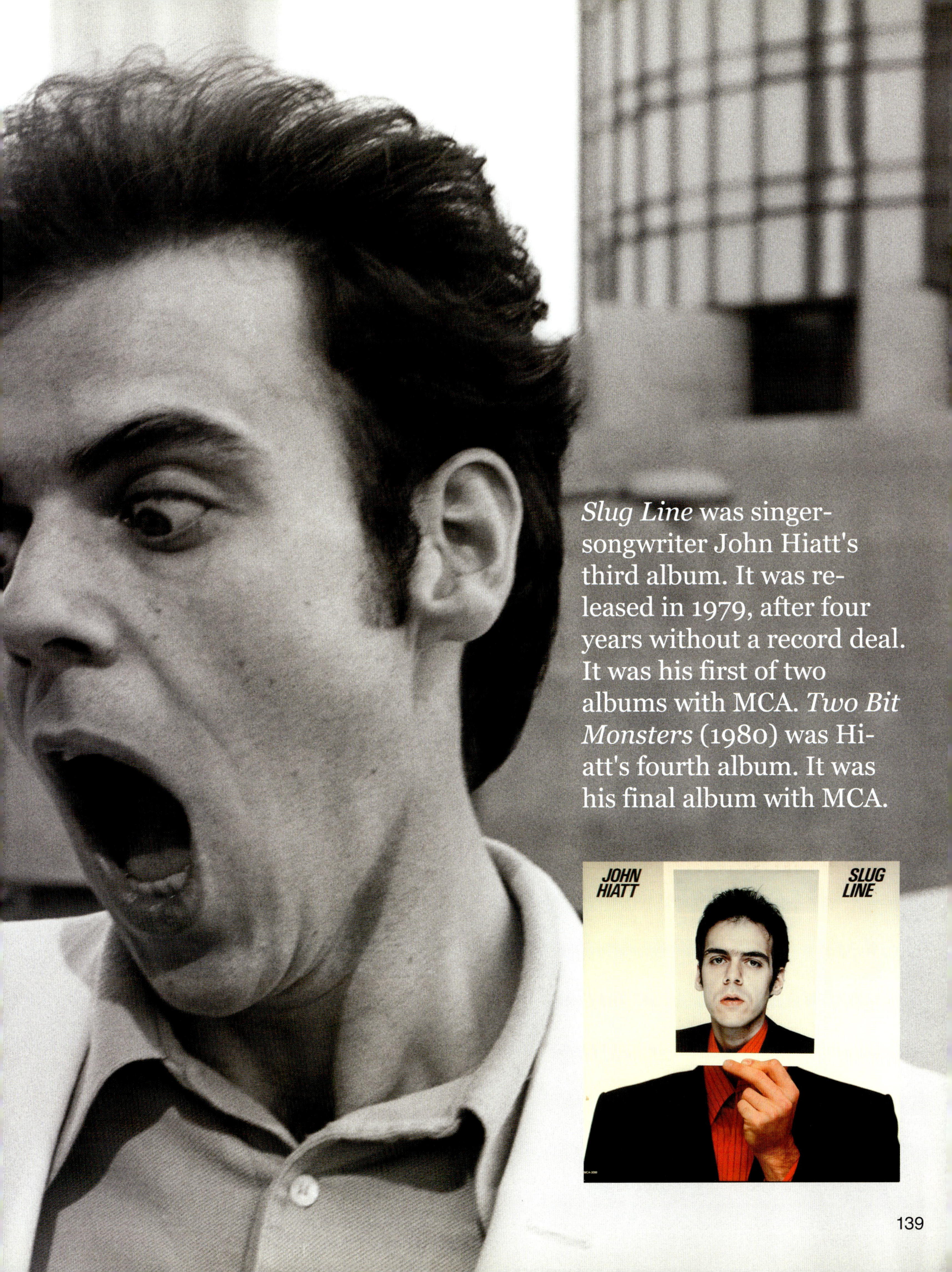

Slug Line was singer-songwriter John Hiatt's third album. It was released in 1979, after four years without a record deal. It was his first of two albums with MCA. *Two Bit Monsters* (1980) was Hiatt's fourth album. It was his final album with MCA.

SELF-PORTRAIT (1980)

I was a photographer, but I created images with other photographers. I was the art director. The medium is the message; the media was conforming to a digital medium, changing the analog world that I once knew as a designer.

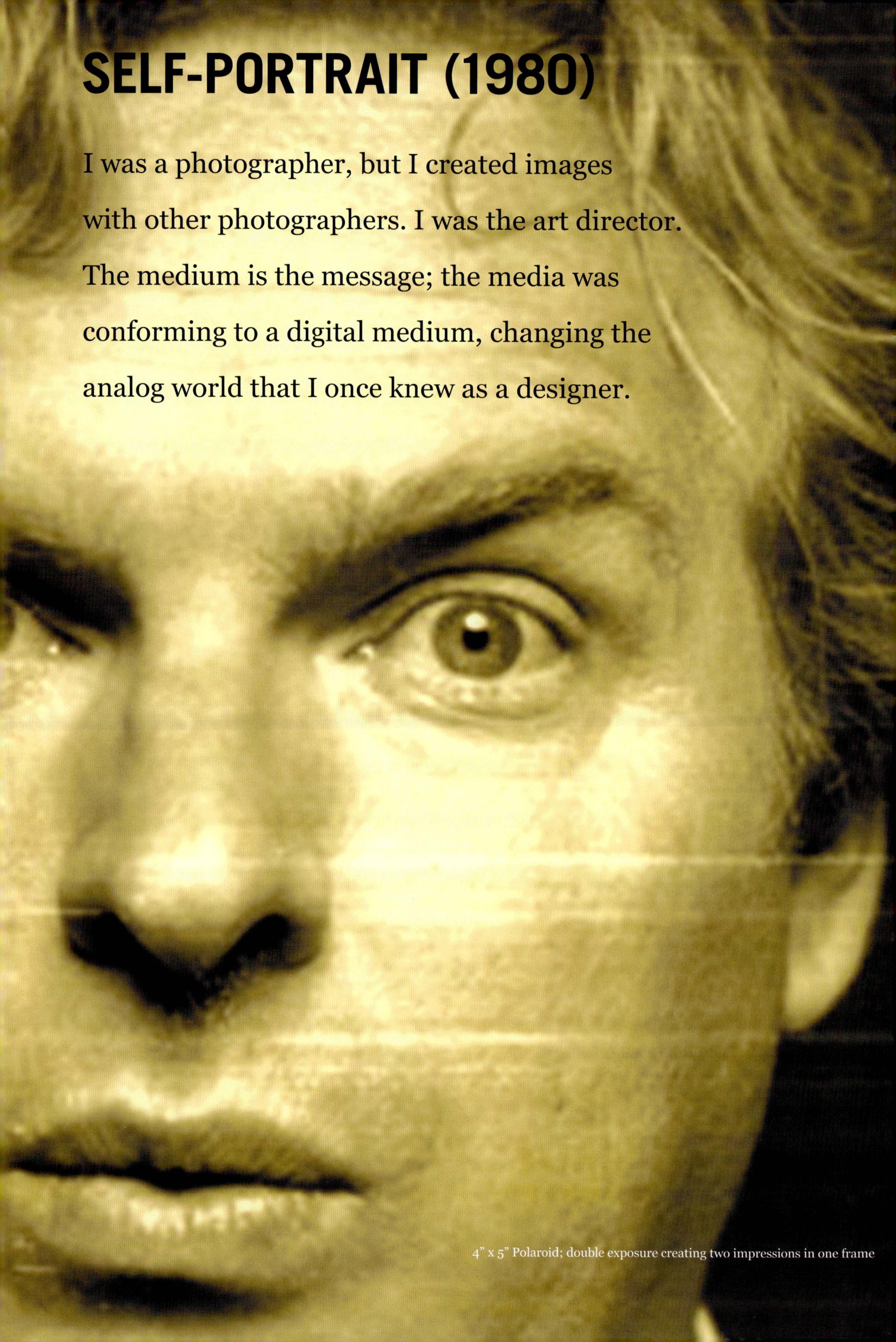

4" x 5" Polaroid; double exposure creating two impressions in one frame

THE END

By the 1980s, MTV was in your living room at the scale of an album cover and live action dances entertained the new generation of rock viewers. I, along with vinyl 12" x 12" inch album covers, became outdated as albums were transformed into CDs as the cultural imaging of time and style was trivalized into a 5 x 5.75 inch format.

For me, the album cover was a great form for making images within the media. I could make symbolic images and have them distributed all over the world through record labels. My multidisciplinary talent, the different studios I worked with over the years, and the people who surrounded me in all kinds of ways helped me form my images of times, places and things. The CD took away the grand record art image that had previously become a part of the listener who had looked at, felt, interacted with, and memorized the image.

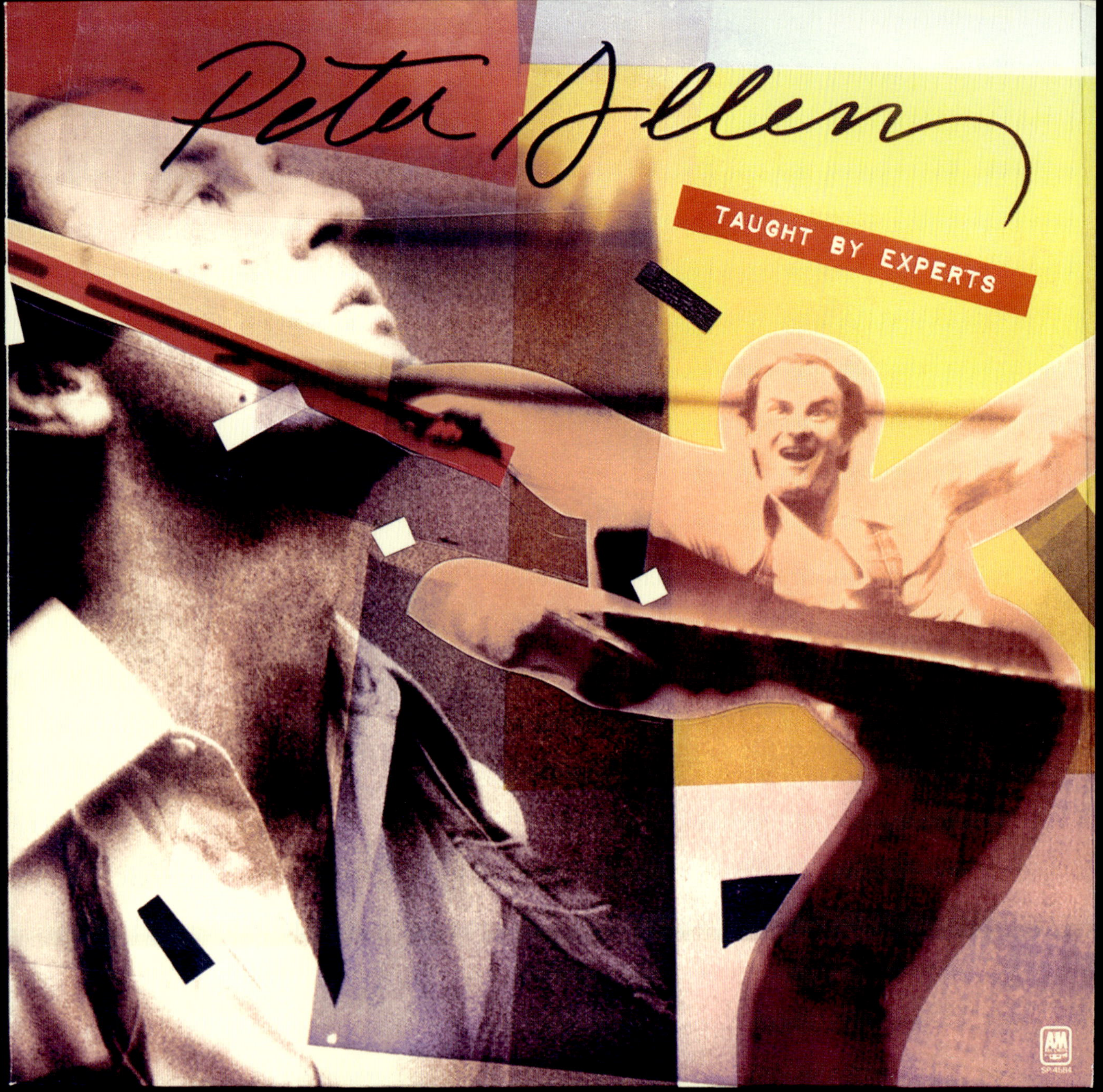

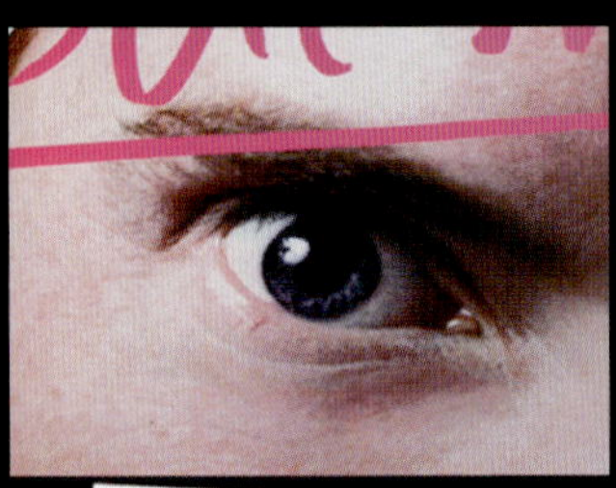

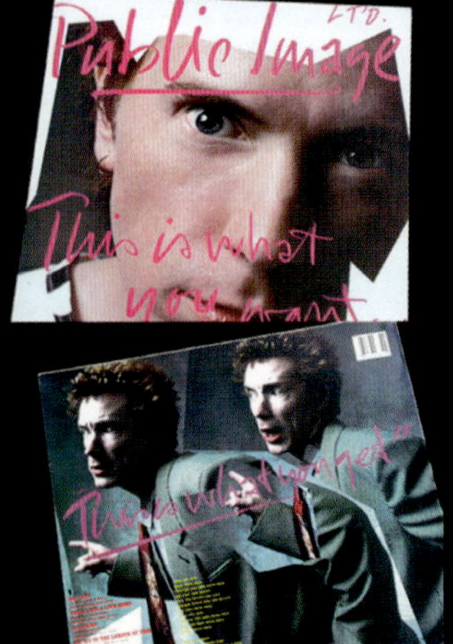

The Peter Allen image (above) was a style of collage, composed of photo film positives, cut paper, and tapes of my rip and tear style of 1972. I had started this style of album cover in 1973, during the begining of the punk music movement. The cover for the Rolling Stones' *Exile* was not what the record business thought was right. My solution influenced a new generation of graphic art, creating and copying to change the look and feel of graphic packaging. Photographer Norman Seeff shot a portrait and video of John Lydon for the manager I was working with through Elektra Records. Seeff gave me photographs and granted me free range to do whatever I wanted with them. This would be my last album cover and campaign for the record business at that time.

By 1984, the music business saw MTV as the go-to media for product promotion. The 12" x 12" album cover was compromised to become a disc which was the final product with a higher price. Basically MTV became the album cover. The John Lydon album cover was made in 1984 for MTV; the Peter Allen collage was created seven years prior.

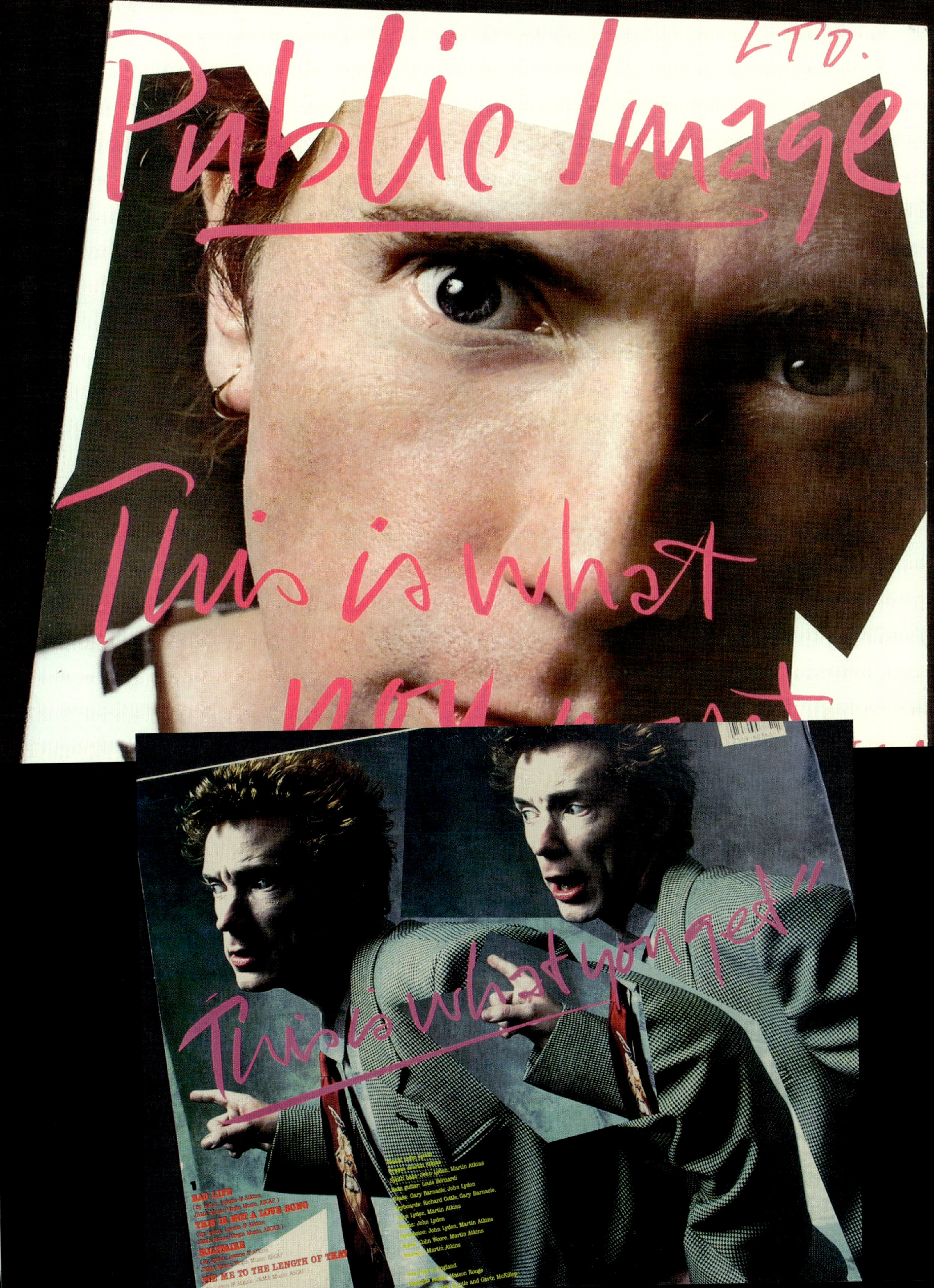

Public Image LTD.
This is what
"This is what you get"
BAD LIFE
THIS IS NOT A LOVE SONG
SOLITAIRE
Synth bass: John Lydon, Martin Atkins
Bass guitar: Louis Bernardi
Keyboards: Richard Cottle, Gary Barnacle.

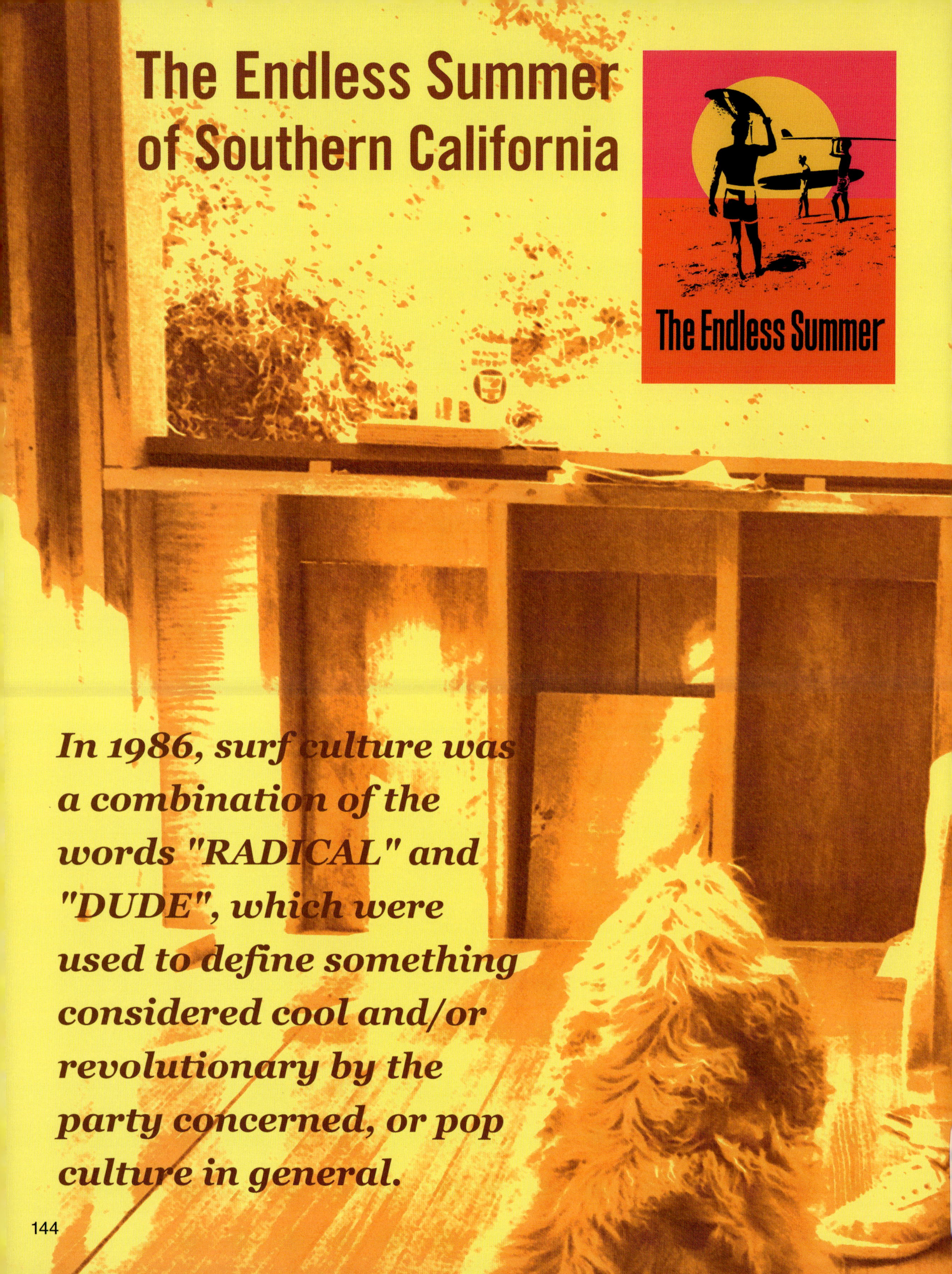

The Endless Summer of Southern California

In 1986, surf culture was a combination of the words "RADICAL" and "DUDE", which were used to define something considered cool and/or revolutionary by the party concerned, or pop culture in general.

The Surf's Still Up for the Men Who Made *Endless Summer*

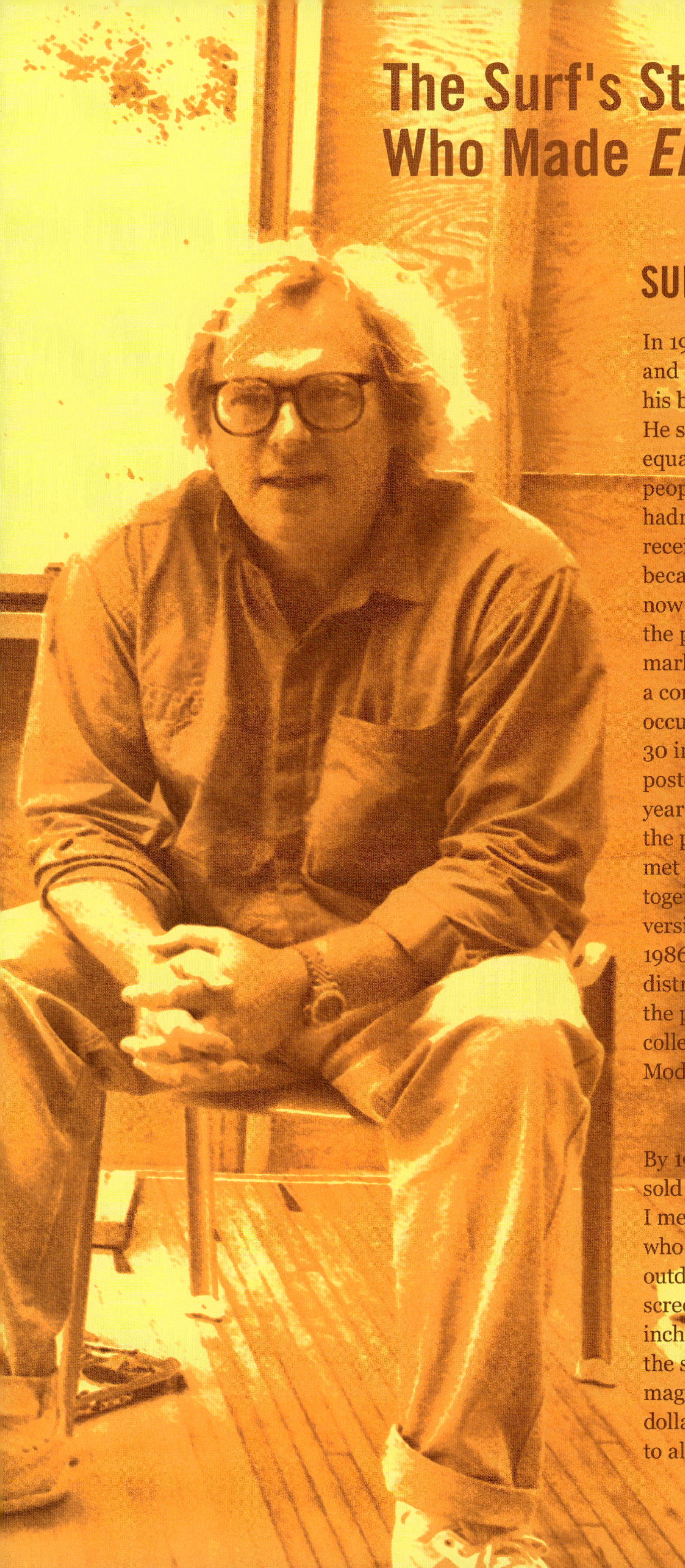

SURFER MAIL ORDER

In 1985, I re-met Bruce Brown, the producer and director of *The Endless Summer* film, in his beach attire at a Malibu legend contest. He said, "The *Endless Summer* poster is equal in value to the movie, and I always tell people you did it." Since 1967, Bruce and I hadn't talked about anything. When he received a check of six million dollars, we became distant as his life changed. However, now he wanted to help—he wanted to print the poster again for the new Eighties market. So, by 1986, we got together to start a contract sharing in the royalties. This occurred around twenty years after the 40 x 30 inch NYC version of the *Endless Summer* poster was released, and around twenty years after the original smaller version of the poster from 1964. Bruce Brown and I met up in Santa Barbara, making a deal together to distribute a screenprinted version of the poster for *Surfer* magazine's 1986 distribution. In 1987, Portal Poster distributed the commercial litho version of the poster, and by then the poster was collected by the New York Museum of Modern Art.

By 1991, the 6,900 silkscreen posters were sold with a subscription to *Surfer* magazine. I met with Gangi Studios Inc.'s Paul Gangi, who specialized in screenprinting line art for outdoor graphics. They had an automatic screenprinting press to print the 40 x 30 inch poster the way I had envisioned it, in the style of the Sixties. Through *Surfer* magazine, the poster was sold for $24 dollars a copy. 6,900 posters were shipped to all parts of the world.

New York City (1986)

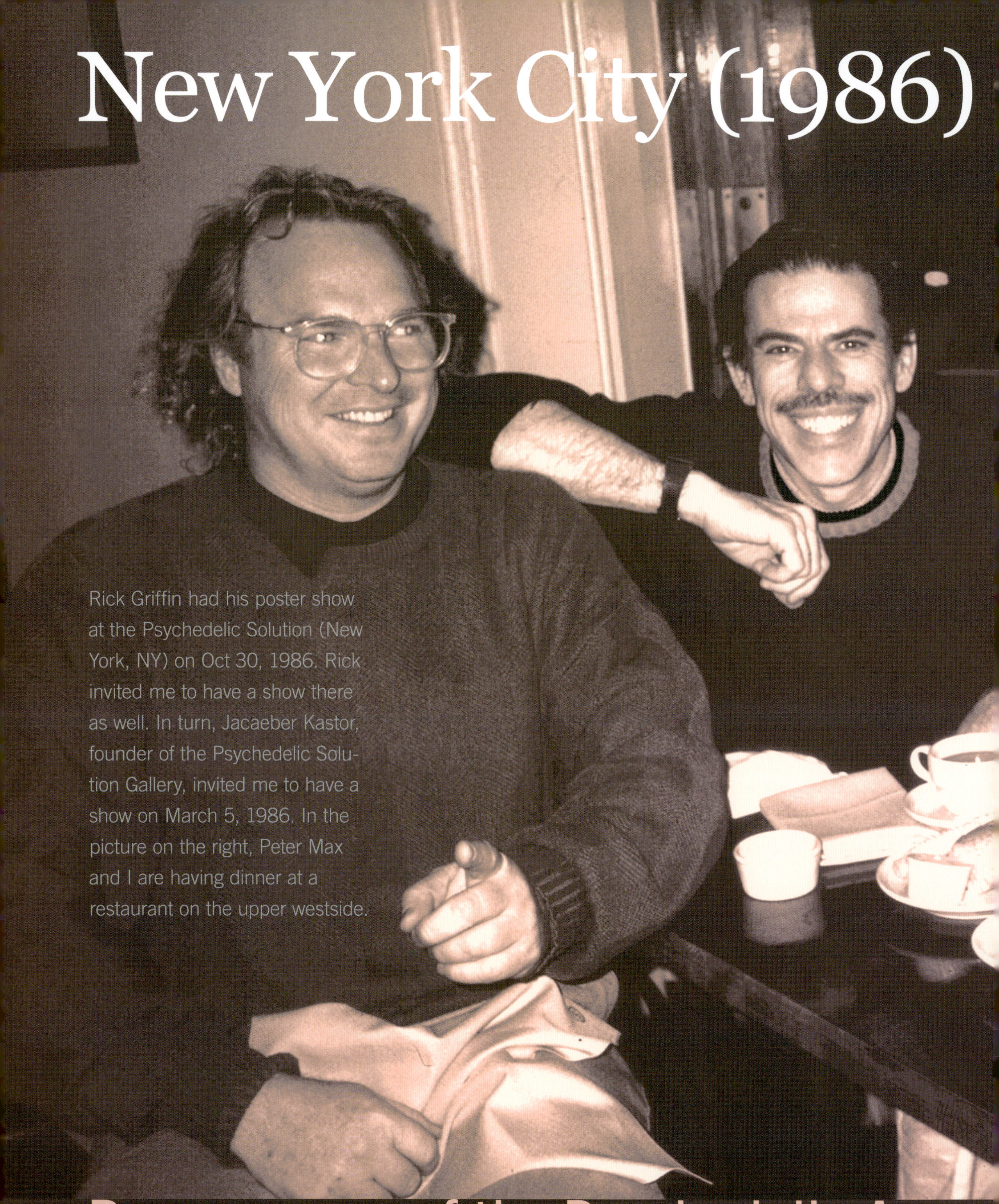

Rick Griffin had his poster show at the Psychedelic Solution (New York, NY) on Oct 30, 1986. Rick invited me to have a show there as well. In turn, Jacaeber Kastor, founder of the Psychedelic Solution Gallery, invited me to have a show on March 5, 1986. In the picture on the right, Peter Max and I are having dinner at a restaurant on the upper westside.

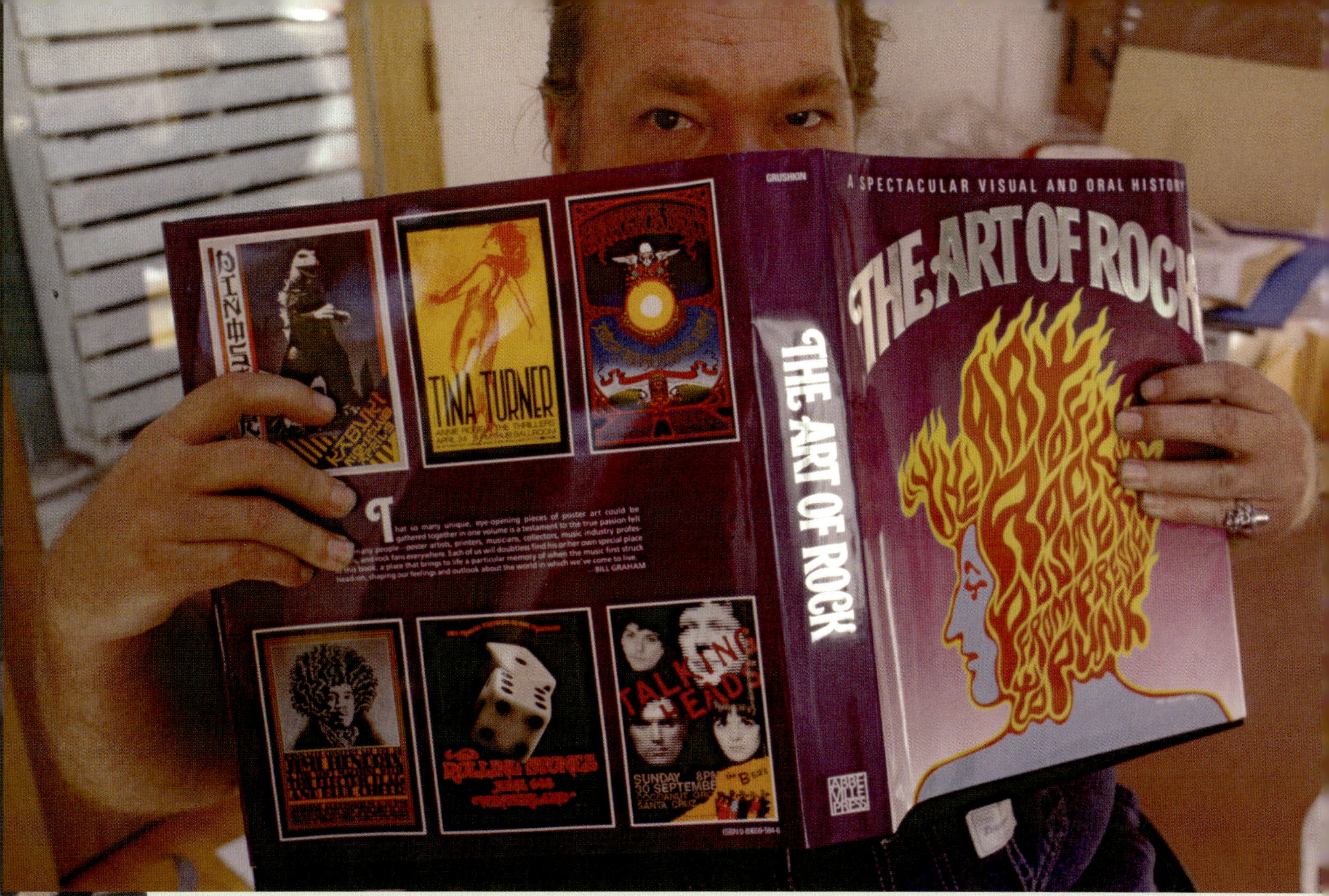

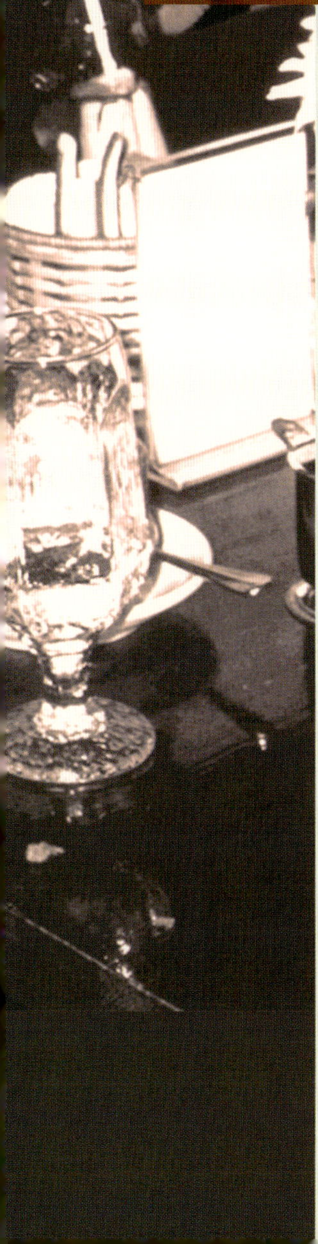

The long awaited psychedelic poster book arrived (I have about 13 pages in that book). Above is Skip Engblom looking at *The Art Of Rock* at the Malibu Tech Hut Studio in 1986. Skip's world in the '70s focused on the polyurethane wheels for skateboards in his shop, Zephyr Skate Shop. His west coast fame comes from having lived during the famous Dogtown days in Venice, CA. Below is the Psychedelic Solution poster store on 8th Street and MacDougal Street in New York.

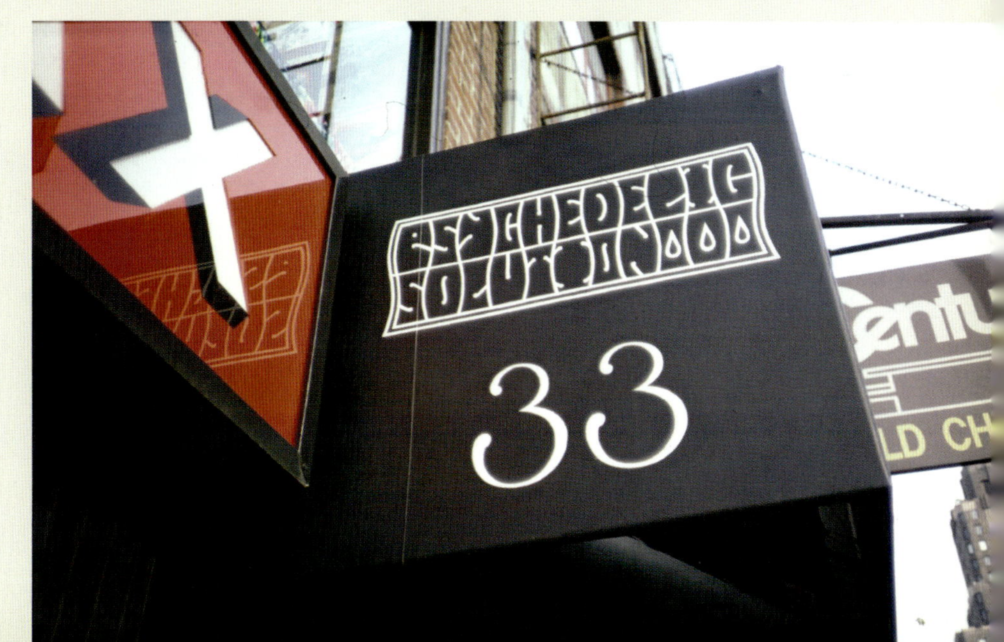

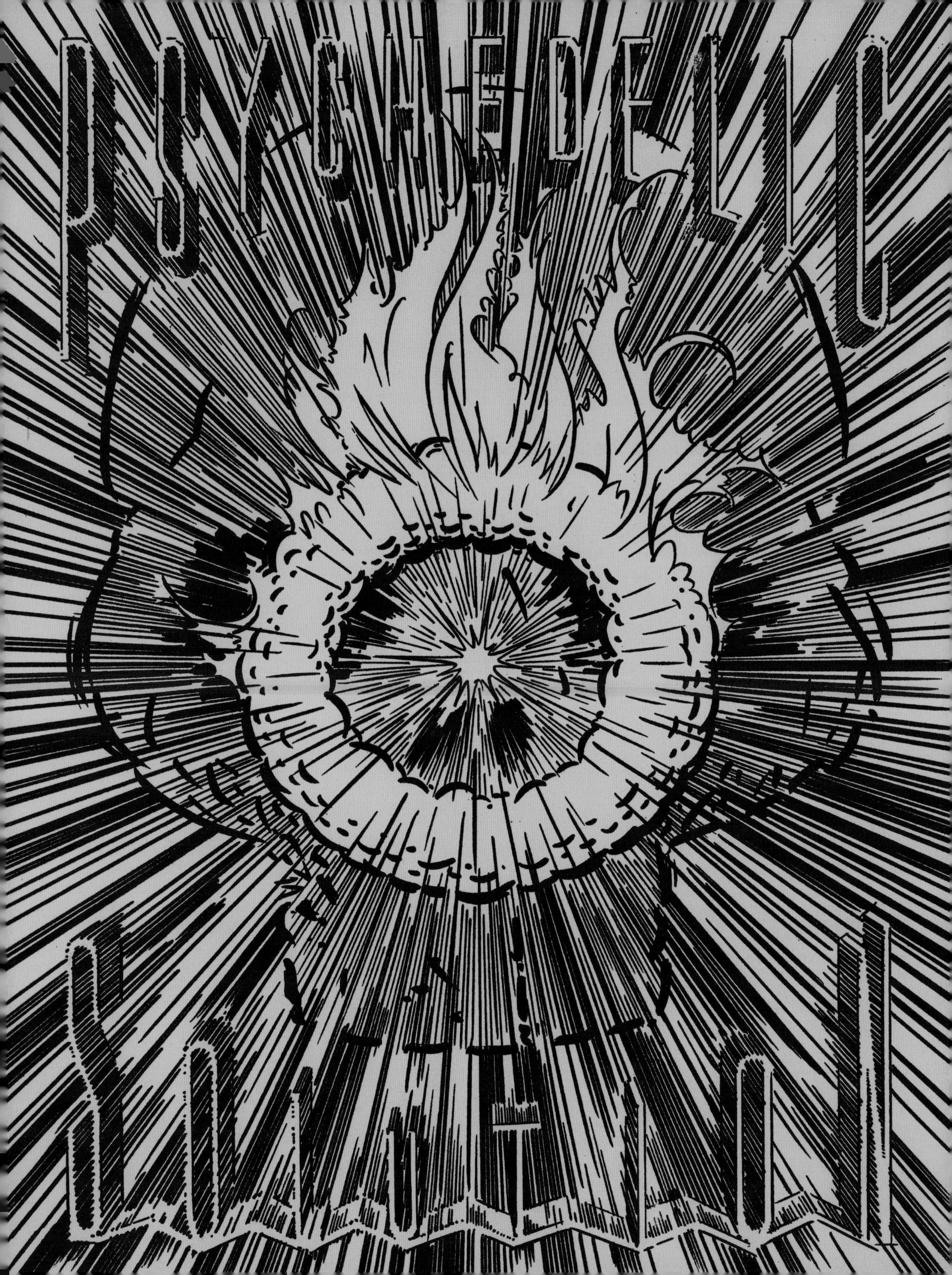
PSYCHEDELIC

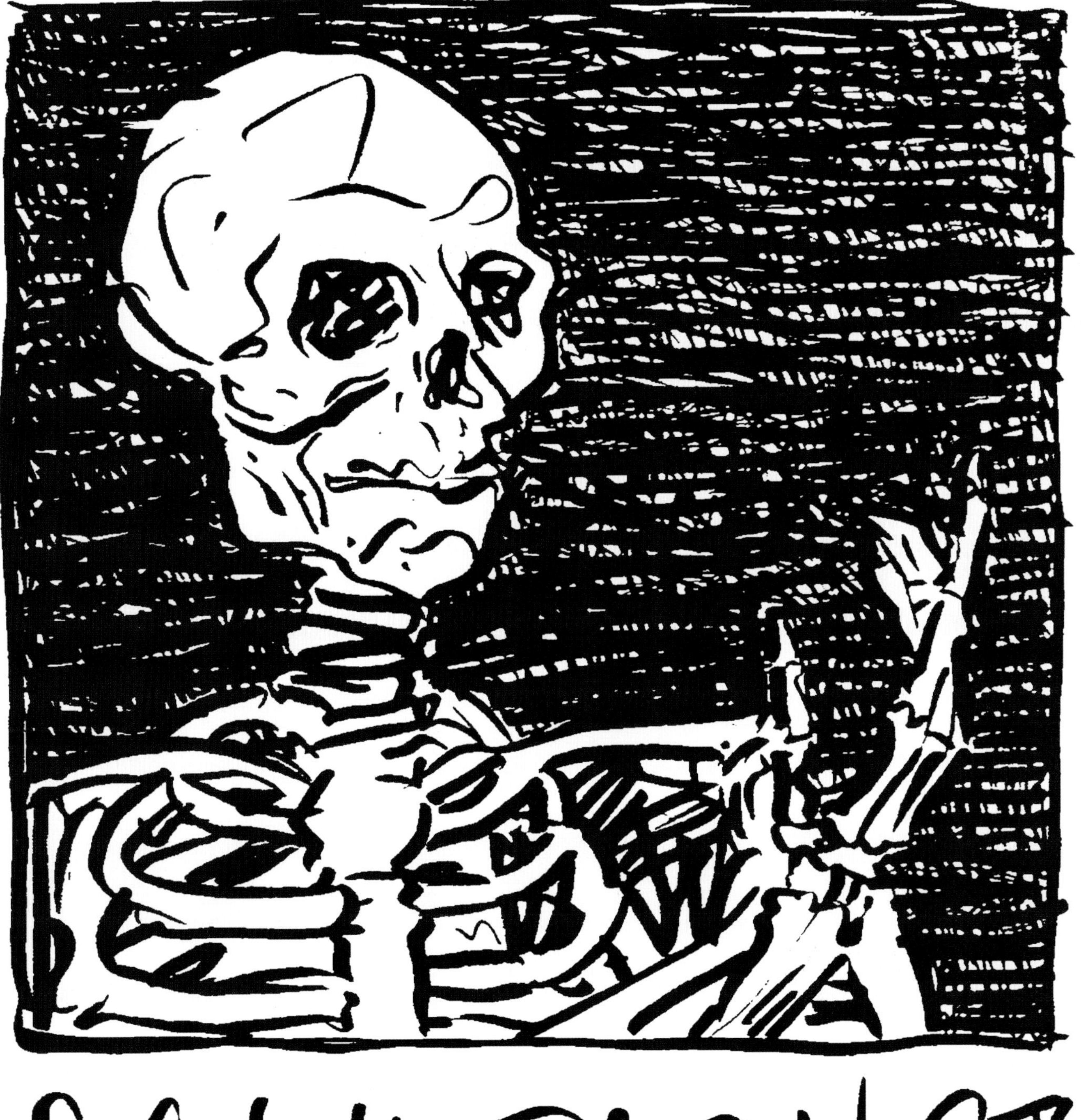

Rick Griffin would call me late in the evening at my Malibu studio and tell me about how he was hanging out at the Psychedelic Solution with Billy Idol. After hearing this, I drew an image for Billy and sent it to Rick. He said Billy loved it. So that was how the image became a poster for my show in 1986. I did the drawing above for the owner Jacaeber Kastor in 1987.

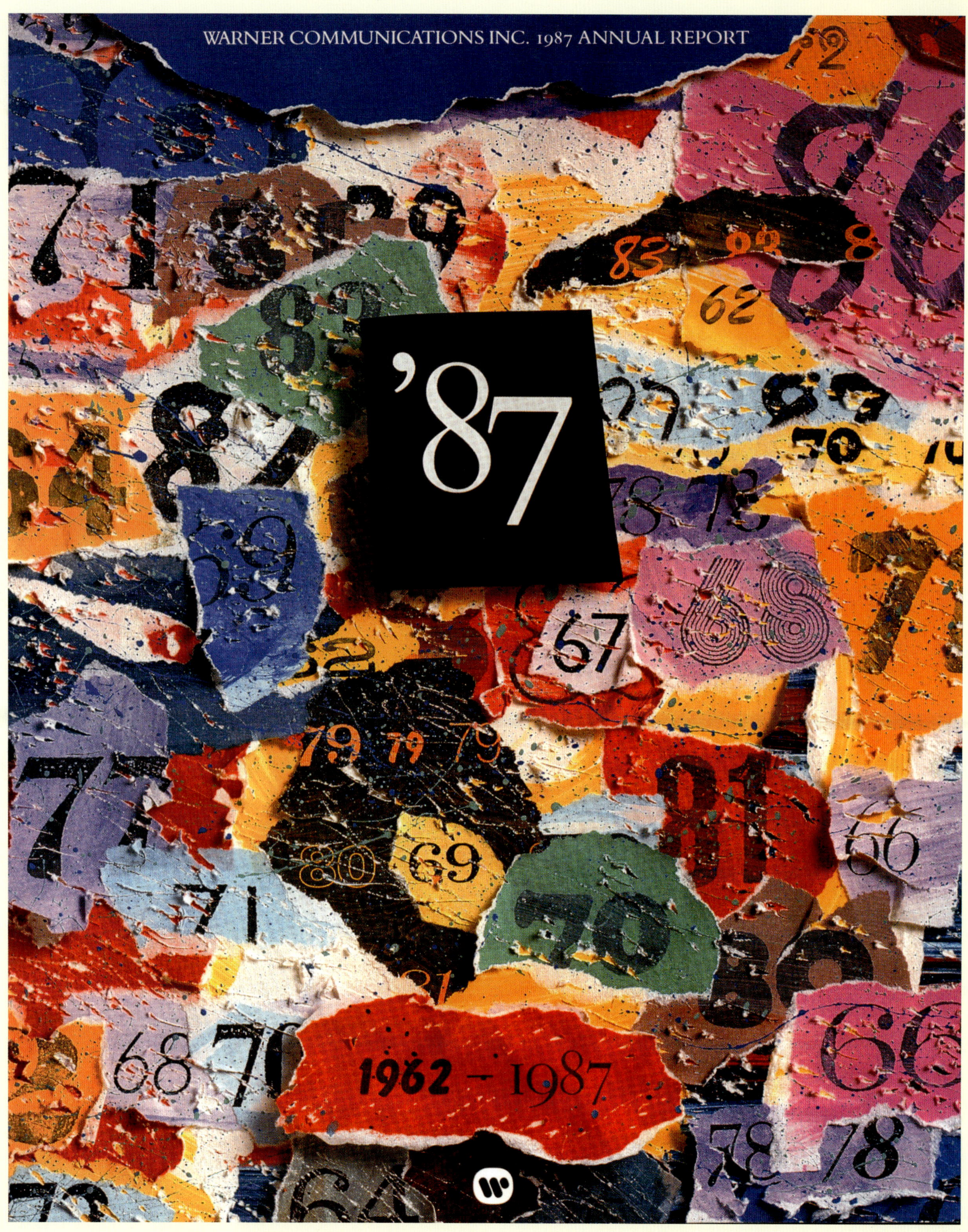

1988: Creating Collage Art for Pentagram, NYC Warner Communicatons Annual

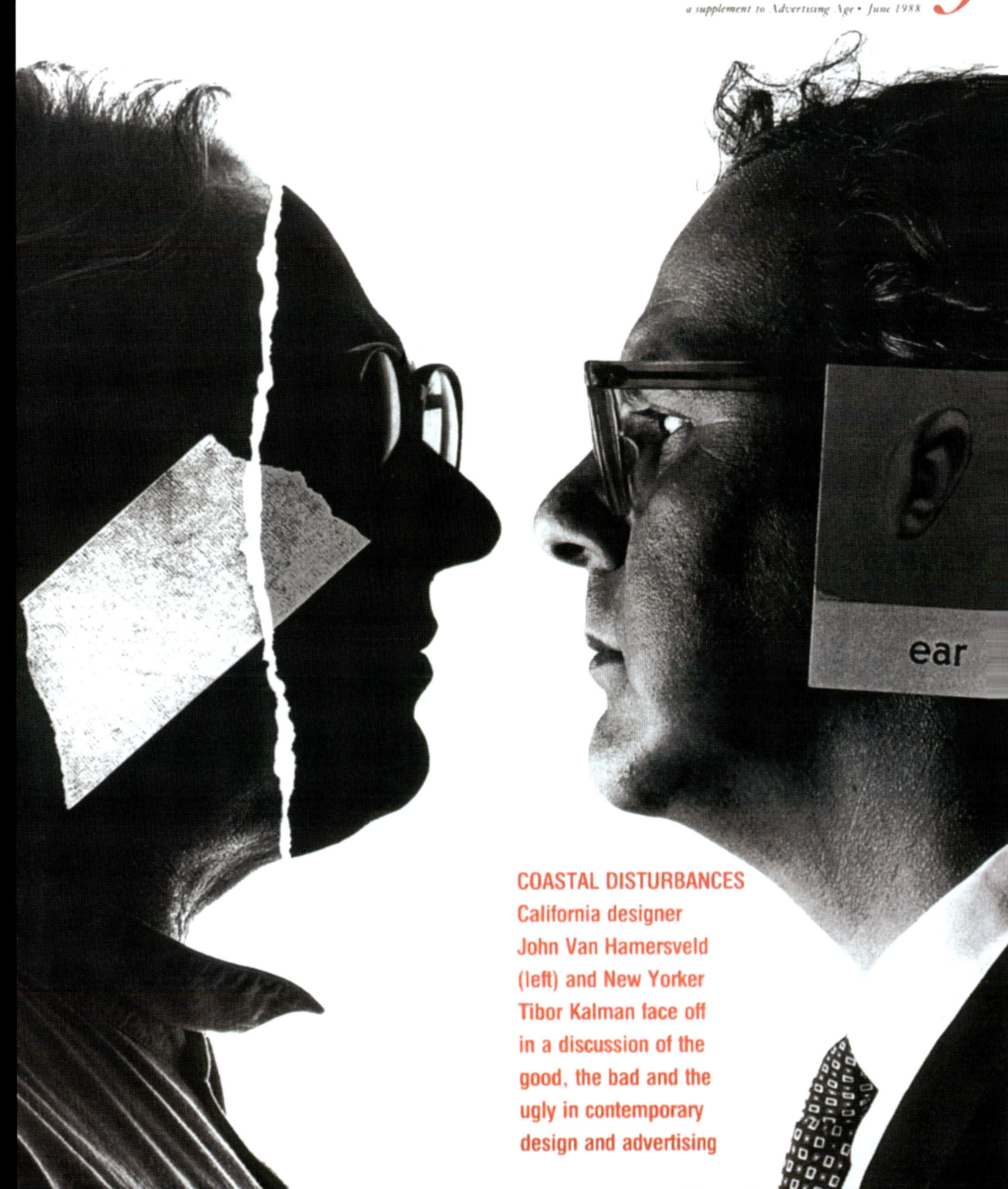

1988: Cover Collaboration with *Creativity* Magazine

Signs and Symbols (1987–1989)

Signs and symbols seem to last an eternity in the business environment

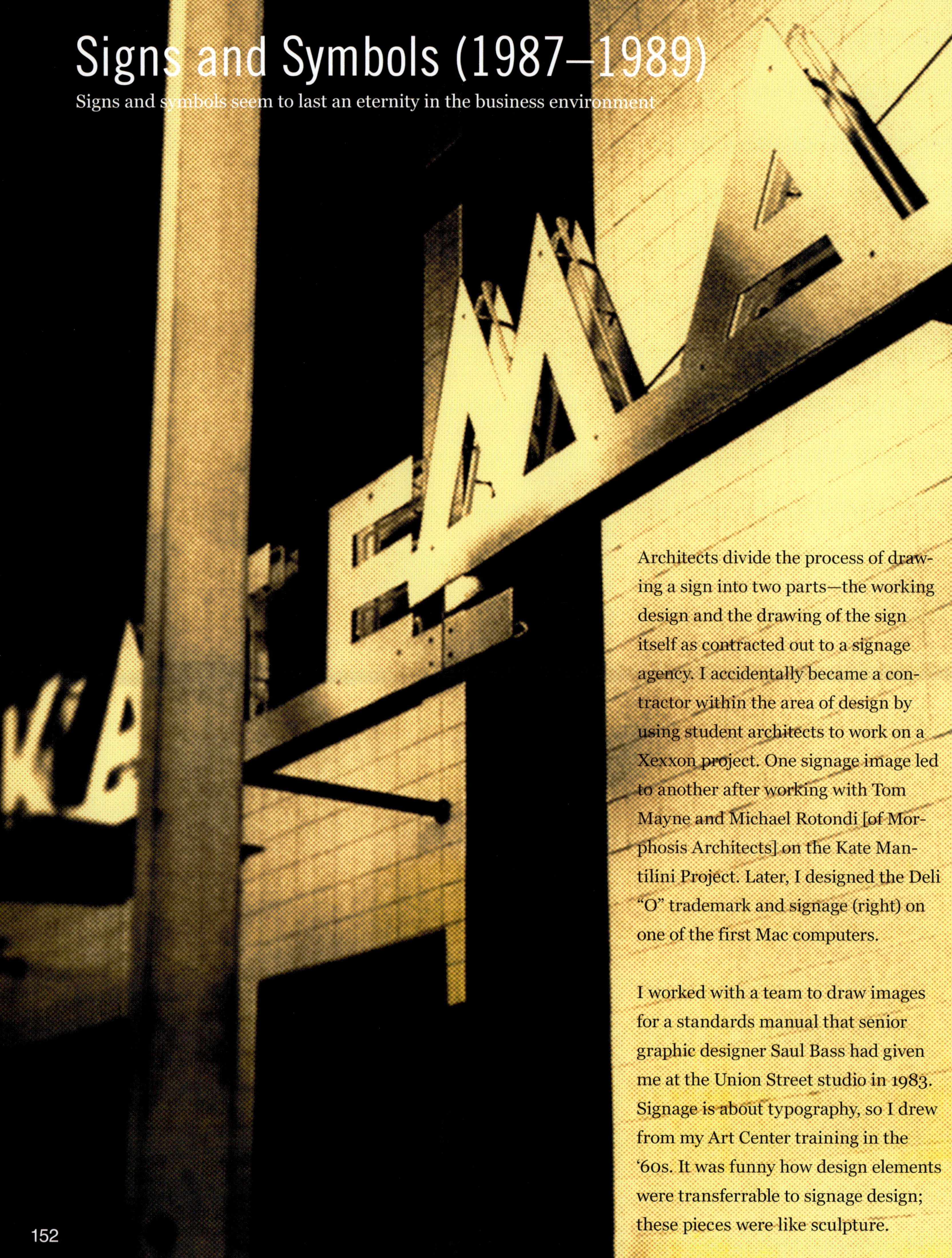

Architects divide the process of drawing a sign into two parts—the working design and the drawing of the sign itself as contracted out to a signage agency. I accidentally became a contractor within the area of design by using student architects to work on a Xexxon project. One signage image led to another after working with Tom Mayne and Michael Rotondi [of Morphosis Architects] on the Kate Mantilini Project. Later, I designed the Deli "O" trademark and signage (right) on one of the first Mac computers.

I worked with a team to draw images for a standards manual that senior graphic designer Saul Bass had given me at the Union Street studio in 1983. Signage is about typography, so I drew from my Art Center training in the '60s. It was funny how design elements were transferrable to signage design; these pieces were like sculpture.

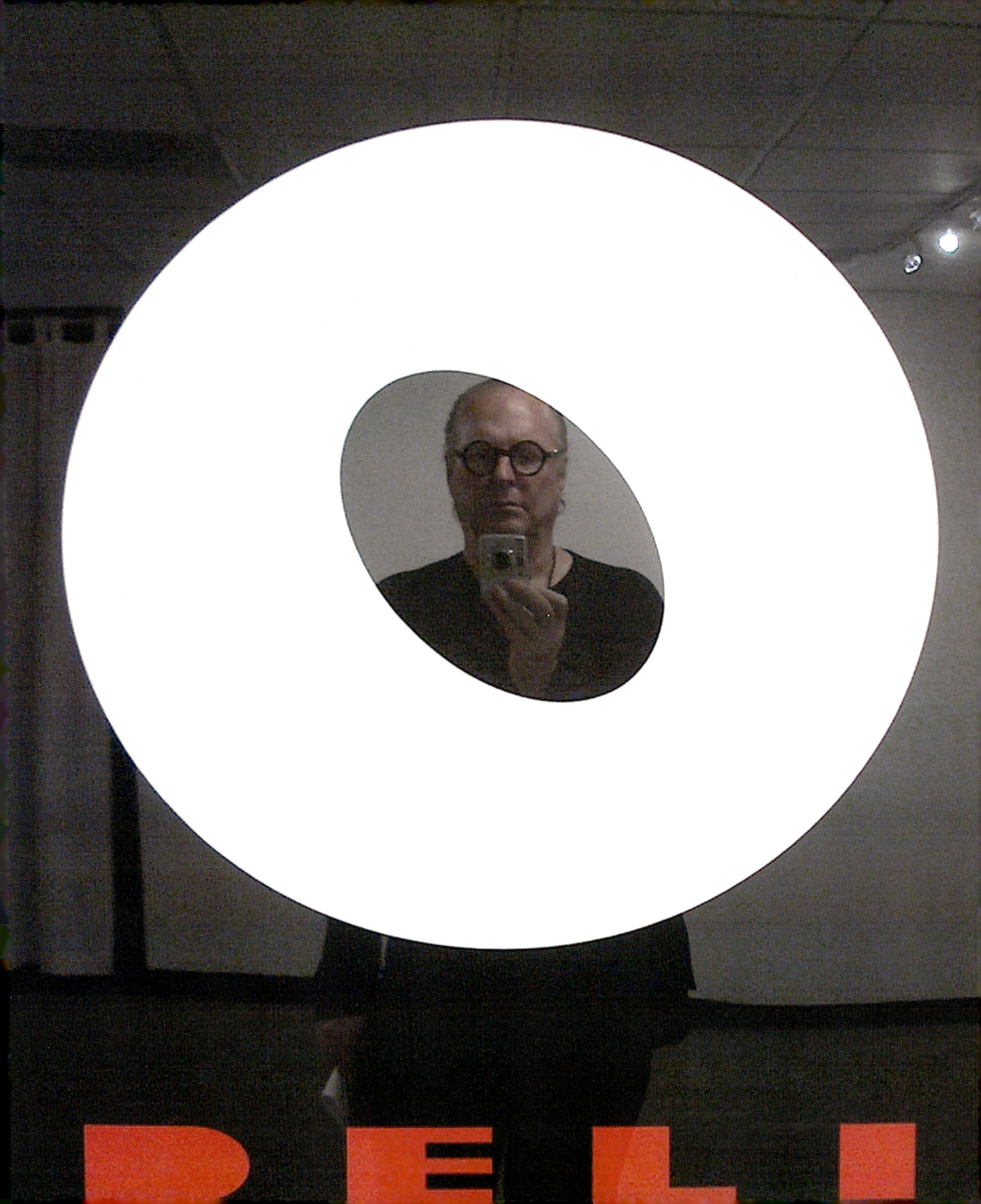

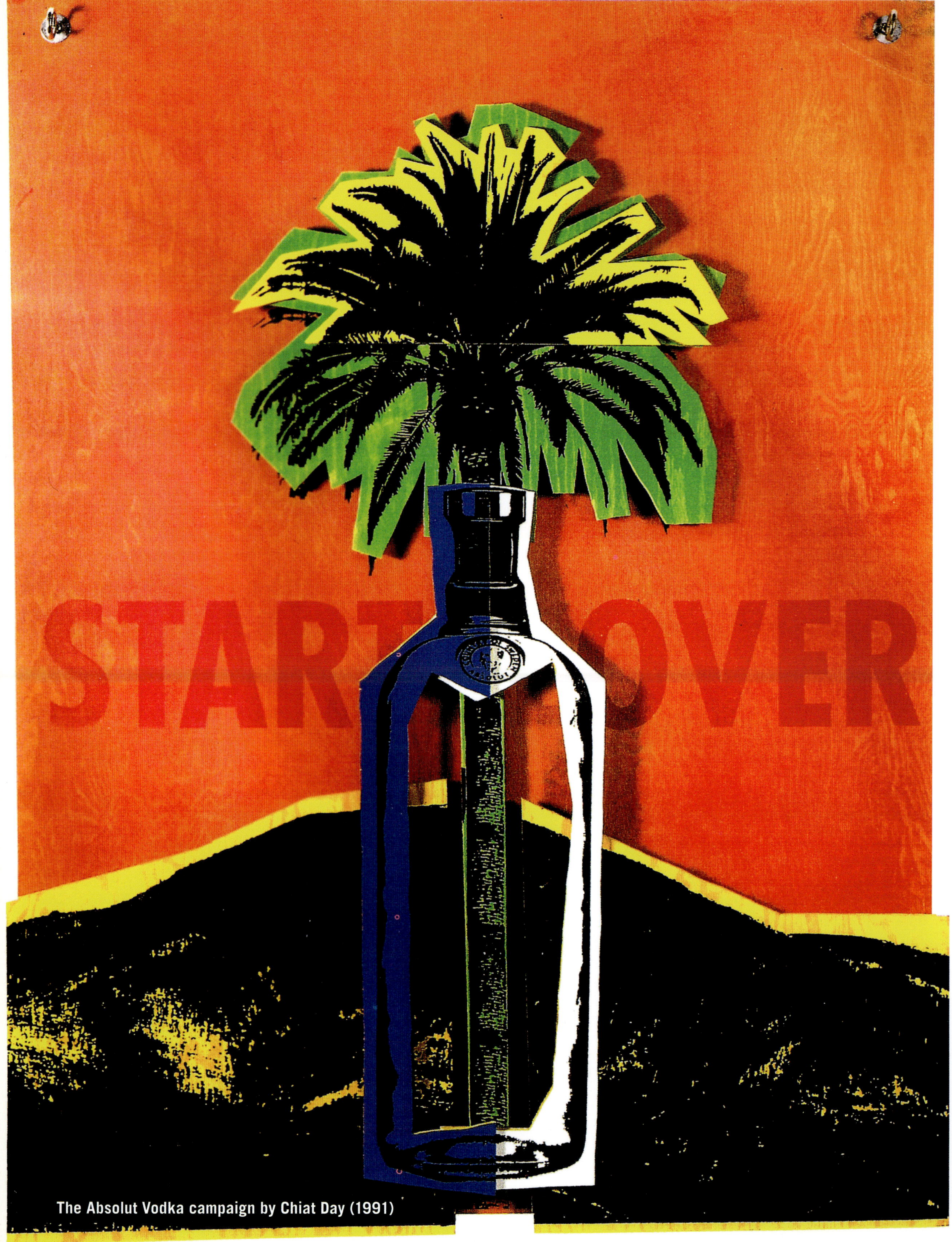

The Absolut Vodka campaign by Chiat Day (1991)

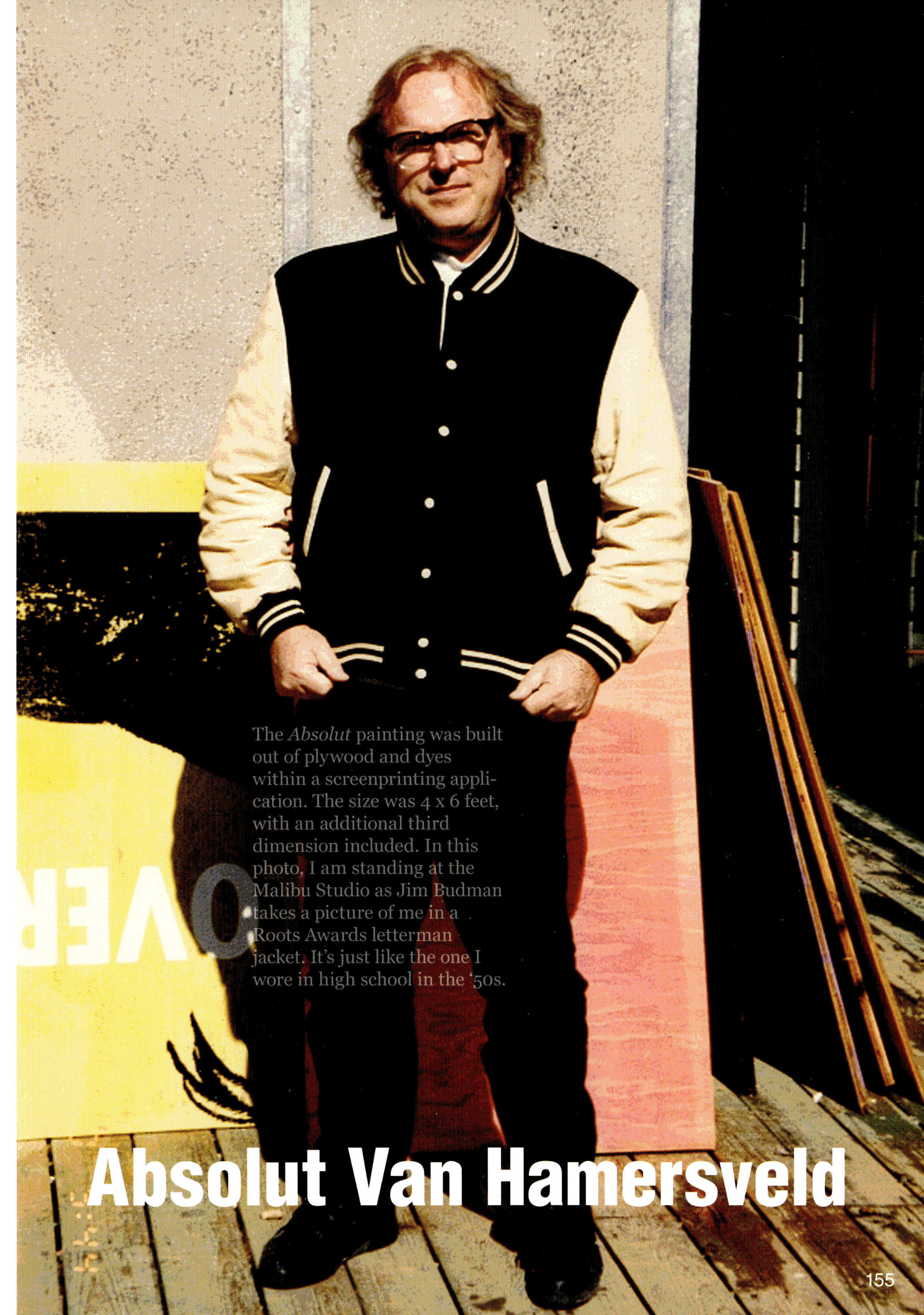

The *Absolut* painting was built out of plywood and dyes within a screenprinting application. The size was 4 x 6 feet, with an additional third dimension included. In this photo, I am standing at the Malibu Studio as Jim Budman takes a picture of me in a Roots Awards letterman jacket. It's just like the one I wore in high school in the '50s.

Absolut Van Hamersveld

Design a trademark for a small company that becomes a big company

CONTEMPO
CASUALS

Morphosis Architects referred me to the theater owner/soft-drink bottler/investment company General Cinema. They owned Neiman-Marcus Group, Inc. (encompassing the Neiman-Marcus, Bergdorf Goodman and Contempo Casuals stores). General Cinema signed the check for my design in 1987. I designed the Contempo Casuals trademark and the initial store facade as the company used the design to create 224 stores in 1990. In 1995, Wet Seal acquired 237 Contempo Casuals stores from the Neiman Marcus Group. Contempo Casuals would continue to use its own name until 2001.

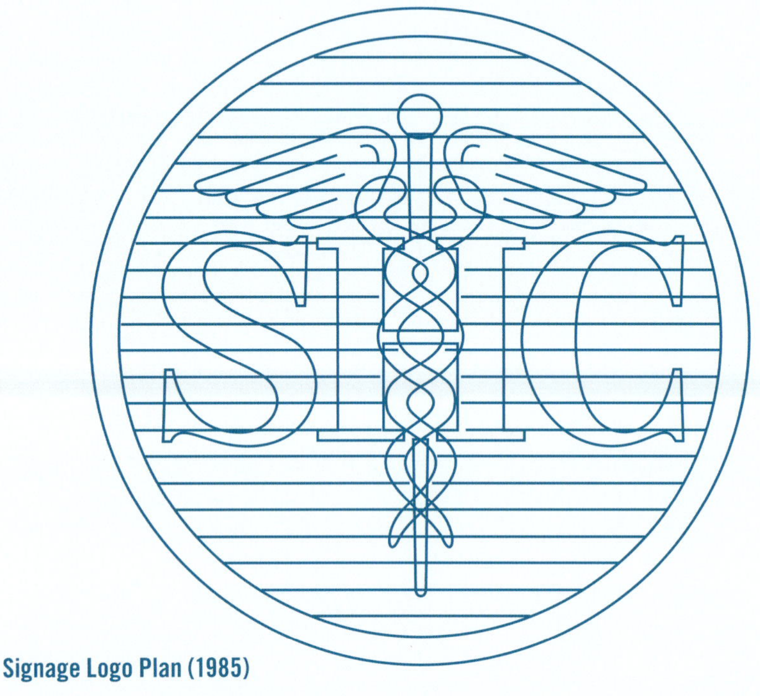

Signage Logo Plan (1985)

Morphosis Architects referred me to Salick Health Care in 1985. I started the trademark with Bennard Salick, the owner, who took the company public and opened its first comprehensive cancer clinic. Moving to New York City later was quite a coup for Salick, and the company had plans to expand into satellite clinics throughout the area. In 1997, its half-owner, Zeneca, bought up the other 50 percent of the company it did not already own. Zeneca had the option to buy the rest of the company within two and a half years from when it purchased half the company in 1995, but it moved up the time frame and purchased the company for $234 million by 1996.

In November of 1990, I met with Fatburger Restaurant's new owner through Chris Blackwell of Island Records, while starting the trademark design program for the Island Trading in New York. I also designed the first seven prototype variations of different buildings that would become stores in the chain. Today there are 100 stores in the chain worldwide that use the original trademark.

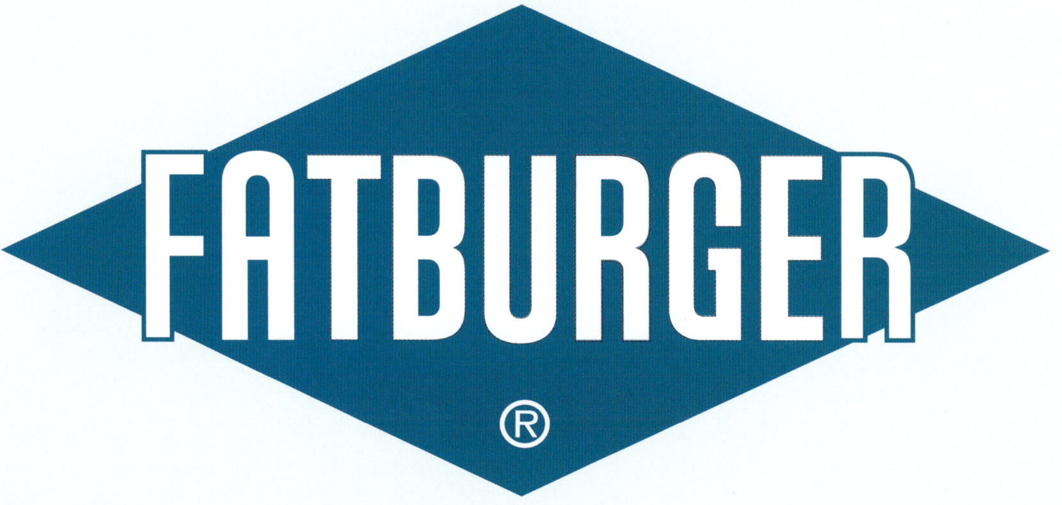

SIGNAGE WARS (1990)

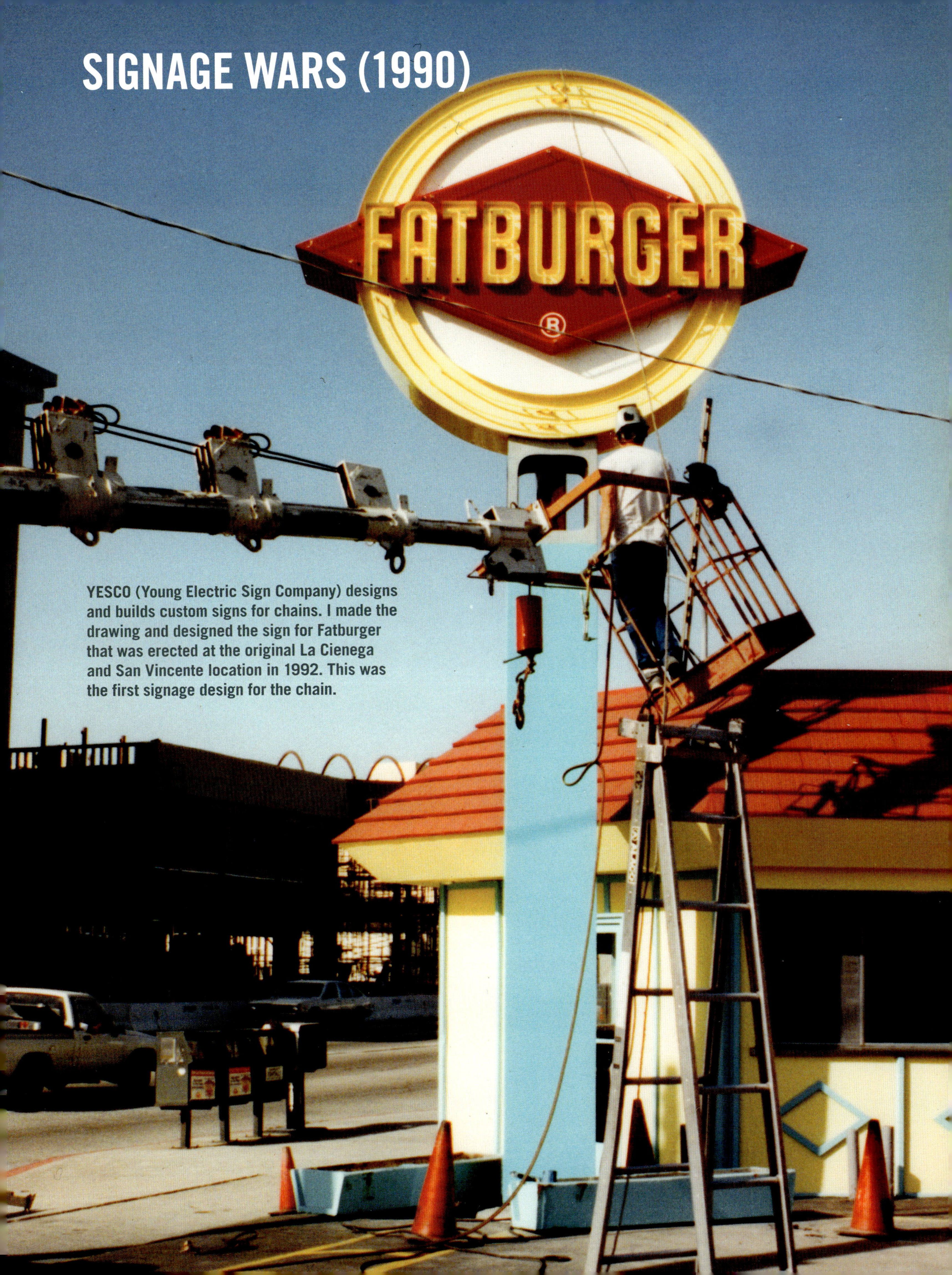

YESCO (Young Electric Sign Company) designs and builds custom signs for chains. I made the drawing and designed the sign for Fatburger that was erected at the original La Cienega and San Vincente location in 1992. This was the first signage design for the chain.

The business of T-SHIRT and ENTERTAINMENT COMPANIES

Rolling Stones, *Voodoo Lounge Tour* of 1994–1995

Here we see my t-shirt design for the Rolling Stones' *Voodoo Lounge Tour*. This is about the administrators of entertainment companies, the acts they represent as commodities in the trade. Funny how the music artist is more important than the packaging designer.

This is my story now, many years later, as recently as coming out of my garage in June 2004, into an alley outside of the 17th Street studio. There is a guy standing in front of a garage, wearing a *Voodoo Lounge Tour* t-shirt. It's been ten years now since I had anything to do with it. I stop to talk with the guy, as his wife comes to his side and I take the picture to the right. The t-shirt is still a part of the environment; people would say they had seen the shirt at many Stones tours over the years.

Here's the story of the t-shirt game as a business

The Rolling Stones image comes to me one night while in line at a Kinko's store in Costa Mesa, during November of 1993. While waiting for service, a funny looking guy is standing in line behind me; he's a musician- and sees my portfolio of in-progress drawings on the counter. We strike up a conversation and he is a screen-printer for a rock band. I leave for Tokyo the next day, and after months go by I eventually get a call from him. He says a band member of his plays at a small shop in Costa Mesa, has a big printing warehouse, has a friend who knows Keith Richards, and he wants to back the business and get a t-shirt deal with the Stones tour. I met with them and they sent me home with a job to develop designs they could sell to the Stones.

Their business is involved with Disney on the *Lion King* project with Wal-Mart. Their business was creating tie-dye looking goods for the work they did in Costa Mesa, as apparel they were selling out for their Wal-Mart orders. They needed a new project for the company. The friend asks for some fantasy image he thinks will sell. So I bend a little to cater to my notions, and give them what he thinks will work, but I threw in that my Stones face-like symbol would work the best, while knowing that will be the one they need to close with when pitching the designs. I told them Jagger never pays for a thing. People just want to get in front of Jagger and ask questions and get involved with him, while others do the deals and pay you. You can get the money out of the other person's business. The Stones bank their money off-shore. Somewhere, that money belongs to them.

I get a call from their buddy stating they are leaving for Toronto for the meeting with Brockum, the merchandiser for the Stones tour. The band buddy returns and says they got the job—Jagger chose mine. He explained his experience of the trip to me. There was a huge room with thousands of t-shirt samples; Jagger came into the room and walked over and chose my shirt. It was in muted colors, rich jewel-like tie-dyed colors, with the design imprinted in black over the color. The shirt was distressed as well, having been pre-washed, thrown in a pile, and made to look wrinkled. Jagger asked "Brockum" the licensee for it, because of its different look. Jagger reinforced his enthusiasm by telling him they should go ahead and manufacture the design and they would see if it would sell better than the tongue logo image, their trademark, influenced by my *Johnny Face* image of 1970. The relationship goes back a long way, when John Pasche designed the tongue logo in 1971 for their label. They ordered 24,000 shirts for the start of the tour featuring my design. The Costa Mesa company was ready to print and deliver.

From there, I established a royalty amount they would pay before the shirt left the manufacturing building. I also had rights to the design. I was at the window of the Newport Studio where I often spent all day before driving to Los Angeles at night to arrange work, when I saw a Ferrari drive up and pull over in front of the condo building. From the window, I see the printer's buddy and his rich partner; they came over to talk about their business. The two of them are standing in front of me, mad as hell, shaking and telling me I have to give them the copyright to the design, or they will lose everything they worked for to get their Stones t-shirt deal with Brockum's distributor.

They tell the story about their problem with the rights and the new deal with Brockum. Brockum believes the artist owning the rights has no place in their deal, that it is the name, "The Rolling Stones," that sells the t-shirt and not the design. Brockum demands to have the exclusive rights, and if he doesn't get them, he will take the 25,000 t-shirts he received out into a field and videotape them as they are lit on fire and incinerated. This is Mr. Brockum, a rock n' roll promoter, managing the Rolling Stones tour of 1994-1995. That was the threat being conveyed from these two Costa Mesa businessmen. What could I do but respond to an agreement signed and sent to Brockum by fax in Toronto.

As the 56-city Stones *Voodoo Lounge Tour* took off around the country, the t-shirt was ordered from Costa Mesa. About 125,000 units were ordered and sold. By the time the shirts got to the stadiums, the shirts were sold to Brockum at $5.00 a piece; Winterland Productions from San Francisco was the merchandiser for their retail stores, and was both selling them for $40.00 and handling mail orders (which sold out). The Stones received $4.00 per shirt in royalties, which rounds out to about $500,000. Brockum made $5.00 per shirt, so he made about $625,000 in total, and the printer and his buddy made a buck per shirt, if that. I made $20,000 off the involvement with the company and their deal. I continued on with my business, they went their way, and I would continue do my sampling with the small shop owner that I met at Kinko's.

Years later, a friend told me how the Stones collected their cash from merchandising products on the tour. The friend's brother was hired at the Miami Airport to unload some boxes from a private jet coming in there. The plane arrives and the Stones hop out. The boxes were filled with cash. The friend tells the story of merchandisers making their payments in cash for the licensed goods sold on the tour. The boxes were assumed to go to a bank in the Bahamas.

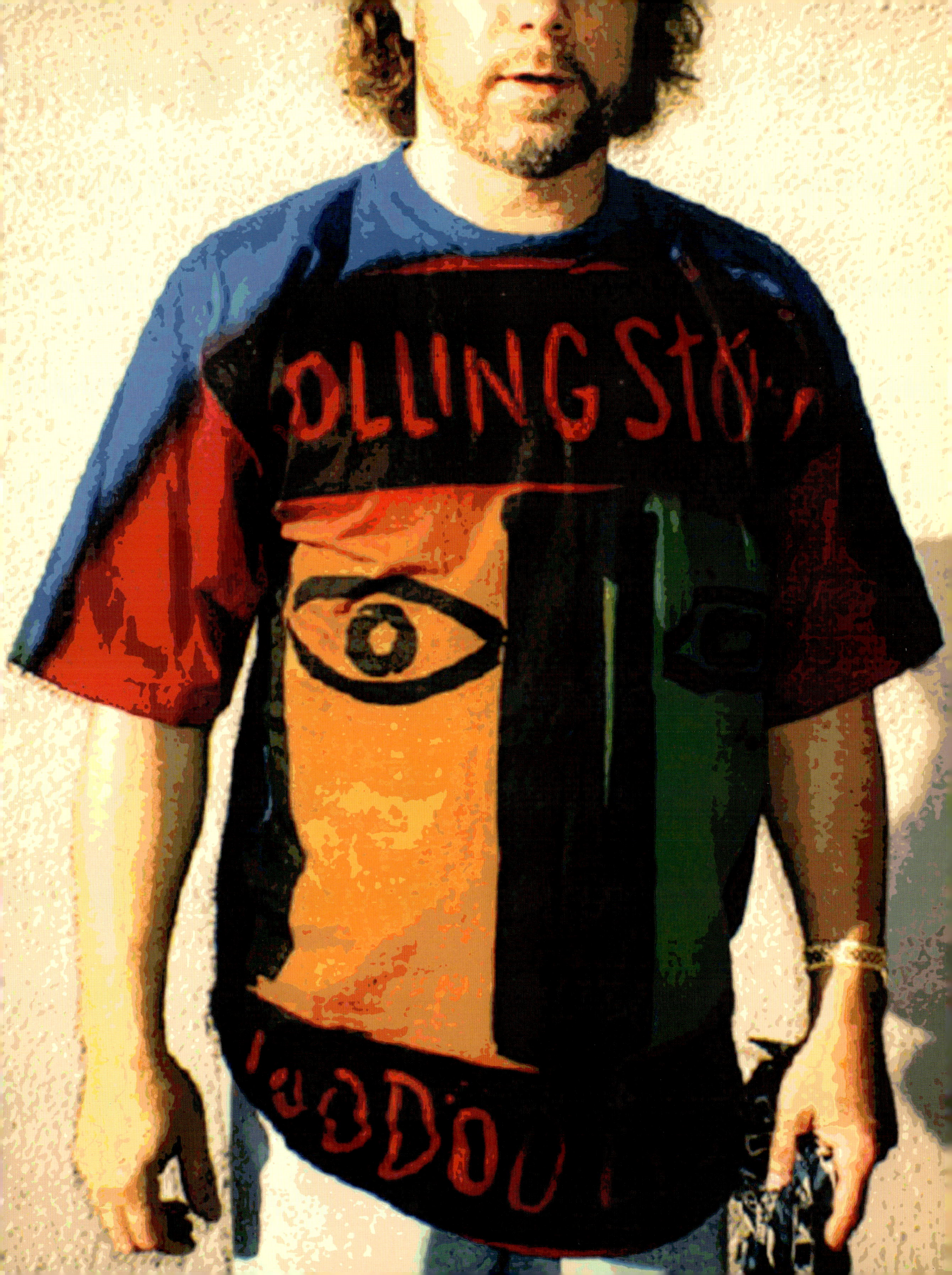
OLLING STO

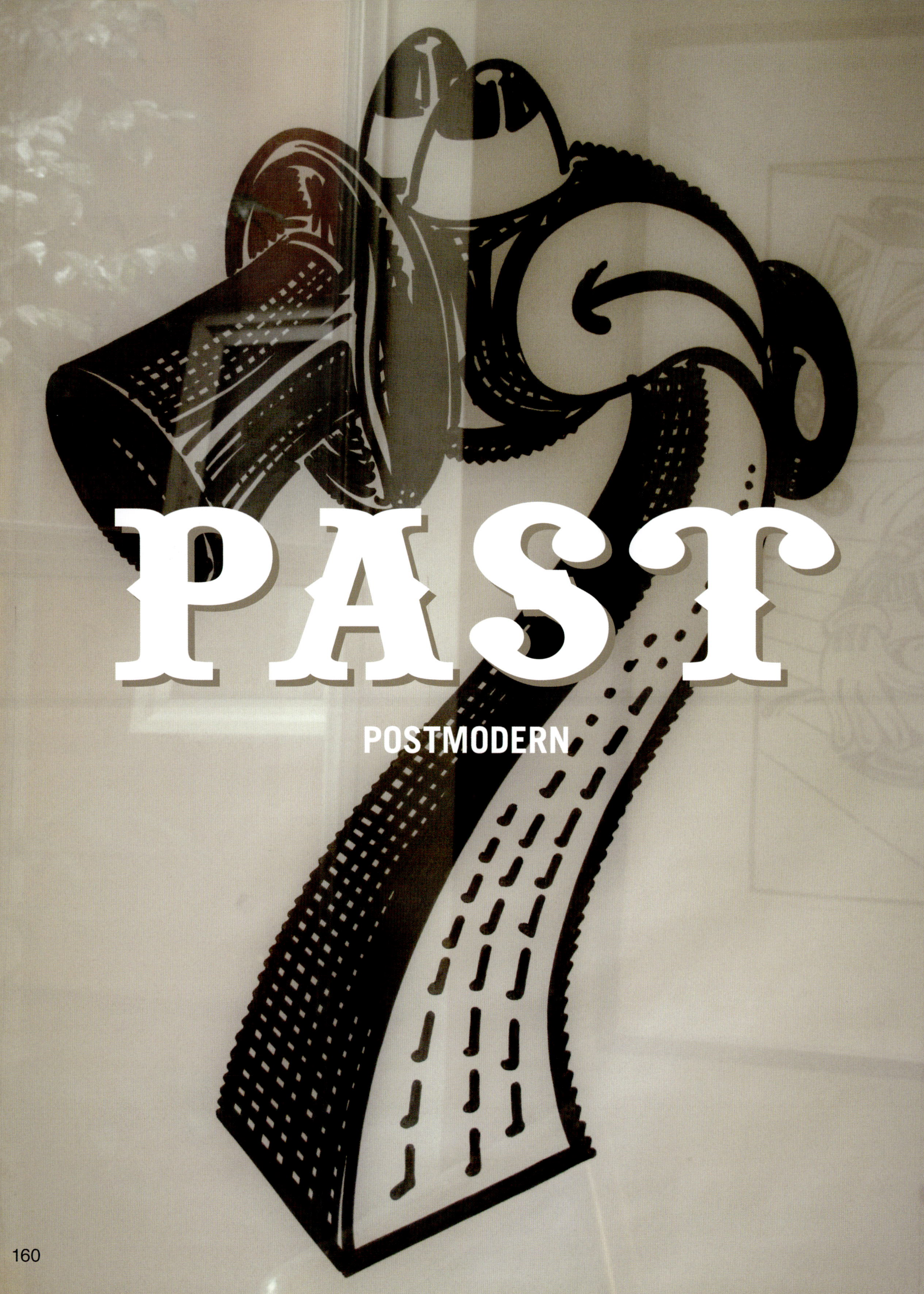

PAST

POSTMODERN

FUTURE

STARTING POST-FUTURE

What is **Post-Future**? The Meaning of 'future': *That which is to be or come hereafter; that which will exist at any time after the present; as, the next moment is future to the present.* In the age of the internet we have become a referential culture. Today I use a keyword like POST-FUTURE for the times we live in. Does the present meet the expectation of what is the future? What do we expect if the future is not the reality, but the past representing the future? "POST" represents the ideas of the past. What is the future today but the past trapped inside a digital Google search for the future as the next search for the referenced, or the referential? If the Internet has become so powerful as to respond to billions of searches a day, the future has become the past by referencing the moment, thus making the moment referential. Every aspect of style in the decades of our existence has become readily accessible so that culture is itself self-referential and instantaneous. All is at a point of convergence as we have entered an aura-free universe in which all eras coexist at once in a state of possible permanence within the atemporality given to us courtesy of the Internet.

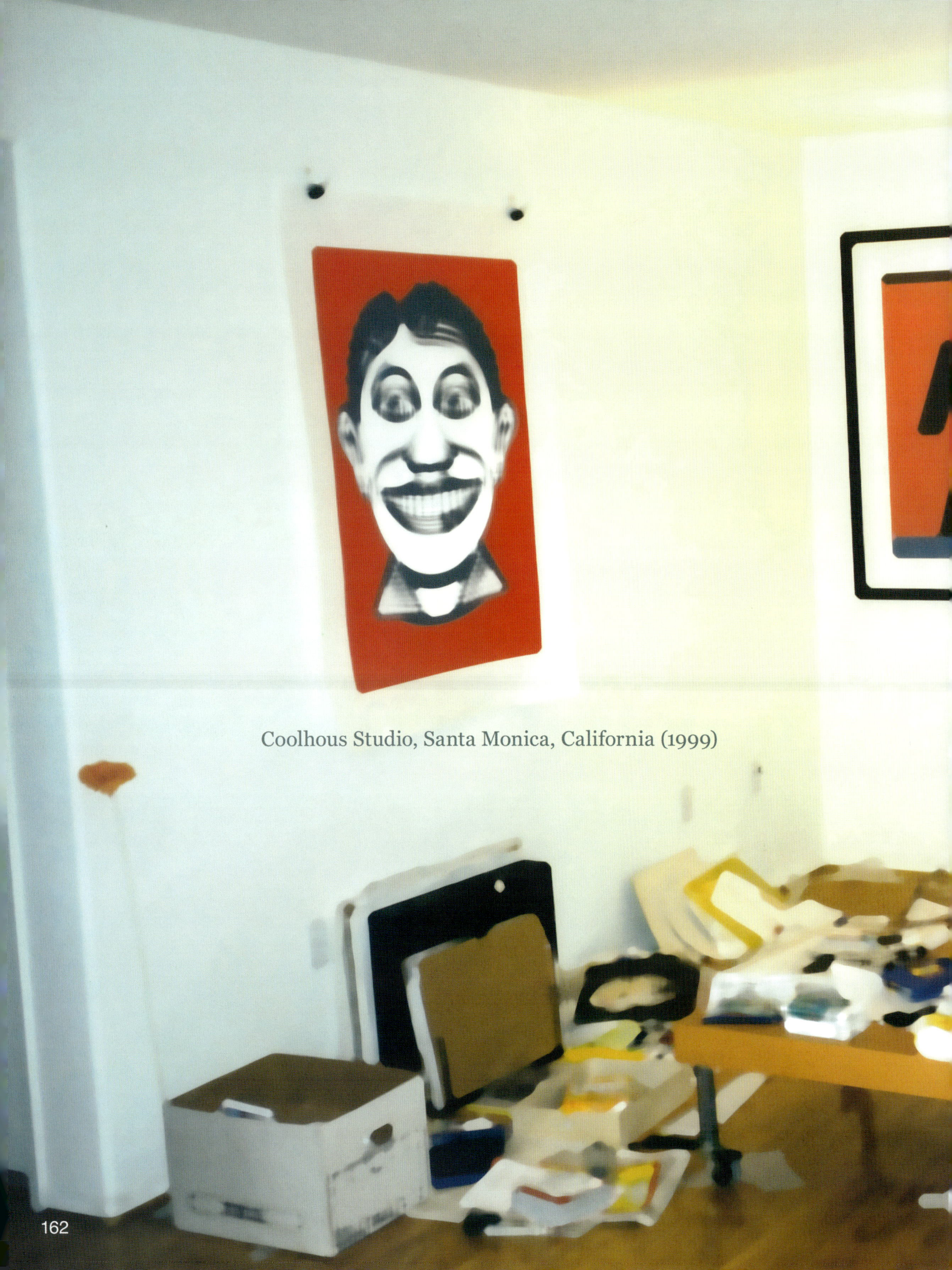
Coolhous Studio, Santa Monica, California (1999)

Starting Coolhous

Dial-up, DSL, and cable had reached the corporate developers and managers, thus spawning the "do it yourself" home jobs of today. Corporations were becoming virtual, like in Toffler's "digital revolution" idea. My analog design consultancy world had dissolved with the keyboard and email which allowed me to reach my client by sending pictures and writings instantaneously. Journalists could begin to brand their stories and be self-marketers. During this period the trend was: down with ad agencies and marketing firms and up with branding and branders. I felt at 59 years that I was being phased out of the media packaging business. The Information Age was everything, everywhere.

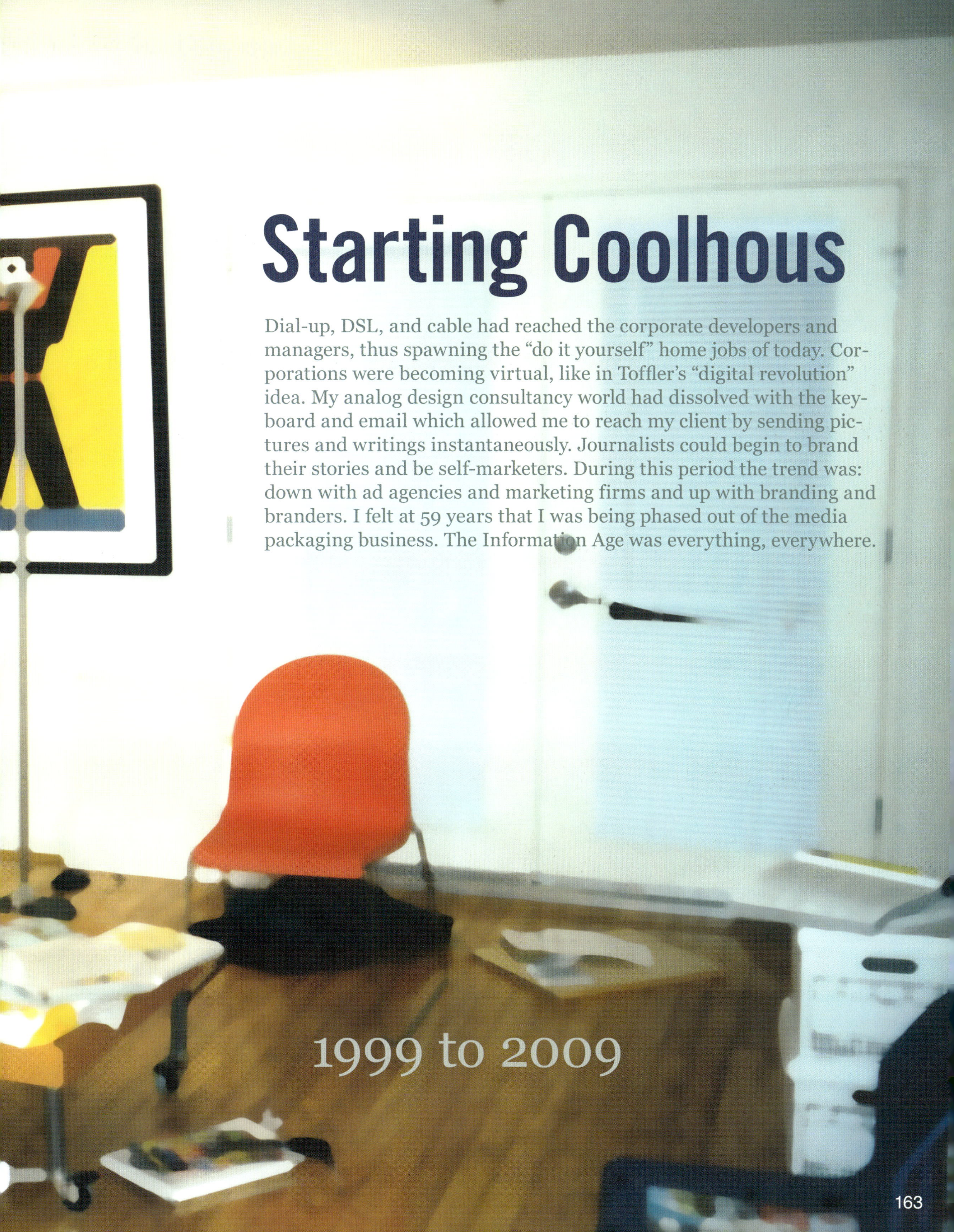

1999 to 2009

In 2000, with my immersion into digital culture, I developed an interest in electronic architecture. I began using a new electronic application that interlinked wireframe designs into an animated movie environment. Using this function, I created a seven minute film titled *Life Star*. The film is an architectural walk through of a medical campus the size of LAX. (3ds Max is a professional 3D animation rendering and modeling software package used mostly by game developers and design visualization specialists.)

3DS-CA-ARCH-DESIGN 2000

Three Dimensional Studio, Computer Assist, Architectural Design 2000

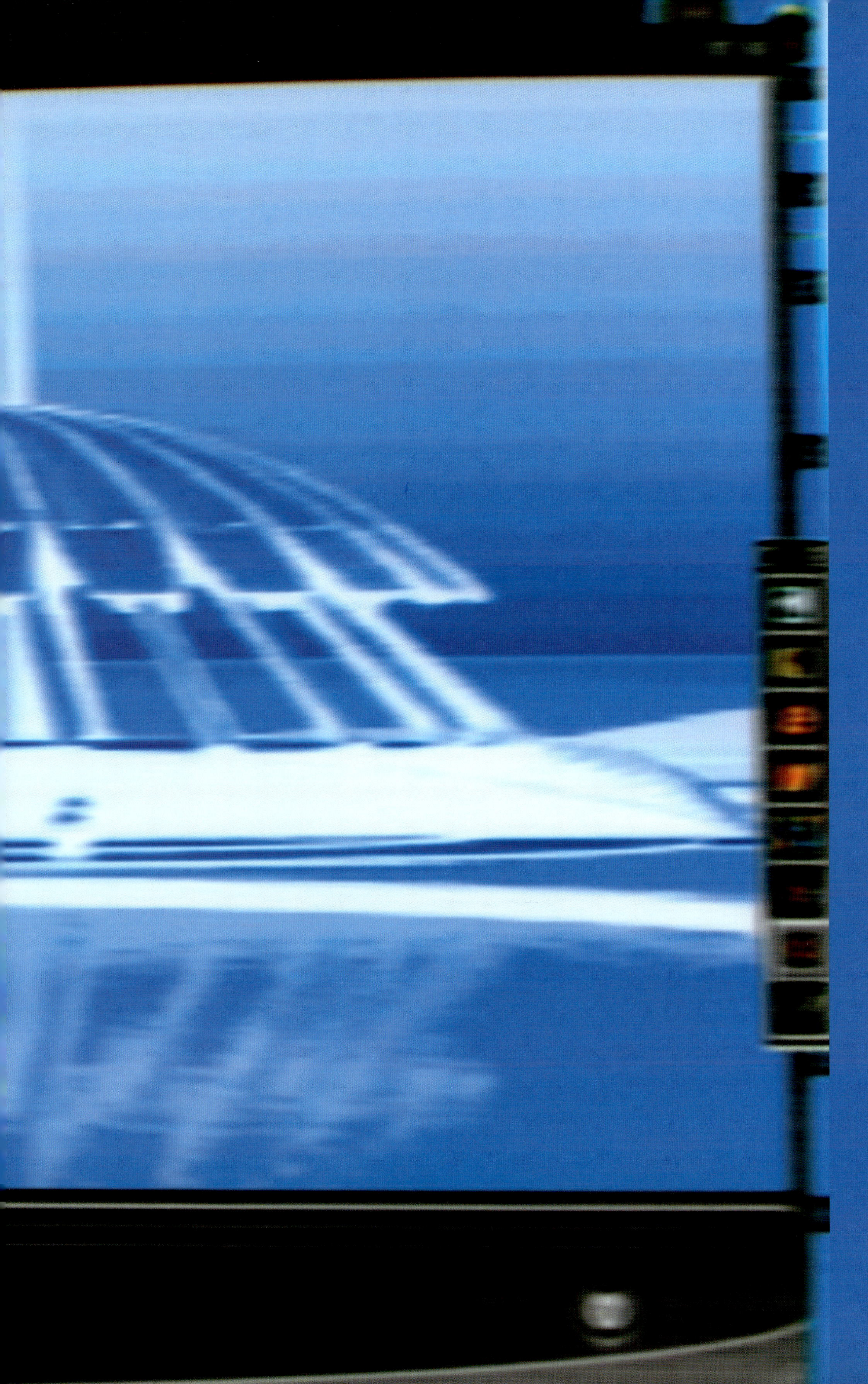

COOLHOUS STUDIO

The year 1999 ushered in the "Communication Age" as a data culture of images and symbols. There were moments where the past became future, and the future was suddenly past. "The Web Network" became everything from everywhere. Objects were symbolic and all signs were forced into the idea of a brand. Everyone had a story to tell, and everything seemed like a virtual world in a plastic universe, between TVs, computers, and cell phones.

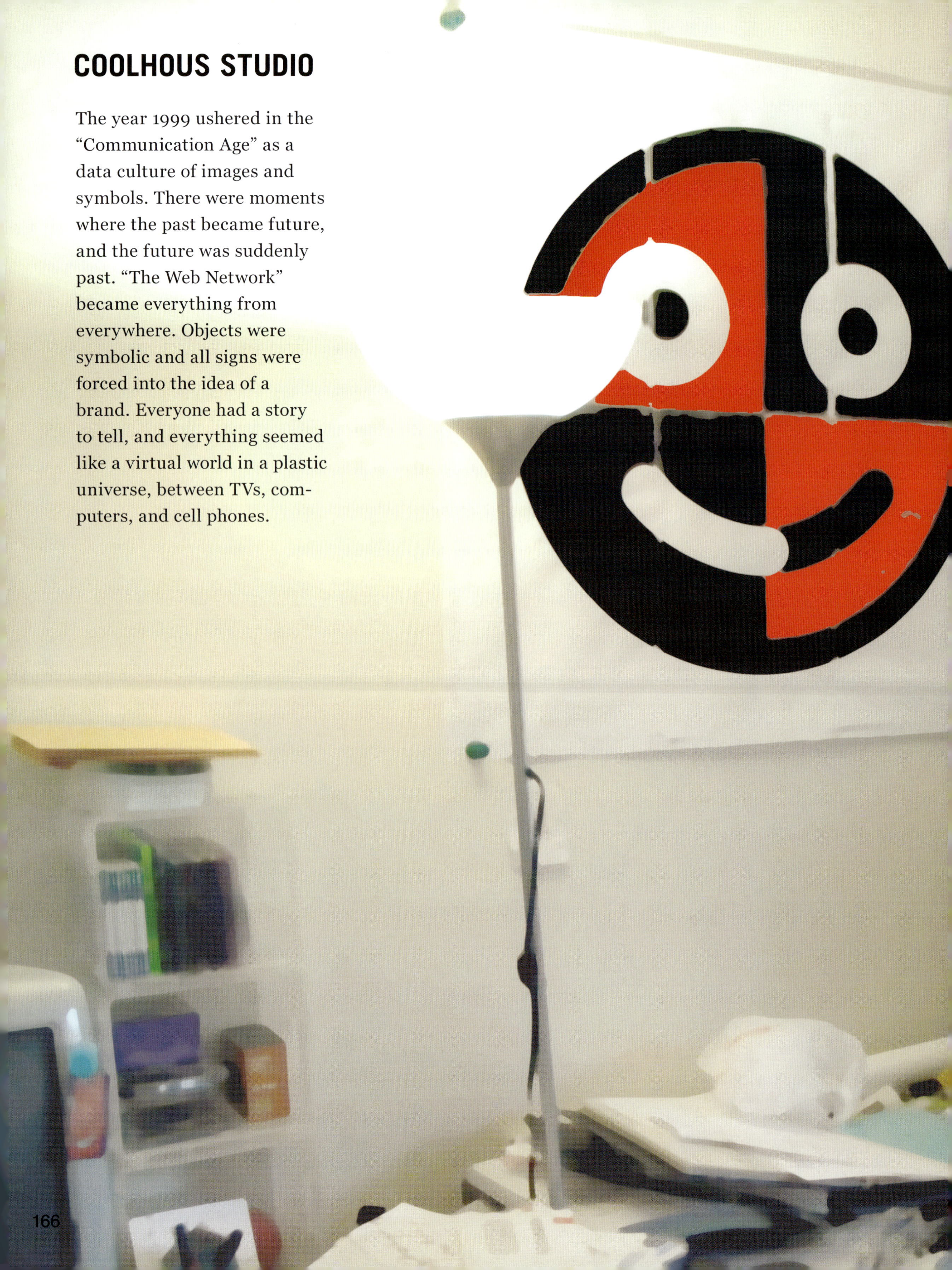

The Plastic Universe of Mac Computers

2000

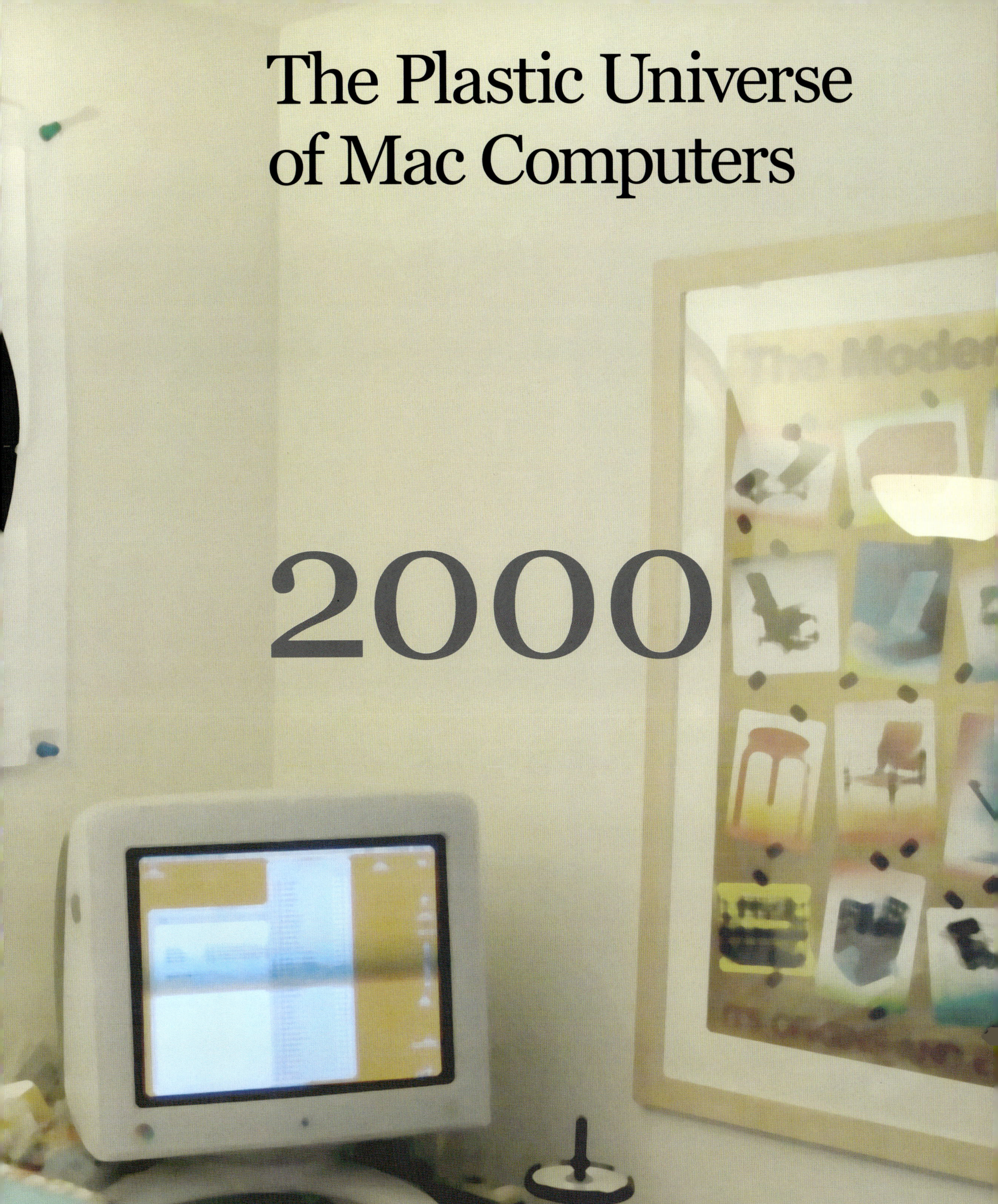

2001

The Postmodern Digital City below is information at your fingertips on the digital keyboard—just run a search on Google! The City Center is designed to help connect the digital community of business, educational institutions, and other leaders who are dedicated to implementing, improving, and advancing their community, business, or organization's broadband technology as a digital infrastructure.

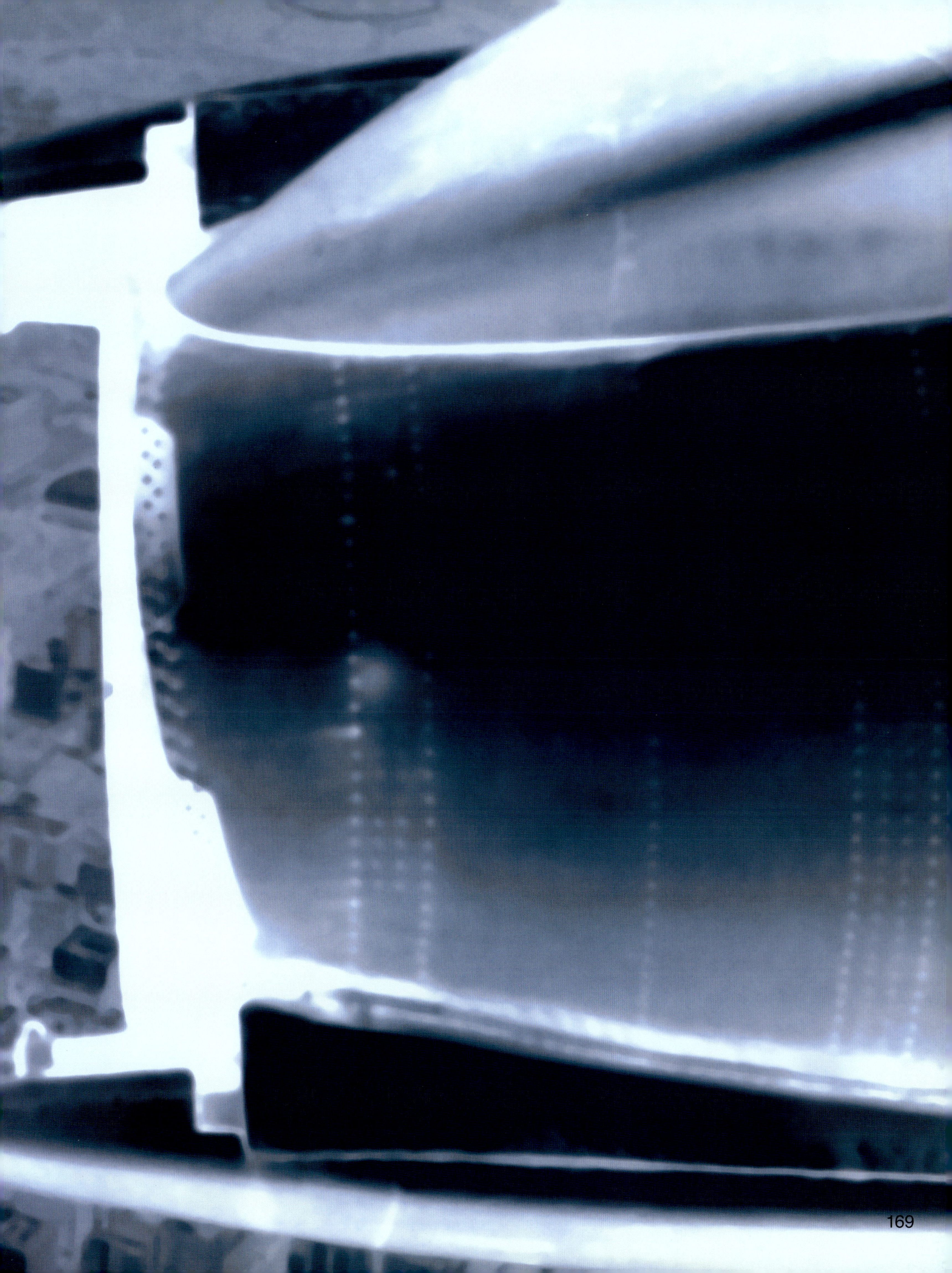

When I look at an airplane in the skies above, the first thing that comes to mind is a vivid image of a 757 disasterously propelling towards the south face of the second tower of the World Trade Center. Ironically, I could imagine a parallel between Osama Bin Laden and a conceptual artist; operating within his subterranean cavern complex as if he were a CalArts student doing an installation at the Whitney Museum. His mark upon our world is unfortunately that of a monolithic catasphrophe, burrowing his abhorrent dogma deeper into our minds and forever altering our impression of the 21st century.

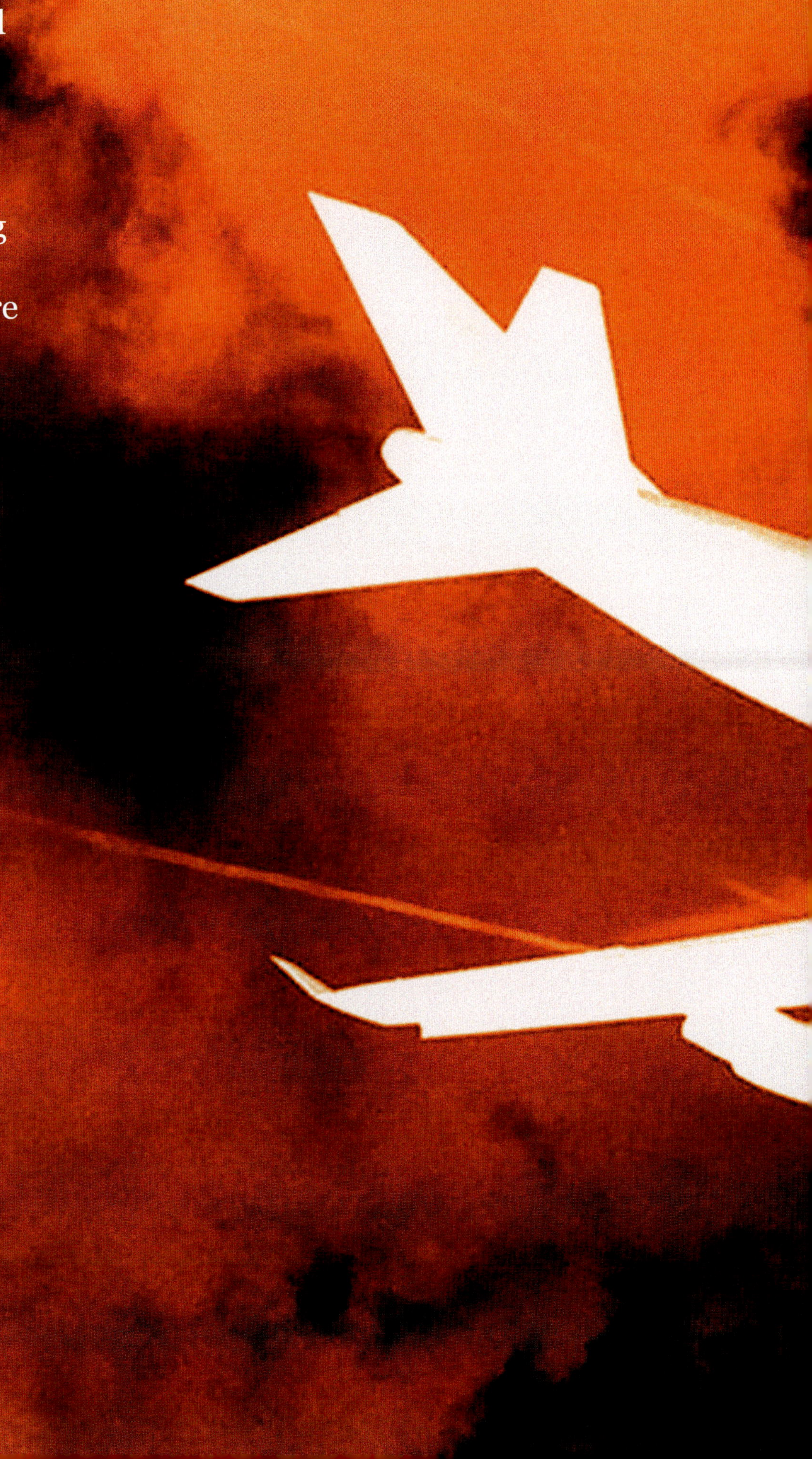

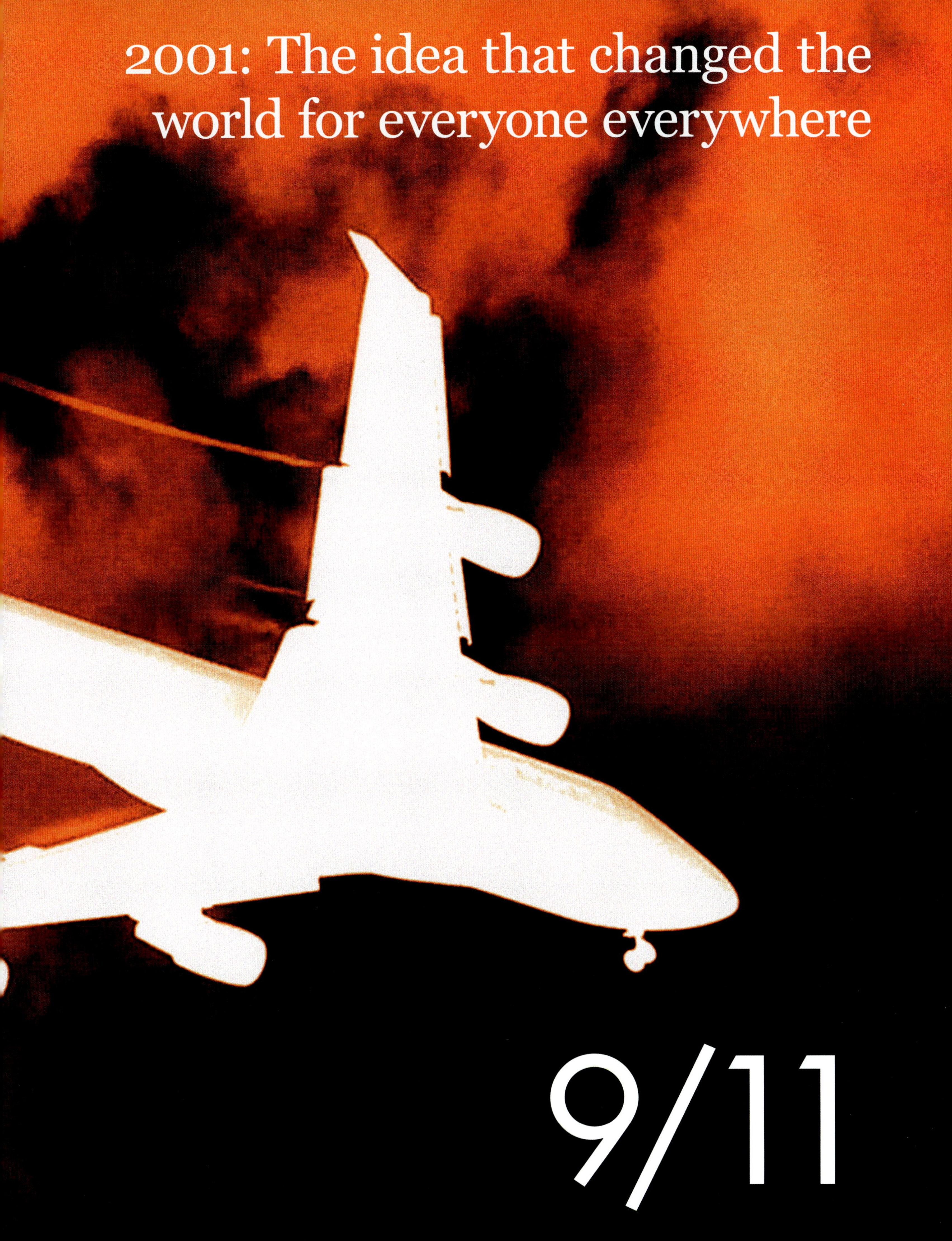
2001: The idea that changed the
world for everyone everywhere
9/11

Getting
Attention
Words
Images
Cellphone
Website
Digital TV

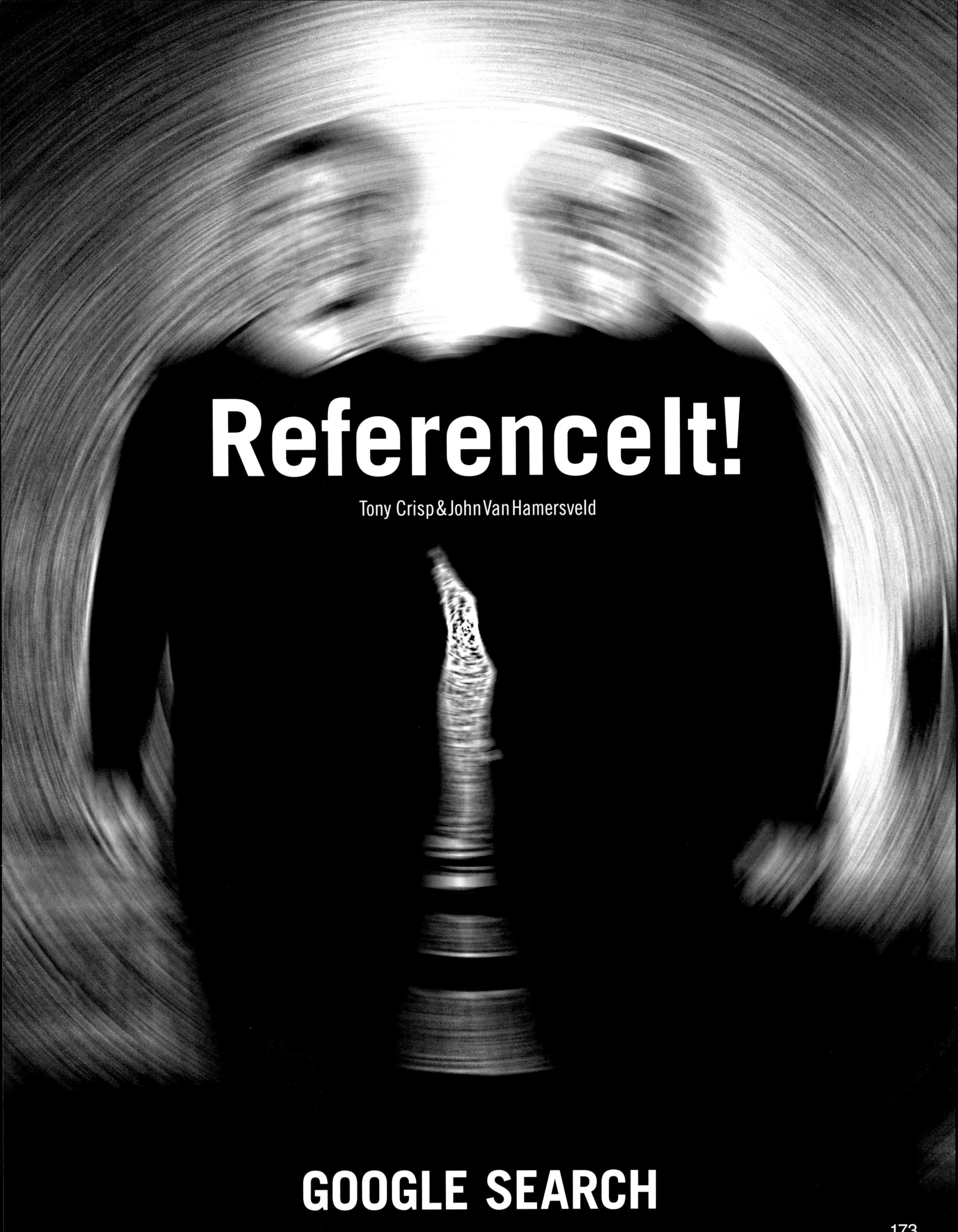

ReferenceIt!

Tony Crisp & John Van Hamersveld

GOOGLE SEARCH

SMART CAMERAS

During my teaching career at CalArts in 1978 I taught a photography class called "Taking Pictures Without a Camera." The class was conceived around the idea of each student using an inexpensive instant camera. There was the simple camera used to capture the idea as a photograph. The photographic image was from the students' "thinking." I wanted the student to visualize the image in their mind and the camera would capture their thought. My hopes were they had studied light and form in their other classes in the curriculum and that they had ideas and concepts in their heads to convey to me.

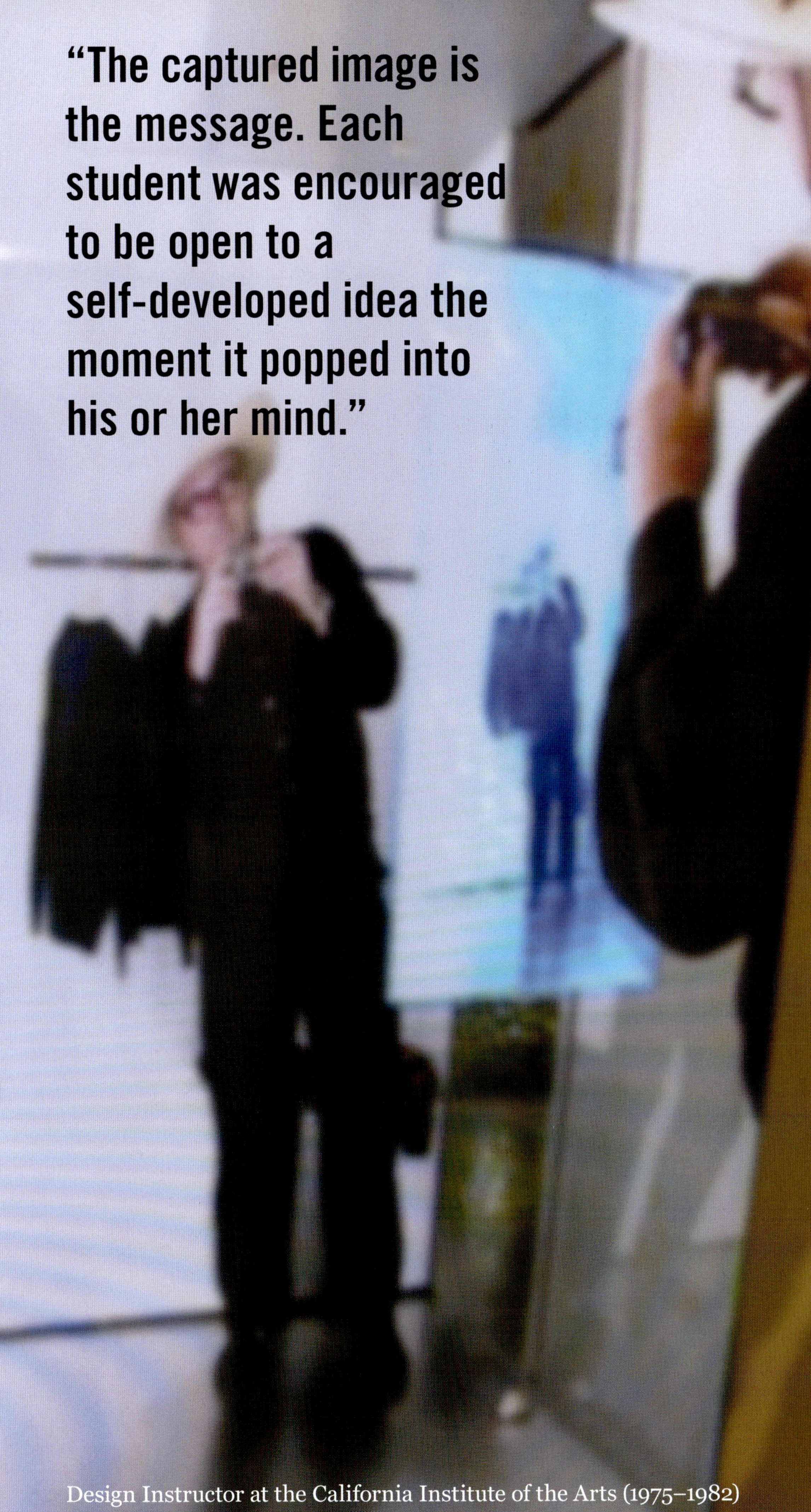

"The captured image is the message. Each student was encouraged to be open to a self-developed idea the moment it popped into his or her mind."

Design Instructor at the California Institute of the Arts (1975–1982)

The student would be the photographer and both live in the moment and capture the moment with a camera. The captured image is the message. Each student was encouraged to be open to a self-developed idea the moment it popped into his or her mind. Since they thought like photographers, there was a delayed shutter response slower than the eye which captured their thoughts as they passed. The lapse of a few seconds that takes place as thought and shutter sync up freezes the moment that is captured with the instant camera.

The negatives were manipulated in the school dark room to create prints of their image as the thought.

PEOPLE: a body of persons that are united by a common culture, tradition, or sense of kinship, that typically have common language, institutions, and beliefs.

PLACE: a particular region, center of population, or location where a figure has a position in relation to others of a row or series.

THING: separate and distinct individual quality, fact, idea, or usually entity b: the concrete entity as distinguished from its appearance; a spatial entity or an inanimate object.

Collect People, Places & Things

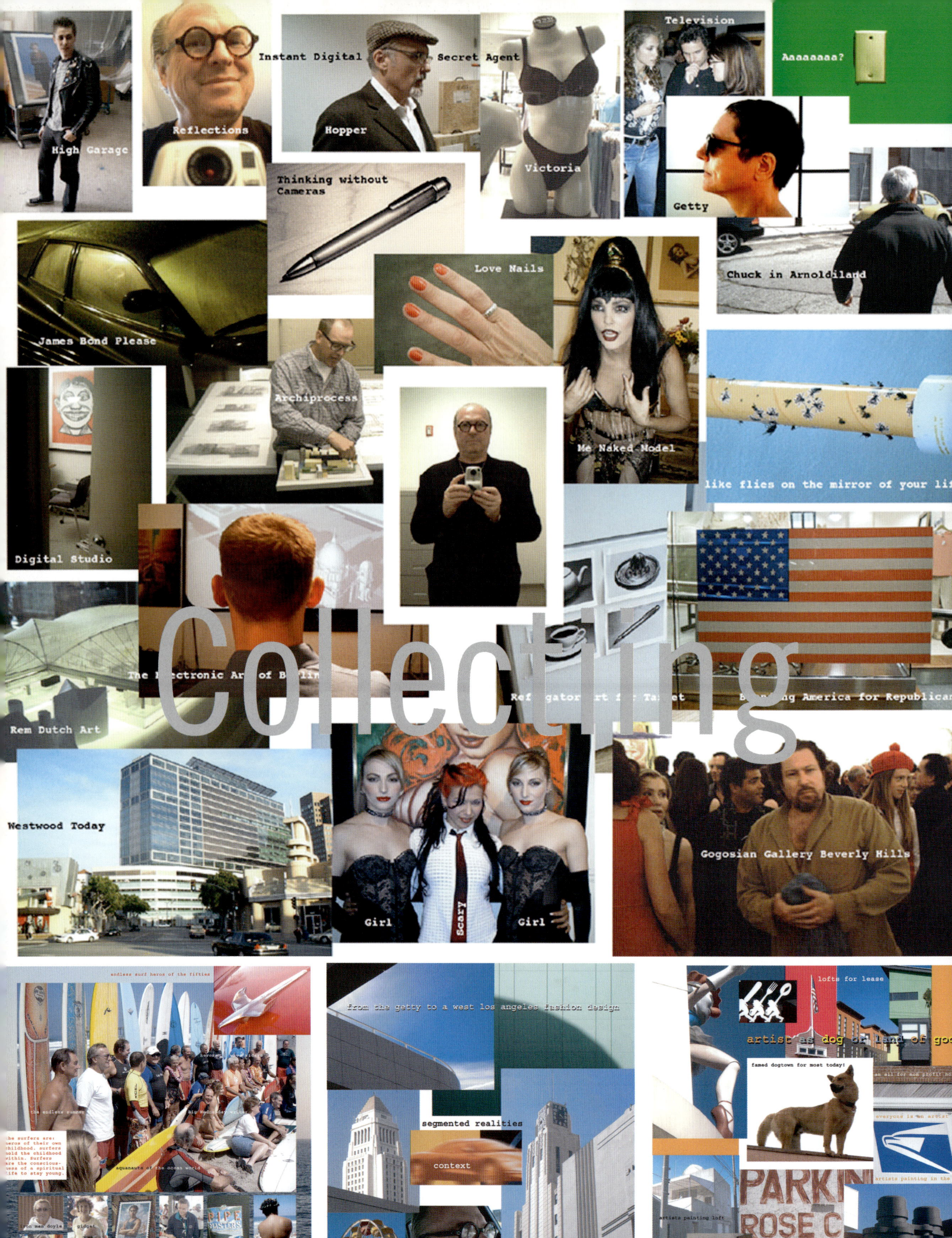

High Garage
Reflections
Instant Digital
Secret Agent
Hopper
Victoria
Television
Aaaaaaaa?
Getty
Thinking without Cameras
Chuck in Arnoldiland
Love Nails
James Bond Please
Archiprocess
Me Naked Model
Digital Studio
Collecting
Rem Dutch Art
Westwood Today
Girl
Scary
Girl
Gogosian Gallery Beverly Hills
endless surf heros of the fifties
from the getty to a west los angeles fashion design
segmented realities
context
lofts for lease
famed dogtown for most today!

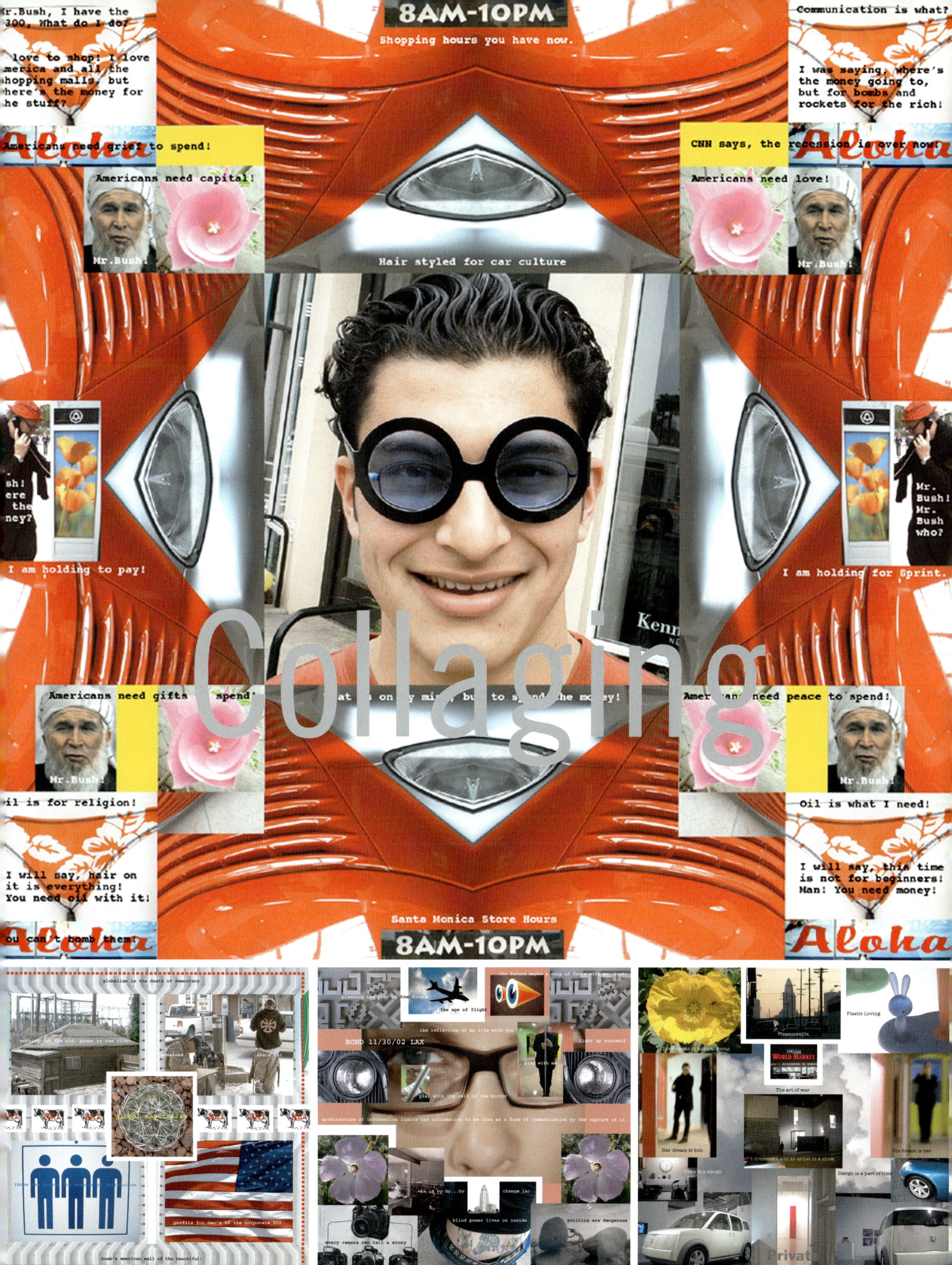
8AM-10PM
Shopping hours you have now.
r.Bush, I have the 300, What do I do?
love to shop! I love merica and all the hopping malls, but here's the money for he stuff?
Communication is what?
I was saying, where's the money going to, but for bombs and rockets for the rich!
Aloha
Americans need grief to spend!
CNN says, the recession is over now!
Americans need capital!
Americans need love!
Mr.Bush!
Hair styled for car culture
sh! ere the ney?
Mr. Bush! Mr. Bush who?
I am holding to pay!
I am holding for Sprint.
Collaging
Americans need gifts to spend!
Americans need peace to spend!
Oil is for religion!
Oil is what I need!
I will say, hair on it is everything! You need oil with it!
I will say, this time is not for beginners! Man! You need money!
Santa Monica Store Hours
8AM-10PM
ou can't bomb them!
globalism is the death of democracy
profits for ceo's of the corporate 500
bush's american mall of the beautiful
BOND 11/30/02 LAX
the age of flight
play with the self in the mirror
every camera can tell a story
blind power lives on inside
politics are dangerous
change is!
Plastic Loving
Pleasureville
WORLD MARKET
The art of war
Her dream is him
His dream is her
Time is a design
Design is a part of time

PERCEPTION

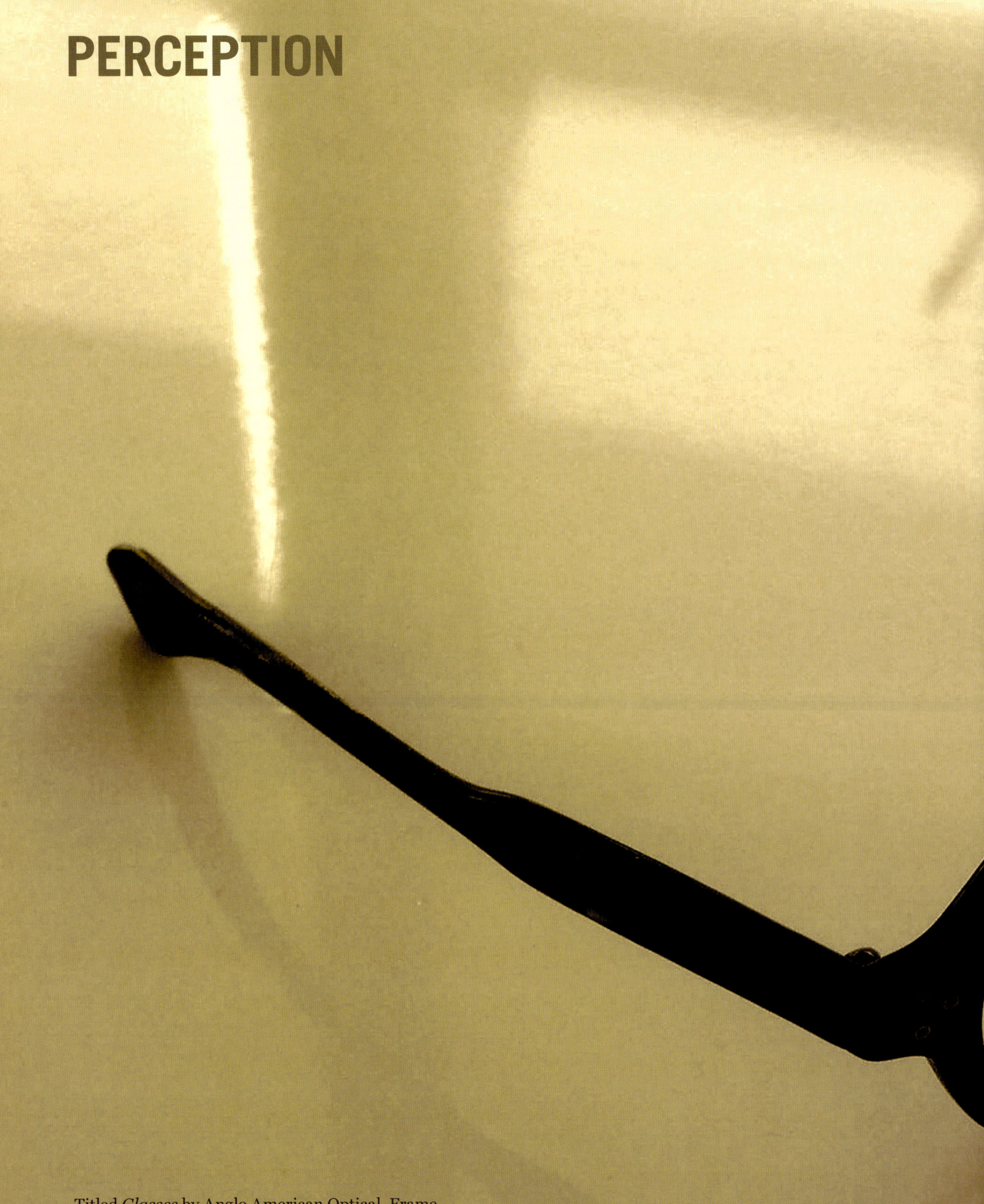

Titled *Glasses* by Anglo American Optical. Frame English. Purchased at Eyes On Main (Venice, CA). Taken with a Leica Digilux 1 camera (2004).

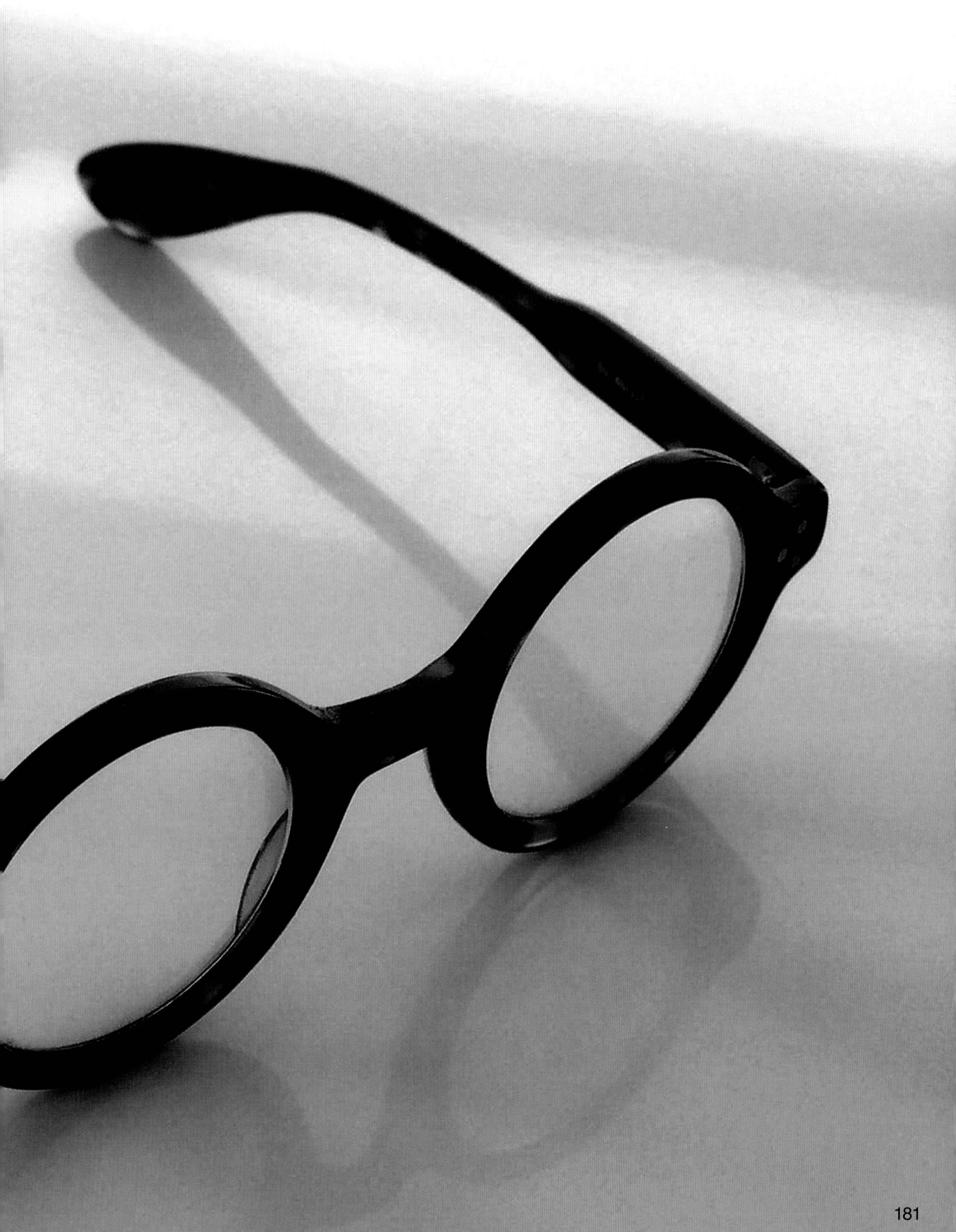

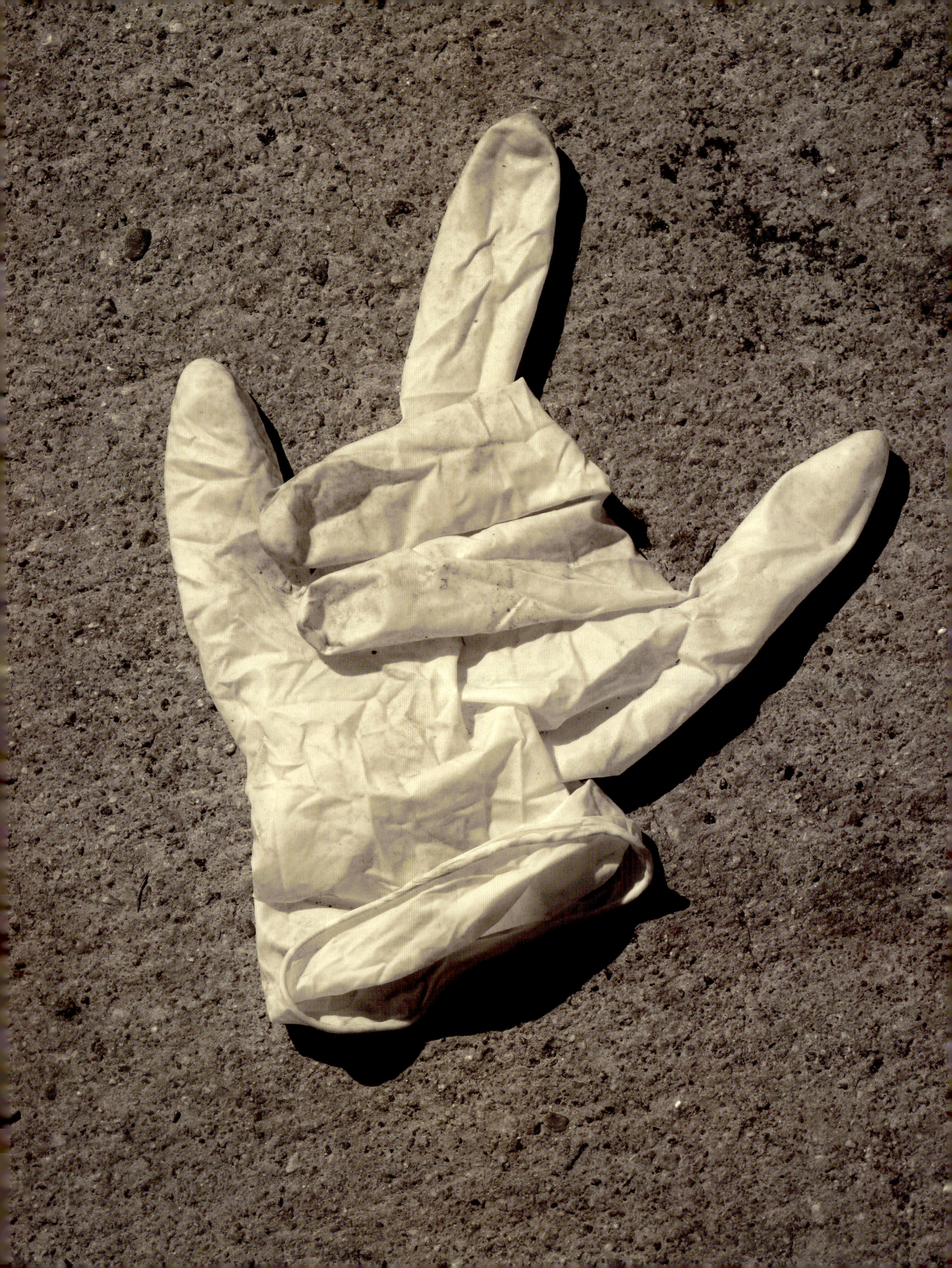

A right handed glove on the pavement (left) coincidentally positioned with the "devil's horns" sign; taken with a Canon G10 (2011). The antique salt shaker (right) was taken with a Leica Digilux 1 (2006); in position at the Patinette Cafe of the MOCA, Los Angeles.

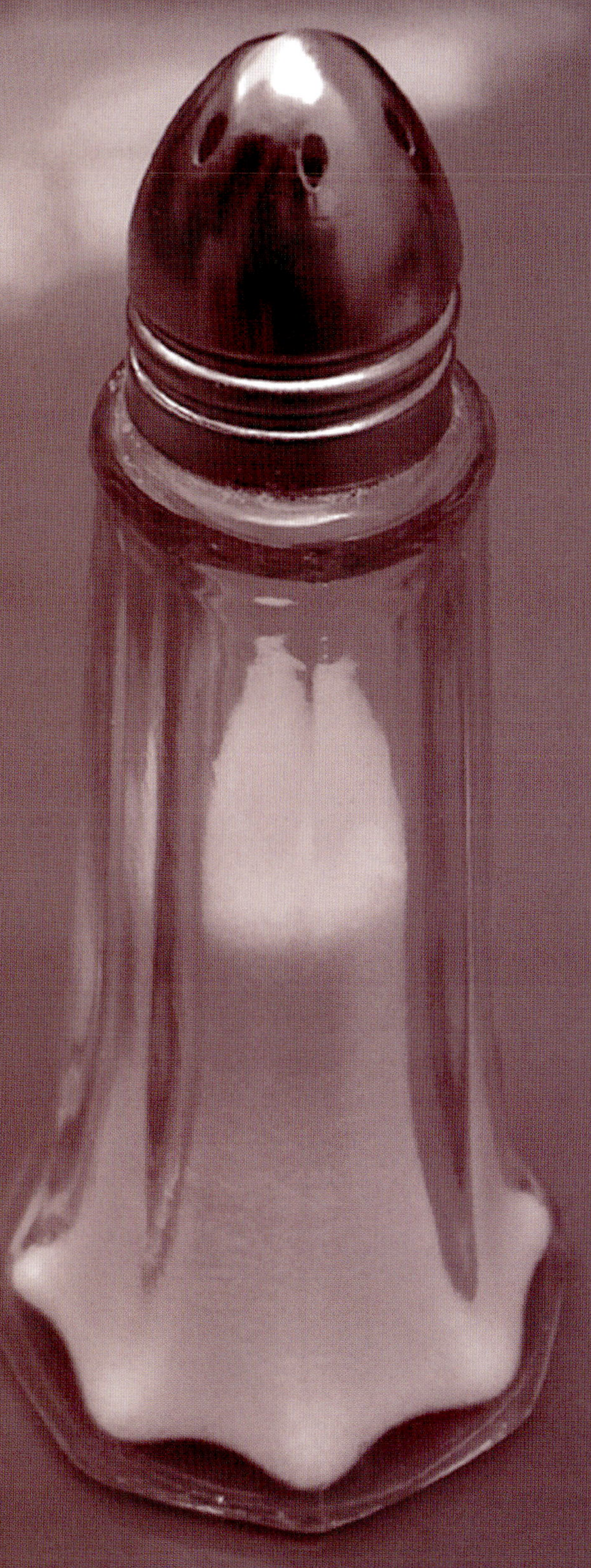

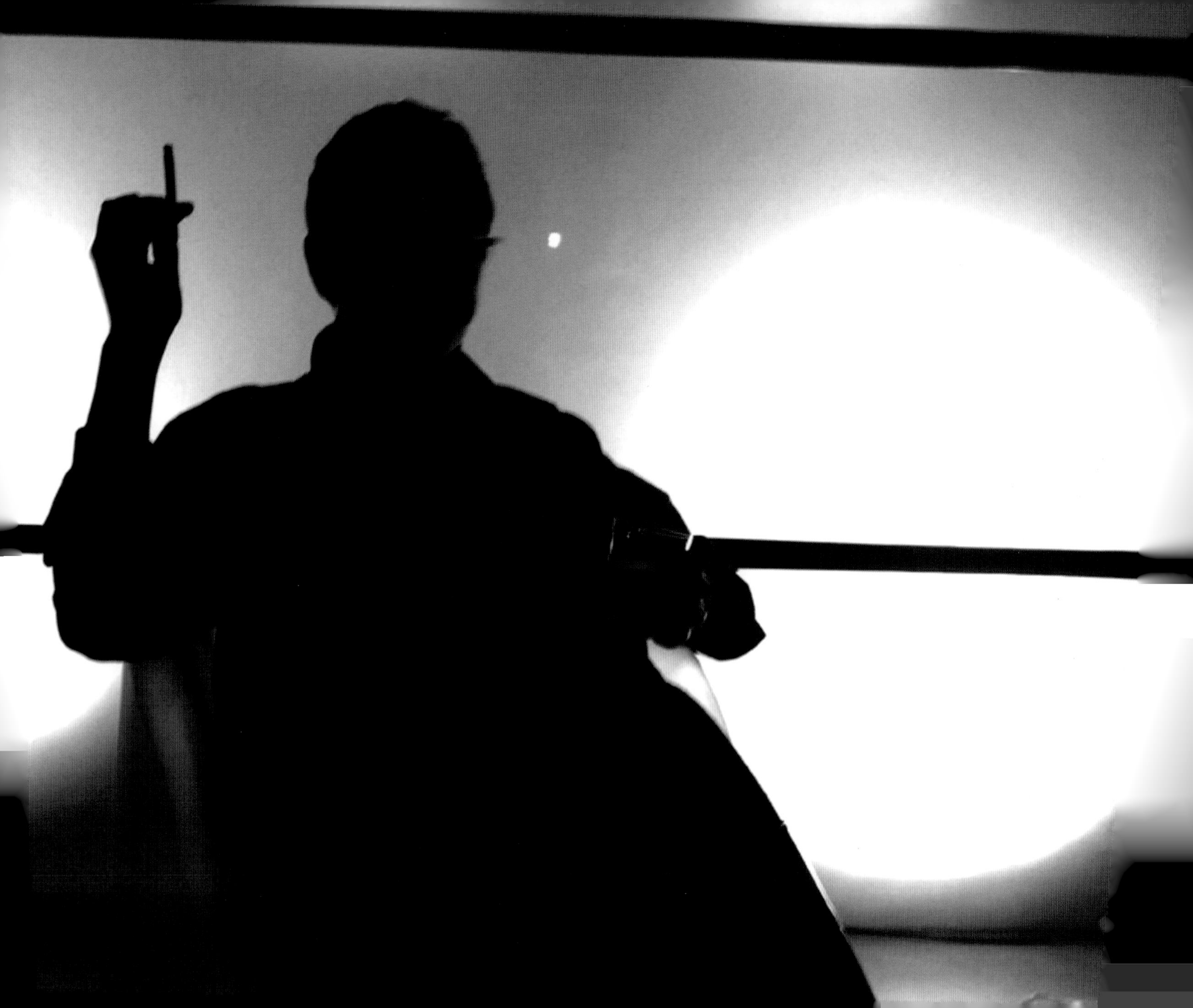

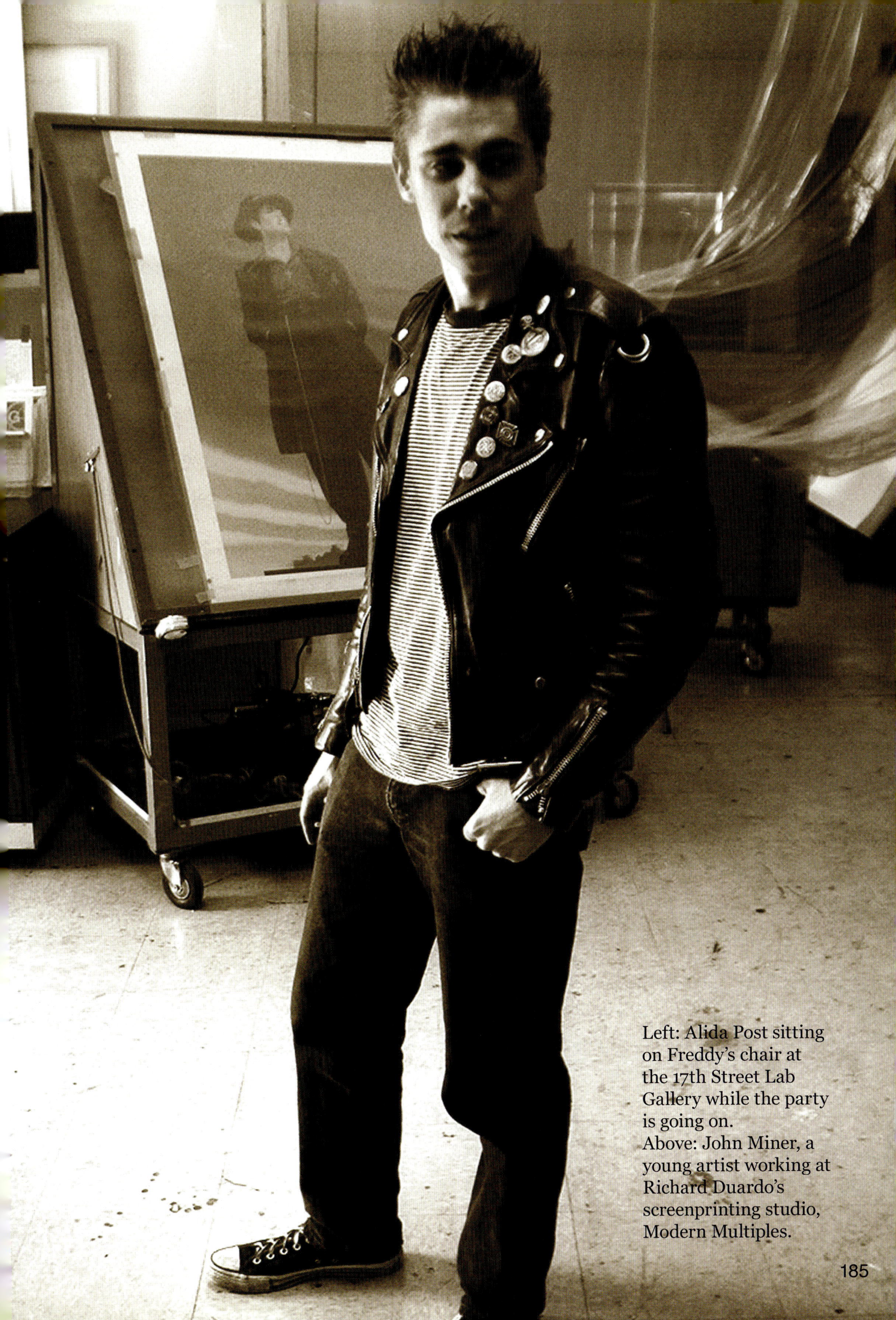

Left: Alida Post sitting on Freddy's chair at the 17th Street Lab Gallery while the party is going on.
Above: John Miner, a young artist working at Richard Duardo's screenprinting studio, Modern Multiples.

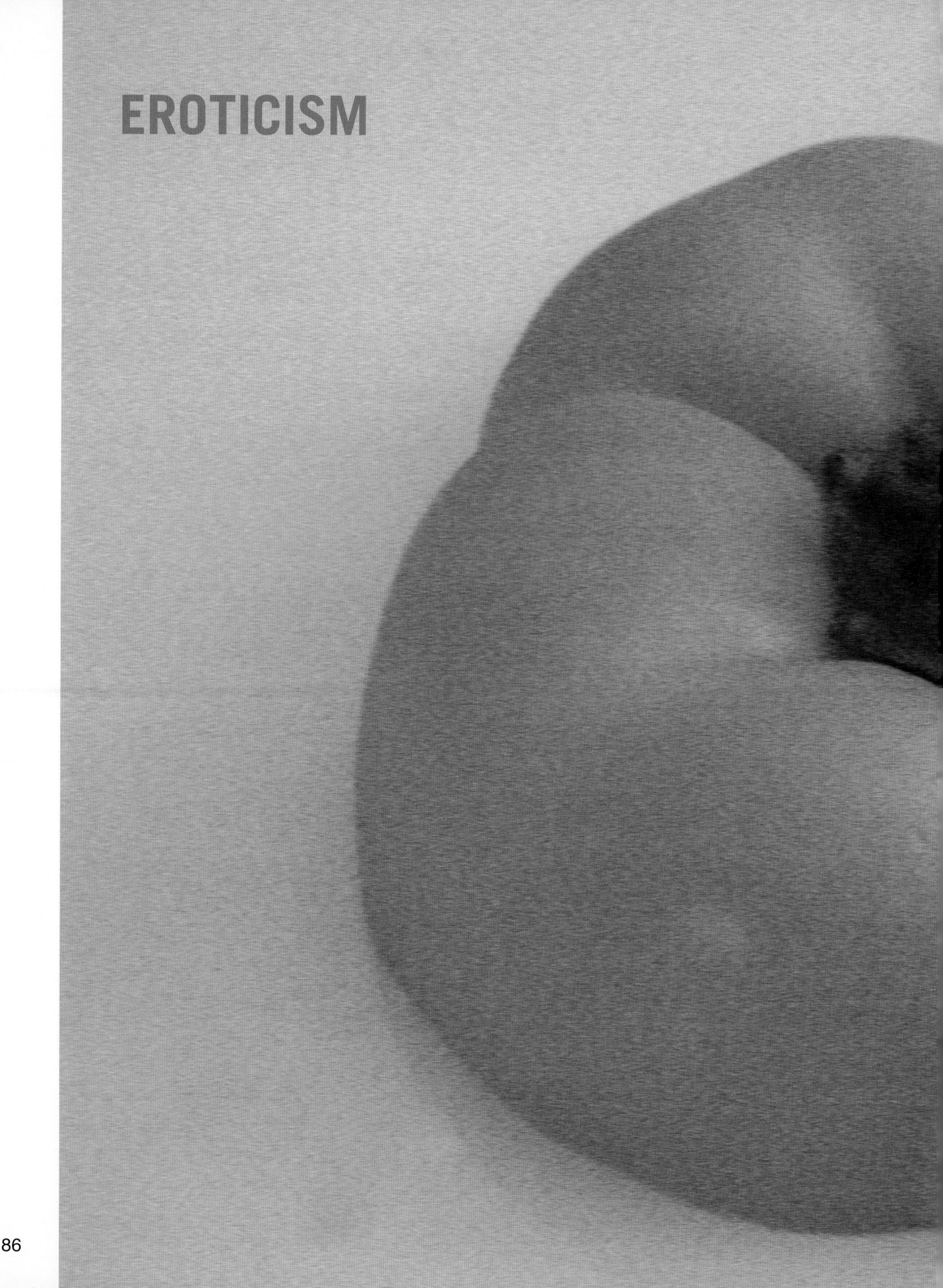

EROTICISM

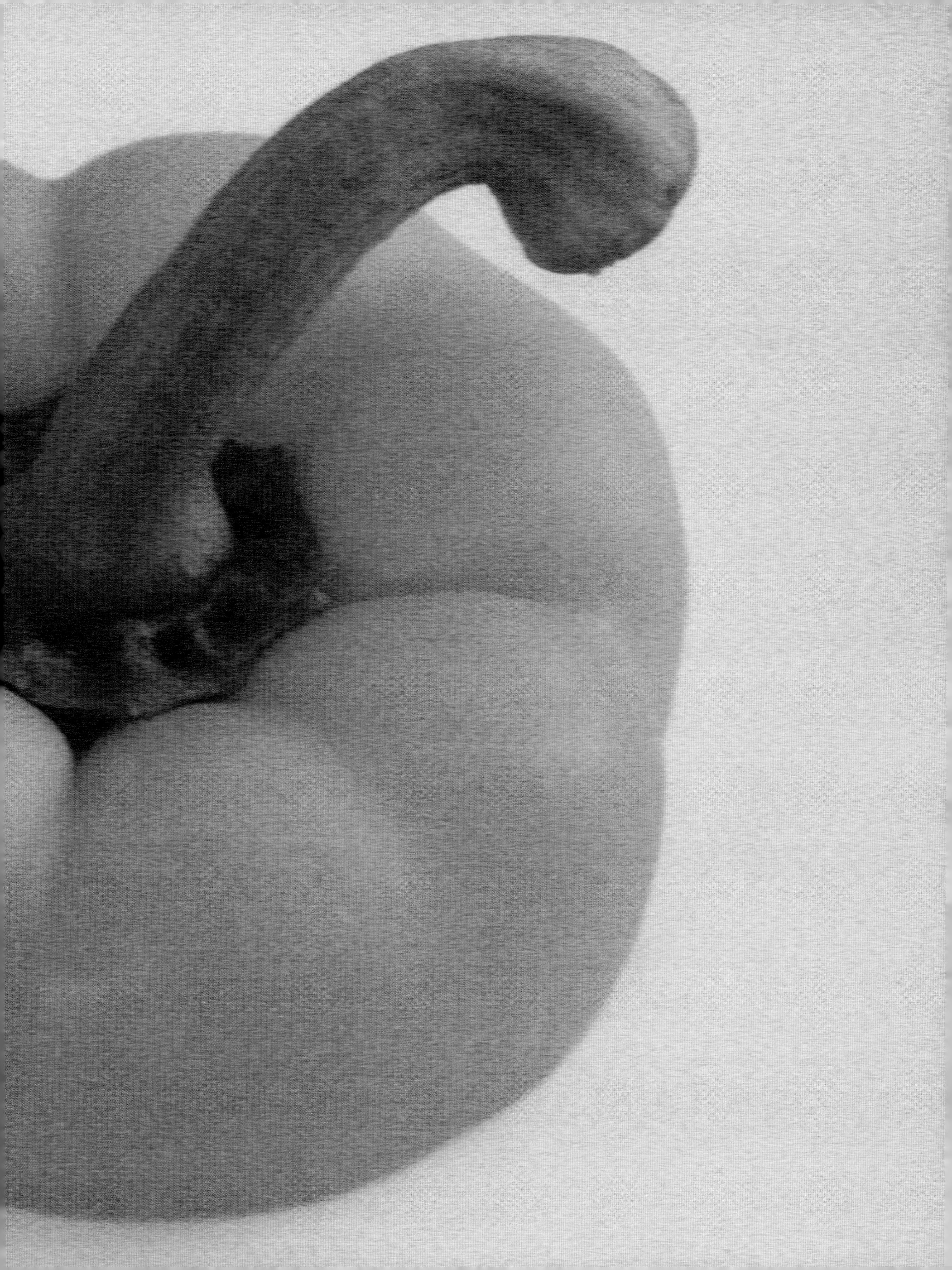

CURATOR

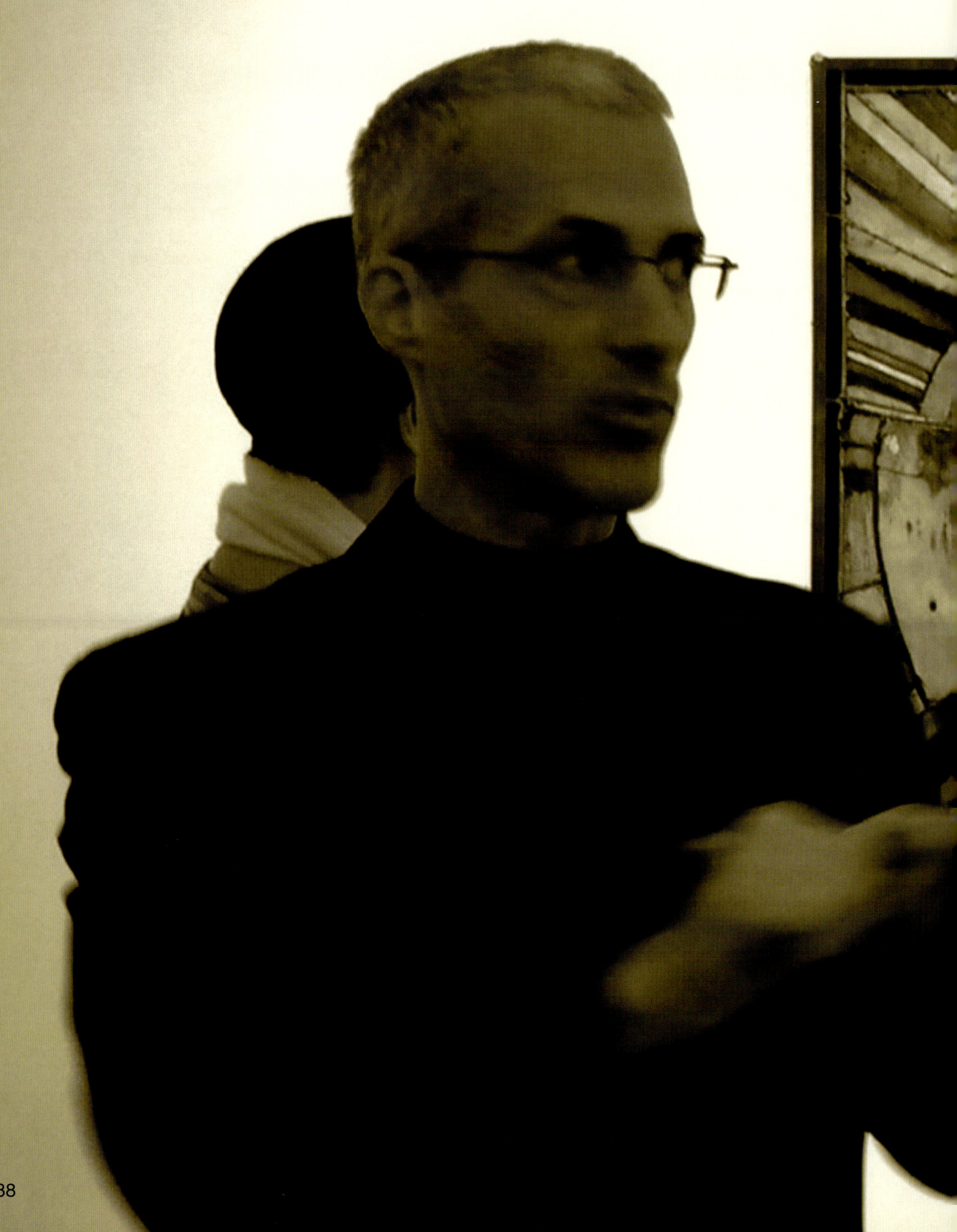

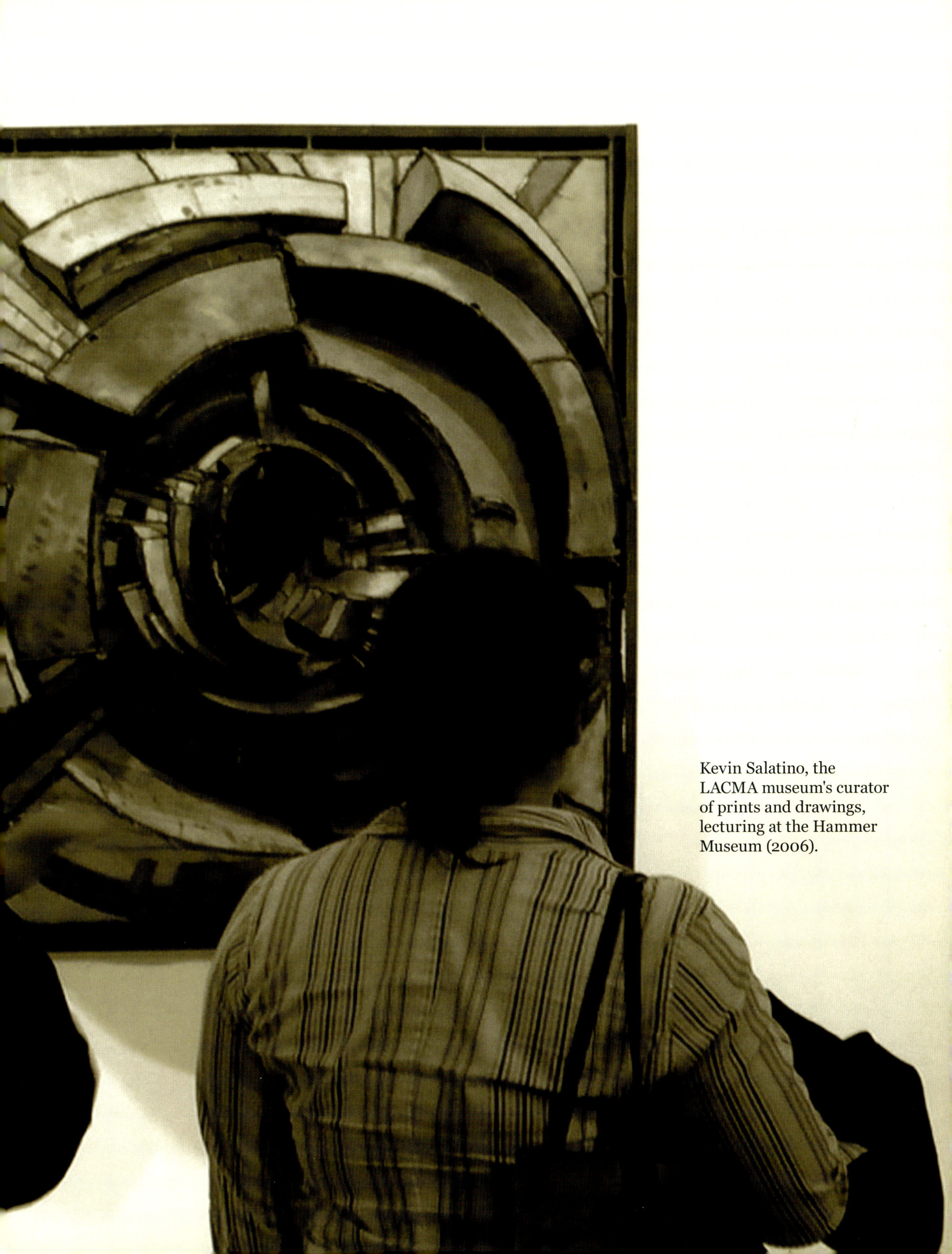

Kevin Salatino, the LACMA museum's curator of prints and drawings, lecturing at the Hammer Museum (2006).

FACADE

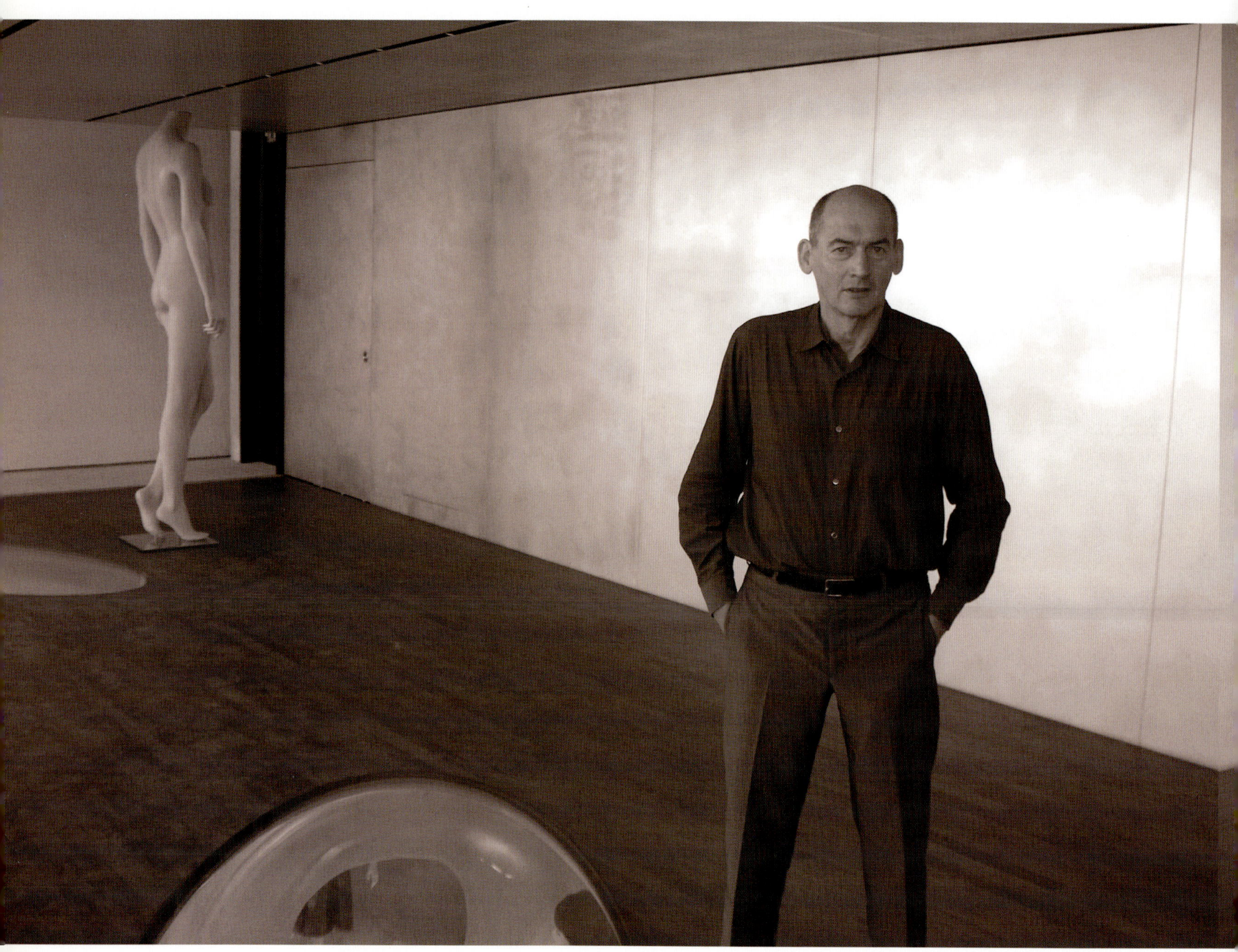

Architect Rem Koolhaas' front facade at the Prada Epicenter (Beverly Hills, California). Taken with a HP Photosmart R967 10 megapixel camera.

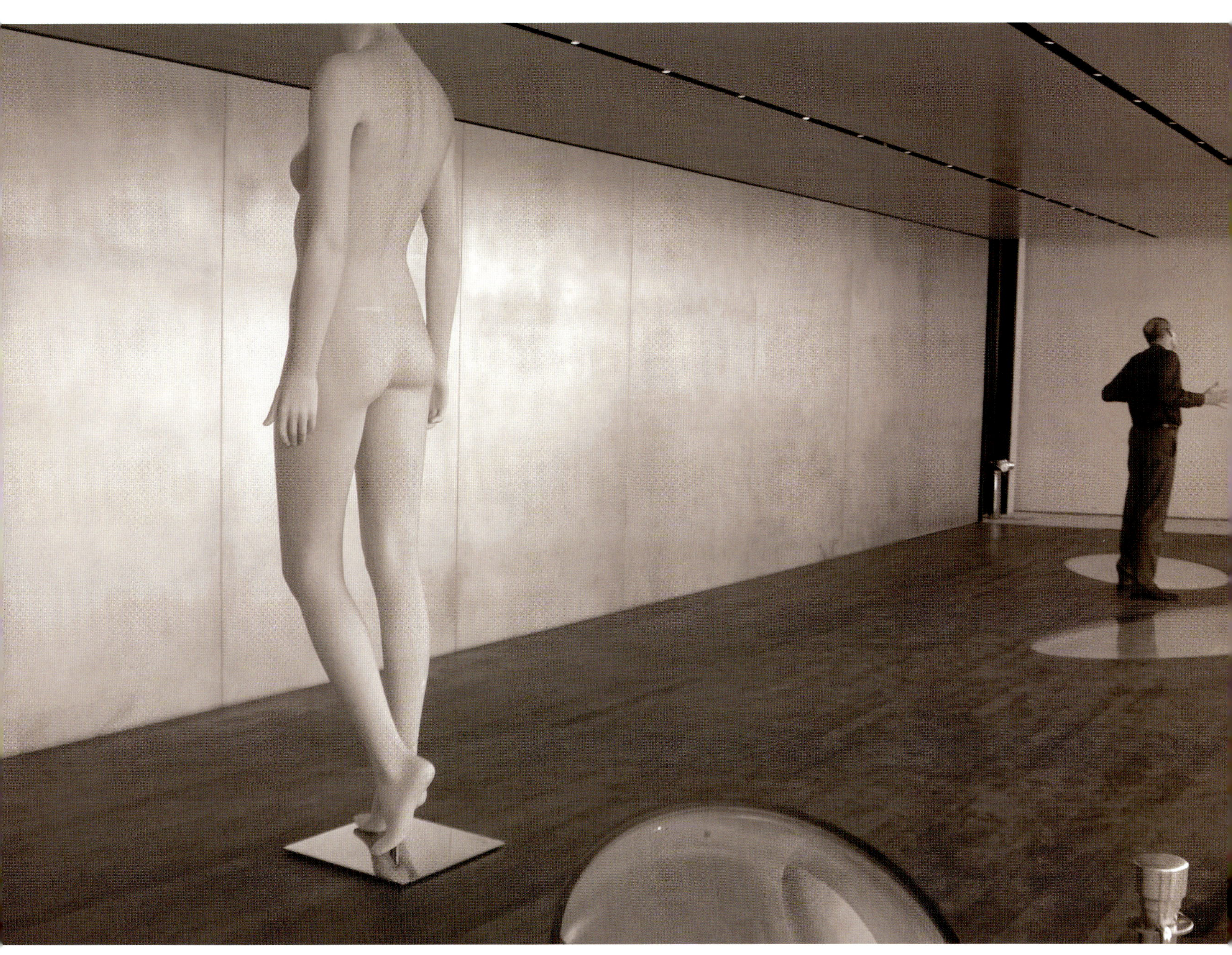

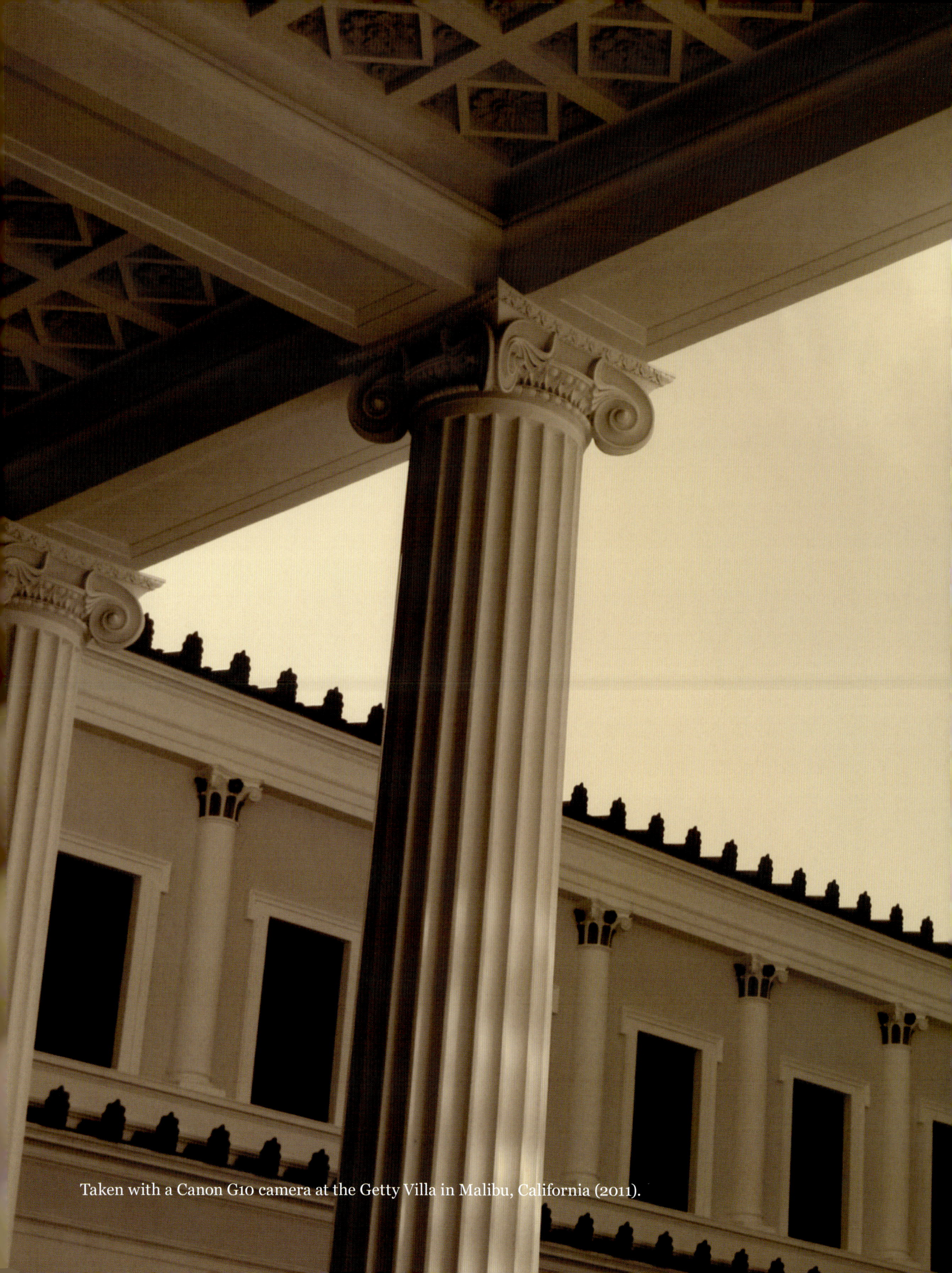

Taken with a Canon G10 camera at the Getty Villa in Malibu, California (2011).

PHILOSOPHY

PHILOSOPHER

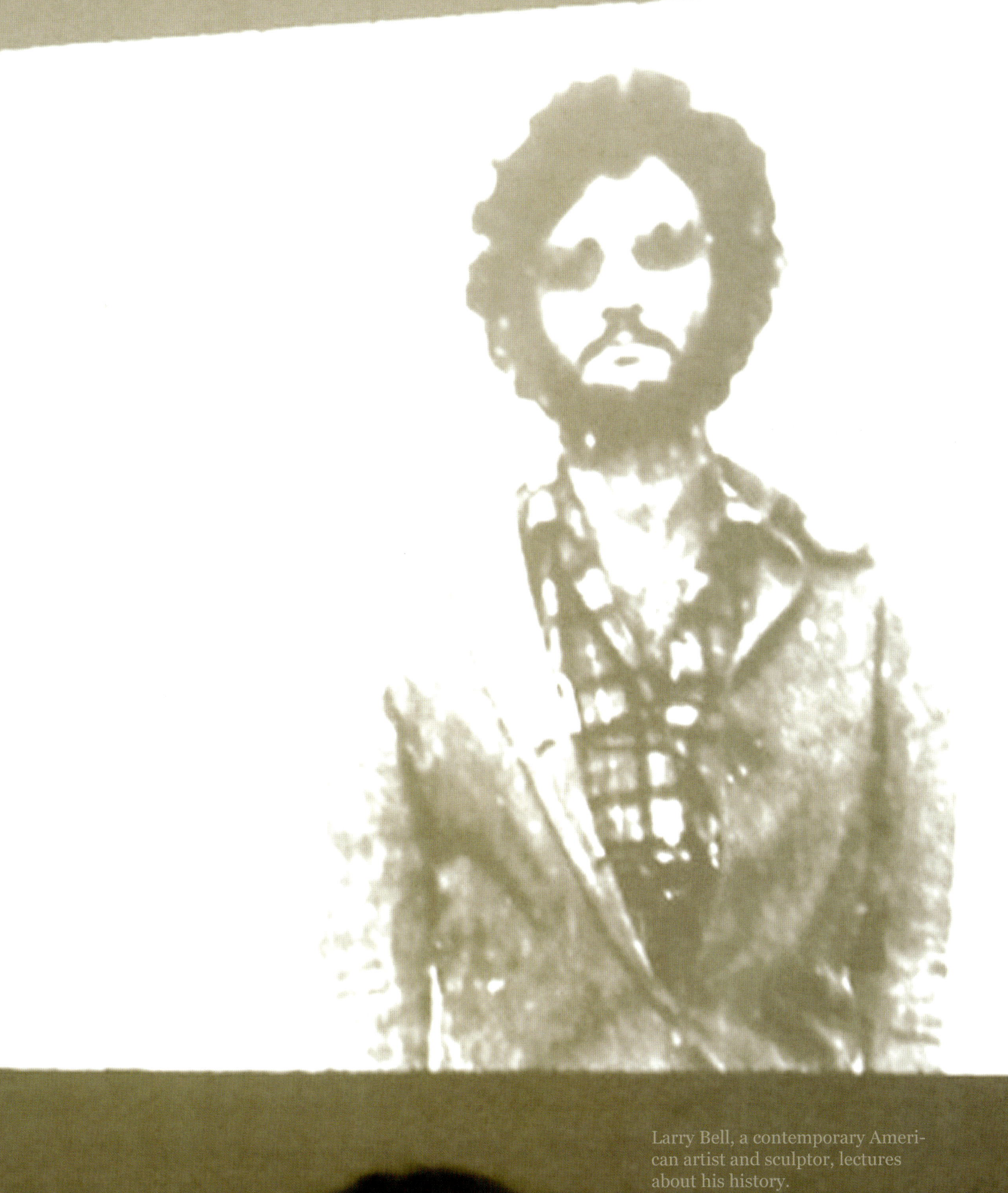

Larry Bell, a contemporary American artist and sculptor, lectures about his history.

The Movie:

The *Endless Summer* poster began its distribution from the Kips Bay theater, where the film had its New York debut as a 35 mm theatrical release in July of 1966. The distribution of the poster then moved on to the famous Personality Poster Store located on 8th Street in the Village. Martin Geisler, the owner of Personality Poster, had a background in advertising. He printed the *Endless Summer* poster with the same original screenprinted colors, crediting its success to the color scheme. The poster was also entered into trade shows and distributed to college bookstores around America.

The Distribution... **Martin Geisler, the owner of Personality Poster**

The Critique of the Poster Icon
"Coastal Confluence: Geography Links the Art in 'Baja to Vancouver,' But It's the Social Landscape That Resonates."
by Christopher Knight
Art Review, 2004
"In his famous poster for the classic 1966 surfing documentary The Endless Summer*, graphic artist John Van Hamersveld posed his faceless tribe of free-spirited beach bums in an otherworldly terrain, engorged with pure psychedelic beauty. Above a vast crimson beach beneath a bright magenta sky, an enormous lemon-yellow sun sat bolted to the horizon. 'The image was the stuff of epic literature, high or low. Three men carrying long boards—silhouettes in the vivid landscape, courtesy of the blackness of a high-contrast photograph, stood facing into the distance, prepared to enact a utopian quest for the perfect wave. The sun, poised between perpetual rising and continuous setting, forged an eternal radiance.'"*

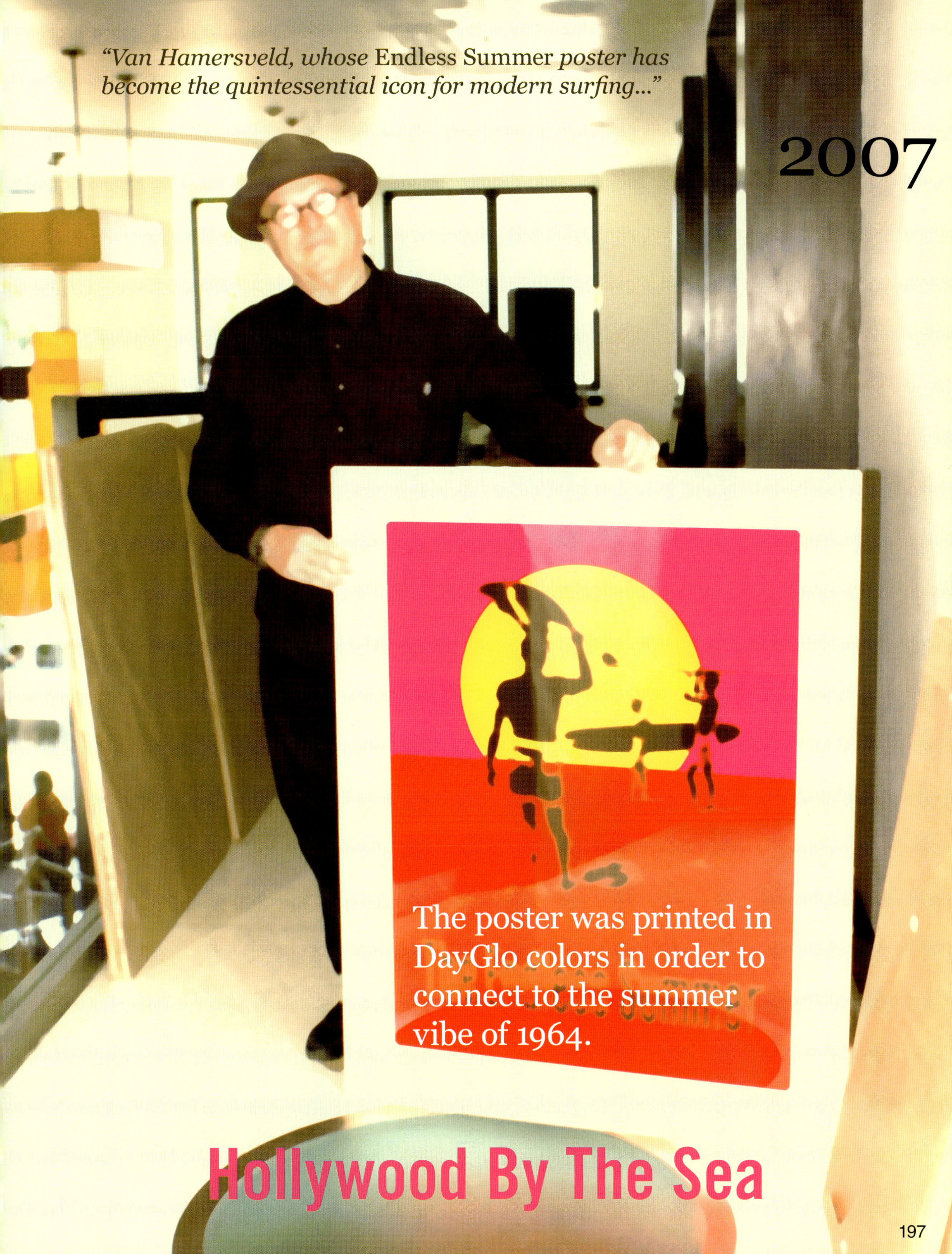

"Van Hamersveld, whose Endless Summer *poster has become the quintessential icon for modern surfing..."*

2007

The poster was printed in DayGlo colors in order to connect to the summer vibe of 1964.

Hollywood By The Sea

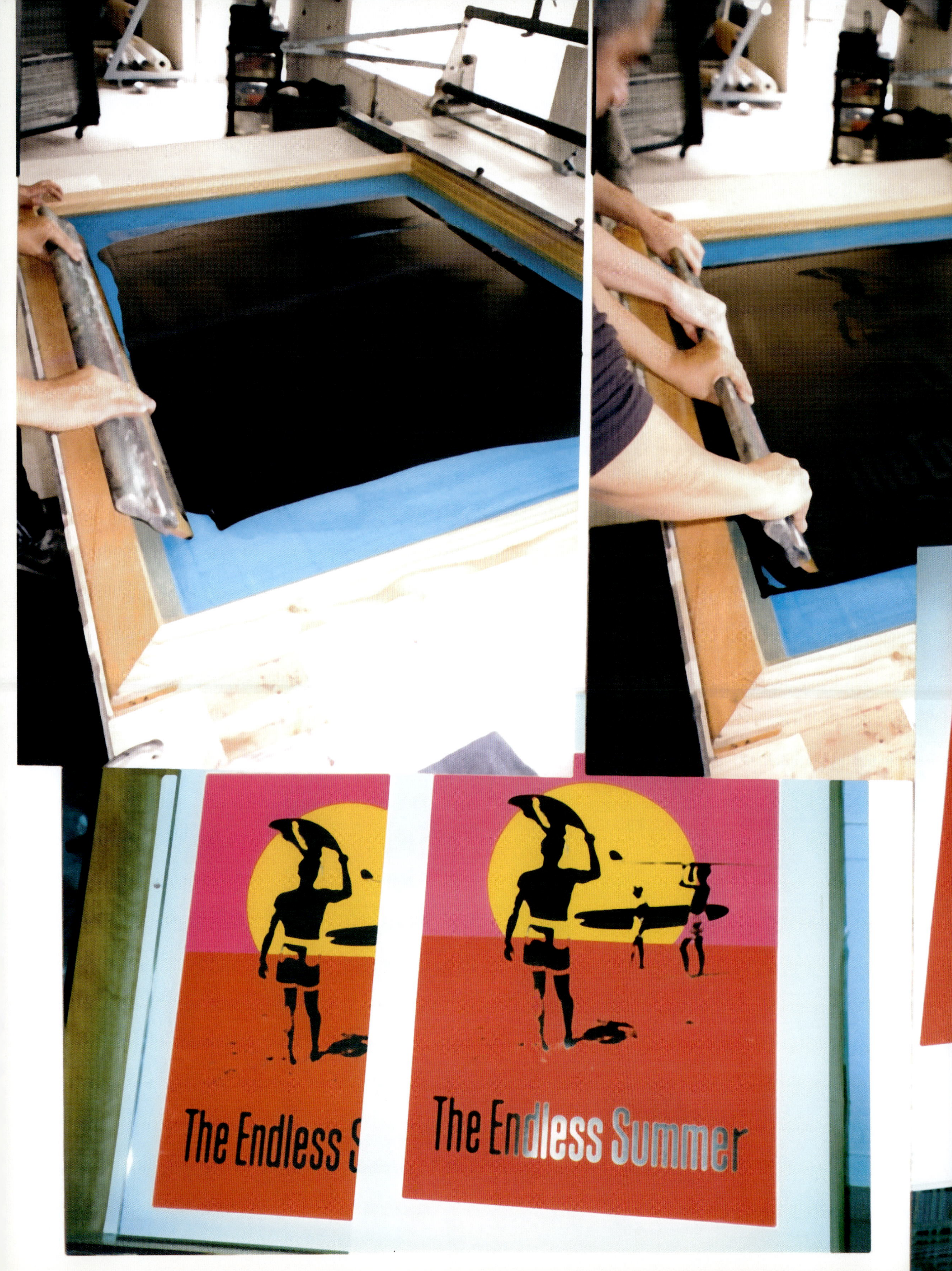

The Endless S
The Endless Summer

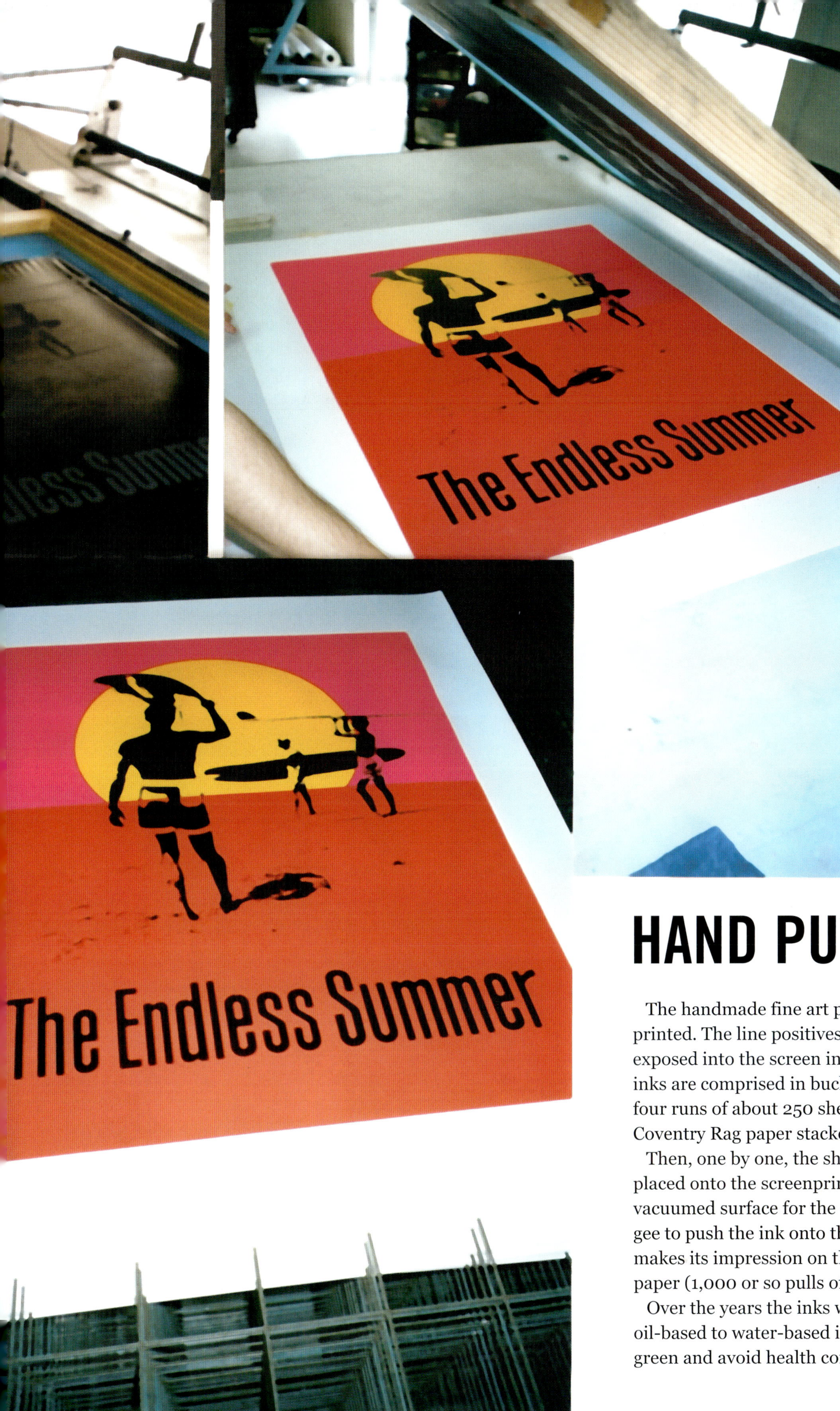

HAND PULLED

The handmade fine art print is screen printed. The line positives are created, then exposed into the screen in the frame. The inks are comprised in buckets. There are four runs of about 250 sheets of Legion Coventry Rag paper stacked in a pile.

Then, one by one, the sheets of paper are placed onto the screenprinting table's vacuumed surface for the one arm squeegee to push the ink onto the paper as it makes its impression on the 250 sheets of paper (1,000 or so pulls of the squeegee).

Over the years the inks went from being oil-based to water-based in order to go green and avoid health complications.

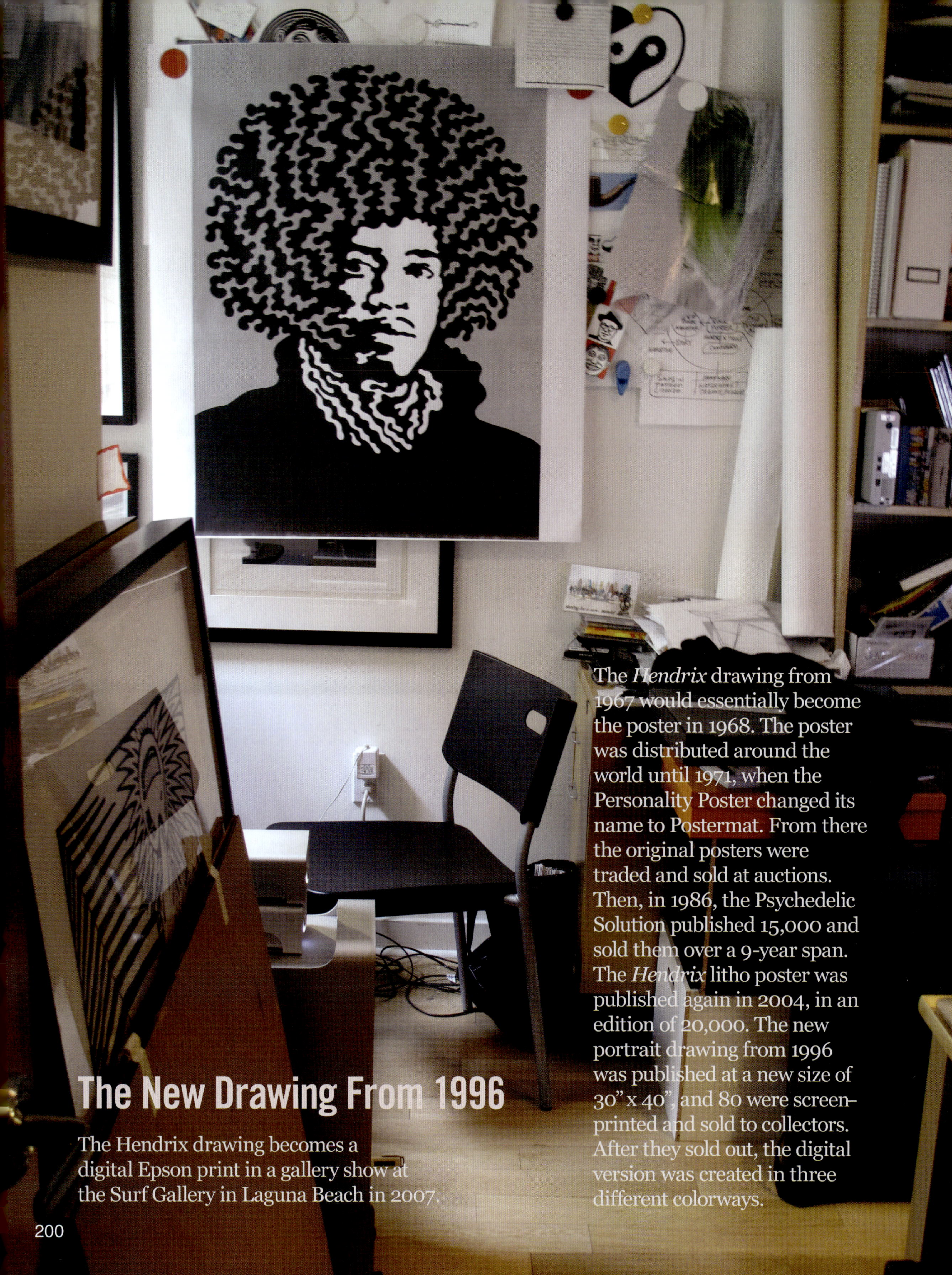

The *Hendrix* drawing from 1967 would essentially become the poster in 1968. The poster was distributed around the world until 1971, when the Personality Poster changed its name to Postermat. From there the original posters were traded and sold at auctions. Then, in 1986, the Psychedelic Solution published 15,000 and sold them over a 9-year span. The *Hendrix* litho poster was published again in 2004, in an edition of 20,000. The new portrait drawing from 1996 was published at a new size of 30" x 40", and 80 were screen-printed and sold to collectors. After they sold out, the digital version was created in three different colorways.

The New Drawing From 1996

The Hendrix drawing becomes a digital Epson print in a gallery show at the Surf Gallery in Laguna Beach in 2007.

Chetwynd Stapylton Fine Art Gallery

PAST MEETS PRESENT AT THE PORTLAND GALLERY (2002)

The New Drawing Becomes Gallery Art

The 19" x 27" Hendrix poster *(1968) is placed in the window alongside both the Beatles'* Magical Mystery Tour *(1967) and the Rolling Stones'* Exile on Main Street *(1972) album covers.*

The Plains Indians held beliefs in multiple deities. They believed that these deities materialized into multiple forms, such as the sun, moon, stars, and anything particularly unusual, like an animal, human, or even a uniquely shaped stone. The Indian men received this god-like power through a series of visions. In order to receive a vision, the Indian would journey into a state of seclusion—total isolation for several days without any form of sustenance. Over time, this isolated state resulted in meaningful visions and the title “Shaman” was given to those who received multiple visual manifestations. These men became known as soothsayers and healers.

2003

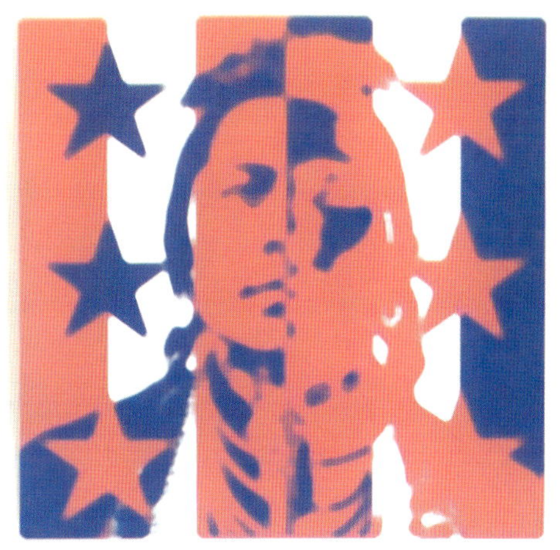

THE NATIVE AMERICAN STUDY

Coolhous Studio, Santa Monica

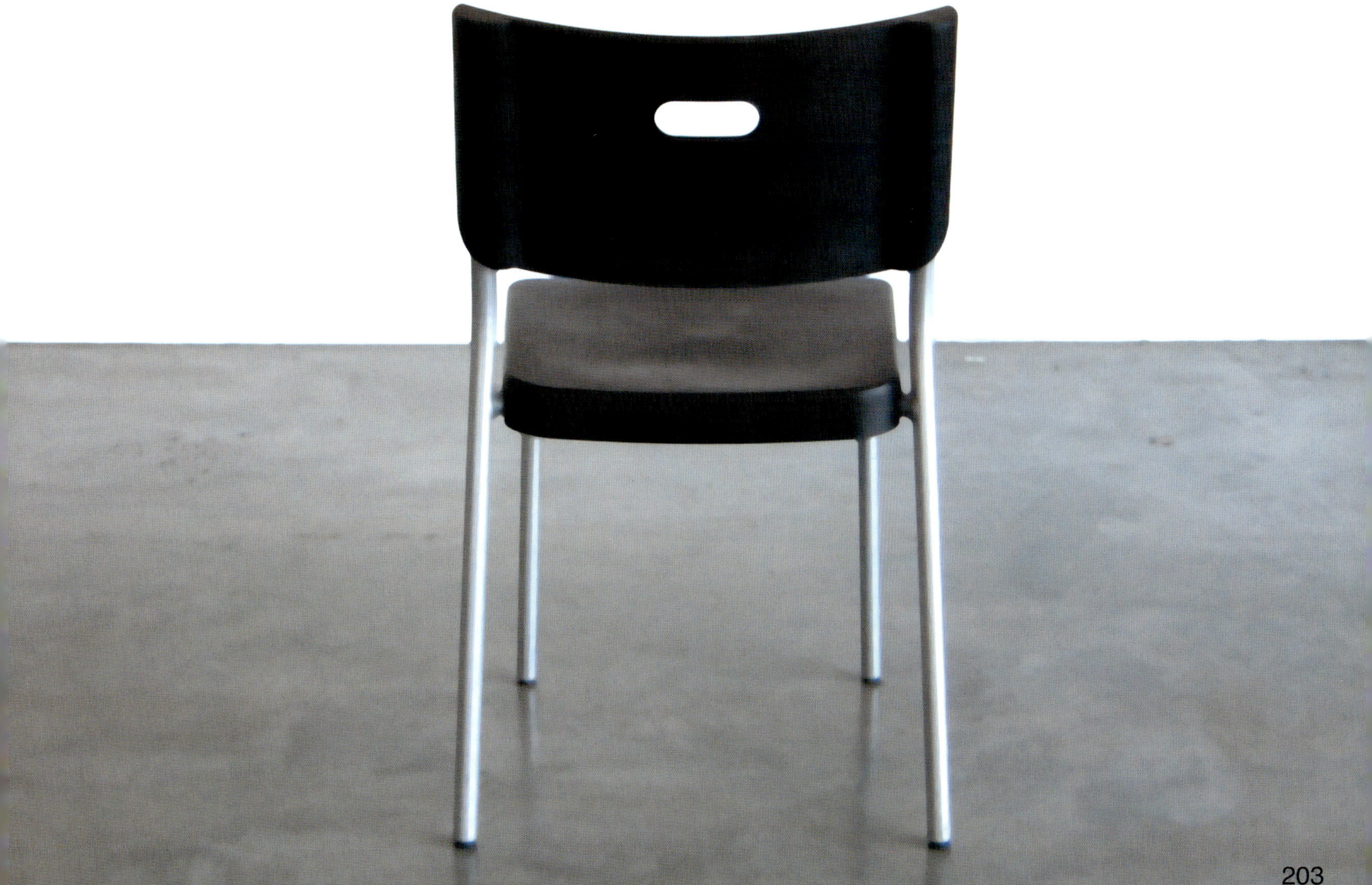

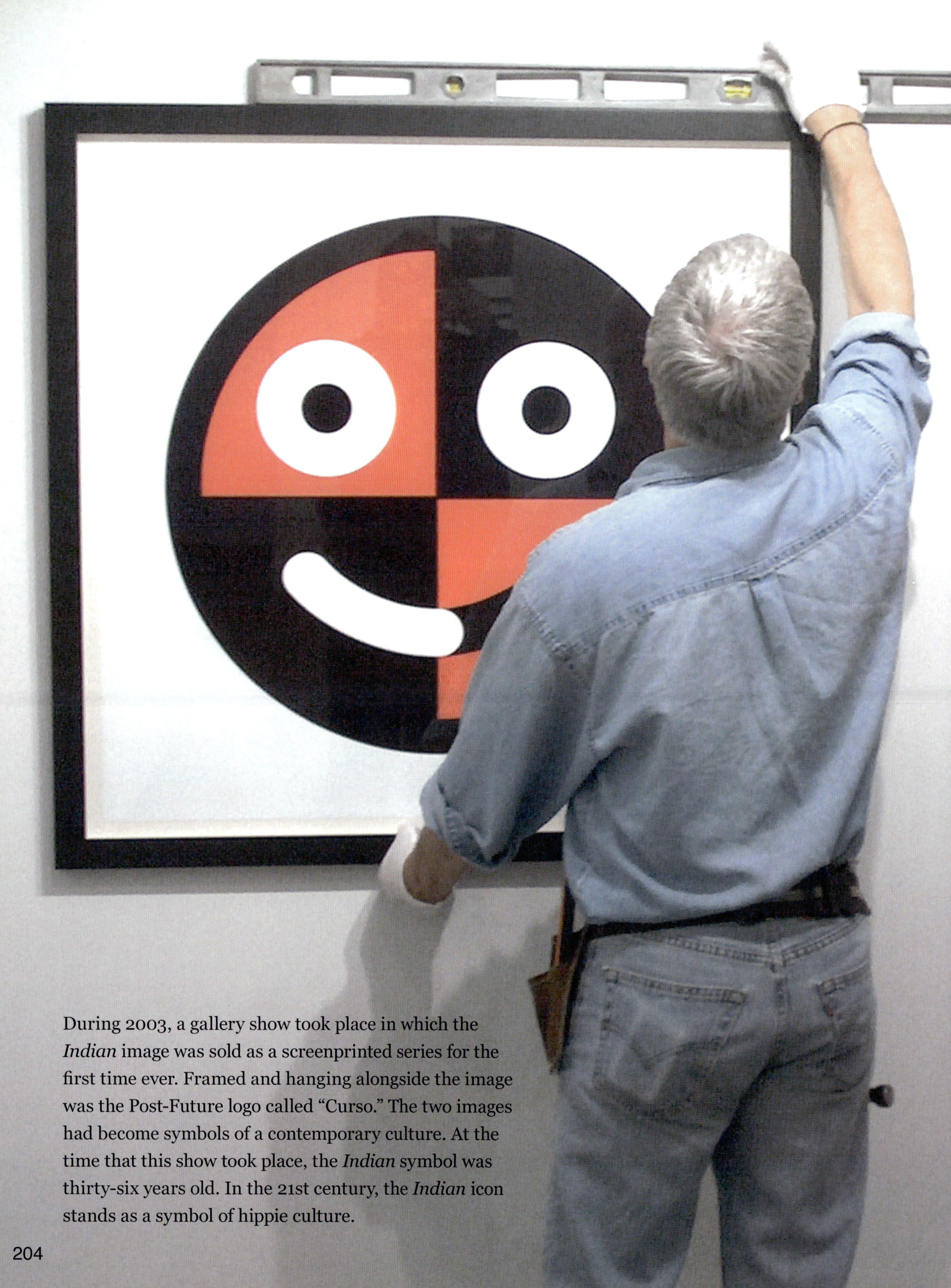

During 2003, a gallery show took place in which the *Indian* image was sold as a screenprinted series for the first time ever. Framed and hanging alongside the image was the Post-Future logo called "Curso." The two images had become symbols of a contemporary culture. At the time that this show took place, the *Indian* symbol was thirty-six years old. In the 21st century, the *Indian* icon stands as a symbol of hippie culture.

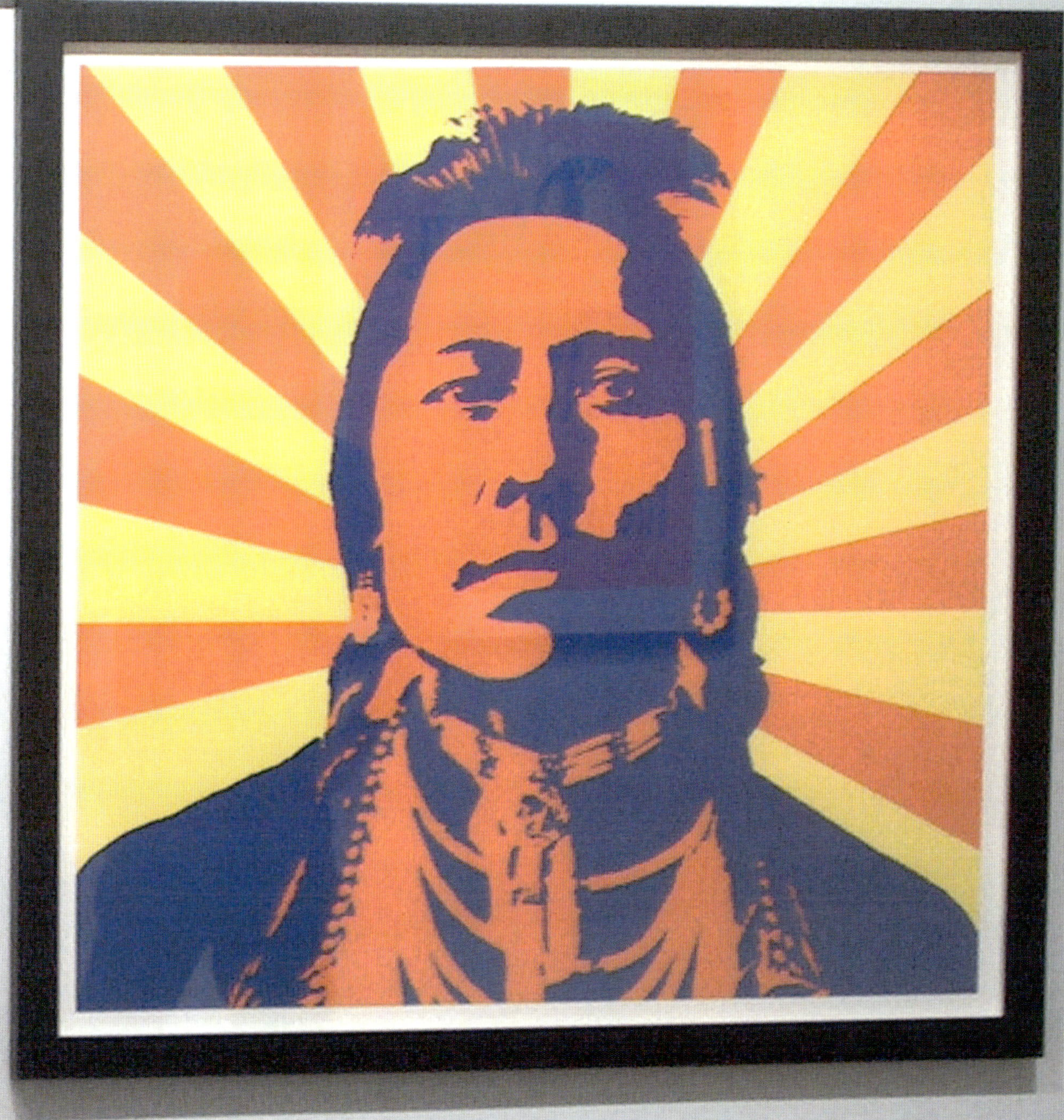

Gallery Installations

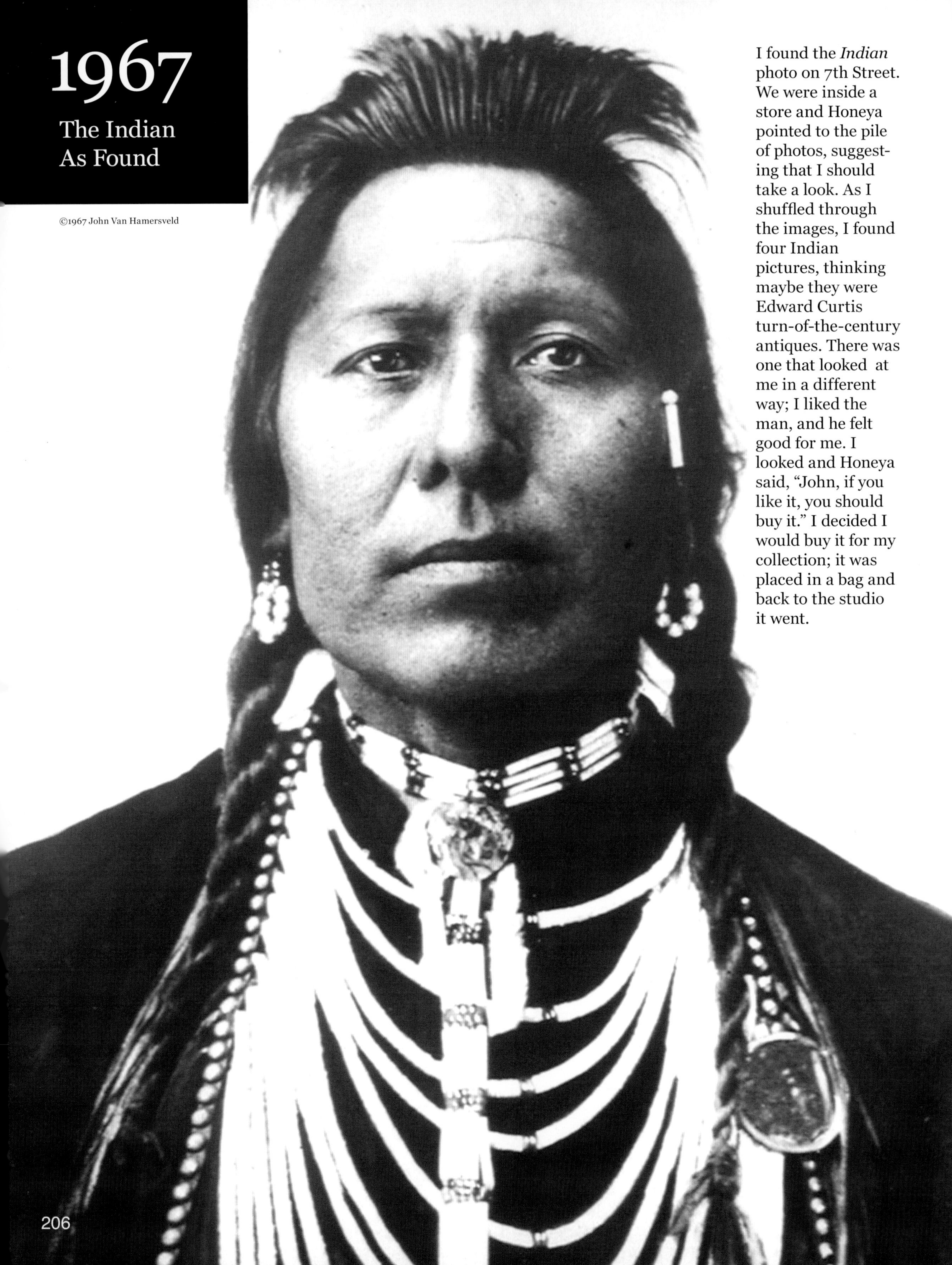

1967

The Indian As Found

I found the *Indian* photo on 7th Street. We were inside a store and Honeya pointed to the pile of photos, suggesting that I should take a look. As I shuffled through the images, I found four Indian pictures, thinking maybe they were Edward Curtis turn-of-the-century antiques. There was one that looked at me in a different way; I liked the man, and he felt good for me. I looked and Honeya said, "John, if you like it, you should buy it." I decided I would buy it for my collection; it was placed in a bag and back to the studio it went.

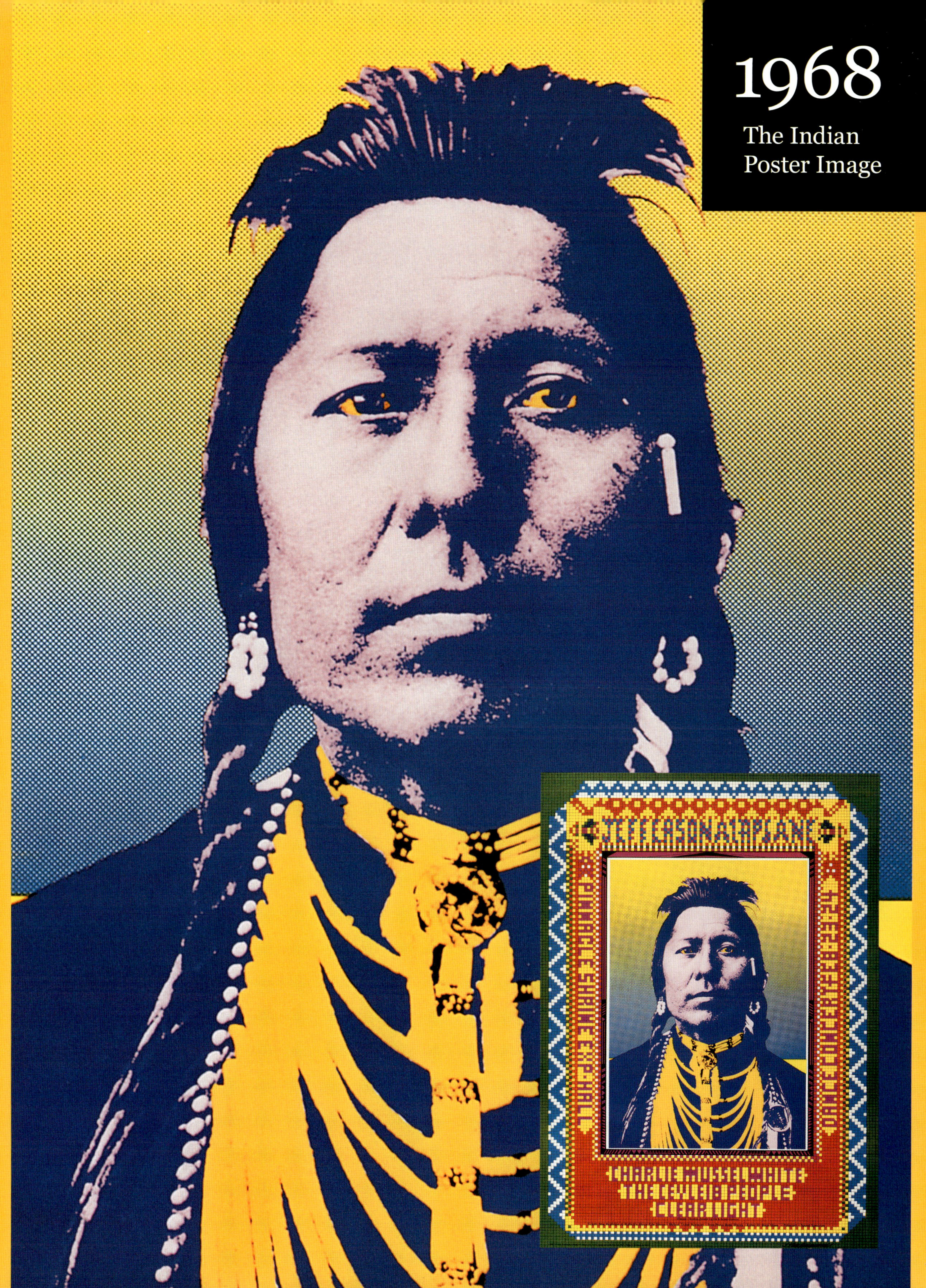

1968

The Indian Poster Image

1968

The Indian Poster/Print

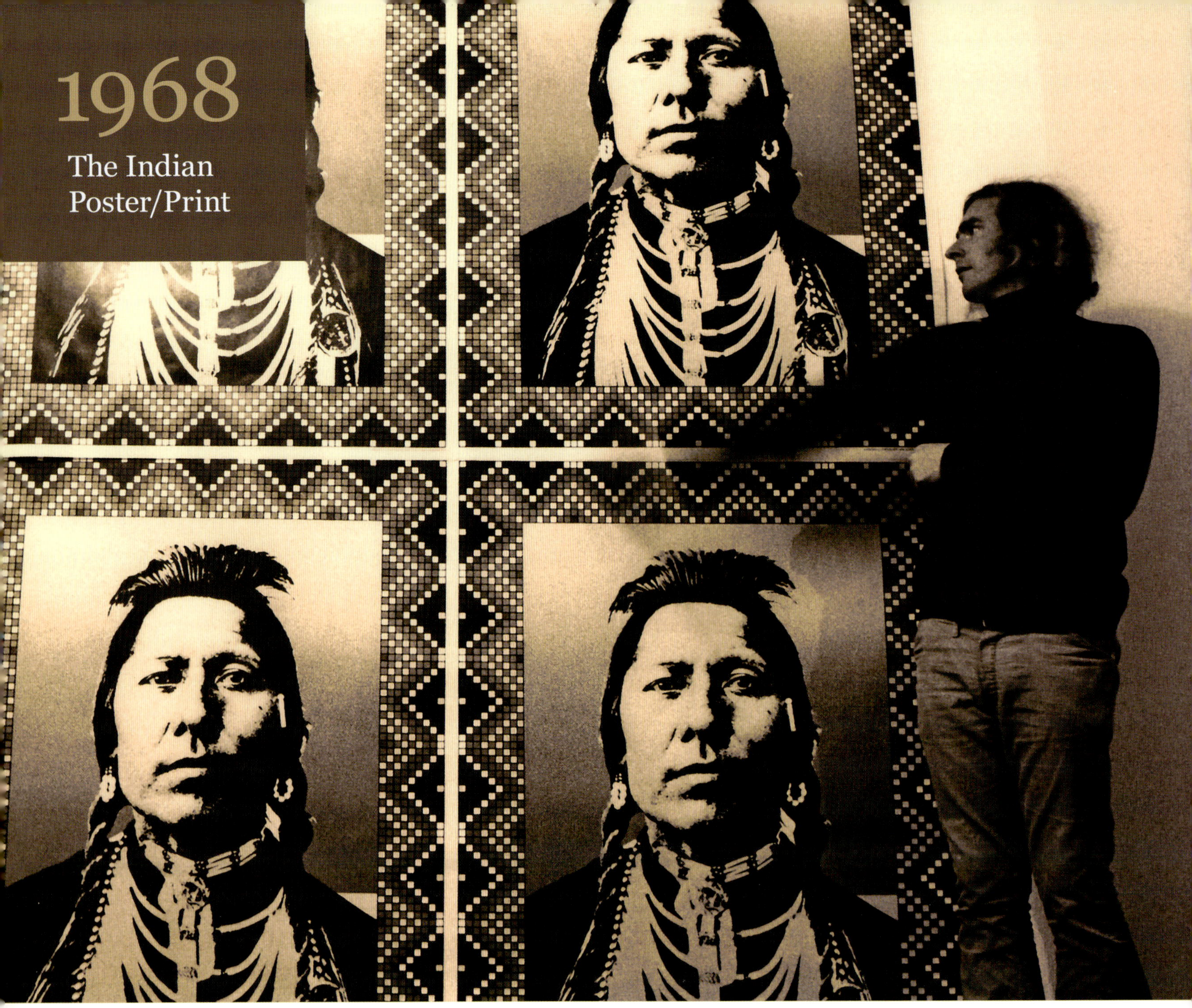

These *Pinnacle Indian* prints were originally photographed by the artist Ron Cooper. The original print was made up at the Hugo Meyer Show printing plant in 1968. Later, there was a second edition made in 1970 that was used by a jeans company. During November of 1968, I was in New York for a Thanksgiving vacation and gave the *Indian* image to Andy Warhol. The print that I gave him is now a part of the Warhol Foundation collection.

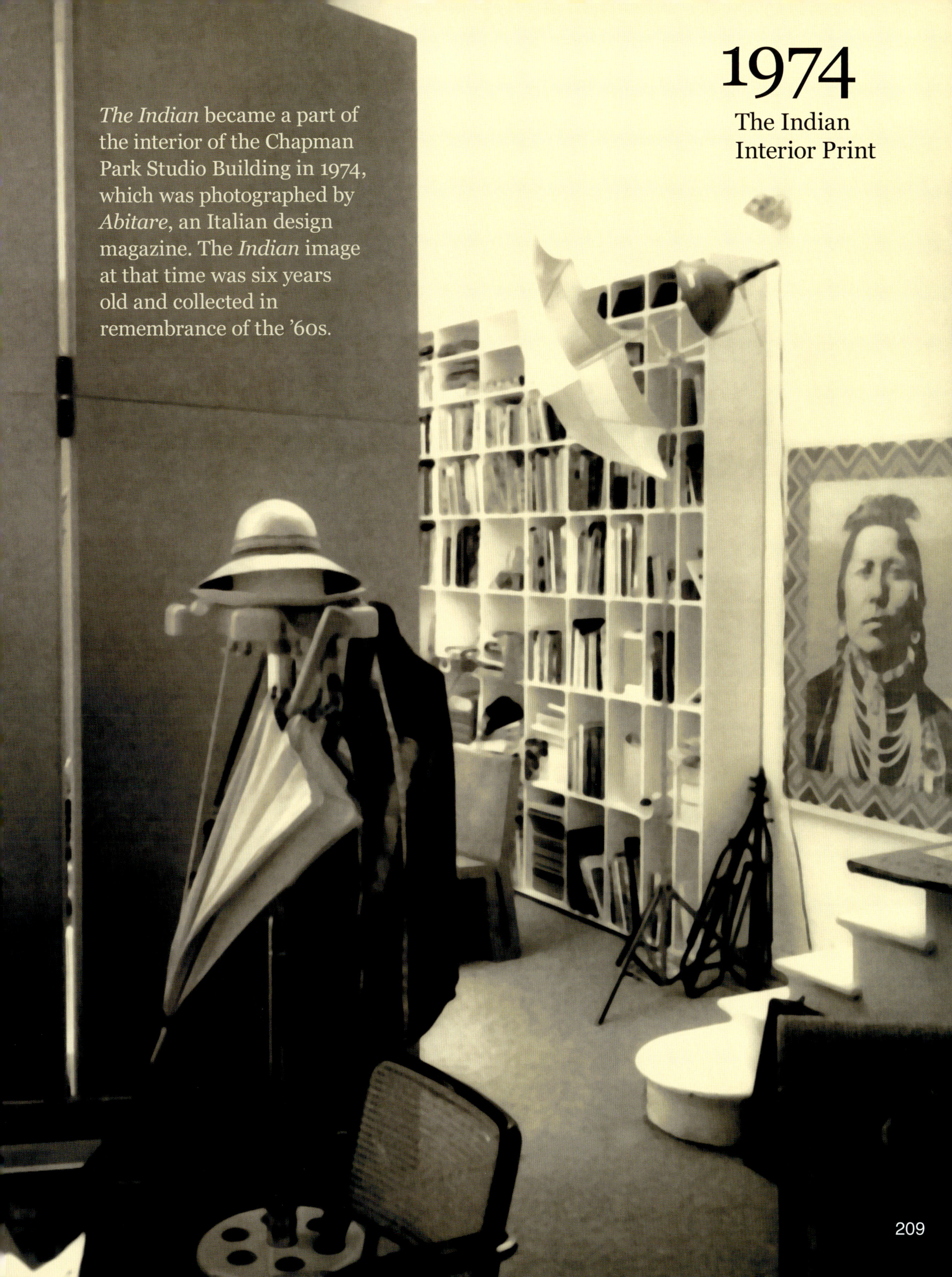

1974
The Indian Interior Print

The Indian became a part of the interior of the Chapman Park Studio Building in 1974, which was photographed by *Abitare*, an Italian design magazine. The *Indian* image at that time was six years old and collected in remembrance of the '60s.

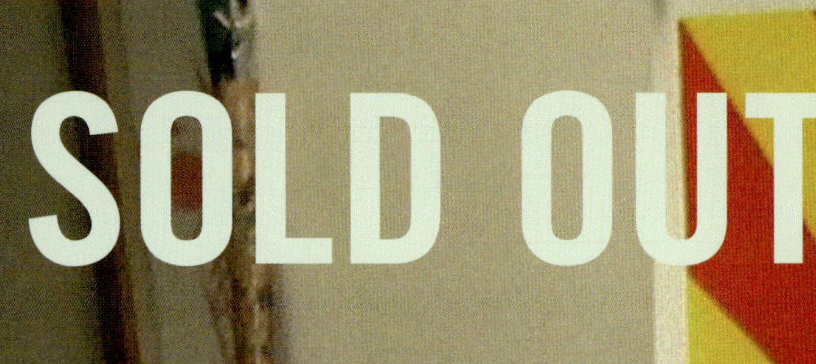

SOLD OUT

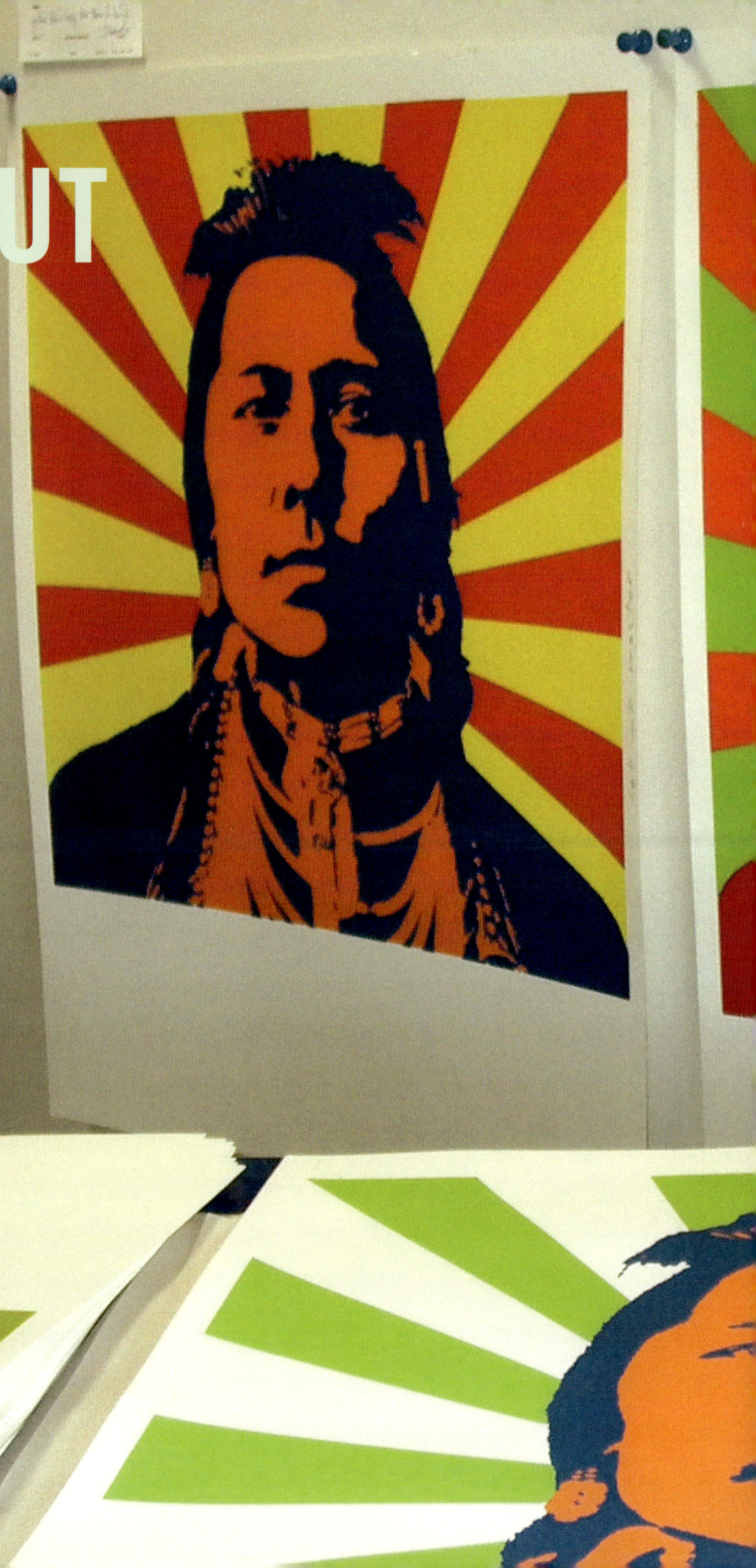

The Native American

The screenprinted *Indian* print is 35.5 x 35.5 inches in size, printed in four colors, in an edition of 30 (very limited availability). As the t-shirt of the *Indian* print continued to sell through the Worn Free company in stores around the world, the print value stayed high as a product. The image as a design combines the ray background and Indian head to create a spiritual feel and hint of rebellion for the now collectible print. The wearable art idea was loved by women all around—especially in red and black.

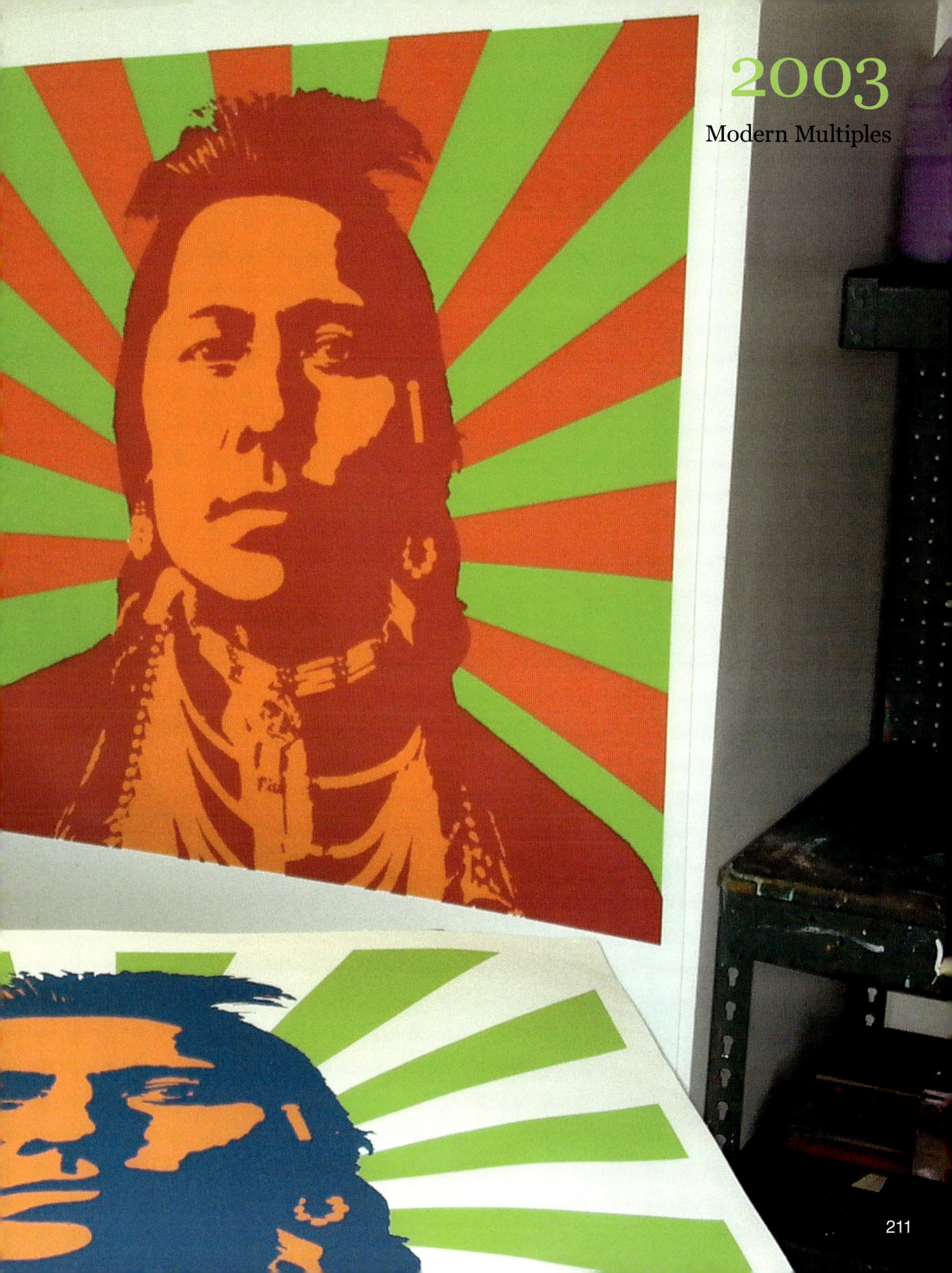

2003

Modern Multiples

2009

Printmaking American Image

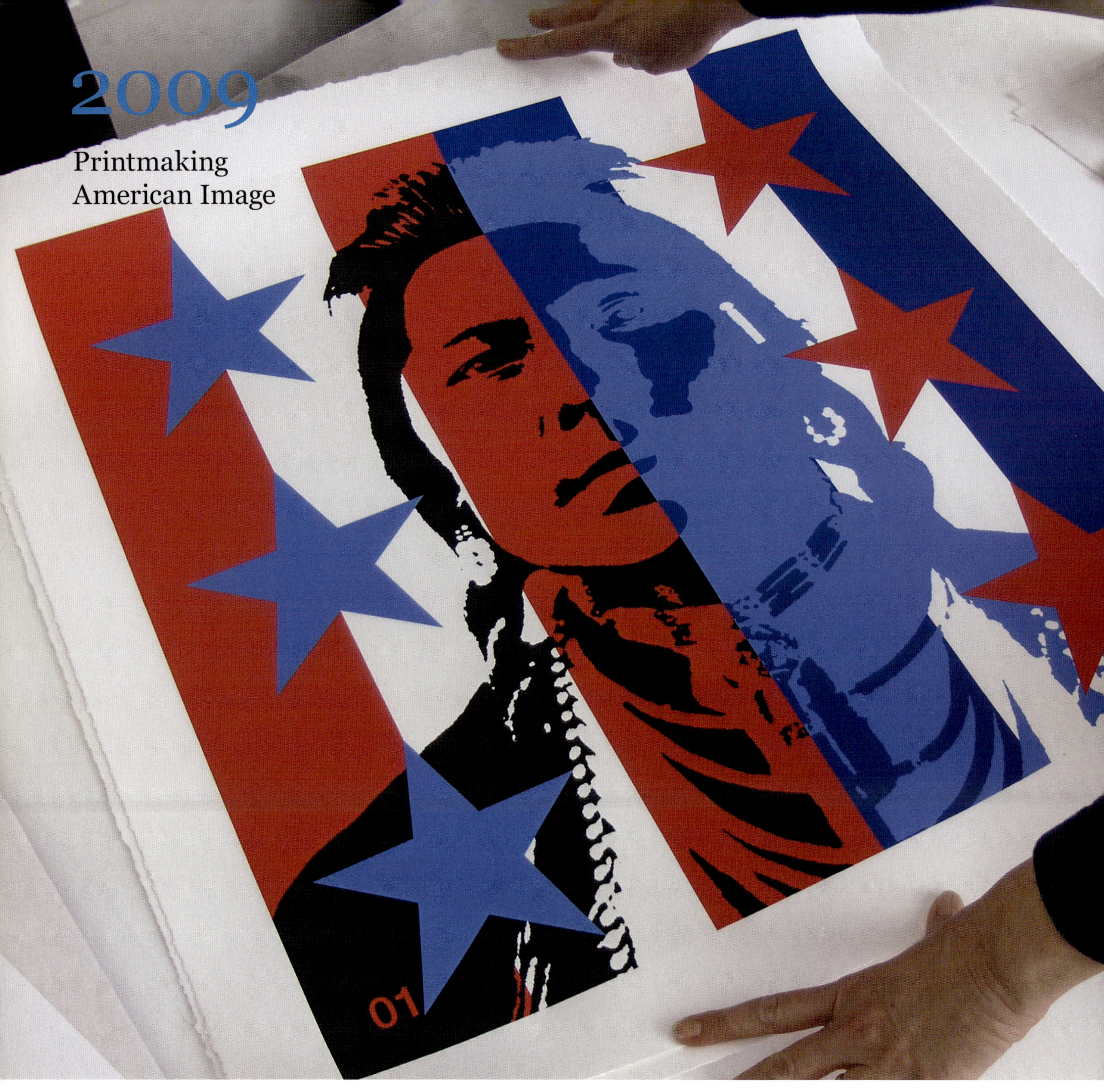

The twelve digital Indian images were created using Adobe Illustrator on a G4 Macintosh computer in 2002. The edition was printed as a digital fine art print. The square juxtaposes the American flag against Thundercloud, who lived in rebellion against the US government. I call it *Indian Number One*.

Shepard Fairey hosted the Subliminal Projects gallery event on March 5, 2009 in Echo Park. This was the debut of these Indians. In my studies of Native American culture, I learned that often Indians would decorate their structures with colored stripes and designs. The twelve digital Indians were decorated in a way that was supposed to reference that tradition.

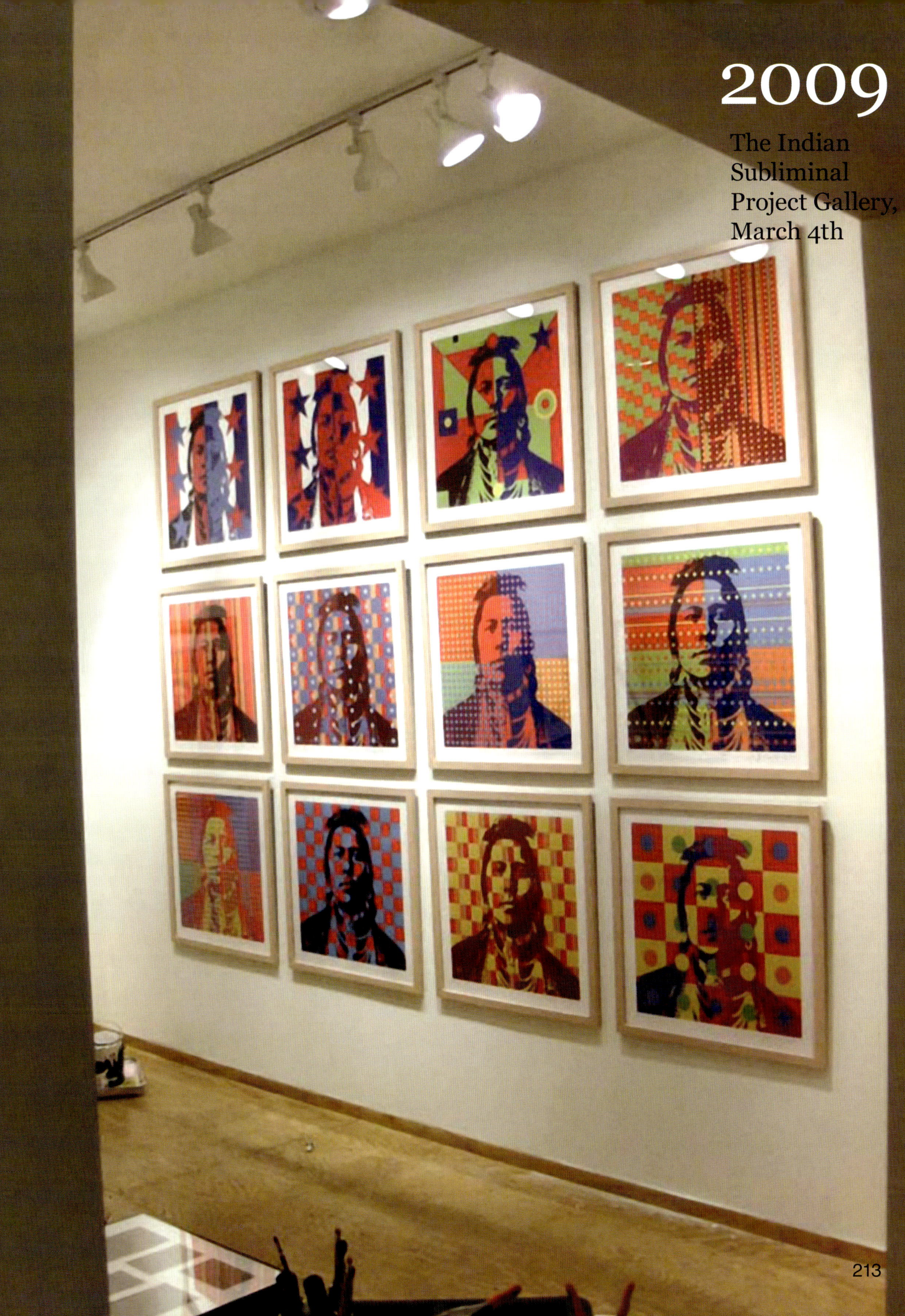

2009

The Indian Subliminal Project Gallery, March 4th

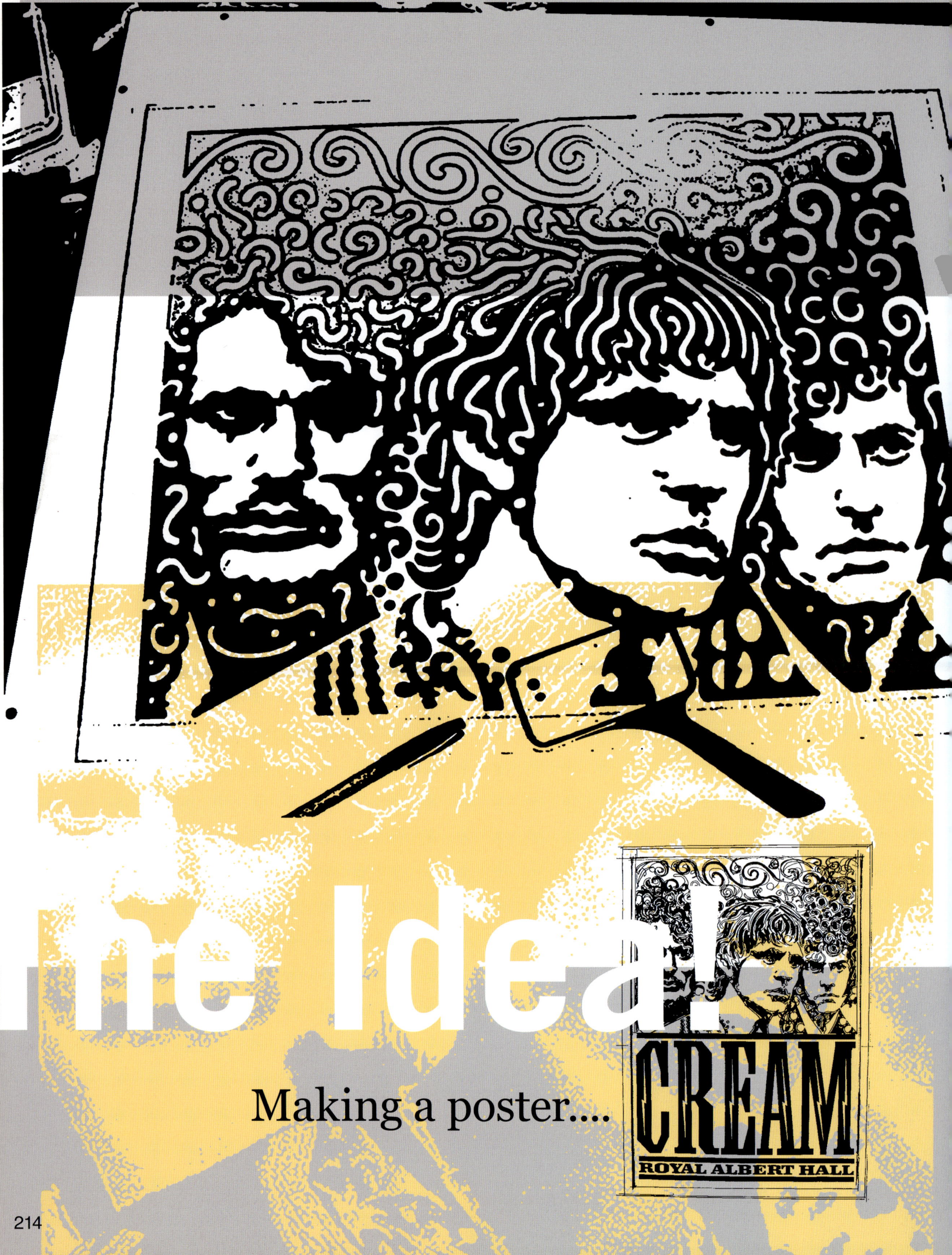

The Idea!

Making a poster....

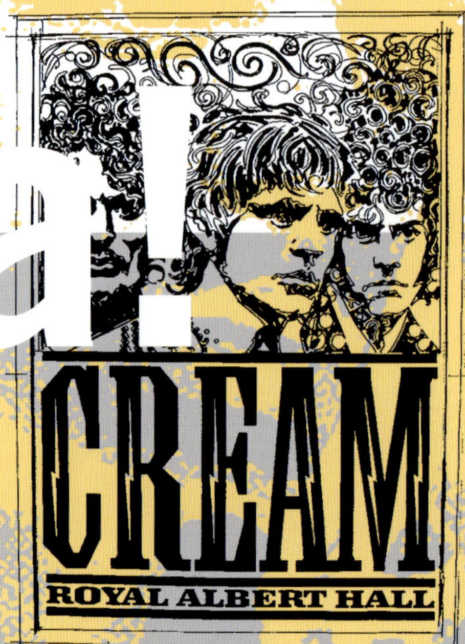

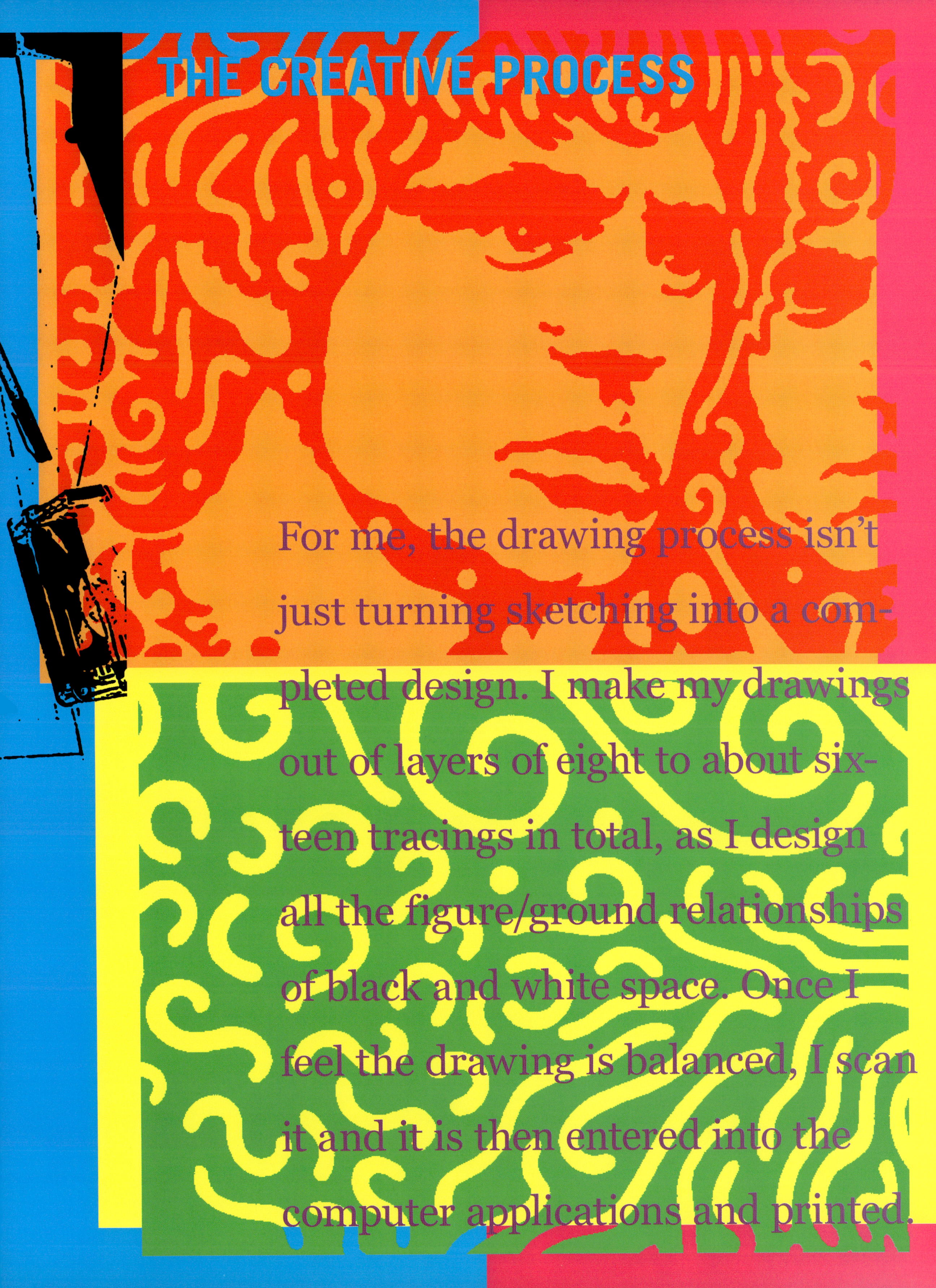

For me, the drawing process isn't just turning sketching into a completed design. I make my drawings out of layers of eight to about sixteen tracings in total, as I design all the figure/ground relationships of black and white space. Once I feel the drawing is balanced, I scan it and it is then entered into the computer applications and printed.

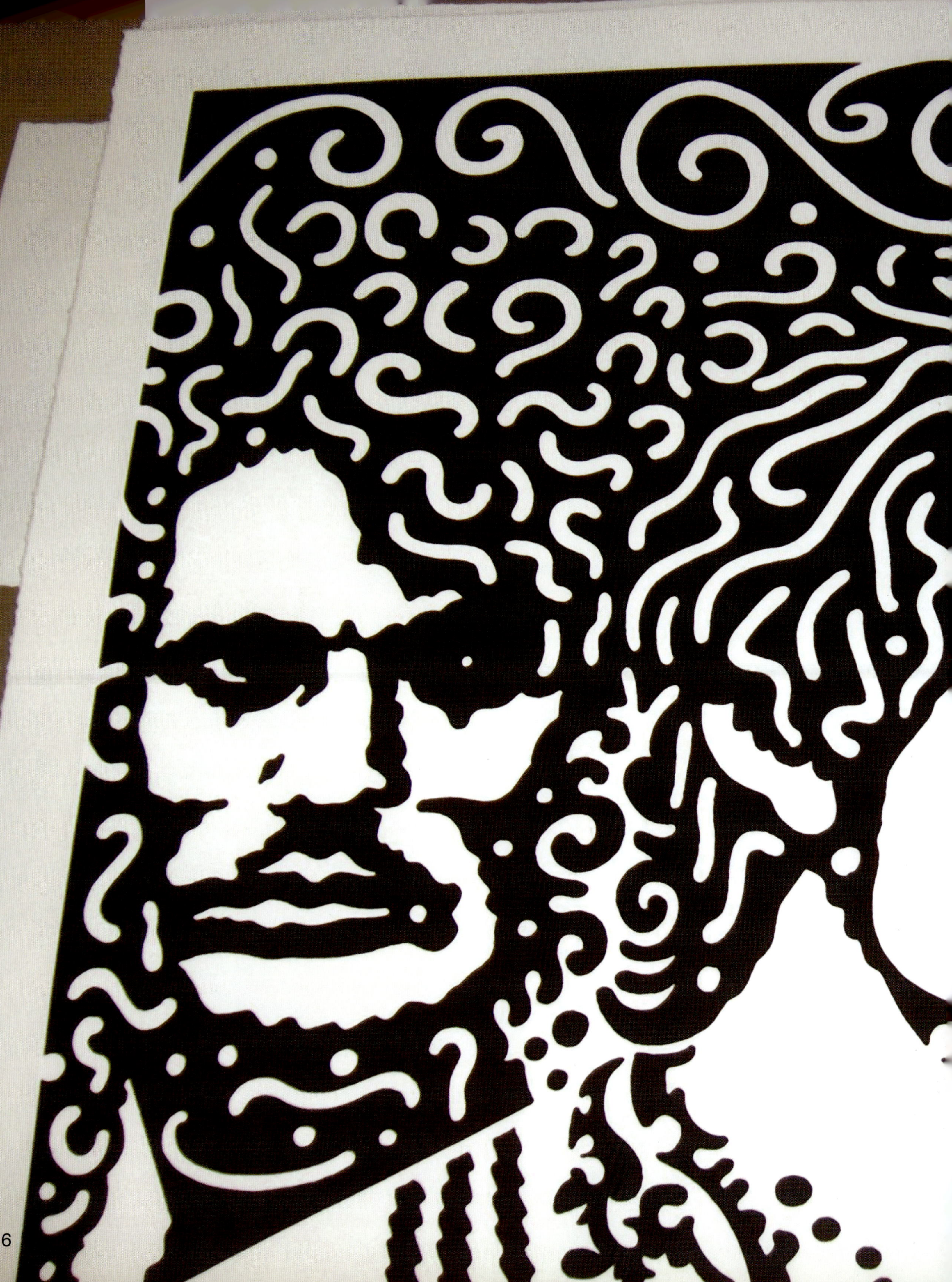

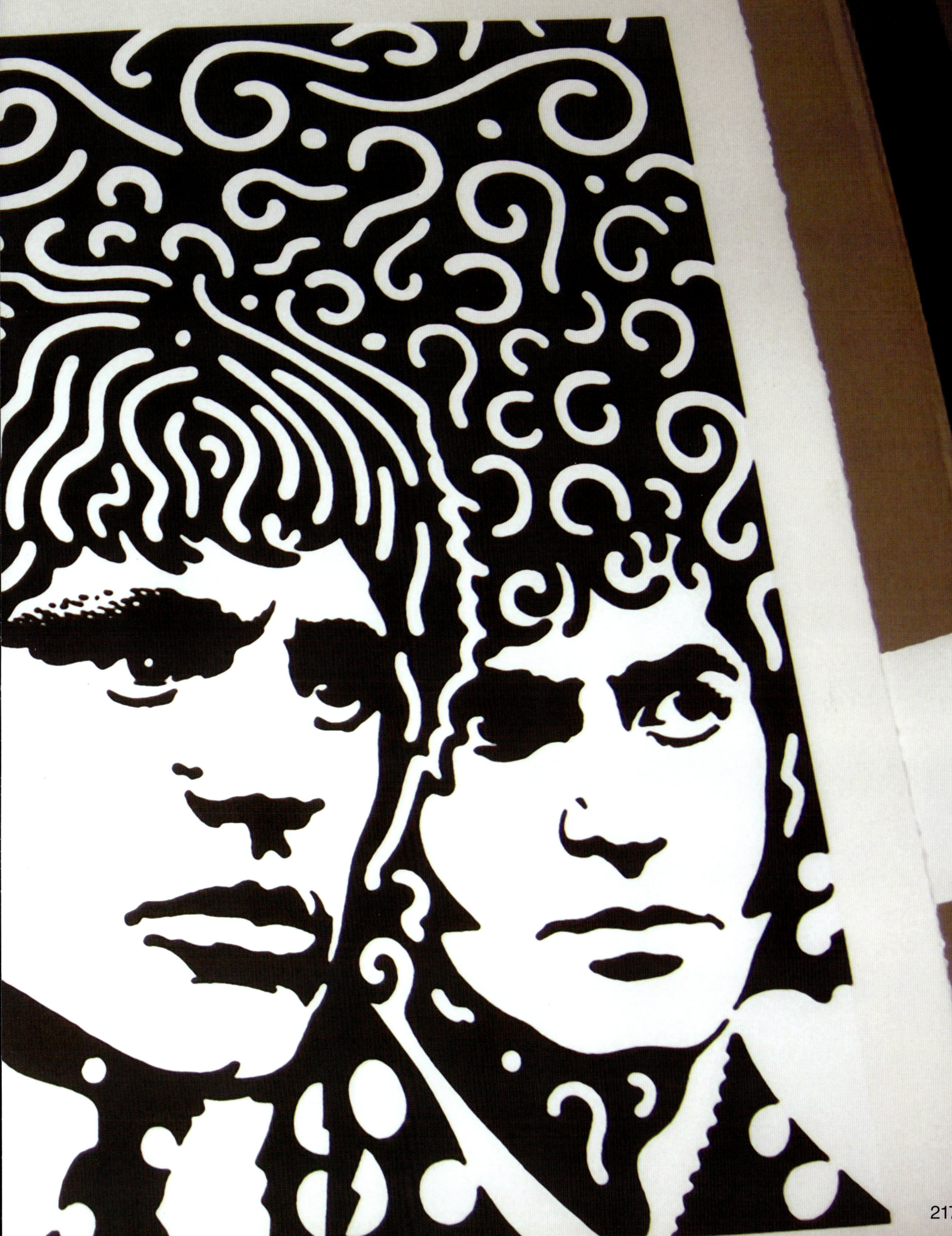

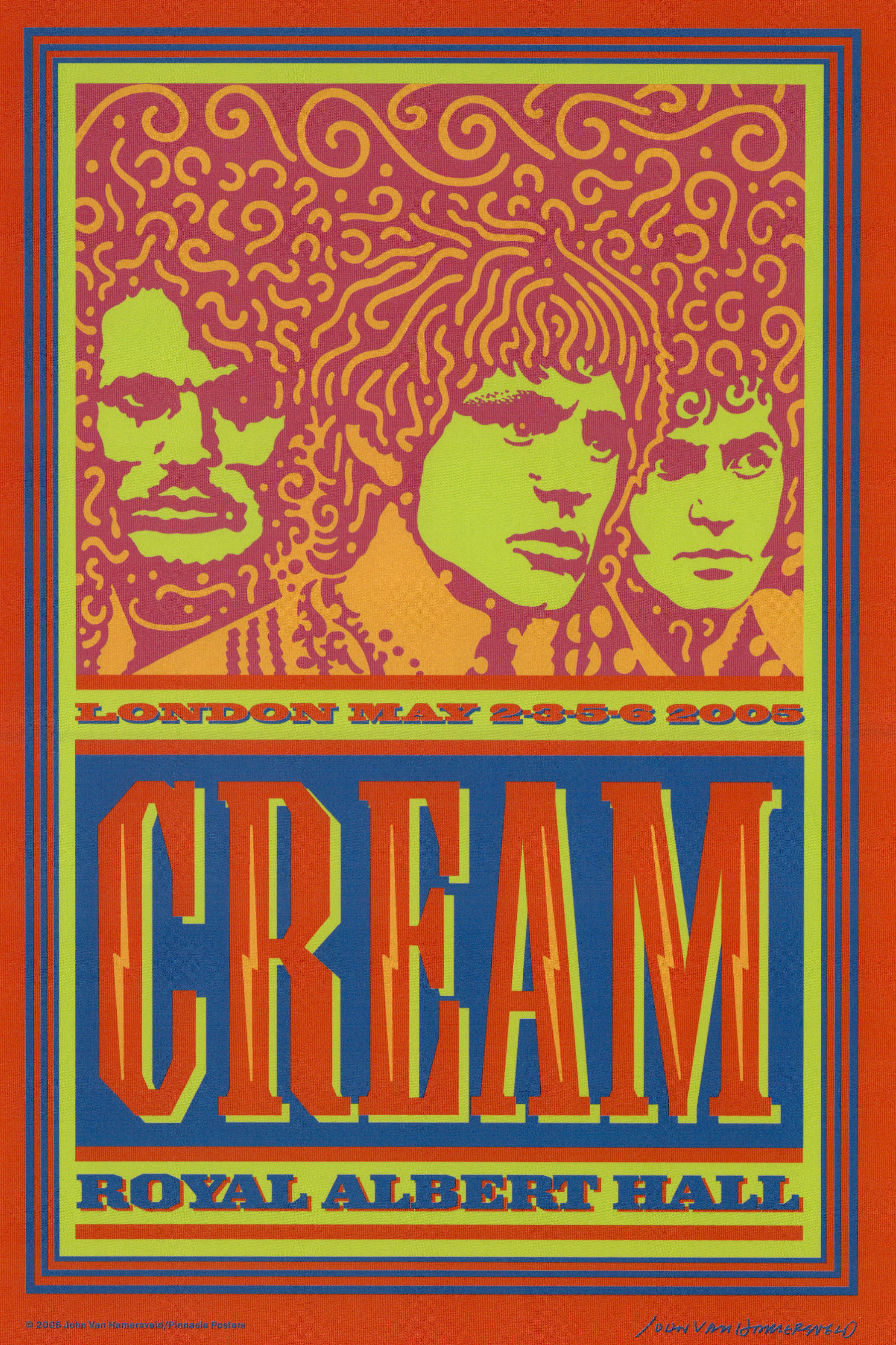
LONDON MAY 2-3-5-6 2005
CREAM
ROYAL ALBERT HALL
© 2005 John Van Hamersveld/Pinnacle Posters
John Van Hamersveld

THE CLAPTON POSTERS 2005–2010

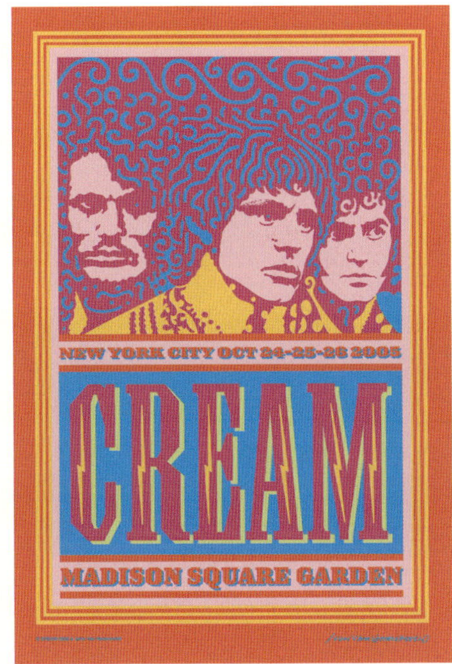

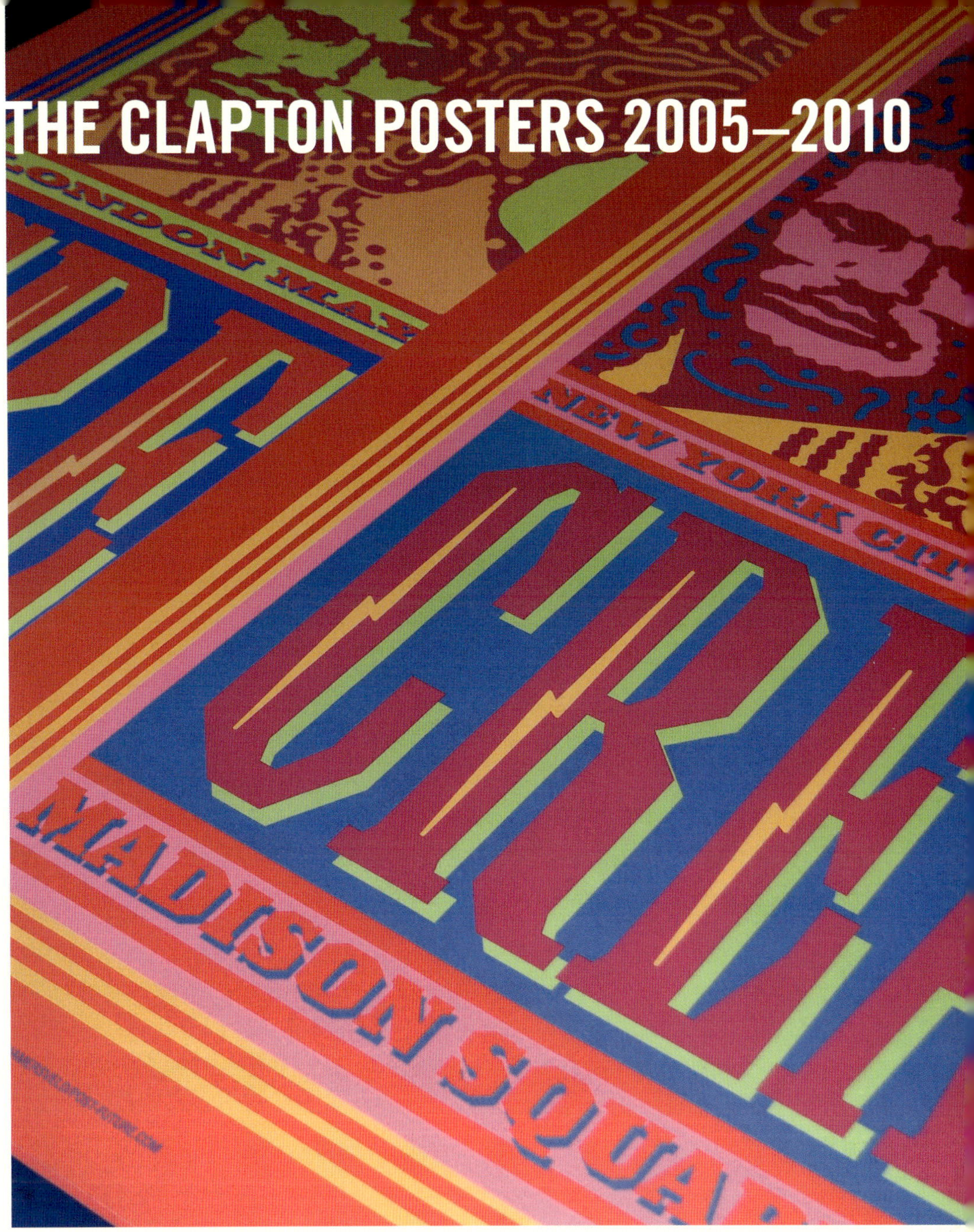

The rediscovery of the *Pinnacle Hendrix* poster in 2004 led to a 24" x 36" production of the *Cream Reunion Concert* poster in 2005 that sold out within 15 minutes of the first day at the Royal Albert Hall. As a result, more were made for the four day event and the new retail price of $70.00 for each poster created a new value for my poster work. Between 2007 to 2010, more poster designs followed over the years during the Clapton and Winwood tours throughout the world.

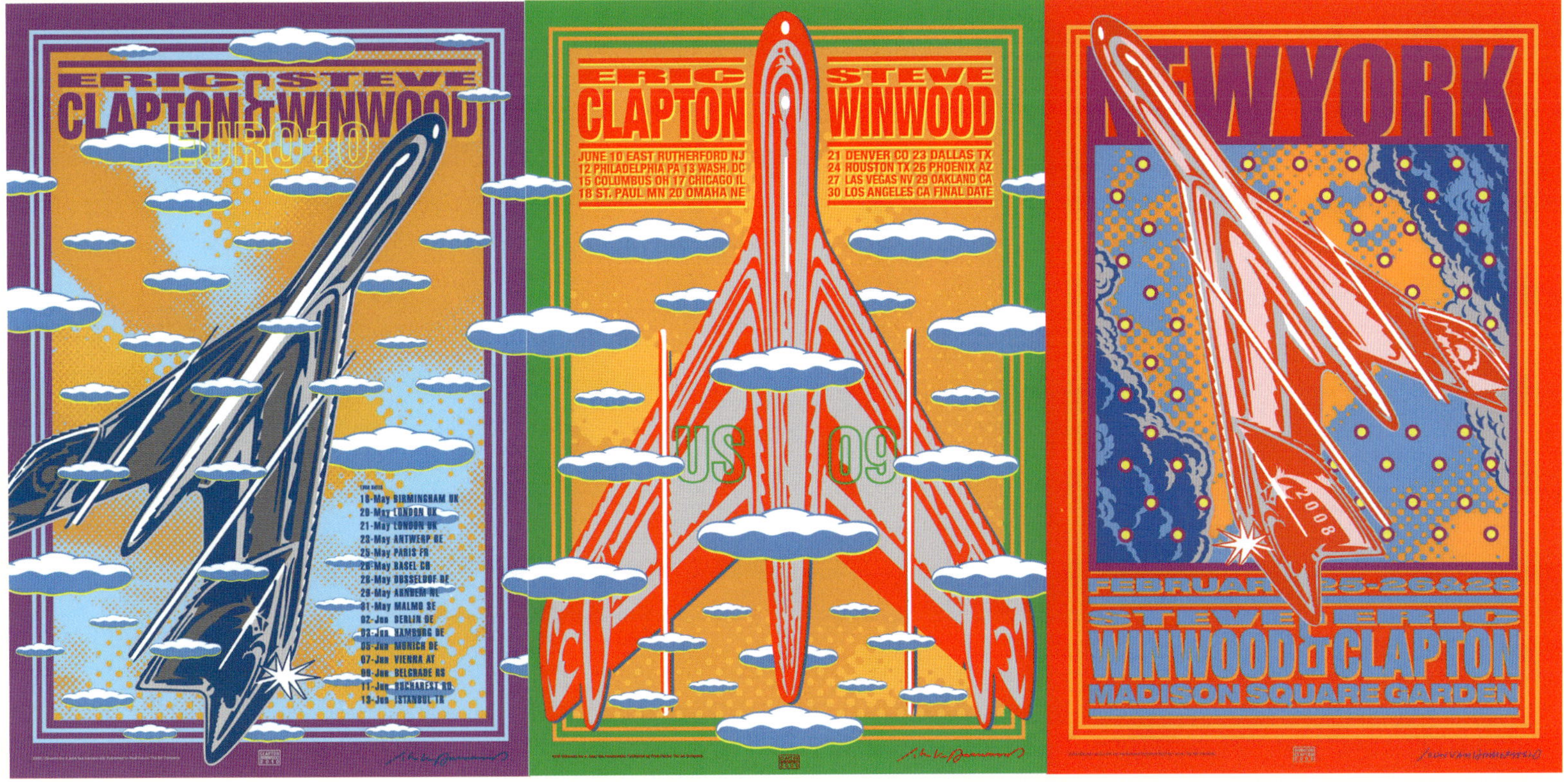

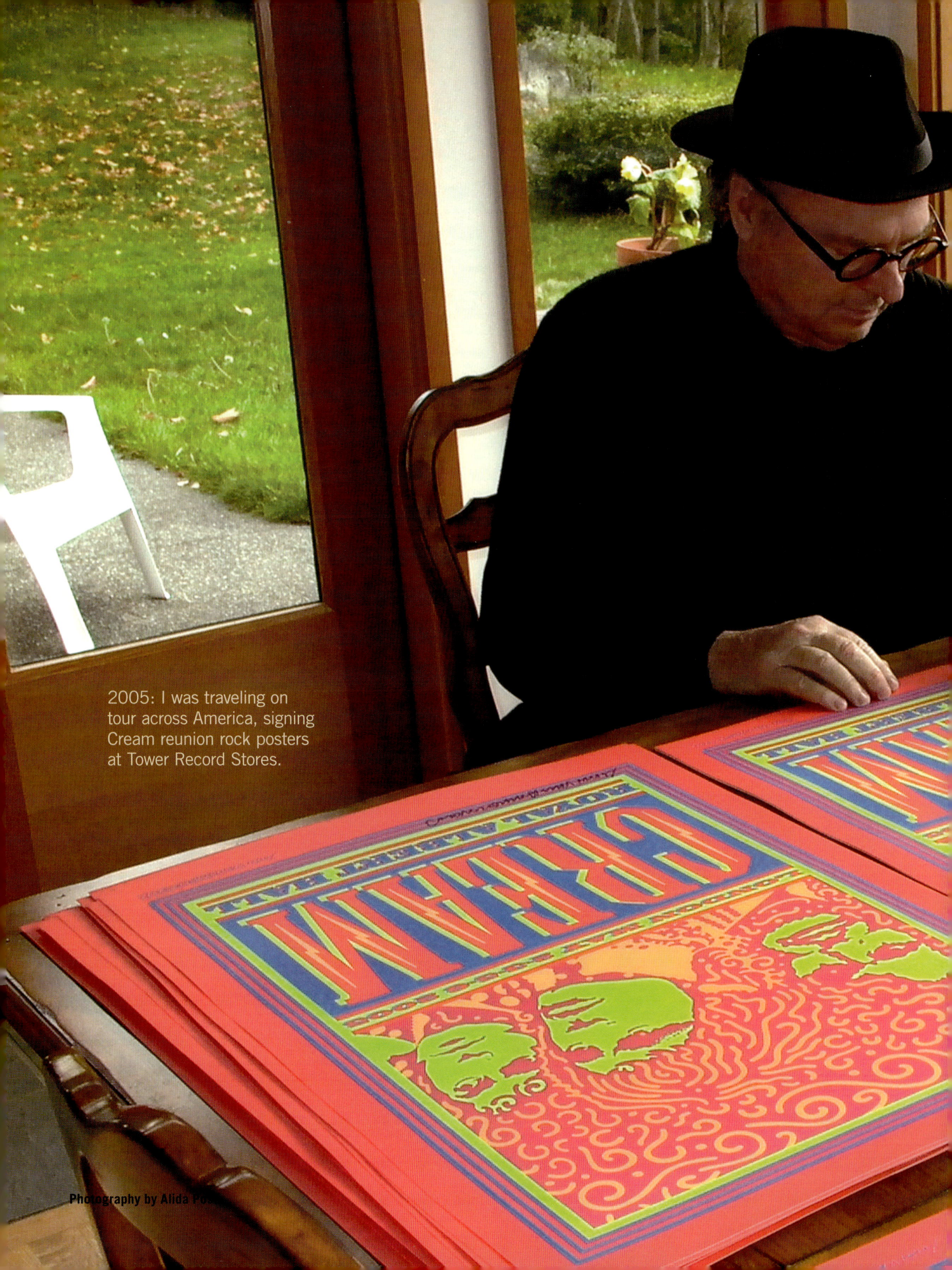

2005: I was traveling on tour across America, signing Cream reunion rock posters at Tower Record Stores.

Photography by Alida Pos

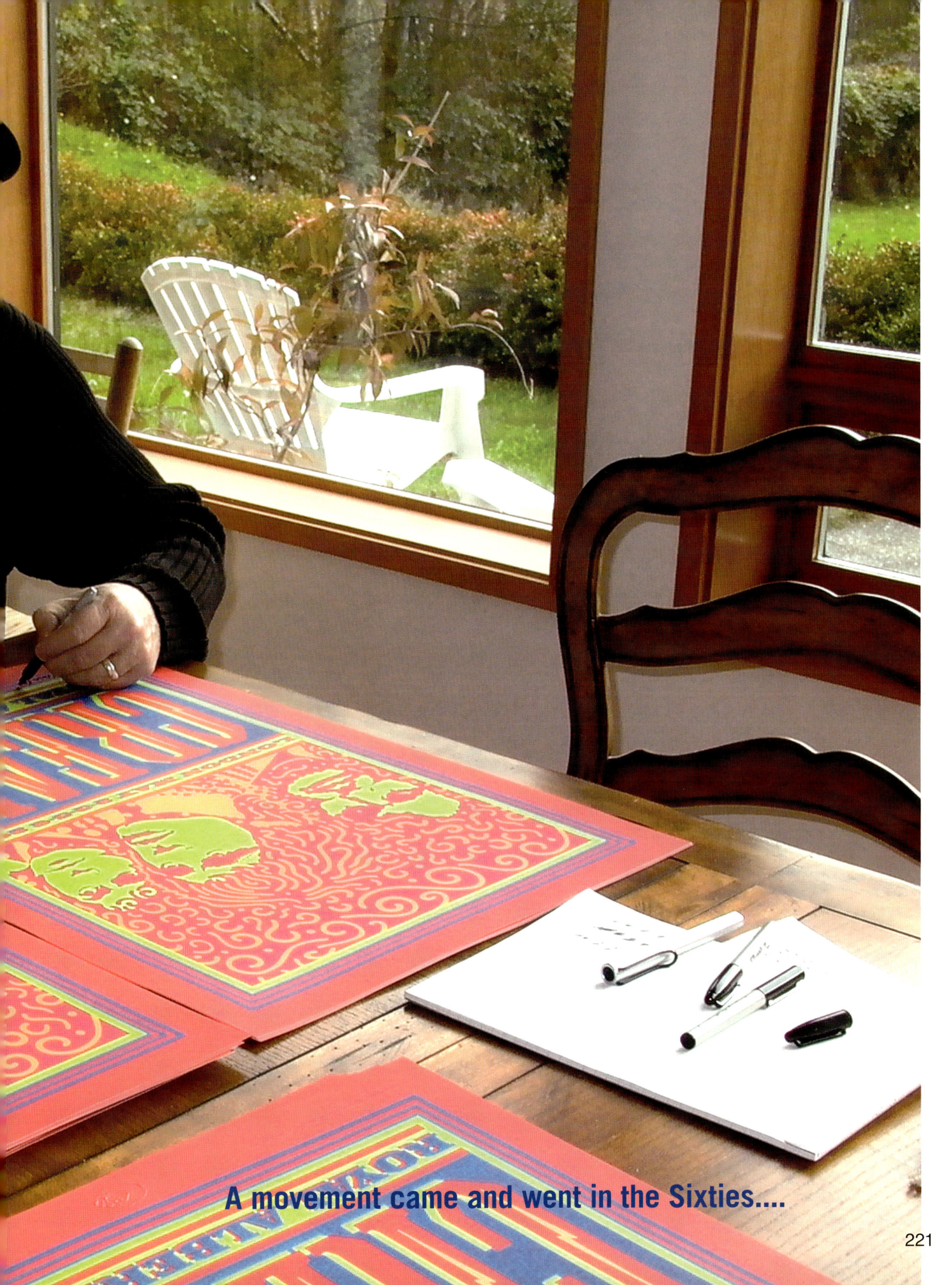

A movement came and went in the Sixties....

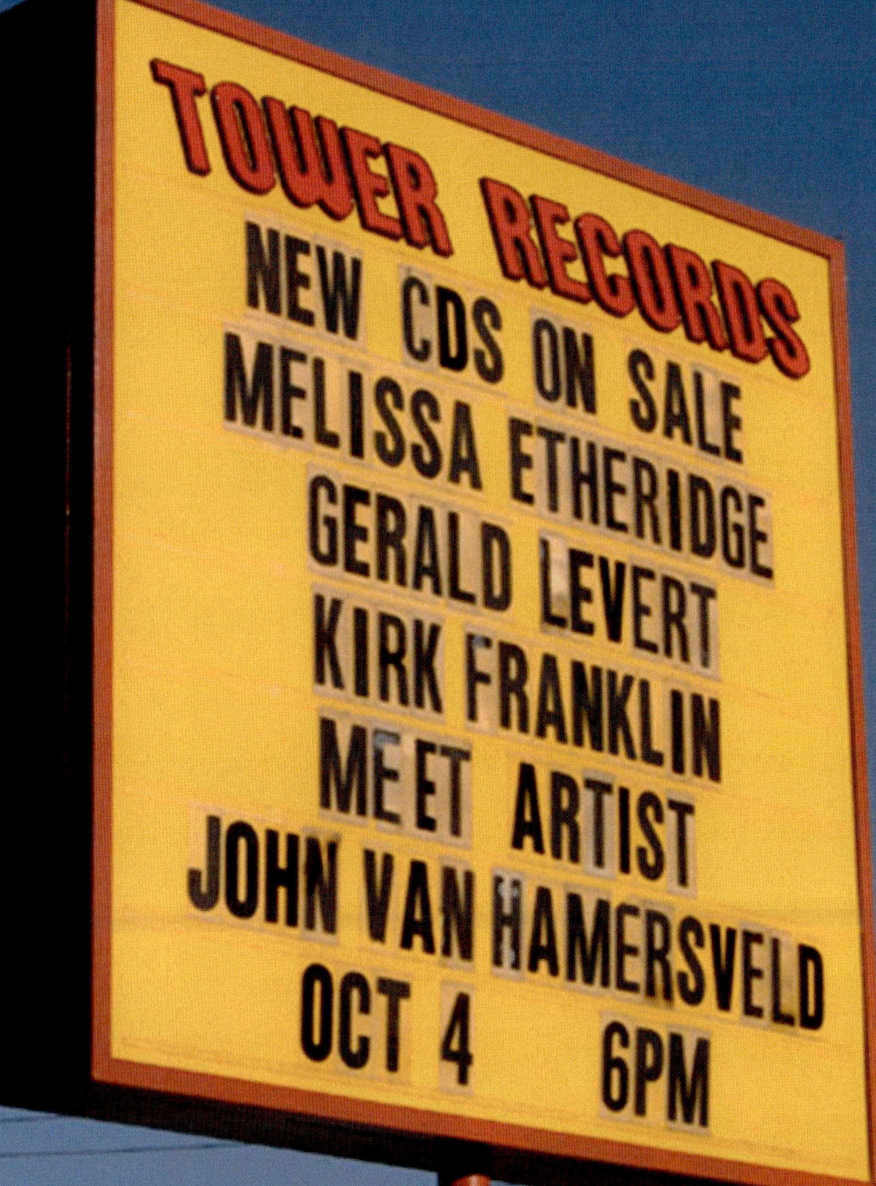

CROSSING AMERICA

12,000 Miles and 38 Hotels

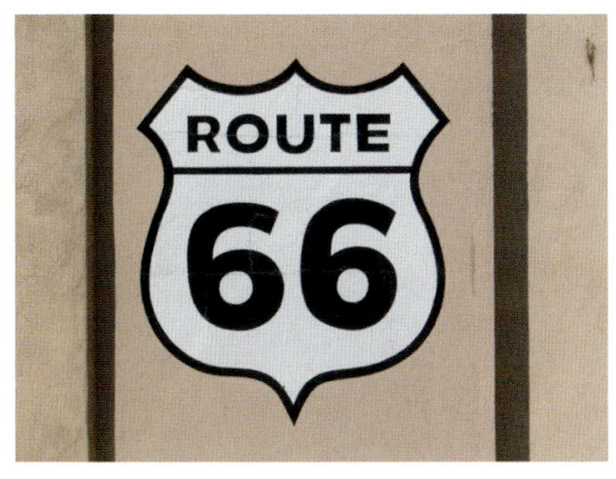
ROUTE
66

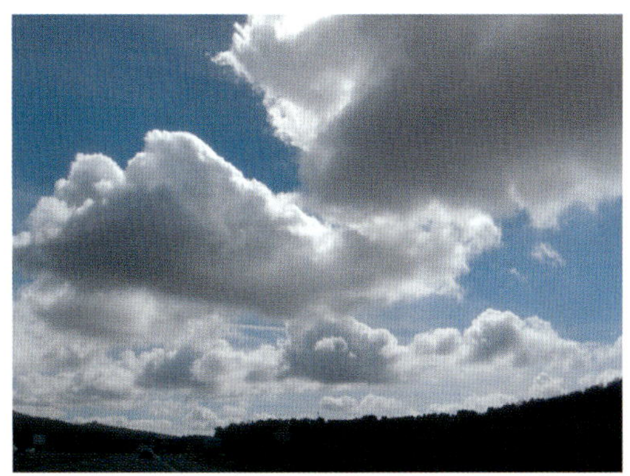

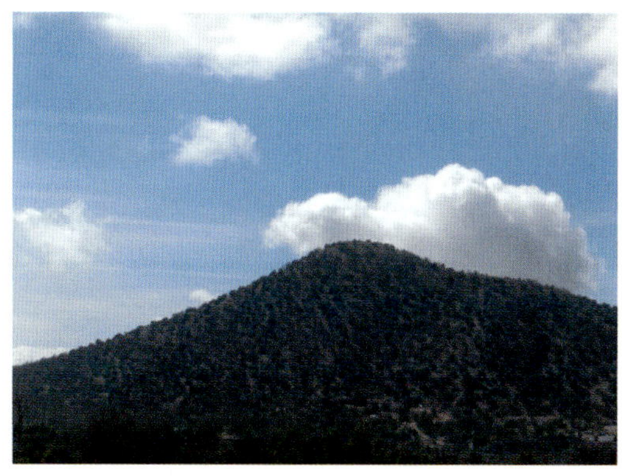

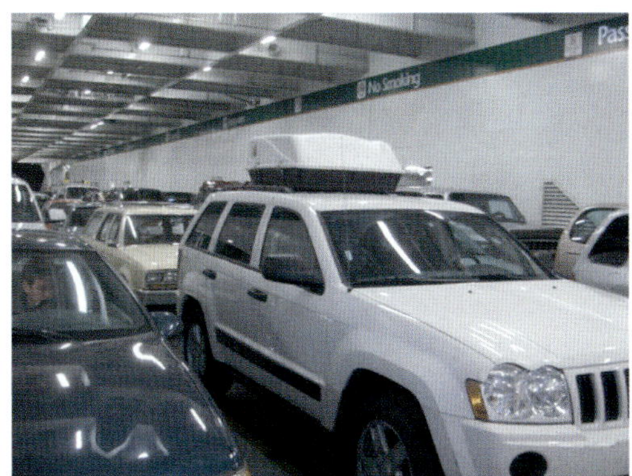
No Smoking

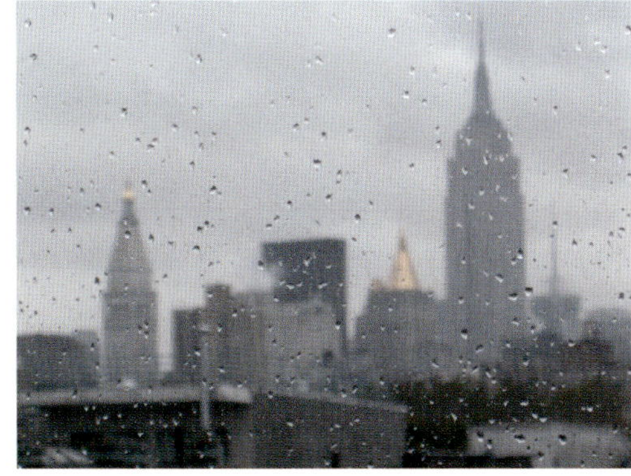

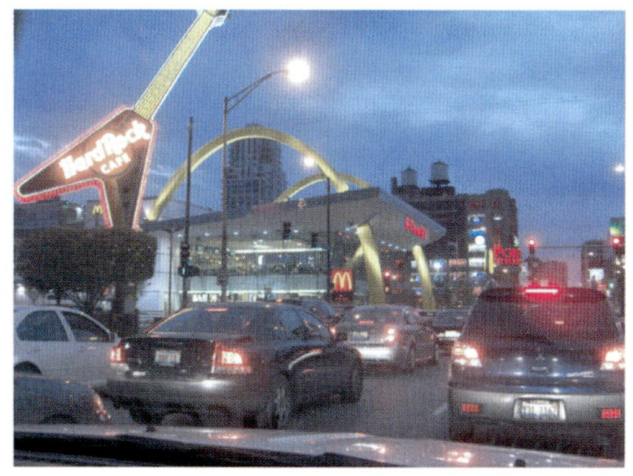

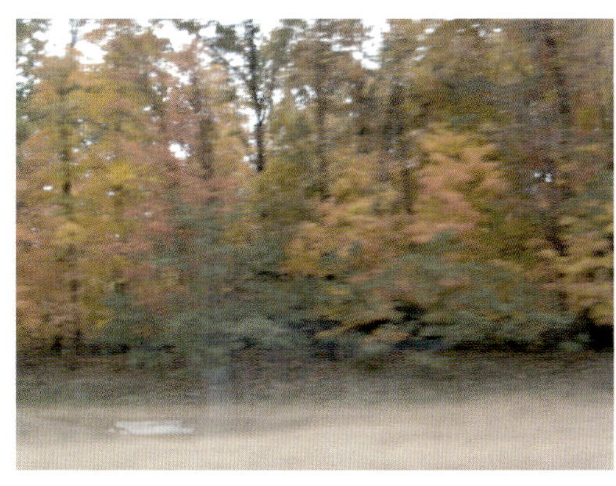

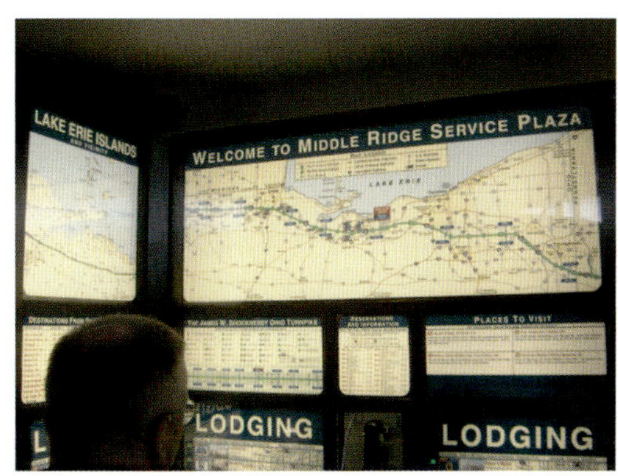
LAKE ERIE ISLANDS
WELCOME TO MIDDLE RIDGE SERVICE PLAZA
PLACES TO VISIT
LODGING
LODGING

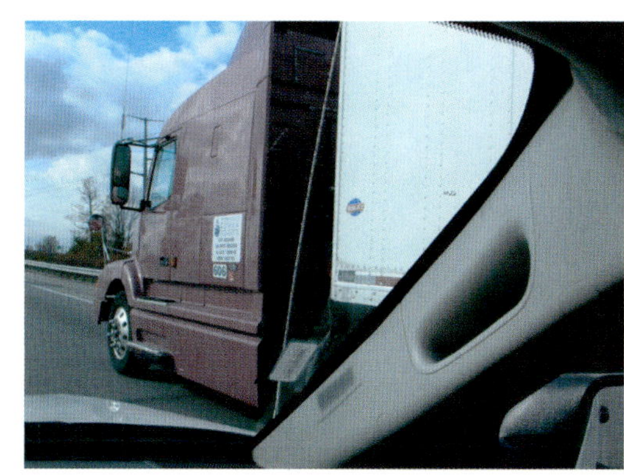

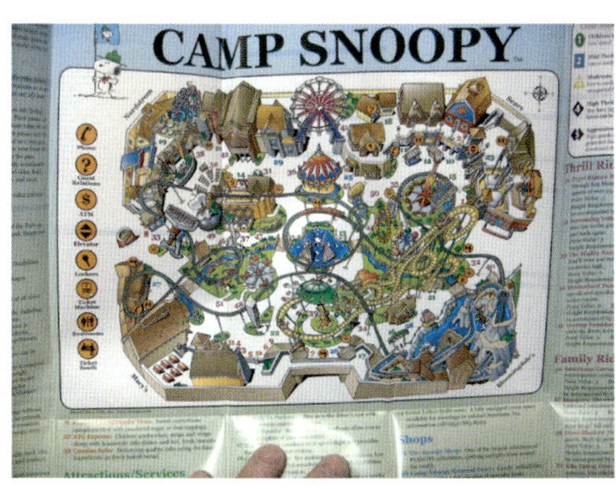
CAMP SNOOPY

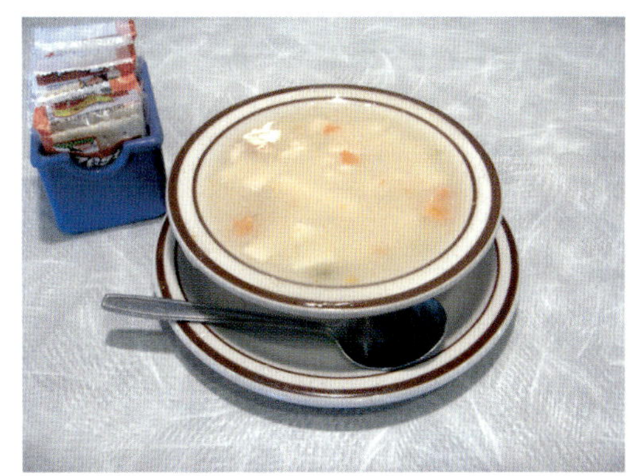

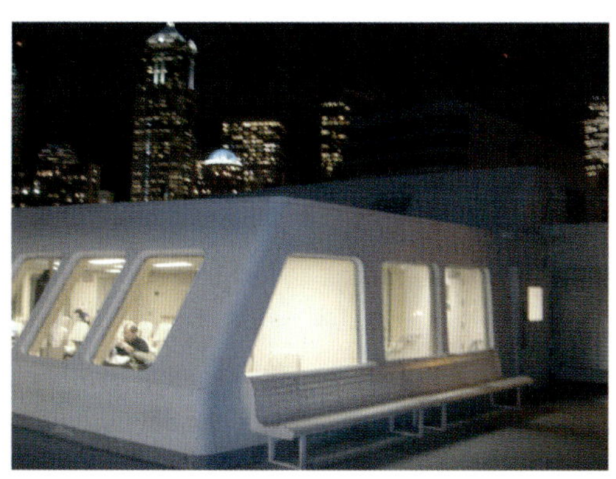

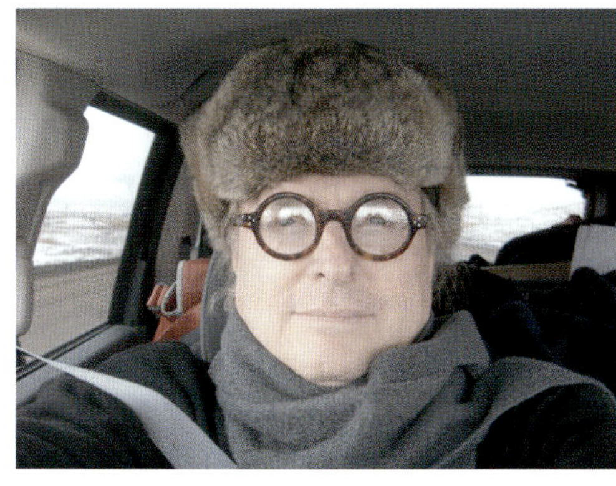

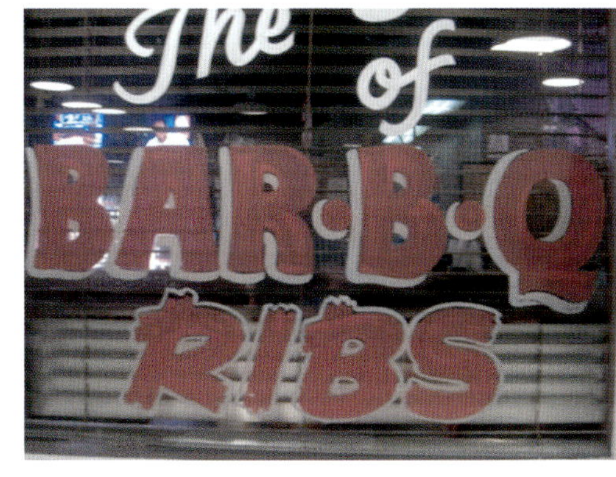
The
of
BAR·B·Q
RIBS

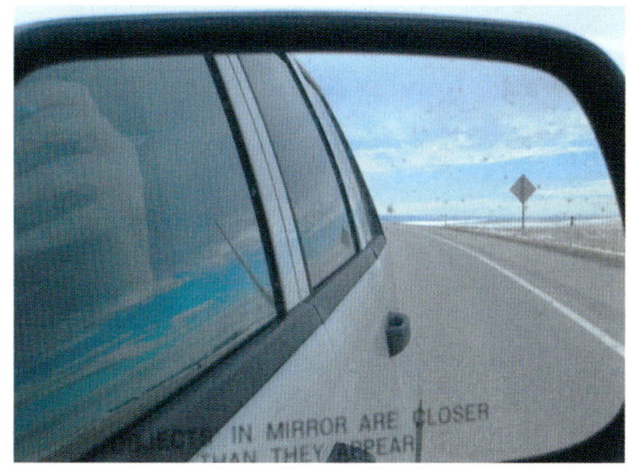
JECTS IN MIRROR ARE CLOSER
THAN THEY APPEAR

"My mind is just blown by the attention this signing tour at Tower Records is getting," said John Van Hamersveld.

SACRAMENTO, CA. 2005 (Tower Records)— Tower Records, America's leading independent music and movie retailer, today announced that it welcomes legendary Rock Poster Artist John Van Hamersveld on an exclusive cross-country Autograph Tour at select Tower Records stores nationwide.

WHO: Famed Poster Artist John Van Hamersveld, who began his rise to fame in the '60s & '70s. John has designed over 300 rock album covers for groups like the Beatles, the Rolling Stones, Jefferson Airplane and many others, and for such well-known records as: Exile on Main Street *and* Magical Mystery Tour.

WHAT: In a first-of-its-kind tour, John Van Hamersveld will appear at select Tower Records locations nationwide to sign Limited Artist's Editions of the Cream '2005 Live at Albert Hall Reunion' concert poster (for which he also designed the CD/DVD art at the request of Eric Clapton), as well as his famed Jimi Hendrix 'Pinnacle' poster, which commemorated Jimi Hendrix's February 10, 1968 concert at LA's Shrine Auditorium, widely considered to be one of the greatest rock posters ever made. The Cream poster is John's first rock poster in 21 years.

"My mind is just blown by the attention this signing tour at Tower Records is getting," said John Van Hamersveld. "It's re-igniting in me a whole new way of looking at the rock art and entertainment scene. Back in the day, Disney bought the art school where I was studying and turned it into an arts and performance school, which led to the Pinnacle concert posters I did and so much more. I feel like this tour is an extension of that... in the new millennium."

—www.top40-Charts.com

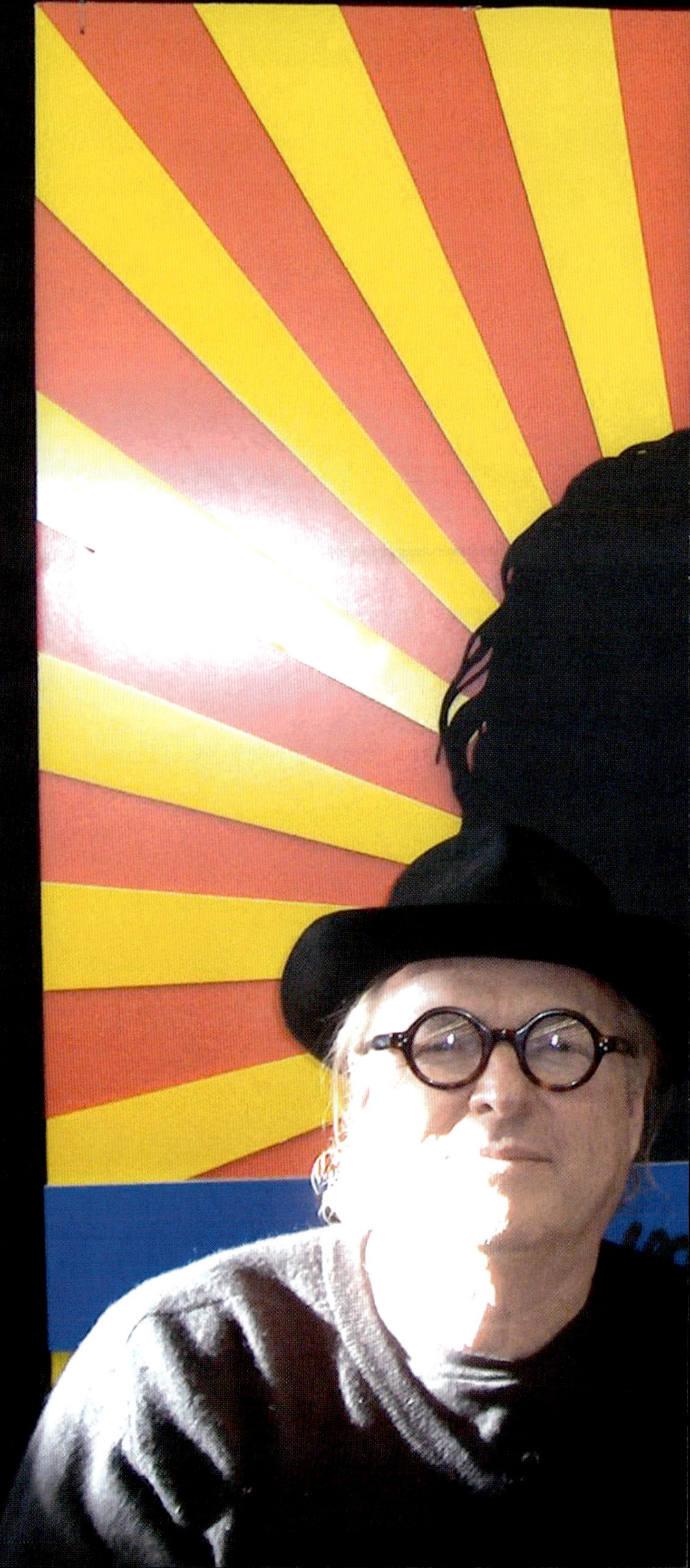

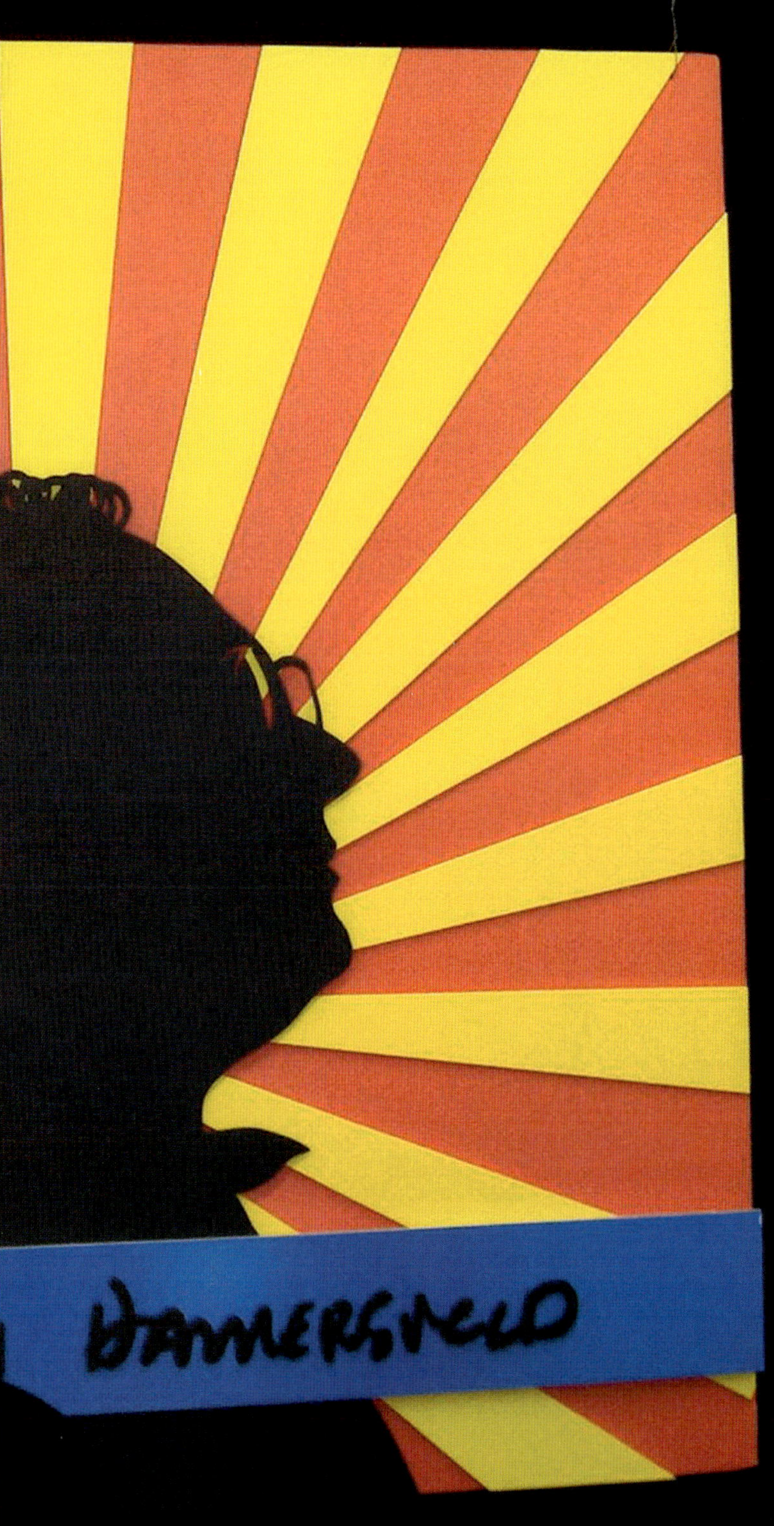

Tour Sites

Watt Ave.,
Sacramento
Columbus & Bay,
San Francisco *
NY Village *
Mountain View *
Washington DC *
Sunset *
Nashville *
Chicago *
San Diego *
Seattle *
LaJolla, California
Santa Monica
Denver*
Las Vegas*
Laguna Hills
Dallas*
Ave. of the Arts,
Philadelphia*
Sherman Oaks*
Atlanta, Georgia*

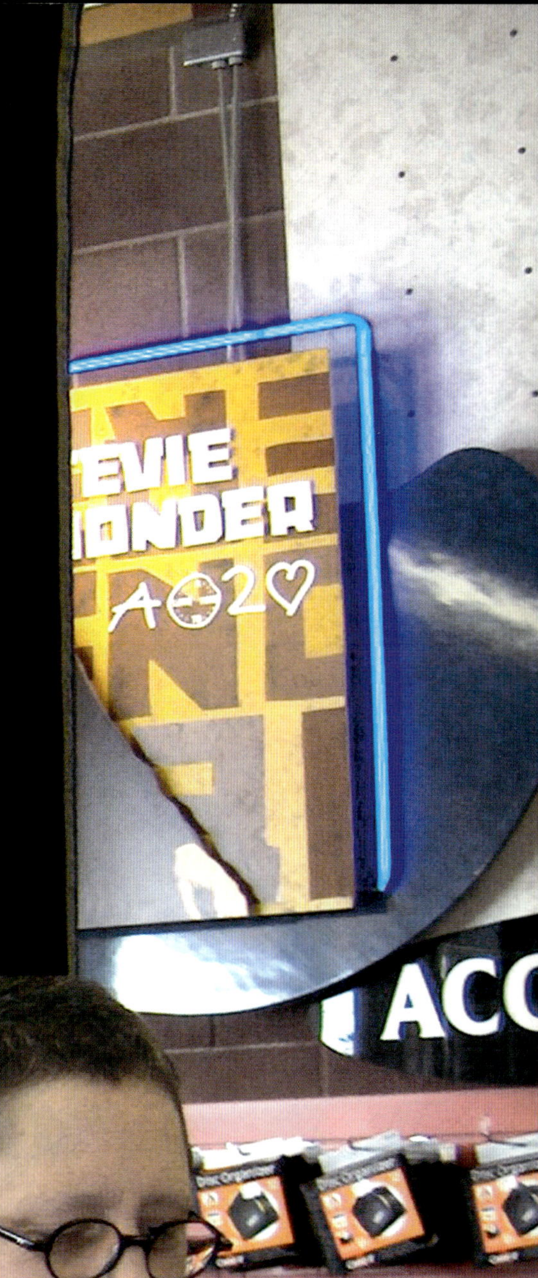

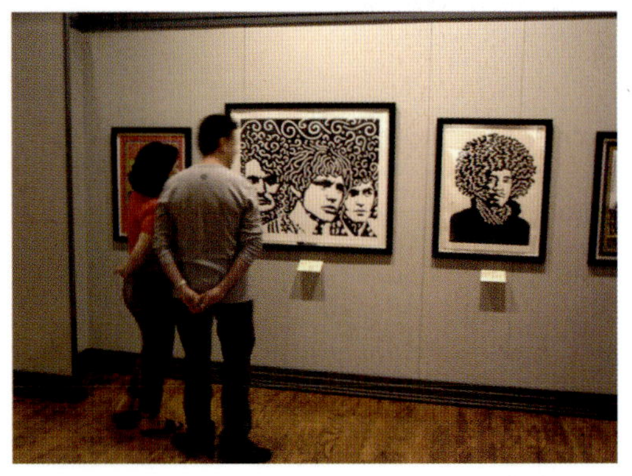

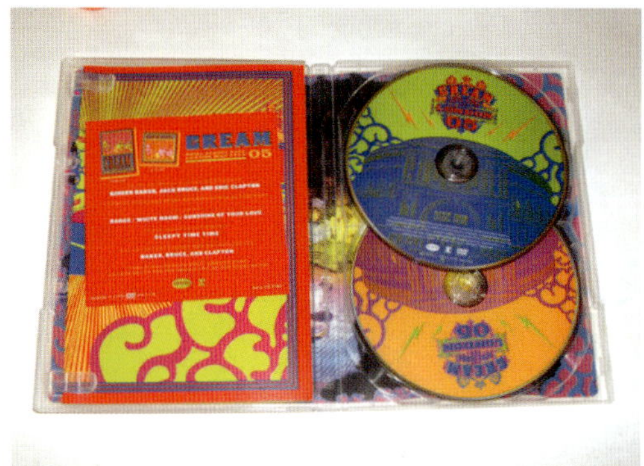

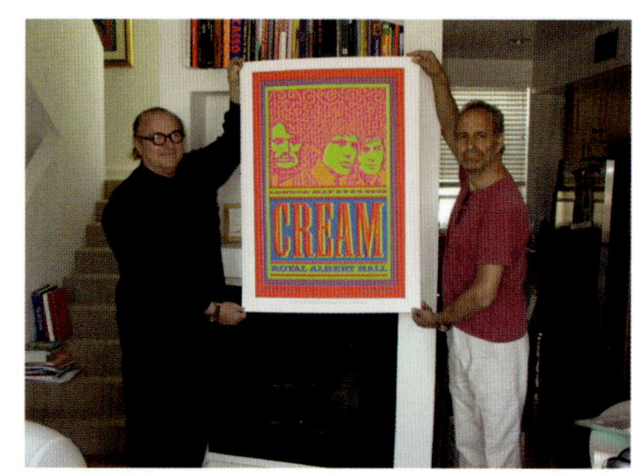

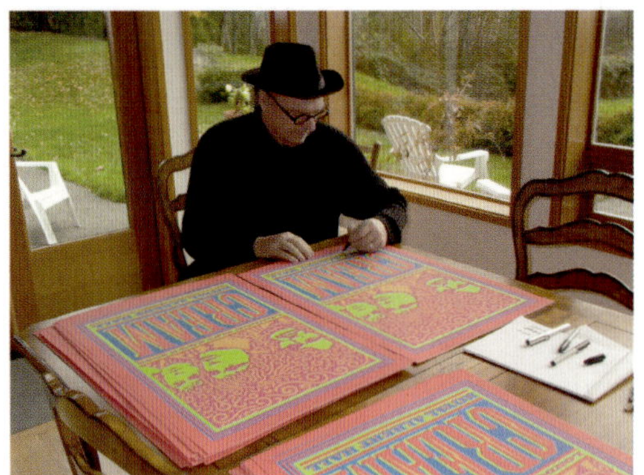

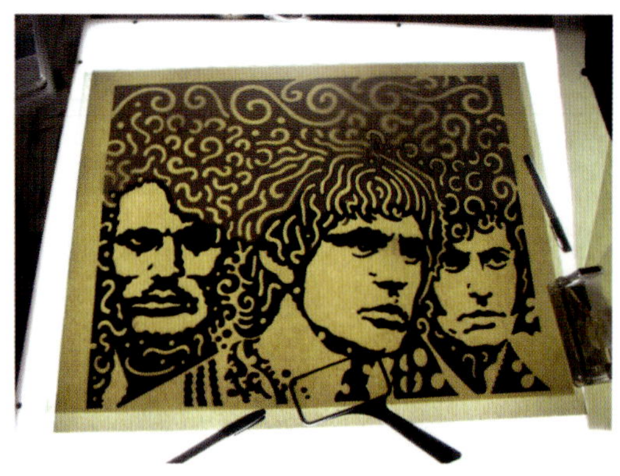

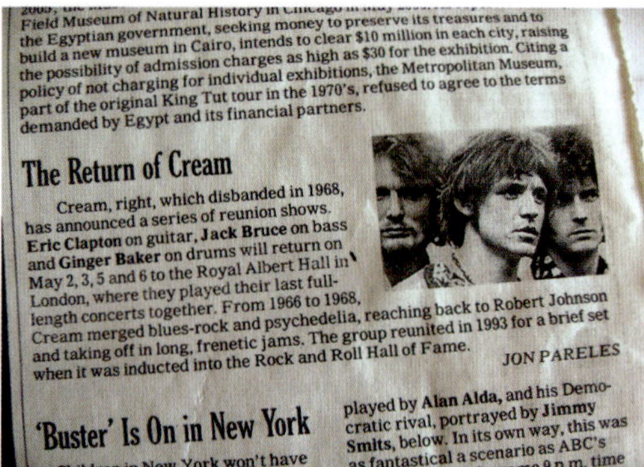

Field Museum of Natural History in Chicago in May ... the Egyptian government, seeking money to preserve its treasures and to build a new museum in Cairo, intends to clear $10 million in each city, raising the possibility of admission charges as high as $30 for the exhibition. Citing a policy of not charging for individual exhibitions, the Metropolitan Museum, part of the original King Tut tour in the 1970's, refused to agree to the terms demanded by Egypt and its financial partners.

The Return of Cream

Cream, right, which disbanded in 1968, has announced a series of reunion shows. **Eric Clapton** on guitar, **Jack Bruce** on bass and **Ginger Baker** on drums will return on May 2, 3, 5 and 6 to the Royal Albert Hall in London, where they played their last full-length concerts together. From 1966 to 1968, Cream merged blues-rock and psychedelia, reaching back to Robert Johnson and taking off in long, frenetic jams. The group reunited in 1993 for a brief set when it was inducted into the Rock and Roll Hall of Fame.

JON PARELES

'Buster' Is On in New York

Children in New York won't have ...

played by **Alan Alda,** and his Democratic rival, portrayed by **Jimmy Smits,** below. In its own way, this was as fantastical a scenario as ABC's "Alias" spins in the same 9 p.m. time ...

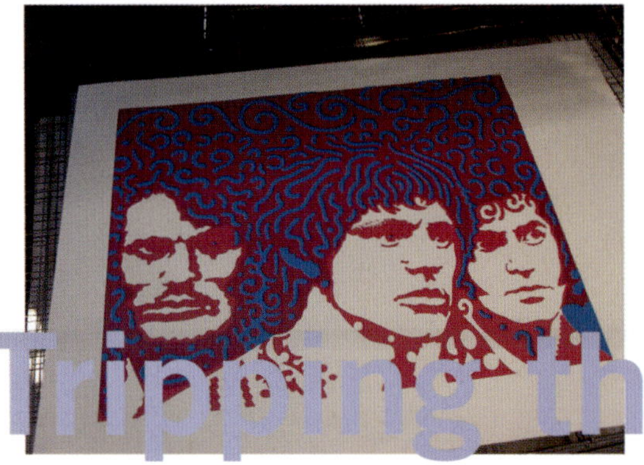

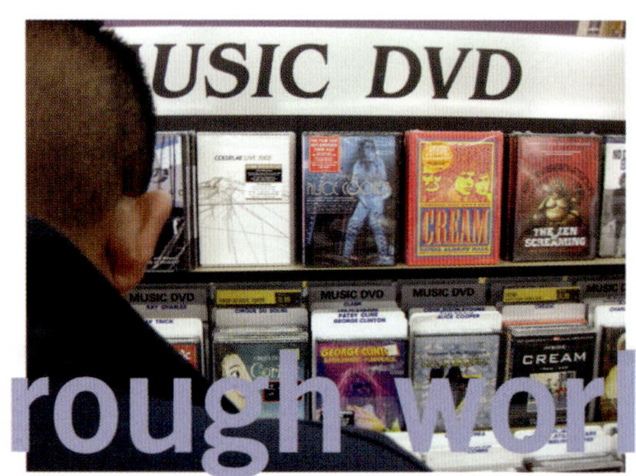

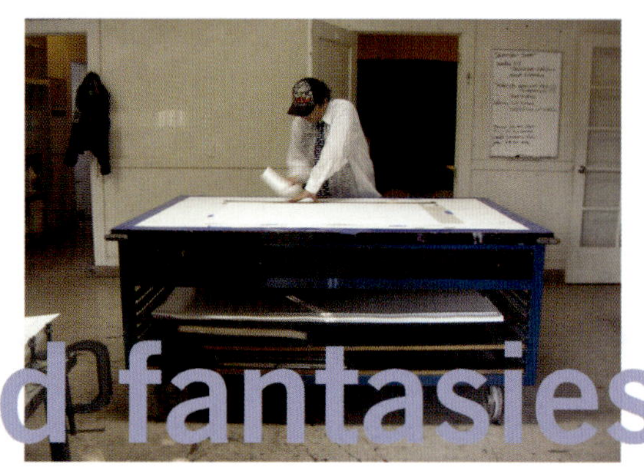

Tripping through world fantasies

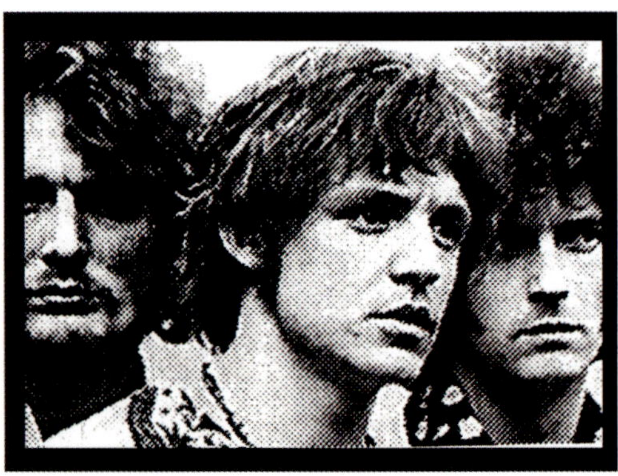

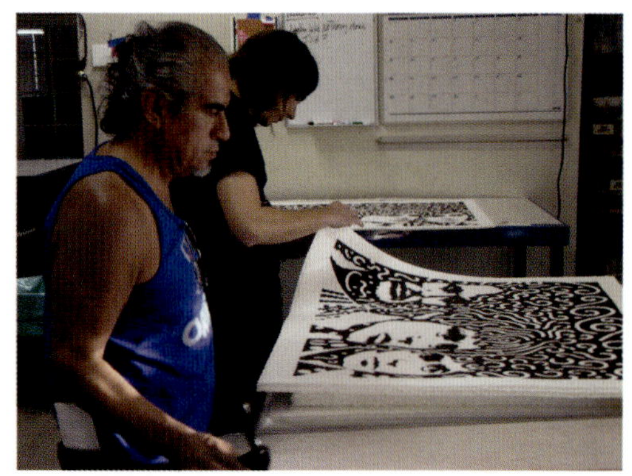

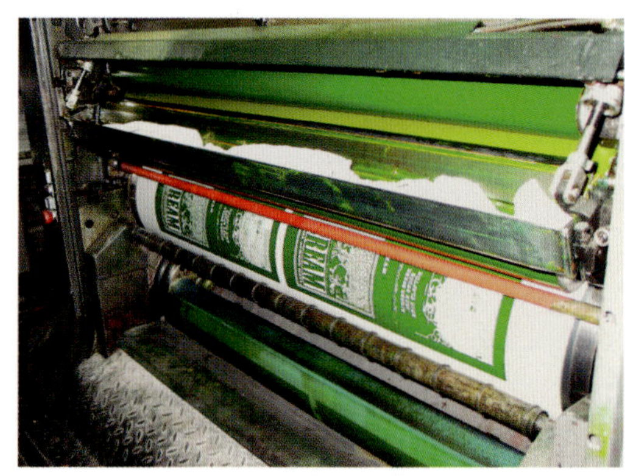

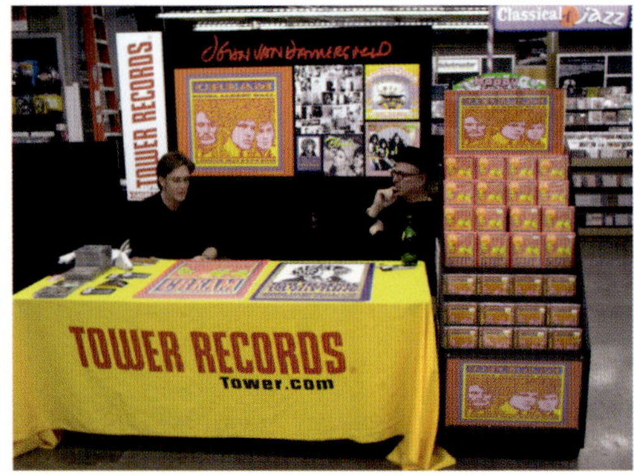

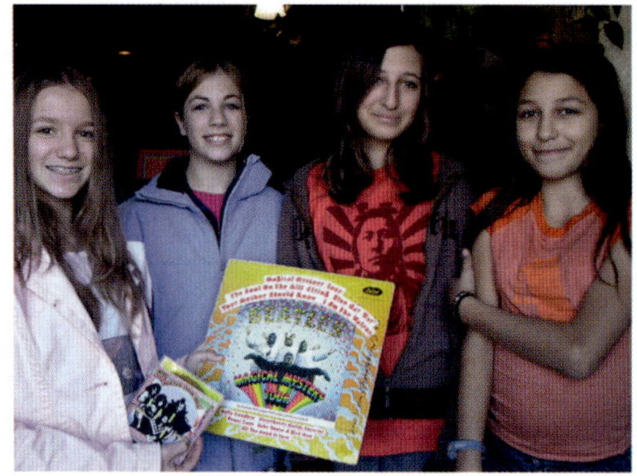

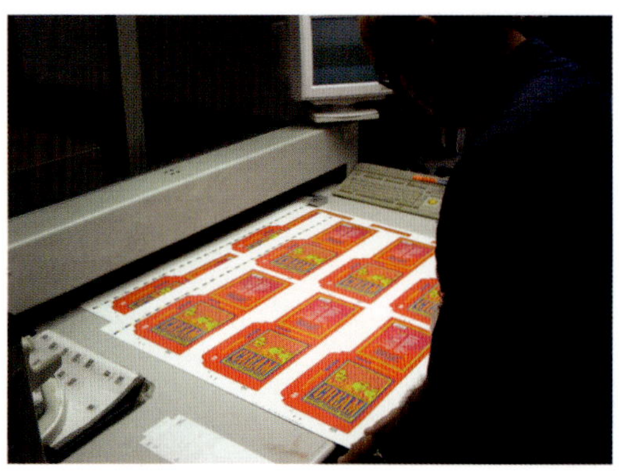

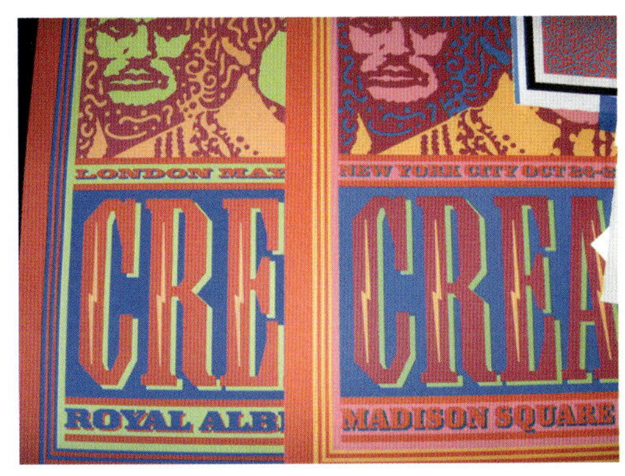

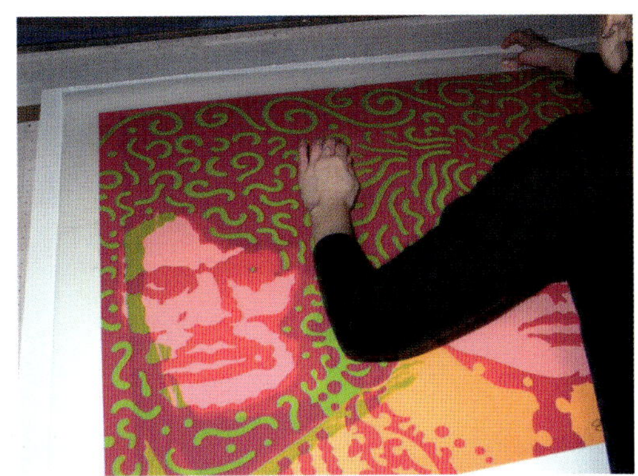

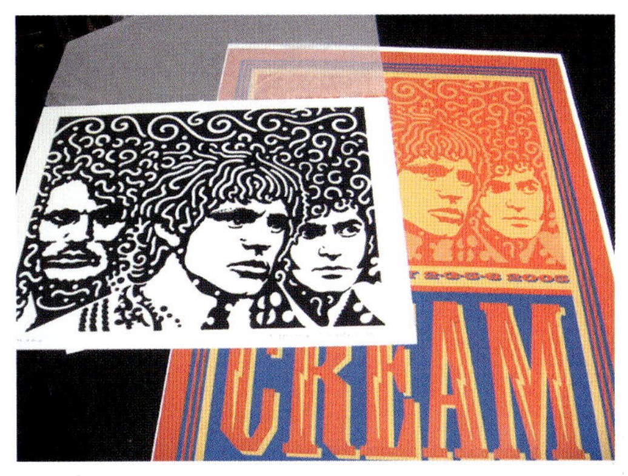

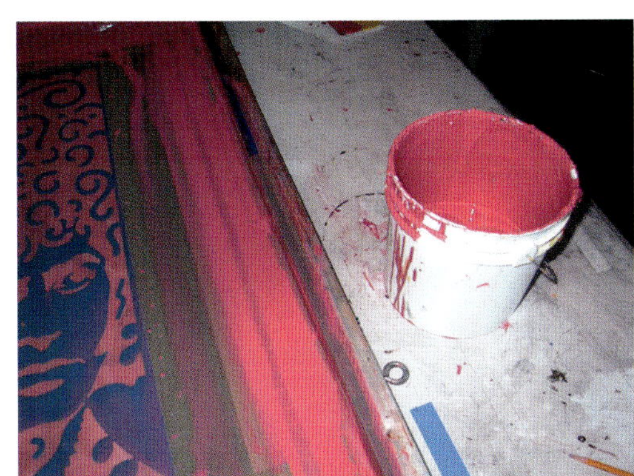

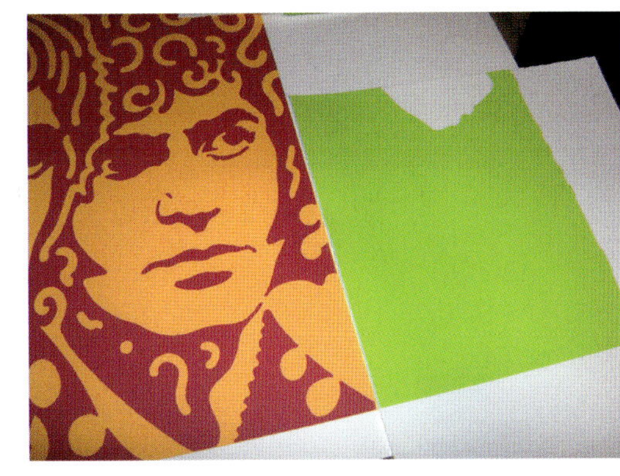

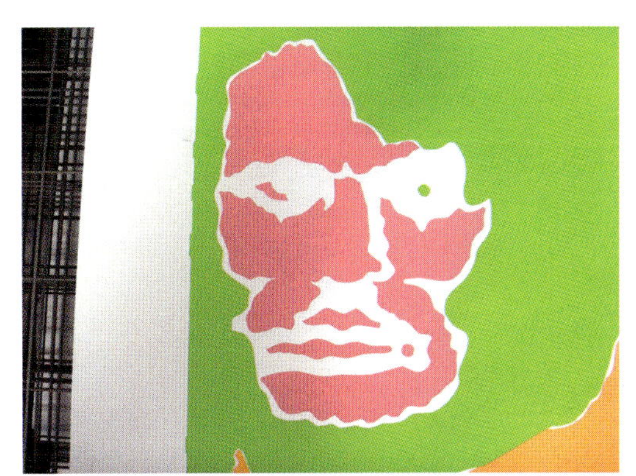

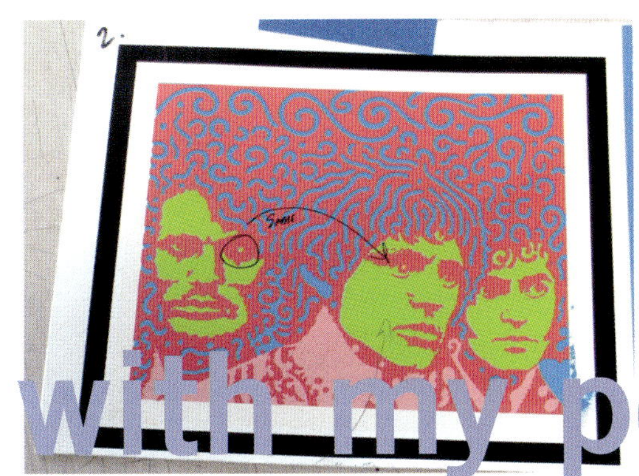

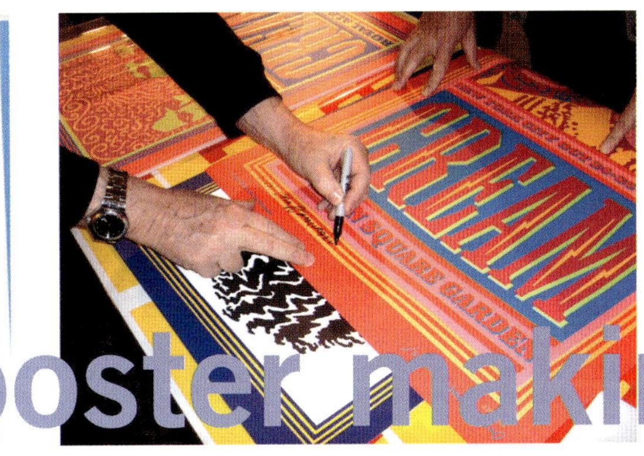

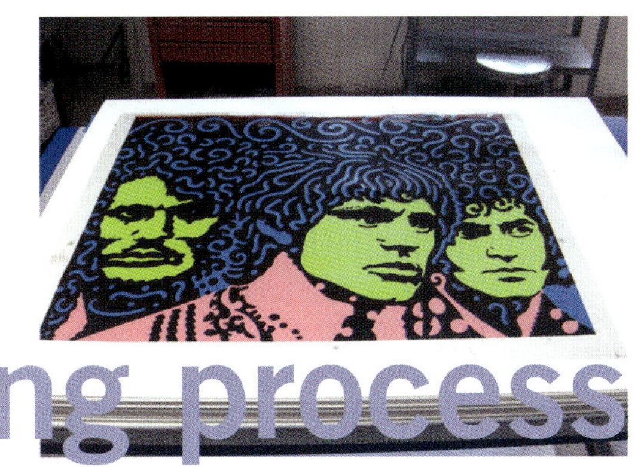

with my poster making process

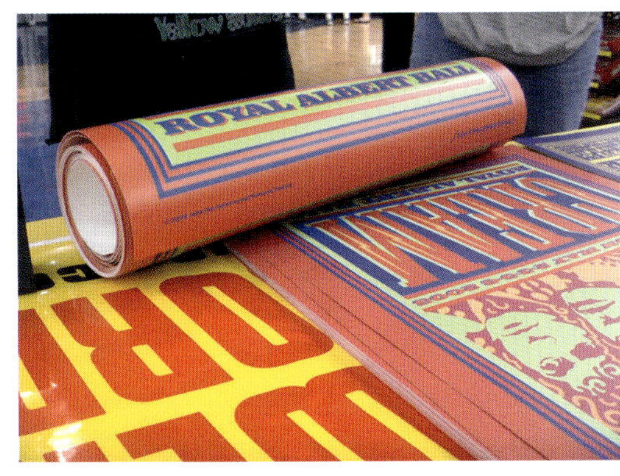

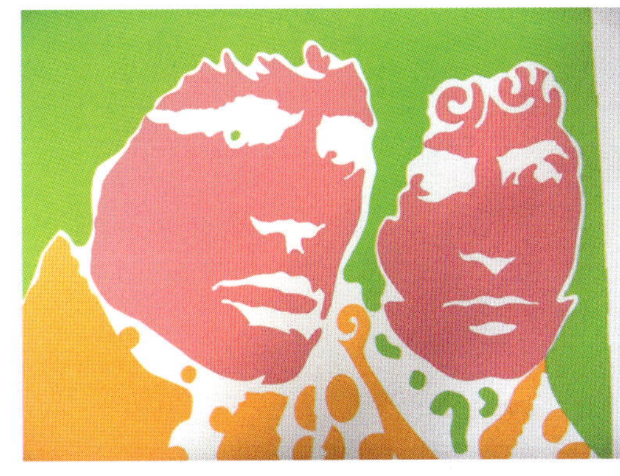

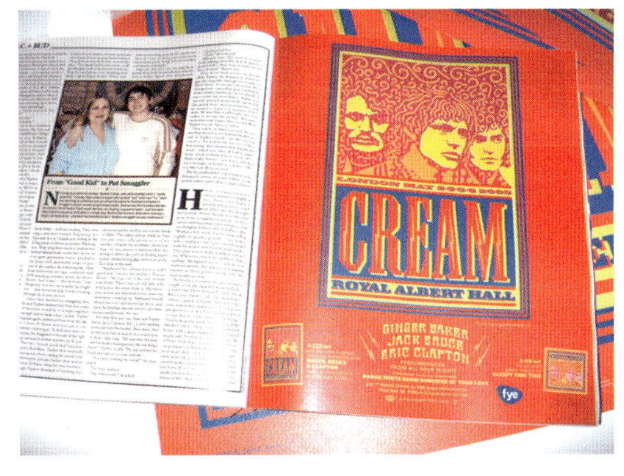

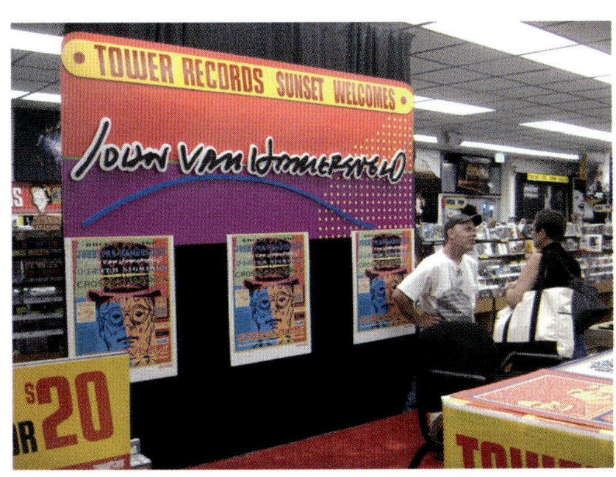

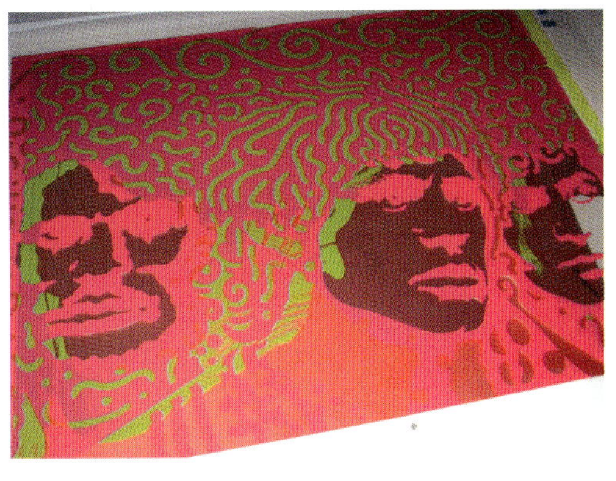

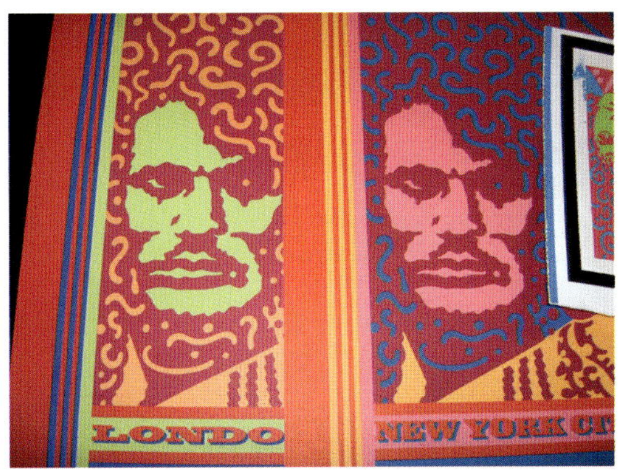

Revisiting the Psychedelic Revolution (2005)

Alida meeting Victor at the Rock Poster Society (TRPS) event in San Francisco, the planet's largest organized group of rock poster collectors.

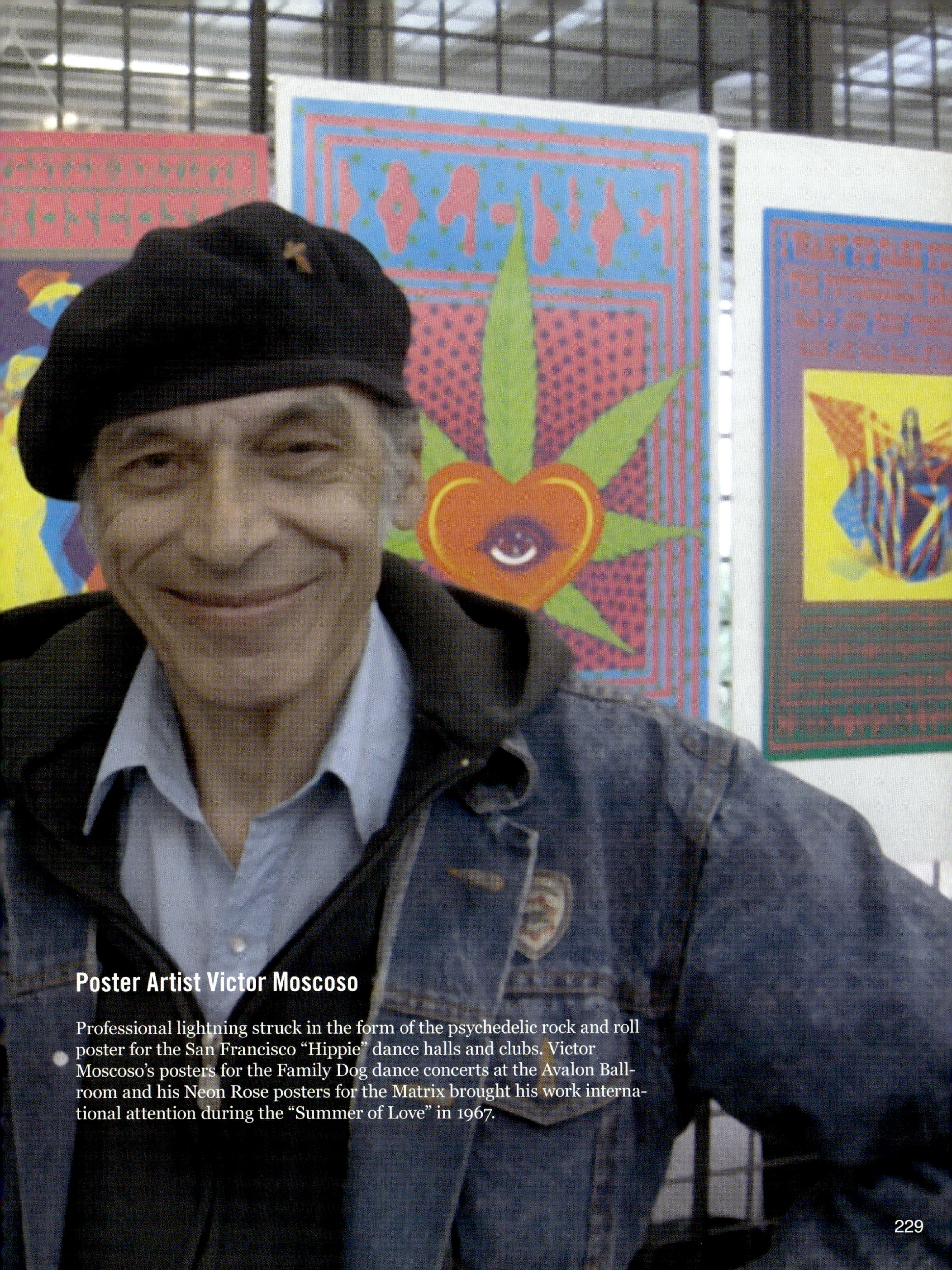

Poster Artist Victor Moscoso

Professional lightning struck in the form of the psychedelic rock and roll poster for the San Francisco "Hippie" dance halls and clubs. Victor Moscoso's posters for the Family Dog dance concerts at the Avalon Ballroom and his Neon Rose posters for the Matrix brought his work international attention during the "Summer of Love" in 1967.

Poster Art Collections (1966)

The Endless Summer and Milton Glaser's *Bob Dylan* poster were both collected by the Museum of Modern Art.

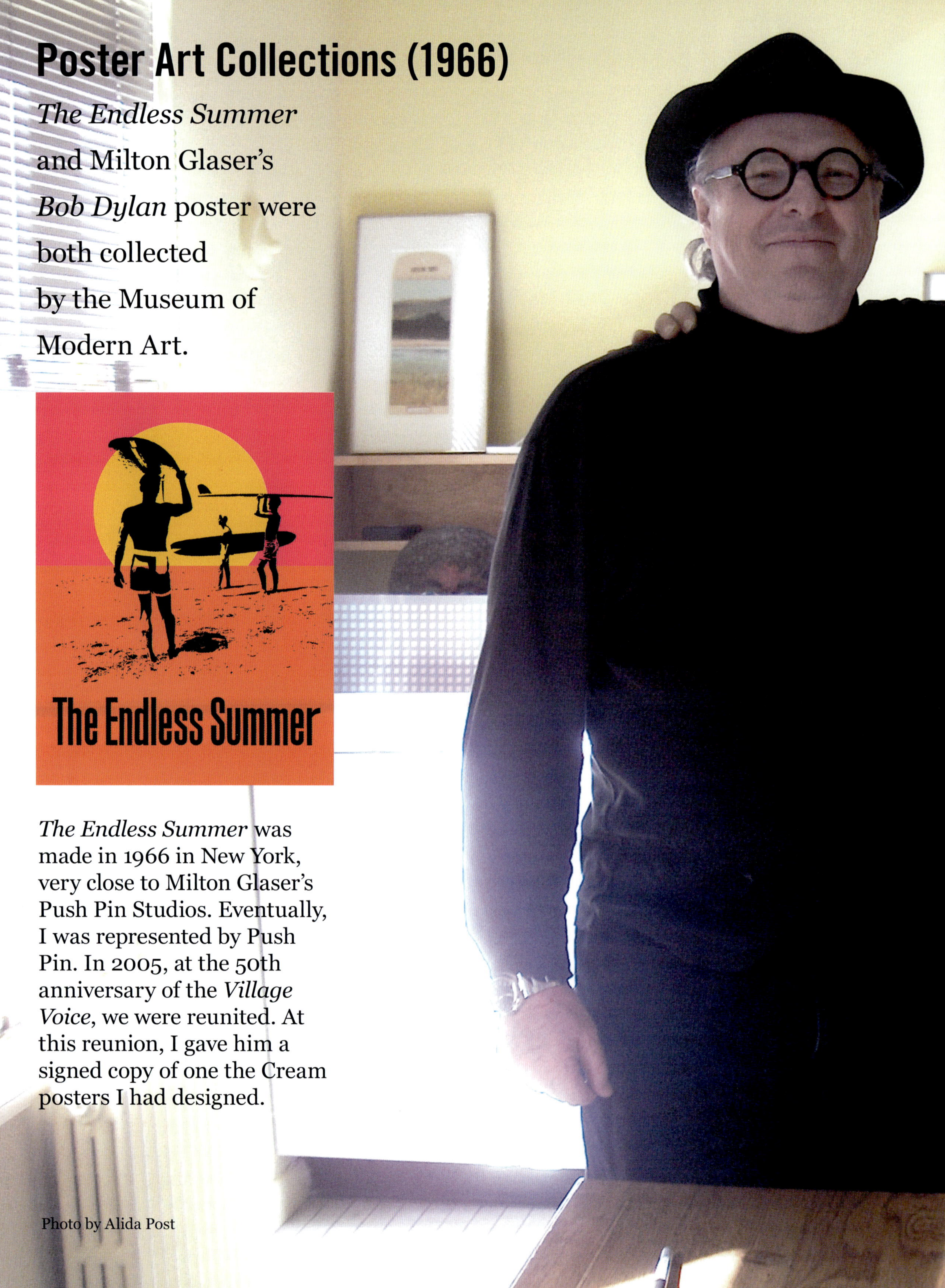

The Endless Summer was made in 1966 in New York, very close to Milton Glaser's Push Pin Studios. Eventually, I was represented by Push Pin. In 2005, at the 50th anniversary of the *Village Voice*, we were reunited. At this reunion, I gave him a signed copy of one the Cream posters I had designed.

Photo by Alida Post

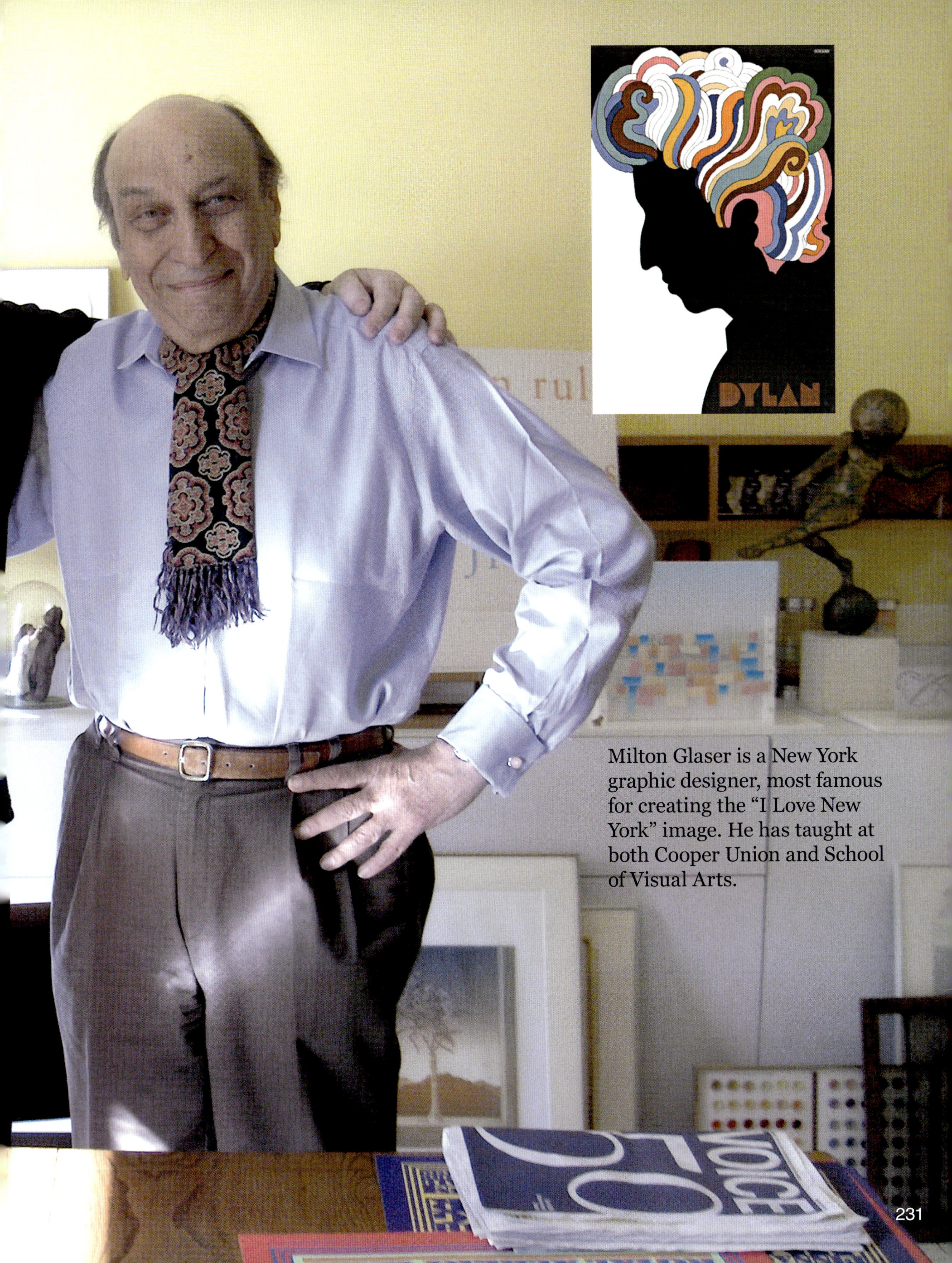

Milton Glaser is a New York graphic designer, most famous for creating the "I Love New York" image. He has taught at both Cooper Union and School of Visual Arts.

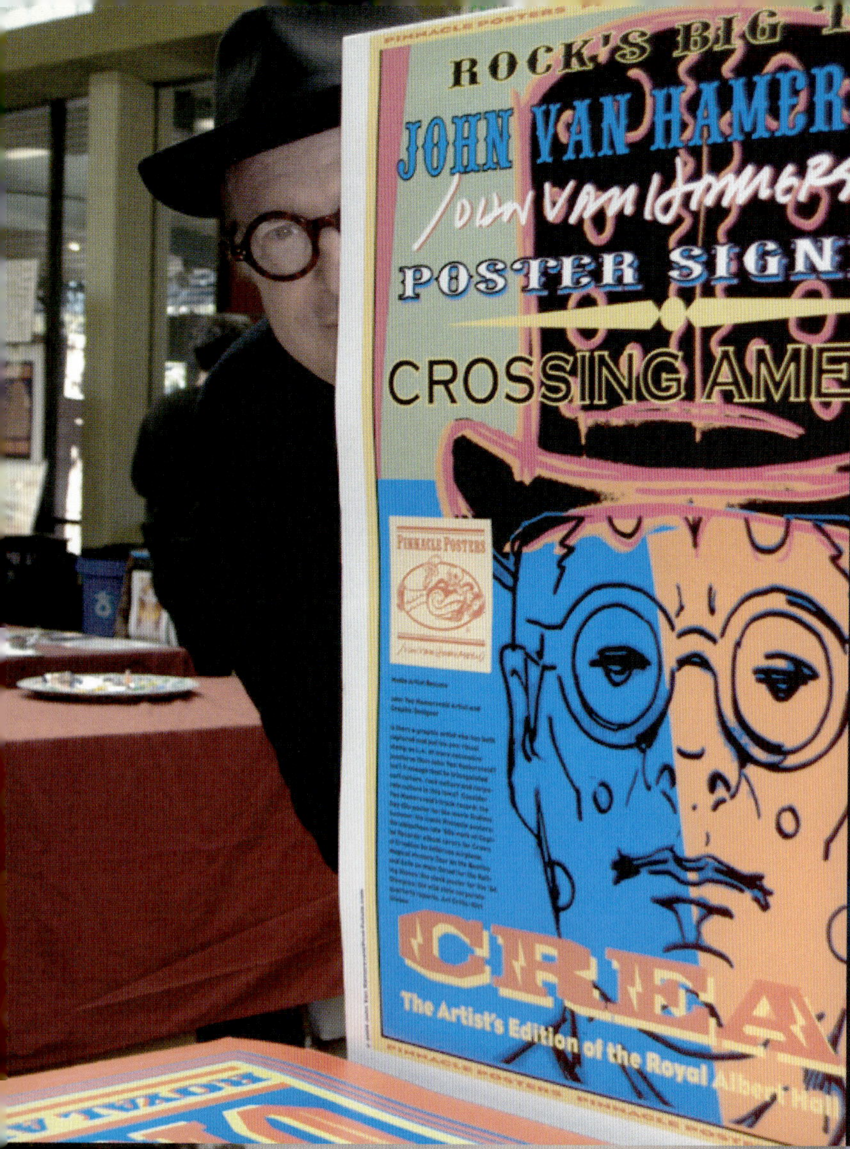

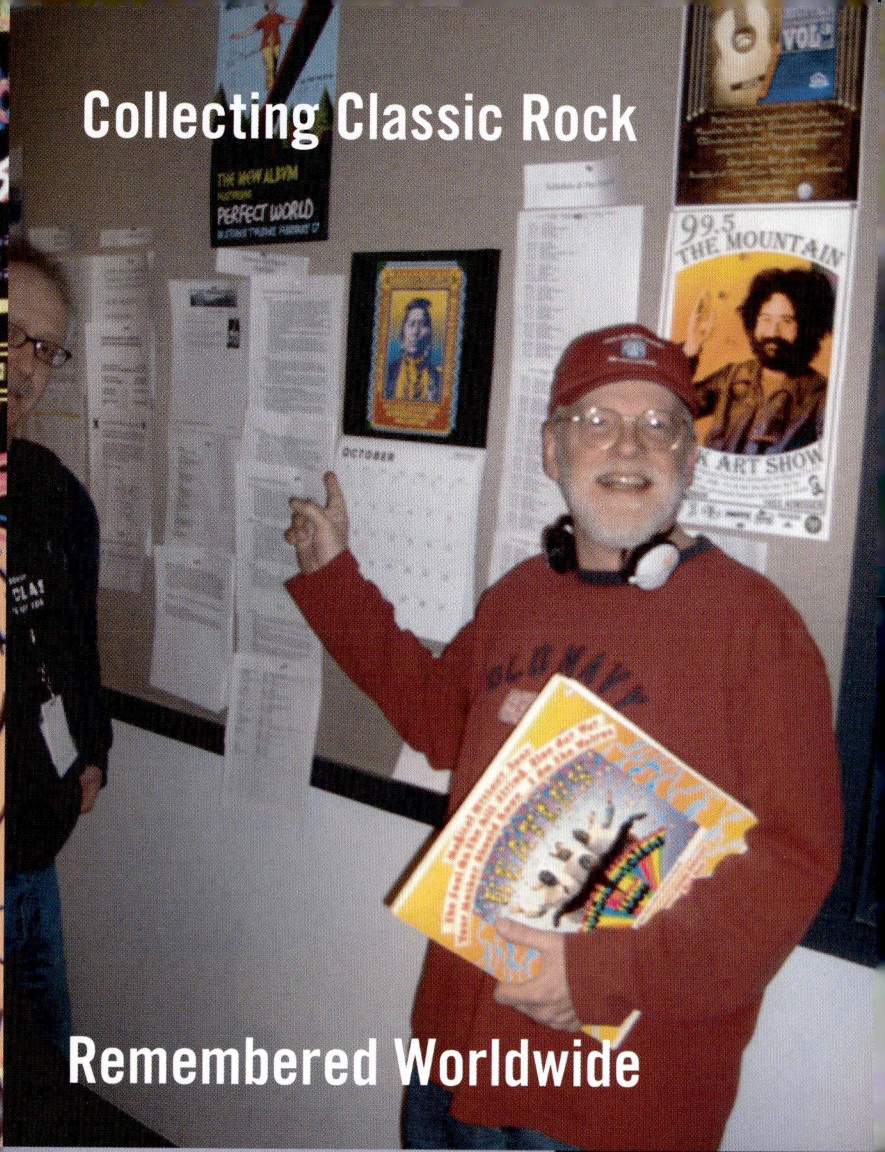

Collecting Classic Rock

Remembered Worldwide

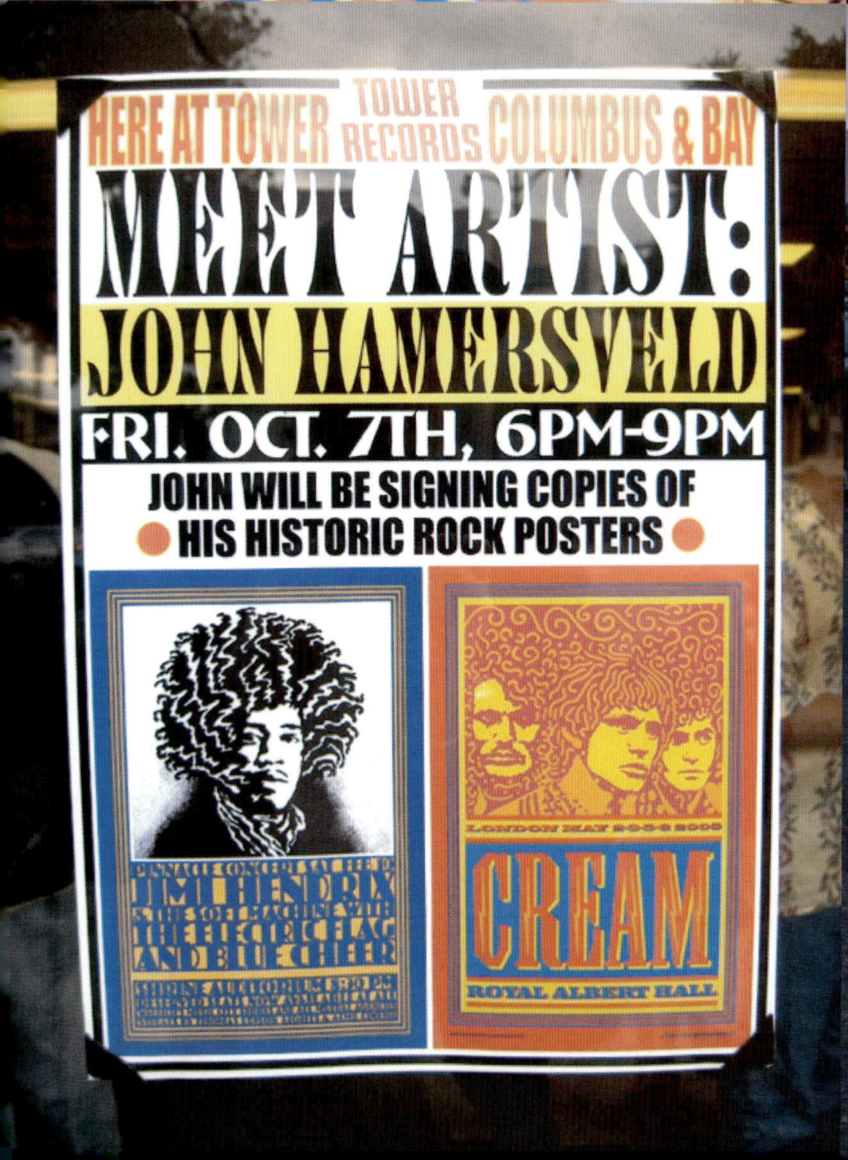

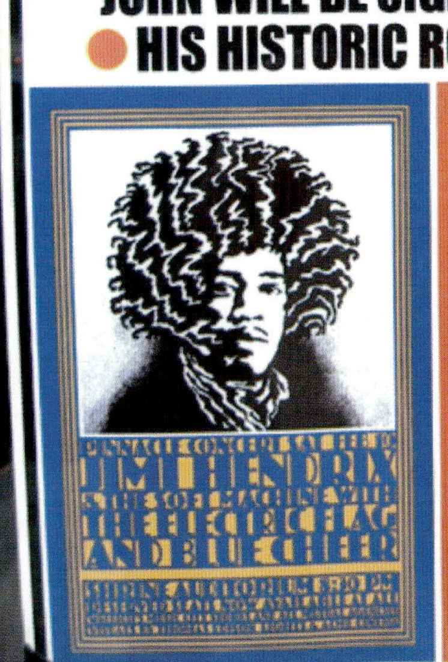

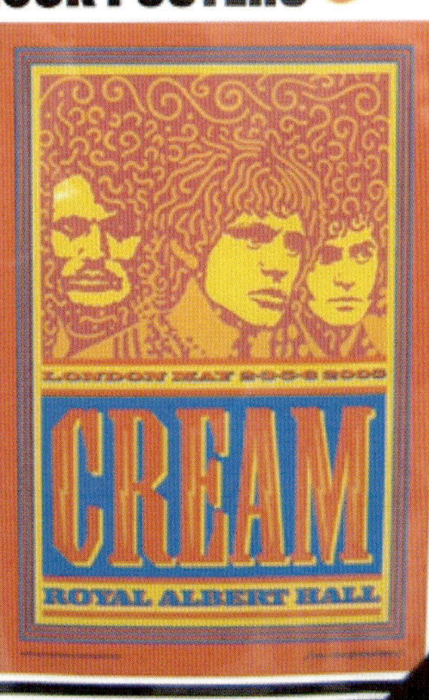

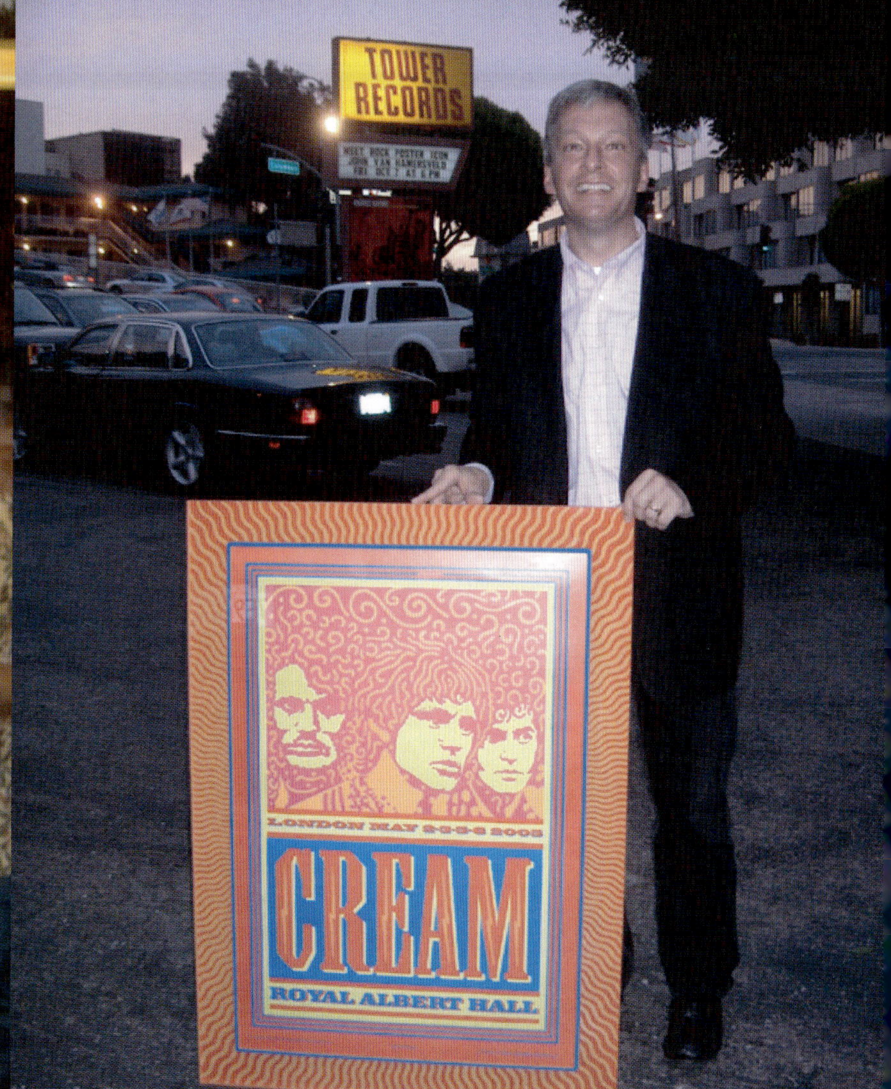

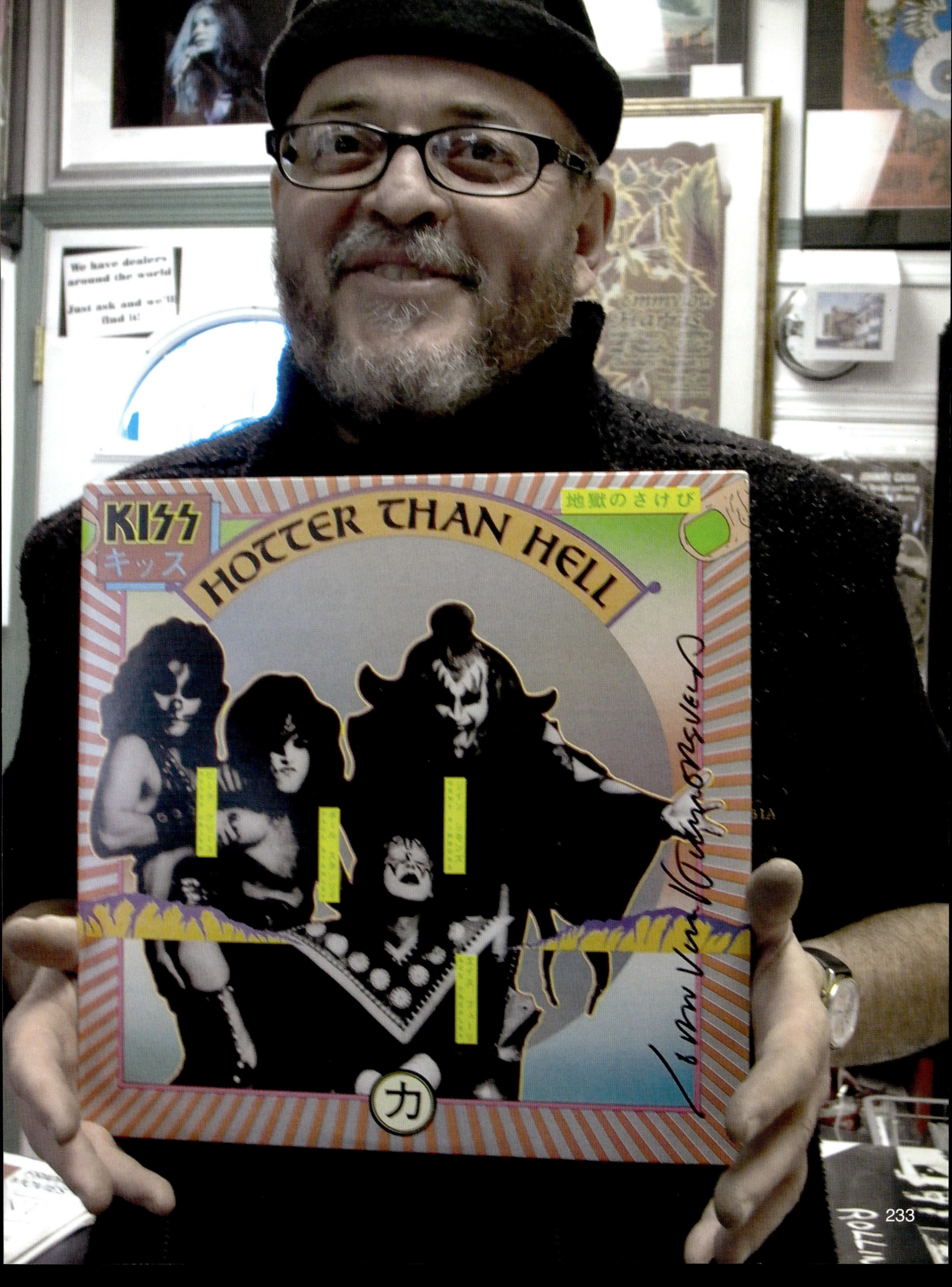
We have dealers around the world
Just ask and we'll find it!
KISS
キッス
HOTTER THAN HELL
地獄のさけび
力

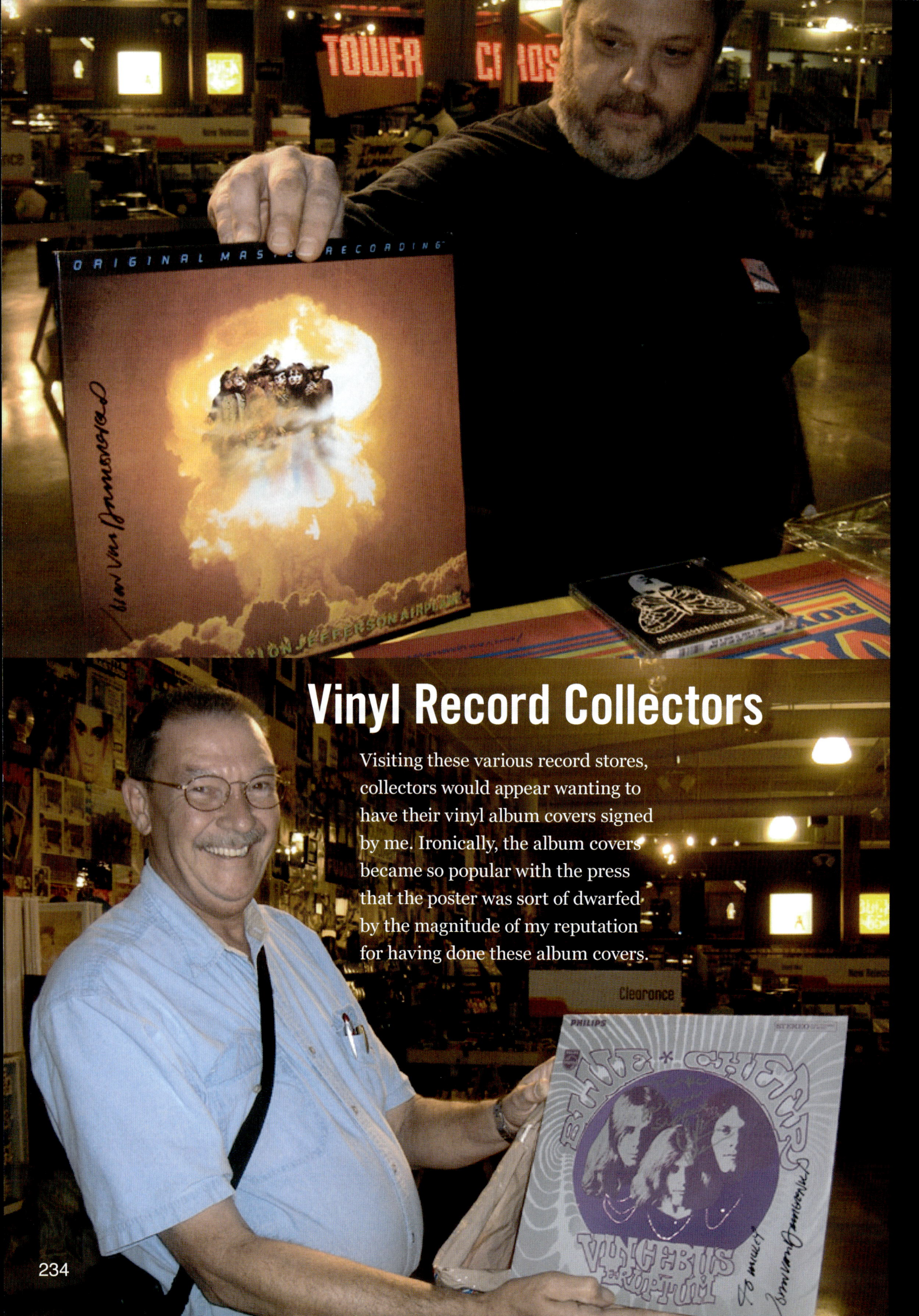

Vinyl Record Collectors

Visiting these various record stores, collectors would appear wanting to have their vinyl album covers signed by me. Ironically, the album covers became so popular with the press that the poster was sort of dwarfed by the magnitude of my reputation for having done these album covers.

music

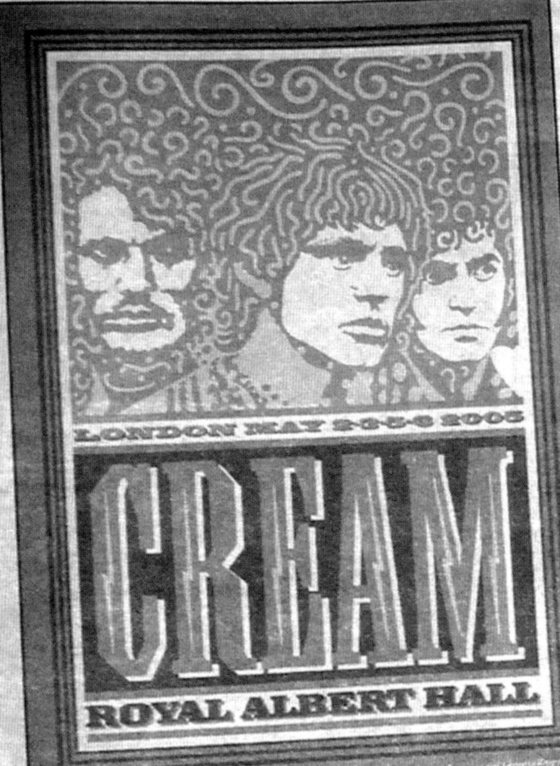

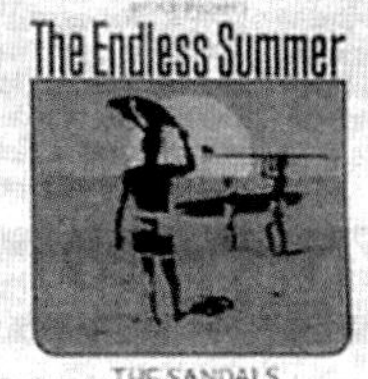

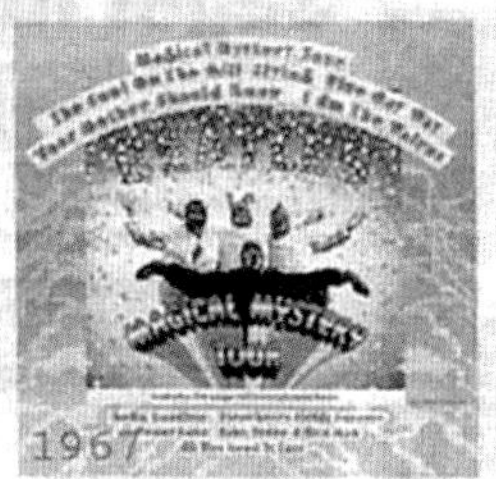

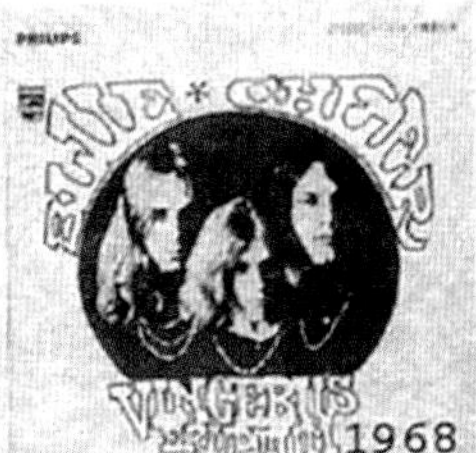

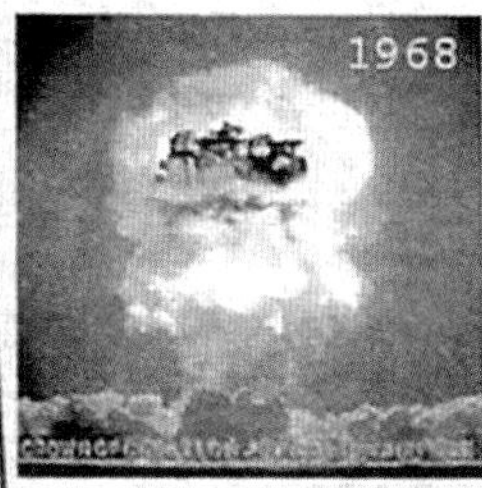

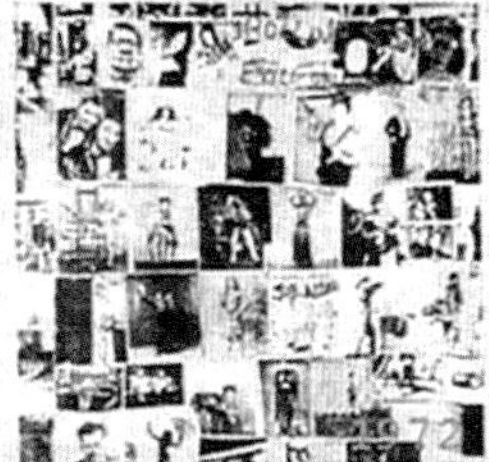

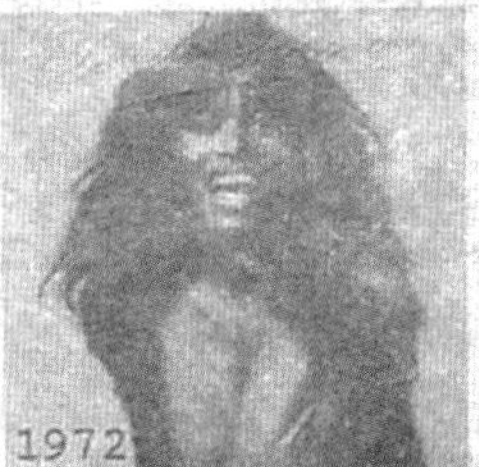

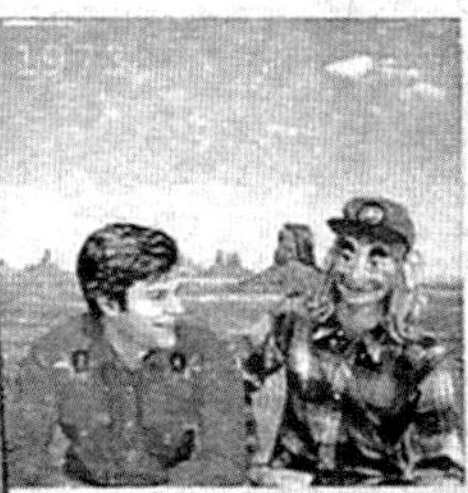

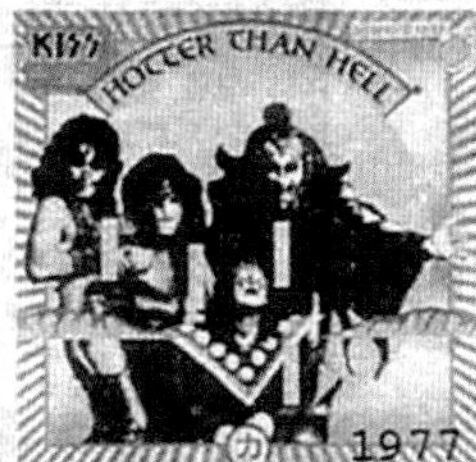

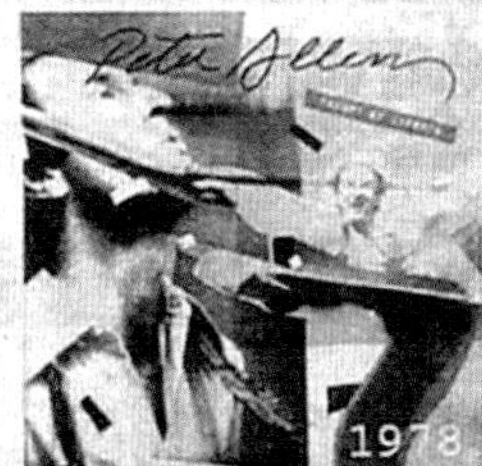

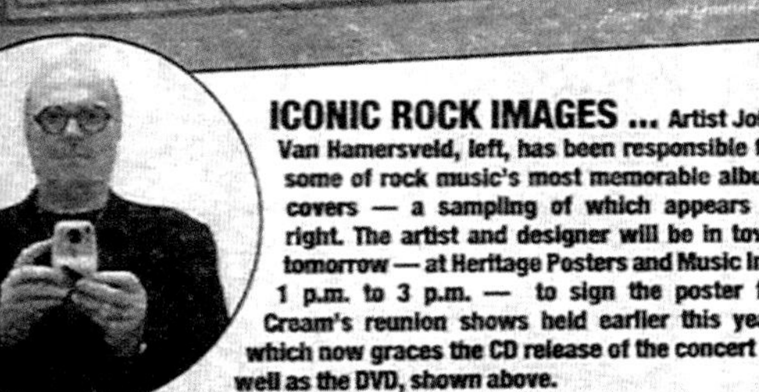

ICONIC ROCK IMAGES ... Artist John Van Hamersveld, left, has been responsible for some of rock music's most memorable album covers — a sampling of which appears at right. The artist and designer will be in town tomorrow — at Heritage Posters and Music Inc. 1 p.m. to 3 p.m. — to sign the poster for Cream's reunion shows held earlier this year, which now graces the CD release of the concert as well as the DVD, shown above.

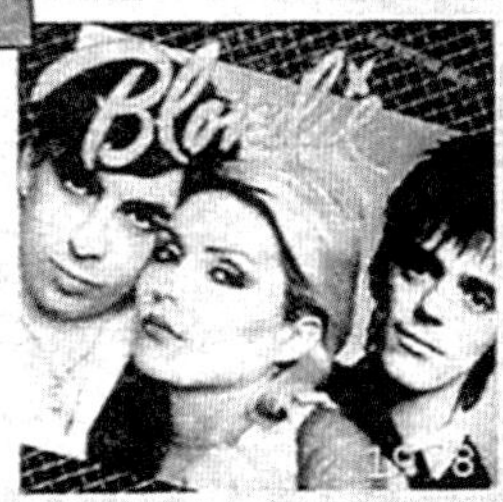

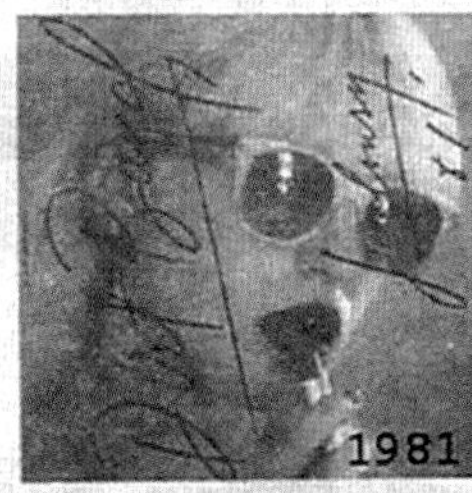

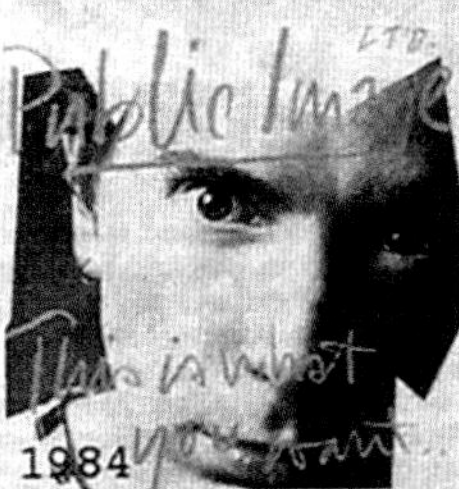

Giving music another look

Designer John Van Hamersveld brings his iconic rock 'n' roll images to Calgary

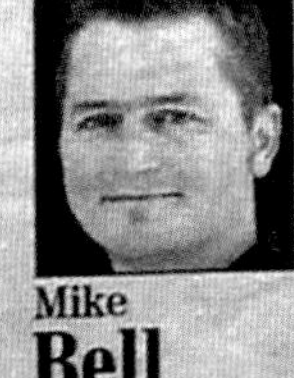

Mike **Bell**

Music

Defining what **John Van Hamersveld** does isn't so easy.

Even to the people around him and know him best.

"My father used to ask me, 'What do you do John?' " says Van Hamersveld during a recent phone interview. "And I would say in return, 'I'm a cultural designer.'

"And that sort of resolved our relationship."

What he's saying, really, is he's more defined by what he's done, which has also helped define people, time, eras, events.

Confused? Well, maybe we'll just go with the usual and call him an artist and designer who has been responsible for some of the most stunning and lasting images of the '60s, '70s and '80s, including posters and album covers that are now iconic. Some of his most notable work in the album vein includes **The Rolling Stones'** *Exile On Main St.*, **The Beatles'** *Magical Mystery Tour* and **KISS'** *Hotter Than Hell*.

Not bad, considering his career as an album designer came about quite casually, when — armed with the poster for the film *Endless Summer*, which is now, itself, a pop culture entity — he walked into Capitol Records on a cold call.

"I walked into the guy's office with my *Endless Summer* print and he went over to his book shelf and he pulled out an *Endless Summer* soundtrack album," Van Hamersveld says. "So it wasn't as if I'd done an album cover before, but my poster had been reduced down to do the album cover."

Two days later, on the strength of that, as well as, his ties with L.A.'s burgeoning '60s rock scene a la his work as a concert and party promoter, he was hired on full time and eventually counted on as a link to the youth culture.

"Here's a record company in the middle of their transition from the '50s where they were in the souvenir business basically for **Frank Sinatra** and **Nat King Cole** ... and all of the sudden they're thrown into this new world," says Van Hamersveld, who was given *Magical Mystery Tour* soon after his arrival.

"All of the sudden they're on top, they have these two major groups (The Beatles and **Beach Boys**) and they're making money, but they still have absolutely no idea of who they are, what they're doing, how to do it, whatever.

"So, I became a person that was a translator for them — a cultural translator."

A short while later, he left the company and went back to work on his own, producing more designs, posters and album art before moving away from pop culture.

Now, after a 21-year absence — which has seen him called back into the rock world thanks to his poster design for the **Cream**'s reunion concerts earlier this year in both London and New York.

So popular was the design, that it's now been used as the cover for the CD and DVD release of the concerts and set him off on a signing tour of the U.S..

Van Hamersveld will be in Calgary tomorrow for his only Canadian appearance signing Cream reunion posters and his famous **Jimi Hendrix** design at Heritage Posters and Music Inc. (1505 11 Ave. S.W.) from 1 p.m. to 3 p.m.

A more complete overview of his work can be found at www.post-future.com and www.vanhamersveldmuseumofart.com.

mike.bell@calgarysun.com

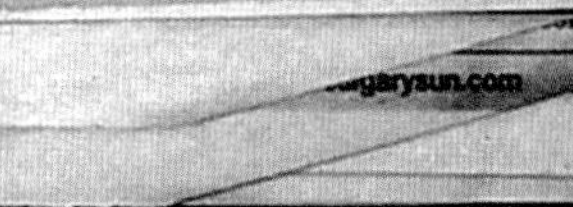

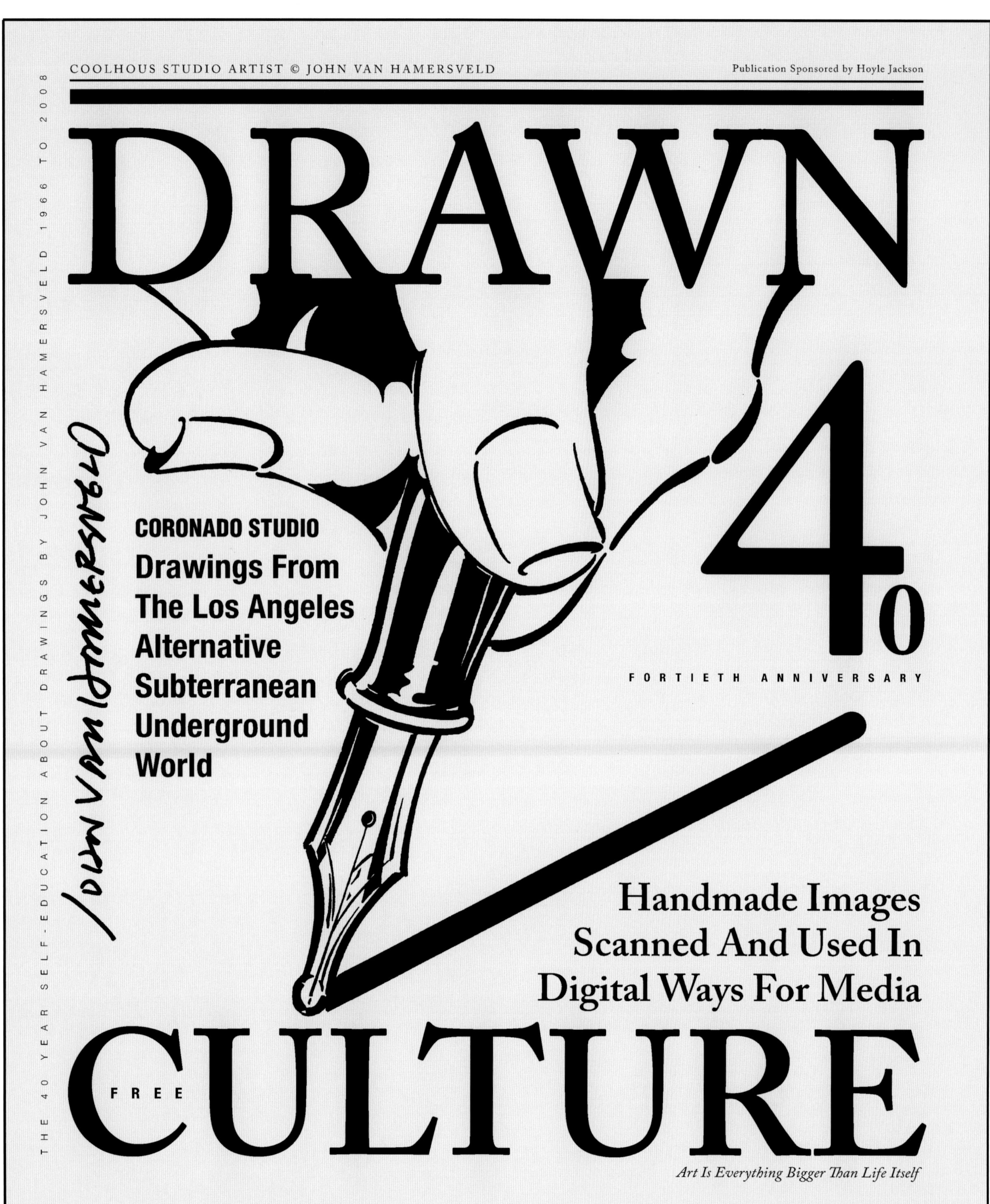

Newspaper as Analogue Communication

Fortieth Anniversary Of The John Van Hamersveld Drawings

Page72

Prints On Paper

17x22

Collectors Editions

Black & White
Contemporary
Giclee Fine Art
Print Editions of
Twenty-Four
Contact Us At
Post-Future.com

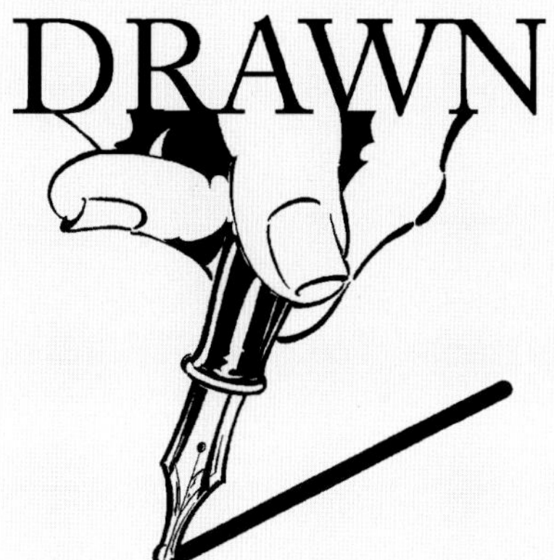

Drawings by John Van Hamersveld 1996 -2008

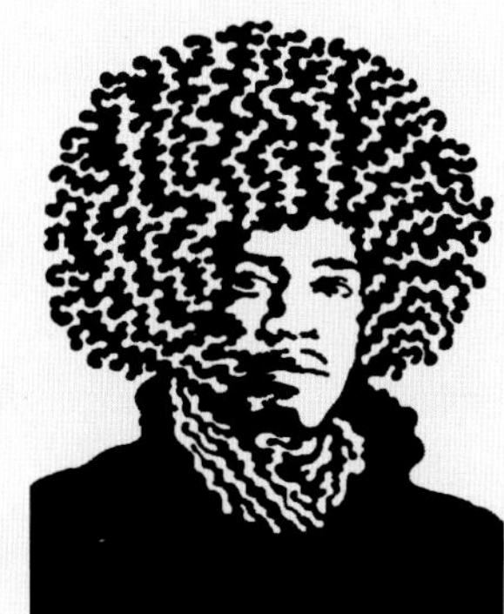

Hendrix 1966

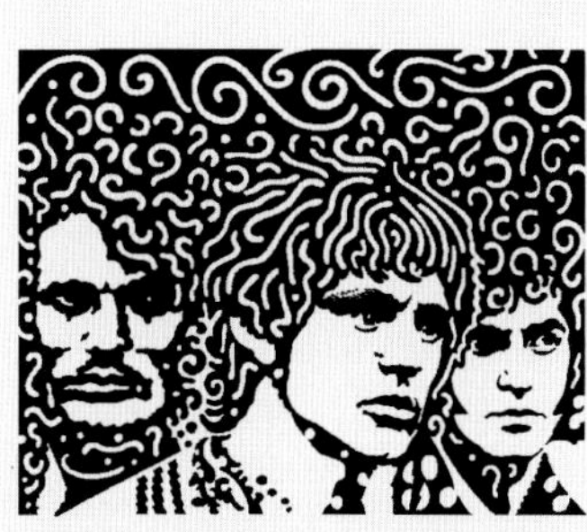

Cream 2005

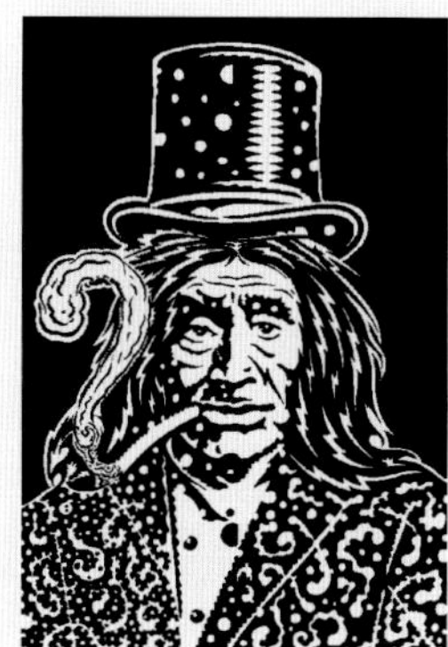

The Chief 2006

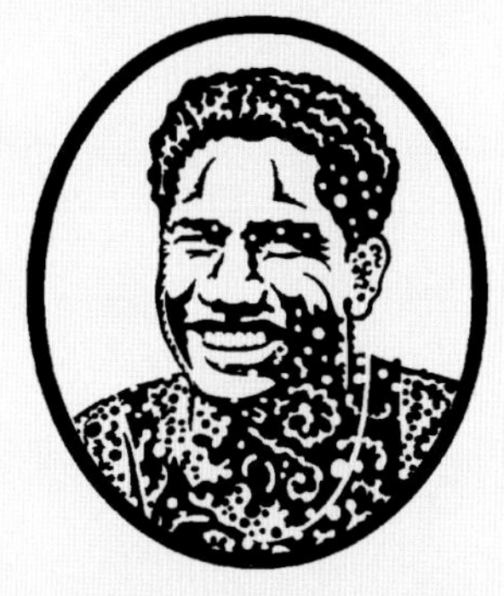

The Duke 2006

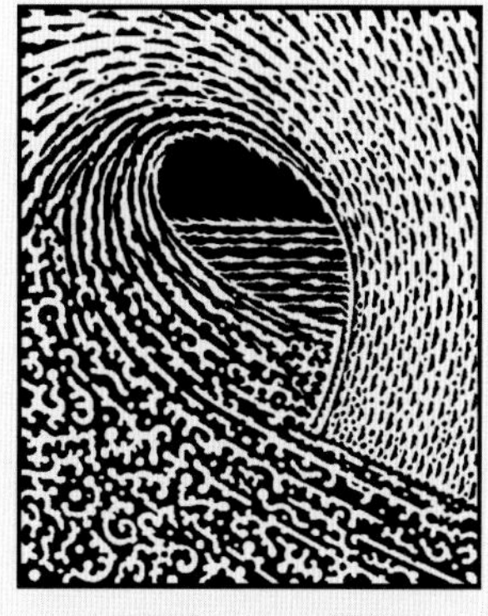

The Next Wave 2006

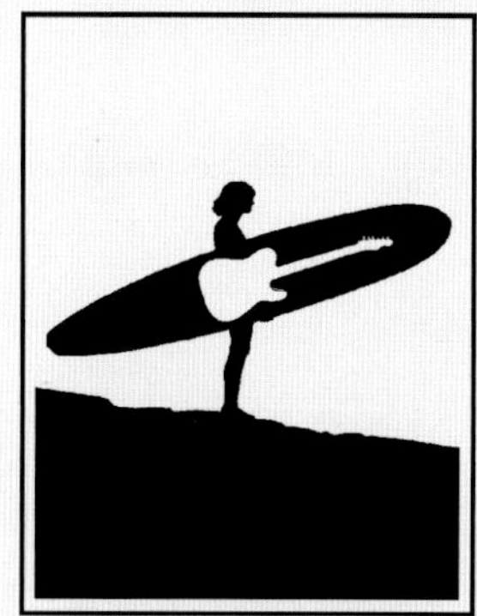

Surf Rock 2006

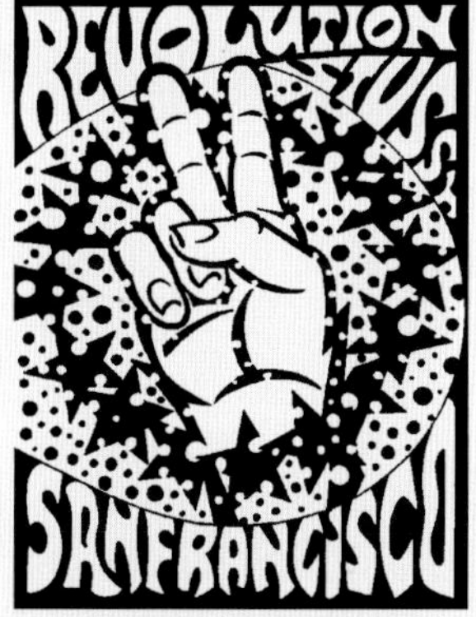

Stussy Revolution 1 2006

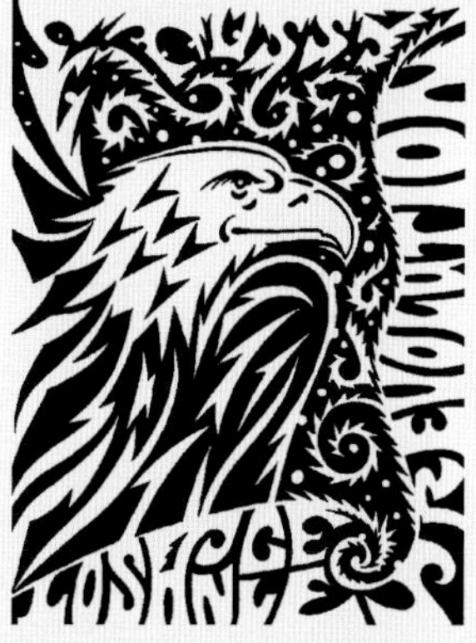

Stussy Revolution 2 2006

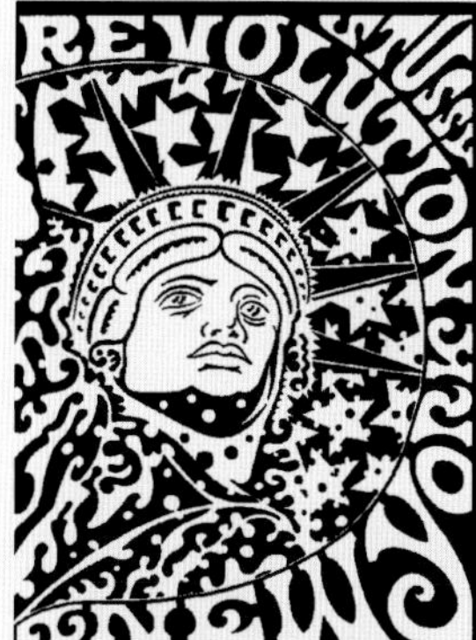

Stussy Revolution 3 2006

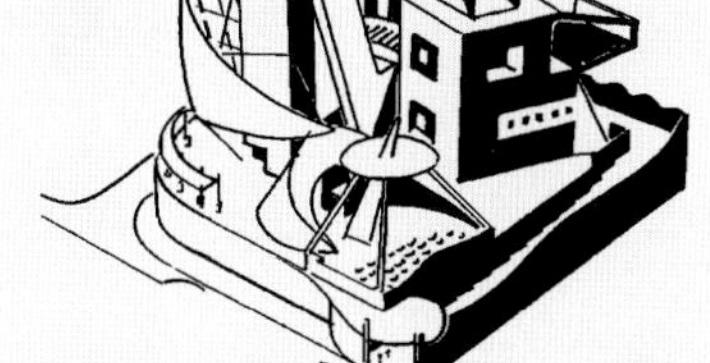

See the virtual museum VHMOA!
VAN HAMERSVELD MUSEUM OF ART, SANTA MONICA

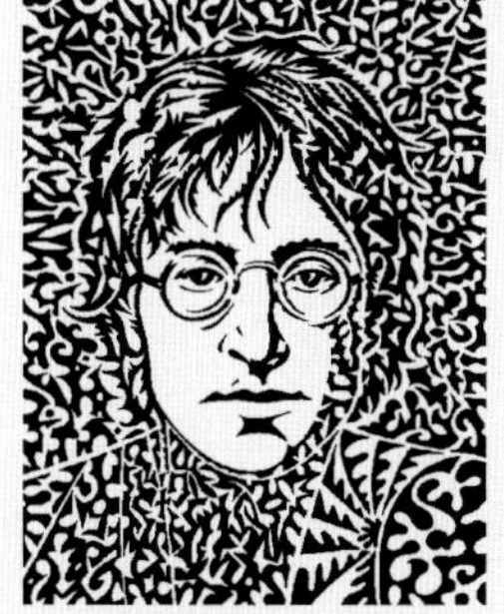

John Lennon 2007

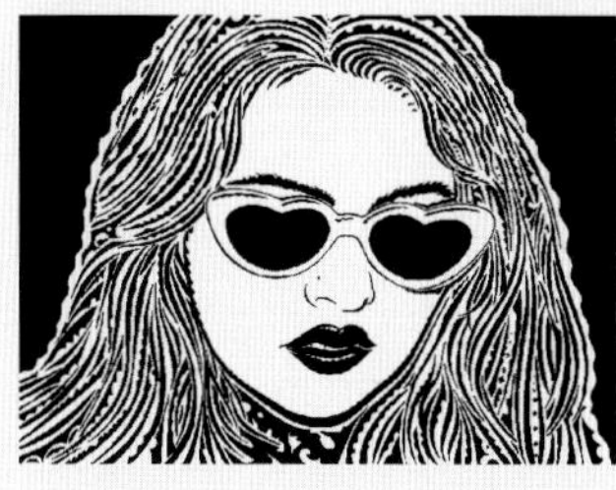

Love Sunset 2008

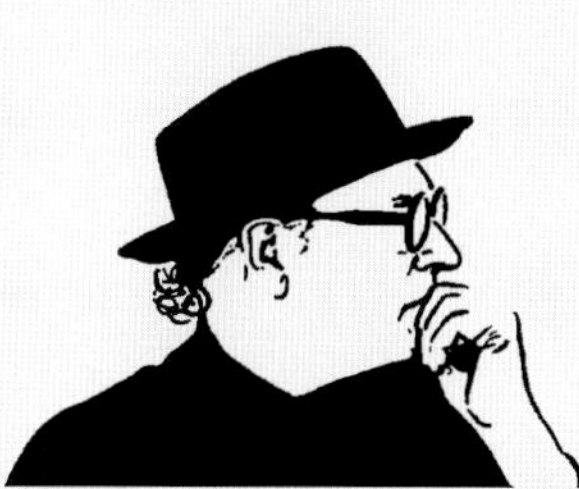

Self Portrait 2008

Communicating 75 Analogue Drawings from 1968–2008

TEES AS COMMUNICATION IN 2004

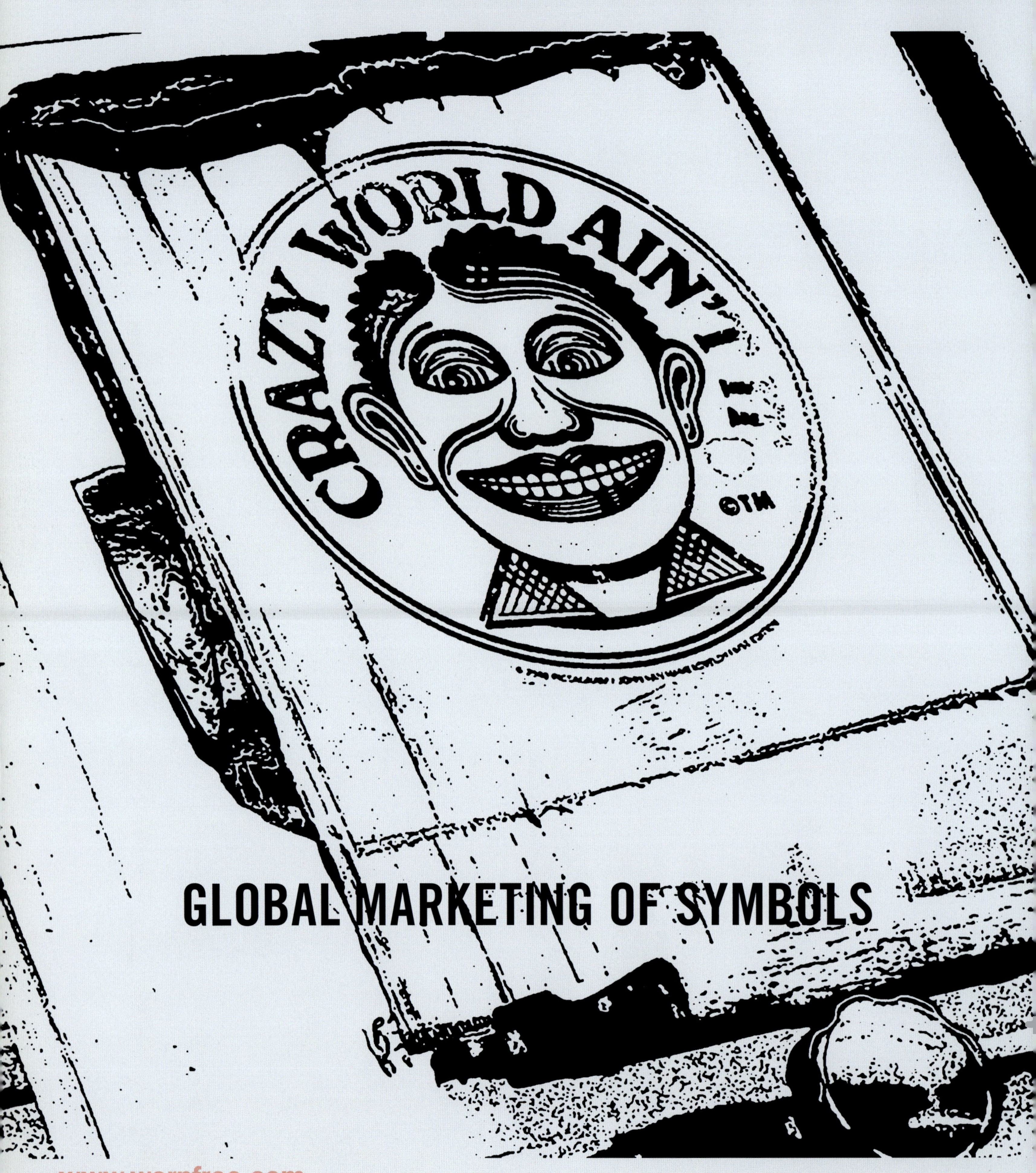

GLOBAL MARKETING OF SYMBOLS

www.wornfree.com

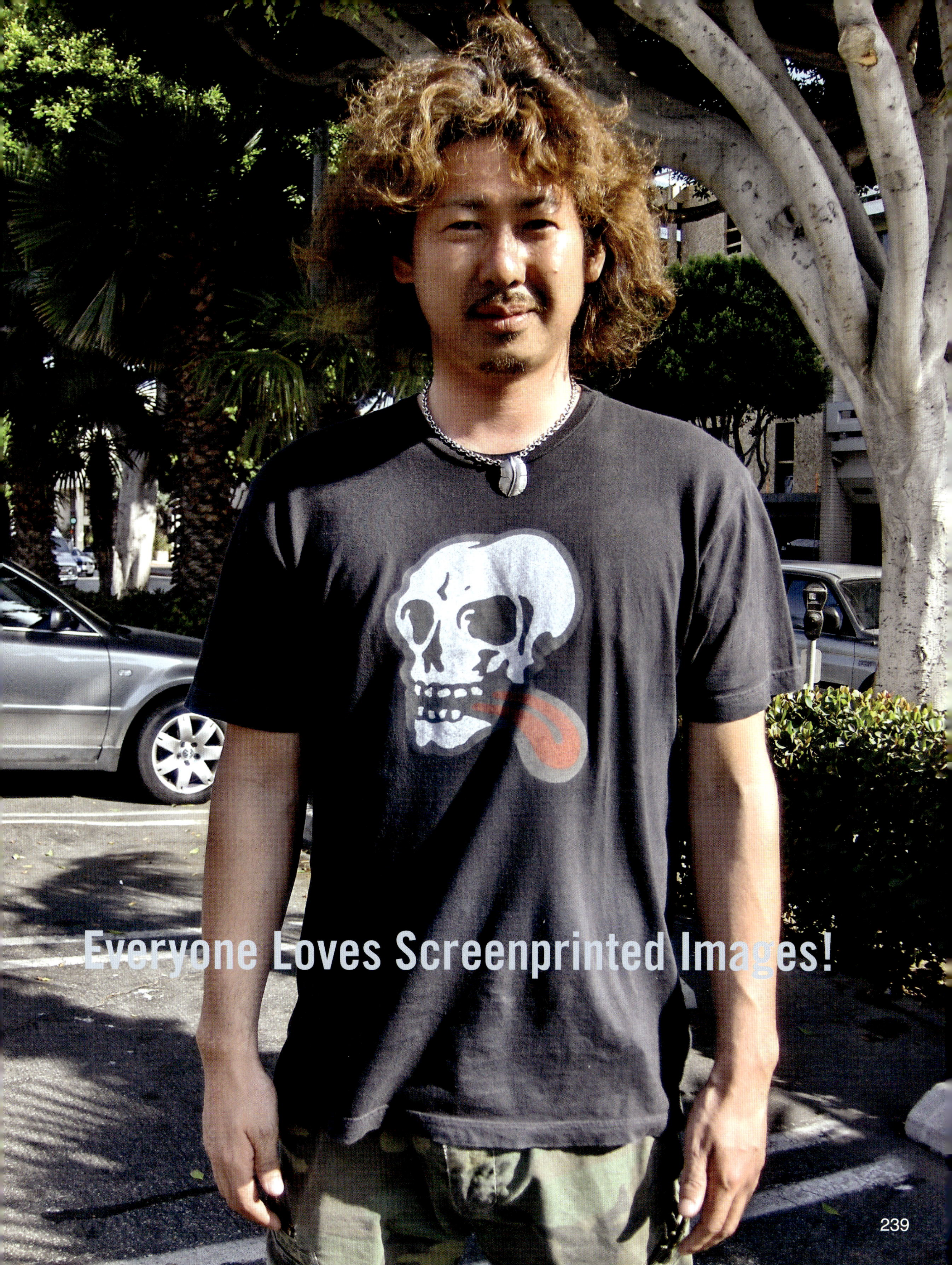

Everyone Loves Screenprinted Images!

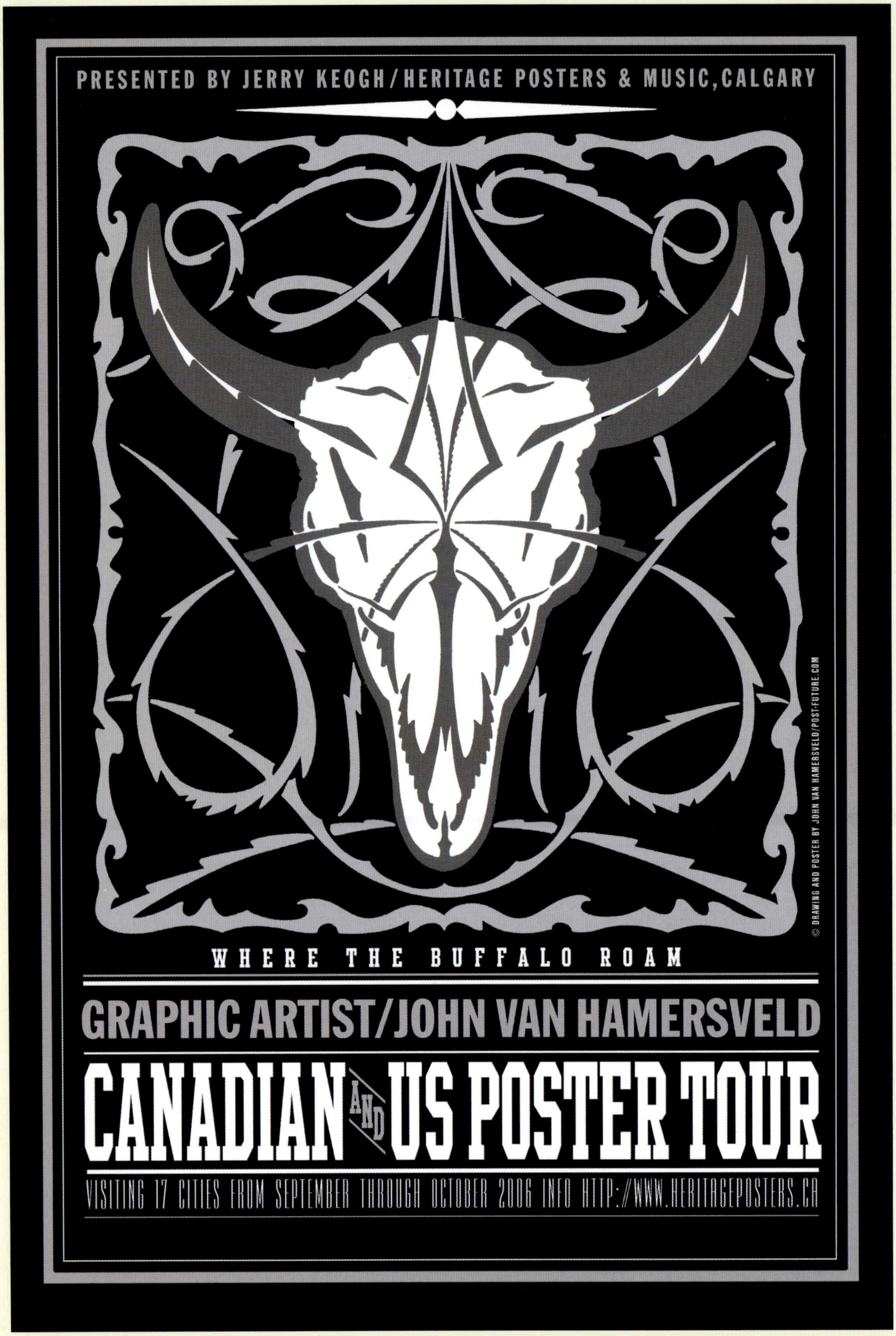

PRESENTED BY JERRY KEOGH/HERITAGE POSTERS & MUSIC, CALGARY

WHERE THE BUFFALO ROAM

GRAPHIC ARTIST/JOHN VAN HAMERSVELD

CANADIAN AND US POSTER TOUR

VISITING 17 CITIES FROM SEPTEMBER THROUGH OCTOBER 2006 INFO HTTP://WWW.HERITAGEPOSTERS.CA

© DRAWING AND POSTER BY JOHN VAN HAMERSVELD/POST-FUTURE.COM

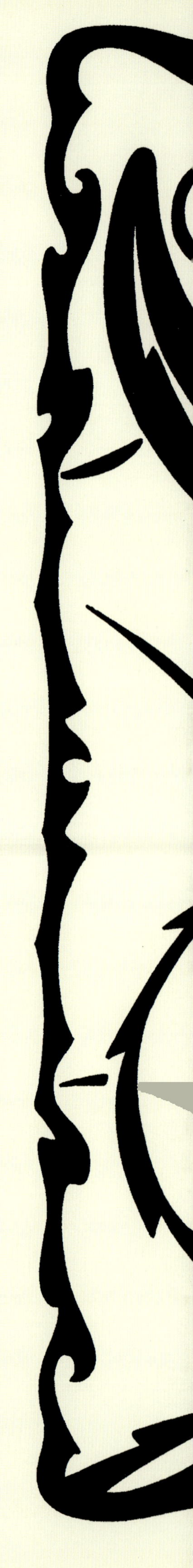

I began drawing a buffalo head after the *Crossing America* poster signing tour. With the *Hendrix* and *Cream Reunion* posters in tow, we decided to plan a Canadian tour. We met Emek and Gary Huston in Seattle at the Bumbershoot show, a poster event with over 95 artists present. From there we continued into Canada, a country with a population of just over 30 million, in contrast to the 311,732,000 people in the US. So the *Buffalo* poster found buyers and with the tour, we ventured into eight towns.

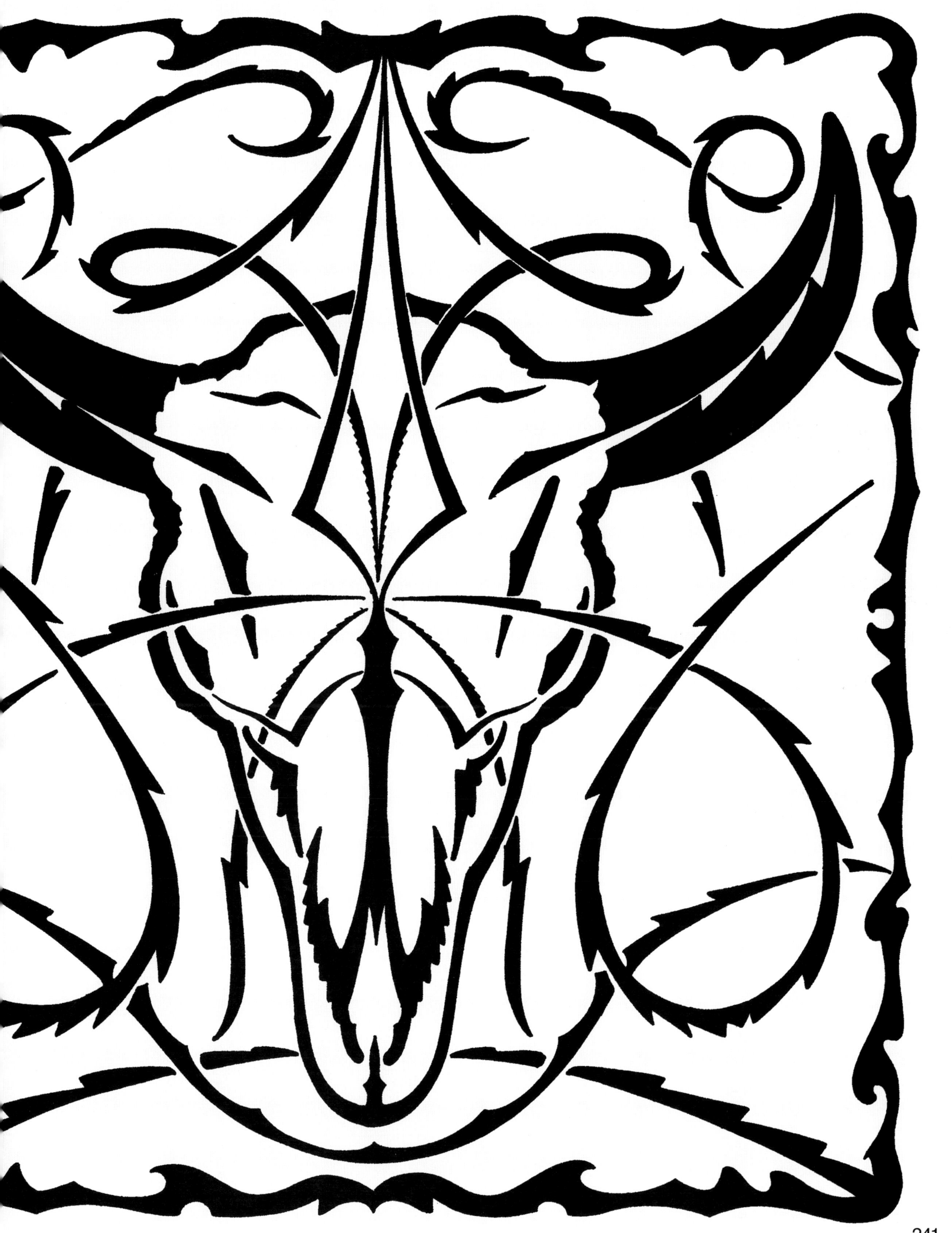

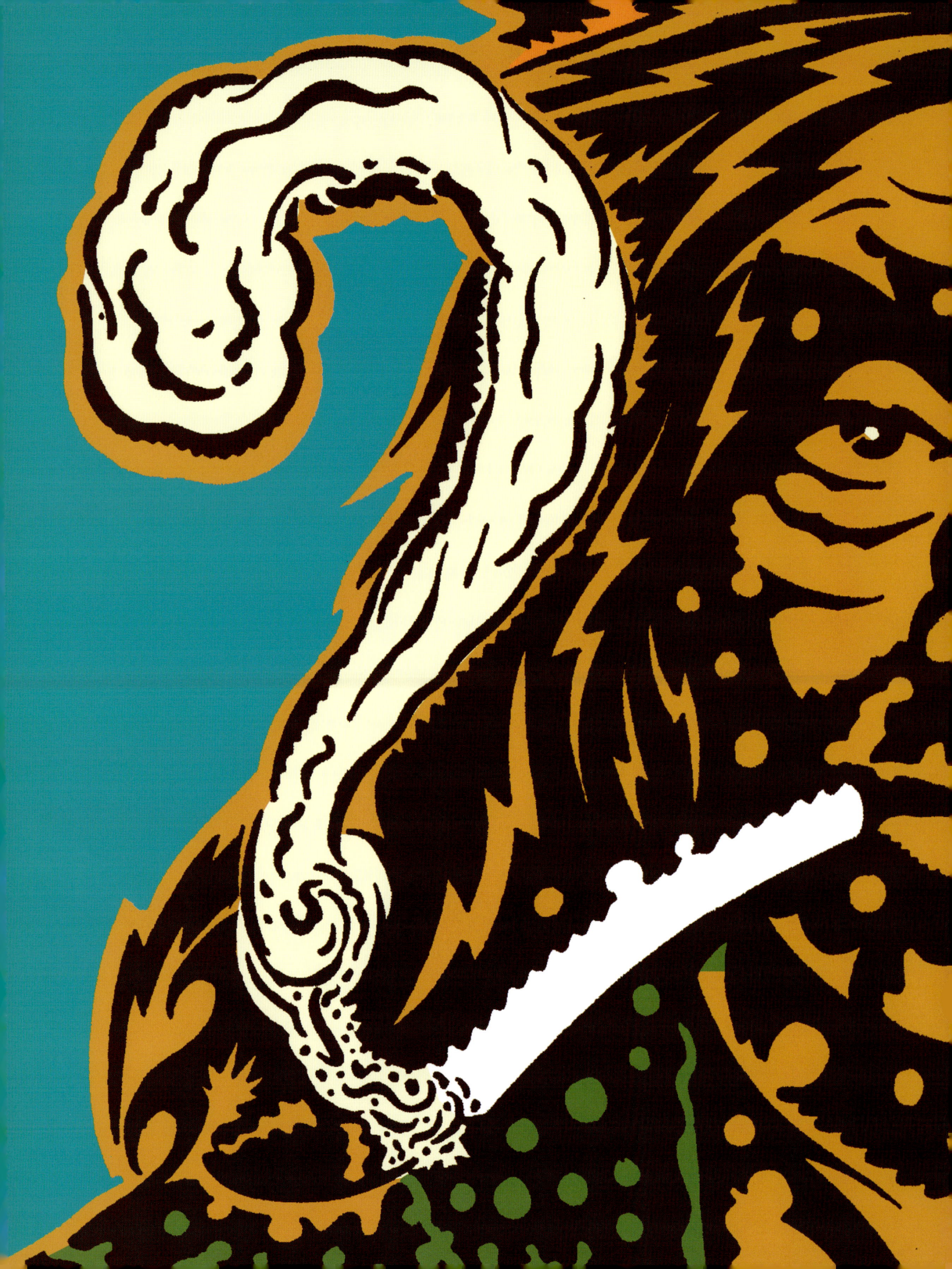

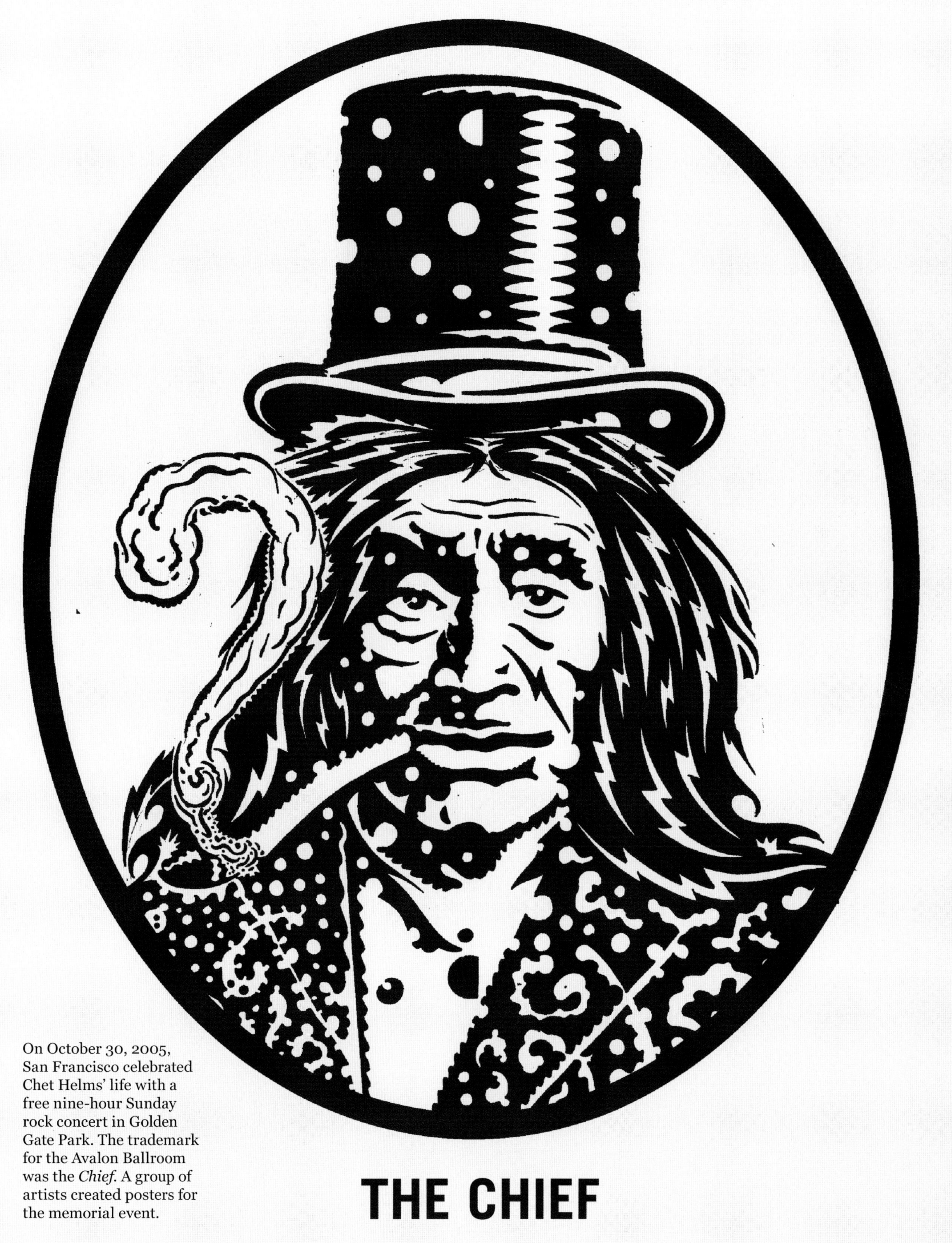

On October 30, 2005, San Francisco celebrated Chet Helms' life with a free nine-hour Sunday rock concert in Golden Gate Park. The trademark for the Avalon Ballroom was the *Chief*. A group of artists created posters for the memorial event.

THE CHIEF

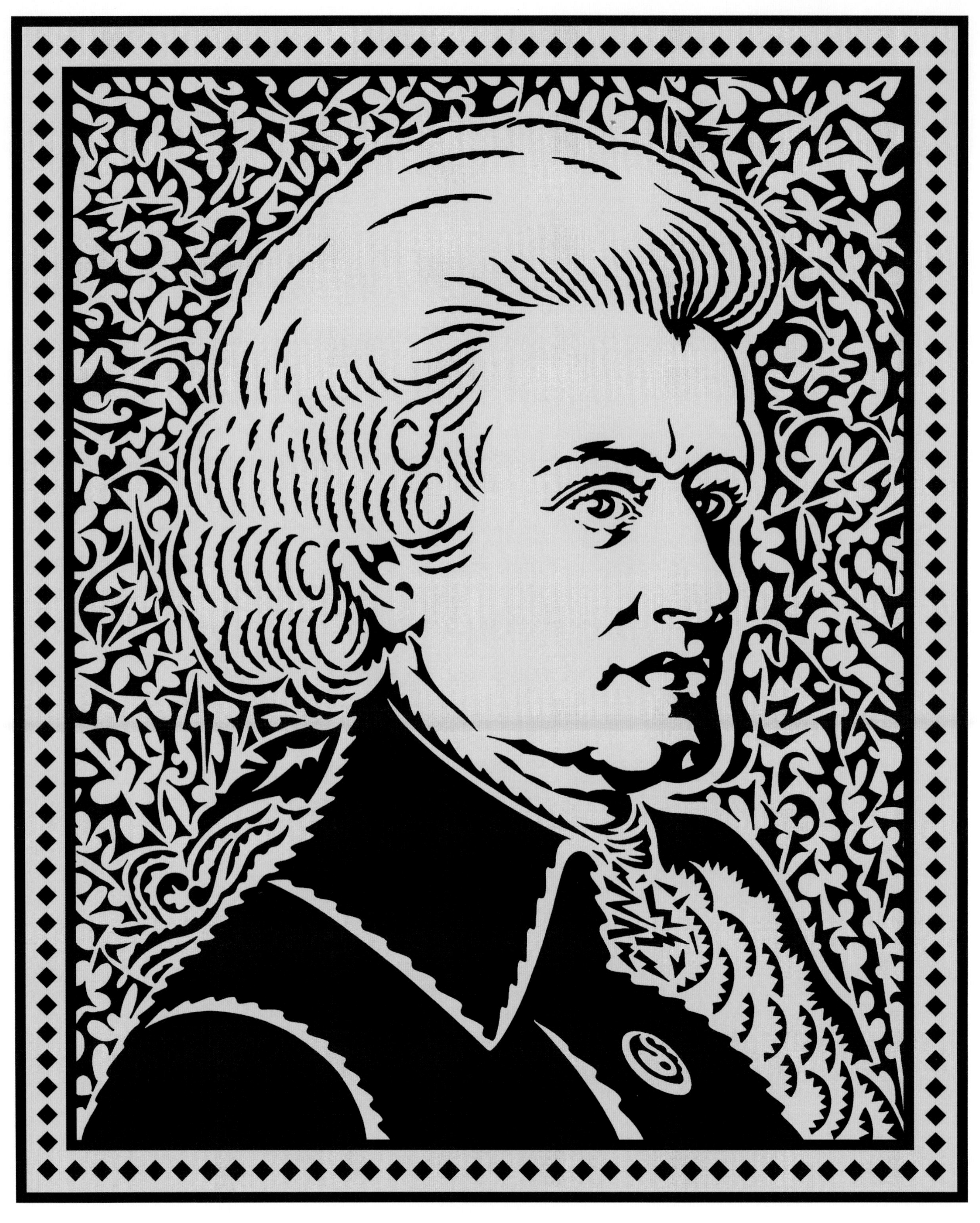

Wolfgang Amadeus Mozart

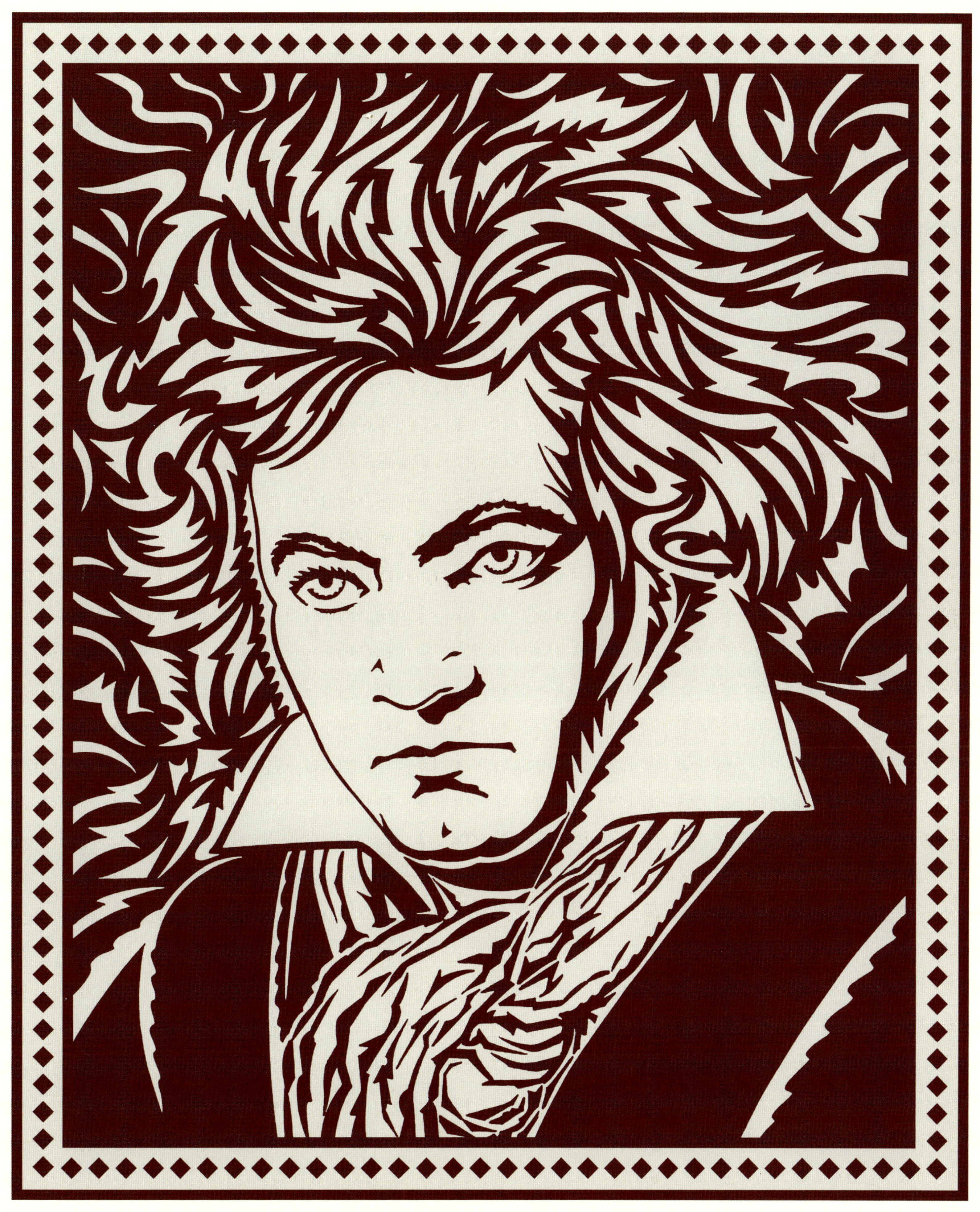

Ludwig van Beethoven

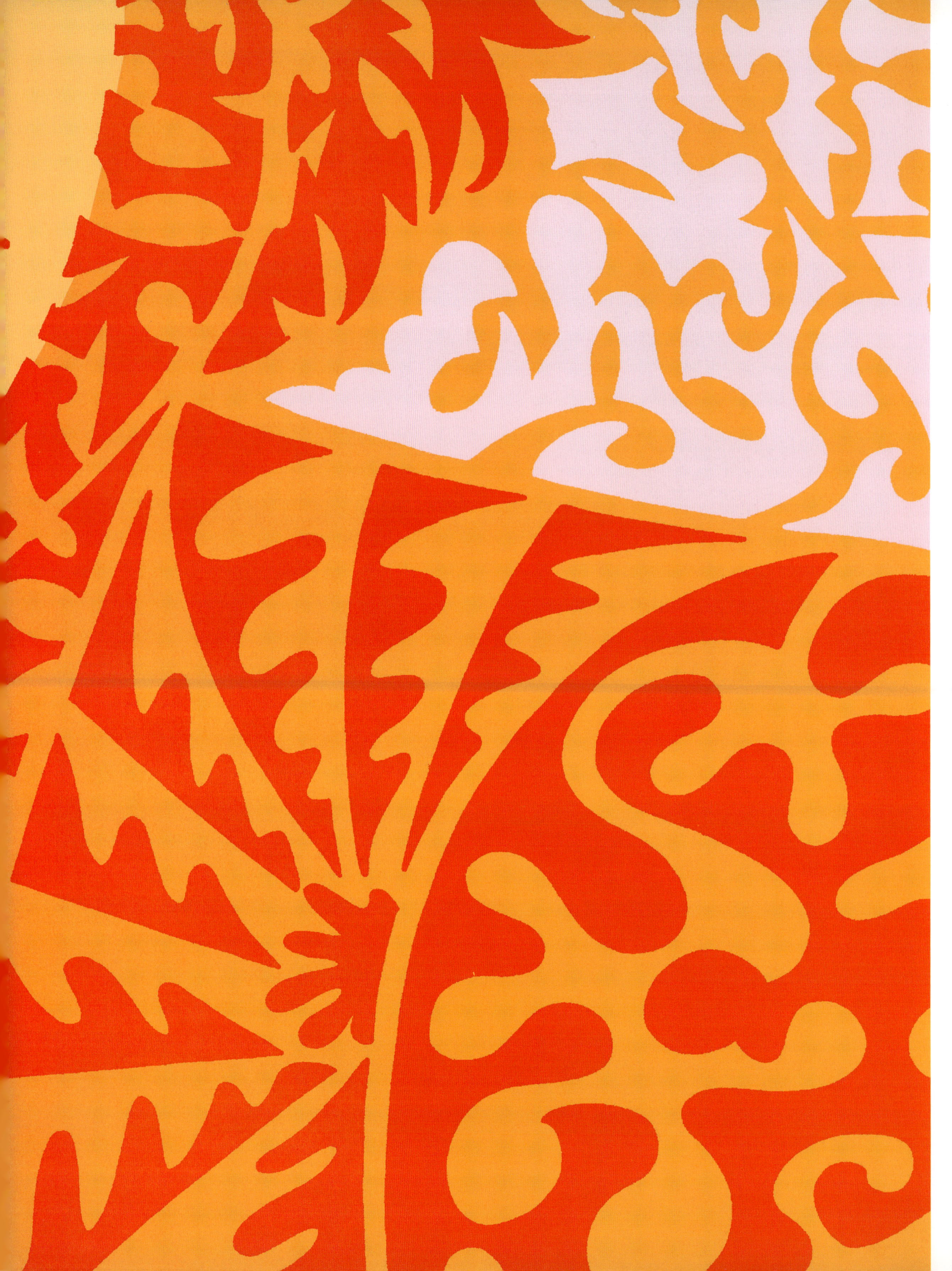

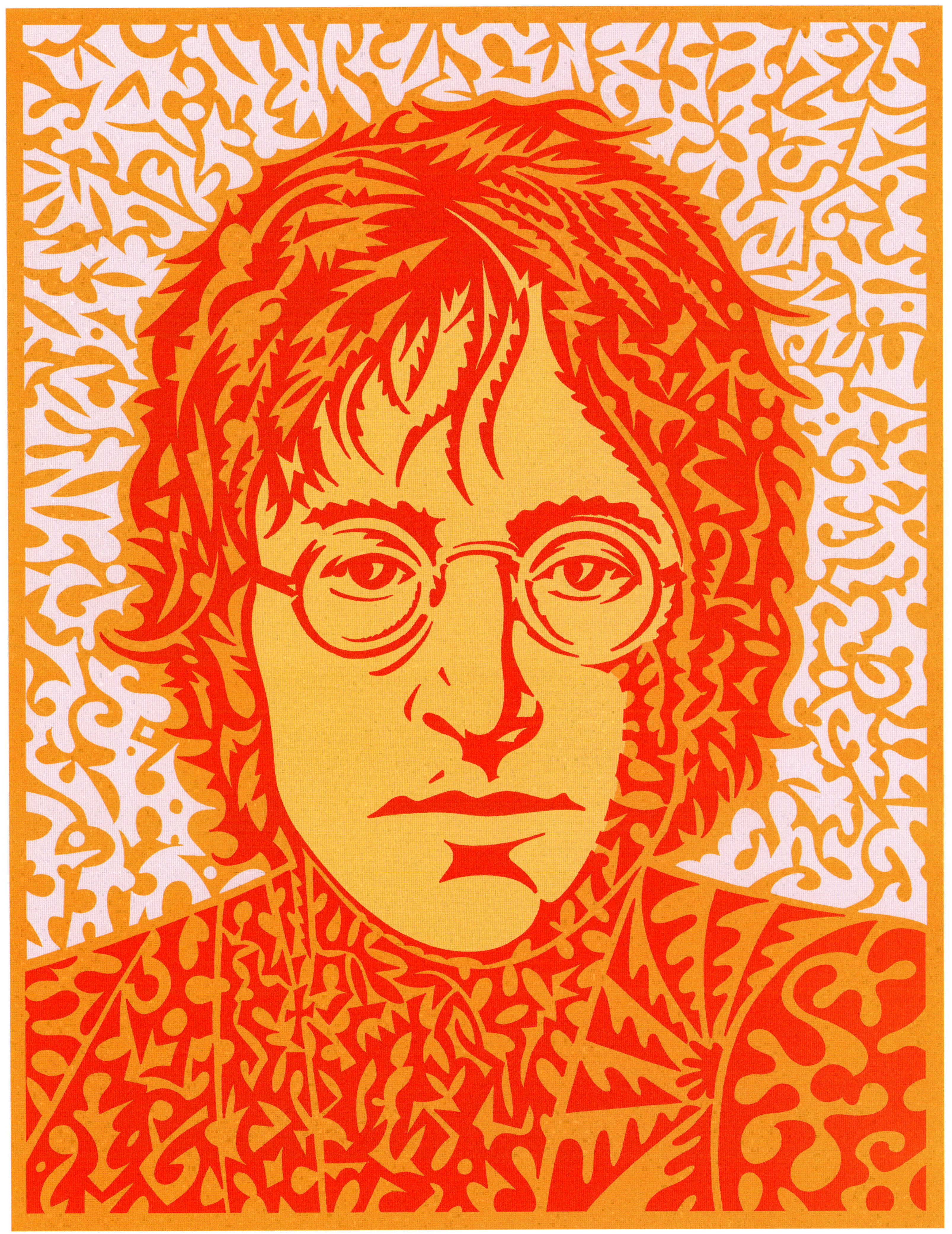

John Lennon (2007)

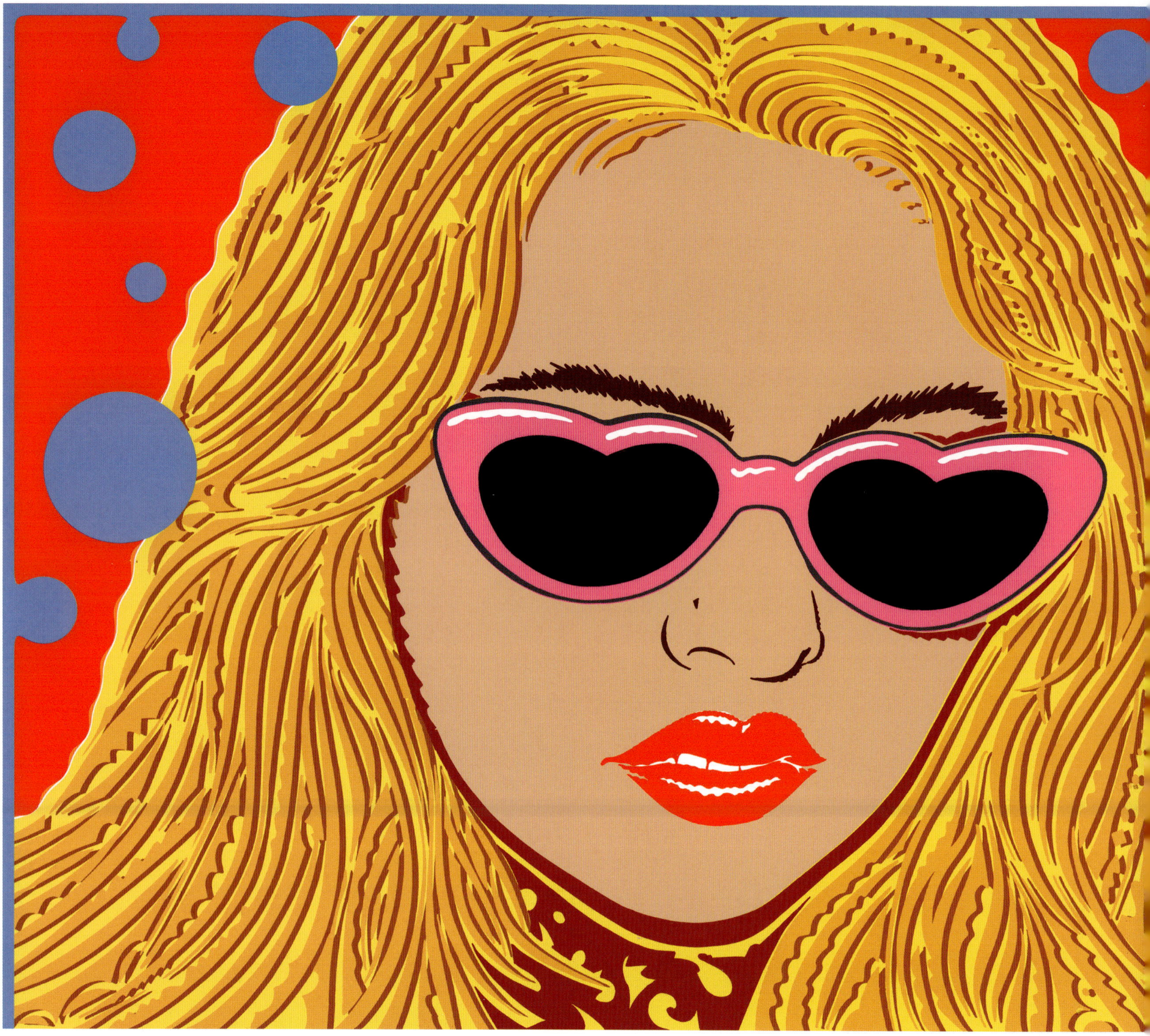

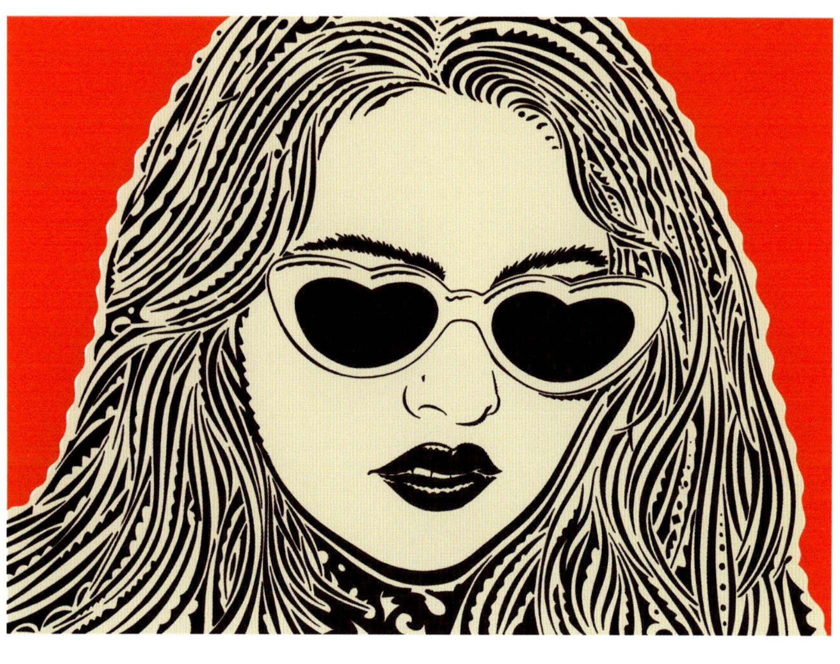

Love Sunset

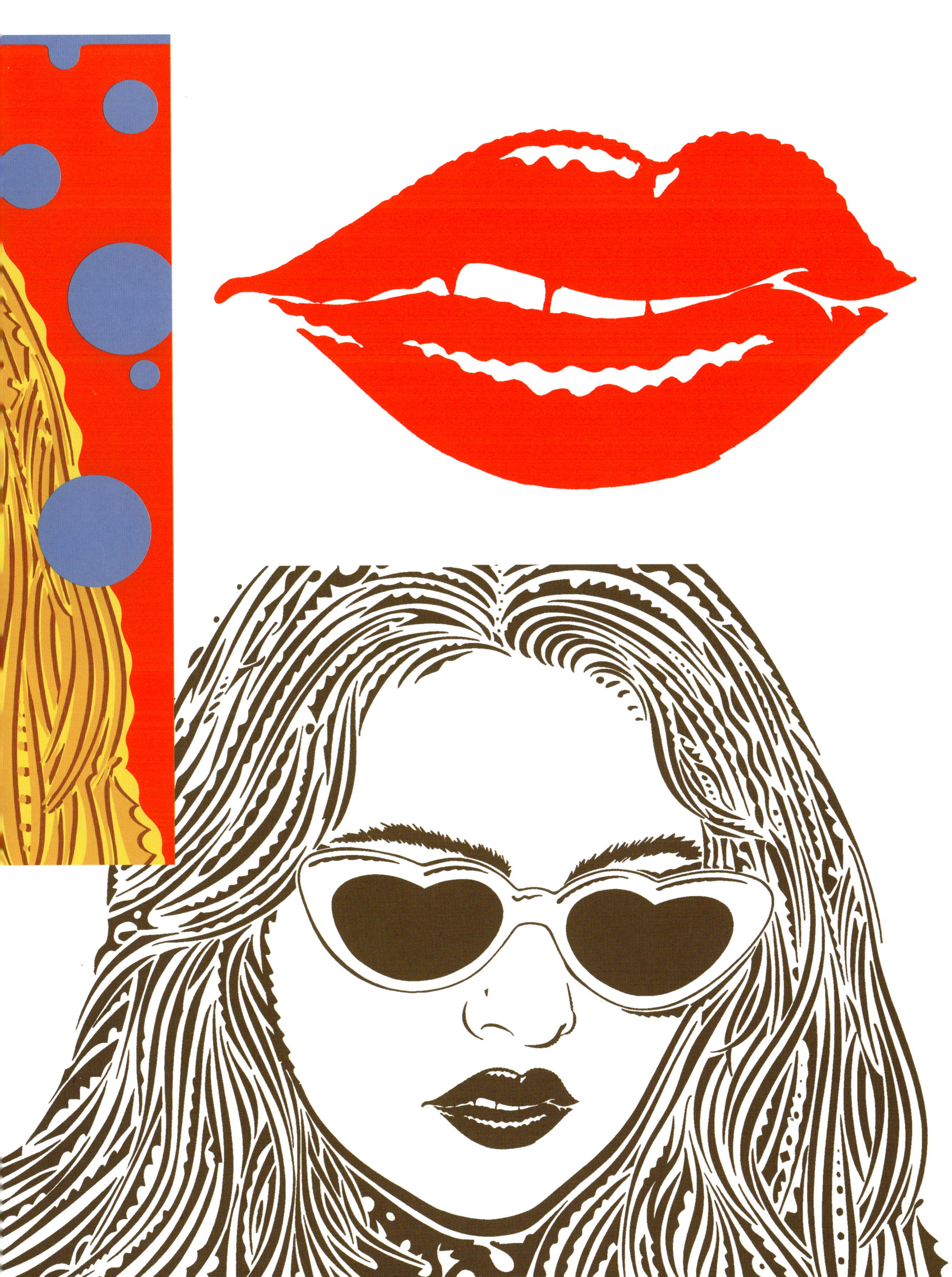

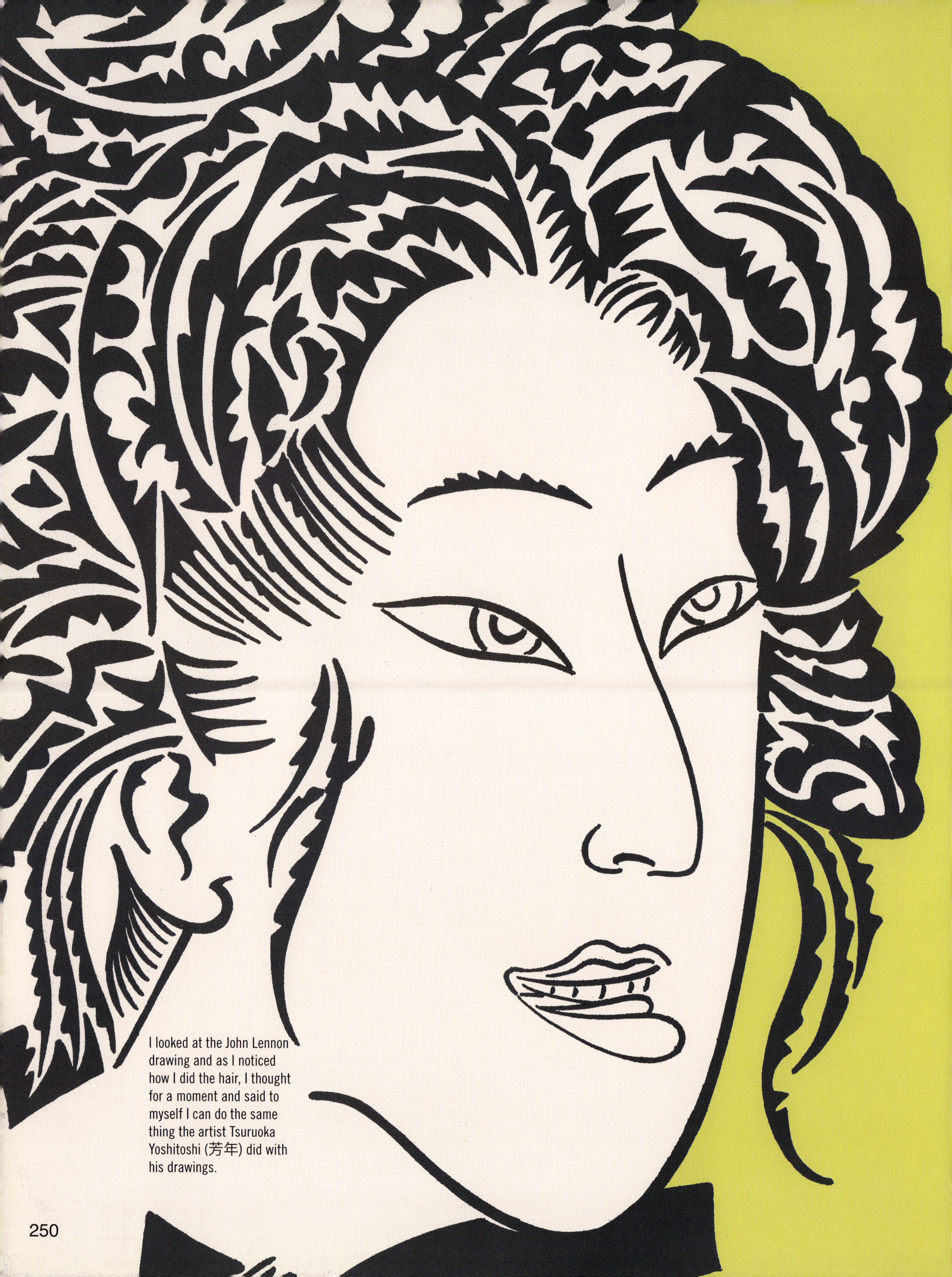

I looked at the John Lennon drawing and as I noticed how I did the hair, I thought for a moment and said to myself I can do the same thing the artist Tsuruoka Yoshitoshi (芳年) did with his drawings.

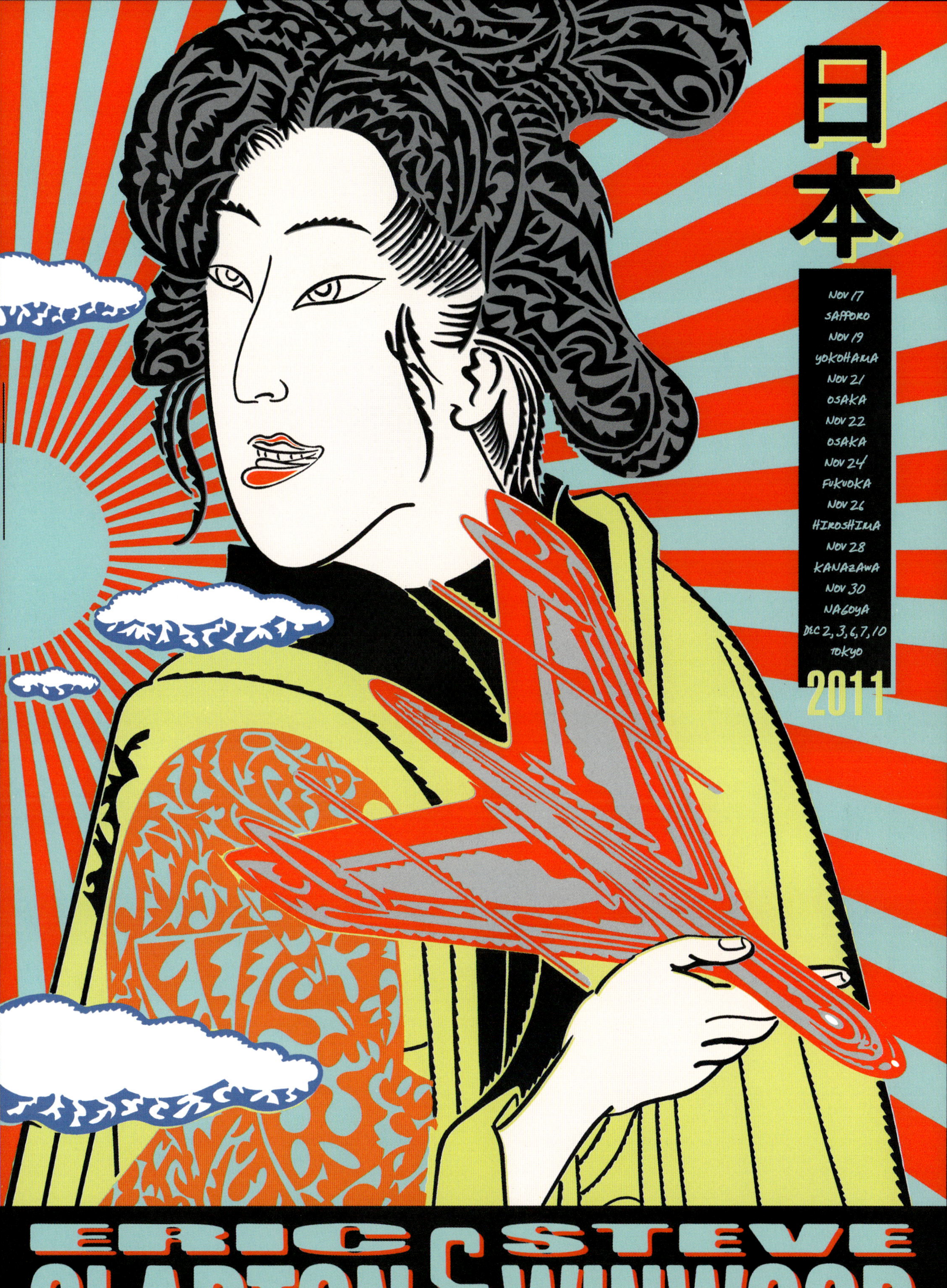

日本
NOV 17
SAPPORO
NOV 19
YOKOHAMA
NOV 21
OSAKA
NOV 22
OSAKA
NOV 24
FUKUOKA
NOV 26
HIROSHIMA
NOV 28
KANAZAWA
NOV 30
NAGOYA
DEC 2, 3, 6, 7, 10
TOKYO
2011
ERIC & STEVE
CLAPTON & WINWOOD

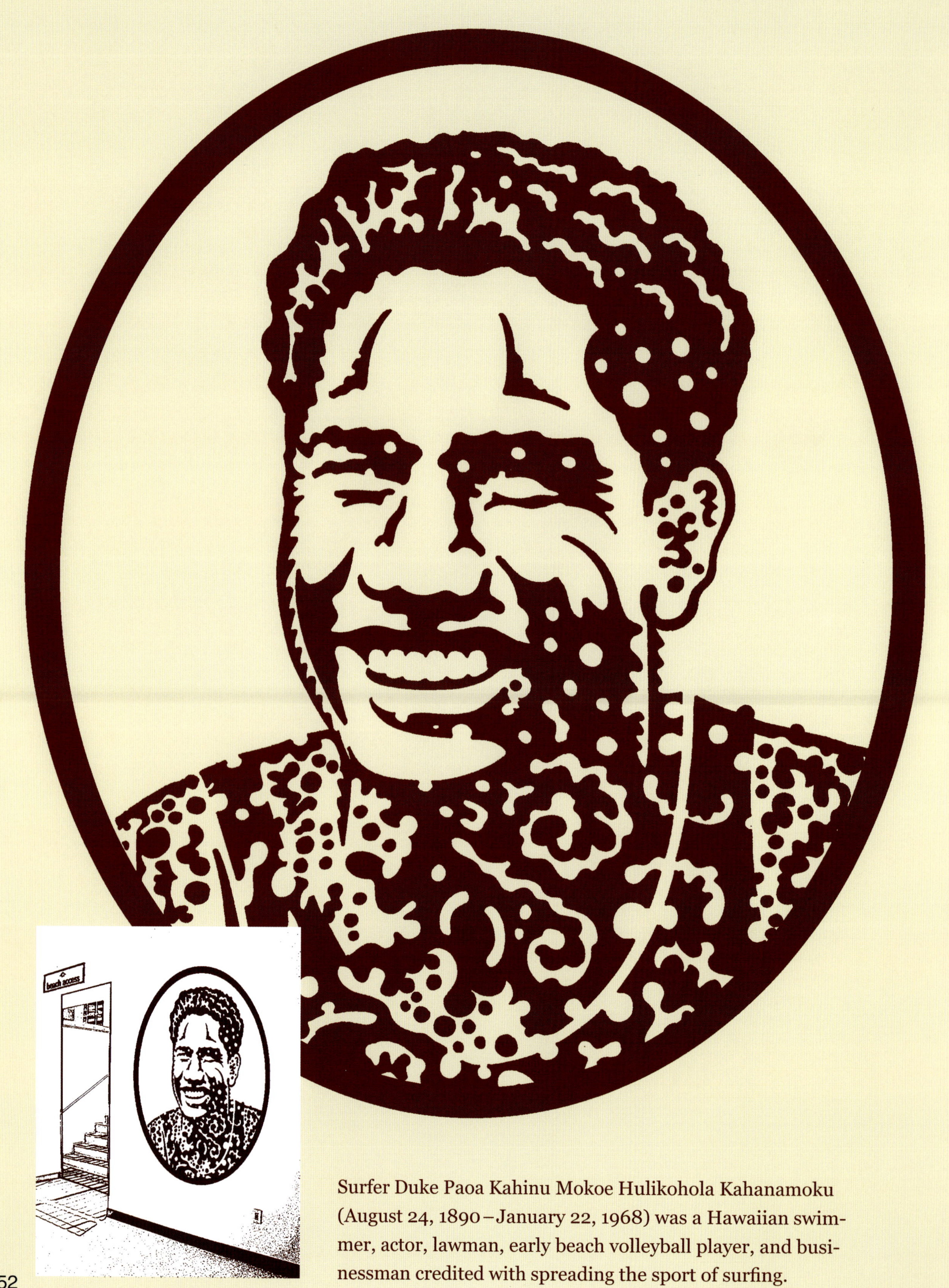

Surfer Duke Paoa Kahinu Mokoe Hulikohola Kahanamoku (August 24, 1890–January 22, 1968) was a Hawaiian swimmer, actor, lawman, early beach volleyball player, and businessman credited with spreading the sport of surfing.

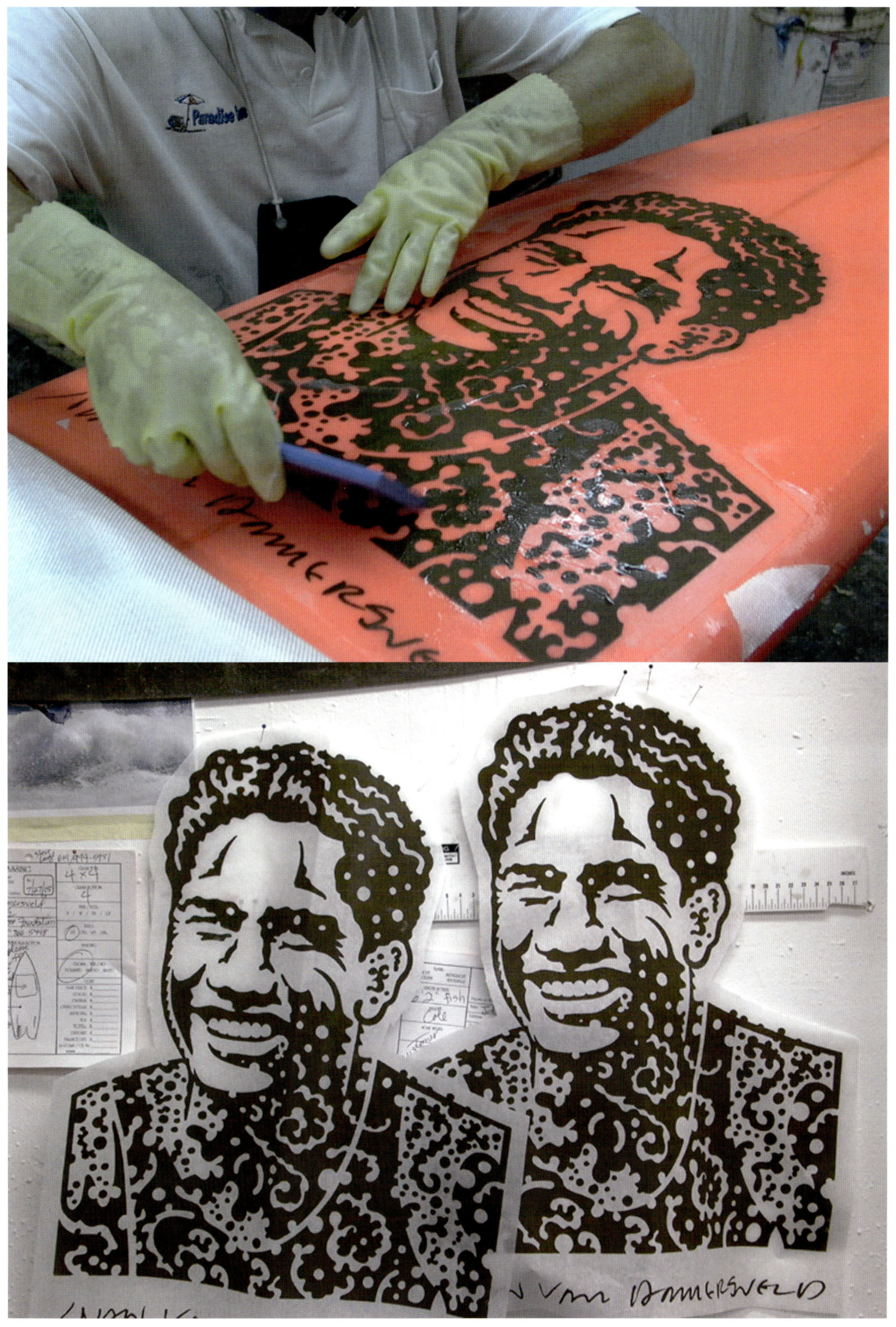

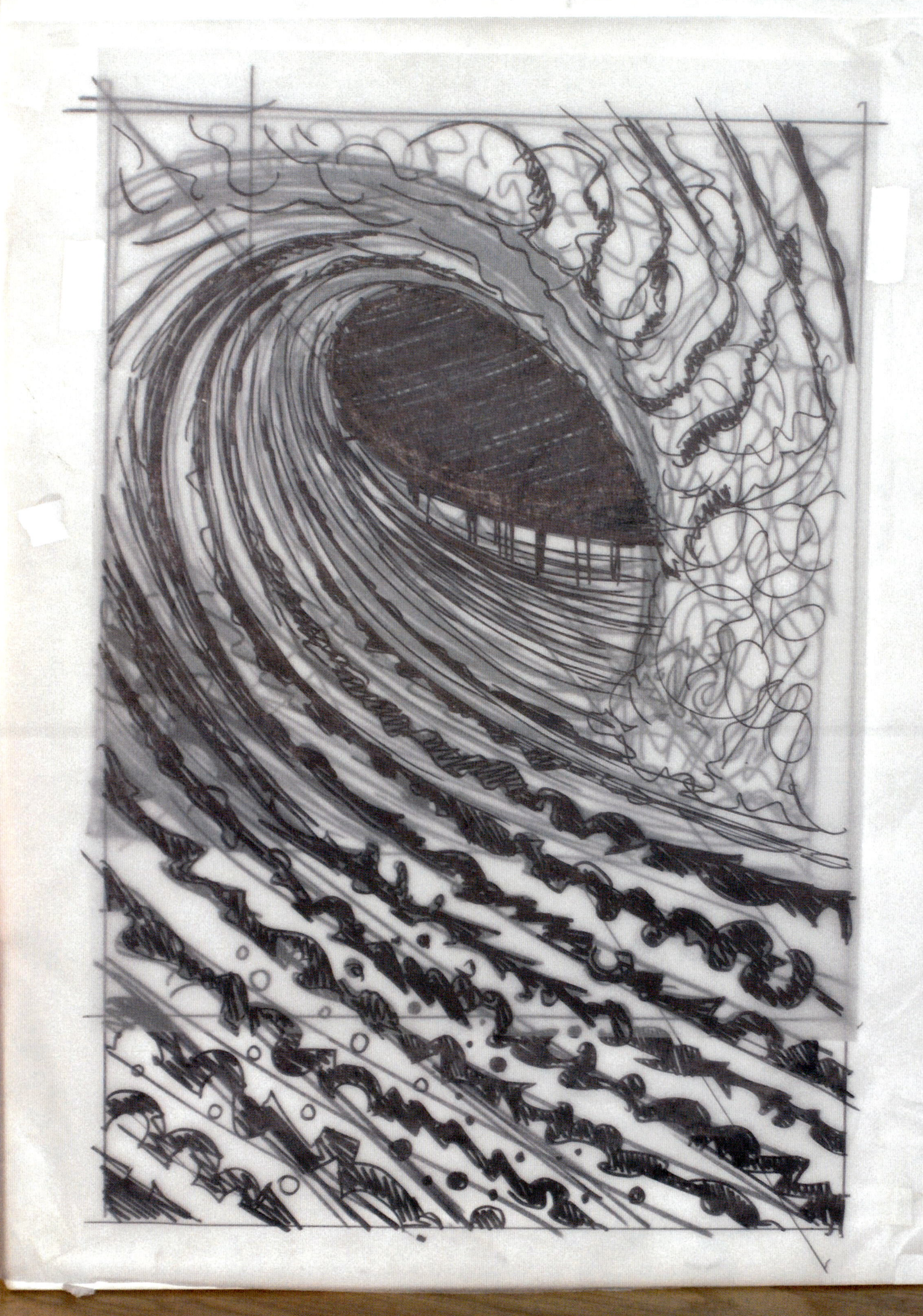

The rough and final drawing of *The Next Wave* fine art print (2006)

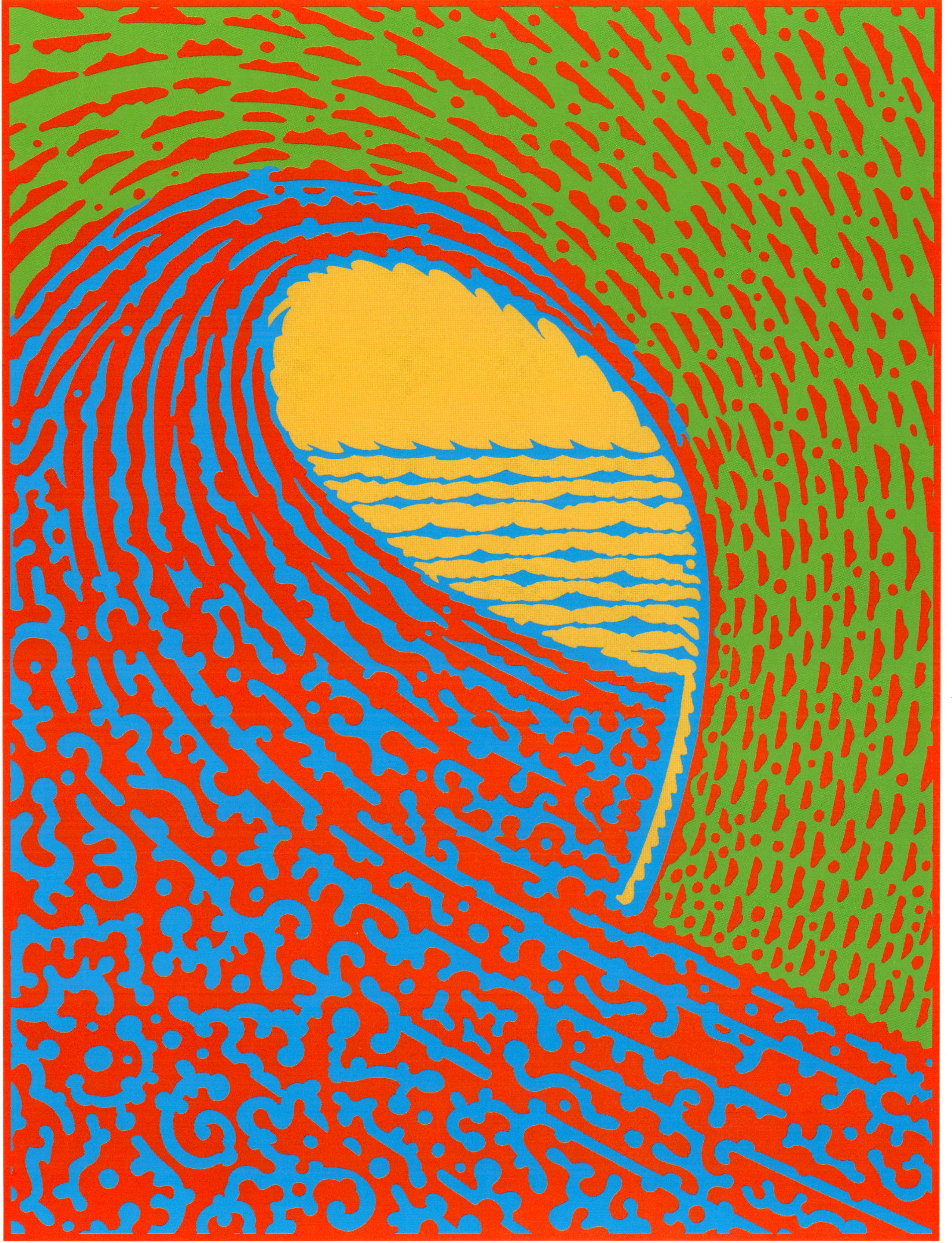

THE BIG WAVE

The Art Of Drawing Waves

During 2006, I drew the *Next Wave*, and to my surprise the kinetic quality of the '60s drawing came to a new level of perception. With the early understanding of printmaking, it seemed I could create a digital block treatment from the ancient world of the "Edo Floating World Style," previously obtained from studies in art school. Katsushika Hokusai (Oct 1760–May 10, 1849) was a Japanese artist, ukiyo-e painter, and printmaker during the Edo period. Through understanding of the printmaking process of Hokusai, I began with B&W, and then proceeded with colorizing.

The Luau wave in color and black and white shows the combining of the color blocks. The Big Wave *(right) is like the Hokusai notion of a huge wave in the sea of Japan.*

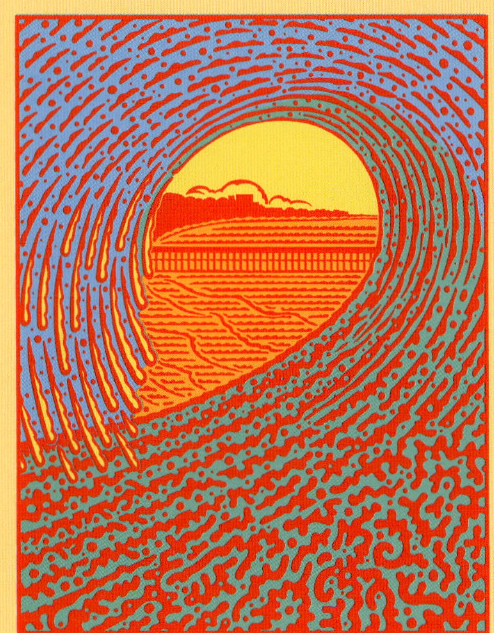

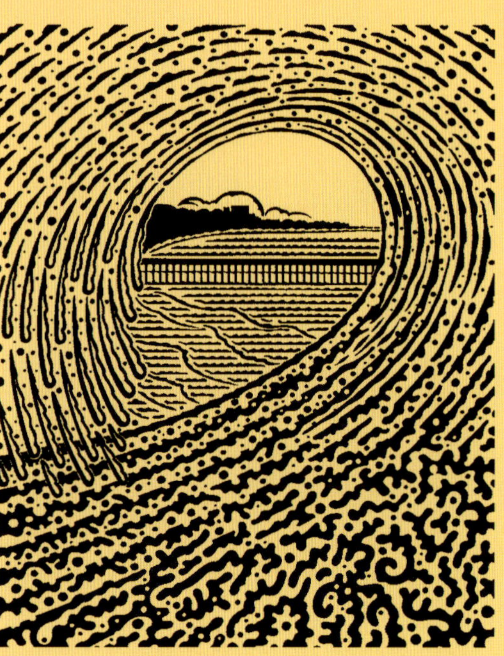

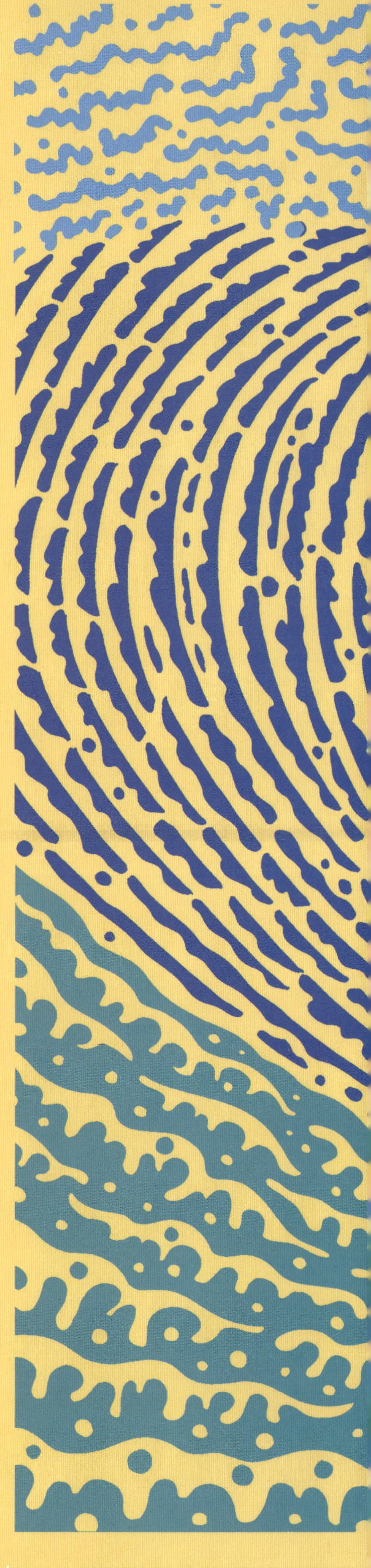

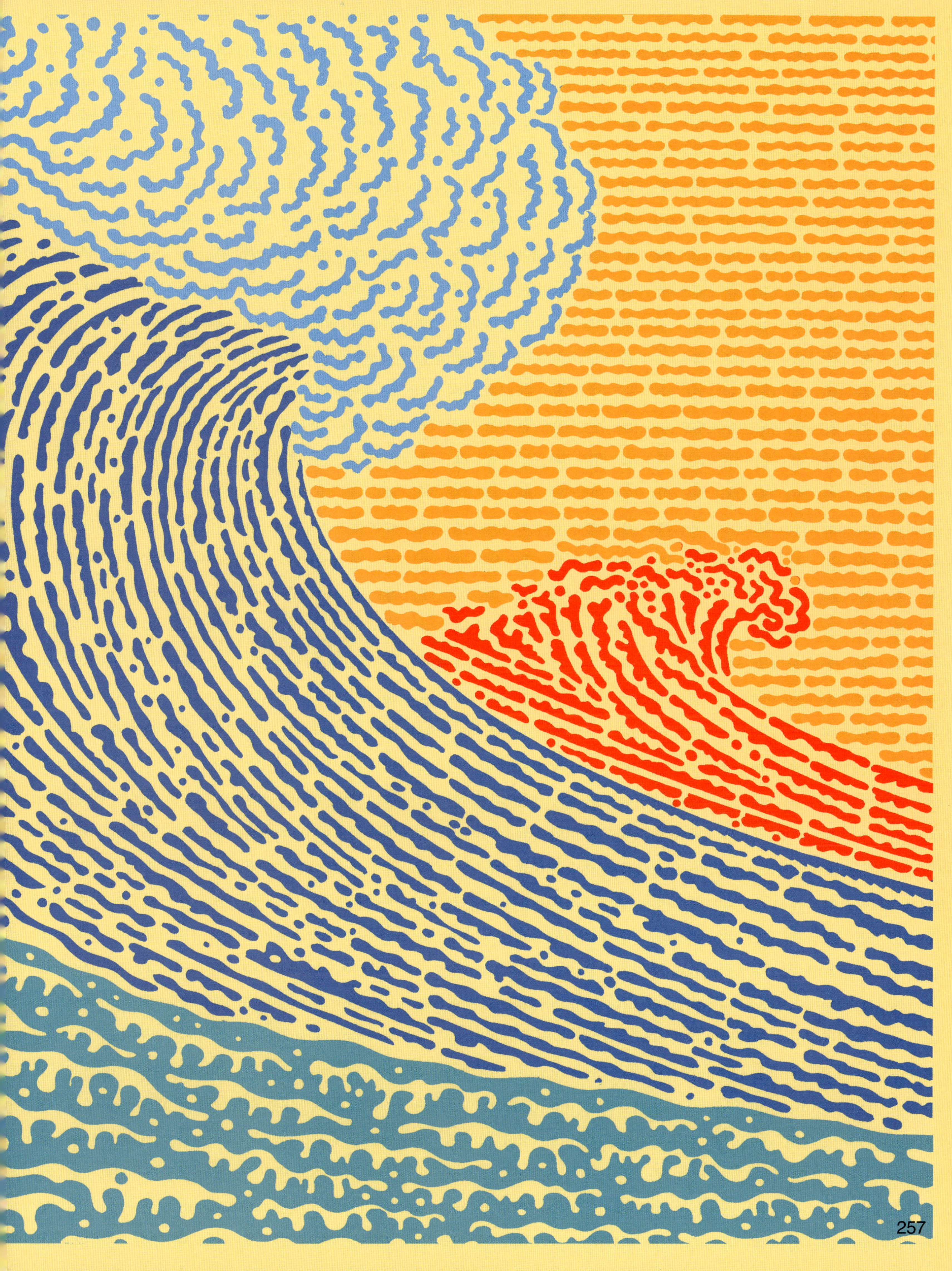

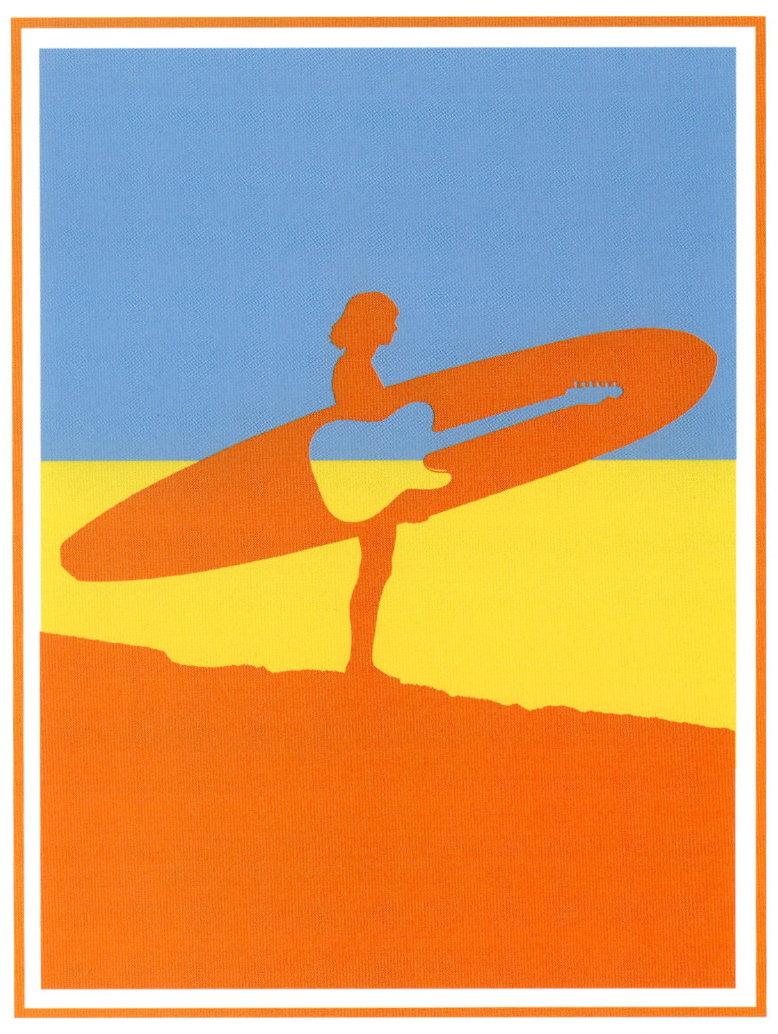
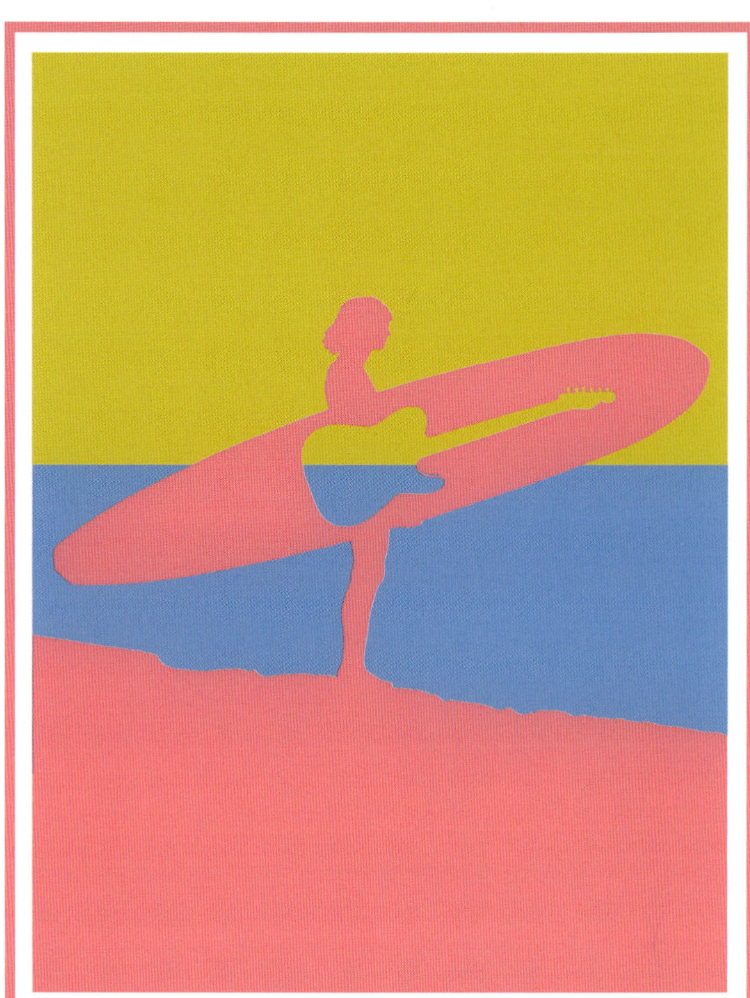
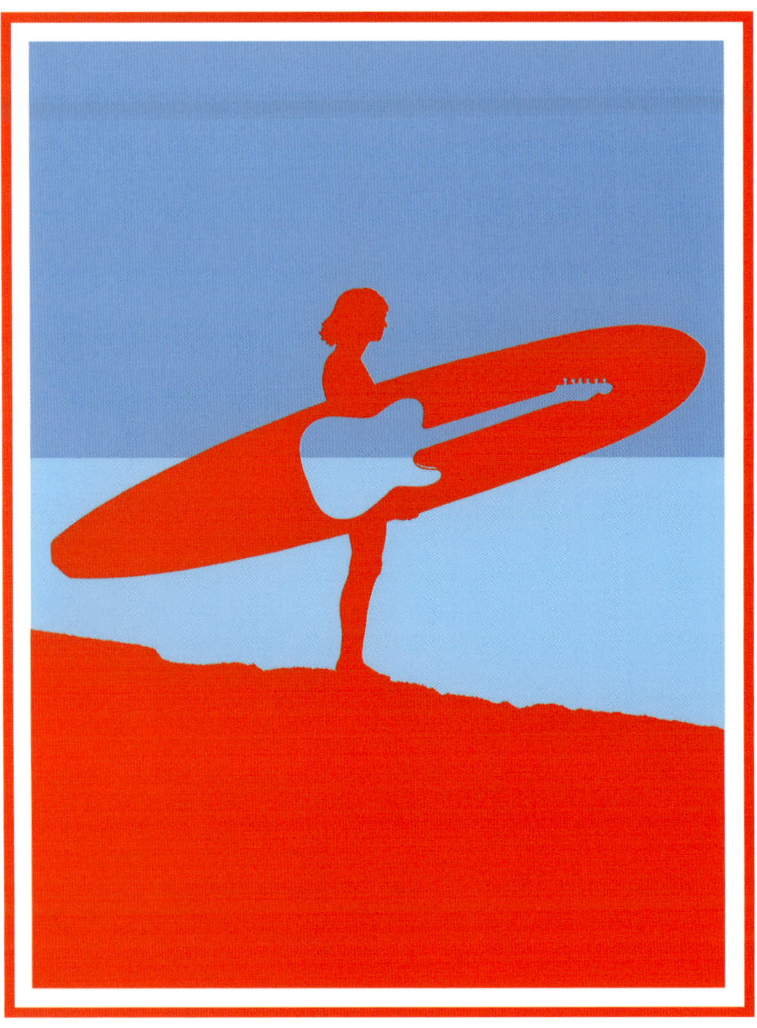
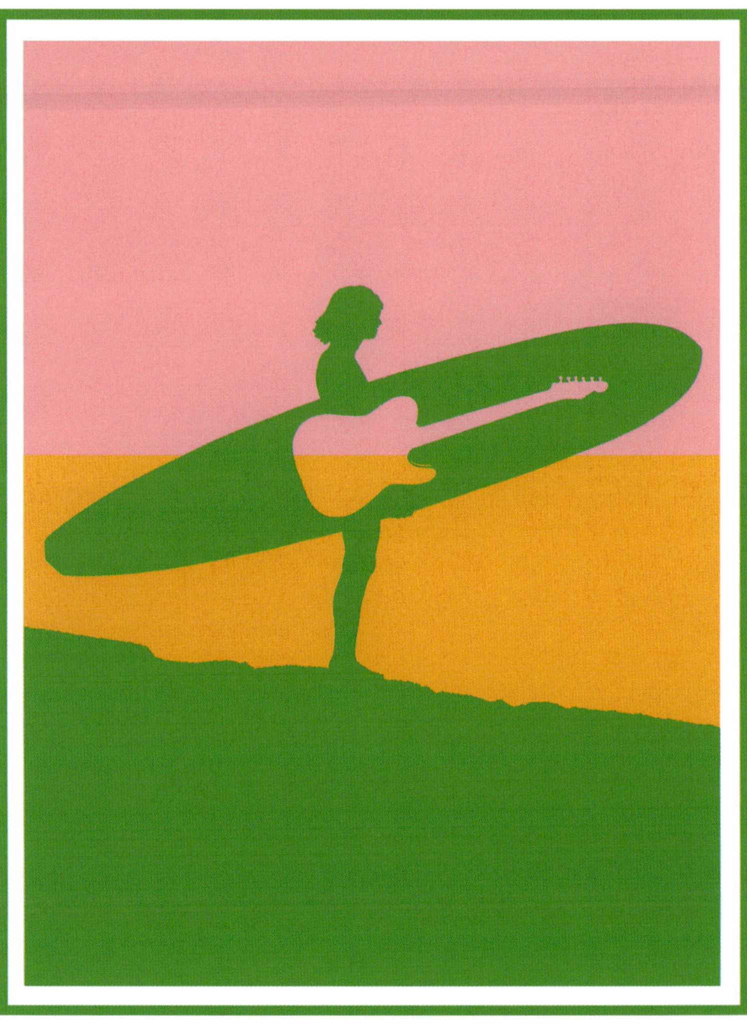

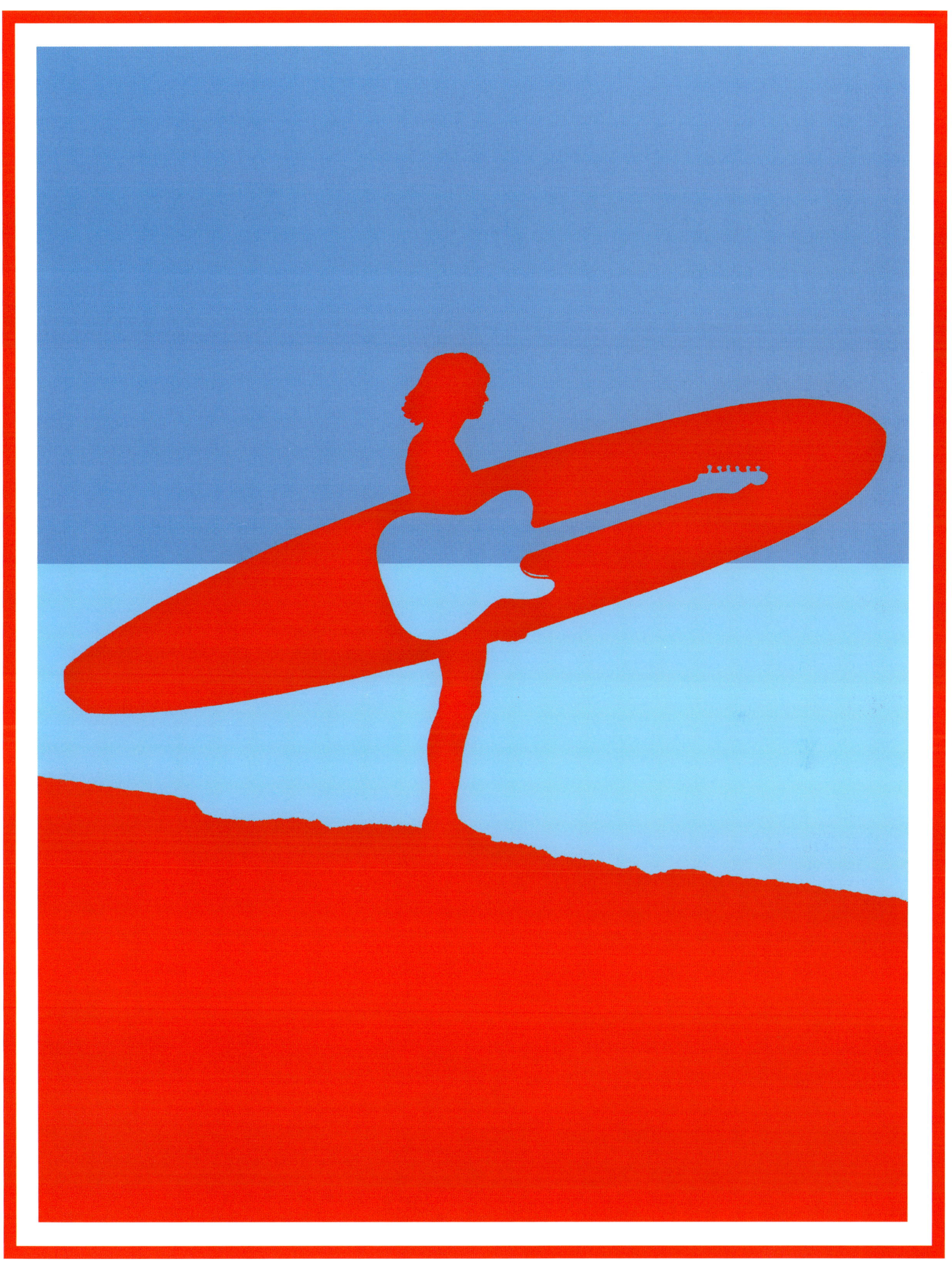

The *Donavon Frankenreiter Avalon* poster was for a benefit concert for Avalon Bay's *Every Drop Counts* — as was the limited edition print above.

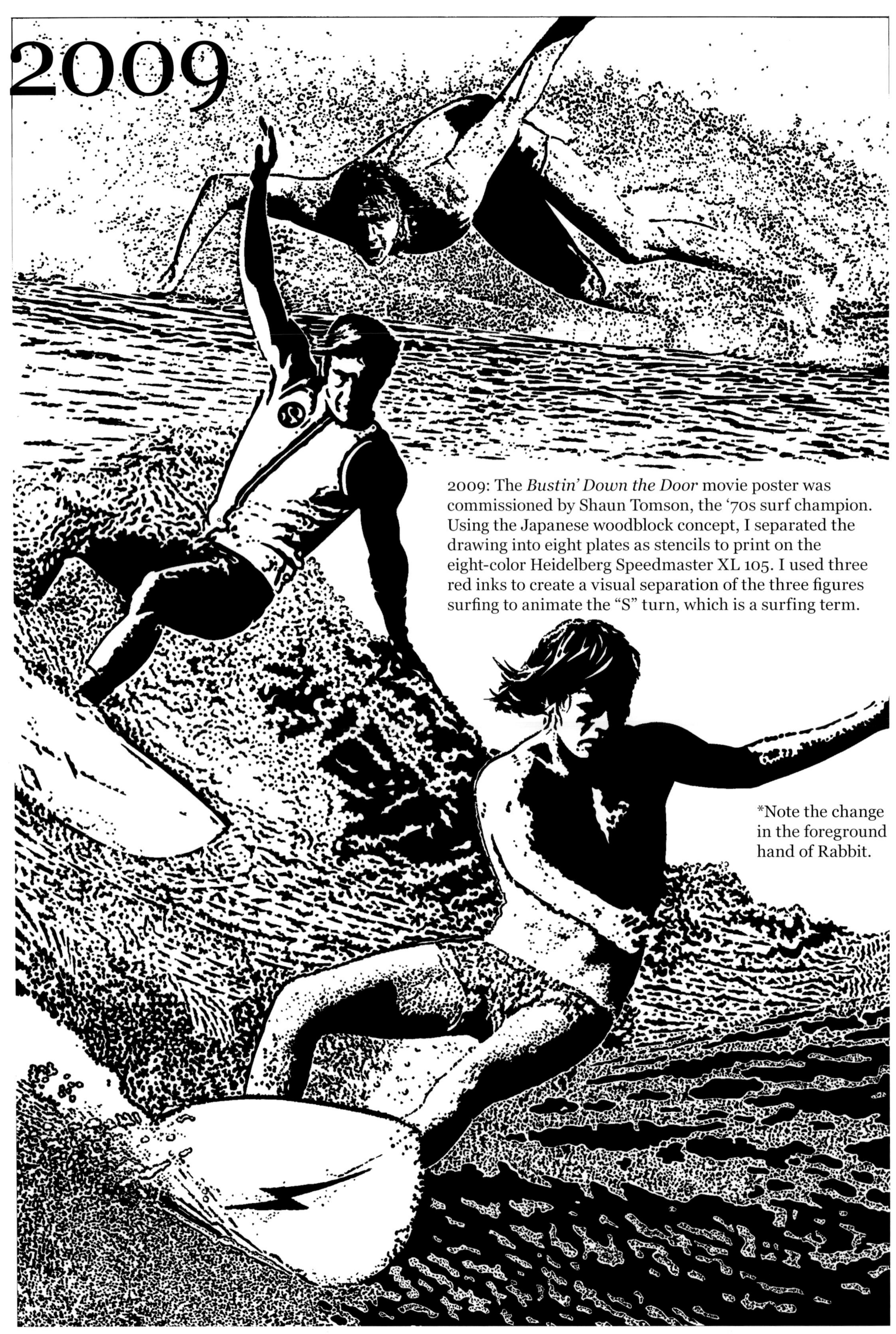

2009: The *Bustin' Down the Door* movie poster was commissioned by Shaun Tomson, the '70s surf champion. Using the Japanese woodblock concept, I separated the drawing into eight plates as stencils to print on the eight-color Heidelberg Speedmaster XL 105. I used three red inks to create a visual separation of the three figures surfing to animate the "S" turn, which is a surfing term.

*Note the change in the foreground hand of Rabbit.

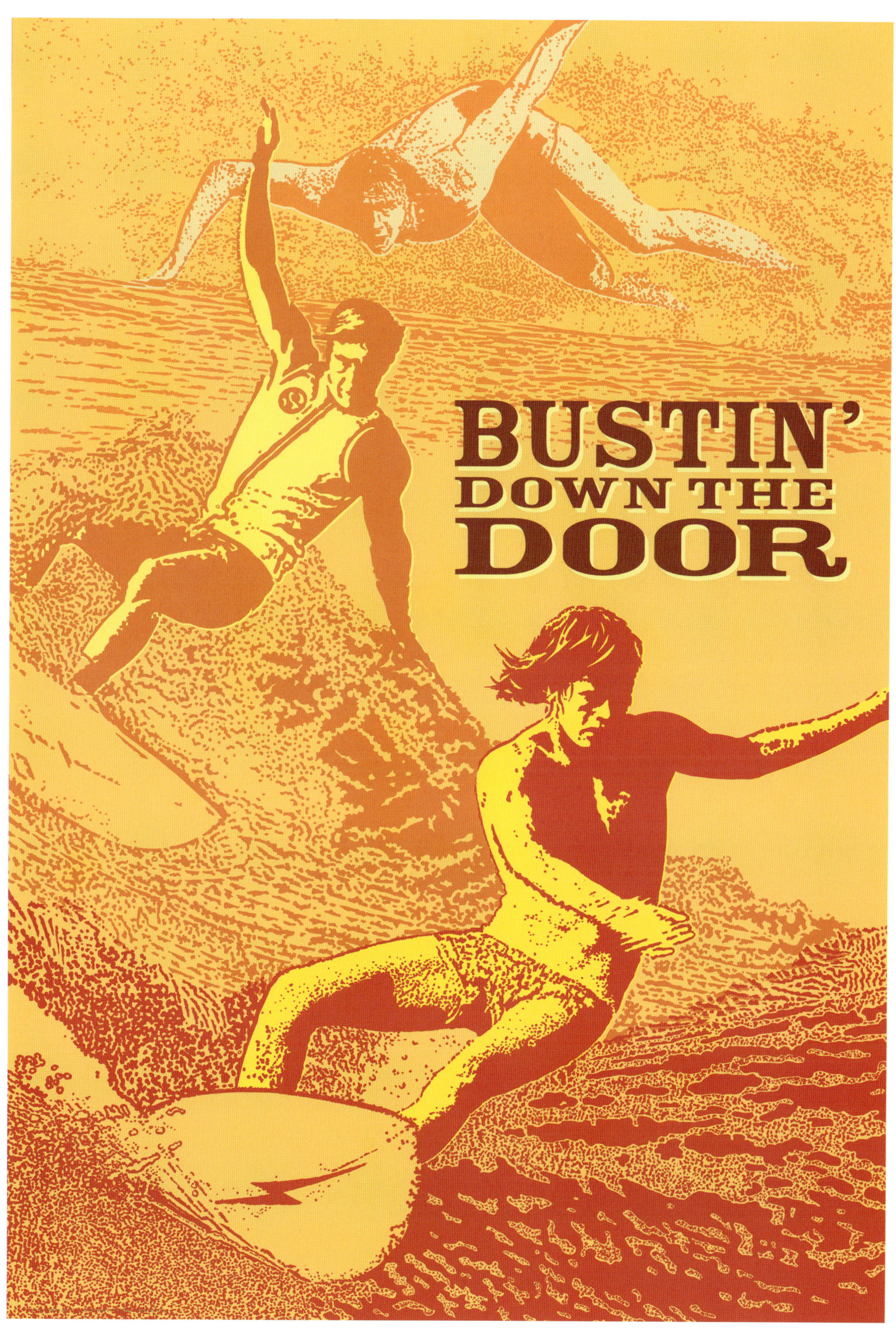
BUSTIN'
DOWN THE
DOOR

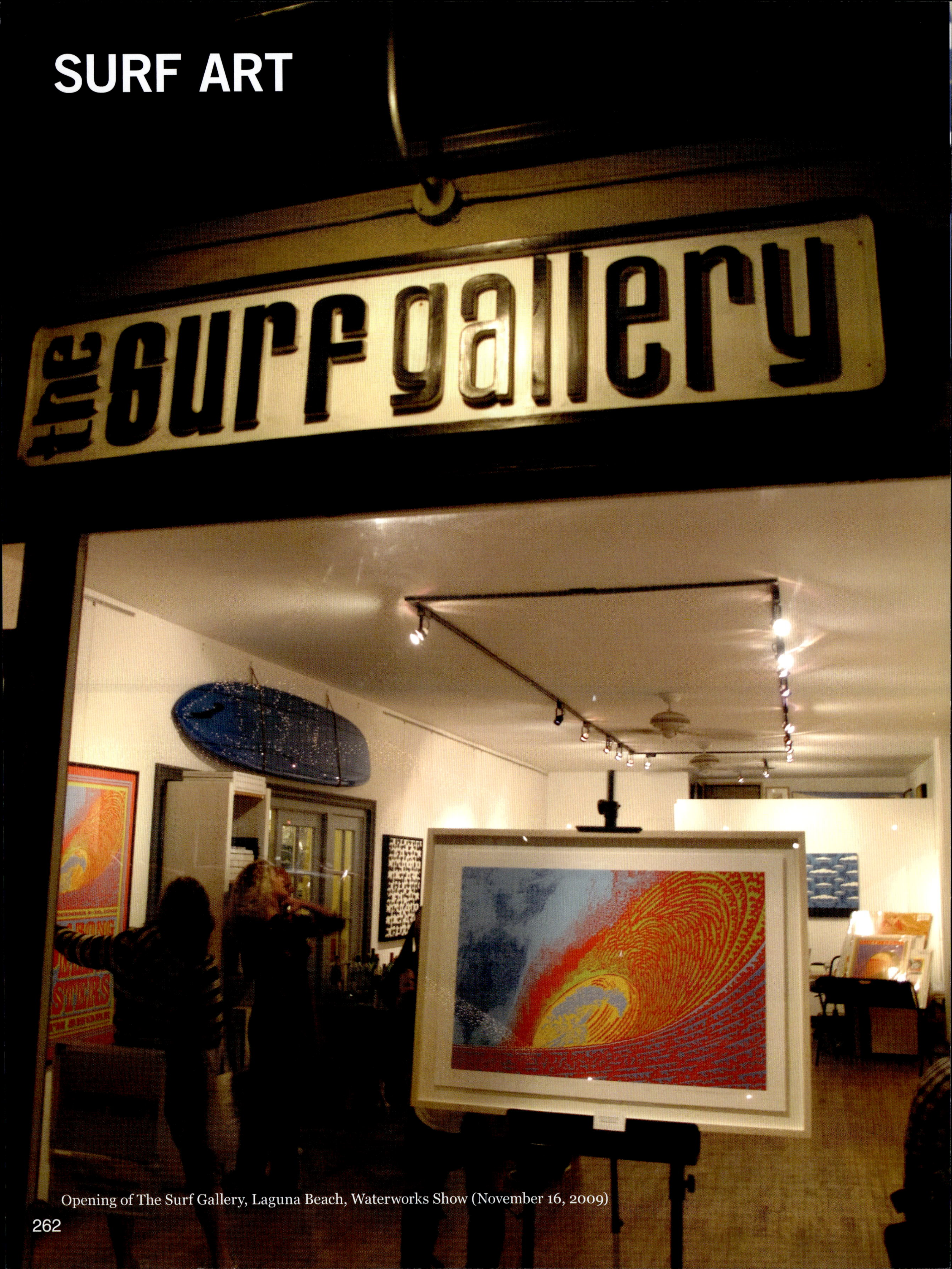

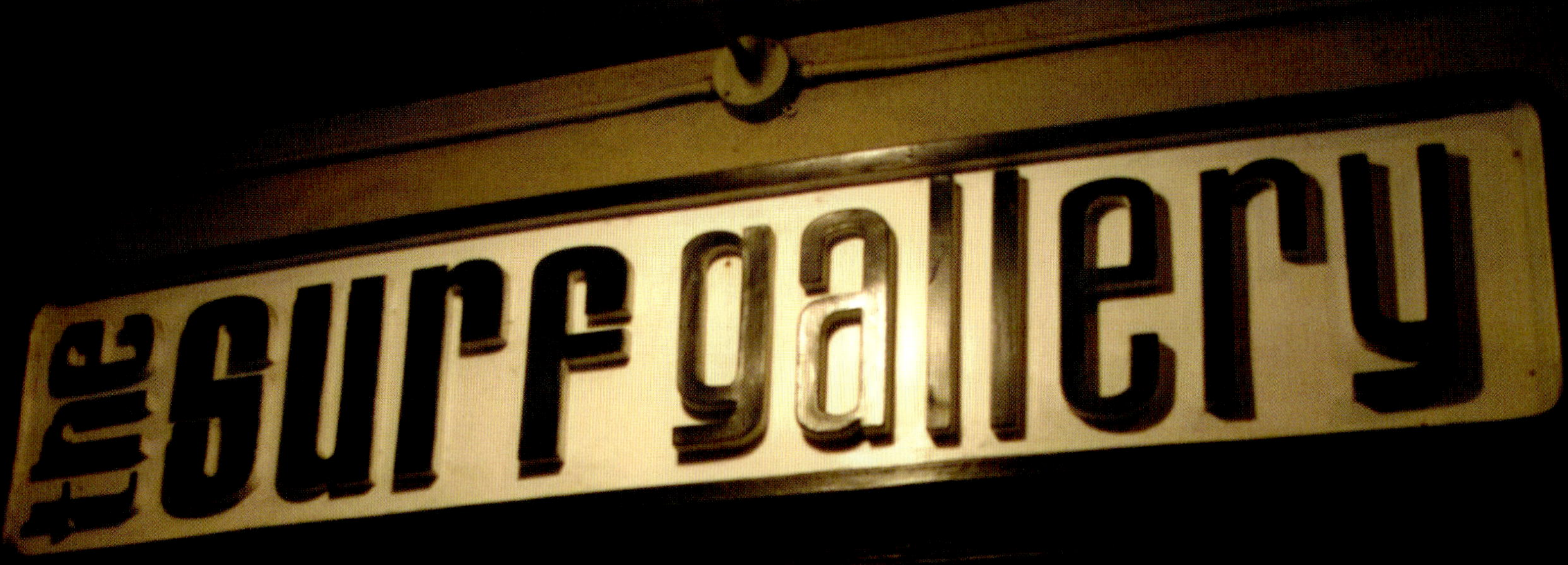

Opening of The Surf Gallery, Laguna Beach, Waterworks Show (November 16, 2009)

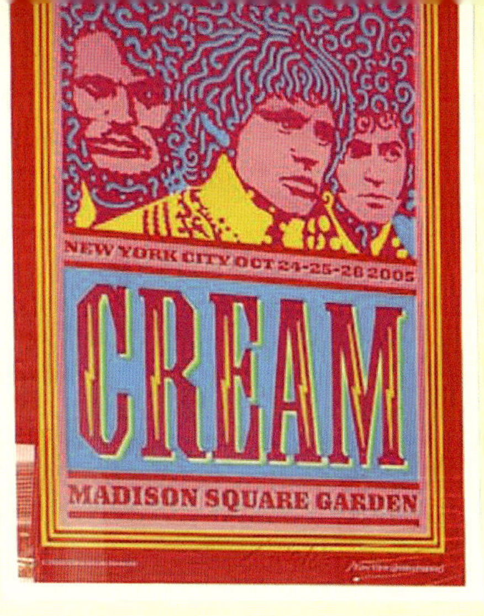

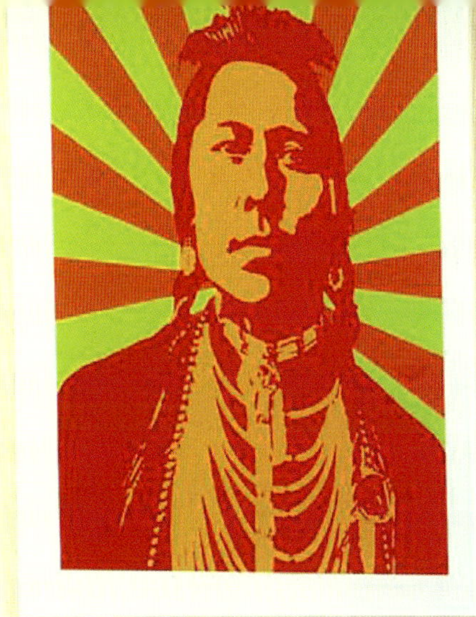

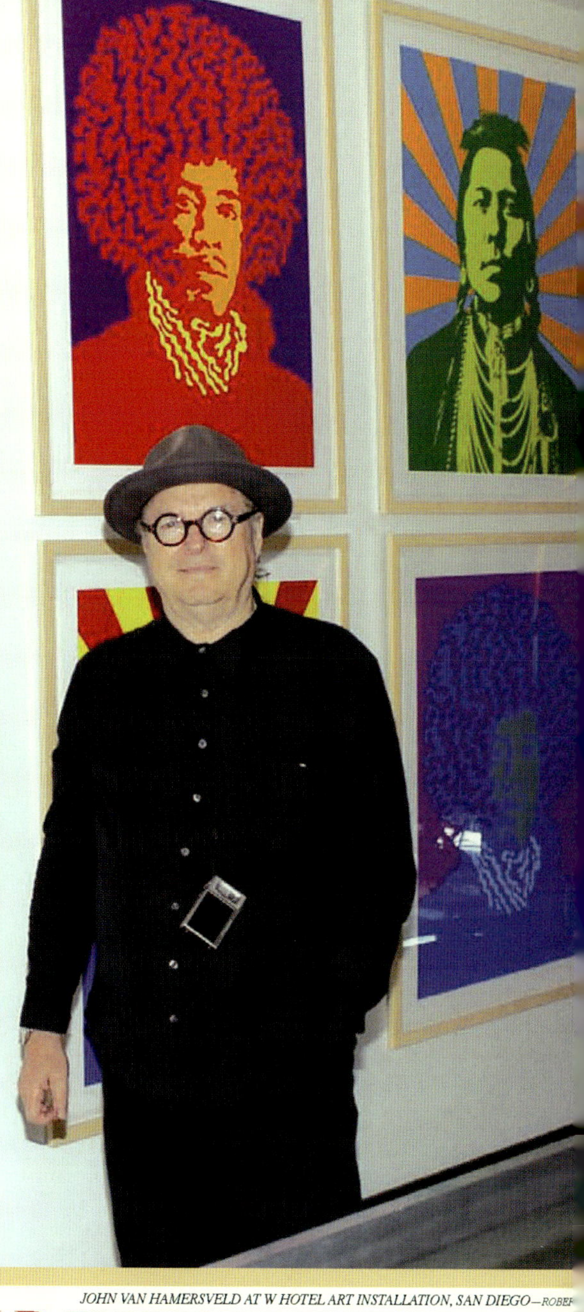

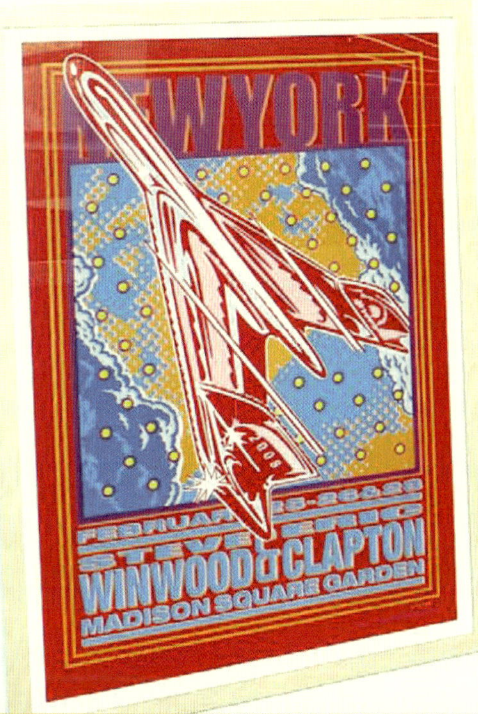

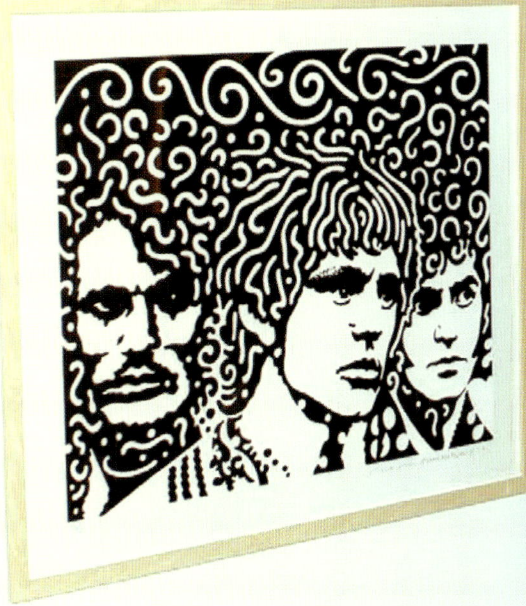

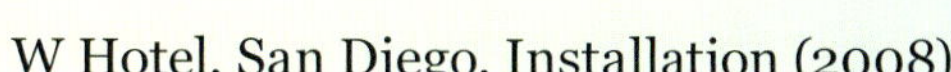

W Hotel, San Diego, Installation (2008)

JOHN VAN HAMERSVELD AT W HOTEL ART INSTALLATION, SAN DIEGO—ROBER

Surf & Rock Art

Authentic

Visual Arts 1960–2010

JOHN VAN HAMERSVELD

DECADES

Robert Wald

You would be inclined to think it is genetically encrypted, a man who can vividly express himself through his yet simultaneously maintain his wits as h a businessman and visionary in the ever-anging climate of popular [illegible]re. Yet es much deeper than that [illegible]llow buzzw[illegible]rd ultitasking" used so [illegible]eely nowadays[illegible] lity of graphic [illegible]st and desig[illegible]r John Van mersveld [illegible] shift changing cultural gears thout [illegible]ing up his conceptual clutch is nething to behold, particularly in an epic eer that has spanned [illegible] than four deles. Very few artists, [illegible]ng [illegible]ead, can lay im to both the enorm[illegible]lent an[illegible] suc[illegible]s John Van Hamersveld.

To truly understand [illegible] ful[illegible]ep[illegible] of [illegible]d n Hamersveld maintain[illegible]popul[illegible]e ough his expression in color and design, e must first trace the lineage from whence came.

His grandfather was an inventor. His far designed and engineered satellites and jet craft. His mother was a fashion model and e art painter and his grandmother a Wall eet investor. It would be an understatement say that Van Hamersveld was immersed ep in an influential well of knowledge from ich he drank deeply, thus carving his own

Born in the East, Van Hamersveld's family migrated we[illegible]t to California in 1950, se[illegible] across the s[illegible]eet from Lunada B[illegible]n Palos Verdes Es[illegible]es o[illegible]erlooking the[illegible]ue Pacifi[illegible] Ocean. T[illegible] ocean [illegible] in[illegible]ediat[illegible] influence on Van Hamersveld's ea[illegible] dev[illegible]opm[illegible]t, mainly because of an ancie[illegible] Hawa[illegible]an sport called "surfing" had arrived in his neighborhood—[illegible] to mentio[illegible] Lunada Bay prod[illegible] an exc[illegible]ent winter [illegible]nt [illegible]eak rivaling t[illegible] of [illegible] world.

By [illegible]e mid-50s [illegible]g [illegible] the man[illegible] uring [illegible] surfboar[illegible] in th[illegible]outh Bay o[illegible] os Angel[illegible] county had [illegible] a [illegible]ong foot[illegible]ld largely due to a man named Dale Velzy who had been designing and building surfboards for a new gen[illegible]on of surfers.

"As high [illegible] kid[illegible] we [illegible]ould see [illegible]urfe[illegible]s from our ne[illegible]ghbor[illegible]ood in t[illegible]e s[illegible]f mo[illegible]ies [illegible] our communities," Van Hamersveld said. "We lived near surf spots; it was the newsreel of our life and the beginning of a new culture."

Working out [illegible] V[illegible], Velzy, overloaded with surfboard orders eventually teamed up with Hap Jacobs establishing the

tom balsa wood surfboard. The cost: $75.

Velzy, staring into Van Hamersveld's sparkling thirteen year-old eyes said, "Hey kid, we [illegible] board for [illegible] more buck. How 'bout it, kid?"

"Yes sir, Mr. Velzy!" The deal was done.

Some months later, (shaping balsa wood boards was a long an[illegible]ous process) Van Hamersveld's mother dro[illegible] him to Velzy and [illegible] brand new sur[illegible]ard [illegible] young [illegible]4, a new e[illegible] had [illegible]st b[illegible]

[illegible] Cal[illegible] tee[illegible] in t[illegible] '50s, th[illegible]e was no more power to be had than in becoming a surfer," Van Hamersveld said. "Being with my famil[illegible] was like being in a cave, in [illegible]e dark, but I remember when I left home and went to learn how to surf with the other boys! I had gained the power to go with the older guys, to stay overnight and surf the next day, sometimes for the whole weekend."

It was thr[illegible]gh th[illegible] critical developmental times in his life Van Hamersveld realized that "questions about the truth, the folklore of

at the end of my street. I did not kn different than what was in front of parents provided me with what they but down at the end of the street I cou everything I wanted to know that my wouldn't tell me. What was sex? W exciting? What wa[illegible]e lik would show up [illegible]e end of th[illegible] street [illegible] the world op[illegible]ed into ocean su[illegible]reak. WOW!"

Being that Palos Verdes did not own high school for the local kids to Van Hamersveld was bused to El High School, miles up the road. Thoug ear the ocean[illegible] really didn't dig it.

"T[illegible]e, h[illegible] school stood as a sy [illegible] par[illegible]ts' au[illegible]rity, with the teacher p[illegible]nts[illegible]ide," [illegible]n Hamersveld said. de[illegible] why I ha[illegible] go down there an class, hearing things taught that I co relate to. In that boring place, my d along with the fact that I was surrou classmates I didn't know because the surf, made me feel like I was drownin discipline and order."

Despite his near drowning in di and order, Van Hamersveld had thre that kept his head above water. One, his art class. Two, there were perfum in hoop skirts and soft sweaters re

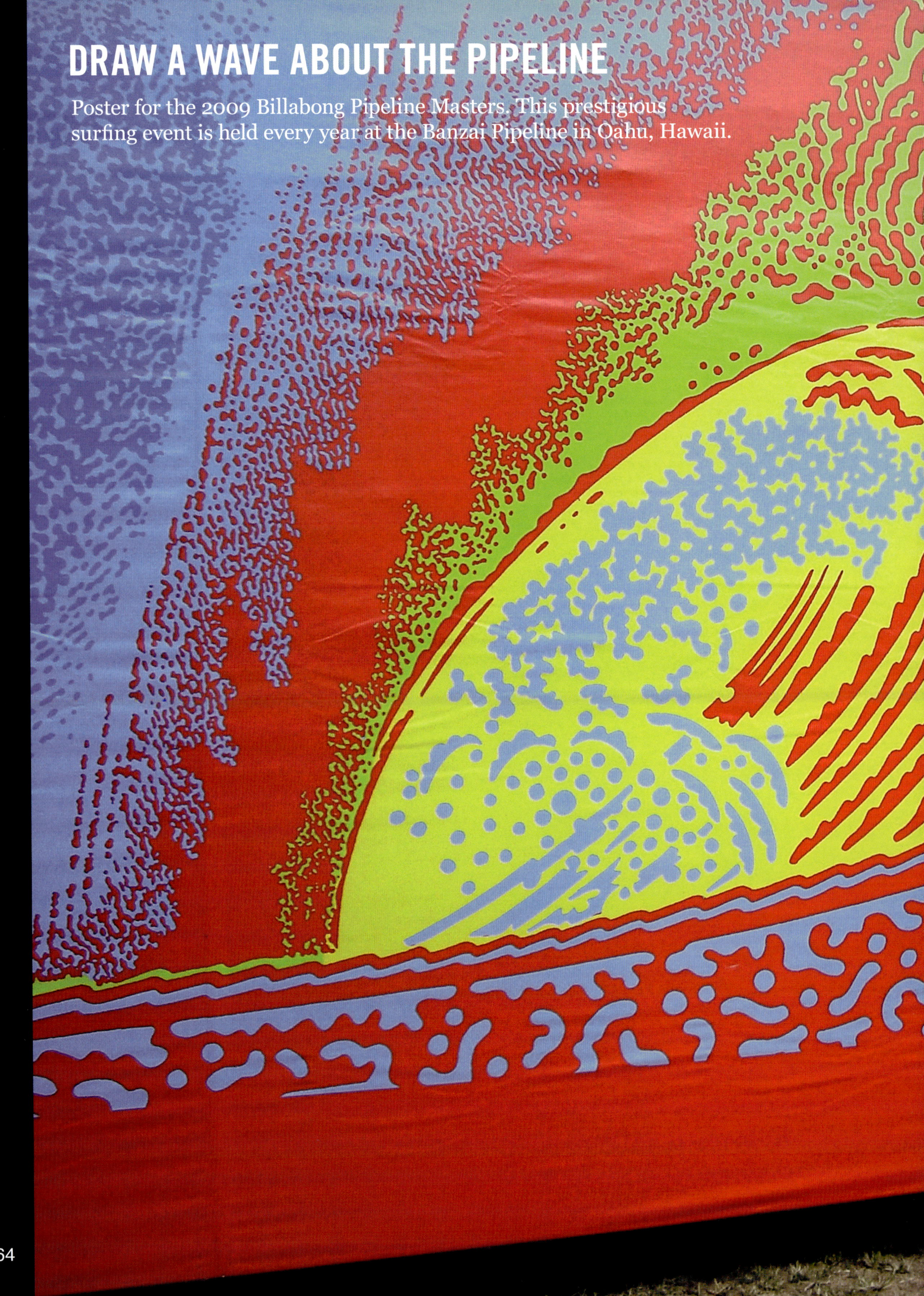

DRAW A WAVE ABOUT THE PIPELINE

Poster for the 2009 Billabong Pipeline Masters. This prestigious surfing event is held every year at the Banzai Pipeline in Oahu, Hawaii.

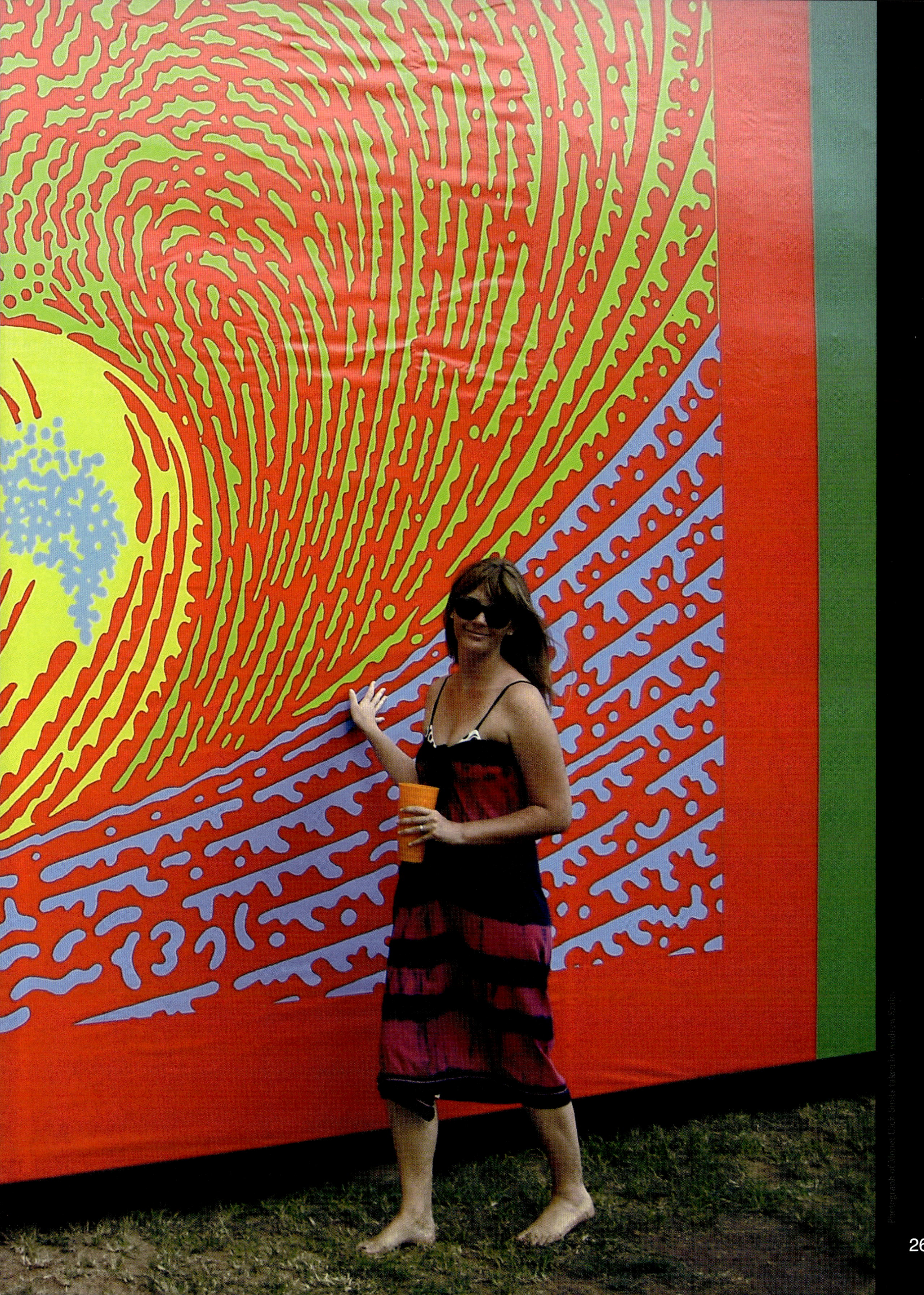

Photograph of Monet Lick-Smith taken by Andrew Smith

WATERWORKS CANVASES (2010)

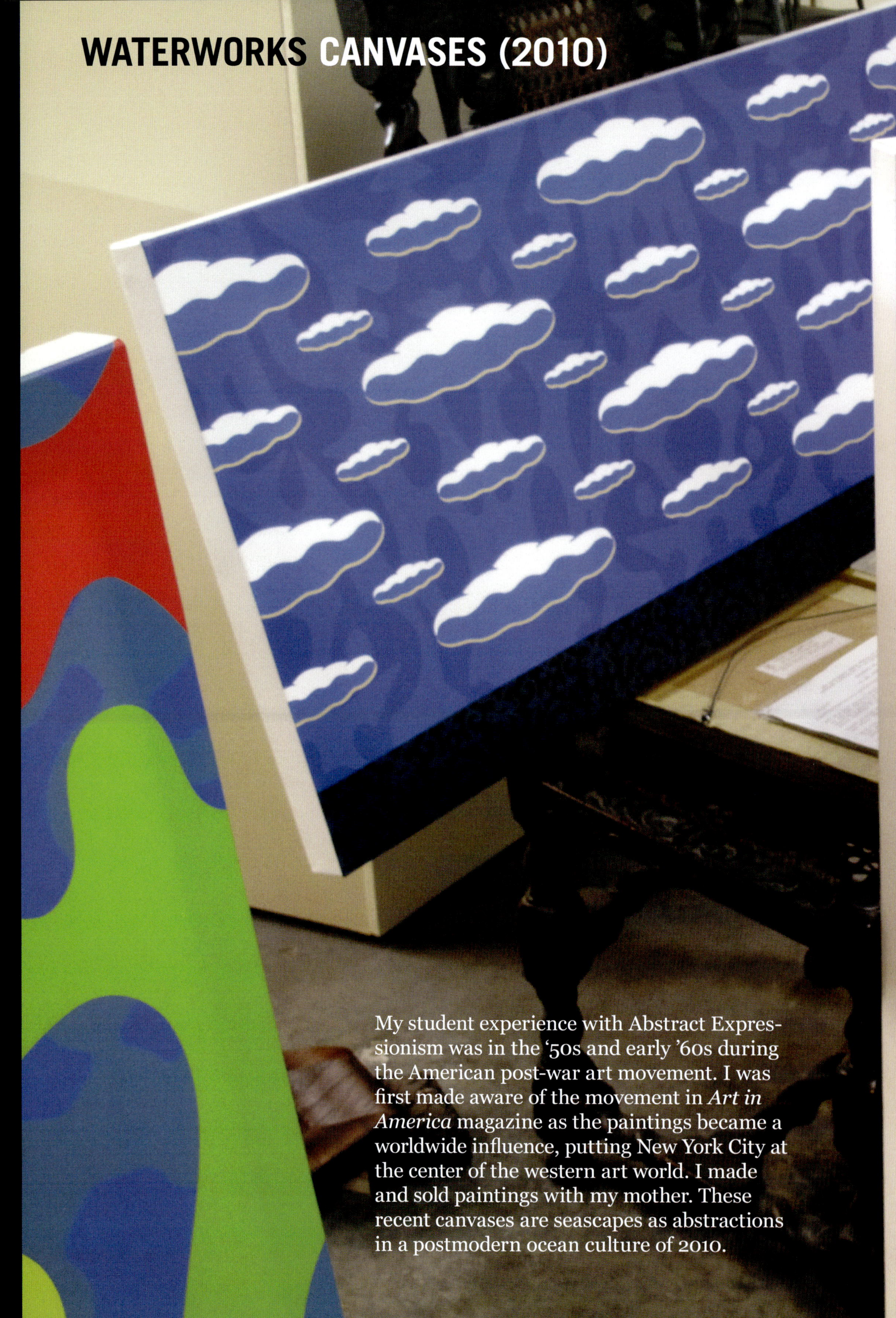

My student experience with Abstract Expressionism was in the '50s and early '60s during the American post-war art movement. I was first made aware of the movement in *Art in America* magazine as the paintings became a worldwide influence, putting New York City at the center of the western art world. I made and sold paintings with my mother. These recent canvases are seascapes as abstractions in a postmodern ocean culture of 2010.

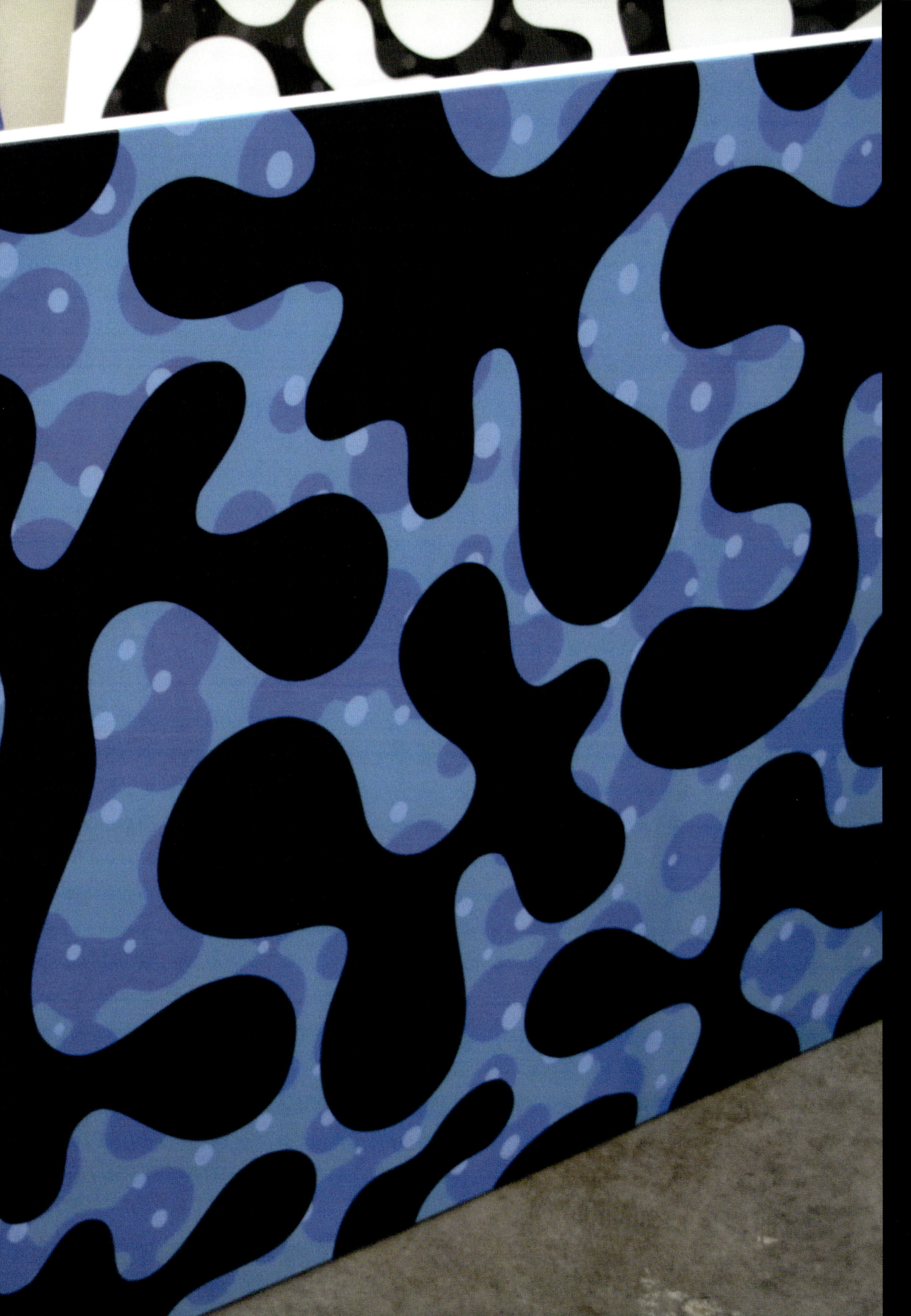

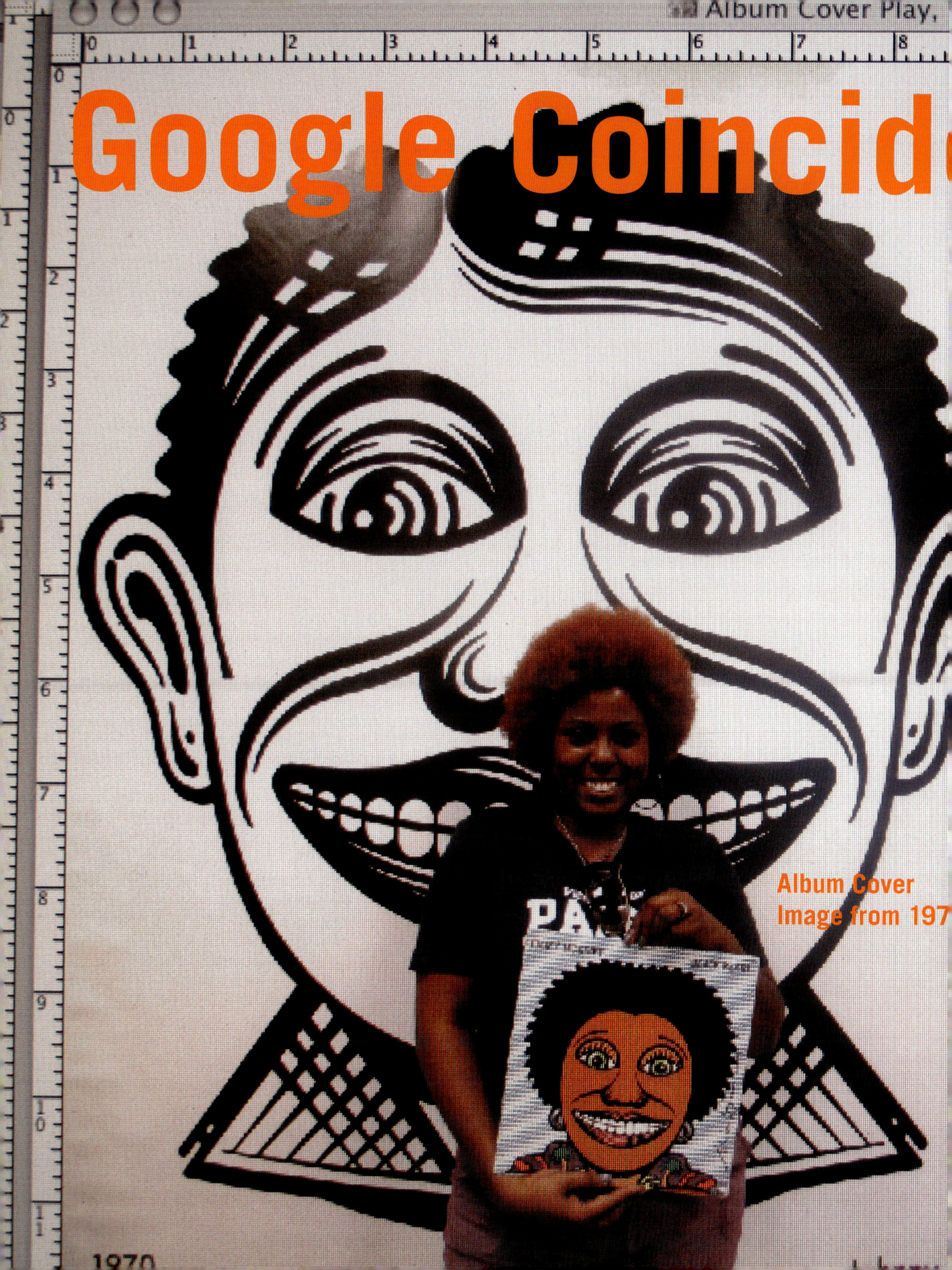
Album Cover Play,
Google Coincide
Album Cover
Image from 197
1970

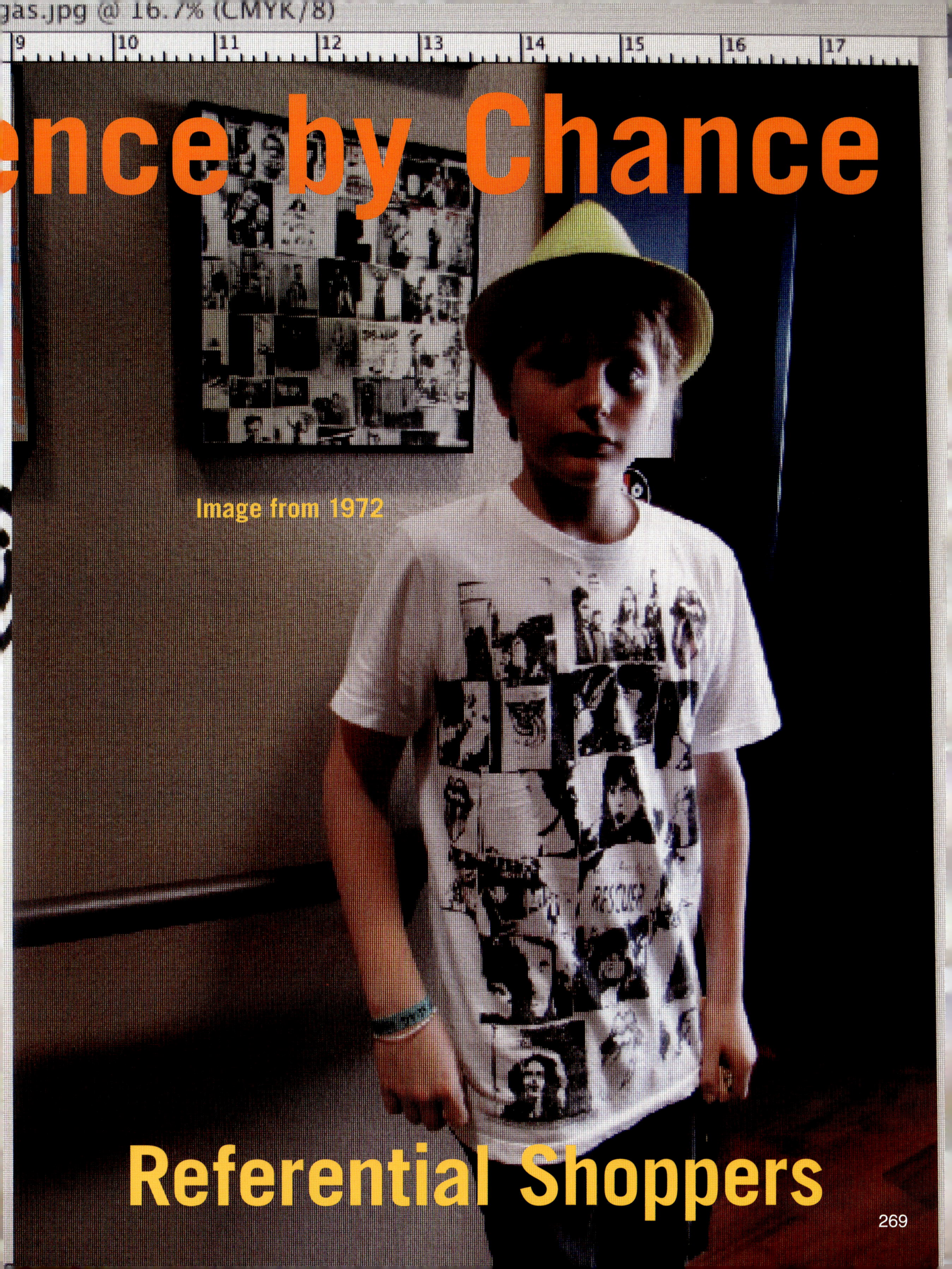

gas.jpg @ 16.7% (CMYK/8)

ence by Chance

Image from 1972

Referential Shoppers

WHAT DOES

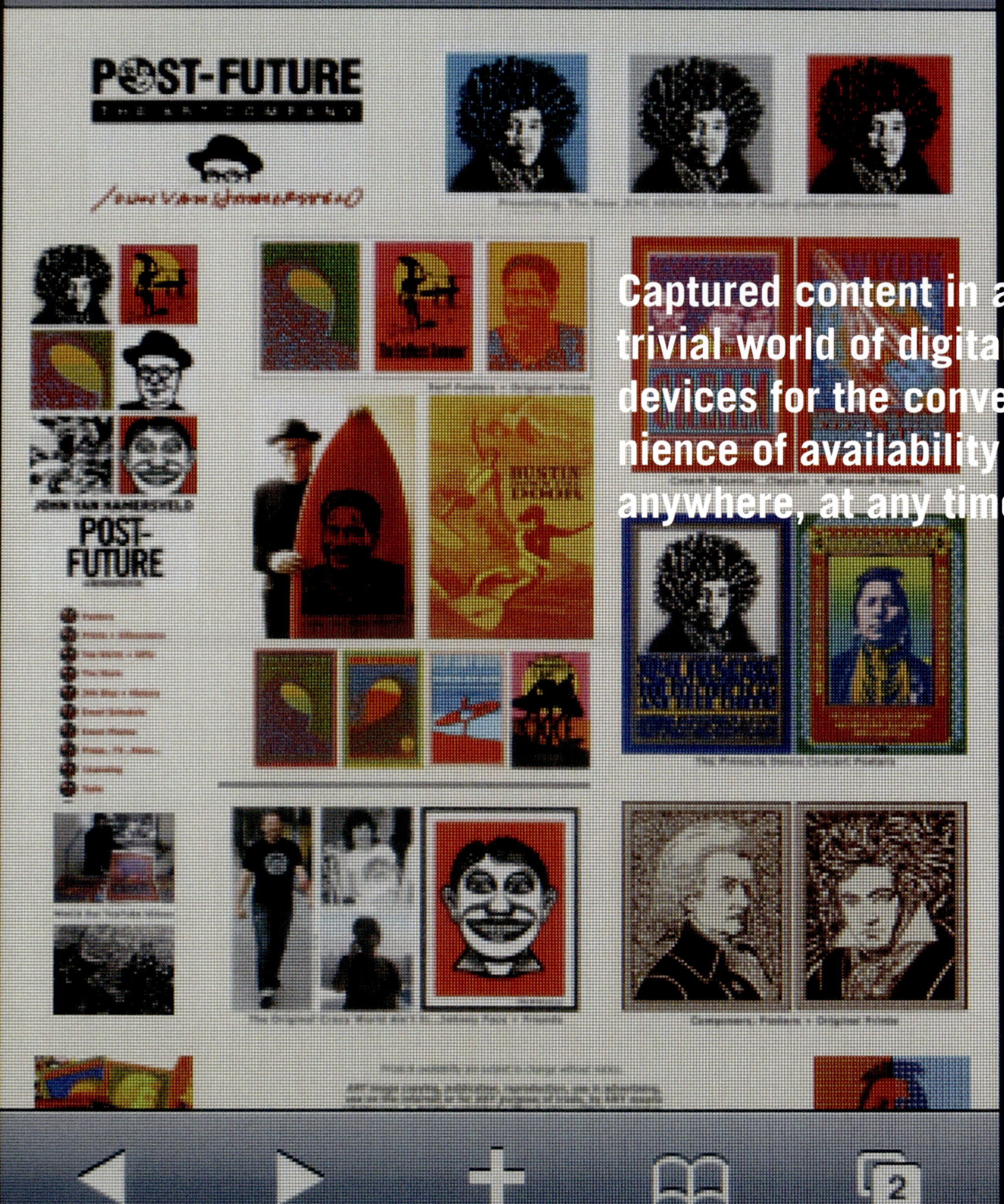

Captured content in a trivial world of digital devices for the convenience of availability anywhere, at any time

Digital Vernacular

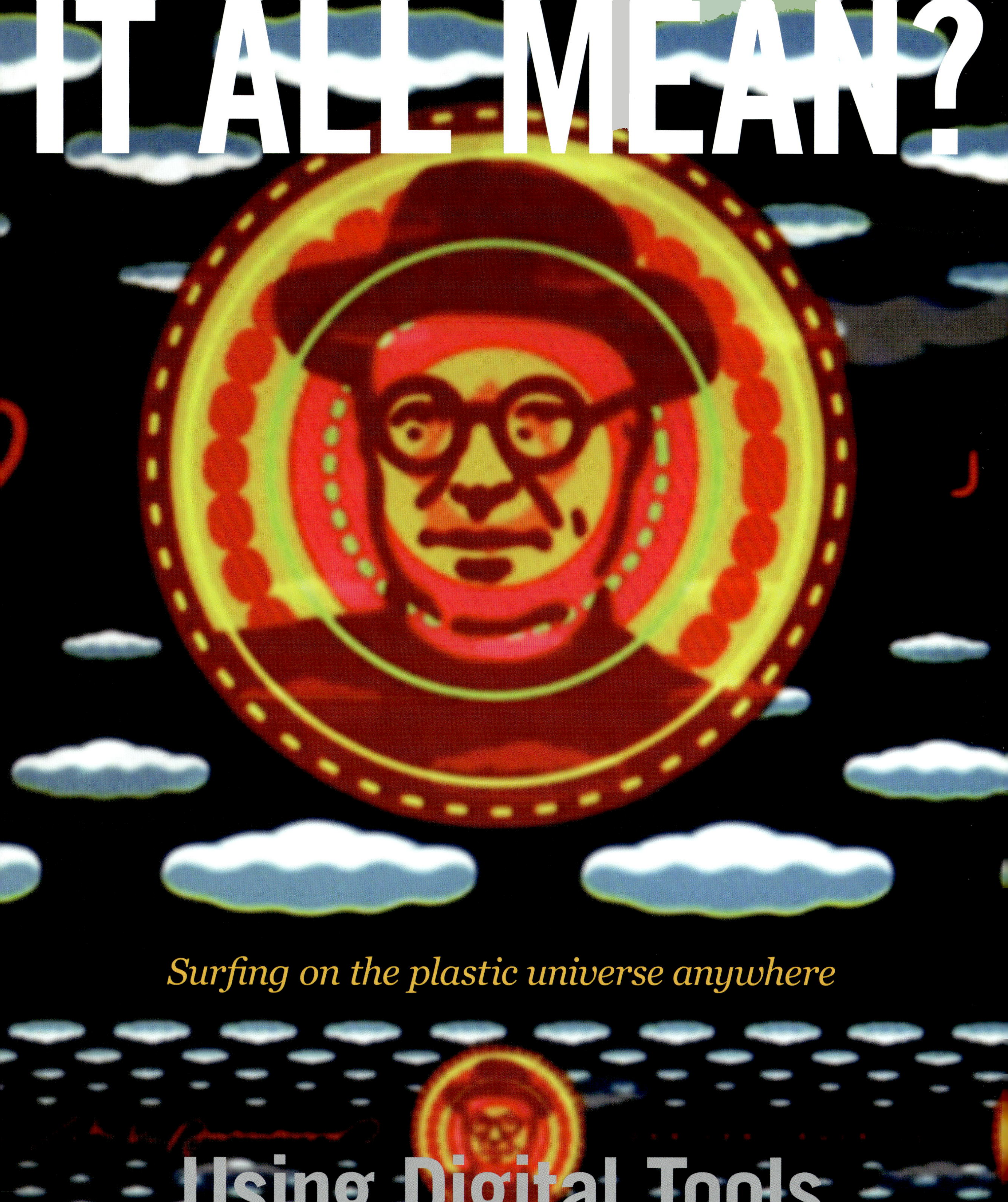

Surfing on the plastic universe anywhere

Using Digital Tools

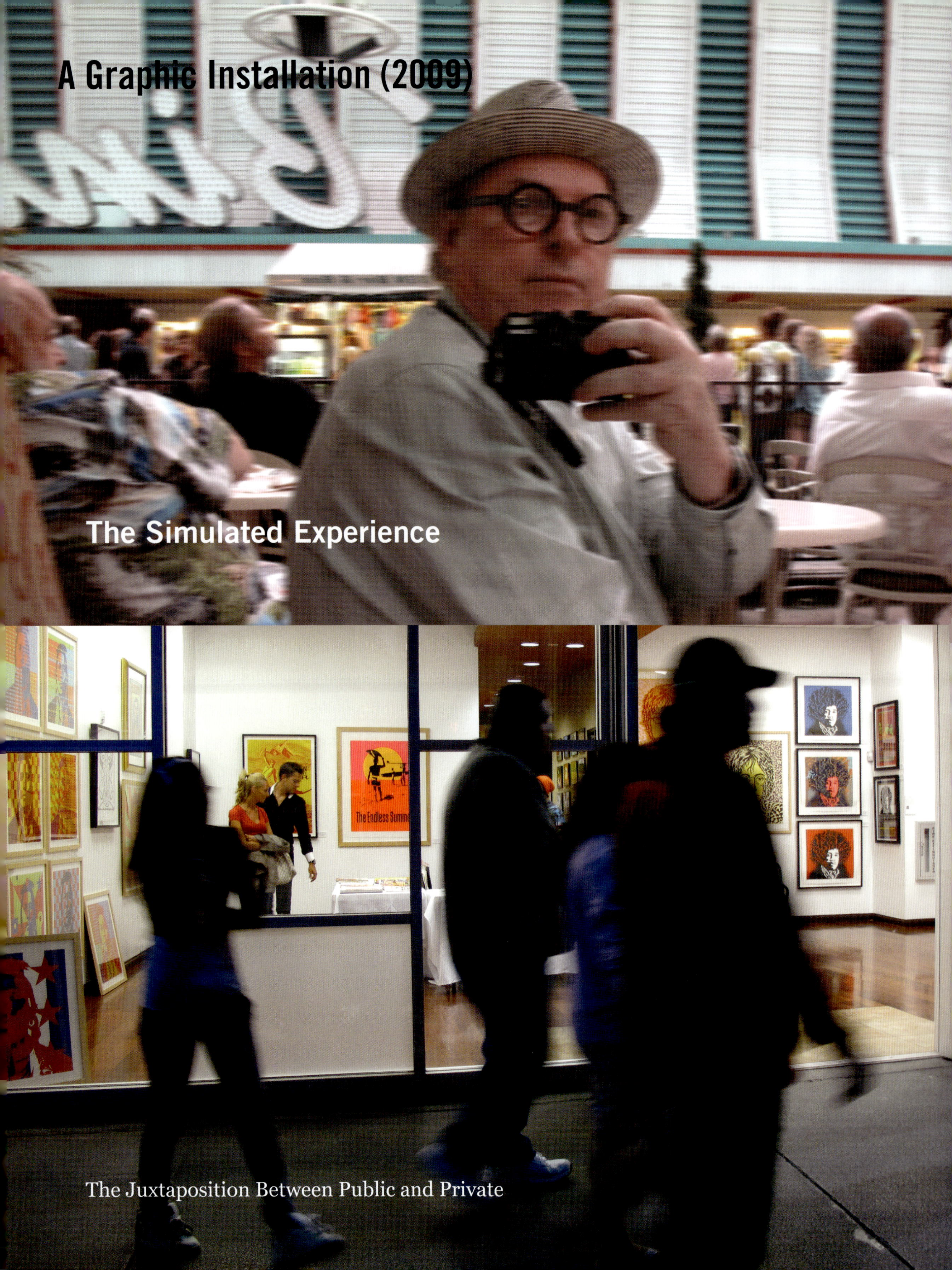

A Graphic Installation (2009)

The Simulated Experience

The Juxtaposition Between Public and Private

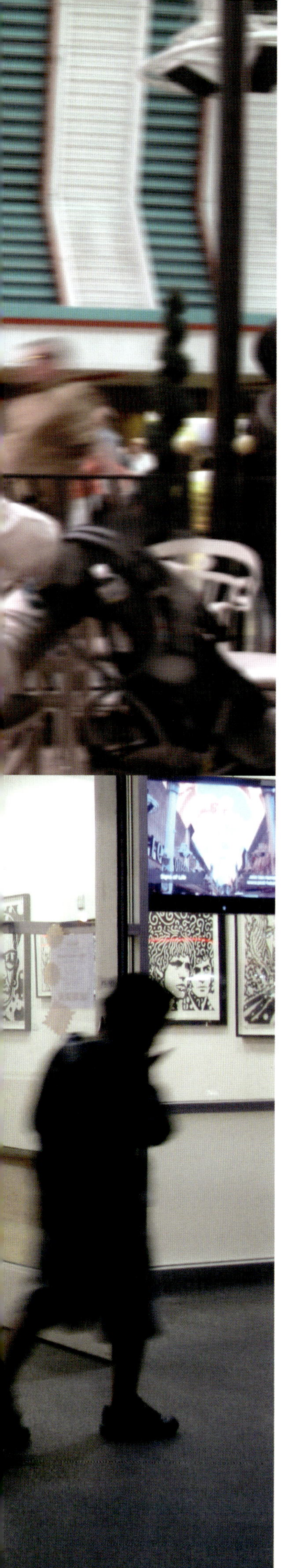

Multimedia Artist/Graphic Designer John Van Hamersveld Named Official Artist of Fremont Street Experience's "Summer Of '69: Vegas or Bust" on June 1st, 2009

Van Hamersveld's Official Artist of Summer of '69 *participation will include the creation of a debut Viva Vision show titled, "Signs of Life," two custom-painted vintage school buses to be used during the summer-long event series and working alongside Fremont Street Experience in design aspects for* Summer of '69. *Van Hamersveld will also open Hippie Nation™ Gallery & Records, an art gallery located at Fremont Street Experience that will sell custom John Van Hamersveld posters, digital prints, original drawings and hand pulled silk screens, in addition to record albums.*

"I feel very grateful and excited to work with Fremont Street Experience on the Summer of '69 *event series," said the world-renowned pop-culture artist.*

"My inspiration comes from a new time introduced to us by President Obama, feeling we need to readjust our needs and values to a time of change. I've custom-created four symbols that represent Summer of '69*: a flower, symbolizing growth; a peace sign, instilling safety within; a heart representing love; and a globe for balance. I feel these emblems truly symbolize the great year of 1969 and bring a fresh, modern approach to these events."*

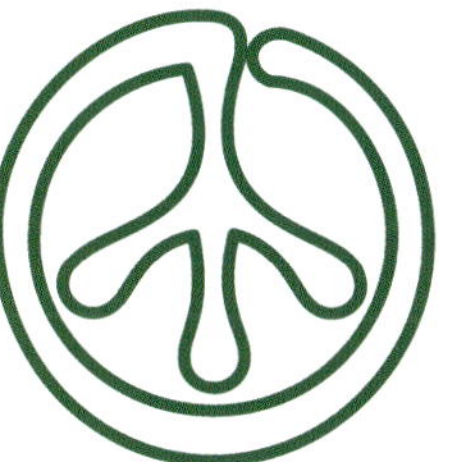
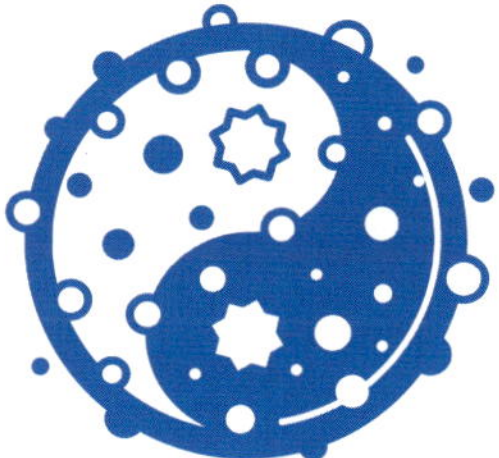
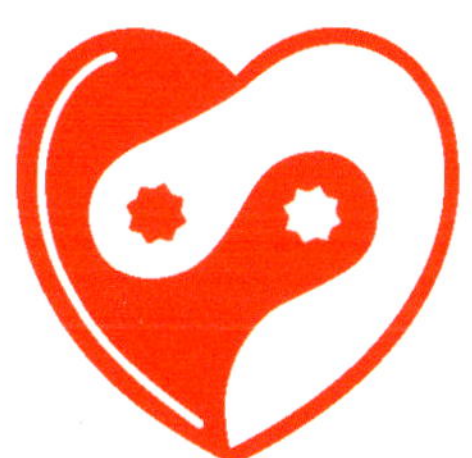
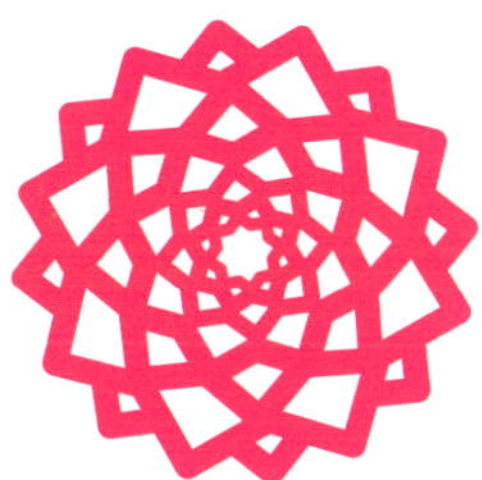

THE "SIGNS OF LIFE" SYMBOLS

"In 1967-1968, I did the Pinnacle dance concerts at Shrine Exhibition Hall with a team of artists and community people," said Van Hamersveld. "It was like artists doing a music event and it turned into a happening. What I am doing with Fremont Street Experience is similar. I have brought all of these pieces of my drawings and my symbols to the party and we have created a multimedia event here."

The custom-painted John Van Hamersveld buses, Hippie Nation™ Gallery & Records and "Signs of Life" Viva Vision show can be seen at Fremont Street Experience's "Summer of '69: Vegas or Bust" event and concert series Memorial Day weekend through Labor Day.

—Preferred Public Relations

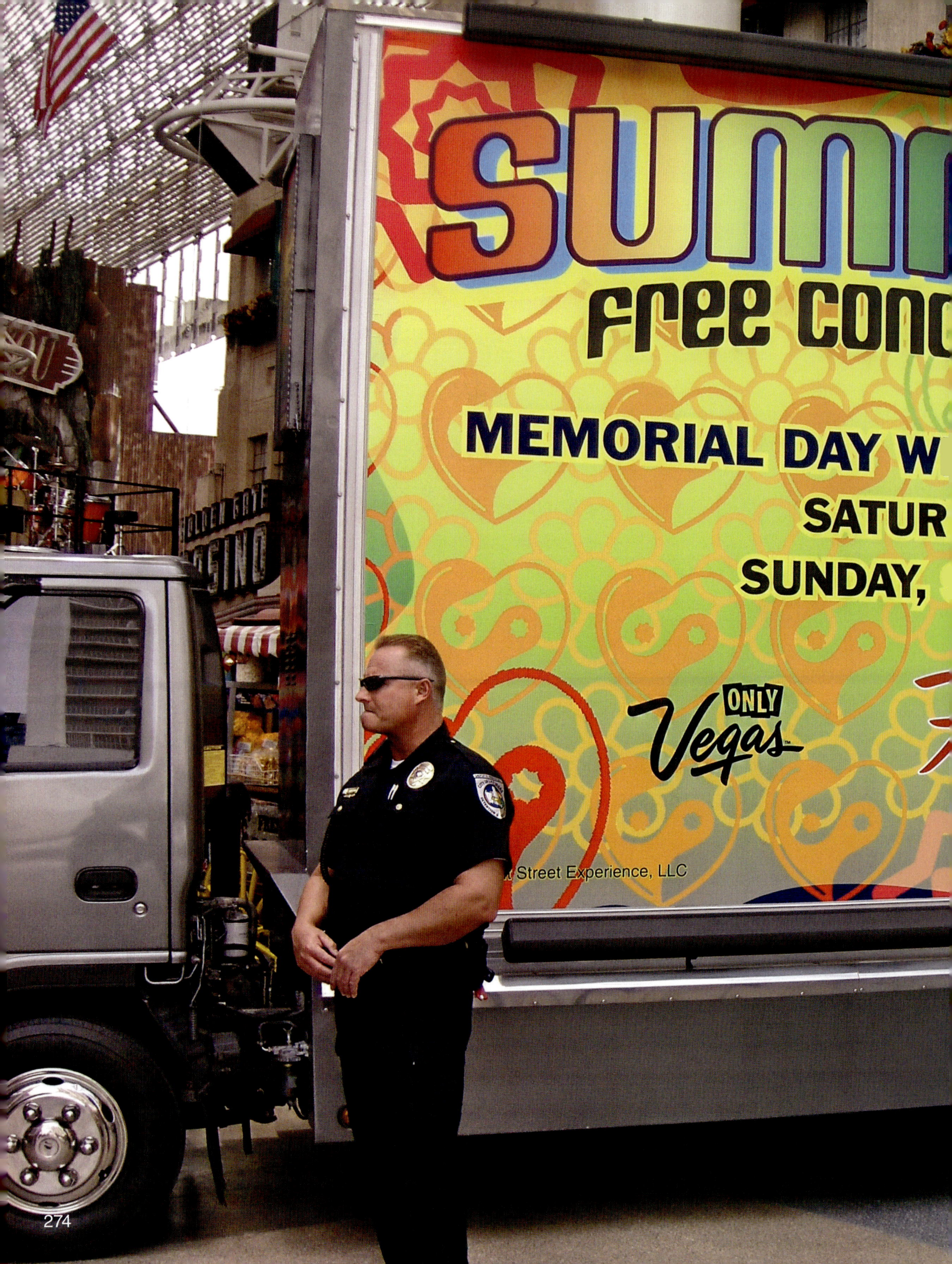
SUMM
Free Conc
MEMORIAL DAY W
SATUR
SUNDAY,
ONLY
Vegas
Street Experience, LLC
GOLDEN GATE
CASINO

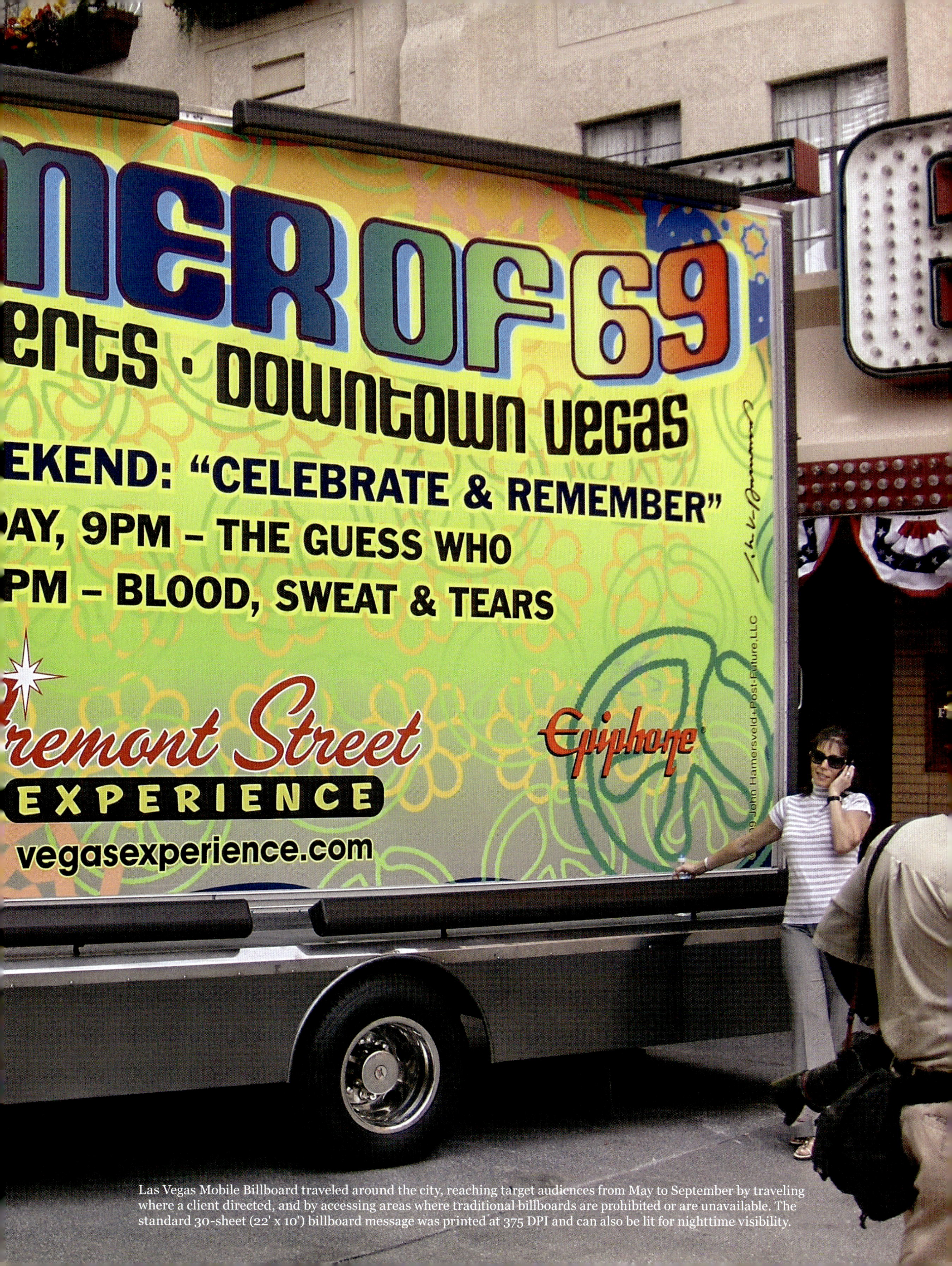

Las Vegas Mobile Billboard traveled around the city, reaching target audiences from May to September by traveling where a client directed, and by accessing areas where traditional billboards are prohibited or are unavailable. The standard 30-sheet (22' x 10') billboard message was printed at 375 DPI and can also be lit for nighttime visibility.

Digital: Signs of Life

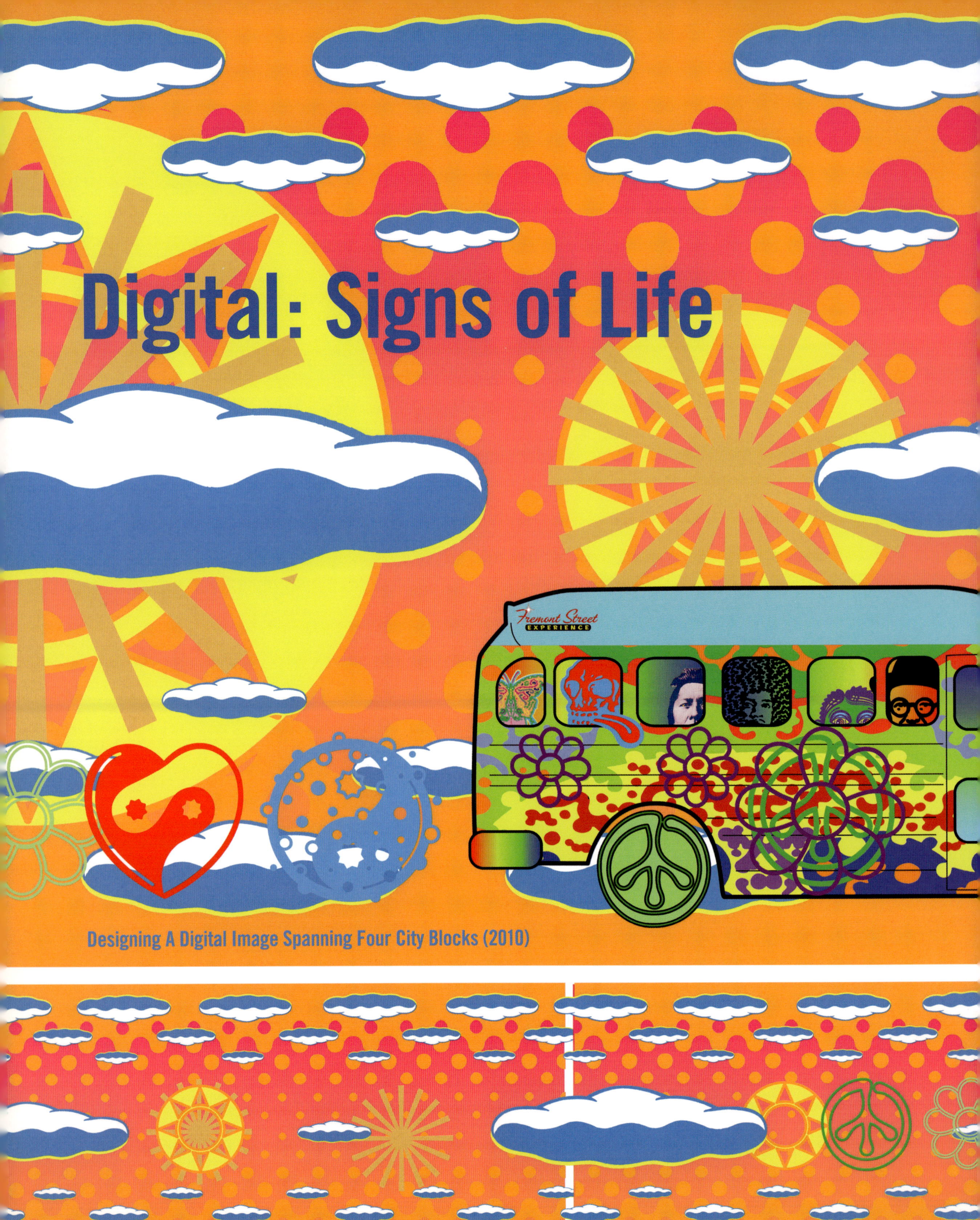

Designing A Digital Image Spanning Four City Blocks (2010)

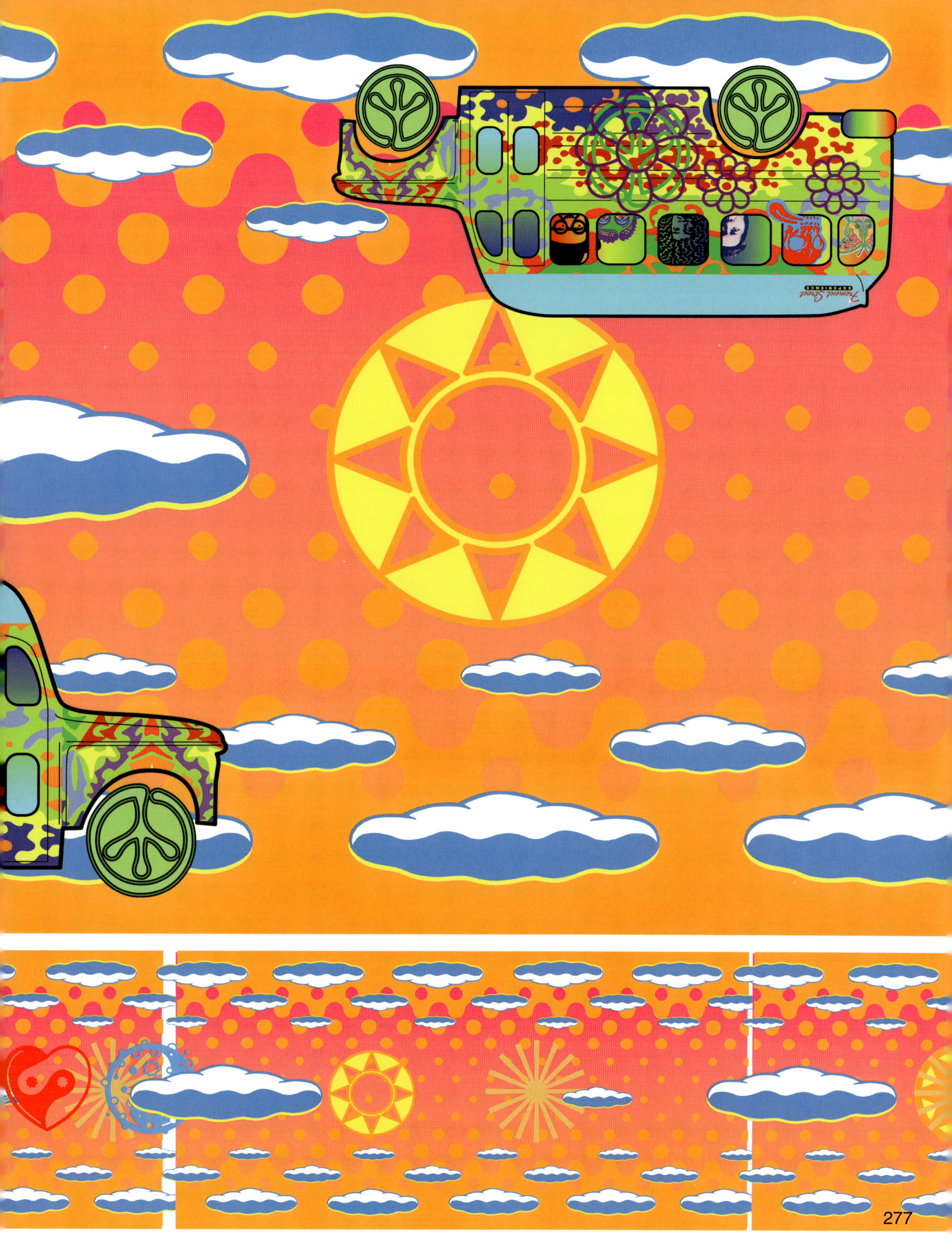

Creating a digital collage with symbols

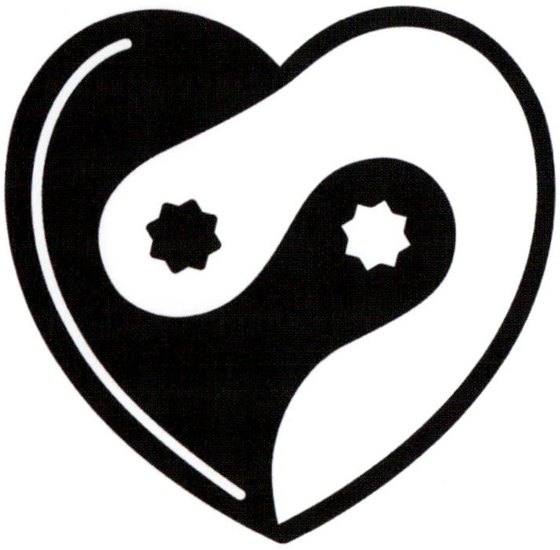

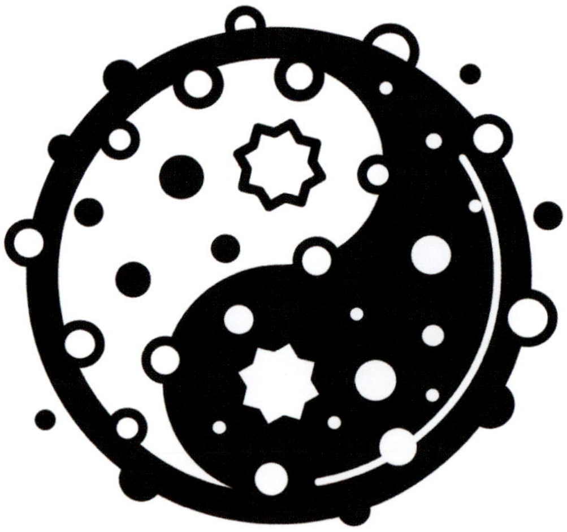

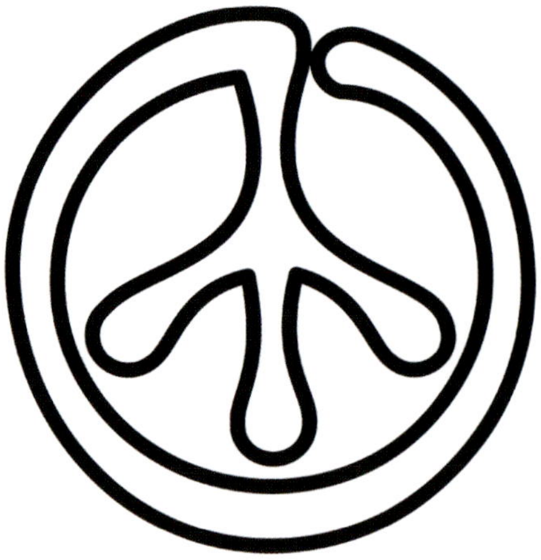

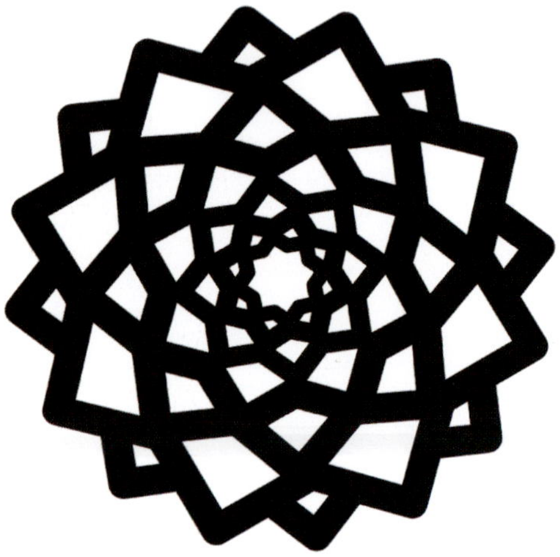

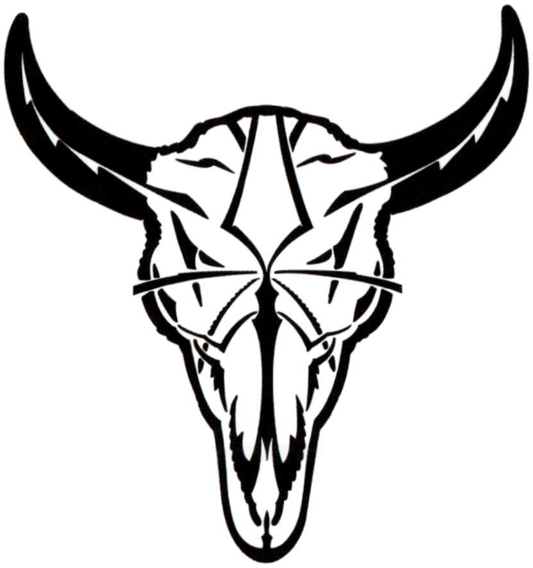

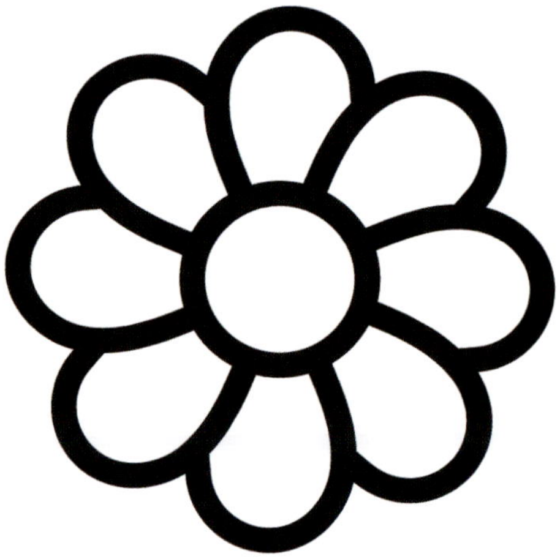

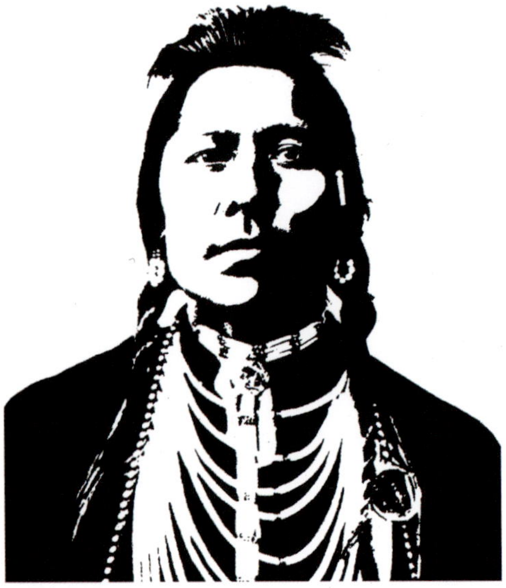

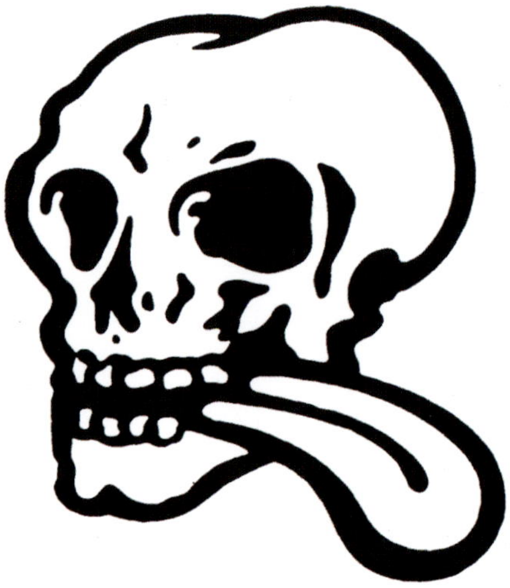

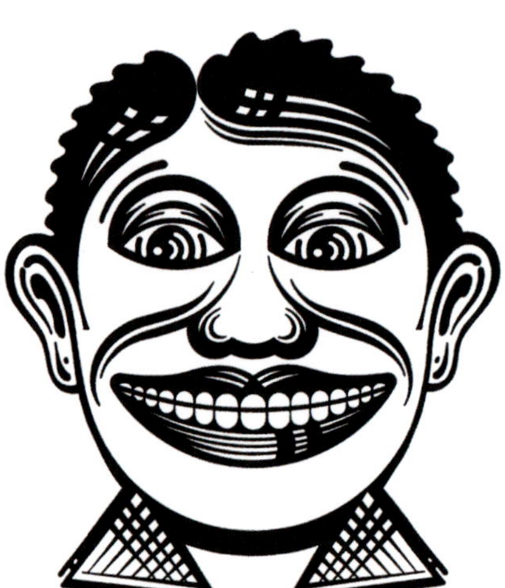

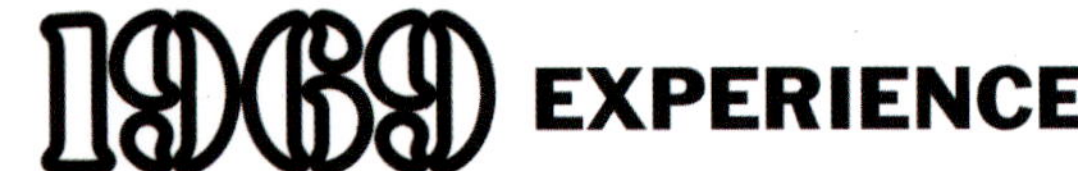

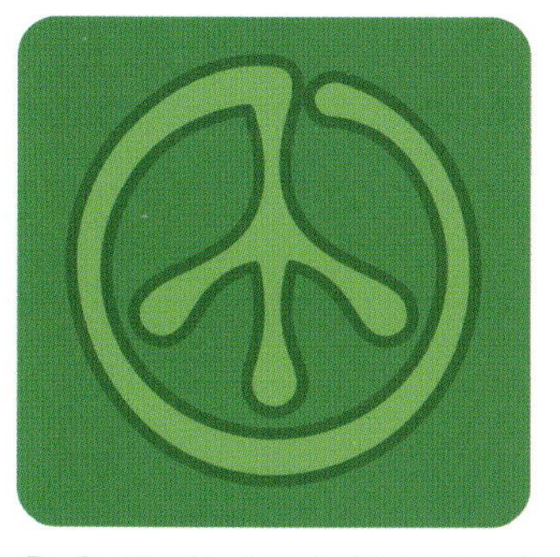

SAFE WITHIN

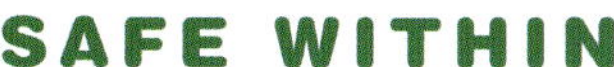

THE GROWING

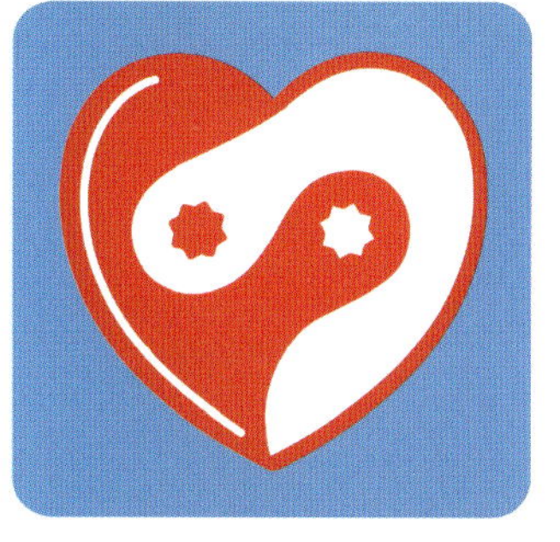

TWO FOR ONE

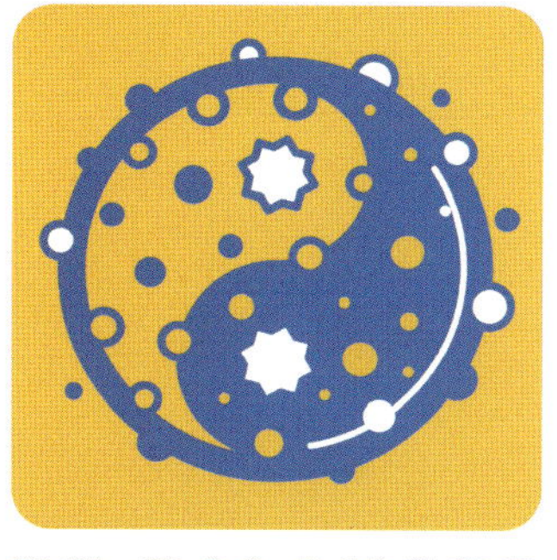

BE BALANCED

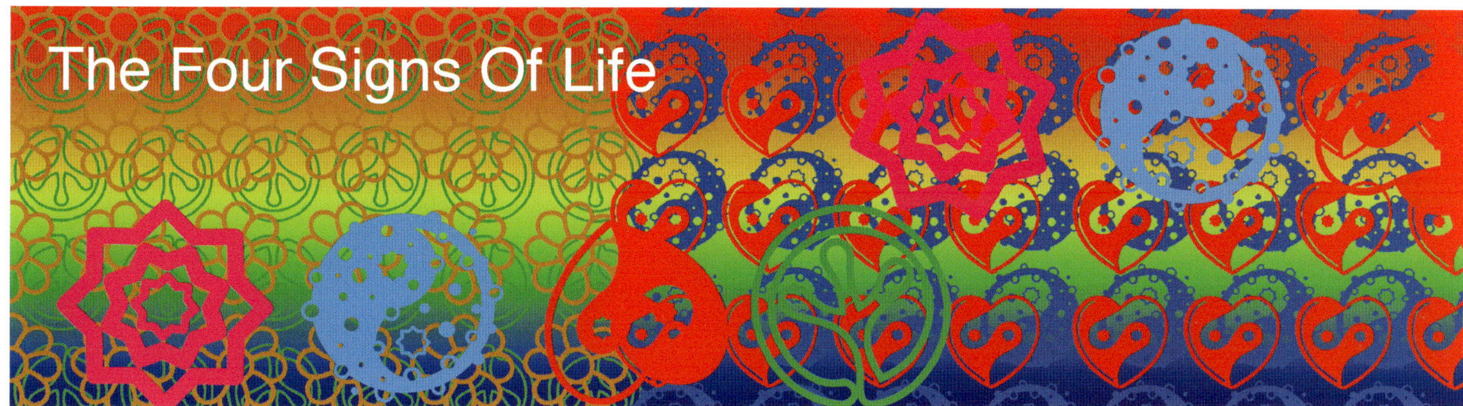

In 1995, Fremont Street was closed to vehicular traffic and a giant screen was suspended 90-feet over the street to display spectacular light and sound shows on its 1,500 foot surface. The 12.5 million lights of the Viva Vision screen dazzle 365 nights a year and make the Fremont Street Experience a one-of-a-kind venue. With direct pedestrian access to 10 casinos, more than 60 restaurants, specialty retail and free nightly entertainment, the Fremont Street Experience attracts millions of annual visitors.

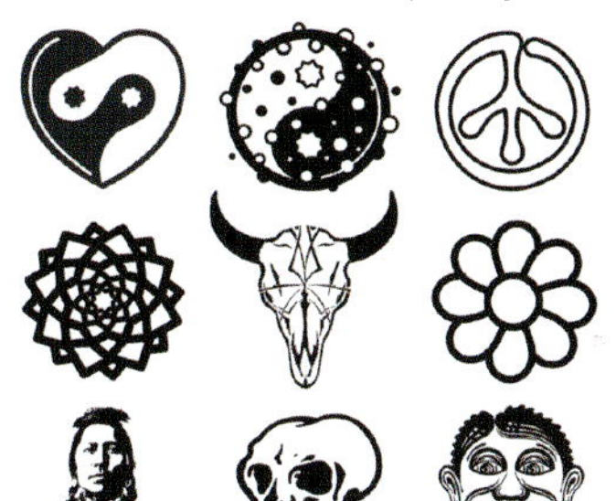

With the other symbols added

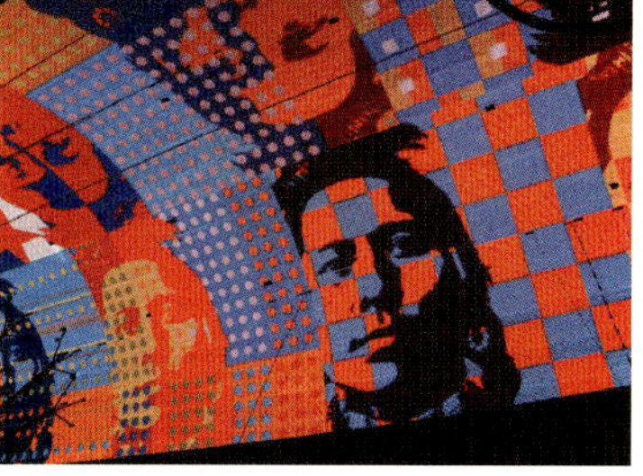

The Signs Of Life Park Signs

The Pinnacle Indian added

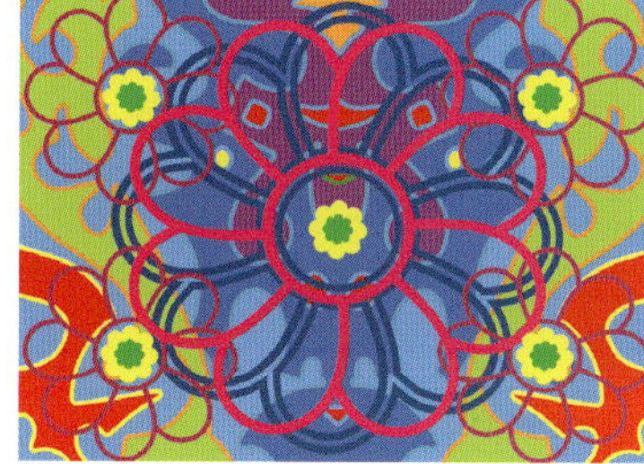

The fabric design as wall covering

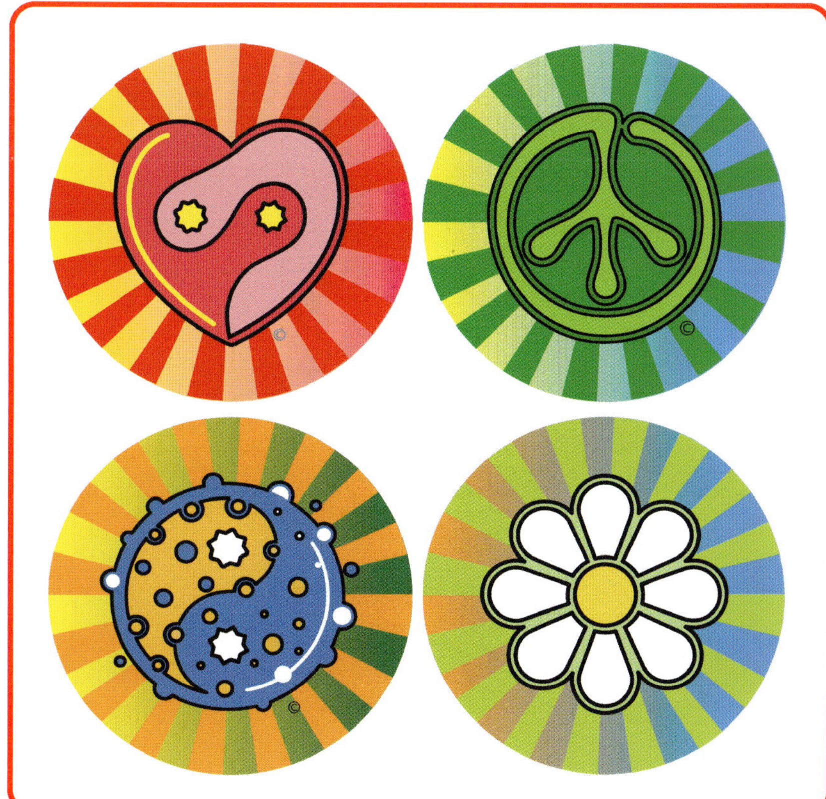

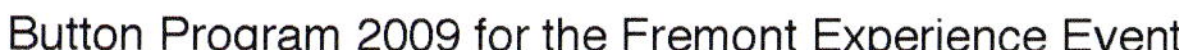

Button Program 2009 for the Fremont Experience Event

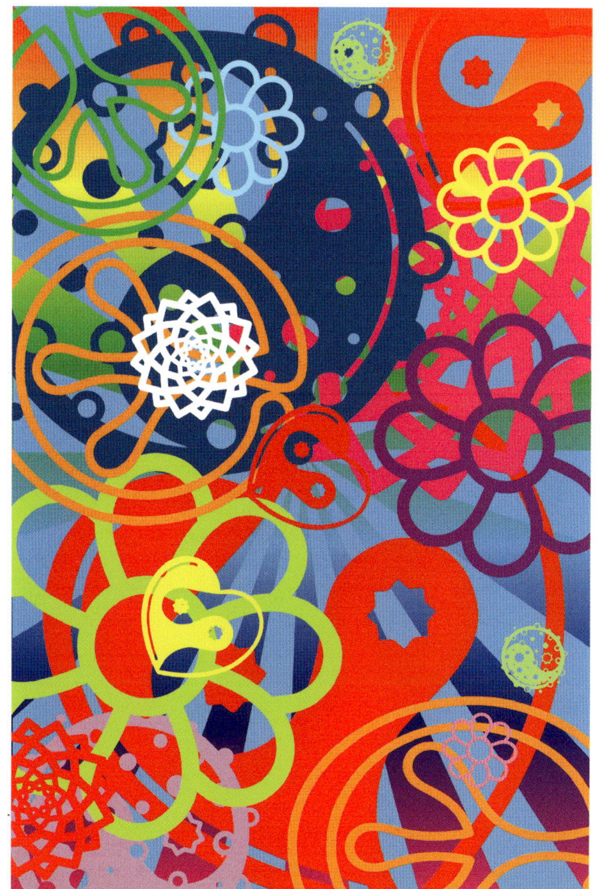

Collage Print Design

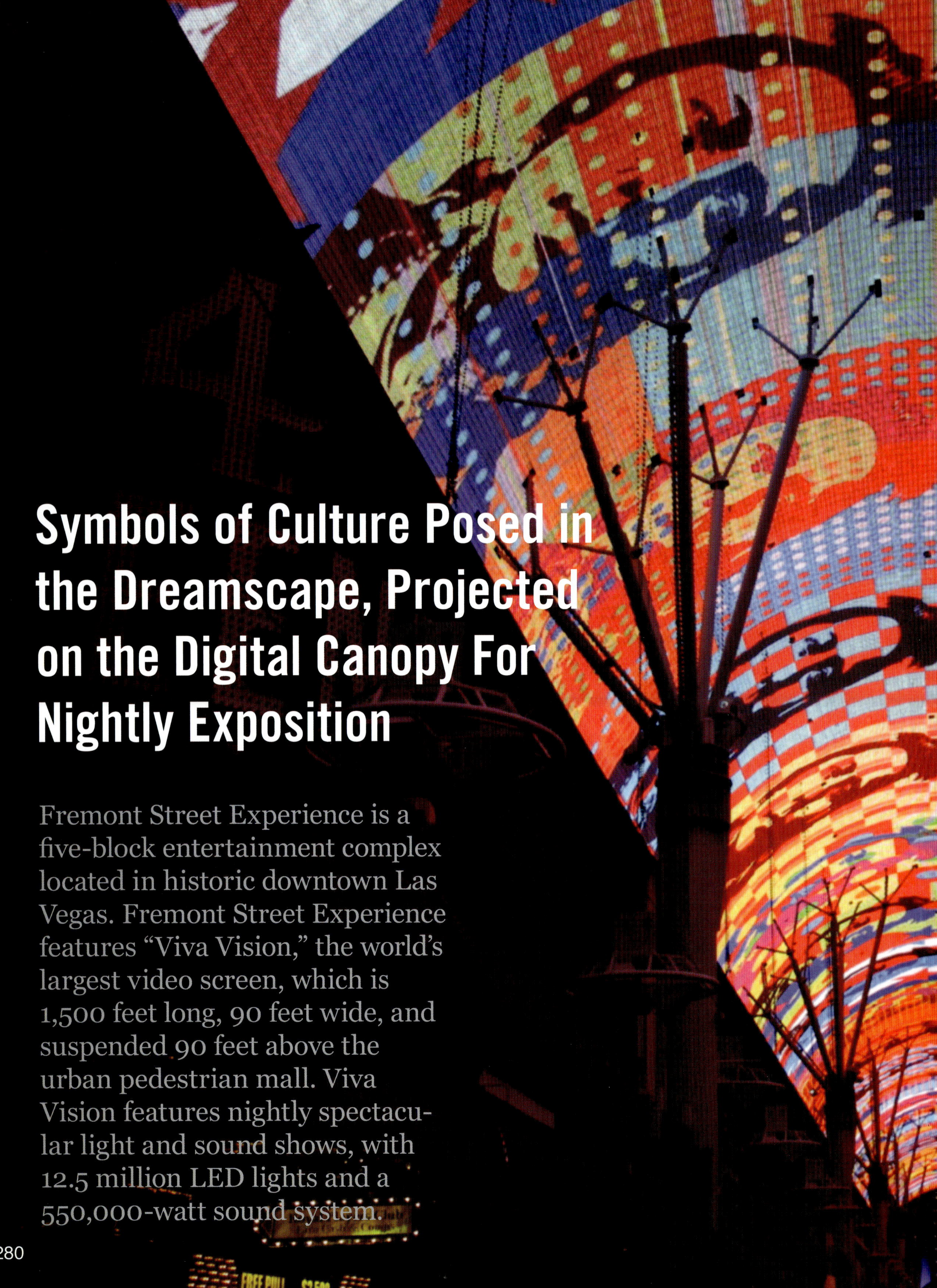

Symbols of Culture Posed in the Dreamscape, Projected on the Digital Canopy For Nightly Exposition

Fremont Street Experience is a five-block entertainment complex located in historic downtown Las Vegas. Fremont Street Experience features "Viva Vision," the world's largest video screen, which is 1,500 feet long, 90 feet wide, and suspended 90 feet above the urban pedestrian mall. Viva Vision features nightly spectacular light and sound shows, with 12.5 million LED lights and a 550,000-watt sound system.

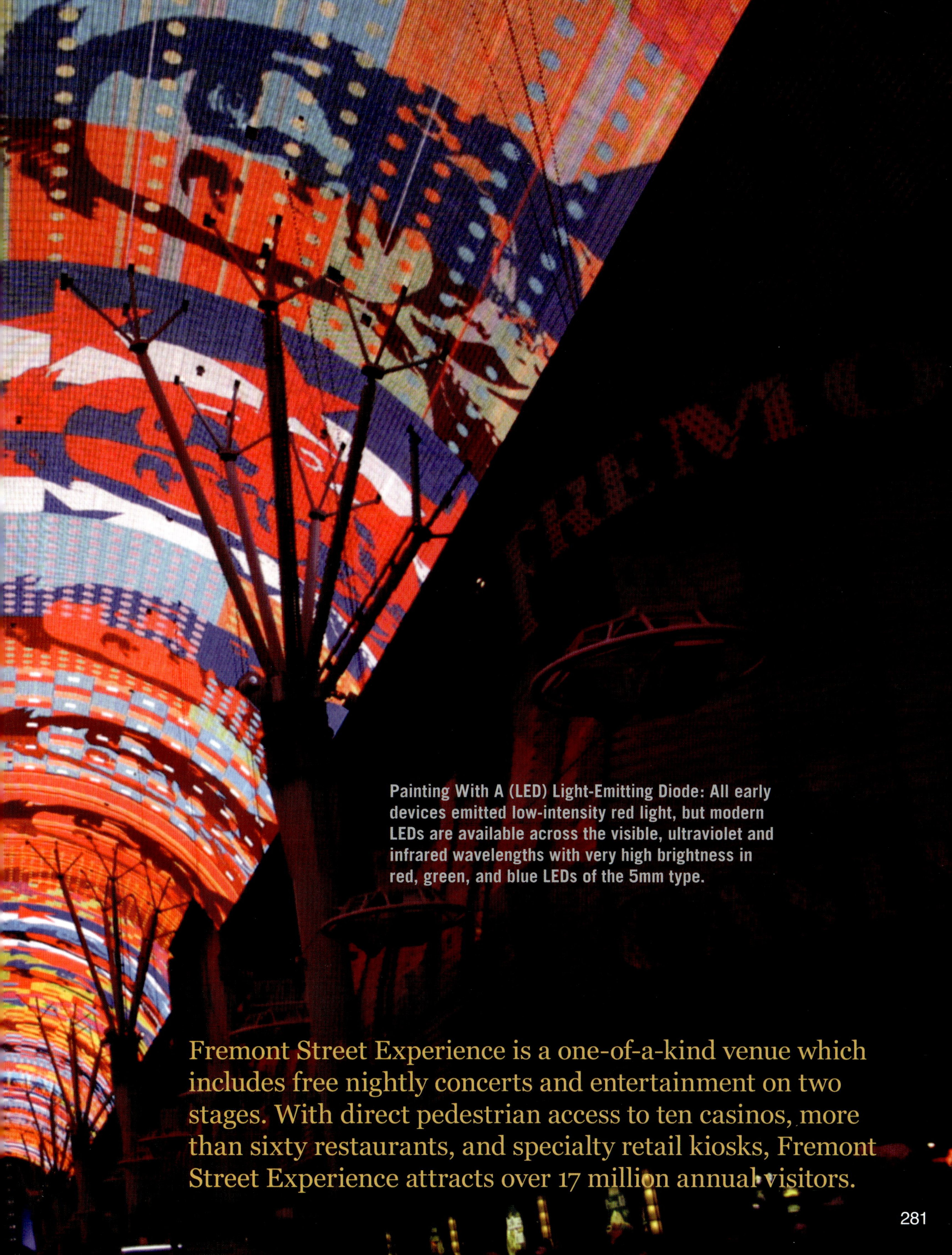

Painting With A (LED) Light-Emitting Diode: All early devices emitted low-intensity red light, but modern LEDs are available across the visible, ultraviolet and infrared wavelengths with very high brightness in red, green, and blue LEDs of the 5mm type.

Fremont Street Experience is a one-of-a-kind venue which includes free nightly concerts and entertainment on two stages. With direct pedestrian access to ten casinos, more than sixty restaurants, and specialty retail kiosks, Fremont Street Experience attracts over 17 million annual visitors.

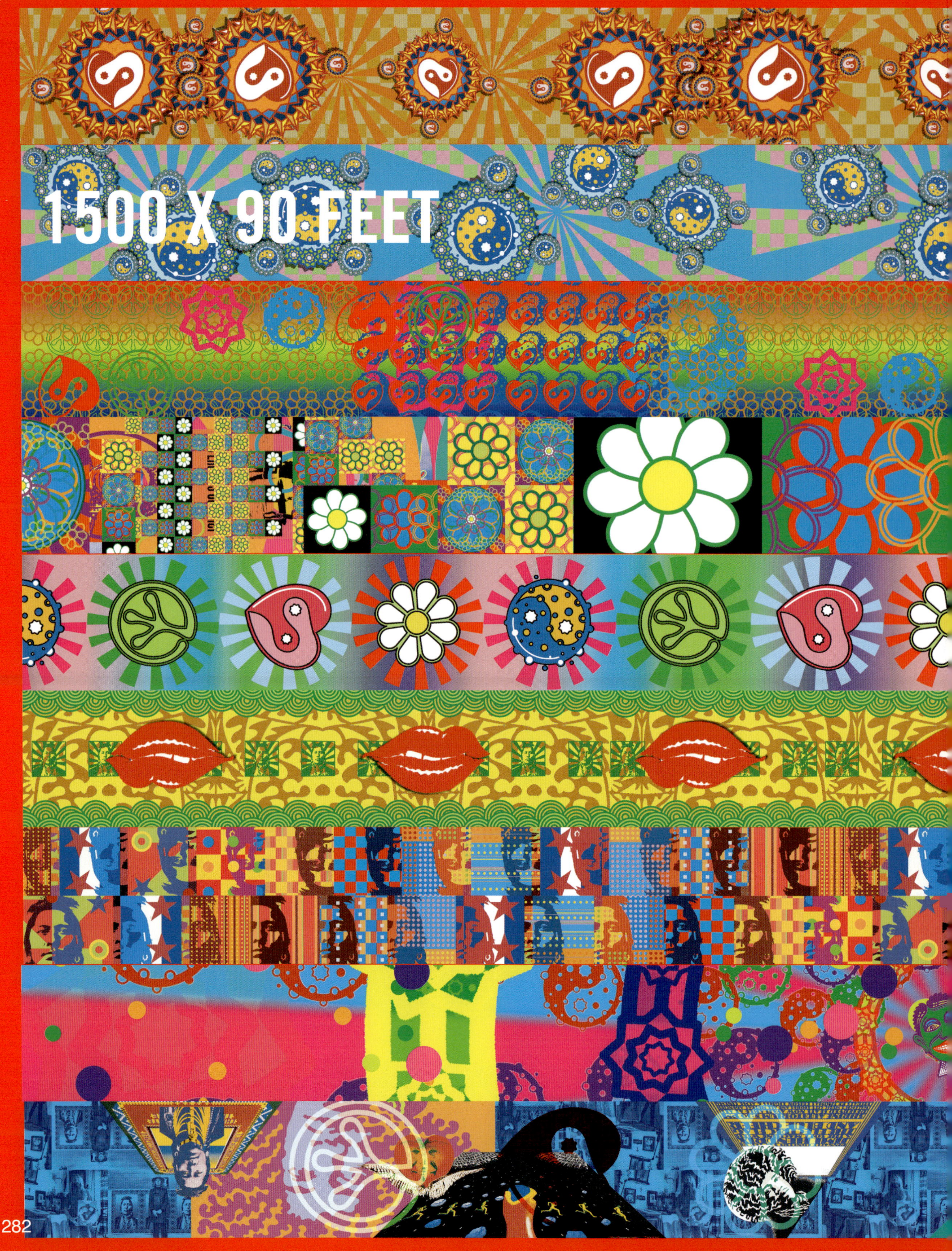
1500 X 90 FEET

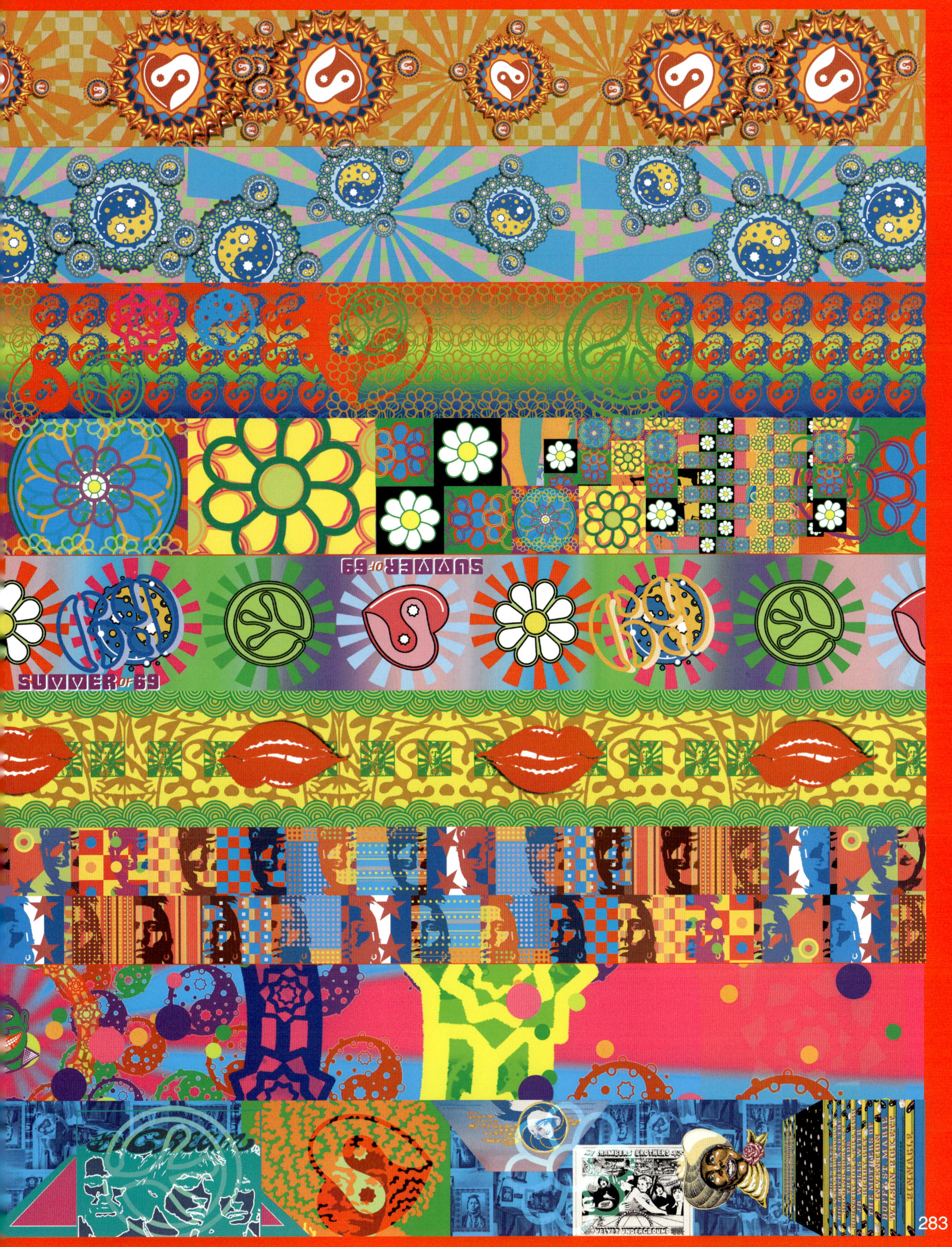
SUMMER OF 69
SUMMER OF 69

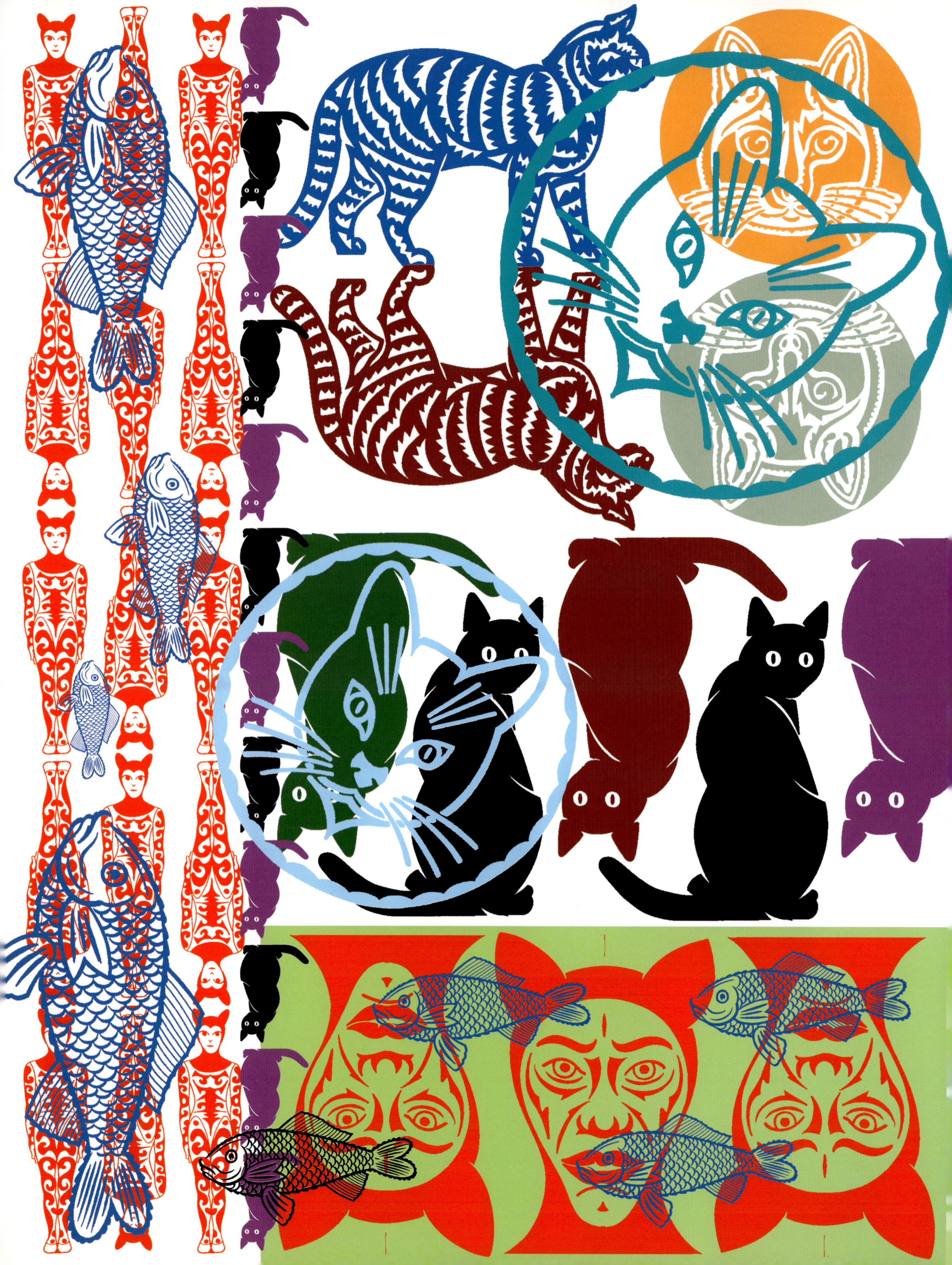

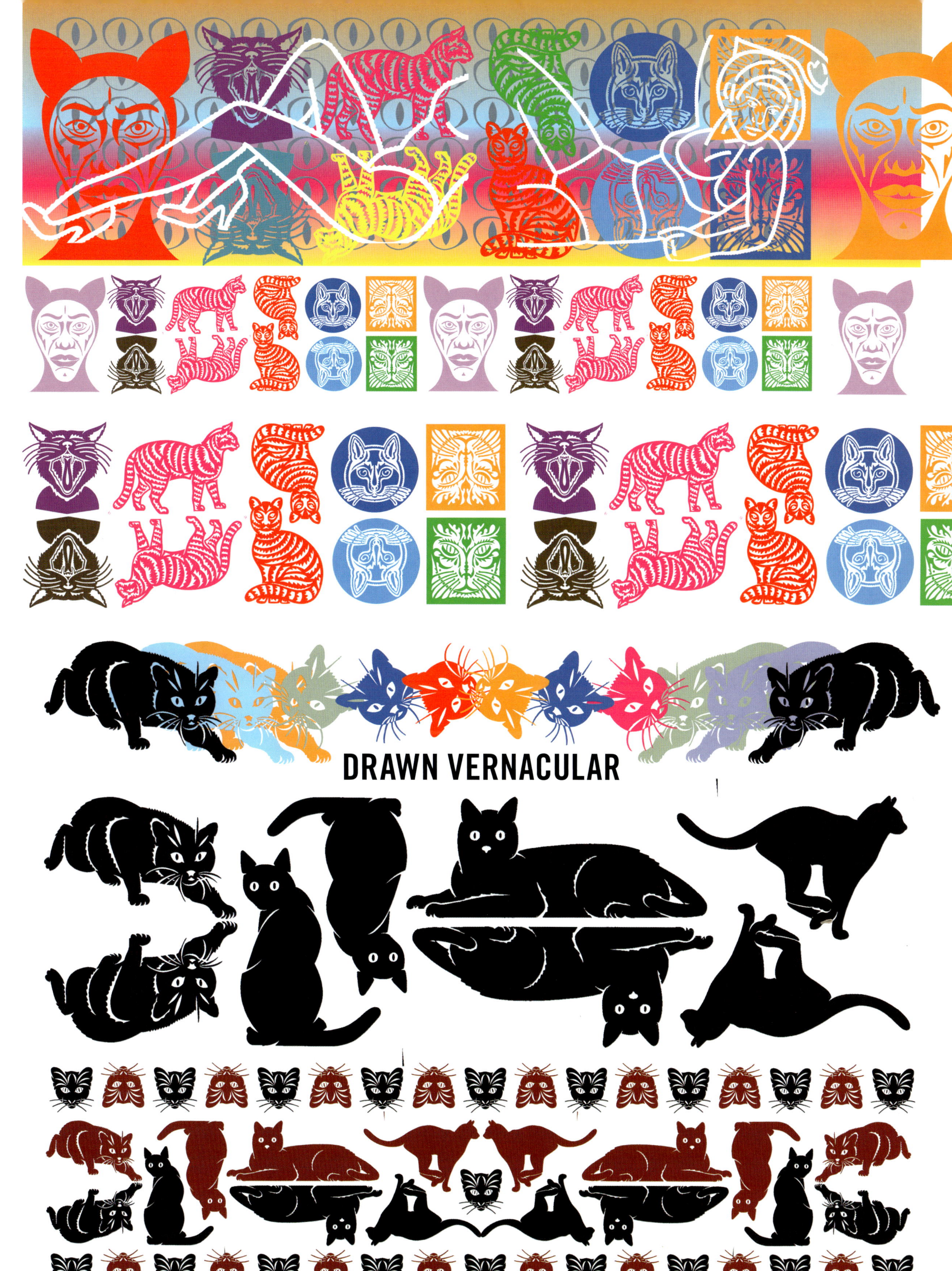
DRAWN VERNACULAR

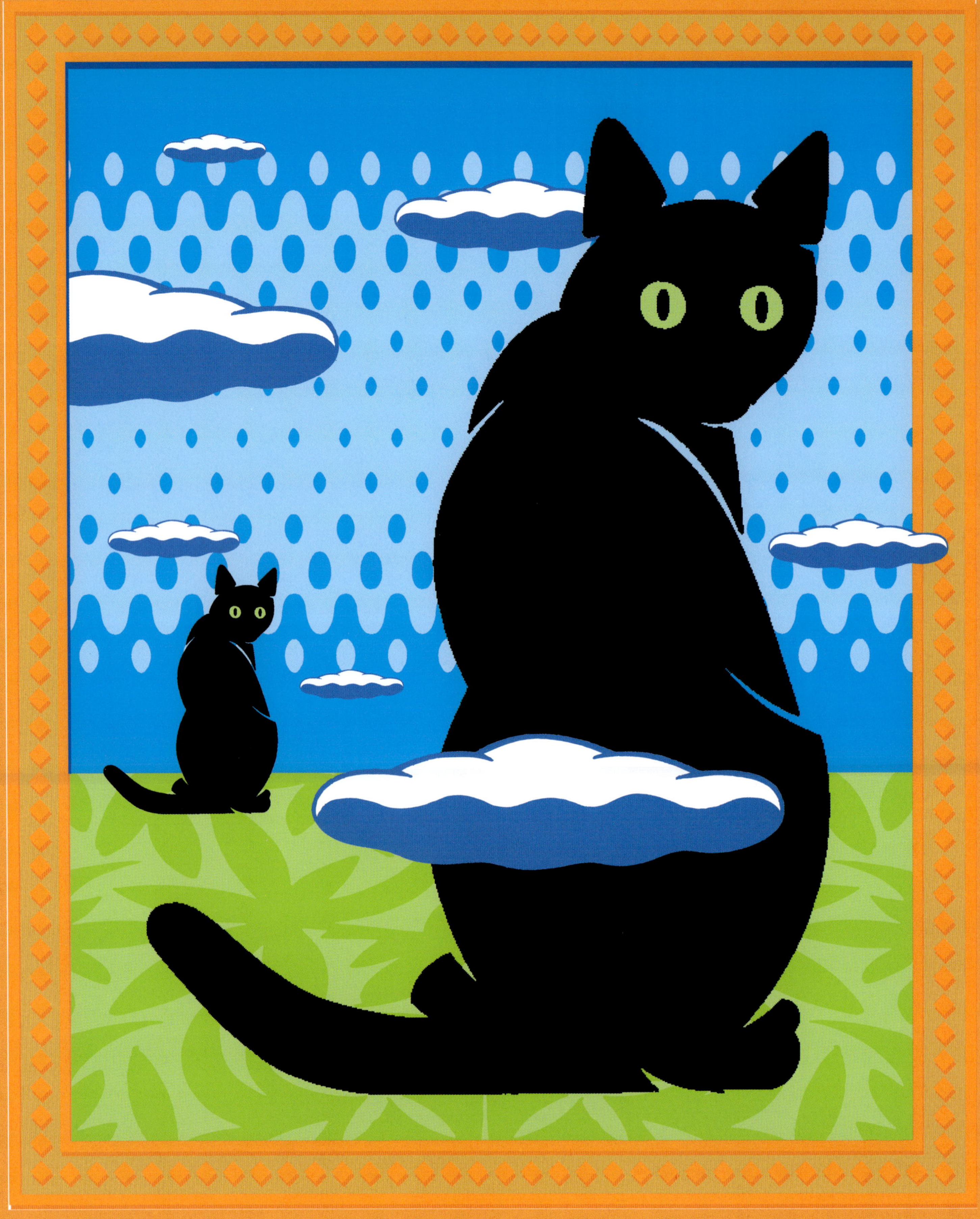

Surrealist Cat

Catmania

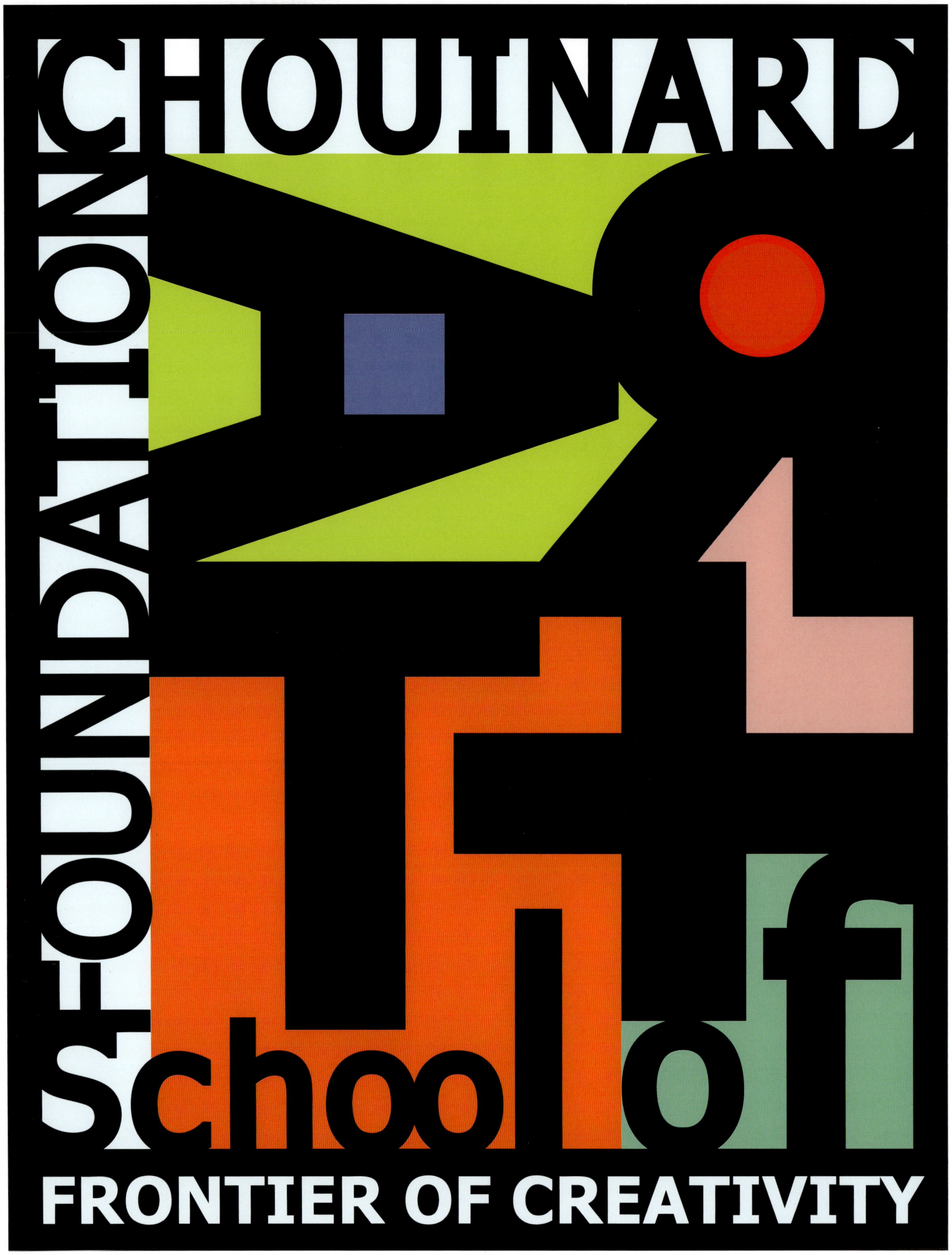
CHOUINARD
FOUNDATION
School of
FRONTIER OF CREATIVITY

Expo Center

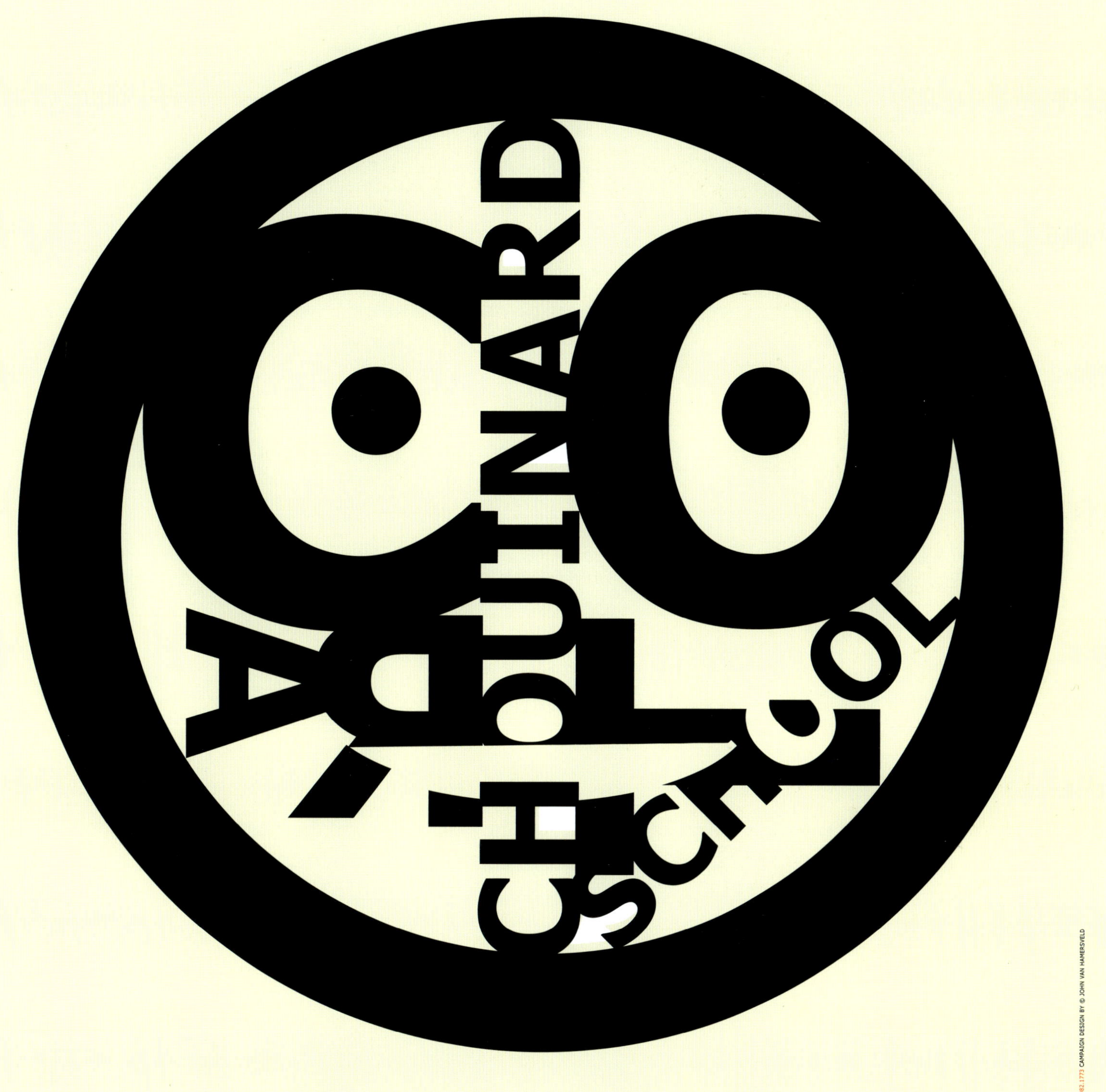

Creative

WWW.CHOUINARDFOUNDATION.ORG 323.982.1773 CAMPAIGN DESIGN BY © JOHN VAN HAMERSVELD

CHOUINARD AT LA REC&PARKS

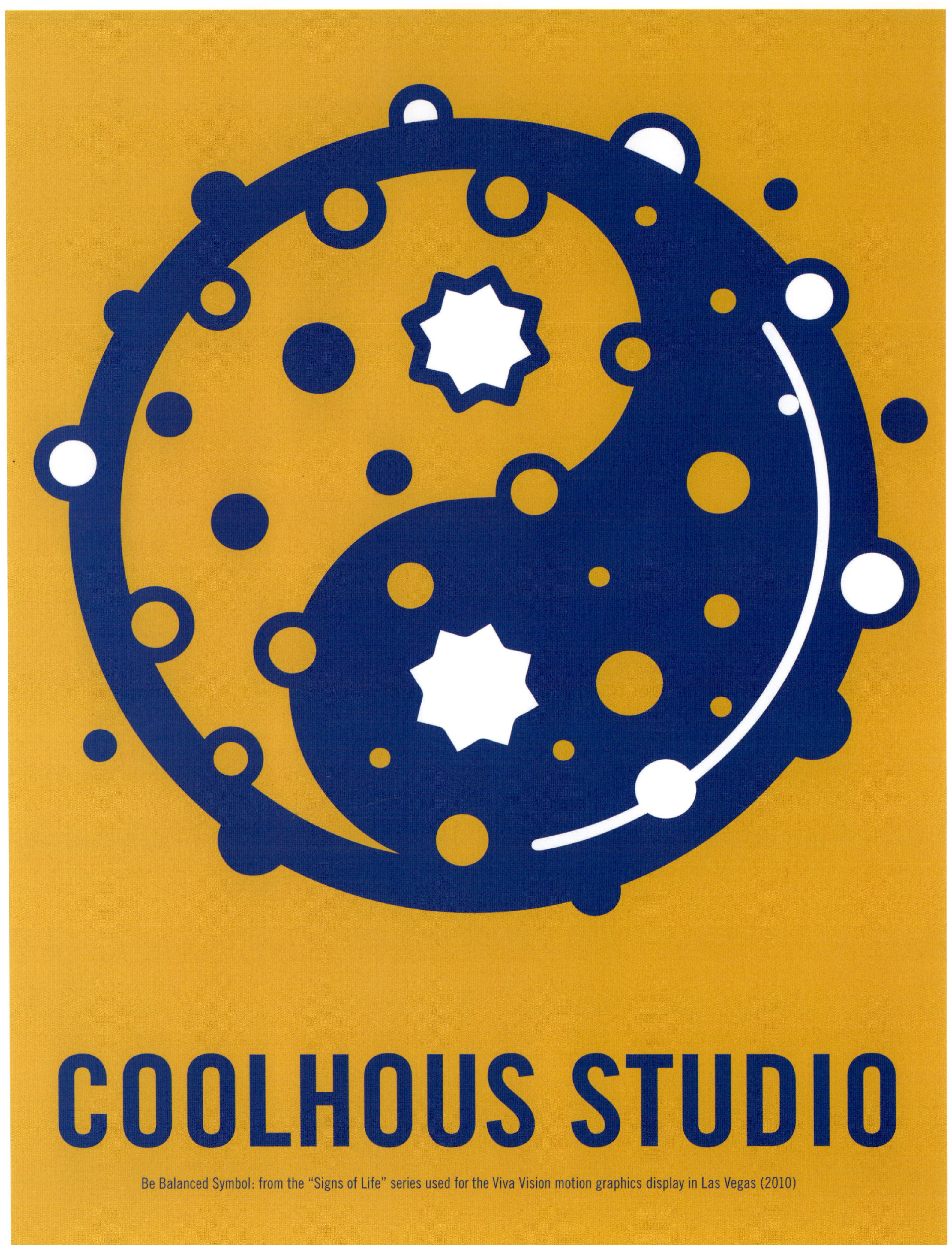

Be Balanced Symbol: from the "Signs of Life" series used for the Viva Vision motion graphics display in Las Vegas (2010)

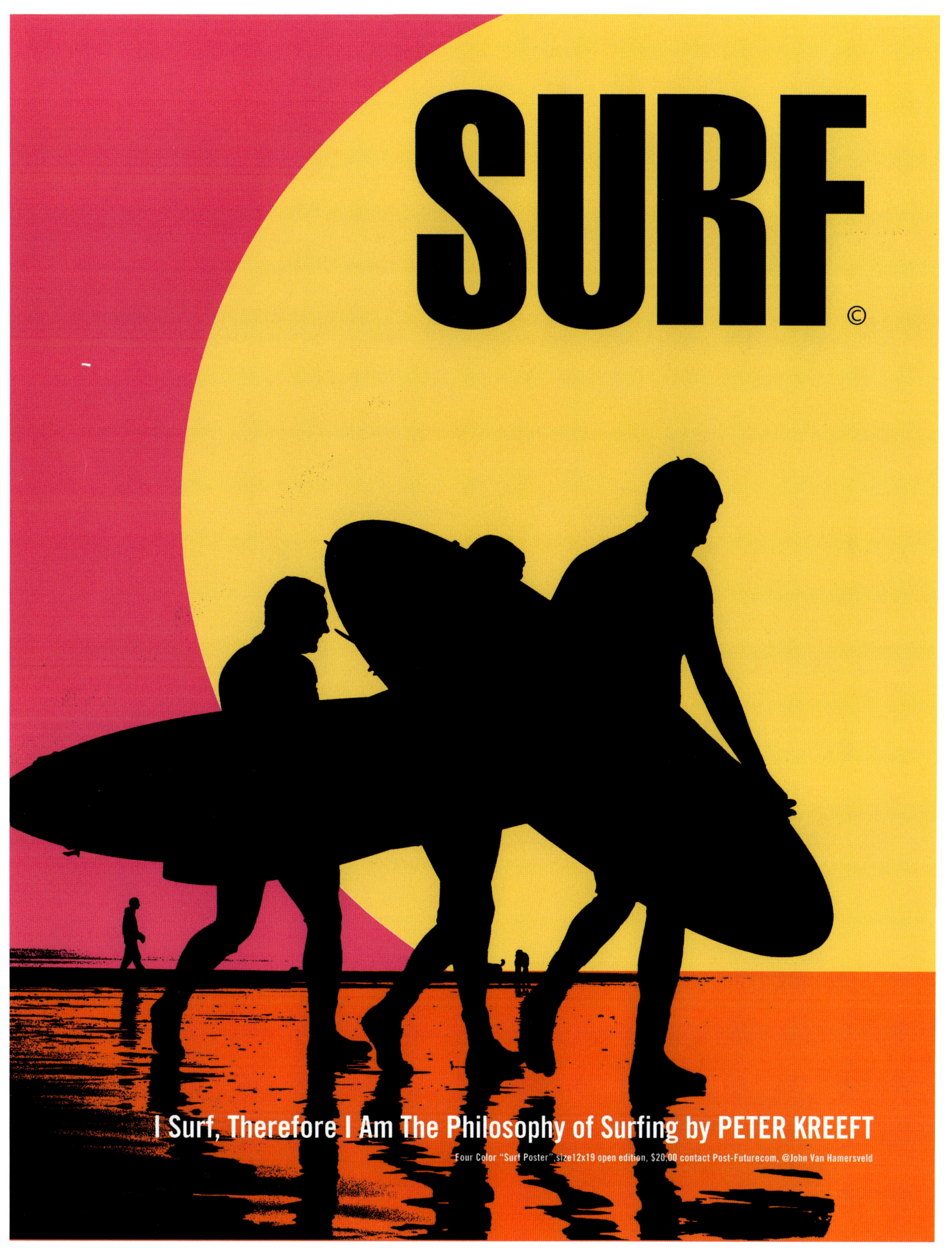
SURF ©
I Surf, Therefore I Am The Philosophy of Surfing by PETER KREEFT
Four Color "Surf Poster",size12x19 open edition, $20,00 contact Post-Futurecom, @John Van Hamersveld

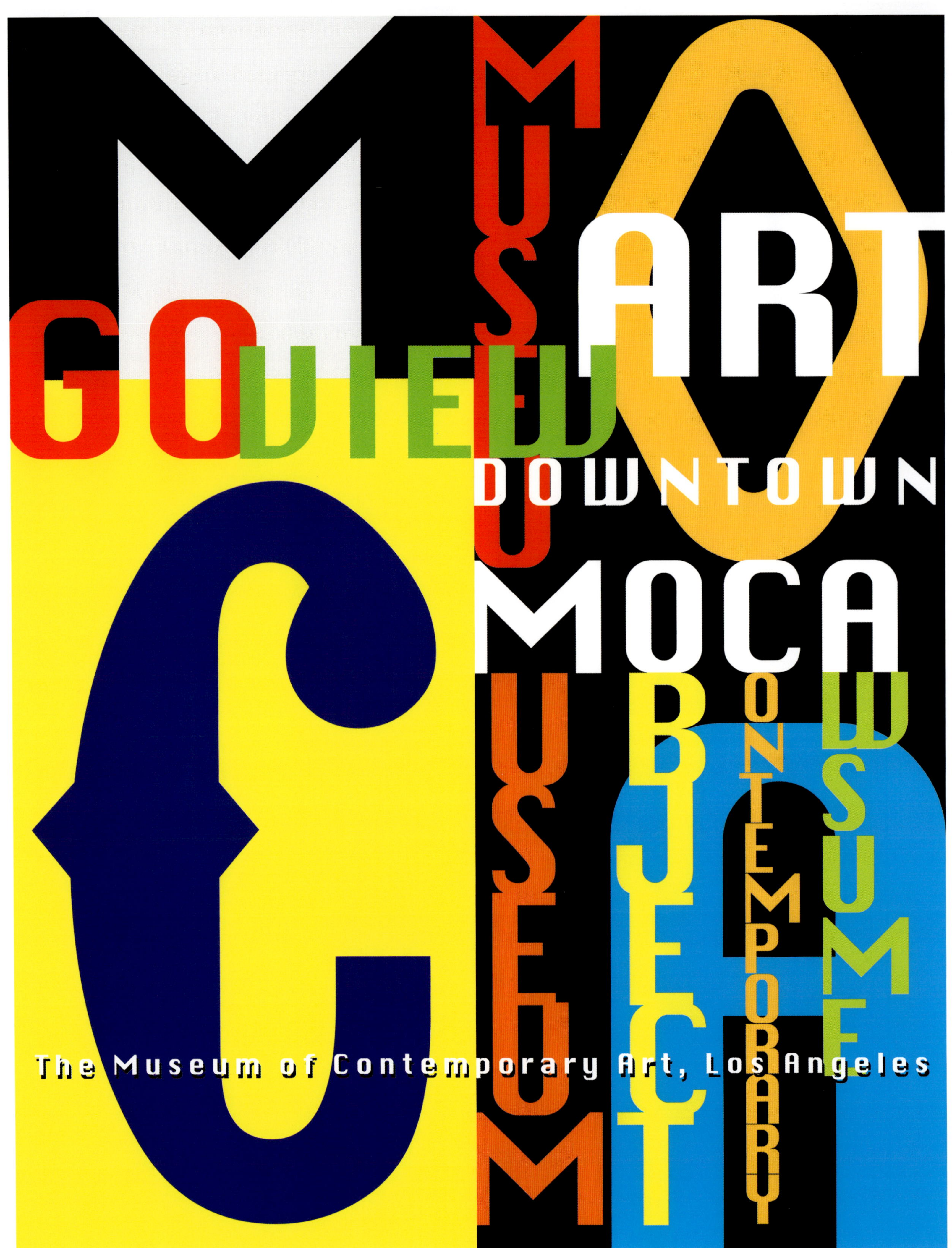
GO
VIEW
ART
DOWNTOWN
MOCA
CONTEMPORARY
The Museum of Contemporary Art, Los Angeles

Draw The Idea

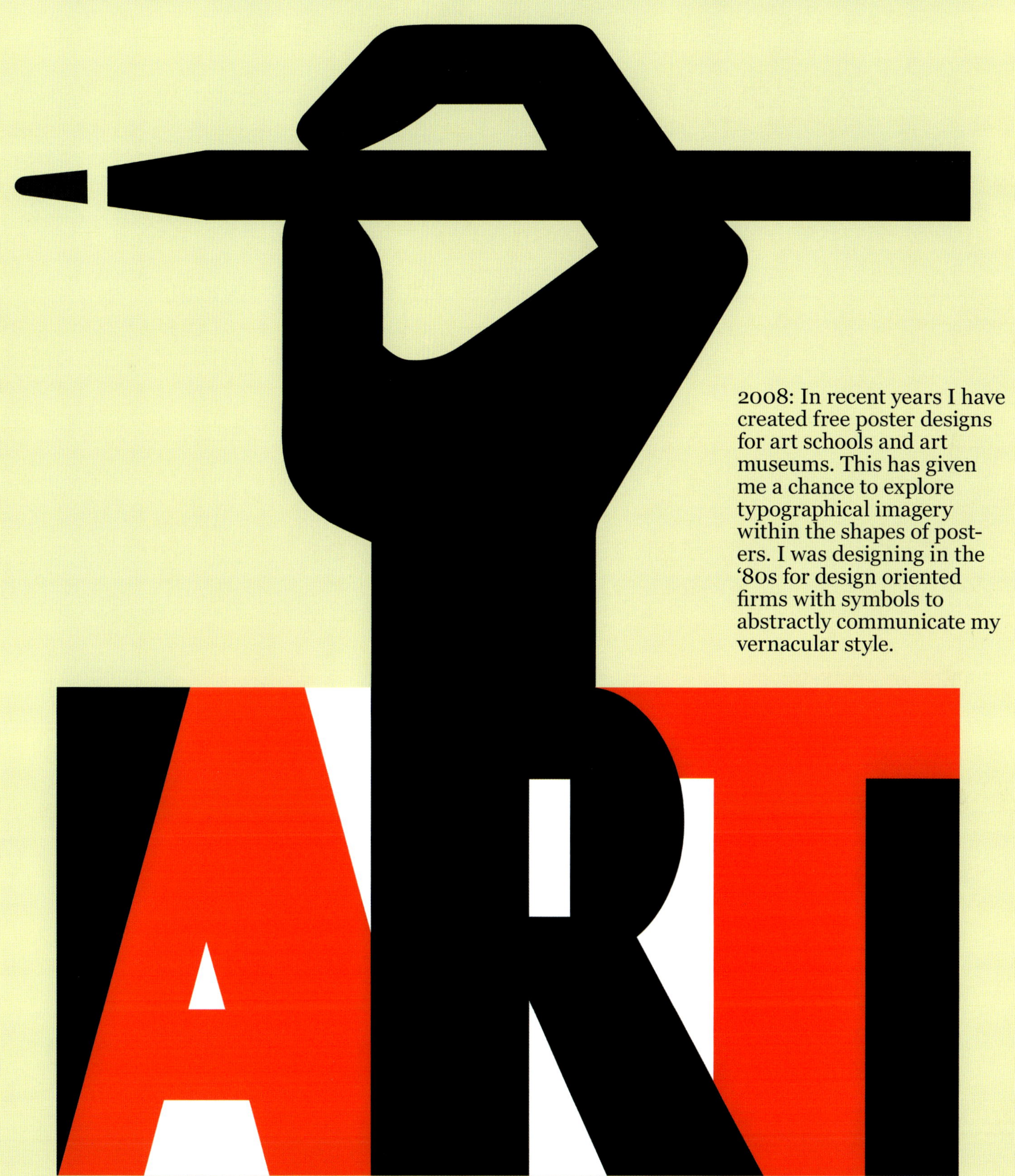

2008: In recent years I have created free poster designs for art schools and art museums. This has given me a chance to explore typographical imagery within the shapes of posters. I was designing in the '80s for design oriented firms with symbols to abstractly communicate my vernacular style.

Sponsored by the Chouinard Foundation and the City of Los Angeles Department of Recreation and Parks

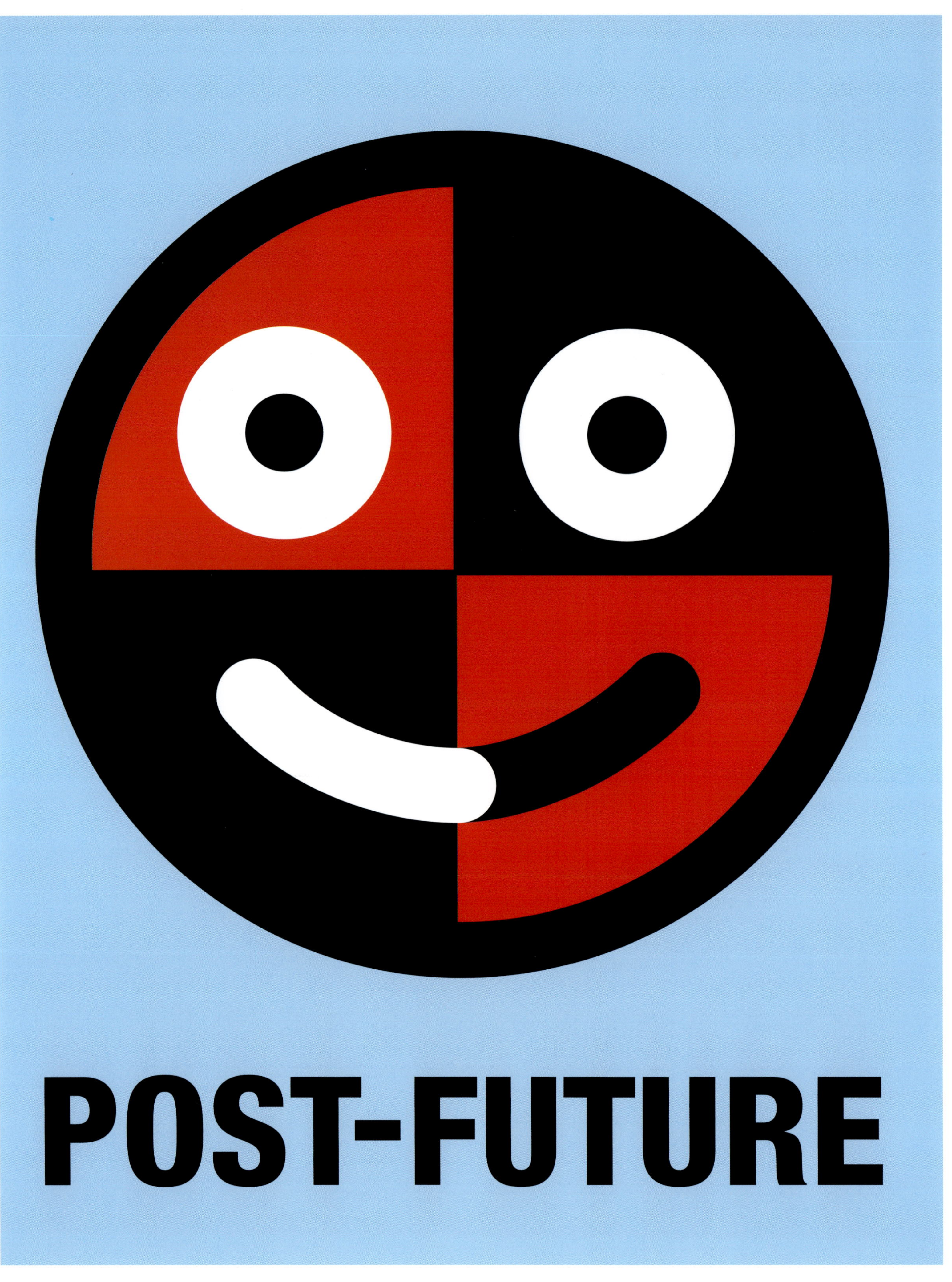
POST-FUTURE

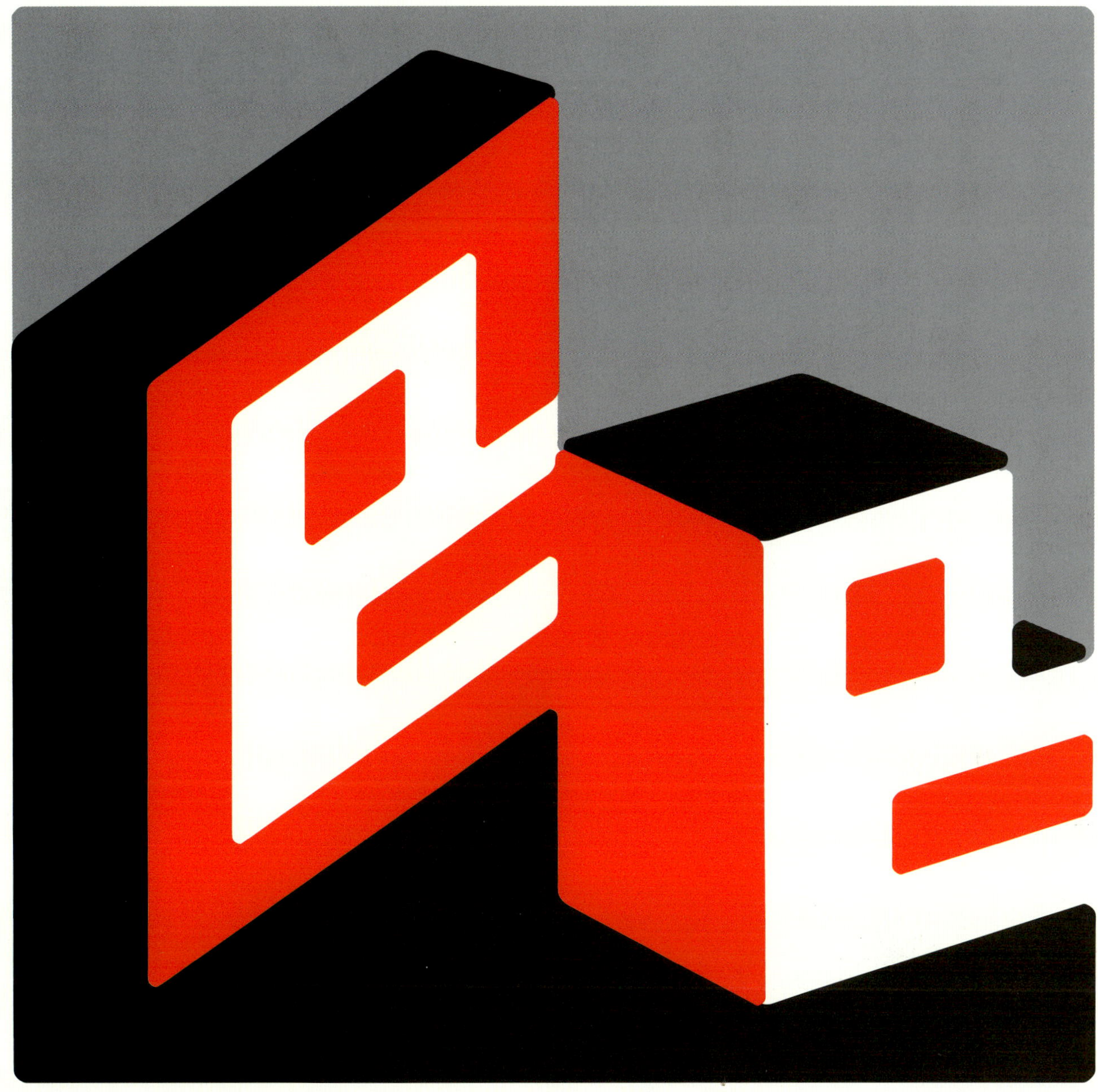

These posters are based off of two trademarks made for the Coolhous Studio brand (2002)

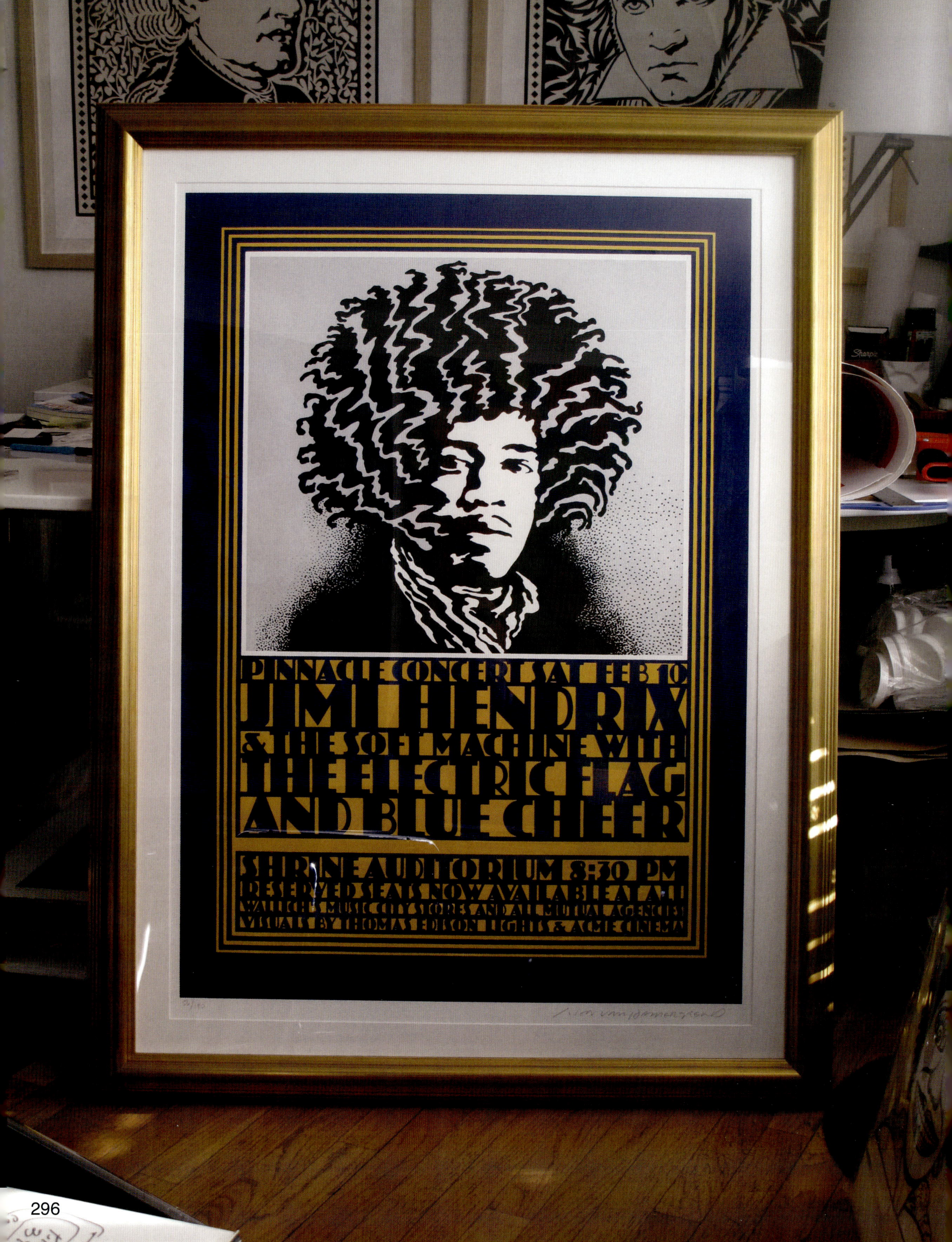
PINNACLE CONCERT SAT FEB 10
JIMI HENDRIX
& THE SOFT MACHINE WITH
THE ELECTRIC FLAG
AND BLUE CHEER
SHRINE AUDITORIUM 8:30 PM
RESERVED SEATS NOW AVAILABLE AT ALL
WALLICHS MUSIC CITY STORES AND ALL MUTUAL AGENCIES
VISUALS BY THOMAS EDISON LIGHTS & ACME CINEMA

BOOK REVIEW

AS AN INFLUENCE

Shepard Fairey picks John Van Hamersveld's "Pinnacle Hendrix" poster, citing it as an influence on his Andre the Giant images. Fairey writes that Van Hamersveld's iconic work possesses all the criteria of a "perfect image," that it's impossible to imagine the work any other way or to improve upon it. Van Hamersveld's posterized black-and-white style informs much of the graffiti, street art and fine art today, including Fairey's images (the Obama "Hope" poster), Banksy and his possibly manufactured alter ego, Mr. Brainwash.

OCKING HIS WORLD: Shepard Fairey cites a poster by John Van Hamersveld as an influence on his own work.

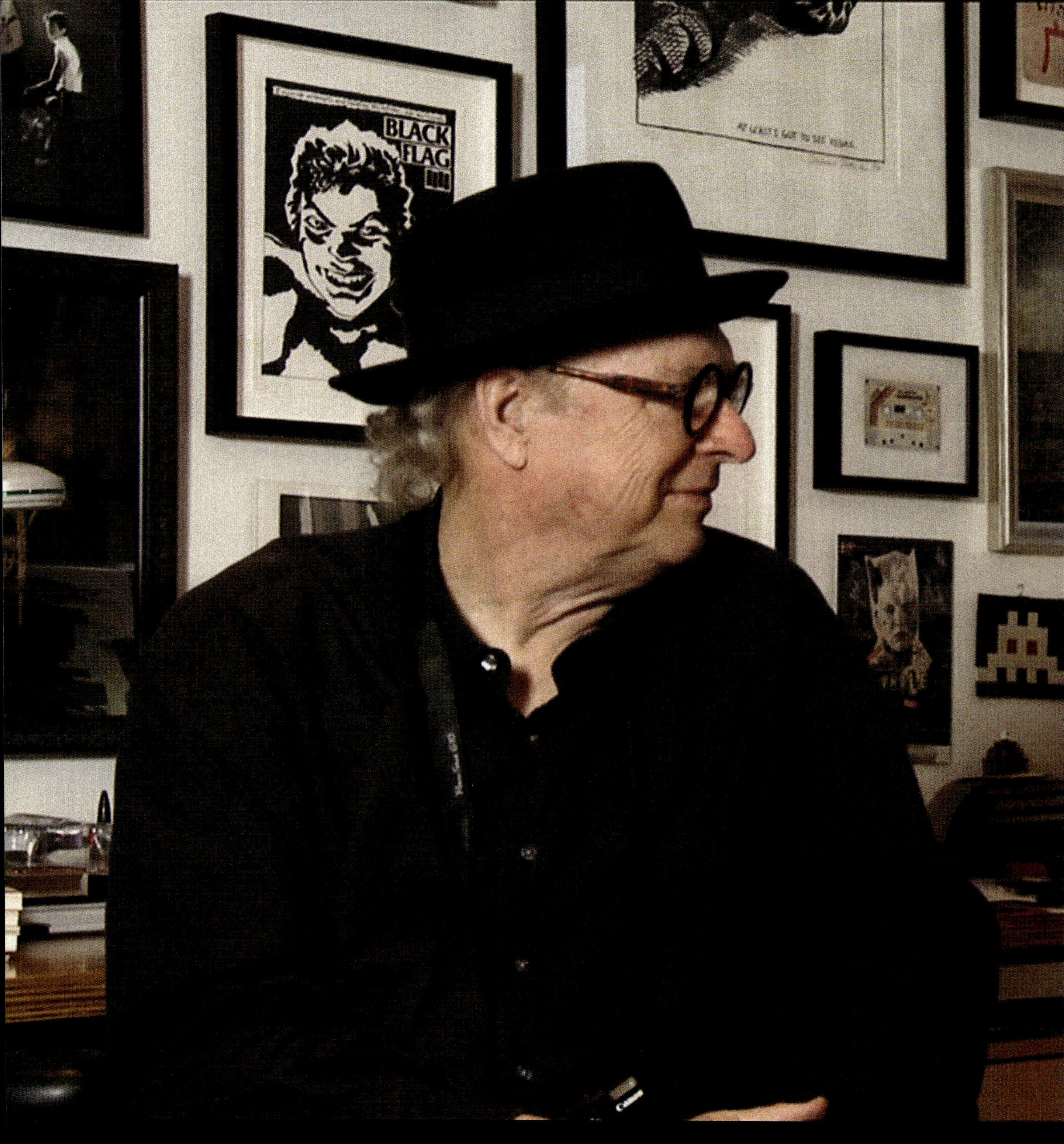

A new world of image making....

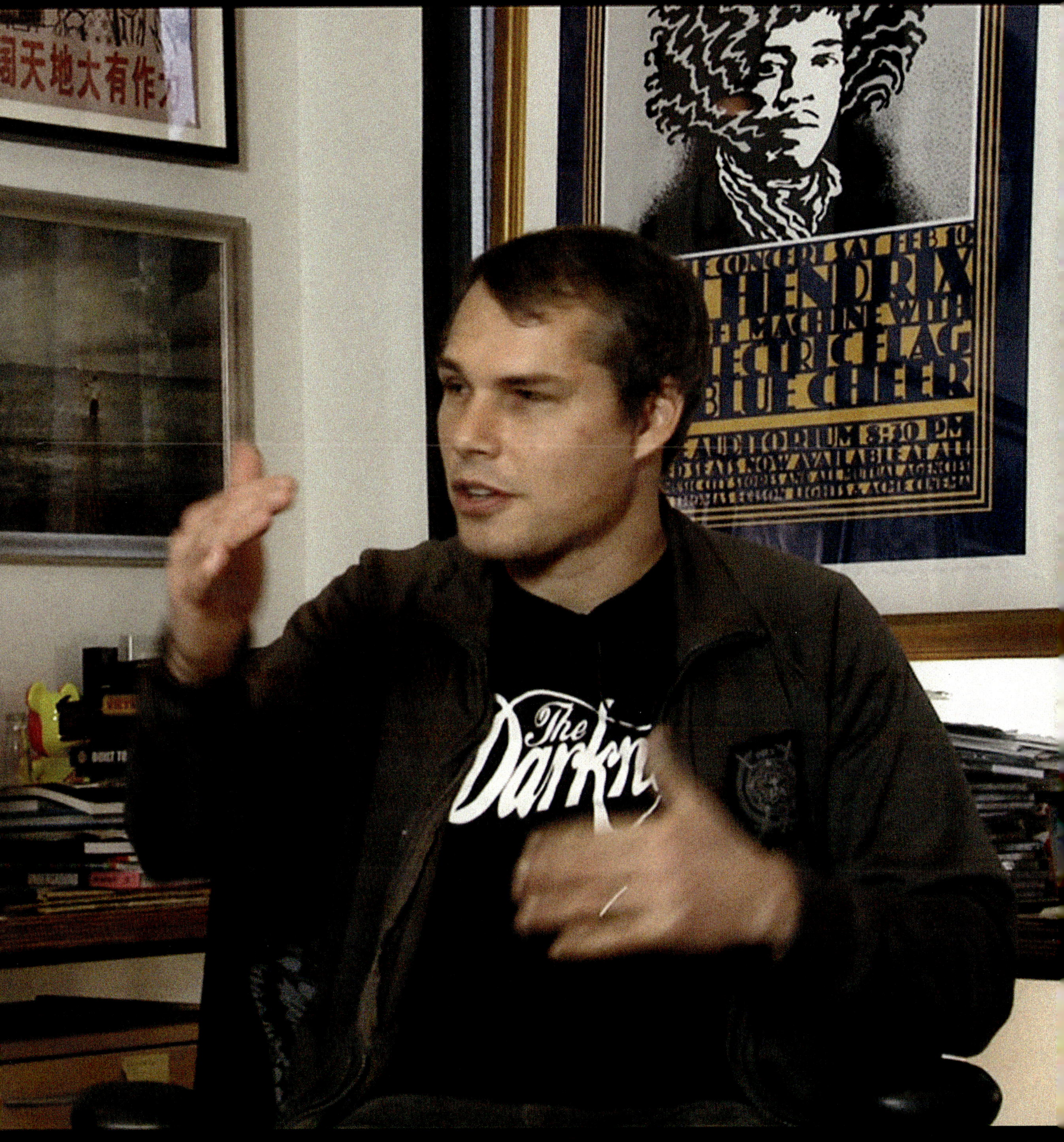
阔天地大有作
HENDRIX
The

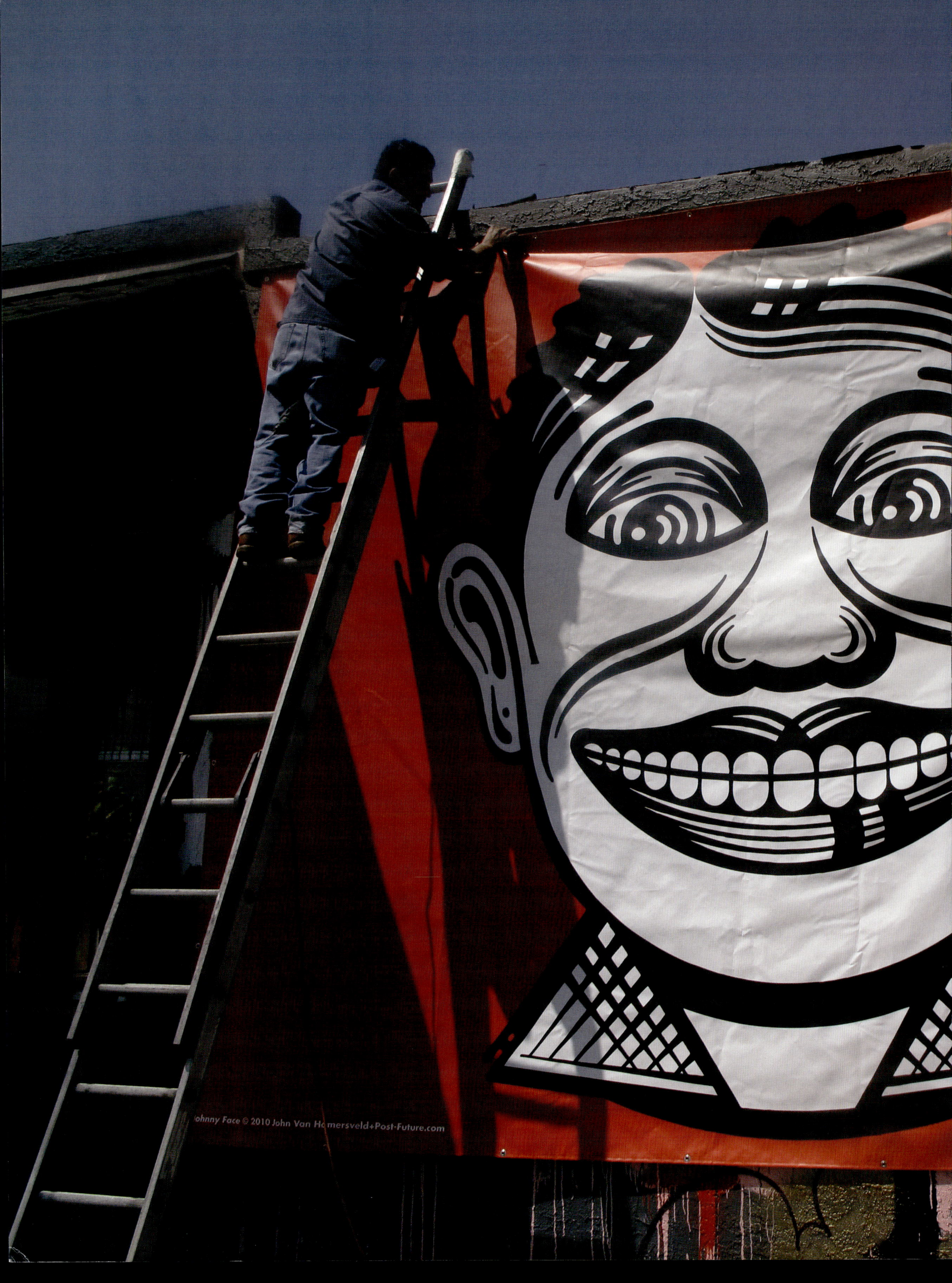
ohnny Face © 2010 John Van Hamersveld+Post-Future.com

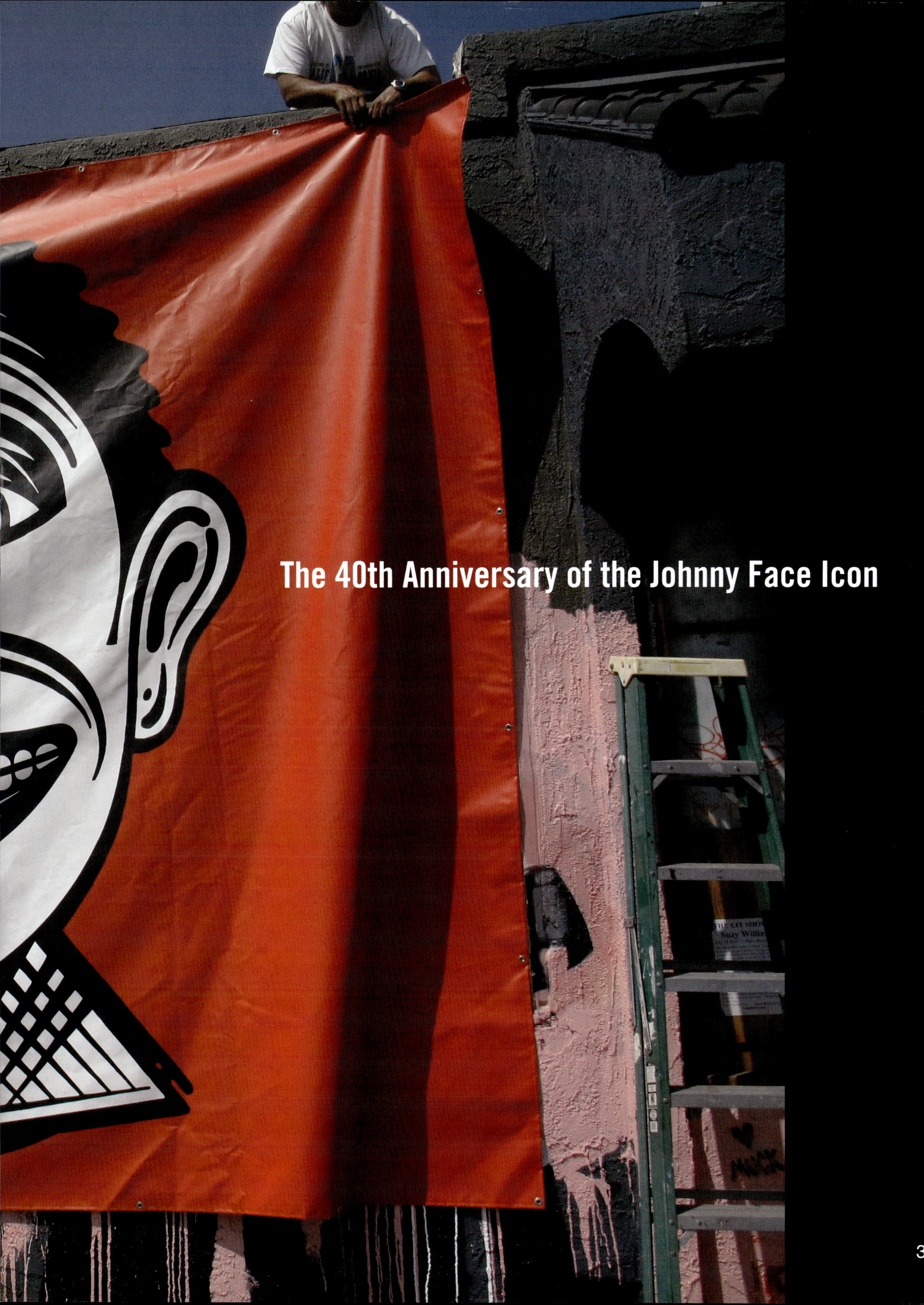

The 40th Anniversary of the Johnny Face Icon

It took almost 50 years to hear that the *Endless Summer* poster was being collected by the Los Angeles County Museum of Art. In addition, the poster was also included in a modern design exhibition put on by the museum, and was published in their exhibition catalog for a show called *California Design, 1930–1965: "Living In A Modern Way."*

Pacific Standard Time is an unprecedented collaboration of more than sixty cultural institutions across Southern California, coming together to tell the story of the birth of the Los Angeles art scene. It was initiated through grants from the Getty Foundation.

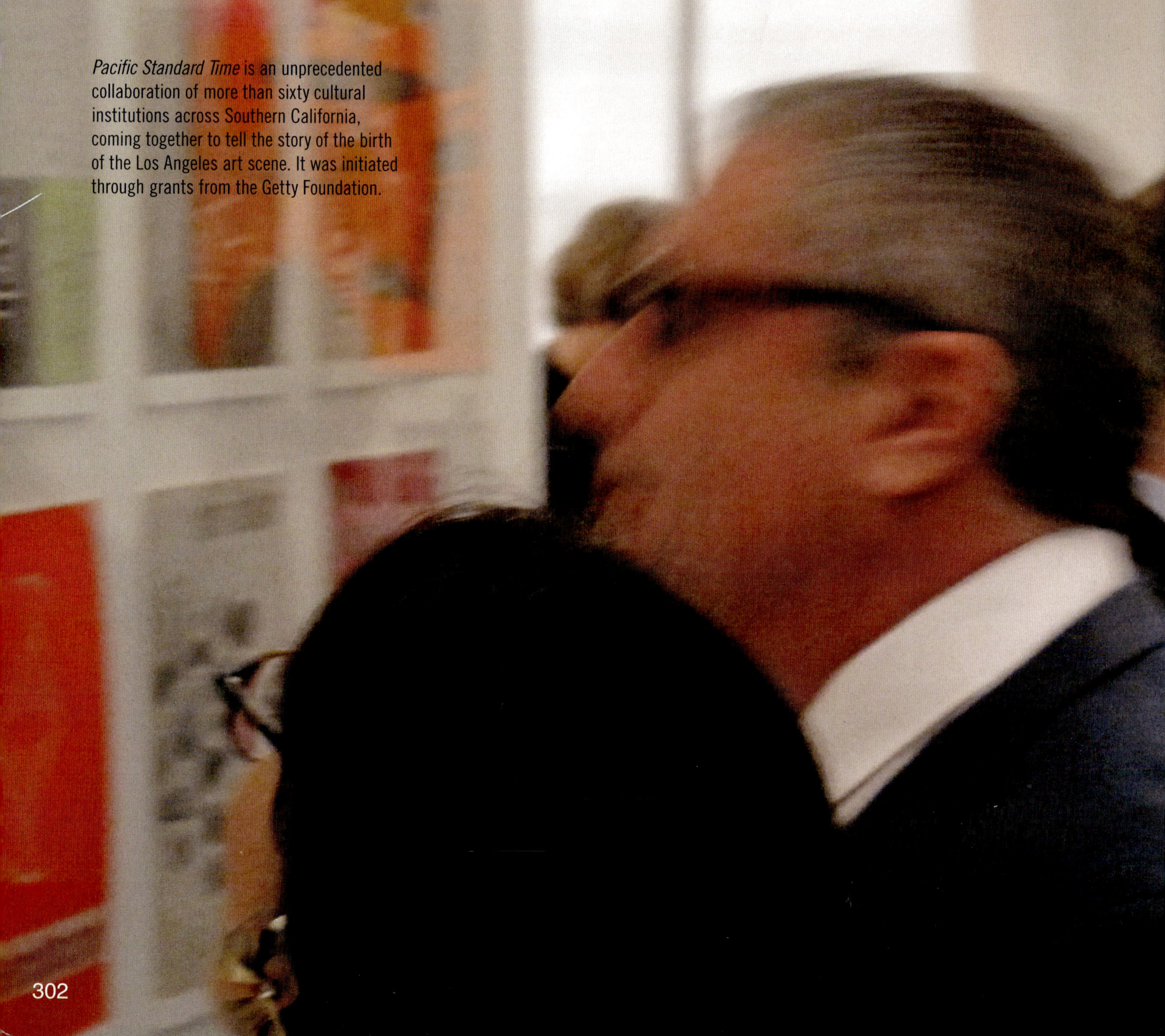

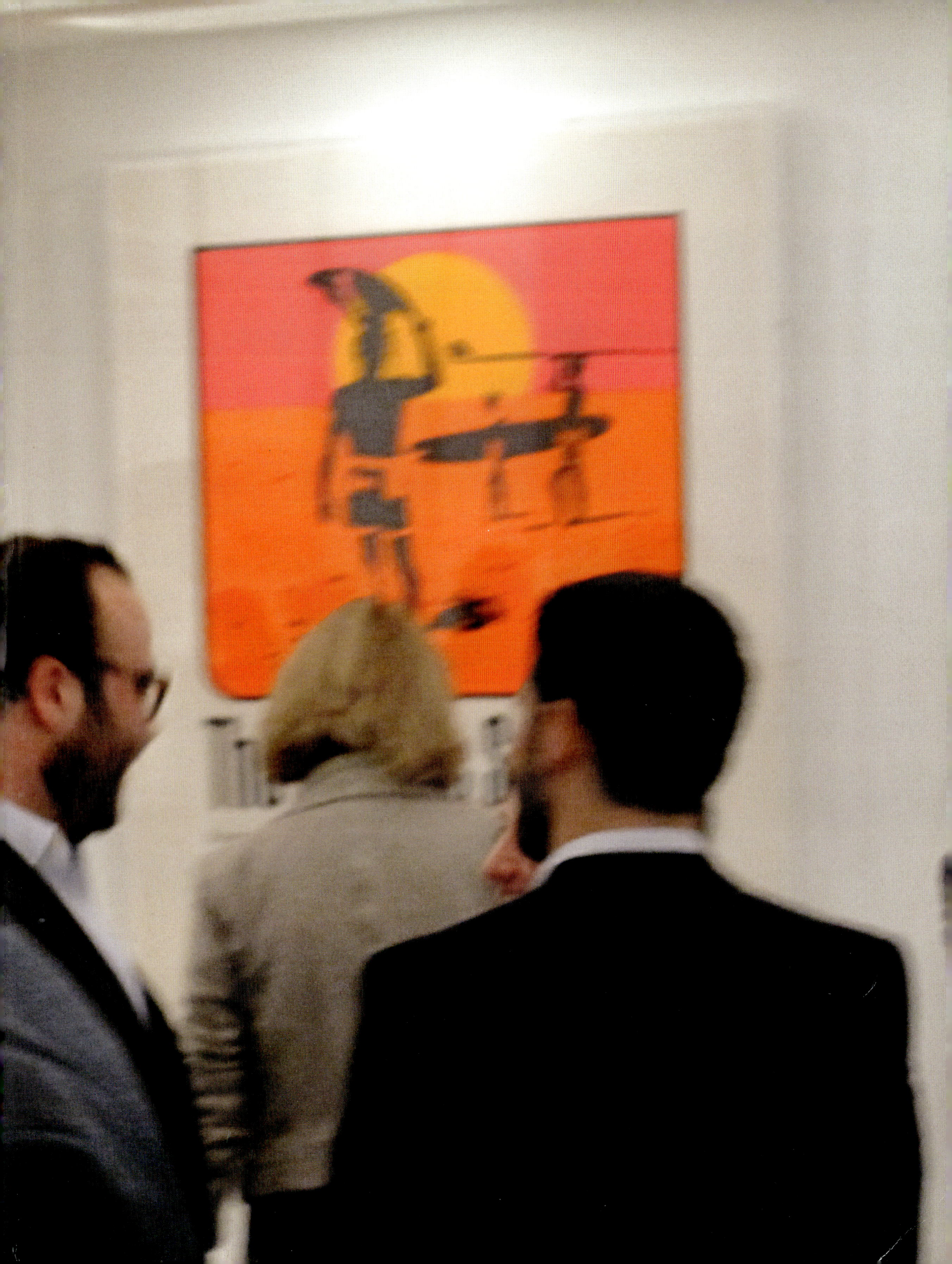

First Published in the United States of America, 2013
First Edition

Published by
Gingko Press
In association with
Coolhous Studio

Gingko Press, Inc.
1321 Fifth Street
Berkeley, CA 94710, USA
www.gingkopress.com

contact: post-future.com
contact: Coolhous Studio, johnvanhamersveld.com

ISBN: 978-1-58423-472-2
LCCN: (2012945611)

Printed in China

Production, design and text editing, Charles Ponce
Additional copyediting by Ellen Christensen